PUBLISHED BY REVELATION RECORDS
P.O. BOX 5232
HUNTINGTON BEACH, CA 92615-5232

LIBRARY OF CONGRESS CONTROL NUMBER: 2009921672

ISBN: 1-889703-02-8

PRINTED IN THE UNITED STATES OF AMERICA

FIRST PRINTING: APRIL 2009
FIRST EDITION

WRITTEN AND ASSEMBLED BY BRIAN PETERSON

BOOK DESIGN BY ROSE NOBLE

FRONT COVER PHOTOGRAPH BY OLE CHRISTIAN PETTERSON

3 5 7 9 11 12 10 8 6 4 2

BURNING FIGHT

THE NINETIES HARDCORE REVOLUTION IN ETHICS, POLITICS, SPIRIT, AND SOUND

BRIAN PETERSON

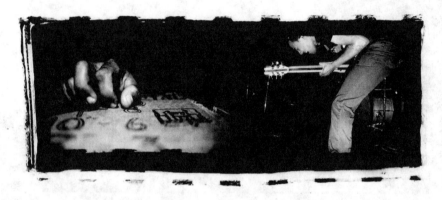

Burning Fight IS DEDICATED TO MATT DAVIS (1976 — 2003), WHO EMBODIED THE SPIRIT OF HARDCORE LIKE NO OTHER PERSON I HAVE KNOWN.

CONTENTS

kids hanging out after show –
Greyhouse/Snapcase

PREFACE

I grew up in the Midwest and spent much of my youth as a fan of hip-hop due to the fact that the artists had something to say. In junior high I had my first taste of hardcore through a friend — Bad Brains, The Circle Jerks, Minor Threat, Youth of Today, and others. I remember chuckling at some of the names and I wasn't quite ready for the screaming. But for some reason this sound stuck with me.

In high school, I felt isolated and devoted myself even more to music. Around the same time, Nirvana exploded onto the musical landscape. They represented a changing of the guard for mainstream rock, and I was fascinated by their sound and overall aesthetic. In interviews they spoke about the hardcore and punk bands that inspired them. I didn't even realize that there was a thriving hardcore scene still going on at the time. But the more I read about the classic bands, the more I found out about the contemporary ones. Eventually I came across an issue of *Maximum Rock N'Roll* and something changed inside of me.

Hardcore was more captivating and passionate than anything else I had heard. The sound seemed to express a feeling of frustration that I felt about my surroundings and our culture. What separated hardcore from everything else was the fact that the individual had the power to take an active role in the scene and claim it as their own. There was no waiting around for others to tell you what mattered — you could define the debate yourself. This changed my outlook as it also did for many of my friends in the hardcore scene, which led to several years of going to shows, reading zines, playing in bands, putting on shows, and driving long distances to fests.

Of course, being from a small town, especially in the pre-Internet days, it was a challenge to really get involved in hardcore. Area music stores didn't carry many records. Bands rarely played our town. We had to drive to Chicago to see most hardcore bands, but the problem was that we didn't know when any shows were going on. As a result, we formed bands and booked shows in our own area while corresponding with kids who wrote zines around the country. Eventually it all paid off as we watched our scene develop over time.

As I became more involved in hardcore, I was exposed to a variety of ideas such as straight edge, animal rights, and human rights. I also gained a much broader awareness of politics, spirituality, and ethics that all ended up playing a major role in my development. Because nineties hardcore played such a pivotal role in my life, I found that I wanted to document what it was that made hardcore so important. After thinking about what the best way to do that would be, I decided talk to people active in the era about their perspectives and compile them into a book. I started interviewing people in 2003. Six years, countless hours of phone, email, and in-person interviews, a box full of micro-cassette tapes, innumerable evenings transcribing interviews, and a ton of typed pages later, the book is finally complete.

Burning Fight is an attempt to document some of the issues, movements, bands, and trends that played an important role in the nineties hardcore scene as I experienced it. Like the generations that preceded it and the generations that followed, nineties hardcore was composed of innumerable bands, zines, records, people, debates, performances, and memorable times. The influence of this era cannot remain unnoticed as it greatly impacted the trajectory of sound, dialogue, and ethical concerns in hardcore. As the editor of this book I see my role as a tour guide, noting relevant pieces of history through the thoughts and memories shared by others. The people and bands interviewed and written about in this book are clearly not the only people who played important roles during this era. There is no "definitive" version of nineties hardcore, just as there is no single objective account of any set of shared experiences. *Burning Fight* is a tribute to some of the bands, ideas, people, songs, and zines that made an impact on me, as well as thousands of others.

Burning Fight examines four of the most prominent debates within the nineties hardcore scene: politics/social awareness, straight edge, animal rights/vegetarianism, and spirituality. In addition, it also focuses on thirty-one bands that helped define the sound and ideas of the nineties scene. It is my intention that the reader acquires a sense (or is reminded) of the impact the ideas, music, and personal connections had on the lives of those involved in nineties hardcore.

I view *Burning Fight* as an opportunity to create an evolving discussion in which we as a community of hardcore kids (once a hardcore kid, always a hardcore kid) can come together and discuss what this music has meant to our lives, particularly the ideas underlying the music. Many people I encountered through the assembling of this book are doing a variety of interesting things with their lives. Regardless of what they do for work or in their free time, it is obvious that hardcore forever changed them. I can't speak for other generations, but I believe this happened for a lot of nineties hardcore kids due to the focus on the unique ideas — be they artistic, ethical/philosophical, or political — that pervaded this era. Although one does not want to dwell on the past, reflection is the key to continual growth. And as I said earlier, there are a ton of great bands, ideas, zines, labels, and people who I unfortunately did not have room to include, so I am looking forward to reading their stories in the near future.

In the meantime, I hope you enjoy these.

FOREWORD

I have never been one for nostalgia. I don't think there has ever been a point in my life where I viewed the past as being more vital than what lay ahead of me. In the spectrum of punk rock and hardcore I always found nostalgia to be oddly misplaced. Wasn't punk rock urging us to forge our path, to look forward and obliterate all that stood in our way? If so, then how or, more importantly, why would we care to live in the past? It has never made sense to me. That isn't to say I don't value the past, after all it is the past which molds who we are today, but I simply saw no reason to yearn for it, and I certainly never wanted it to be more important, or even almost as important, as what was to come. In terms of the hardcore/punk scene, I have watched friend after friend over the past 20 plus years become enthralled and almost obsessed about the past and how much "better" it was. You know what that told me? That hardcore/punk was now dead to them. There is a fine line between nostalgia and appreciating the past. To me it's as simple as remembering that if things don't evolve then they die. If we cannot appreciate the evolution of our scene then it is no longer ours.

For me the early to mid-nineties was a special time. The mid to late-eighties saw the hardcore scene really narrow itself down in terms of ideology and sound. There was, of course, diversity, but when you looked closely at the hardcore scene, the popular bands almost always fit the same mold. If you fit in with the ideologies and mentality of that period, it was great, but after a few years the entire scene had collapsed. Literally within months shows went from 500-plus kids to under 100. The combination of so many of the popular bands breaking up, almost the entire straight edge scene growing out of the ideology it was based on and the rising violence that became prevalent at most shows was a death knell to that era. It was almost as if everyone grew old and gave up at once. Many of the seminal clubs closed or stopped doing hardcore shows, most small labels were known for not sending kids the records they paid for rather than excitement over the new up and coming bands they were releasing records for, and large labels started to poke around. It was an awkward time.

For those who survived it all there was a sense of urgency to do something different. Bands weren't restricted by a certain sound or ideology and were inspired to create their own sound and express their social and political inspirations. Kids focused on doing shows in small clubs, VFW Halls, and basements where new bands could make their mark and the vibe was that of shows for kids and by kids. Labels prided themselves on selling records at a fair price and in being known for the bands and ideals they embraced as opposed to the amount of kids they screwed over. Fanzines stopped asking the same questions and started to take on a more expansive role in talking about the climate of the scene and how we related to the world we all lived in. What was occurring was the polar opposite of the scene it followed and it felt exhilarating.

Personally, the best part about this era of the hardcore scene is that diversity of the bands, venues, labels, and fanzines was encouraged and embraced. I remember one particular show in Washington, D.C. with Shelter, Rorschach, 108, Assuck, and Lincoln as this show, to me, represented the antithesis of the scene that had now developed. No matter the bill at any given show you always knew everyone who attended would say what they wanted to say and many times, like this particular show in Washington, D.C., the bands would have messages that were practically diametrically opposed to one another and although disagreements were many it didn't result in people being intimidated; rather, the tensions seemed to further encourage people to speak out, to be themselves, and to push one another to be accountable for what we said and how we treated others.

Brian has taken on the unenviable task of writing *Burning Fight: The Nineties Hardcore Revolution in Ethics, Politics, Spirit, and Sound*, which covers many of the bands and debates from this era. To be perfectly honest I don't know that anyone could capture the feelings and urgency of this time. For every band represented here, another is missed; and for every remembrance recorded, a dozen more are lost. Still, this book stands as a document of a special time in the hardcore scene. Like the scenes both before and after it, what made it special is also what led to its demise. In the case of this era things became so calculated politically, socially, and even musically that many of its entities were ultimately suffocated by their own sense of politics, ethics, and sound. Still, it was a unique time in hardcore and punk history that is worthy of several books to celebrate, remember, and appreciate a special era in our scene.

If this book says anything it is that the scene is what we make it. Our desire to evolve, to express our heart and soul, to make our history what we want it to be, and disregard all that stands in our way is the life's blood of hardcore/punk. The nineties were no more important than the seventies, eighties, or what's to come. Every era has its story, the things that make it unique, and it is only because of these differences and the evolution from one era to another that there is still a hardcore/punk scene to speak of. So here's to a special time and all of the people who played such important roles in it and, more importantly, here's to a scene that is as vital today as it ever has been or will be.

Robert Fish
December 16, 2008
Ressurection, 108, and The Judas Factor

INTRODUCTION

Although there are different definitions of hardcore, most people agree that it's a loud, intense, and often abrasive form of music that usually contains personal or political lyrics and a rejection of the status quo. Its roots come from punk rock, an underground musical and cultural movement that started in the late seventies, but hardcore became its own sub-genre as the music was often faster and more extreme than much of the early punk was.

Like any music-based subculture, hardcore is also more than just a sound. It's a community, a feeling, a way of life. Here are a few perspectives on what hardcore means:

LIFETIME

VIC DICARA (108, INSIDE OUT, BEYOND): Defining hardcore is like defining falling in love — definitions really miss the point. You don't need a definition to know if you're in love or not — you just *know* it. You just feel real hardcore when you experience it.

RYAN MURPHY (UNDERTOW): Hardcore is first and foremost a form of music. That is to say that there are hardcore bands out there that have nothing at all to say, and there are others that have more to say than music to play. Additionally, I believe that there are more components to hardcore other than the music.

KATE REDDY (108, KRSNAGRRRL FANZINE): I wasn't attracted to radio music; it just didn't ring with any sort of authenticity. But I loved that you could go to a hardcore show and it was kids running it. I felt like such a part of the music that was actually happening.

AARON TURNER (HYDRAHEAD RECORDS, ISIS): For me, hardcore is more about spirit or a set of ethics than it is a sound. Black Flag is an obvious example of what I think the roots of hardcore are and the perfect example of what it has been about in terms of how I've run Hydrahead Records. But Black Flag evolved quite a bit. At every point in their career they basically said "fuck you" not only to the critics but even to their fans a bit. They always did what they wanted to and didn't play by anyone else's rules. One of the best things about hardcore is that it has kind of a free spirit, which has brought about a variety of amazing music sounds and lyrical ideas.

CONVERGE

TAYLOR STEELE (FOUR WALLS FALLING): Hardcore is a release of aggression through music. It's based on what motivates you to not do the "normal" thing with music. Whether you're talking about straight edge, political hardcore, or even the "tough guy" attitude, it's about some type of some emotional release that is prompting you to play that type of music. It's a community, as well. There are different sub-communities within that one broad community, but they all intersect in one way or another.

TIM SINGER (DEADGUY, KISS IT GOODBYE, NO ESCAPE, BOILING POINT FANZINE): Here's this entirely independent music. We didn't need MTV or radio or glossy magazines. You put on your own shows, make your own records, take your own pictures. That's an amazingly empowering environment. A lot of people [who] grew up in that D.I.Y. culture took that attitude with them to their lives outside the scene.

AARON BURGESS (WRITER): To me, hardcore equals iconoclasm; it means I'm not playing by anyone's rules but my own (and, sort of ironically, by those of the people who come to identify with me); and it means I'm not making my musical or social/political/moral statement because this subculture or that activist or some other scene figurehead dictates it's the way you do things. At the same time, it's a complex way of living, behaving and creating that, even at its most iconoclastic, has its own very specific set of rules. To get even more out-there with this definition, hardcore is to people like me what Zen is to Buddhists; it's an anti-system piece of a larger systemic puzzle that affords people like me enough freedom to discover themselves within its very loose boundaries. At the same time, it provides a very clear path toward what I guess you'd call "enlightenment," in that you exit "the scene" totally aware of who you are, while at the same time never really being able to exit the scene. I'm not there yet, but I feel more comfortable of my own relationship to hardcore at age 32 than I ever have.

IAN MACKAYE (MINOR THREAT, EMBRACE, FUGAZI, DISCHORD RECORDS): The word hardcore is ambiguous. I don't think it has a single definition. Sometimes it can be a divisive term; sometimes it can be very complimentary. Historically speaking, in 1979 and 1980 when I first got into punk rock, there were two basic definitions: there were "new wave" people and punk rock people. We definitely did not want to be considered new wave because it was this party kind of thing. But the problem with the word punk rock, even though it was something we connected with, at that time the way the media had treated the Sex Pistols the word came off as this nihilistic and very fashion oriented, self-destructive, Sid Vicious kind of image. We didn't see ourselves like that at all. It's funny because you can see these kinds of stereotypes that really played out. The other day I was looking at this new, glossy "punk rock" magazine and the people in the magazine had a certain style to them; it was as if some point *People Magazine* back in the seventies declared "This is punk," and that has become the template visually for people. So, we didn't want to be new wave and we were into punk but didn't want to be called "punk rock." We opted for the term hardcore punk. Our idea was that we were kids and we were serious about our music and our scene and we were really into powerful, fast music, so we definitely saw ourselves as being super hardcore. We were hardcore punks. Right around this time D.O.A. came out with a record called *Hardcore '81* and around the country people began to refer to themselves as hardcore punks. So, at some point the word punk got clipped off and it just became hardcore.

In the late seventies and early eighties, bands like Minor Threat, Bad Brains, Black Flag, Necros, Circle Jerks, 7 Seconds, S.S.D., D.O.A., M.D.C., Dead Kennedys, Negative Approach, Agnostic Front, and many other hardcore groups cranked up their amps and helped create an intense new form of music. For many hardcore bands, song structures were straightforward, almost always extremely fast, and devoid of solos. For a lot of people, these factors were seen as essential for punk and hardcore because they rejected the artistic pretensions of mainstream rock and the less complicated songs made playing in a band more accessible. This fast, raw simplicity repelled adults and more mainstream-minded kids who worshipped the carefully assembled structures of commercial rock.

A related aspect of hardcore was a do-it-yourself (D.I.Y.) ethos. This idea came about partly by necessity and partly from the desire for independence from outside influence. The idea was that people in the

WORLDS COLLIDE

scene should do their own bands, write their own zines, and put out their own records without the involvement of "big business" (for more about this topic see Chapter One: "Politics and Social Awareness").

The content of the lyrics has always been equal in importance to the aggressive music style in hardcore. Hardcore kids (a term that has more to do with being a part of the scene than your actual age) were able to voice their opinions in a public forum whether it was on stage or in the pages of a fanzine. Consequently, if you felt out of sync with mainstream society you could likely find acceptance in the scene. That formed the basis of a feeling of community, which is a key component of hardcore.

ROB PENNINGTON (ENDPOINT, BY THE GRACE OF GOD, BLACK CROSS): I was intensely unhappy during my teenage life. I didn't feel like I fit in during high school. I got into heavy metal in middle school, which was kind of my first rebellion. [laughs] Then I had a friend who had gotten into punk and he started turning me on to music. I started delivering papers with this guy and we started talking philosophy and bigger issues and at the same time I was transitioning out of heavy metal music and into this music that seemed to address certain issues with me. The kids in this scene accepted me for who I was, and I just felt drawn to it. I wanted to fit in so badly as a little kid and here was a group of people I felt I belonged with. I met a group of people who needed each other — the music came second. Maybe that's why I've been able to maintain interest in it for so long. It's still cathartic and a place to express what I can feel.

QUICKSAND

PETE WENTZ (BIRTHRIGHT, EXTINCTION, RACETRAITOR, ARMA ANGELUS, FALL OUT BOY): The people in the bands would hang out and you had these interpersonal relationships. It was a family type of thing. You're this disenfranchised person and you find these communities and they start telling you, "These are the reasons you are feeling disenfranchised" and there is solidarity. And that's what lured me in — I felt like I found a place for myself.

JASON ROE (KILL THE ROBOT FANZINE): Young people in hardcore were doing their own thing. No one told us we had to do this or that. We decided what hardcore was and what it would be. The best part was that there wasn't some executive trying to tell us who we were and that we had to buy this product. There was an amazing pureness to hardcore. The anger and the attitude helped, as well. Being able to express the rage I felt was great — anger at society, anger at my own shortcomings. Anger at everything!

JOHN "PORCELL" PORCELLY (YOUTH OF TODAY, JUDGE, PROJECT X, SHELTER): When I first got into hardcore it was such a small underground thing. You had bands like Dead Kennedys that wrote lyrics that really blew my mind and changed my life. They introduced ideas to me that from my suburban house in Westchester I would probably never have heard otherwise. That band made me really question things I had never even thought of before.

BRENDAN DESMET (GROUNDWORK, ABSINTHE): Most of us were looking for something to identify with — people, ideas, fashions. There were a lot of nasty things happening in the world at the time, so it was somewhat easy for me to be drawn toward music that was angry. I also wasn't really happy with my home life, so getting into the escapism that hardcore offered was attractive, too.

SEAN CAPONE (POSITRON FANZINE): I was turned on to punk in the eighties through movies like *Repo Man, Suburbia*, and, uh, *Return of the Living Dead*. [laughs] Where I lived in suburban Texas didn't offer a lot of windows to the outside culture, so I dressed and acted like a poseur until I started meeting other kids who did zines, had better record collections, and knew about the local scene. My friend took me to my first show in Dallas — Bad Brains *I Against I* tour, can you imagine?! — where I got the crap kicked out of me by skinheads my first time in the pit. It was the most fun and intense thing I ever experienced, so I was hooked. Also, it was obvious to me that punk and hardcore were tools that could allow me to be a creative, expressive, and hopefully smarter and more self-defined individual.

MIKE KIRSCH (FUEL, TORCHES TO ROME, BREAD AND CIRCUITS): There weren't a lot of ways I knew to express myself at a young age that felt very good — hardcore was something that felt a bit better than the rest. We had something to say and we found a way to say it. It wasn't a question of whether we wanted to do it or not — we *had* to do it.

SCOTT BEIBIN (BLOODLINK RECORDS): At one point I thought hardcore was pretty dumb. [laughs] I was already straight edge and vegan but turned off by the macho, alpha-male thing that was going on. I went to shows at The Anthrax in the late eighties and it was kind of hard to fit in. Then something happened, I'm not sure exactly what it was but I ended up shaving my head and I was already involved with animal rights and Amnesty International stuff — I was a big fan of the Weather Underground and the Yippees. The positivity was what really clicked with me — the idea that we could do anything if we put our minds to it was liberating. There really are glass ceilings. Not everyone can achieve everything they want to because of racism and classism, so the positivity might have been a bit naïve, but I wanted to dive into that naivety and not feel like a total jaded asshole. I put aside a lot of my own prejudgments about people. The music took a while to grow on me. But to me the most interesting thing about the scene wasn't the music; it was the personalities of the people involved. Hardcore attracts extreme personalities.

SNAPCASE

FREDDY CRICIEN (MADBALL): Hardcore was always a tight knit family. Going back to my first experiences as a little kid going into the city and hanging out with my brother [Roger Miret, vocalist for Agnostic Front]. I got to meet all these different characters from the New York hardcore scene. These guys were literally living in the streets and squats on the Lower East Side. That was my first dose of the lifestyle before the music aspect. I went to a club to see my brother's band Agnostic Front play in 1987 when I was really young. It was pretty crazy, but everyone knew each other. Everyone was a rebel in some way and that's where everyone related. It was like a family. People were into rebelling against society in the early days, and there were some issues going on at home for a lot of kids. People didn't want to conform. It was the punk mentality, but instead of Mohawks they were shaving their heads.

DANIEL TRAITOR (RACETRAITOR, ARMA ANGELUS): I went to my first couple of shows and it was so amazing! It seemed really romantic, like a scene from a movie — you go into some club, you're like 16, everyone else seems older, cooler, tougher. Going to a hardcore show was so cool because that was around the time of the first Gulf War. I remember seeing Billingsgate and they played this song called "Not My Blood," and I remember realizing that the song made a lot of sense — just hearing I'm not going to die for somebody's oil company, and coming from a family of coalminers. I was like, "Yeah, *fuck* that!" So, the anger, the aggressive music, that was somehow a positive alternative at the same time. It felt like enlightenment. [laughs] It allowed me a new place to be myself.

DAVID MOORE (SPLIT LIP/CHAMBERLAIN): Well, early on at least, I don't know that I had any concept of a "scene" or "movement" — not in any codified sense. The movement in those days was nebulous like a whisper — clusters of young people like me who were searching for an antidote to the world that we had inherited. Like any other movement, it was spawned from a need to heal the collective wounds we had been born into. Personally, my first leanings toward the counterculture came through my desire to be an artist and a writer and to surround myself with like-minded wildly creative individuals. It just so happened for me those people all had a common thread that held them together and that thread was music. I was drawn to others who were searching to make sense of their interior and exterior world through the paramount power of creativity. It wasn't until later that I realized we were all part of something larger and more complex.

ROBERT FISH (108, RESSURECTION, THE JUDAS FACTOR): To me what separated hardcore from most other genres was that it has very little to do with music. The way I see it is that what made a hardcore band or record great was not the music alone. It was a combination of the music, the time, the people, and most importantly the investment that both the bands and the listener invested in every chord, song, and show. Political and social issues play a tremendous role, if not an absolutely critical role, in the foundation of hardcore. Not necessarily that all bands spoke or need to speak specifically about political and/or social issues but there has to be that reference point to qualify as punk or hardcore music.

Many hardcore bands in the early to mid-eighties spread a message about personal or social injustices. Groups like Dead Kennedys, Minor Threat, 7 Seconds, Youth Brigade, Articles of Faith and many others addressed issues like abuse of government power, consumerism, and a general rejection of mainstream society. Not every band sang about the same issues, but their anger and desire for change was shared and proved to be contagious. Fans connected with this and channeled it into their lives, many of them picking up instruments and starting bands of their own.

BRENDAN DESMET: People in the hardcore scene were often folks who were looking for something completely different than the norm. For instance, dying your hair, going vegetarian, or listening to shrill music that seems so contrary to the mainstream pushes people's comfort level. Hardcore is an opportunity to satisfy their needs to live a life outside the lines of what is considered normal. For the most part hardcore turned people's minds on to other issues that stuck with them long after their interest in the music itself.

GAVIN FREDERICK (STICKFIGURE RECORDS/DISTRO): I think [caring about broader issues] had to do with perceptions of what punk/hardcore meant to a lot of us. And that meant using music to help change the world for the better. The idea was that music is a great way to spread a message about important issues, whether those were personal, political, social, or otherwise.

JEN ANGEL (FUCKTOOTH FANZINE, CLAMOR MAGAZINE): Like many people, I was politicized by punk and hardcore. I just realized the other day that what led me to the people and the music in the first place was my attempts to distinguish myself from my family and community, and some of the first people I interacted with that helped me establish my own identity were punks. I didn't like the first music I heard, but some of the music, like Minor Threat and Fugazi, I was really drawn to, and they were definitely political. So, in part, I think that early political bands helped set the tone, and also once I was engaged and conscious of this political world, I felt that others in the scene were as well and I could talk with them. It was a real community in the sense of shared values/ideals, and I definitely didn't feel that from my family or school. I got into writing and reading zines around the same time, and I would put as much importance on them as on bands in developing my political awareness. The impact that both had on me were that I felt that I was empowered to become a more active person, to speak and define my own voice, and that my ideas and opinions were valuable. This was not being encouraged elsewhere in my life, and it definitely set me on a path to being politically active and outspoken the way I am today. I am still involved in punk and in activism.

SCOTTY NIEMET (MORE THAN MUSIC FESTIVAL): Growing up in the Reagan/Bush era, most of us came of age piecing together and seeing the effects of a government ran into the ground by trickle down economics, the rise of the Christian right, and by the end of my high school career the U.S. in war. I grew up in a working class family. I still remember the day my dad came home to tell my mom he was laid off. I had never seen my father cry before. My early attraction to punk and hardcore had me questioning things by the age of 12. Sitting in my room listening to and reading the lyrics of Dead Kennedys, staying up 'til two a.m. on Sunday nights watching *120 Minutes* on MTV taking it all in, skating a launch ramp with "I saw your mommy and your mommy's dead" blaring from the garage.

DUNCAN BARLOW (ENDPOINT, GUILT, BY THE GRACE OF GOD): Rites of Spring made it okay for me to cry. Teen Idles made it okay for me to stay sober. Black Flag made it okay for me to be angry. Youth of Today made it okay for me to be vegetarian. Bad Religion made it okay for me to think critically. Void made noise beautiful. I could go on forever.

Hardcore's originators were dealing with the world of Reaganomics, fear of nuclear war, increasing class and racial divisions, in addition to personal problems like harassment from parents, jocks, or rednecks. Many in the scene addressed these and other issues

through music, zines, and discussion. Bands like Dead Kennedys, M.D.C., and Bad Religion created a dialogue about political resistance and social revolution that continues to the present. Sometimes sub-groupings within hardcore also developed as a reaction to problems they saw within society that also were present in the scene. Straight edge, a belief that advocated a rejection of alcohol and drugs, started as an idea that D.C. bands like Minor Threat wrote about and grew to become a mass-scale movement in the years that followed (for more about that see Chapter Two: "Straight Edge"). There were other movements as well including a fairly politically conscious crust punk/hardcore scene that was centered around anarchist principles. Many involved in this part of the scene lived in and supported squatted housing and were inspired by early British anarcho-punk bands like Crass and Conflict.

THE LOCUST

Eventually the first wave of hardcore gave way to a second one. Some people took hardcore in new directions musically whether it was through changing their bands' sound or by forming new bands altogether. Along with these new musical influences and directions, new ideas were also presented through lyrics and conversations at shows. Dozens of bands like Husker Du, the Meat Puppets, and the Butthole Surfers formed and migrated or broke away from conventional hardcore sounds despite being associated with the scene in some way. Other bands kept the idea of hardcore evolving by incrementally adding elements to the music including many that added a slightly more metallic edge to their sound. By the mid eighties another group of bands like Uniform Choice, Youth of Today, and Justice League formed and attempted to keep traditional hardcore sounds alive, but they also added other musical and lyrical elements either consciously or unconsciously. These, of course, were just a few of the diverse range of bands that existed in the scene at this time.

As the eighties progressed, hardcore continued to diversify in sound as many veterans of the scene gave birth to new projects similar in intensity yet strikingly different in atmosphere and approach. The D.C. scene in the mid to late-eighties is the most prominent example of this trend. It ushered a more philosophically divergent brand of hardcore and post-hardcore by way of the melodic yet often dissonant sounds of Rites of Spring, Embrace, Dag Nasty, and Nation of Ulysses, among others. These bands and other scene members directed scathing social critiques at the hardcore scene itself, as well as society at large. Unsurprisingly, these attitudes and ideas prompted a strong reaction from hardcore traditionalists, but they also became popular and had a wide and lasting impact on what direction the scene was headed as the nineties approached. This intentional restructuring of the underground in D.C. was itself a reaction to the levels of violence, turmoil, and predictability that had, as they saw it, plagued hardcore.

KENT MCCLARD (HEARTATTACK FANZINE, EBULLITION RECORDS): Initially, hardcore was about this crazy anger and then around 1986 it just kind of got dull for a time. That outward anger wasn't working as well. It was about 1988 where you saw this resurgence in hardcore and it had a lot to do with straight edge. It was about looking back and trying to figure out how we were going to define ourselves. We weren't just going to thrive on anger and hate. We were going to concentrate more on what we were doing. The D.C. hardcore scene of the mid to late eighties was extremely important in that bands like Embrace and Rites of Spring were attempting to redefine that anger which fueled the hardcore of the early eighties and make it more about effecting change both within and in a person's community. Also, the whole straight edge scene you associate with Youth of Today and Judge and bands like that definitely had a political mindset. A lot of the people in those bands had been around in the early eighties and were looking to implement changes and make it more of a progressive movement.

Ideas that become widely accepted in hardcore usually provoke re-evaluation at some point. Straight edge was one example. It had become one of the largest movements within hardcore toward the end of the eighties, but as that decade came to a close, the number of those who championed straight edge messages began to falter. Many distanced themselves from the term whether or not they continued to believe in the idea, as they felt it was too limiting a label to live their lives by or felt that the idea had become associated with a movement they weren't comfortable with. Similarly, a lot of bands — the majority of their members were still in their late teens or early-twenties — felt confined by others' definition of hardcore, and wanted to construct bridges to alternate musical and social landscapes.

HEROIN

second nature

number one

These and other factors led to some changes in the scene as the nineties arrived.

MARTIN SORRONDEGUY (LOS CRUDOS, LENGUA ARMADA RECORDS, LIMP WRIST): By the late eighties and early nineties a lot of the older people just left, or died or were junked up. In Chicago, for instance, the scene changed. People were trying to separate from the older scene to create something different. Musically things went all over the place into sub-genres where in the past everything was all under one roof. In the past you didn't have a separate youth crew scene or a fast hardcore scene, it was just all in one place because everyone gathered there. But things had grown so big that people were able to branch off and do their own thing.

MICKEY NOLAN (SHOW PROMOTER, WRITER): Hardcore is a pretty finite thing in that there are only a few characteristics that define it. There are few allowed deviations before you become something that isn't hardcore. You have this really narrow definition of what this hardcore is and what it means, yet people evolve so the nineties were different than the eighties because you had people trying to come up with something different under those somewhat rigid parameters. If you wanted to play hardcore music then you had to expand the subject matter.

CURTIS MEAD (SPLIT LIP/CHAMBERLAIN): I think the late eighties was the developing period of hardcore and where punk turned into hardcore. It was just figuring itself out. The nineties found people pushing boundaries and the whole thing was still growing. There were also more people involved, which brought about more influences.

Social, spiritual, and political upheaval played a primary role in development of the nineties hardcore scene. A variety of philosophies had been sung, written, and talked about since hardcore's inception, yet the nineties would put such an emphasis on lyrical content, activism, and D.I.Y. ethics, as well as sonic dynamics, that hardcore would be irrevocably altered.

Whether it was the animal rights movement, the re-emergence of straight edge, the fresh sonic excursions pioneered by a wide variety of bands, social-political debates, emotional catharsis, or spiritually rooted lyrics, these various ideas and artistic concerns, as well as the dialogue elicited by them, were the life's blood of the nineties scene.

DESPAIR

SCOTT BEIBIN: In issue 89 or 90 of *Maximum Rock N Roll* it featured every tendency that was going to be in hardcore for the nineties. It was the issue when Ray Cappo came back from India and was interviewed. This issue had letters that had Sam McPheeters and Sick of it All debating, there were letters from Sean Vegan Reich in there, there was an ad for the Sleeping Body tour, there was a review of the Downcast record, Norman Brannon had a letter in there. So there were all these things happening and you can look at this issue and see the direction where everything was going to go from that point on. Keep in mind what had happened at this point was kids weren't as interested in going to CBGB's shows anymore because it was too violent — it was overrun with skinheads and there was that whole tough guy scene going on.

KIM NOLAN (BARK AND GRASS FANZINE, CHICKS UP FRONT): To me, the nineties look more like a progression from the late-eighties as the audiences grew and the interactions of that created and integrated new influences: musically as people explored or brought in new styles — like metal and grindcore, and hip-hop — and let's face it, learned to play better, politically, as we pushed each other on racism, sexism and class, and culturally as the influences included outside frames like Krishna and veganism. These to me are indicative of growth and evolution of the earlier expressions, not necessarily marks of a new form entirely.

SCOTTY NIEMET: We seemed to be in a limbo by the time Clinton came to office, all of our youth crew icons were selling out and doing "post hardcore." We had a Democratic president, but things around us were still pretty fucked up. New York hardcore bands were playing huge shows with metal bands...the early nineties were leaving us kind of without an identity. But with me hearing bands like Downcast, Born Against, and Struggle, I realized my frustration with the limbo had a voice again. I was motivated to take on politics because it was always in me. It's what I always felt punk and hardcore were supposed to be about. And here was a growing voice of others saying, "Hey, we need to take on these political views, things we feel affect us on a personal level. Things we can approach and actively apply to our everyday lives to make an immediate change for the better."

MIKE KIRSCH: I started to see, as the nineties came around, that it was true that when a handful of freaks and weirdos put a lot of energy into something they can turn it into something that has a massive influence on popular culture. Hardcore was a resistance to capitalism and the mechanisms of capitalism. What you started to see was that it was getting bigger and was still threatening in some ways, but bands were starting to get signed to major labels and the culture was being pulled out from under it in some ways. When something like hardcore gets big it changes the whole culture around shows and you start to see this process by which stuff is deteriorating and this thing that was once so small you start to see its influence everywhere. Many of the people and places I sought refuge from in the first place were starting to claim it as their own. To me, hardcore was a reaction to that. People realized it was going to take more than political slogans to really change stuff; it's going to take long term commitment. And with that it's like we have to go deeper underground — we have to take the stuff that matters about this and make it more relevant and more threatening and more on fire and part of who we are. We have to take the elements that feel authentic to us and not worry about the rest of the shit that's going on.

CHRIS BOARTS-LARSON (SLUG AND LETTUCE FANZINE): It was a formative time for me. I was living in New York City, was in art school, and was heavily involved in the hardcore/punk scene, and for me the slant was on the anarcho-punk side of things, so, yes, politics was huge. I was exposed to a lot of city politics, the politics of housing and squatting in particular. That was a very unique time for the Lower East Side. I was also photographing the city, the streets, the punks, the squats, and the general urban decay. The entire atmosphere politicized me. There was a huge housing crisis and homeless problem and Tompkins Square Park was at the center of that with a tent city and soap boxing orators on a regular basis. Then there was the first Iraq War and a surge of resistance and protest surrounding that. Being involved in a politicized community also opened up information to many topics and various struggles both local and international.

ADAM NATHANSON (BORN AGAINST, YOUNG PIONEERS): [Born Against was antagonistic] because we were emotionally charged up people not entirely focused on the "real enemy" or who the true creators of problems were. We'd focus on other bands and how they did their bands, which was not the real problem. The war in Central America was still raging on at the time with U.S. advisors and dollars and lots of people were being killed with U.S. equipment and training, which are things much more worth being outraged about. So, there was some misguided outrage in our demeanor. That said, I hope we made some sort of an impact. We took our cues from other people in music we thought were really smart who put together some good music. Bands like M.D.C. and Conflict opened up our eyes to be able to understand why things were so fucked up in the world. That's where that influence for wanting to have some sort of message or to ruffle some feathers comes from. Being political that way in our music was an outgrowth of that. Also we were trying to conduct ourselves in the scene the most ethical way possible, and so we took inspiration from things that Dischord Records were doing. All in all, because we were inspired by these amazing bands and people, we felt it necessary to try and do the same.

GREG BENNICK (TRIAL): We saw the same thing happen in the eighties. Reagan was in office and two things happened: punks got really politicized and punks started drinking more heavily and gave up. There were more bands than ever singing about political issues and more bands than ever who didn't seem to care at all. The nineties saw resurgence in this split, but with different social influences as the cause; for instance, bands signing to bigger labels and looking for bigger audiences led people to want to oppose that or fully support it. Lots of bands had signed to bigger labels before such as Bad Brains, Youth of Today and others signed to labels like Caroline, but until Nirvana, Rage Against the Machine and Quicksand, the major label thing was a bit out of the question. Once those floodgates were opened, people on both sides of the debate pushed for what they believed in. It was great! D.I.Y. was never stronger, and for those influenced by that mode of thinking, there were lots of people to share ideas and strategies with.

DUNCAN BARLOW: I think the biggest difference between the eighties and the early nineties was the influx of female voices. The eighties were pretty much a boys' club. Granted I loved many of the bands, but there was a serious lack of female involvement, which proved to be very problematic as it didn't create a necessary dialogue that was desperately needed in the scene. I was sixteen when I first played a show with Fugazi; Ian MacKaye gave an amazing introduction to their song "Suggestion" where he directly confronted the threat of the male gaze on women. Several old scene guys heckled him and Ian turned on them and confronted them, as he always does so aptly, on their

masculinity. I had never seen anything quite like it. Rob Pennington, the singer of Endpoint, was entirely shaped in certain political ideals by that moment. I could see the change in his eyes; it was outstanding. In the early nineties we started seeing more groups confront masculinity and we saw bands, zines, and political movements like the Chicks-Up-Front Posse develop around the Midwest and East Coast.

AARON BURGESS: If I had to pinpoint one event that dramatically separated [hardcore] bands [of the eighties and nineties], I'd point to the widespread information explosion, mostly via the Internet, that shrank the gap between bands of the new school and bands of the old; and even this wasn't an overnight event — in fact, it's still ongoing. After a while, the old regional differences between bands and scenes started breaking down, to the point where being a "New York hardcore band" or a "Boston hardcore band" or a "Chicago hardcore band" or a "Washington, D.C., hardcore band" simply meant you came from that area; it didn't really signify any of the old ideas people used to associate with those scenes; you know, where bands from a certain area would have their own musical "dialect" or worldview, or other sorts of cultural/social rituals or traits that were theirs exclusively.

KEN OLDEN (WORLDS COLLIDE): The biggest difference was the continued divisions in the scene. In the eighties things were younger, fresher and the shows had a mixed crowd. The bands were mixed too — you'd have punk, hardcore, skinhead, sometimes metal bands and fans all coming together. Things got a little violent at times, but mostly kids were there just to enjoy themselves. In the eighties you had arguably a bigger exchange of ideas because kids were exposed to different ideas, different types of people. As we got into the nineties, the scenes started to split up. And musically there were lots of changes: hardcore music began to be more and more influenced by metal and emo styles.

A lot of people in the nineties scene came to have extremely radical views on topics like animal rights, gender, D.I.Y., race, spirituality, and many other subjects. These ideas were around in the eighties, but many people became even more focused on them in the nineties.

In fact, some people began to feel that others were too extreme in their views on these issues. Militancy played a role in all of these debates, which led to arguments that the scene had become overly judgmental.

SEVAPRIYA BARRIER: I think the most important debate was whether you could drink caffeine and still be straight edge. No, really, that's what I think, because it highlighted how really out of control people's sense of self importance was, how much they felt entitled to judge others and how impactful they saw their every action.

JOE EPSTEIN (WRITER): Music in general was far more political in the nineties. Art wasn't driving politics, though. It was rhetoric overload. If you compound that with the requirements of being a hardline, straight edge, vegan, Krishna then you get people wondering, "Why can't I just go to a barbecue?" [laughs] At some point it became too cumbersome for many. "I don't need to save the world with this shoe purchase decision — can't I just vote?"

DANIEL TRAITOR: The nineties straight edge scene contained a lot of militancy, which in retrospect maybe wasn't good on one level, where people were condemning others for their lifestyle, instead of trying to embrace them into a new lifestyle, or supporting them through hard times. I don't think it helps to condemn and alienate people from anything. And that was kind of the tone a lot of the time in the nineties.

JOHN HENRY WEST

NORMAN BRANNON (TEXAS IS THE REASON, ANTI-MATTER FANZINE, SHELTER, RESSURECTION): Hardcore is a youth movement and young people do and say stupid shit. We were all taking ourselves way too seriously. The nineties were weird because it was like someone flipped a switch and there was no middle ground. You were either Vegan Reich or you were Born Against. [laughs] The dichotomy was so broad.

For those who took to these issues, the political and ethical focus in the nineties hardcore scene was vital. A lot of people, in fact, pursued these ideas outside the scene and made them their life's work. However, as the late nineties came around the number and intensity of debates that were once wholly integrated into the scene had diminished. One major factor for this occurrence was that many who promulgated much of the dialogue took their ideas into areas outside the scene. Others blamed the heated and sometimes divisive discussions for pushing people away from the more political and substantive aspects of hardcore.

By the end of the nineties, and into the next decade, corporate interests also took a greater hold. Business has played some sort of a role in hardcore and punk even from the beginning. However, the nineties saw this relationship becoming even stronger, which alarmed many who were dedicated to the idea of hardcore remaining a completely underground scene. They worried that the scene's authenticity and political credibility could be undermined by these outside interests and the bands that worked with them.

MOE MITCHELL (CIPHER): In the mid-nineties, hardcore bands would not get accepted if it seemed like they were trying to sell out and be too marketable. Now that's not exactly a big issue. Even if a band wasn't overtly political, their process was intentionally counter-cultural. So, even if your band didn't take political positions, what you were doing was a political act in itself — making your own show flyers, pressing and recording your own records, doing your own design, writing, distributing, and marketing your own music. All this stuff is autonomous, collective economics. The hardcore scene was and in some ways still is about building viable alternatives to mainstream institutions.

KIM NOLAN: Bands were politically outspoken in the nineties because they still could be. People used music as a medium to express what they were thinking about and they found people to be mostly receptive. Around 1995, punk and hardcore bands began to sign to major labels, and that in itself was a big debate. Then some hardcore kids got picked to do A&R at some majors, and suddenly we were inside the music business, and the industry was interested in us. I'm not going to say that that's not something that people who have spent their lives making music and only want to get paid to do it forever should not go for that. But it will be controlled by other factors rather than what the music is, like will it sell? And can it be carried by major stores? And what does it have to look like so that will happen? One good example is that Racetraitor can't have a record called *Burn the Idol of the White Messiah* and expect to be on Sony Records, they just wouldn't sell it, or Vegan Reich for that matter, but Andy [Hurley] and Pete [Wentz] can get rid of the political content and then get a record and Hot Topic merch deal with Fall Out Boy. Which I guess is okay if that is what they want, but it explicitly means it can't be political. That's the trade off.

SCOTT VOGEL (TERROR, BURIED ALIVE, DESPAIR, SLUGFEST): I could care less if someone downloads my band's music, but no one makes a fucking lyric sheet anymore, which to me is killing what hardcore is! Half the meaning of hardcore to me is reading the lyrics, seeing what the band had to say, the artwork — the whole package needs to be there! Now when you get a record there's nothing to it but sound, and hardcore is more than just a sound.

TODD GULLION (TIME IN MALTA, ICE 9): I really think it's the infusion of capital that changed hardcore in the nineties. All of a sudden labels like Victory and Revelation were creating an international stage for some pretty fantastic and controversial bands, out of just the simple fact of selling tons of records. After this initial "explosion" of the rebirth of hardcore, it seemed to stem a slew of original projects that I will always be deeply affected by. But with all breakthroughs of genius or imagination in history, deterioration follows. Through advertising and institutionalized example, the new generation has been trained to consume and regurgitate this "morphed" and "safer" version ad infinitum.

RYAN MURPHY: When I first started going to shows, hardcore was really "ours" and we protected it. We didn't have to worry about sharing it with the outside world because they wanted no part of it. Now we see hardcore bands on Warped Tour or on Headbanger's Ball and it's like the outside world has tapped into our form of music and we have to share it now. But for the most part, they will never "get it." Hardcore was always about doing things yourself. The D.I.Y. ethic was a huge part of hardcore for me. We didn't need MTV to play *our* music, and we didn't need Warped Tour to help gain acceptance by the mainstream. Hardcore was all of the above; an ethic, an ideal, a feeling, a way of life, all rolled into a form of music, but most importantly we felt like we owned it.

JOHN "PORCELL" PORCELLY: A lot of bands cater to the lowest common denominator to become popular. If you look at what is popular in America — McDonalds, strip malls — I have always been against all that. Now you can play punk or hardcore and get big as long as you don't take a stand on anything. You can play this really sugar coated, loud-guitar punk and be huge. I've always hated stuff that tried to be popular because it caters to people who don't think and don't question and who are led through life by what the media tells them.

JACOB BANNON (CONVERGE): In some ways we are better off without the agendas. Although it was hard to co-exist, it was nice to know your enemy, now they are harder to spot. Bands have cashed in their religion and spirituality for more commercial accessibility. Their motivation is still there, it's just no longer public. The communication is there, but people aren't saying anything anymore.

INK&DAGGER/HATEBREED/BREAD&CIRCUITS

Although the prominence of politics and ethics in hardcore appeared to wane, they of course did not totally disappear. As with every era in hardcore, new generations react to the old. In the process, new issues that arise from the current times are explored. But no matter what new directions the scene heads, it will also likely be influenced by what transpired in the past.

ROBERT FISH: I don't necessarily believe that hardcore is any less political or socially relevant today than it was in years past. The sound and the different fashions may be very popular these days, but I always believed that punk rock was just more than those surface level notions. It may be harder to find and identify amongst the thousands of shitty rock bands that look or sound "punk," but it still lives in many kids garages, recreation halls, and small clubs.

D.J. ROSE: You can't kill hardcore. People have really tried to exploit what we like in this culture. That doesn't mean it's over, though. It'll never be over unless you let it be over.

AARON BURGESS: It would be presumptuous to say D.I.Y. has disappeared from hardcore. I mean, people are still doing much of the work themselves; it's just that the type of work they're doing has changed immensely since Black Flag was running all over L.A. slapping up their own fliers with wheat paste. Today, to be "D.I.Y." could just as easily mean you've registered your band as an LLC; it's all in the mind of the individual. But many independent bands, label owners, booking agents, managers and club owners are all D.I.Y., in the sense that they're all independent business owners who are in some way connected to a larger system of independently owned and operated businesses, which collectively make up an industry that both operates outside of the music industry and mirrors a lot of the practices that have made people leery of having anything to do with the music industry.

VIC DICARA: Maybe it's changed for us, but I realized that if you really want to enjoy it you can't just sit in the back of the room, you've got to get right up near the stage. I remember seeing The Promise not too long ago and I was having a conversation about this topic with a friend of mine outside and that's exactly what I told them. But then I realized that I'm being a hypocrite because I'm telling them to do that and I'm standing outside the show myself. [laughs] So, I went inside and got right up on the stage. All of a sudden, I had this amazing time watching these dudes in The Promise just tear it up with at least as much fury and passion as anyone who ever tore it up! Hardcore is not really a musically sophisticated art form; it's not like you can just put it on at a low volume and appreciate it. That's not what it's about. The essence of it is the passion and how can you feel the passion if you're not actually a part of it? Maybe we think the hardcore scene has lost its soul because we're not as much a part of it as we used to be.

Hardcore is arguably more popular now than ever in terms of the sheer number of people involved in the scene. But even though it has become more accepted, the ideas and the feelings expressed in the scene affect people the most. The impact of the ideas behind the music has always been far more important to hardcore fans than the number of people who take part.

SPARKMARKER

GREG BENNICK: Hardcore is the ultimate combination of passion, intensity and energy. Find me another example that encompasses all of that and I will gladly jump on board. Music gets into your bones. It runs deep. I am surrounded by it constantly and it moves me all throughout every day. I find so much inspiration in hardcore and in music in general. I always have and I always will.

SCOTTY NIEMET: Seeing things in my eyes at age 35 by decisions I made at such a young age puts a grin on my face. I think we truly created a youth movement pure and full of heart. I will always be a hardcore kid. It's molded a mindset that I can't even really describe. It has made it difficult at times to relate to others my age. It has added a high value to questioning the world and not taking anything as truth. It has made for an independent man, a man who still cooks food out of Soy not Oi!

ROB MORAN (UNBROKEN): For me hardcore is an escape, education, and emotion. There is not sound that is "hardcore" in my opinion. To me, it is the feeling I get from reading lyrics, seeing a band live and knowing I am involved in something that people on the outside would never understand. I learned more with hardcore than I did in school. Labels like Three One G, Ebullition, and Bloodlink had something to say to me. P.E.T.A., Mumia Abu Jamal, corporate run government, and Rod Coronado, were all things I learned about by being involved with hardcore. Hardcore is a feeling, ethic, an ideal — it is what you make of it.

SCOTT BEIBIN: Hardcore is an idea. It's an idea that if you set your mind to something then you can achieve your goals. It's also the idea that you can work with other people to achieve your goals, too. For me it was a very positive state of being and it's something that helped me get through a really tough part of my life. It's too simplistic to say hardcore changed my life, but the rethinking of my position in society — which was prompted through hardcore — was the thing that did it for me.

MING FIGHT: THE NINETIES HARDCORE REVOLUTION IN ETHICS, POLITICS, AND

POLITICS AND SOCIAL AWARENESS

Revolutionary politics and anti-government ideas have played a fundamental role in hardcore and punk since their inception. In the late seventies, punk rock started as an iconoclastic cultural movement that rejected most mainstream beliefs and ideologies in a way that was often intentionally offensive. Punk's imagery was often meant to shock. Many punks dyed their hair, had body piercings, used lots of drugs, and generally spurned the norm. Punk rock music was also loud and aggressive, which was the opposite of much of the popular music of the time.

Hardcore was an offshoot of punk, though early hardcore scene members saw themselves as punks who rejected the more fashion-oriented "new wave" direction some people in the early punk scene gravitated toward. In response, hardcore became faster, more aggressive, and took even more uncompromising political stances. Regardless of the level of political or social awareness a band conveyed, nearly all made some sort of comment on politics or society at one time or another — otherwise it might be hard to define them as punk or hardcore in the first place. Early hardcore bands were often characterized by boldly speaking out against the Reagan/Thatcher era conservatism that was prevalent in the political and social climate of the time. Bands like Dead Kennedys, M.D.C., Articles of Faith, and many others wrote overtly political lyrics and encouraged scene members to take action against the culturally conservative atmosphere.

From the mid eighties into the nineties the political bent of bands varied widely. Instead of just a general rejection of mainstream culture, bands started to take on more alternative ideas. Eventually, various sub-scenes were formed that sometimes exclusively aligned themselves to political or ethical principles like straight edge, D.I.Y., anti-racism, animal rights and anarchism, though there was plenty of overlap among most of these. This differentiation of issues continued into the nineties as grassroots factions deepened their focus on these topics and continued to introduce new ones. Inspired by the revolutionary ideas present in previous eras, nineties bands like Born Against, Los Crudos, Spitboy, Go!, Downcast, Econochrist, Endpoint, Trial, Struggle, His Hero is Gone, Code 13, Drop Dead and zines like *HeartattaCk, Slug and Lettuce, Inside Front*, and *Profane Existence* were just a few of many that addressed such issues. The exposure to these different points of view and an overall broader cultural and political awareness that was present even in more mainstream circles in the nineties helped create a larger political consciousness in this era.

For many, the nineties cemented the notion that hardcore should be equated with substantive ideas.

KENT MCCLARD (HEARTATTACK FANZINE, EBULLITION RECORDS): Hardcore isn't about a musical style; it's about emotion and anger and hope and you can express those feelings in a variety of ways and not necessarily rely on traditional hardcore sounds.

ANTHONY PAPPALARDO (IN MY EYES): You're getting educated by a kid a year or two older than you. You read an article in a zine and there are no sources and it's pretty much, "Capitalism sucks." But that's really special when you're 16. The dudes in your class aren't thinking about that shit. They are eating a burger after school and driving around in their cool car. Even as primitive as it was, it was rad.

BRIAN DINGLEDINE (CATHARSIS, INSIDE FRONT): We inherited a punk/hardcore that had always touched on issues — maybe not "politically," but there was always talking between songs. I came into it from a sort of tough guy hardcore scene, but even there it was expected that bands would talk about how tough shit was. Everyone talked between songs, you know? And in the course of that talking, especially in a countercultural underground space with lots of room for experimentation, eventually people figured out a lot of things that were important to them.

MICHELLE (TODD) GONZALES (SPITBOY, INSTANT GIRL): Hardcore is about exchanging ideas and making people think about issues they hadn't thought of before. I was attracted to hardcore because you could find substantial pockets of people who cared about making a difference and changing society in a positive way.

JOHN MCKAIG (PHOTOGRAPHER, SHOW PROMOTER): People were accepted in the hardcore scene for who they were and their ideas were valid, so people felt comfortable enough to speak from the heart. When there's that acceptance, you feel empowered. It wasn't about what you danced like. We were more concerned with what was in your heart and mind.

Many of the people interviewed for *Burning Fight* were greatly impacted by the dialogue in hardcore. The exposure to alternative political ideologies and other new viewpoints prompted them to take an active role in political and social issues. In turn, they formed their own bands, wrote their own zines, and made their voices heard about the things that concerned them.

MARTIN SORRONDEGUY (LOS CRUDOS, LIMP WRIST, LENGUA ARMADA RECORDS): I didn't like all the music in the nineties, but it was the first time where there was this incredible amount of dialogue happening and there were all these amazing voices being heard in punk and hardcore. It was important to see that and be a part of it. There was a lot being talked about and a lot of workshops and activism became huge. It was like music was secondary and the message was the primary thing, which was amazing!

RYAN PATTERSON (BLACK CROSS, COLISEUM): I remember getting the *State of the Nation* comp that Dischord put out in the early nineties which had all these awesome D.C. bands of that era on it. It also came with a booklet and it was this big photocopied zine that had all this dis-information. It had facts about McDonalds and oil companies and women's issues. It also had facts about the lies that America spreads and it just blew my mind!

NATE WILSON (MONSTER X, DAS OATH): I'm not sure what happened, but I know that it scared a lot of the eighties kids who might have been on their way out anyways to actually get out of the movement. Bands like Drop Dead, Born Against, and Los Crudos were influenced by what was happening elsewhere in the world politically and socially. They started taking certain ideas or concepts that were happening in Europe or abroad and brought them to the attention of the kids in the U.S. The end of the Cold War and Reaganomics meant the end to politics to some involved with eighties and nineties hardcore. People just thought things were okay now, and bands started singing about more personal issues. It's very fortunate that the bands mentioned above had the intelligence and insight to realize the world was still a fucked up place.

BRIAN LOWIT (LOVITT RECORDS): Shows back in the nineties either seemed to find the band talking about politics between songs, having tables of information about issues, or people just discussing things. There was a band in Greensboro that used to pass out a lyric sheet before they played so you knew what the lyrics were, since they were screaming, and it also had a thing about what each song meant. After they played a song, they would talk to the audience about the song and open up a discussion on the issue.

MARK MCCOY (CHARLES BRONSON, DAS OATH): No matter how far you remove yourself from society, you still have to give a fuck about something. If you're alive, if you deserve to be alive, you must keep an eye open to the world. You have to accept and be aware of changes on any scale. For me that's politics.

JUSTIN PEARSON (SWING KIDS, THE LOCUST, STRUGGLE, SOME GIRLS): Music is the only effective form of communication — it goes beyond language, class and gender and everyone can tune into it. At the same time it's just music; it's not like you're starting some revolution in society. It is part of a community and a musical community can change the world. But did we really do all that much? I'm not sure. I see all these jaded assholes now doing stupid shit. At least people were informed — I learned all kinds of stuff in the early nineties and it made me a better person and if it wasn't for that I'd probably just be some shit-head hick living in Arizona or something.

SEAN MUTTAQI (VEGAN REICH, CAPTIVE NATION RISING, PRESSURE, UPRISING RECORDS): Ideas are one thing, but if there isn't some type of action then you're never going to deal with the issue firsthand. If you're saying that some sort of action needs to stop and the one or two percent majority elite that control the country are behind it then it doesn't matter if you get 60 or 70 percent of the country who feel it's wrong. Until they do something about it then nothing is going to change.

Since the beginning, the number of social and political issues in hardcore has been so large that there would be almost no way to touch on them all in a reasonable amount of space. This chapter of *Burning Fight* is just an overview of several issues that have been discussed in the scene since the early days but became focal points for many in the nineties. In addition to the subjects of the other chapters in this book, anti-corporate self reliance, race, gender equality, sexual orientation, and the so-called "P.C. backlash" are subjects that came up in most of the interviews conducted for this book. Each of these could probably warrant a book of its own as could the many others that are not covered here.

D.I.Y.

The do-it-yourself (D.I.Y.) ethic has always been a vital issue in hardcore and punk. Independence from the corporate world is seen as important to maintain the ethical integrity of the music. Although some early punk bands' albums were released by major record companies, hardcore's early bands, labels, and fanzines were created without the backing of large organizations. They defined their own music, issues, and positions and were free from the influence of commercial record companies and publishers. This simple concept went beyond the boundaries of the scene and became a general philosophy of taking your personal ideas, beliefs, and ultimately your life, into your own hands.

KATE REDDY (108, KRSNA GRRRL FANZINE): We didn't call it D.I.Y in the eighties. It was just what you did. You'd glue your seven-inch covers together. You were stoked just to print 1,000 records. [laughs] There was no expectation or desire to go outside the scene or make money. It was really in its most essential form at the time.

JOSH GRABELLE (TRUSTKILL RECORDS, TRUSTKILL FANZINE): D.I.Y. is the essence of hardcore. That's the blood line. You can't name a record label or band or even a booking agency that exists in this scene that didn't start out as D.I.Y. If they did start out as something bigger they probably fell on their face.

ADRIENNE DROOGAS (SPITBOY): It's always been about D.I.Y. It's all coming from your heart, strength, emotion and energy. Anything that comes from all those places is going to be so clear and interesting. There was a lot of energy that people wanted to put into everything — music, lyrics, zines, booking all-ages tours. All of those things held meaning and strength and people wanted to cherish it.

MIKE KIRSCH (FUEL, TORCHES TO ROME, BREAD AND CIRCUITS): D.I.Y. was a reaction to larger forces trying to co-opt the larger punk and hardcore scene, so there was this need to take things and find some place to throw anchors down in a more underground fashion. People had nothing to lose. Those kinds of situations free you up because if you're playing music just because you enjoy doing it then you're going to play what you like playing, which ended up freeing up people to exploring and pushing new boundaries.

RECLAIM YOUR LIFE

SUPREME COURT

FUGAZI
BIKINI KILL
SPEAKERS FROM
WASHINGTON
PEACE CENTER
DC SCAR
RIOT GRRRL
EQUAL JUSTICE
AND MORE...

NOON
JULY 25
US CAPITOL

PUNK PERCUSSION PROTEST AT THE REAGAN/BUSH SUPREME COURT

BRENDAN DESMET (GROUNDWORK, ABSINTHE): A lot of kids were just looking for something to do as they lived in an area that was somewhat isolated. As the scene progressed in the nineties there was an explosion of ideas. That was a period of time when the mainstream came knocking for the first time in a long time. Sonic Youth, Nirvana, and bands like that brought a wider audience, which brought some level of homogenization. At the same time there was a group of kids who banded together to attempt to reinforce what exactly hardcore meant to them, trying to "keep it real." That reinforced the D.I.Y. ethic. The idea that people could do things on their own as opposed to relying on some big label was a very liberating thing for the era.

STEPHEN BRODSKY (CAVE IN): The sense of accomplishment D.I.Y. gave was marvelous. To acquire one of those V.F.W. lodge places required a lot of energy. Being a 15-year-old kid trying to convince an adult with no understanding of our local music scene to rent it out for a hardcore show was a feat in itself. Most of these people would immediately associate such a thing with drugged out kids trashing the place to pieces.

DAVE MANDEL (INDECISION RECORDS): D.I.Y. allowed people to go out and experiment and try stuff. How many fanzines existed because people said, "I want to do something"? Anyone in the scene could contribute. I have no musical prowess whatsoever and I've spent the last 20 years contributing to the scene because I can.

SCOTTY NIEMET: The explosion of D.I.Y. zines is by far one of the most important elements of this era. You have a scene of all these kids figuring out how their lives are impacted by "the man" and how they can, in turn, make some positive changes to neutralize these pressures. It was insane how many kids were voicing their opinions. It created this alternative media that was easy to understand, gave resources to things like how to become vegan, how to scam corporations, and simple "you are not alone" topics. I guess having our own media and our own resources to pull from, we kind of shut out the world that we hated and the bullshit we felt they were feeding us. I still to this day come across movies, songs, TV shows from the nineties that I swear I have never been exposed to before. That's how removed from the mainstream a lot of us became. We consumed our time with these social issues. We spent endless hours molding our daily lives, our social time and our money around a lifestyle fueled by making a difference.

POLICY OF 3

SCOTT BEIBIN (BLOODLINK RECORDS): The hardcore scene wasn't just passive consumers — it was kids putting on shows, making zines, creating music and artwork. They were figuring out how to make things work either with their parents' money or their own money or no money at all. We were able to get stuff out there because we were getting copies for free from a certain corporate-owned copy shop. I was also a bit of a hacker kid so I transferred those ideas from one thing to another, too. At the time it was very expensive to make phone calls and there were suddenly these lists of calling card numbers floating out there. And as soon as one ran out there were 10 more. Kids used these to organize tours. I found it necessary to help bring in scams to help build the scene. Scamming copy businesses, calling cards, and dialers are the very things that brought the hardcore scene from nothing to it being a sustainable scene. If it wasn't for that subsidy hardcore never would have become as big at it did.

As hardcore moved from the eighties into the nineties, the issue of D.I.Y. became even more important in maintaining what many felt was the underground, anti-corporate, ethos so ingrained in hardcore. Bands with a punk rock or hardcore lineage such as Sonic Youth, Nirvana, and Green Day signed to major labels and became mainstream successes in the early-nineties. The success of these larger bands brought even more major label attention to the underground music scene of which hardcore was a part.

Most viewed this as corporate colonialism. At the time, several prominent hardcore bands either flirted with or actually signed to major labels, which caused a lot of controversy. These trends prompted many in the scene to become more defensive about maintaining its independence from big business. Some saw these major label deals as an act of treason while others were sympathetic toward bands that aspired to get their music to a broader audience. Unsurprisingly, the debate against major label involvement and the position taken those who defended a band's decision to sign with such labels divided the scene to a certain degree.

IAN MACKAYE (FUGAZI, MINOR THREAT, EMBRACE, DISCHORD RECORDS, THE EVENS): I think of music as sacred, so when I think about music being handled by people who care only about profit it is so discouraging. Music is organic and it's created by people for people and should be supported by people. The major label is not interested in music. Let's be honest about it. If they were interested in music don't you think at least once in the history of that charade known as the Grammys that at least one independent record was better than a major label one? But it's just an advertisement for themselves. If you're on the outside and you're looking at it you can see it and it is clear. If you roll around in shit you don't smell it after a while, but if you're walking down the street with you're eyes open you don't step in shit — you see it and you avoid it and that's the way I look at it.

RYAN DOWNEY (BURN IT DOWN, SUPERHERO FANZINE): I always believed that if you had a message you should reach as many people as you can. I have known far too many "D.I.Y." people who are rip-offs and con-artists. And why should a band be chastised for asking for a guarantee at a show? So the promoter can make all of the money? There are so many sides. Business is business and art is art. You should approach your art in one way and the business around your art in another.

WALTER SCHREIFELS (QUICKSAND, GORILLA BISCUITS, RIVAL SCHOOLS): Selling out is something that you don't have to sign to a major label to do. It's when you establish yourself as a certain thing and people believe in it, and then you become something else that you are not in an effort to be popular. If you make a good record and you're on a major then who gives a shit? Why would I want to deprive a good band a chance to continue playing music? Being in a band is really difficult and there is no money in it and people ultimately have to quit. If you can get a little success then the world is rewarding them for their work and you get to play longer. It's a philosophical thing. Do you believe in yourself and your own creative direction? If you believe in that and you stick to it then you're not selling out. If you do something because other people want or expect it from you then people will smell it. It doesn't necessarily have to do anything with money.

KENT MCCLARD: My big thing is hardcore is our musical movement and anyone who tries to take it away from us should be burnt down. I don't give a shit what the message is; it's the medium that's so important. Hardcore is a movement in which, for the most part, there weren't corporate controlled labels and interests. Anyone could do anything. A band could do whatever the fuck it wanted to — the only thing that could stop you would be your talent, and sometimes that didn't even stop people. You could be anything you wanted to be and that's why it's so important to fight for every day. When that goes away the whole thing is completely meaningless. The idea of being on a record label where some guy in a suit is calling the shots has nothing to do with hardcore as far as I'm concerned. I think we should be controlling it. If money is going to be made then it should be made by the people involved.

CHRISSY PIPER (PHOTOGRAPHER): We took it personally sometimes. It was like, "We support you, why do you need to go to corporate America to get your music out?" [laughs] It was our thing, why would we want someone else to have their hand in it? Some bands did it and got burned while others were okay. It went both ways.

JOE EPSTEIN (WRITER): The attitude toward bar codes was endemic of how people wanted to keep this music separate from the mass communication that fed the mainstream.

Youth culture at the time was more "us against them" so it went right along with that attitude. It was an attempt to keep it for the people who cared about it so deeply. But in terms of economics when there is a small economy a larger one will always come. I could never begrudge anyone for making a living. There is a degree of romanticism in the scene about the blue collar work ethic. Let's face it: All bands worked hard. I don't think these bands signed and were immediately doing coke off strippers' tits. Look at a band like Helmet — they had a three record, million dollar deal and after all the expenses they were left with about $20,000 a piece.

DUNCAN BARLOW: I have always been a fan of the underdog and as long as artists are trying to generate art, especially subversive art, I try to support it. It's important to recognize the structures of power within systems. The nineties seemed to be a time when bands realized the power structures existed and worked against them; however, it would seem now that many of the people that led the counter movements were some of the first people to become a system of their own. What is the point of subverting a system if you become a power structure with limitations, marketing schemes, and discourse within the larger global economic system? I am not saying that artists should reject capitalism, although the idea is rather appealing at times; rather, I'm saying that there is no point in challenging the structures of power if you become a new structure of power.

CHRIS LOGAN (CHOKEHOLD, GOODFELLOW RECORDS): Chokehold had no beef with the bands or the people in the bands, but when a promoter would come to us in tears because she wasn't making enough to cover these bands' guarantees, we were floored. I had never heard of a hardcore band demanding money from a promoter at that point. It just didn't occur to me that those things happened in our community. You came, you played, and you got whatever the kids could give you. But in came the riders, the guarantees, the contracts... it was fucking insane! This eventually led us to speaking out against it and us getting into awkward situations with friends in bands on Victory. But we said what we said and didn't let it stop us. These things I mentioned are commonplace these days and a band is considered insane to tour without having contracts for shows. So I guess we were insane for trying to stop the money revolution.

BRIAN DINGLEDINE: Hardcore isn't an aesthetic, it's an independent space for kids to develop their own culture. You can't have that with corporations running the show. Every time any band has signed to a big label, they've basically left the hardcore scene, or it [has] left them. Hardcore is made up of the spaces the kids control and those are outside the grip of corporations — and, I'd like to think, also outside the grip of religious institutions, fascists, etc.

SCOTTY NIEMET: I was pretty consumed in the D.I.Y.-ness that I didn't put too much care into what bands were "trying" to accomplish with making a living at their music. My annoyance with the whole thing was when it came to booking for the More Than Music

Fest and general shows. It seemed every month that went by fewer and fewer bands were booking their tours, which is not all in all a bad thing, but with that came guarantees and stupid shit. Over the years I as a kid that did shows in my house and also spent over eight months out of the year organizing a fest, I felt I and my friends were pretty fair minded and giving when it came to helping bands out. I mean, we never took money out for our utilities, although there were some weeks in the summer that we would have six shows, 50 showers, and 10 meals provided by us. And all of a sudden we would be getting calls by some random person asking random demands and bands showing up and making us feel guilty for not fulfilling our end of the "deal." It's not a coincidence that this all happened when bands stopped talking and sharing themselves.

ANDREW KLINE (STRIFE): If you turn on MTV or the radio would you rather have a crappy band you couldn't care less about or would you rather have something that you actually liked? If a major label is willing to give you money to make the record you want to make then more power to you. There were kids who were quick to cry sellout, but they weren't the ones who worked so hard over the years to get to that point. If it added to what the band was trying to do then I didn't have a problem with it.

IAN MACKAYE: People asked us (Fugazi) why we wouldn't want to sign to a major [label] and there's only one reason I could think of: Money. It's been my experience that things that are done for money are almost uniformly bad, whether it's bombing another country for oil or signing to a major label and casting away your sense of autonomy. The point is that [major labels] didn't show up until there was money to be made. I'd been in bands since 1980 and Fugazi had been playing for four years by the time Nirvana hit. By 1993 almost every big label attempted to contact us, but to be honest we didn't even take a lunch. There was just nothing to discuss. It just seemed like such a boring story. I mean, how often have you heard the story of a band that had strong principles but then they signed to a major label? And how many times have you heard of a band that actually did stick to its guns? That to me is interesting. I'd rather have on our gravestones "they never gave up!" I also think a lot of people operate on the idea that a major label can sell twice or three times as many records as an independent. I think at the time we were selling a couple hundred thousand records and people were telling us, "Hey, you guys could sell six hundred thousand records!" But I would submit that we would sell fewer records on a major label because we would break up. The band is a relationship and our connection, like any, had its fragilities.

KENT MCCLARD: People saw there was money to be made and people wanted it, and it makes sense because that's what our society is about in some ways. I've made money as well and I'm not saying that I'm above wanting to run my label smart. But the difference is what people are willing to do to get over. I don't care if people make money. I just wish the money could stay in the scene itself.

MARTIN SORRONDEGUY (LOS CRUDOS, LIMP WRIST, LENGUA ARMADA RECORDS): So many people started out D.I.Y. when they had an audience, but when it was no longer convenient for them they kicked punk and hardcore to the curb. How many times all these years have I heard kids scream about revolution and then walk away because they have the ability and the privilege to do so? That really bothers me. We can't walk away from our neighborhood. We know that when we go back home we go back to what we were singing about. That was cute, your rant about revolution and changing the world, but where are you now?

CHRIS BOARTS-LARSON (SLUG AND LETTUCE FANZINE): Hardcore is all about "doing it yourself." It is at the core of the heart of it all — taking things into your own hands, going outside the system, creating something that you believe in with what you have available to you, taking control back into your own hands, expressing yourself honestly and passionately. Whether it is a reaction to the mainstream, whether you are doing it yourself because no one else would do it for you, whether there was no other outlet, most of the punks and hardcore kids in the eighties and nineties were misfits in one way or another who found a place where they could belong and connect with other misfits or other like minded outcasts. That was the heart of it. Then in the mid-nineties punk and hardcore got so popular, suddenly our underground community was financially viable. There were those who were very successful running their record label, distro, show space, or band. Suddenly they were making a living off of their hobby and having to make unique financial decisions. Some people had to make their "business" legit and pay taxes because there was too much money to just squeak by under the radar. Ultimately the scene caught a lot of attention, whether from record labels who saw the buzz and money, or because suddenly there were punks who had jobs in positions to help out their friends with some real money. The bottom line is that for a whole variety of reasons, some smart, some smarmy, some out of necessity and some out of greed, hardcore and punk became a sellable commodity and where there is success and potential for money there are always those who will jump in and reap the reward. And so things got sticky, weird and complicated.

JESSICA HOPPER (HIT IT OR QUIT IT FANZINE): I try not to judge people for signing. Some people I know in bands came from shitty towns or have no education and music is their skill. But certain people are selling not only their bands but also offering up in-roads to their entire community and they are offering up things that are not necessarily theirs to give and I understand why people would be upset with that. The other thing is that sometimes bands are good and they sign and they end up sucking because they bend over backwards to make bucks. The other thing is that it legitimizes the major label tactics of profit over the artist. Most of these bands that sign only make 11 cents per record sold even though it might be selling for $16.99 at Best Buy.

JACOB BANNON (CONVERGE, DEATHWISH, INC. RECORDS): There's always been a potential for profit in hardcore. The punk community was driven by major labels in the seventies and eighties. The nineties were the first time that the D.I.Y. ethic was embraced as an ideology, not a means to an end. Now you have a turbulent time when bands and labels are more transparent than ever in their business practices. Sadly, more and more kids are no longer caring about it.

CHAKA MALIK (BURN, ORANGE 9MM): If I had one thing to do over again relating to hardcore and my place in the music and myself as a potential model, I would have kept the money out of my mind and just stuck with what got us there. A lot of bands on big labels are great bands, but often they are trying to be something they're not. It was a necessary good and evil. It was like a fake marriage of sorts. Now all bets are off.

RACE

The issue of race was also heavily discussed in hardcore. From the eighties into the nineties, many in the scene spoke of racial unity and the promotion of cultural awareness, often as a way to push back against white power skinheads that were sometimes on the fringes of the scene. Despite this anti-racism focus, a number of people felt that some in hardcore and punk had, even if subconsciously, racist sentiments at times or at least expressed some racial insensitivity. Some also felt that because the scene was predominantly Caucasian, there was somewhat of a built-in lack of cultural awareness.

On the other hand, people from all backgrounds were often drawn to hardcore because of the political and ethical concerns voiced in the scene. Bands like Downcast, Los Crudos, and Racetraitor examined issues of white privilege, gentrification, and a perceived Eurocentric attitude some countries had in matters of economic policy and international diplomacy. Such bands occasionally drew criticism if their members did not come from disaffected minority groups because some thought that these discussions should be led by those most directly affected by those issues. Others, however, felt that as long as the issues were being discussed in a sincere manner, the ethnicity of the person doing the talking was not important.

MOE MITCHELL (CIPHER): Race in hardcore was glossed over in general. There were plenty of people with anti-racist buttons and stickers and anti-Nazi stuff. Everybody knows Nazis are bad. What about taking accountability and recognizing your own racism? That was frustrating. I've developed better strategies for dealing with it. I used to feel silenced. Now, I attempt to be consistently vocal about chanting down oppression. It's perfectly valid and needed for white folks to discuss white supremacy and for men to discuss patriarchy. The people who benefit from and keep a certain system alive should certainly be talking about it.

TAYLOR STEELE (FOUR WALLS FALLING): Hardcore is dominated by white males, so you definitely don't want to lead on an issue that someone else should be leading on. You want to express yourself but you want to realize your place in the issue. I've read tons of books to look at the issue of race deeply over the years, but I'm never going to understand what it's like to be an African-American, so I'm going to defer to them and let them define what their experience is and go with that and support them 100 percent.

CHAKA MALIK: If I'm a kid that needs to hear that message and it's a beautiful message of race relations or something beautiful that helps promote understanding then who cares who writes those songs? Is it valid? Of course it's valid! Anytime you are asking people to be more humane in any way is valid. Would I rather have you write something negative? Nobody has a monopoly on anything. We're lucky to be here and the smart people learn from other people. You can try and criticize and say who is or isn't important enough to be saying these things, but why? Just shut up and deal with it or don't deal with it.

KEN OLDEN: I grew up in a very mixed area, so I was used to being around blacks, whites, Asians, Mexican people, so I always felt comfortable. I never thought, "Damn, there's a lot of white people here" or whatever. [laughs] There's no doubt that the style of music is very white male dominated, but so is the entire country! I mean, look at any corporation or the government. I don't think hardcore is any different than mainstream America in that way. Any effort made by one group to understand another group is a positive thing. So if white men are trying to discuss or deal with race issue, I say that's all good. Most white people are probably not as aware of the ongoing racial problems in this country. I think most people see racial problems as minor, and why shouldn't they? I mean, if you're white, they don't affect you in any kind of day-to-day way, and depending on where you live, they may never affect you. For others it's a daily struggle. Overall, I think it's cool for people to reach out to others and make people think about a different perspective.

KIM NOLAN: Anti-racism was always a part of hardcore and punk, and in Chicago it was especially relevant because in the mid-1980s there had been a large Nazi skinhead sect that eventually had been driven underground or out of the city, and Anti-Racist Action was supported by a lot of the skinheads that I knew. The debates over white privilege were pushed most by Racetraitor and by Mary and Erica, two Riotgrrrls who moved to Chicago from D.C. and began to push the issue with the kids who eventually became Racetraitor, who in turn were working with N.P.D.U.M. (National People's Democratic Uhuru Movement) on the south side of Chicago and were more aware of issues like community self-determination, police brutality, race segregation, gentrification, and so on. These were important debates, but they were informed in turn by outside influences as well. For example, a lot of us went to DePaul University, took the same classes, and were involved in the same student groups and brought those ideas to the scene too.

DANIEL TRAITOR (RACETRAITOR): There were some very different reactions to our band [Racetraitor]. Some kids from African-American or Latino descent loved what we were saying because they felt like they could never say that stuff as they were also minorities in the punk or hardcore scene as well. It's more dangerous when you're a person of color and you are trying to confront a majority white peer-group. Some people embraced what we were doing because it spoke to their experience and there were others who were like, "Why are you guys saying this stuff. We should be saying it!" I guess overall we received some good support. How I view race now and how I viewed it back then is quite different — race is such a dynamic thing, there is a lot of heterogeneity within racial groups, class, gender, sexual orientation and life experience… we're all human beings and we have different experiences and race is a general category to look at some larger issues in the world and it doesn't explain the entirety of someone's experiences nor should you expect it to.

ROB MORAN: Growing up a minority in hardcore was very odd for me, because for the first time in my life, I felt accepted by outcasts just like me. Nobody cared that I was Mexican. People just saw someone who, like them, didn't fit in with the "real world." Aside from gangs in my neighborhood, punkers were the only ones that made me feel that there was something else to live for. I imagine that is how other "minorities" I've met around the world have found their way to hardcore, as well.

JAMES SPOONER (AFRO-PUNK): I never really heard anything about race outside of "fuck Nazis." I was always like, "Big deal. Fuck Nazis? Yeah, duh." No one was talking about anything [along the lines of race] that I could relate to. The only band that really made a powerful statement about race was Los Crudos, by the sheer fact that they wouldn't sing in English. There were also some bands that talked about white privilege, which is important to mention. I think Downcast and Heavens to Betsy did the best job at that. In a scene filled with white kids, that's really the best you can hope for.

GREG BENNICK (TRIAL): I think that any time that anyone discusses race/gender issues, with intent of diminishing racial/gender violence or opposition, that they deserve support regardless of their race or their gender. A few years back I asked Carrie Dann, elder of the Western Shoshone Nation, what she thought of all the white kids supporting the Western Shoshone in their land rights struggle with the United States government.

She said "I don't care what color they are! We need all the help we can get." Dialogue is critical. Anyone who thinks or thought otherwise is and was short sighted.

MICHELLE (TODD) GONZALES: Most people spoke out about issues in earnest. There were definitely times, though, when people were talking the talk but not walking the walk. People weren't always living out their ideals as articulated by songs or in interviews or whatever, which is always disheartening. What really bugged me was that there wasn't much of a conversation pertaining to people's own privilege. Everyone in hardcore or punk has the idea that, "Well, I dress weird, so everyone hates me." But almost no one understood if they were white and middle class, or even upper class, they were privileged. It didn't matter whether or not you had your punk uniform on, you were still a privileged person. That conversation did not happen because people did not know how to discuss things at that time. But I thought it was weird that we were bold enough to have all these other conversations, but we didn't have the conversation about people of color within the hardcore scene and where they fit in. Maybe their perspective wasn't the same as everyone else's.

JESSICA HOPPER: It's one thing to have a song about gender or racial equality, it's another to do larger work within the scene to actually make it a comfortable place and open up dialogue rather than going, "Hey, Puerto Rican people, we want you here." Just having songs about wanting equality and not doing things to change the space socially and to make people feel welcome and feel like hardcore is a place for people who aren't white and male.

MIKE KIRSCH: There's a time and place for that to be a valid criticism, but there's also something important in putting it in a larger context. One of the things that happens sometimes is you get people saying, "We're going to crusade on behalf of these victimized people. If we can evangelize in this place where these people are the other we can save them," which is bullshit. Malcolm X said even thinking about the term minority in a place like the U.S. is a white power way of dealing with things. If you look at the way congressional districts are gerrymandered then of course people can seem like a minority. But if you look at white people in America who have resources that's such a small sliver of the planet's population. The discussion about that kind of stuff was kind of clunky in hardcore. It's pretty hard for 400 people to have a conversation at once. But you've got try things out. It's better to try and initiate a conversation than to not try at all.

MICHELLE (TODD) GONZALES: I remember we (Spitboy) titled our seven-inch *Mi Cuerpo Es Mio*, which means my body is mine. There was a Riot Grrrl in Washington who was going around and saying that Spitboy had culturally appropriated Spanish for our own benefit. The irony of her saying all that pushed me over the edge. I wrote her a letter tearing her apart basically. I remember putting into the letter how everyone was so absorbed with their identity as a punk rocker or a hardcore kid that nobody is seeing anything else. Nobody noticed that I was Mexican. I was invisible, and I had done it to myself, because I allowed it to happen. That's when I started speaking out. But that was a very painful experience to realize. People looked at me and saw "Oh, that's Todd from Spitboy" and nothing else. My ethnicity was invisible to them. After that I started speaking more about it, and I didn't want to do it to separate myself from my band or my friends, but I also felt like it was a conversation that needed to happen.

KIM NOLAN: In hindsight, it was a bunch of kids trying to make sense of their world, and trying to find ways to talk to each other about it, which is always valid. And the interrogation that went along with that was also totally relevant even if we didn't always know what we were talking about or knew how to express ourselves. I still draw on the conversations I had with kids on what it means to be white, and I think those experiences surely changed how I think about race now. We were trying to learn from each other.

GENDER AND SEXUALITY

Women have been involved with some aspects of hardcore since the beginning, but many felt marginalized by the ratio of males to females involved in the scene. Like many other music scenes and sub-cultures, men have largely outnumbered women in hardcore. Women formed bands, wrote zines, booked shows, and took part in other ways, but male perspectives were always the most prominent. Many saw this as a contradiction as the scene is theoretically a place where everyone should be able to have their voices heard. It wasn't that men always actively excluded females (though females who were in bands were sometimes heckled at shows, and some experienced more overt forms of sexism), but rather there seems to have been a culturally ingrained notion that females should remain in the background.

The nineties, however, found females more visibly involved in the scene. Female bands like Spitboy and loosely organized female groups such as the Chicks Up Front Posse, not to mention many male voices in bands and zines, voiced their concerns about the lack of focus on gender and sexuality issues. Many of these people were inspired by other nineties underground movements like Riot Grrrl, which had become established in nearly all facets of alternative music and art.

Openly gay voices were also rarer than one might expect in a supposedly "alternative" sub-culture. The scene has also had its share of homophobic slurs in lyrics or in the banter at shows, which is likely a by-product of the macho overtones that can often accompany the music. Consequently, these ideas and behaviors made it appear that the scene was, at the least, not concerned with gay issues.

Things started to change in the nineties though as a variety of zines that dealt with homosexuality like *Positron* and *Kill the Robot*, as well as many prominent members of the scene coming out about their sexuality, helped make gay issues an important part of the dialogue during this era. Homophobia became less acceptable as the years passed.

Although these topics were sometimes met with prejudice and misunderstanding, the conversations fostered a broader awareness of issues pertaining to gender and homosexuality in the scene.

VIQUE MARTIN (SIMBA FANZINE, SIMBA RECORDS): In 1989, I would often be the only female at a small straight edge show in London. If there were 50 people there, then there were likely to be only one or two girls. And the others were always girlfriends who didn't seem to really like the music. But by 1992, I was regularly traveling to the USA, and things seemed to be improving. I found other women who loved hardcore as much as I did, so the male dominance didn't bother me. Nothing mattered when standing with my girls screaming along. Holding on to SevaPriya's hand and yelling "You sicken me" during Into Another's feminist anthem. Standing next to friends that were crying while Rob [Pennington of Endpoint] sang about date rape. Chicks Up Front in full effect for Four Walls Falling's pro-choice song, feeling so passionate and empowered. These are the moments that bring a lump to my throat when I think of them. These are the times that exemplify this time period in my life, and they illustrate what hardcore means to me.

VIC DICARA (108, INSIDE OUT, BURN, BEYOND): When punk split into new wave and hardcore in the very early-eighties, most of the females gravitated away from hardcore, which latched on to aggression as a primary trademark to distinguish itself from new wave. Hardcore hit its nadir, in terms of the least female involvement, in 1986-1989. That whole youth crew straight edge scene was an extremely homogenderal sweat festival, where the one or two women who were involved had a very difficult time being accepted in any important capacity. When the nineties came in, things began improving gradually. Some non-macho artistic elements began to make their way into hardcore music, and this attracted and nourished female participation; for example, violence at shows became shunned, musically the scene opened up to more sophistication and less brute force, ideas of spirituality and vegetarianism became important. Very soon into the nineties I remember the first incarnations of female-oriented hardcore in the shape of the Riot Grrrl and similar offshoots.

DAISY ROOKS (CHICKS UP FRONT): I noticed that as it got toward the mid-nineties it was sort of in vogue in the straight edge scene to at least pretend you were down with feminism or choice issues regarding abortion. People gave lip service to it, which was good because men were talking about these issues, but in terms of overall core behavior I didn't see a lot of change during my time in the scene.

NORMAN BRANNON (TEXAS IS THE REASON, ANTI-MATTER FANZINE, FOUNTAINHEAD, RESSURECTION, SHELTER): Hardcore still is a white, male, heterosexual playground. Any way you cut it, it's the truth. In that sense, hardcore is still as progressive as it can be, but it's still a reflection of the mainstream society, which is run by white, heterosexual males. In that greater society there is such a long way to go with these issues, so the hardcore scene has similar problems. It might run on a faster track in hardcore, but it's still perhaps not as progressive as it would like to think it is.

CHRIS BOARTS-LARSON: In the early-nineties, when ABC No Rio was first getting started, there was a hard stance of not tolerating racism, sexism, or homophobia. That

CHICKS UP FRONT

was largely because the New York City scene prior to that was rampant with all of those aspects and the community at ABC No Rio was truly formed as an alternative. No bouncers, no thuggery — it was all D.I.Y. and self-run. Being involved with that scene did definitely change my perspective on gender issues, which absolutely were a huge issue in the nineties and still are. But the nineties were definitely a time when it was hotly debated, talked about, and brought to the forefront of conversation, attitude, and policy. I was raised to not be limited by my gender, to go after what I wanted, regardless. And so I did. I was, and still am, actively involved in the punk/hardcore scene — I was going to shows, setting up and promoting shows, I have done a zine for 20 years now — and while I have absolutely fought for my equality, I have also never really gotten too hung up on it. Sure, I can tell some stories, but in general I have always felt like there were tons of rad female role models from the early-eighties on. I sought them out; I looked for bands with women, zines made by women. There were always tons of girls at shows, maybe not always in equal number, but I usually didn't feel a lack of representation.

JEN ANGEL (FUCKTOOTH FANZINE, CLAMOR MAGAZINE): For a large part the level of sexism depended on where you lived. I felt that there were real regional differences in how communities were comprised. Where I lived in Ohio, there were women in the scene, but only a few were really active in bands or writing zines. A lot of them just went to shows and hung out, and that was cool, too. I was fortunate to have a few really good female friends, and I was really influenced by female-made zines like *Slug and Lettuce*, *Cooties*, and a ton more. I did feel like it was a boys' club, but I also felt that I could assert myself if I wanted to, though that was difficult. I remember there was a lot of discussion around competition among women in the scene and I definitely felt that, which may have been real or perceived. I felt that it made it difficult for me to really make strong friendships with women, with a few exceptions, and I had to work to overcome that so I could build new relationships with amazing women and not feel threatened by them.

ADRIENNE DROOGAS: There is sexism in punk and hardcore and we're all guilty of perpetuating stereotypes, but I hung out with a very political group of people and so everyone was constantly trying to challenge stereotypes and the issues within their own hearts. Also, I never felt like I was fighting against a boys' club mentality in the scene because I hit the ground running. I was doing whatever I felt like doing and nobody was ever attempting to stop me. My friends and my peers were incredibly supportive and I found myself drawn to people, women and men, who were incredibly motivated and on fire with the need to express themselves in artistic and creative ways.

JASON ROE: When I was 15, skinheads were still beating up gays in D.C. I was a very small guy and this made me pretty scared. So I became friends with them. Everyone treated me well. At some point most people realized that I was gay. I never had any problems with anyone. Before I went to college I had been doing some zines, one of them being *Kill the Robot*. Part of my focus was being a queer straight edge kid. Honestly, at this time being a gay teenager was crazy! No one was out. I knew maybe five younger gay guys. None of them were into hardcore or anything like that.

SEAN CAPONE: I think the homophobia in hardcore was a simple, uncreative, "don't drop the soap" style homophobia. A queer in the pit was a threat to the normative sublimation of hetero-male aggression that can only come from physical contact with another man. People took my arrival with a certain grain of salt. It's not like "queer-edge" was some movement dying to be born. Why the lack of discussion? Well, straight

guys will begrudgingly accept feminism in their scene; after all, it's their sex lives on the line at the end of the day. But there's no real personal stake in having to accept gays, I guess, which may be a bit reductive, but I was astonished at the appalling credulity of people in the face of blatantly untrue rumors and calumny. I'll be honest, I wasn't out to start a sexual revolution within hardcore with [*Positron* Fanzine], I just wanted to have fun and annoy some people, which I did, and find some boys to date, which I was less successful at.

CHRIS BOARTS-LARSON: Homophobia was even worse than racism as an underlying issue that was ingrained into people — whether from family or society — that was in turn mimicked in the scene. I think it was very hard for people to be "out" in the late-eighties and that in the early-nineties it did become a hot topic and it was a very positive thing. For me it went hand in hand with gender, sexism and racism — all of them were bad and it was important to educate people about [them]. Homosexuality and homophobia was one of the biggest topics of the time period of the early-nineties at ABC No Rio. Mike Bullshit, who was one of the people organizing the initial hardcore matinee at ABC No Rio, was gay, and he felt very ostracized in the NYC hardcore scene. I think that he was in the closet for a long time, and finally around this time came out and it was therefore one of the essential foundation issues of the time and place. If you couldn't deal with it, essentially you weren't welcome at ABC. I have tons of respect for Mike for what he did at this time, I really can't begin to say I know anything about what he went through, but I know it was hard and putting yourself out there like that is hard and he caught a lot of shit, even amongst those who should have been and were expected to be more understanding. But it definitely opened up a door for a lot of other people to talk about their own experiences and feelings and I know that a lot of other people also came out around this time.

SCOTTY NIEMET: I came out at the first More Than Music Fest publicly. I already had a good, supportive group of friends locally that I had come out to...I did it through my zine at the time *Let Me Live*. I never felt back then that the scene was homophobic. I mean is being a hard-ass New York hardcore dude automatically mean you're homophobic? That's up for debate seeing that some figures from that era have since come out. Does being a small town Earth Crisis worshiping redneck with the conservative views of your environment mean hardcore as a whole is homophobic? I don't think so. But what I found confusing and frustrating within the scene is the unconditional support for being "out" in the scene. All I wanted was that support and it was there for me. The problem was, "Where do I go from there?" Sure, I met other queer kids in the scene. But for some reason I had so much shit going on in my head I could never get a grasp on how to fit being queer into my daily life in Columbus, Ohio. After a while it ate away at me and I couldn't figure out my place. I started exploring the gay scene in Columbus. It was new and exciting but all it did was make it apparent that I didn't fit in to that culture, full of excess, money, and snobbery. I was left feeling I was living a double life, trying to balance the two. So after years of feeling isolated and trying to figure myself out, I think I have settled on this...I'm a 35 year old queer man who will never relate to mainstream America. The gay male community as a generalized whole bores me. It has created a culture with rules and mannerisms that mirror those of mainstream America and puts things such as wealth, career, and beauty as signs of success. I'm a punk kid and I will not compromise those values.

JASON ROE: People responded to me and *Kill the Robot* pretty well. Being queer was maybe 20 percent of my zine, so a lot of people who weren't gay read it. I got a lot of letters of support and a lot of letters from kids telling me that it helped them come out. That was a pretty great feeling. At that point before the internet there was such isolation. No gays on TV. Nothing. I'm glad that we are where we are now. I don't know if I ever felt not part of the scene because I was gay. Just being young made life scary. I remember at some of my first shows being freaked out about walking across the floor. I just didn't want to draw attention to myself. Obviously that goes with time.

KIM NOLAN (CHICKS UP FRONT, BARK AND GRASS FANZINE/COOKBOOK): I definitely felt like there were few women into hardcore, and because it was so aggressive it wasn't exactly the magnet for more women to show up at shows. The way I saw it was that because the aggressiveness in the music was masculine there ended up being roles that everyone was supposed to play, which mirrored more traditional masculine/feminine family roles, which I got into hardcore to get away from. I could handle being one of a handful of girls at a show, but I surely didn't want to be seen like I wasn't fully committed to building the community because I was just someone's potential girlfriend. I didn't want to have to hold someone's coat and stay on the sidelines while they jumped on the pit, and I surely didn't need to be protected if it was me that was in the pit. The roles that I felt I was being assigned made me like half a participant in it, and that was the problem. I felt like this was my scene too, but since there were so few women that we weren't being allowed the same access, or participation.

DAISY ROOKS: My sister [Margaret Rooks] and I started Chicks Up Front to pretend there was this huge movement of straight edge women, so we created this mythical group and we always referred to it as though it was something real, and then it turned into something real. At one point there was about 30 or 40 women that were affiliated with it and would run around and scream at people. It was a way to confront some men in the scene and voice our opinions on some issues we felt were neglected.

NORMAN BRANNON: One of my best friends was part of Chicks Up Front. I remember the first time I ever saw her I was at a show in Middlesex College in New Jersey and here comes this girl in a pink t-shirt, blue denim overalls and she's carrying a pink baseball bat that says "XChicksUpFrontX" on it. She is the first person in the front of the stage and was grabbing the mic every chance she could and screamed her guts out. And this is a high pitched scream that you could hear outside the college! [laughs] I remember thinking to myself, "I want to be friends with that person." I had so much respect for that.

KURT SCHROEDER (BIRTHRIGHT, CATALYST RECORDS): Chicks Up Front was one of the best things to ever happen to hardcore because that's an issue that is still around in the hardcore scene now. There is such a privilege for white males in the hardcore scene and it was awesome to see both females and males questioning the macho attitude that has been around since day one. There was a backlash of "girls don't belong in the pit," but it seemed for a while that there were a decent amount of girls in the scene who were super involved in all aspects.

KIM NOLAN: At first Chicks Up Front was just a few people: Daisy and Margaret Rooks, Vique Simba, Moon Morse, and me, and it spread from that as we met other girls and gained allies. At first it was just a way to meet other girls who were into hardcore, but we all started to see the same treatment or attitudes from the "boys' club," so it began to become more than that. It was a statement about hardcore and how hardcore wasn't much different about its treatment of women [than mainstream society]. One of the things we were known for was taking up the stage front and banding together up front at shows to sing along, to have fun, and to protect each other from getting kicked in the head, but also to show that we were active participants in the scene. We knew all the words, we could throw fists too, and don't try and patronize us. At the same time that Chicks Up Front was starting to find each other, Riotgrrrl was starting up in D.C., and Margaret knew those girls and was really into it, Daisy less so. They didn't like Daisy so much because she was totally into hardcore and didn't understand why she wanted to be identified with such a masculine scene. For me, I knew what Riotgrrrl was doing and I was supportive of that, but to me the bands associated with Riotgrrrrl sounded like folk music compared to like the Cro-Mags, so it wasn't something I wanted to do. Instead, we kept with Chicks Up Front and tried as a group to become more visible than any one girl alone. We forced the scene in general to take stock of how hardcore thought of women, how women were treated at shows, and how this was our scene, too. There were a lot of fights over who was acting sexist, whether or not it is ok to hit girls at a show, what roles should be and so on, mostly played out at shows, but also in the zines we all created and through the alliances we made with guys who understood us, and with bands that supported us. I think in the end the Chicks Up Front won the fight in some ways, because the scene really began to interrogate sexism, and in turn hardcore became more accepting of women's participation, whether or not more women got into hardcore.

MICHELLE (TODD) GONZALES: A lot of female bands did eventually start coming out to provide some alternative to the boy bands. Of course, most of the male bands weren't singing about blatantly sexist things, but the scene itself seemed so boys' club. Hardcore is very hard and aggressive and loud and what most think of as male, and it's going to attract people into that who are mostly guys. At the same time, I'd been involved with punk and hardcore for a long time — I liked hardcore and I wanted to play it. Some guys had the idea that girls couldn't play hardcore. I was just like, "Look, I've been playing music since I was in third grade. Hell, I can read music, which most of you can't even do!" [laughs] So, I never had any idea that I couldn't play in a band.

SCOTTY NIEMET: Women started taking a voice through zines mainly. This was a way to express thoughts on their own terms. There was this amazing contribution women made with the zine culture. They propelled this creative and fun approach. In what seemed like a parallel universe was the rise of Riotgrrl. Of course these scenes overlapped and I think the confidence of Riotgrrl made it easier for girls to start criticizing and opening up debate in the hardcore scene. With the debate open, the hardcore scene had a lot to answer about how females were viewed within our scene. But to be honest the debate [was] too naïve. Here we

were, 16-21 year olds trying to solve the culture of sexism in one breath. Here we had a group of boys finding the energy and excitement of something to hold dear to their hearts, and then we have girls finding their strength as young women with voices and the eagerness to apply their new love of feminism. The outcome led to some cheap shots and immediate defense modes.

GAVIN FREDERICK (STICKFIGURE RECORDS/DISTRO): Hardcore definitely was a male dominated scene in the nineties and it still is. Looking back, I honestly feel in that area those of us involved were definitely a bunch of idiots. Hardcore's very nature is aggressive music, which fits the profile of men more than women since men tend to be way more aggressive. Those women who were present in hardcore bands I now feel were able to be there because in many ways they were more like men than a lot of the men present in hardcore. Most women tended to take more "supportive roles" — such as booking shows, promoting, feeding the bands, stuff that is just as important, if not more important, than being in a band or running a label, but a lot of the men at the time weren't that interested in doing such jobs. This issue really is the Achilles heel of hardcore, in my opinion.

AARON BURGESS (WRITER): Forget the nineties, and forget hardcore — when has the majority of people making rock music not been white males? I have a lot of personal feelings about young white men who attempt to discuss these sorts of issues in public, but I don't know that simply because I happen to feel this or that way, those feelings are valid; they're just mine. I mean, listening to young, straight white men in hardcore bands decry racism, homophobia, sexism or any other sort of social problem always struck me as laughable and sort of disingenuous — not disingenuous to the cause, per se, but to the individual championing the cause. I feel like very few white males in hardcore bands have examined the issue of what it means to be a white male in a hardcore band, because to do this, you have to have some sort of outside perspective and comic distance; you have to be able to laugh at yourself. A lot of the reason I feel this way stems from the fact that I, too, am a white man, and I, too, have dealt with the sort of guilt and existential navel-gazing that comes from pondering one's own position of relative social privilege.

SEAN CAPONE: As in all things this is a reflection of culture at large, isn't it? Men have a natural tendency to form units, to conform to each other, to follow orders, to compete and be aggressive. It's the thread of our culture, from sports to religion to the military to government. My question is: what form would an independent music scene take, created solely by women, that wasn't a response to the male-ness of hardcore? Would it be equally loud, bellicose, and combative?

TARA JOHNSON (DISEMBODIED, MARTYR A.D.): I think that if I were more of a "girly girl" I would have been treated differently, but I was just like one of the guys. I don't think people liked Disembodied just because there was a girl in it. I did everything that the guys did — drove, loaded and unloaded, fucking rocked out just like the rest of them. I always appreciated it when girls would come up and say that I influenced them or made them want to start playing the guitar or whatever, but I really never paid much attention to being a girl in a band. I didn't feel like hardcore was a boys' club because I didn't give a fuck. I didn't ever feel like I needed to be a spokesperson for girls in hardcore. They have always been involved, but there just weren't very many girls in bands like there are now.

KENT MCCLARD: The world is a boys' club! You can look at almost everything and that's the case. It has to do with the fact that our society just isn't producing young women who think they can do anything. When I was 15 I thought I could do anything and apparently most young women don't feel that way. I can't make a woman go and do something; they have to do it themselves. The hardcore scene has to try and support women who do their own thing. In some ways I think hardcore makes more sense for women than for men as they have much more to be angry about. The things they have to be angry about are socialized at such an early age. Over time you see more women involved but it's a slow process. By the time someone gets to be 16 or 17 and the age of wanting to play in a band, a lot of that socialization has already happened. It takes a lot of guts for a woman to be in a band. Their whole lives they've been taught they are second best. I don't know how any musical genre can break those barriers down effectively. All musical genres are this way. It's a shame because I definitely want to have an integrated community.

KATE REDDY: I still consider myself a feminist, which is funny considering the irony of the hardcore scene where, at least at first, you had no girls doing anything. [laughs] Girls were virtually not a part of the scene when I first got involved. The big complaint of the scene in a society in which we've never had a woman president and where women have been disenfranchised is that women supposedly weren't being "treated right" in the Krishna Consciousness movement. I felt like saying, "Hello?!" [laughs] There are many devotees who still are sexist. But Gaudiya Vaisnavism is not inherently sexist at all. In fact, if you learn about its roots, it is quite female, goddess centered. Judeo/Christian/ Islamic religions have no female representation of God's energy at all. So, I found this very liberating to see Radha standing next to Krishna representing a holistic view of God. But there was a lot of complicated psychology around living in a tight knit community/ *ashram* that led to all kinds of inequities. We are still struggling to unravel all of those knots. And as I said earlier, there was a lot of [sexist] accusation of the Krishnas, but if we are honest, hardcore wasn't all that liberating for females. Just the opposite.

DUNCAN BARLOW: Sure, it had its moments where it seemed very balanced; however, whenever I stepped out of our small group of friends, I noticed the total inequality of the scene. I cannot say that I was totally innocent of it either. I was young and I had gender expectations as well as anyone; however, I think that I was always open for change and ready for a challenge. Many of my feminist friends were good enough to talk with me about things I took for granted and really opened my eyes on the matters. That is what I loved most about the scene was the open dialogue between the community members. Granted, it often ended up in a yelling match, but there was communication and that was so very crucial to the vitality of the movement.

DAISY ROOKS: There were definitely bands working on a lot of positive issues, but a lot of the issues you saw emerge were closely connected to the fact that it was a pretty conservative time. Hardline was closely related to lots of anti-abortion sentiments articulated by some bands and not really being questioned a lot, so I think a lot of women in the scene felt, "Why is a 15-year-old boy who has never been in a serious long-term relationship, preaching to me about what my rights should be with my body?"

CHRISSY PIPER: It was cool that people were bringing up issues that were thought provoking, even if it was a male dominated scene. At the same time it was kind of strange to see men singing about women's issues. It made you wonder, "Where are all the women at?" [laughs] But there were great bands like Spitboy that were around to even it out a bit.

BRENT DECKER (RACETRAITOR): It was good when I was challenged about my ideas about gender. Not even that they were my ideas but just subconscious thoughts that are pushed on you by this culture. I'm sure a lot of women involved felt like it didn't have an effect. But in that scene people would get challenged either by women or by bands. Shows would be shut down! I know people look back at that with some disdain, but it was actually cool. And it wasn't shut down for fighting, which is what happens now. Shit used to get shut down based on ideas and for its time it was cool.

MIKE MOWERY (GOOD CLEAN FUN, PHYTE RECORDS): Issues are not black and white. It's not so much about the specifics of issues like if you spelled girl like gyrl or woman as womyn. The most important thing is that females are respected, right? People would often get hung up on little rules.

VIQUE MARTIN: We all felt at the time that to be taken seriously you had to work much harder than the boys. If you didn't do a zine, put on shows, know all the words, etc.... then the boys wouldn't respect you or something. But there was this undercurrent that some of the girls took even further, kind of as a direct result of not wanting to be seen as "merely" a girlfriend, so a lot of sexuality was denied. I had been sexually active before finding hardcore, and most of my gender politics defined when I was 12-15 and had devoured anything and everything I could find on feminism. I was also a year or two older than most of the girls and far less compromising on this topic. In *Simba* I discussed my sexuality in an unapologetic manner and attempted to confront the issues that I felt were very ignored in the scene. As a woman I feel that my sexuality and my sexual activity are perfect examples of how the personal becomes the political. Through discussion of my thoughts, emotions, and behavior in relationships, I attempted to open dialogue about the politics of sex and love. I think *HeartattaCk* also really helped to open up these ideas. I totally understand why Kent and Lisa stopped doing it, and I'm still amazed that they continued for as long as they did! But it makes me sad that it's no longer around. I think an era of our scene died when it was laid to rest.

DAISY ROOKS: It seemed to be okay to create a cult of personality about yourself. I got accused of doing that in a small way with helping create Chicks Up Front...being really focused on creating a cult of personality around a small group of people — I'm sure I did it to some extent, but it seemed like that's what you had to do at that time; you had to put yourself out there as a "controversial" person and try to impact people to get people to think about issues that were important to you. Maybe in retrospect I wouldn't have been so crazy about what I was doing. [laughs] People would do these outrageous things so people were forced to have an opinion about something.

"P.C. BACKLASH"

Throughout the nineties, the focus on political and ethical dialogue inspired people to think and act. However, others insisted that this atmosphere also brought about a large amount of peer pressure that compelled people to take positions on these matters regardless of whether or not they actually cared about them. In addition, sometimes the ideas were presented in such a confrontational way that it was difficult to engage in an open discussion without it turning into a yelling match. These factors led toward cynicism from some, which sparked a backlash against the presence of that dialogue.

Because of this division it seemed that many who were deeply involved with issues like animal rights or social work became less concerned with hardcore and channeled their passions into those areas directly. At the same time, hardcore's mainstream acceptance also continued to grow as the nineties progressed and corporate interest in the scene increased. A number of bands signed to major labels or larger indies while still trying to present a personal or political message. But some felt that corporate involvement took away from the focus on substantive issues.

This tension pushed a number of people to become firmer in their views about politics and its role in hardcore. People struggled with these ideas so much that it often forced people to question their very involvement with the scene.

SCOTT BEIBIN: I championed an uncompromising way of looking at things, but the reason why the nineties scene ended in 1996 or '97 was because a lot of the debate got out of control. All of a sudden people were coming to this realization in the scene that there was sexual assault in the scene and how do you deal with it? It spawned two or three years worth of letters to *HeartattaCk* and no one could put a cap on it. Most just got alienated and walked away from it and went on to do other things. There were a lot of kids who had this deep seething anger and this helped drive to break apart everything that had been built. It's important to have a valid critique of capitalism, but it's also important to understand how people think, feel and emote. That was the one thing that was rarely taken into account in a lot of the political scene, and that is exactly what tore it apart. Personal vendettas disguised as political inconsistency were what brought it down.

KENT MCCLARD: There were so many people that expected *HeartattaCk* to be judge and jury of some pretty intense situations, which was so difficult. I honestly don't believe in truth or right and wrong. I think everything that we believe is just made up. I have a really hard time judging other people and trying to come up with answers to these situations. And you're also dealing with so many third party people. I remember being confronted once by a woman at a show asking me what I was going to do about the situation, and I was like, "Look, I don't know these people. Someone wrote me a letter and I don't know if they're telling me the truth." Part of the problem is that people were looking for *HeartattaCk* to be some kind of authority. Just because I have the balls to put out this magazine doesn't mean I know everything. [laughs] It's crazy. Because I do believe right and wrong are just things we make up then you have got to convince people to agree with you. You can try and make a world where if people have a racist thought you can jail them, but that's not going to get rid of racism. You have to get out there and communicate with people and make them believe that things are right or wrong. Nobody is born racist or sexist, they decided it was the right thing based on their experiences. I think it's our job as people to constantly be out there articulating and communicating and hopefully we'll all grow as people.

DAVE MANDEL: I liked the politics, but at the same time maybe that's one of the things that brought about the whole anti-discussion backlash. Once it got to the point of talking about stuff for sake of talking then the idea became dead. For example, I loved Downcast, but I also liked to dance at a show. You're playing music — it's a show, not a speech and debate. Downcast was amazing and had great things to say but then it just became a spectacle. Kevin would sit on the floor and say they wouldn't start playing until everyone sat down. I was like, "You guys are insane!" [laughs] But whatever side of the fence you were on at least people were talking about issues.

JEN ANGEL: The real issue is that though countless people were/still are politicized by punk/hardcore, the scene I experienced didn't offer a good mechanism for allowing political growth or challenges. Many people, and I include myself to some extent, were politicized and then moved on/out of punk/hardcore to do real organizing work in other social movements — many [got involved] in unions, the environmental movement, or nonprofit organizations, for example. It was a limitation of punk/hardcore that much of the culture was so inwardly focused and didn't really encourage organizing outside of immediate social scenes. Punk/hardcore did give me some tools which helped me in my later political life, but I experienced the scene as being somewhat resistant to mobilizing or engaging in any significant way around political issues. I'm sure other people had different experiences.

BRENT DECKER: A lot of people who were serious about their ideas seemed to have this mass exodus out of the hardcore scene. It wasn't because they were against the scene per se, but they had aged a little bit and had passed the high school and college age and got a job or became a full-time activist and that drew them out of it. What was left were people who didn't really care about those issues, and they ended up taking the forefront and went around saying, "Good riddance you P.C. faggots." Interestingly enough that's when you started to see hardcore become very profitable. So, there was this simultaneous thing going on when the politically minded folks left the bands that didn't have much to say got a lot bigger which leads to what we have today.

SCOTTY NIEMET: There were a few things that happened by the late nineties: First was "burn-out" — the self policing and picking of fights became such the norm at fests that no one wanted to contribute anymore to "that element." People would prepare themselves to create a conflict. Calling out people became witch hunt mentality. This shit still is pretty unsettling with me. I watched a well meaning, sincere community at war with itself that in the end destroyed itself. Second was "personal discovery" — I think a lot of us got super active in politics and figured out how to fit it into our lives before we were able to fit our personalities into our lives. Being teens still, we were going away to college reanalyzing

our political views, falling in love, getting our hearts broken. The mid-nineties was a time of figuring out what the fuck we were. Third was, "Where do we go from here?" — so we have friends all over the country, we travel and invite people into our homes on a regular basis, we live a very open and free life shared and dependent among others. What happens when you don't want to share anymore? When your band is asked to sign to Sub Pop? When you can't afford your rent? When you graduated college? Fourth was "political graduation"—there are some who were involved in the scene that discovered that their involvement in some part of radical politics needs to move beyond what the hardcore scene can offer. They left the scene and the political voice left with them.

CHRIS BOARTS-LARSON: Some people definitely got burnt out. A lot of people who were very vocal about certain topics felt like they were repeating themselves to people who already understood and were of a like mind. You get to a point where you adopt certain things as a part of your lifestyle and then you stop talking about it as much. But then what happens, especially with the high turnover rate in the punk/hardcore scene, is that when the dialogue is no longer there, people are not being exposed to things they maybe wouldn't come upon on their own, and there are fewer discussions about issues and ideas. Some of it was definitely reactionary. There were always those who were tired of hearing about all the "P.C." stuff and consequently were "anti-P.C." Then all of a sudden you have a whole faction of kids who get behind that line of thinking. So, whether people got burned out, people stopped yelling so loud, or people got reactionary and lazy, things and times changed. I think there was a very strange twist in things at that time too, which did coincide with the depoliticizing of the scene. I'm sure a lot of people were turned off a lot by the debates and the airing of some specific personal issues. Many lives were changed. I think some people were intimidated, probably scared that they would say or do the wrong thing and get publicly accused. It got pretty intense, and there were some aspects of it that just plain sucked. But at the same time, if in the end there is an awareness that comes about and an understanding of respect for other people, then I think that something is gained, too.

BEN DAVIS (SLEEPYTIME TRIO, MILEMARKER): You know what is interesting to me? The whole phenomenon that developed for like two years of the mid-show rant/therapy sessions when the bands started passing the mic to the audience. It was funny, sad, good, and drawn out when you start hearing at every show people speaking their minds. It evolved from the obvious political rants about moshing and war and vegetarianism — to stories like, "My dad never told me he loved me."

ANTHONY PAPPALARDO: Whenever nerds get power it's a bad thing. [laughs] Why was Revenge of the Nerds Two shittier than the first film? The nerds didn't have power in the first one and when they get power in the second they do everything wrong because they are nerds. Sometimes people take things too far. For a while it was, "Yo, no band can play on stages." Everything had to be priced a certain way. You couldn't distro New

Age stuff at certain shows because this show was too D.I.Y. It became a parody of itself. How come I can't go to a show and enjoy it? These collectives were running shows in Boston and we had to have a debate about what bands could play and if their styles were varied enough. I couldn't believe there was an independent party governing my scene.

GAVIN FREDERICK: Quite frankly, what happened was we grew up. Remember, hardcore is a scene of kids finding out who they are and where they fit in the world. Once you know who you are and what you want to do are you really that interested in arguing with everybody about it? Of course not. Additionally, the scene became more commercial as a result of becoming bigger. Bands were making more money, shows were bigger, more records were being sold and the idea of getting rich or making a good living off of hardcore became something that too many people seriously considered, which resulted in the scene becoming more mainstream in order to increase its money making potential. The end result was that ideas became more superficial and watered down.

CHRIS COLOHAN (LEFT FOR DEAD, THE SWARM, CURSED): The thing that made that era so unique was also the thing that killed it to death — the overload of dogma in the hands of such a young bunch of people. I don't think any of the things we were all talking about or fighting over were at all stupid or pointless. They were definitely more dramatized than they needed to be, but pointless? Never for a minute. It's just that no one accounted for time or space in any of it, or the possibility that the arena for all that dialogue could itself just not be there one day. And college ended, and I think it left a lot of people with nothing else they could do in light of their real lives but to resent it or write it off.

BRIAN DINGLEDINE: I think what happened toward the end of the nineties was the usual split, where the bands and kids that were really into politics went one direction and the kids who were just into fashion went the other way. Part of it may be that the politicized kids started focusing less on music and more on activism. From 1999 to 2001 there was a huge surge of activism and protest that took the place of punk/hardcore in many people's lives, [which] left the music scene to the kids who only cared about fashion. I think the appearance of the internet around then made a big difference in what happened next — suddenly message boards and then MySpace made it at once easier and less meaningful to "do it yourself." Without zines, actual fliers, and the original touring circuit that just got overloaded by billions of bands, the D.I.Y. hardcore scene collapsed, while the bullshit corporate imitation expanded more and more.

MARK MCCOY: There wasn't any importance stressed on the individual [at this time], which annoyed me. Ironically, the scene in the nineties was actually only a mechanism for championing the group mentality ethos. Self-development was a non-issue; there was always a political agenda at hand that was far more important. At the core of the whole scene was a rampant sense of insecurity, transforming everyone into guilt-ridden victims. People were very dry and serious. If you weren't sympathetic to the status quo, you were dismissed as a heretic or some sort of goofball. A band couldn't just play music and sing lyrics about what they were interested in; you had to be part of a charity that required long meandering speeches for people to excuse their self-hatred. Being at shows was really like suffering through a church potluck. People were very on edge about slipping up and saying the wrong things. I recall someone telling me, "Well, if you don't have something to say, then you shouldn't be playing music." I just thought, "You're pretending to care because you need an interest in something. You can't be alone for five seconds. You're at every fucking show."

SCOTTY NIEMET: I started looking deeper into the politics of violence and with that I started connecting the dots with sexism, homophobia, and abuse of power. The conclusion I came to was that if I was feeling all this frustration with how society treats people and controls our lives, I must try to dig at the root of it and not be like them. Cliché as it seems, I consciously changed my actions and how I resolved conflict. So through others coming to the same conclusions in zines, late night talks, fest workshops, and talking in between songs, lots of us seemed to make our lives a bit more sensitive of others' feelings and how our actions affected others. One of the pinnacle events of this new approach to what we as a community will do to address the maleness of the scene came with the rape accusation of Scott, the bassist of Promise Ring, at the More Than Music Fest. The fest was put to a screeching halt for well over four hours. The open mic discussion forced the scene to face our personal views, our level of commitment and tested our attention spans. To be quite honest, looking back at events like that, we were 16-21 year olds discovering the amazing world of feminism and wanting to put what we have been learning into practice. I think it made people once again have to make a decision on what path they wanted to take within the hardcore — do you want to go through the scene very confrontational at every show or do you want to be productive and create a community you can feed of each other's energy? It pitted friends against each other on very static stances. I watched a couple fests later, as two friends' relationship/break-up became a fest meeting topic as to if the cheating boyfriend should be "blacklisted" from attending the fest due to his bad choice in sleeping with another girl. He was deemed sexist and an abuser of women. I witnessed the takeover of the fest committee by people who had no real investment in the hardcore scene. These were people from the anarchist/radical politics scene. They

exploited the failings of our scene, things we were trying to mend and understand, and shattered it. Most of us allowed them in with welcoming arms, some of us walked away in disgust. That year of the womyn centered More Than Music Fest was the year I lost my hope in real productive change for the hardcore scene. I still feel this deep-seated male guilt that I "just didn't get it"...I watched a huge venue be cut up into numerous "safe spaces" (womyn, people of color, queer). I witnessed a boy who was not informed that he was on the blacklist be wheeled away on a dolly off the venue's property to applause. I lost years of trust from dear friends because I truly disagreed with this fiasco of putting this type of politics into practice. I still have people who won't talk to me because I didn't agree with what happened. I spoke up and had three womyn with fingers to my face telling me I had no say in any of this. The movement I felt we had died the

<u>LINCOLN</u>

day after that fest. We continued doing the fest and we made some strides to bring back a sense of community but by then it seemed the ties were being broken. The scene went in so many directions.

SONNY KAY (GOLD STANDARD LABORATORIES RECORDS): The Internet became most people's priority. It expanded the human concept of "community" to the point where true one-on-one, face-to-face communication is no longer essential, and much of what inspired hardcore's spirit of debate and confrontation went with it. You could even argue that the Internet reduces productive communication in some ways. It also encourages spectatorship when one can ingest an issue or topic at home, alone, with little real-time discussion or interaction.

JASON ROE: At least people had some beliefs and they were going for it. Better than just sitting at home doing nothing. Being passionate is a great part of the hardcore scene. People are either going to believe or not. Maybe some kid's attitude will turn you off to their ideas, but maybe it will make you think. Plus, all that adrenaline at shows made things exciting.

PERSONAL IMPACT

Frustrated with their lives, environment, social setting, and government, many came to hardcore as an escape. But instead of simply offering an alternative social setting to the mainstream, hardcore created a dialogue that impacted not only the scene but drove people to try to change the world they originally wanted to get away from. Many people's entire political or personal consciousness was shaped by the debates that occurred. For them, hardcore wasn't just a rebellion for rebellion's sake — it was about learning something and making a change in response.

GREG BENNICK: Hardcore in the nineties came off the heels of the eighties which was a highly politicized time in punk and hardcore. We had lived through the first blood-for-oil Gulf War and were all questioning what we heard and what we'd been told on all fronts. I think that as bands started to form in that climate, they took those lines of questioning and made them part of their lyrics and discussions. I know that we (Trial) certainly did. The most heated debates we got into were about the hot topic of the nineties: selling out your ideals to sign to larger labels, versus not being able to reach as many listeners on smaller labels. Everyone talked about that all the time, and I don't think I ever want to discuss it again. [laughs] The most interesting debates for me were always the ones about what to do with our suffering: What is the best way to admit that we are hurting and share that openness with others? How do we get past defense mechanisms and insecurities, and is it even a good idea to try? Lots of good conversation there.

BURN IT DOWN

BRIAN LOWIT: This is something that I think about from time to time as it is quite noticeable that politics and the debates of the 1990s are not seen in the music scene as much today or at least not in the same way. People used to get really upset when a band "sold out" and signed to a major or if a band charged too much for a show, etc where now that stuff seems to not be too important to most people. I think part of that is because a lot of punk/hardcore/indie labels are basically acting like or having funding from major labels so it is hard to really tell the difference and there are very few underground things anymore. The underground became more mainstream and acceptable. With the politics and debates, I think that some bands are afraid to alienate or offend people so do not say too much about how they may or may not feel. On the other hand, there are bands like Radiohead that make political statements from stage and in their lyrics but would not be considered a political band. I think a lot more "underground" bands trying to make it now than ever or maybe there are just more bands than before. I think it is amusing sometimes what major labels pass off as punk music or that a band on a major can be called indie rock.

VIC DICARA: In general, bands always wanted to be on big labels, seventies, eighties, nineties, makes no difference — fuck the bullshit, that's the truth! The only difference is that today it's very possible for it to actually happen, so it becomes more than just a passing fantasy and becomes more like an actively pursued goal, which might be the cause of a lot of the deterioration in the quality of the music. Mainstream music is always safe, and when you start to pander to getting a slice of the mainstream pie, you start to care about being safe, not causing any issues or being too controversial. To me, the whole point of being in a band was to be controversial and cause a stir.

STEVE HART (DAY OF SUFFERING): Politics plays a huge role in hardcore. Every aspect of our lives is controlled by the government. It governs what we say and think and how we live. Government controls the distribution of what we eat and what goes into what we eat. It controls how we live our lives and where our place in society is as people, and you're a fool if you don't believe that all drugs, including alcohol, tobacco, and especially hard drugs, aren't controlled by the government. They also control the mass production of everything, including factory farms. These are all the things that most nineties hardcore kids were against.

SEAN CAPONE: I always viewed hardcore as more of a stepping-stone to living a more ideal life. Did I live up to those ideals? I'm not sure what values I was exposed to that I would not have arrived at on my own, but I probably wouldn't have made any other choice. Hardcore was my window to a larger world, but once I came out as gay, I have to say that I hit up against the scene's limitations pretty quickly.

DAISY ROOKS: Hardcore definitely had a huge impact on my lifestyle politics in terms of still being vegan and straight edge so that was a huge part in shaping how I wanted to live my life. In terms of my personal and political development, punk sort of stopped there for me and once I stopped focusing on consumption issues and began to focus on things on a larger scale like being involved politically with people who weren't necessarily white, vegan, Converse shoes wearing, patch wearing individuals... if I wanted to engage with different kinds of people then I had to really think about the difference between lifestyle politics and broader politics. That's when I decided, "Look, I'm going to continue to be vegan and straight edge, but I'm not going to be an animal rights activist for the rest of my life, I want to work on women's issues and labor issues and other larger issues."

PETE WENTZ (RACETRAITOR, BIRTHRIGHT, EXTINCTION, ARMA ANGELUS, FALL OUT BOY): Hardcore in the nineties was more political. But the whole thing is so cyclical and it's such a microcosm of American culture. When the country swings right, hardcore goes right. When it goes too far right it swings back left. It's not the counter-culture that I thought it was. I love hardcore and it means the world to me, but once you get outside the bubble of it you can look at it and ask, "Why are these dudes calling people 'fags' on stage?" But if you look at where the country is sitting now, it's the same thing.

DON CLARK (TRAINING FOR UTOPIA): I believe that being into hardcore does imply a level of political awareness/consciousness. At the time, most hardcore bands used straight edge, veganism, animal rights, gay rights, Krishna, Christianity and even Satanism as their platform. What was interesting about the scene is that everyone had an open ear. Sure, you had your standard hecklers and naysayers on every side of the fence, but for the most part it was an unspoken respect. We didn't all agree in our beliefs or priorities, but we respected each other. We made some amazing friends that way and I cherish those experiences.

MICKEY NOLAN (SHOW PROMOTER, WRITER): Nineties hardcore shaped my entire adult consciousness. I don't say this to be snobby in any way, but people who were exposed to this era of hardcore and allowed themselves to be fully immersed into it were given a set of experiences that guide everything they do now. No one else will probably be exposed to the depth of emotion or political consciousness or spirituality that we were.

VIQUE MARTIN: Hardcore is still just as much as a hotbed of politics and debate, just in a more underground way than the "hardcore" bands that are sold in Hot Topic. Vegetarianism/veganism, homophobia, racism, sexism, homelessness, animal experimentation, abortion, violence, rape — these are all issues that are still discussed, learned about and argued over. It's just a different generation doing the discussions. Remember, it is a youth culture.

AARON BURGESS: There has always been as much ethical and political bankruptcy in independent music as there is in the musical mainstream (and you only need ask any band that's been burned by a "friend" at a record label to understand this); it's just that it happens on a smaller level when the culprits are indie, so we choose not to recognize it for what it is because we can't accept that the enemy often looks just like we do. As for how things have developed, I think the type of politics has changed, and the ethical questions have changed slightly, but in general, I feel like we've entered an era where politics, morals, and ethics are incredibly prevalent in much underground music, hardcore or not, and in some ways even more prevalent — or maybe I should say "visible" — on a mainstream level. Regardless of how the elections turned out, Punk Voter mobilized thousands of people to take political action in 2004. Take Action — a tour many underground-music purists would snub solely because of its aesthetics — took its message all the way to Capitol Hill in 2005. These are obvious, mainstream examples, but I bring them up for a reason: The sort of social and political activism that's long been a part of punk and hardcore has done just what people involved in those scenes cynically never thought it could do once it got out of their hands — it hit the mainstream untainted, and people responded.

CATHARSIS

JEN ANGEL: Punk/hardcore was not only instrumental in helping me become who I am today, but also for turning me on politically and giving me a community in which I could play a more engaged role. I truly believe that I would not be the political activist I am today without my experiences in the nineties scene, when I was forming my ideas about what kind of world and society I wanted to live in, and what I thought was possible. Even just the basic suggestion that there is another way to live than what is fed to us by dominant culture, despite our replication of some of those very things, was enough to plant a seed in me.

GREG BENNICK: Cynics say that discussing politics in music will never amount to anything? Neither will apathy. Artists transform the world and give it back to us in new forms. They represent the world, but let's look at that word "represent" for what is really going on with the artist: they re-present the world. They take an idea or an event or an issue, they interpret it, and then they present it back to us in a new form or from a new angle or with a new inflection or interpretation. We need artists to help us interpret the world around us, including social and political events.

NEERAJ KANE (SUICIDE FILE, HOPE CONSPIRACY, EXTINCTION, HOLY ROMAN EMPIRE): You'd have such a backlash about things you didn't like about society, which is pretty typical for a person in his or her late-teens or early-twenties and healthy for any youth culture, which the hardcore scene embodied to a great degree. As you grow up you realize you're not that hardcore kid for the rest of your life. You still have that passion within you and the love for the music, but you start to express yourself in other ways, possibly changing society in ways outside the realm of the "scene." Some of the "politics" I was exposed in the hardcore scene as a teenager made me who I am today, and I am sure it affected many other people as well.

STRAIGHT EDGE

By definition, straight edge is a personal decision to reject alcohol and drugs in order to better oneself and pursue a more fulfilling life. But this definition varies widely among those who apply the term to themselves. Most reading *Burning Fight* will have some familiarity with straight edge due to its long presence in the hardcore scene, but one must examine its history to see how a personal belief developed into a full-fledged movement in the eighties and continued to evolve through that decade's end. This evolution continued into the nineties and, as with many other ideas underpinning hardcore, its definition was expanded to encompass other topics like animal rights, politics, and various ethical concerns, though not everyone agreed that these other topics should be included in the concept of straight edge.

Ian MacKaye, bassist for Teen Idles (1979 — 1980) and later the frontman for Minor Threat (1980 — 1983), and some of his bandmates and friends are credited with coining the term "straight edge" to describe their non-use of drugs. They felt that intoxicants had a negative effect on many of those around them. Whether it impacted social circles, family members, the punk scene, or society itself, this group that originated the idea of straight edge was dismayed with the excesses of drinking and drugs, which they saw as a hindrance to living a productive life.

They were also frustrated that many punk shows were held at bars where underage people weren't allowed in. According to Michael Azerrad's *Our Band Could Be Your Life*, when the Teen Idles went on a short West Coast tour in 1980, they were not going to be allowed inside a San Francisco venue because all of the members were under the legal drinking age. In order for the band to play, the members agreed to wear black Xs on their hands so bartenders would know they were under age. The members took the idea back home with them to D.C. where the "X" became identified with this group of "straight edge" kids who rejected the idea of using intoxicants altogether.

Not too long after that Teen Idles tour, MacKaye formed Minor Threat along with drummer Jeff Nelson, bassist Brian Baker, and guitarist Lyle Preslar. Minor Threat was a seminal hardcore band whose fast and intense music and thought provoking lyrics made them one of the most influential in the history of the genre. The cover of their 1983 record *Out Of Step* featured a simple drawing of a black sheep straying from a flock of white sheep. It was a visual representation of the proverbial "black sheep" being at odds with mainstream society—a feeling which the band expressed in the title song of that record along with several other songs, such as "Straight Edge" (*"I'm a person just like you / But I've got better things to do / Than sit around and fuck my head / Hang out with the living dead"*). The lyrics are as much a statement of rebellion against mainstream society and many of the negative behaviors people exhibit as they are about drug use.

IAN MACKAYE (MINOR THREAT, EMBRACE, FUGAZI, DISCHORD RECORDS): When I wrote "Straight Edge," the point of it for me was that I'm a deviant. I don't partake in what society partakes in, which makes me consistent with the other punk rockers—even the drug users and people who were drinking. The point was they were also deviant but for other reasons. I felt more comfortable with people who were living different types of lives and I felt like we were all outsiders for different reasons. My point of view was I believe in community by *inclusion* and not community defined by exclusion.

Some accused Minor Threat of trying to push their views on others. Suggesting to others how they should live their lives was a sensitive topic in a scene that many joined because of its lack of rules. However, the band repeatedly pointed out that they weren't trying to force mandates on others. They clarified their message by re-working the aforementioned song "Out of Step," one of their well known songs that advocated a straight edge lifestyle. In an effort to rectify any potential misunderstandings, the band added the following spoken word section during an instrumental break: *"Listen, there's no set of rules / I'm not telling you what to do / All I'm saying is that I'm bringing up three things that are, like, so important to the world / That I don't happen to find much importance in."* This is an expression of the "it's a choice, not a label" position that many adopters of straight edge took.

Straight edge became widely discussed in hardcore as many saw value in what MacKaye was saying, although there were also many others who liked and respected Minor Threat's music and message generally but felt alienated by the concept of straight edge. Straight edge ideas were present in the lyrics of several punk bands and other early D.C. hardcore bands like Teen Idles, S.O.A., and Government Issue, but Minor Threat, having coined the term, is usually given credit for the concept.

Over the years that followed, people began to apply the term "straight edge" to themselves whether they were already drug-free or newly adopting the philosophy. The concept of straight edge was regularly debated in the scene throughout the eighties. In particular, one of the most discussed issues was whether or not straight edge should be a self-identifying label or whether it should be simply a personal choice. Many also felt that the scene must be united and that factions would weaken the movement and hamper any change it engendered. While these debates did have an effect on individuals and the scene as a whole, as more people adopted the straight edge philosophy, it became a distinct movement within the hardcore scene. This brought further criticism from many who considered themselves straight edge but believed it was a choice and also from those who had no stake in the idea or rejected it outright.

Members of Boston bands like S.S.D. and D.Y.S. applied the term to themselves as bands and as individuals and were among the first to write about straight edge in a more militant manner. While many felt these bands attempted to make straight edge its own regimented movement in hardcore, Al Barile, guitarist of S.S.D., wrote in the 1982 photo zine *My Rules* that straight edge was something that should be interpreted by the individual rather than a specific code of conduct, which is similar to MacKaye's point of view mentioned above. California bands such as Stalag 13 and America's Hardcore also referred to themselves as straight edge. California's Ill Repute and Idaho's Septic Death were loosely affiliated with the ideology. The influential early Reno, Nevada punk/hardcore band 7 Seconds didn't clearly define themselves as straight edge, but befriended Minor Threat and supported some of the ideas behind straight edge in their lyrics. During this time people involved in the scene usually considered themselves punk or hardcore first and straight edge was secondary to their identity. Hardcore was a movement that was seen as a way to reject mainstream society and often as an alternative to it. This was the primary concern but many also felt that destructive and negative behavior wasn't helpful and saw straight edge hardcore as a way to reject society without harming themselves.

Another major factor in the propagation of straight edge was fanzine coverage. Especially in places like California that were far from D.C., zines often played as large a role as bands did. *Flipside*, one of the most widely distributed hardcore/punk zines, ran an article on D.C. and Dischord and regularly covered straight edge bands even though it wasn't their focus. Smaller zines also played a big role: *Touch and Go* (by Tesco Vee and Dave Stimson), one of the first punk fanzines in the U.S., came from the Midwest and covered the D.C. bands very early on. Barry Henssler from the Necros did *Smegma Journal* which covered hardcore and touched on straight edge. *Leading Edge* (by Martin Sprouse, Jason Traeger, and Pat Weakland), *Think* (by Billy Rubin), and *Ink Disease* (by Thomas Siegal and Steve Alper) all had features on D.C. bands and other hardcore including straight edge bands. Boston zines such as *Suburban Voice, XXX*, and earlier issues of *Forced Exposure* covered some straight edge bands, focusing on the Boston scene in particular. There was even a zine called *Straight Edge*. Especially after Minor Threat broke up, zines were one of the only ways to hear about straight edge until more touring bands formed.

For the next few years, there were a lot of bands that were influenced by straight edge and either had members or collectively identified themselves as such, like Rhode Island's Verbal Assault, Holland's Lärm, or Connecticut's Violent Children. However, it started to become a wider movement by the mid-eighties with bands like Arizona's Youth Under Control, California's Justice League and Uniform Choice and Connecticut/New York's Youth of Today who each made straight edge a defining point for themselves and pushed the sub-genre of music and attitudes further within the scene. Along with their friends' bands like No for an Answer, Gorilla Biscuits, Chain of Strength, Bold, Unit Pride, Brotherhood, and many others, Youth of Today is widely credited with transforming straight edge into a nationwide underground phenomenon. Youth of Today's vocalist, Ray Cappo, agreed with Minor Threat and other earlier straight edge bands and wanted to get even more people to rally around the idea as he and his friends had. They felt that by living a moral and drug-free lifestyle, hardcore kids could make a positive impact on their community and society as a whole.

With the fast growth of the "movement" aspect of straight edge came more diversity and some divisions drawn along the line "are you or aren't you straight edge?" The band Slapshot from Boston was probably the first overtly militant straight edge band although to many they seemed tongue in cheek at times. MacKaye, who had since stopped talking about straight edge in his lyrics, remained committed to living a "straight" way of life, but he grew alarmed with what he saw as an exclusionary attitude as espoused by many of these mid to late eighties straight edge bands—an outlook he felt had nothing in common with his original idea for writing about the topic in the first place.

IAN MACKAYE: My concern with where straight edge started to go was that it appeared to become much more of a factioned thing. I started to perceive those factions as communities defined by exclusion—in other words carving out what they are by cutting other people off. I think what was going on in the eighties was a reaction to what we inherited; what was going on in the late eighties and into the nineties was a reaction to what those kids inherited. I'm not saying one era is better than another. It's just interesting to examine from a sociological perspective.

RAY CAPPO (YOUTH OF TODAY, SHELTER): We were into [the idea of] starting a movement because if I find a good idea then I don't want to keep it in the basement. Why not tell the world about it? And people appreciated it. People make it sound like a negative thing, but Minor Threat had songs and records about it. [Ian MacKaye] didn't want to start a movement but he's singing, "I don't drink, I don't smoke, I don't fuck, at least I can fucking think." That's a statement! If you create something and get up on stage and say something and people can appreciate it, whether you want to start a movement or not you're a spokesperson and people will follow you.

MEAN SEASON

Cappo and many of his peers saw straight edge as a positive message that should not just stay in the confines of local hardcore clubs. Youth of Today and other bands from the late eighties "youth crew" era took their straight edge message across the United States, Europe, and other parts of the world and created a mass following along the way. Many bands from this period promoted straight edge as a moral lifestyle. Most youth crew bands spoke between songs at shows about the virtue of drug-free living and also the idea of being positive. Many from this era also viewed straight edge as a fraternal community that a person could "join," but others still saw it as an individual lifestyle choice within the broader hardcore scene. Again, these attitudes varied from person to person.

In addition to the criticism, some felt that straight edge was laughable for various reasons. Some thought that complete abstinence from drugs and alcohol was overly cautious to the point of being silly, some just thought that the straight, clean-cut attitude was square and had no place in punk or hardcore. In the later eighties some bands expressed their mixed feelings about straight edge in the form of parody. Crucial Youth was a popular straight edge band that poked fun at the trappings of the youth crew movement and had lyrics that took straight edge to extremes that were intentionally ridiculous. There were several other bands that had lyrics that were tongue-in-cheek, mocking, or generally poking fun at the moral, positive image that some straight edge bands portrayed. Bands like Project X and Grudge, and, later on, Good Clean Fun are a few examples.

Although many hardcore fans from in the mid to late eighties agreed with the ideas underlying straight edge, there was a sizable number of people who felt that it was becoming actively exclusionary. In some scenes the tension between straight edge and non-straight edge factions increased as the arguments pertaining to these lifestyle choices continued. By the late eighties, militant bands like Judge, A Chorus of Disapproval, Confront, and others formed and took a more hardnosed approach to issues relating to drugs and alcohol. While these bands were popular in many circles, they were also disliked by those who saw this next evolution of straight edge as even more of a reason to not be associated with that part of the scene.

While straight edge bands wrote about a variety of topics, many were known to address issues long familiar to the genre like friendship, betrayal, scene unity, and, of course, the virtues of living a drug-free lifestyle. On the other hand a number of straight edge proponents took a more progressive view and felt it should be an ideology that inspired people to evolve ethically and emotionally as well. Like some of the politically motivated bands from eighties hardcore and punk like Crass, Conflict, and M.D.C., some straight edge bands started to write lyrics about concepts that addressed animal rights and human rights. Youth of Today wrote a song about vegetarianism called "No More" on their 1988 album *We're Not in This Alone.* Other bands associated with straight edge like Turning Point, Insted, Beyond, Raid, Forced Down, and Amenity wrote about a wide range of political, cultural, and personal issues. The inclusion of such concerns, however, varied from band to band.

While many of the eighties straight edge pioneers had toned down their message or even completely rejected it altogether as the nineties arrived, the legacy of what they accomplished, as well as a broader awareness the concerns they tried to spotlight, influenced many nineties straight edge hardcore bands and scene members. Many who played roles in the nineties hardcore scene saw straight edge as a powerful choice amidst a culture that is known for excess. The nineties, in fact, would see straight edge heighten its connection with animal rights, political and moral issues, and social concerns. In many ways the incorporation of these various perspectives diversified the straight edge scene, but some felt these other issues just divided people further.

Bands like Earth Crisis, Culture, Abnegation, Birthright, and Day of Suffering were strong advocates for veganism, weighed in on moral issues like abortion and sexuality, and encouraged their fans to become animal rights activists. They were influenced by anarcho punk bands like Conflict and Crass and hardline bands (this topic is mostly covered in Chapter Three: "Animal Rights") from the late eighties and early nineties like Vegan Reich and Raid, and linked straight edge with political, diet, and environmental concerns. For many of these bands, straight edge was just the first step toward a greater impact on the environment. They organized protests, worked for animal rights (sometimes through direct action), and used zines and the newly formed Internet to get their message out. By the mid nineties the phrase "vegan straight edge" was a fairly common way to identify oneself in the scene. While vegan straight edge was popular, it was also more militant, which turned off those who felt these messages were too rigid or extreme.

While the vegan straight edge scene became its own faction within hardcore, there were also political bands like Trial, Racetraitor, Chokehold, Downcast, By the Grace of God, and Los Crudos that had straight edge members but their lyrics usually covered social concerns. Many of the members of these bands grew up on straight edge and had remained adherents, but they felt compelled to sing about issues like race, gender, sexual orientation, immigration rights, D.I.Y., corporate greed, and a host of other topics. A good number of these bands also had vegan or vegetarian members, but didn't necessarily speak about those issues on stage.

There was also a straight edge "revival" movement in the mid to late nineties that recalled the spirit and outlook of many of the late eighties youth crew bands. Bands like Mouthpiece, Strife, Battery, Good Clean Fun, Floorpunch, and In My Eyes took a more traditional approach to hardcore and straight edge both lyrically and musically. There was some congruence with bands like these and the other factions, but they often differed widely on their definition of what role straight edge should play in one's life and outlook.

Another change that occurred in the nineties was that of more females becoming straight edge and also playing a larger role in the scene. Although females were involved in the eighties, the influx of new voices and the focus on such a variety of issues brought about a focus on topics related to gender and feminism. While there weren't many all female straight edge bands in the nineties, there was at least one that comes to mind—The Doughnuts—but there were several bands that had female members who were straight edge. Additionally, women from this era wrote zines, put on shows, organized protests, and voiced their concerns in more visible ways. A variety of individual women, as well as collective groups like the Chicks Up Front Posse, a small politically active cadre of straight edge women, were a notable presence in a scene that was still predominantly populated by males.

One could argue that these facets of the nineties straight edge scene, as well as some of the changes that occurred in the eighties, forever altered the intentions of the originators. Even as straight edge continues to endure new challenges, it has managed to become a movement larger than anyone had imagined. Like hardcore itself, straight edge is cyclical. It is constantly moving forward while maintaining an

HARVEST

influence that is informed by its past. Its definition, as mentioned earlier, means many things to many people, which has been the cause of controversy but possibly also attracted people to the idea from the start.

Many of the people interviewed for *Burning Fight* had a variety of perspectives on straight edge. Some have been adherents for a good portion of their lives, others were straight edge for shorter periods, and still others found the concept unnecessary altogether. Most were influenced in one way or another by several eighties straight edge bands, but some also saw it as a personal or political reaction to something that occurred to them earlier in life. Whether or not these people actually lived or permanently maintained a straight edge lifestyle, the impact of what was once just something referenced in a song elicits strong opinions to this day.

MIKE KIRSCH (FUEL, TORCHES TO ROME, BREAD AND CIRCUITS): When I was pretty young I was fortunate to come across people who saw the value in having a degree of sobriety in your life. To tune out and not be aware of your situation in the world is to accept a lot of bullshit. When I was a kid straight edge was a way for me to say, "No, I don't want to be a part of this other stuff."

DUNCAN BARLOW (ENDPOINT, GUILT, BY THE GRACE OF GOD): I walked into a record store and saw the Teen Idles seven inch, which had two fists with X's on them. It occurred to me that staying sober was the most rebellious thing I could do in my life.

KATE REDDY (108, KRSNAGRRL FANZINE): I was completely attracted to straight edge from day one. I had older brothers who were kind of preppy kids and they would go and get drunk on the weekends and I would say, "That's not punk, that's what my parents do." [laughs] I wanted to do something different. Not that I'm a complete non-conformist, but I just had a different idea about human relationships and ways to have fun.

JASON ROE (KILL THE ROBOT FANZINE): Like a lot of other people I experienced what substance abuse could do at a very young age. Sitting in my bedroom reading the Minor Threat lyric sheet, I couldn't believe that Ian MacKaye was expressing these feelings that I had. I hated alcohol and drugs and what they did to people. From my family history I was always afraid that I would turn into an alcoholic. Straight edge was something that helped me maintain my sanity in a world where everyone seemed to be using or drinking.

NORMAN BRANNON (TEXAS IS THE REASON, ANTI-MATTER FANZINE, FOUNTAINHEAD, RESSURECTION, SHELTER): I remember being at a party in Long Island with a bunch of metal heads. I had gotten drunk a bunch of times when I was about 12 or 13—pretty much everyone in my neighborhood was experimenting with alcohol at the time. I soon found out that I didn't like being drunk and it wasn't fun. I'm kind of a control freak so the idea of not feeling I can stop this sensation at any point really bothered me. I remember listening to *Crucial Chaos* one night and it was around the time the *Can't Close My Eyes* seven-inch came out and Ray Cappo was on the show and talking to the host about straight edge. My very first impression had nothing to do with the scene, I just remember listening to him and saying, "That's exactly how I feel." I immediately went to the record store and bought the Youth of Today seven-inch and remember thinking how exciting it was and that now I had a cool excuse not to drink.

CHRISSY PIPER (PHOTOGRAPHER): In junior high and high school most people drank. So, straight edge for me was a form of rebellion. It made me feel stronger about it knowing there were other people out there that felt the same way. Finding Minor Threat was like the sky opening up. It was rad to see hardcore kids not drinking and avoiding those punk rock stereotypes.

JOHN COYLE (OUTSPOKEN): My introduction to being straight edge came at an early age. At a family party, my uncle gave me a huge amount of whiskey while we were playing pool. I ended up with severe alcohol poisoning. That was it. I must have been about 12. Years later when all of my friends started drinking I had no interest. I would go to parties just to hang out and people would just freak out because I would not drink. People would get violent because I would not join in. That was around my freshman year in high school. It seems stupid now, but I went out and had a hat made that said "Milk Rules," would get a gallon of milk and sit right in the middle of the parties and get in fights with all of the people who couldn't deal. I didn't care how many people couldn't stand me. Every weekend I went to shows and saw bands like Uniform Choice or 7 Seconds—that was were I belonged.

JIM GRIMES (STORMTROOPER FANZINE, EXTINCTION): The main reason I got into straight edge was probably looking at the cover of *Break Down the Walls*. I remember thinking, "What is this?" These dudes with X's on their hands and everything. I had heard the term before, but I didn't know what it was exactly. I only drank a few times, and it was boring to me. At the same time, my dad was an alcoholic for the most part and the main cause of the breakdown of his marriage to my mother. I should be a super bad alcoholic because my dad was, but I wasn't going to go down that road. That's why to this day I haven't changed as opposed to people who, say, did it because of some Earth Crisis lyrics. I call myself straight edge but when you get to a certain age it really doesn't matter anymore. It's a pretty natural, ingrained part of my life.

CHRIS COLOHAN (LEFT FOR DEAD, THE SWARM, CURSED): When I started going to shows, I drank a lot and did all that teenage stuff and I don't ever regret it. I was young enough to get away with being fucked up all the time but old enough to see that it was going to make for a really pathetic adulthood if it kept up. I didn't ever get into straight edge, it just boiled down to the fact that I am really shitty at moderation and have a tendency toward self-destructive behavior. There are better forms of self-destruction in my life that give me more to show for my time and energy, like just not stopping when I should, when stress and time and life is shutting me down mentally and physically, just to spit at it and do it all that much harder. I get more out of that than any bottle I ever emptied.

DEMIAN JOHNSTON (UNDERTOW, NINEIRONSPITFIRE, KISS IT GOODBYE, PLAYING ENEMY): When I got into straight edge I considered that subversive. I liked punk rock, but I didn't want to self-destruct in an intellectual closet somewhere in a house downtown. I felt like disciplining myself and wanted to write songs and go on tour as opposed to drink. My parents drank and smoked all the time, so I saw that and felt like the mistakes they made while young messed up their lives. My dad was part of the left-wing culture in Seattle and did a bunch of protesting, but then he got into the lifestyle of just going out to the bar every night. He used alcohol and drugs to keep up with the youthful things he did. He dodged a lot of responsibility. I felt like if I went the way my parents did then I'll be stuck in a factory job until I died.

PETE WENTZ (RACETRAITOR, BIRTHRIGHT, EXTINCTION, ARMA ANGELUS, FALL OUT BOY): At my school there was this thing called "Cancer Corner" and people would sit there and smoke. One day I found a bunch of flyers there left by a local straight edge kid. It was pretty much straight edge propaganda which is pretty laughable, but at the time something about it made me think. A lot of my friends were into metal and that scene was so saturated with smoking and drinking—the most punk thing to do was to be like, "Fuck you, I'm straight edge."

DENNIS LYXZEN (REFUSED, INTERNATIONAL NOISE CONSPIRACY): I traded my Napalm Death *Scum* original pressing for *Break Down the Walls*, and that's pretty much the only thing I listened to in the summer of 1988. Looking back now at the record, sure the lyrics are a bit corny, but at that time it meant a lot. They talked about being outsiders on an even bigger scale. They weren't drinking or eating meat and I got really excited about that. I drew strength from them because when you are already an outsider you can become energized by bands like that who advocate living your own way. So, by the time 1989 rolled around I claimed I was straight edge. What that meant I didn't totally know at the time, as I only knew a little about it. [laughs]

SEAN CAPONE (POSITRON FANZINE): In those days I wasn't looking for an escape; I was looking for an intense way to engage and connect with the world. I thought it was cool that there was a movement of kids in punk and hardcore who were trying to provide an alternative to the alternative — that is, the perception of punk as nihilistic, empty, self-destructive. To me it wasn't about a set of rules or judgments that policed one's body, which is a very reactionary and conservative reading of straight edge. It was about changing your mind about how you react to the negative stuff in the world, and finding respect for yourself.

So, what exactly was the appeal of adopting straight edge? For many it was independence. With an overwhelming number of hardcore fans being in their teens and early twenties, the scene was full of people cutting the proverbial cord from their families, making their own lifestyle choices, and formulating their own ideas. Straight edge provided a community in which people shared their concerns, expressed their ideas, and made their own decisions independent of the mainstream. Since the nineties era was often focused on issues outside of the traditional rejection of intoxicants, this eventually led to many changes in ethical and political stances for these people, as well as dietary changes such as vegetarianism—all of which would play important roles in this politically-charged hardcore era.

KENT MCCLARD (HEARTATTACK FANZINE, EBULLITION RECORDS): That whole "youth crew" straight edge scene of the late-eighties you associate with Youth of Today and Judge had a political mindset. Initially, hardcore was about this crazy anger and then around 1986 it just kind of got dull for a time. That outward anger wasn't working as well. It was about 1988 where you saw this resurgence in hardcore and it had a lot to do with straight edge. It was about looking back and trying to figure out how we were going to define ourselves. We weren't just going to thrive on anger and hate. We were going to concentrate more on what we were doing.

STEVE REDDY (EQUAL VISION RECORDS): Some people jump on the bandwagon and might not be there for the right reasons, but some people might also get it and it might really help them. If you think about it, drinking is such a huge part of society. Diverting yourself from reality is the number one priority for human existence whether it's intoxication or anything else. The dynamic of escapism is so funny. Even if you drink in moderation, you could have a drink or two and hang out standing in a bar for hours. If you hang out in the same place and you're sober then it seems ridiculous. If you see someone who is homeless due to drugs or alcohol—that was no one's plan when they were 13 years old. No one ever says, "Oh man, there's going to be pot and drinking at this party. I'll probably parlay that right into homelessness." But it does happen, and it's random who it happens to. You're taking a chance and for what? Are you afraid to act outside your bubble? You have the ultimate excuse to pass off any kind of behavior. "I was drunk!" I drank when I was in high school and I remember that was a reasonable excuse for most people. "Dude, you got down with my girlfriend!" "Oh, man, I was drunk, though!" After 9/11 people were up in arms, for obvious reasons. But how many people died, 2,500? How many people die every day from alcohol related incidents whether it's alcoholism, drunk driving, fetal alcohol syndrome, or spousal abuse? It *way* surpasses that number.

D.J. ROSE (PATH OF RESISTANCE): When I was a kid my dad was in Vietnam and he ended up coming home addicted to drugs. When I was about five my family won the lottery for $50,000 which was a lot of money for 1973. Money doesn't actually solve people's problems so he just ended up using the money to buy more drugs. My parents separated because of it, and I think that had a profound impact on me as a young person. As a kid I remember being exposed to my mom having a drinking problem and she used to smoke in the car, which isn't fun being in a car in upstate New York during the winter. So, I remember being confused why adults did

these things. It's funny, I remember people saying to me, "It'll make sense to you when you're older." Some things do make sense to you as an adult, but other things just never did. I remember telling myself I'd never smoke or drink and I've actually never done it to this day.

KARL HLAVINKA (RACETRAITOR): I was never straight edge to be part of some cohesive, male fraternal group. Later on, and currently, being drug free started to make even more sense as you start to learn how drugs are produced; how civilization is absolutely dependent on them to keep functioning; how they destroy cultures; how they're used throughout history and the present as mechanisms of control in colonial situations, and how willing people are to get enmeshed in them with phony ass urban legends of it being "natural." Alcohol, for example, seems to be predominantly related to sedentary, agri/pastoral societies, whereas in nomadic hunter-gatherer ethnography no anthropologist has seen it being produced until forced settlement began. Forced settlement came and with sugar used for producing alcohol, we see the same model again and again emerge. Murder rates and violence increase. This model occurs all through European contact from trade or as its tentacles of capital reach into its periphery.

NEERAJ KANE (SUICIDE FILE, HOPE CONSPIRACY, EXTINCTION, HOLY ROMAN EMPIRE): I got into straight edge as me and most of my friends were so into skating and listening to music that we just never cared about drinking or whatever most of the kids did in high school. Eventually we realized that we never really liked that whole party scene and we never understood that culture. Straight edge was such an antithesis of that attitude that we just got into it even more. And now we could label ourselves and be a part of something larger whereas before we were just skaters who didn't drink or do drugs.

MICHELLE (TODD) GONZALES (SPITBOY, INSTANT GIRL): I respected straight edge, though I never was. I grew up in a home where people were abusing drugs and alcohol like crazy. To know there was a movement out there to keep kids from going down that road is totally comforting. Even for the kids who weren't straight edge, just the exposure to the idea of you don't have to get drunk to have fun and you don't have to get wasted to be hardcore. It was an alternative to the party lifestyle that often went along with punk and hardcore.

SCOTT BEIBIN (BLOODLINK RECORDS): The way I carried out straight edge was to add a goofy element to it. A lot of kids went with this militaristic or macho type of thing, but I thought straight edge was fun. When I put the Frail record out we all came up with the phrase "Make your own noise." When kids were moshing violently at shows I would encourage people to sit down in the pit to discourage the violence dancing. Instead of doing windmills, why not fight capitalism or be an activist? Do something more productive. That's what I tried to get kids to see.

STEPHEN BRODSKY (CAVE IN): I had a very straight edge attitude even before I became involved with the local hardcore scene. I do remember feeling a bit of pressure to adopt the title, and in this case, it's sort of a natural thing to experience. In small communities of musically active people, anonymity of any kind is harder to have, especially when those communities are focused so much on identifying themselves with certain politics or ethics to perhaps establish or "prove" why they belong. Simply supporting local music wasn't enough, by some standards. You had to stand for something with a statement or a term to back it up. And I remember people not knowing what to make of it when I would say "I'm not straight edge—but I don't do drugs." That kind of political ambiguity can really freak people out, which always intrigued me.

MANI MOSTOFI (RACETRAITOR): The reason I was straight edge was the same reason I was into hardcore—I didn't like the youth culture scene and the way things were going in the world. It was like when Henry Rollins said, "People come up to me and ask me, 'What are you angry at?' My response is whatta ya got?'" [laughs] The whole idea of everyone converging to be the most mediocre person possible was just fucked. So, the way to rebel is to not let them and here's this one thing they push on you to try and pacify you. Drugs and alcohol keep you slow and weak and make you destructive. If you really want to rebel you shouldn't be about self-destruction but about building a new sort of human and that's what I thought straight edge offered.

RAY CAPPO: I thought straight edge was great! I know for a fact that it saved people's lives and even changed the face of the world! Do you know how many people became vegetarian and vegan after their initial exposure to straight edge and saved thousands of lives because of that? I think of how many thousands of animals I would have eaten if I wasn't vegetarian, not to mention the thousands of fans that listened to us over the years. So, if you can radically change the world like that and save some lives—that's a legacy!

While straight edge impacted many lives in a positive manner, some people felt that it also brought rigidity and moral dictates to a scene that was, supposedly, all about living one's life to the fullest in whatever manner he or she chose. Many, including some who were straight edge themselves, were alarmed by the somewhat cliquish mentality that often came along with straight edge, as factions and crews formed and made other non-straight edge hardcore kids feel out of place within the scene. Some of these groups existed in the eighties, but they became more widespread in the nineties. They would occasionally commit acts of violence against show goers who had a beer or cigarette in hand. Some of the more militant adherents also denigrated those who stopped being straight edge as "edge breakers," which also sometimes brought about violent disputes. The fact that some took straight edge to such extreme levels was a source of alienation for people who felt hardcore shouldn't allow for inflexible rules from within its own ranks.

JESSICA HOPPER (HIT IT OR QUIT IT FANZINE): There was this attitude of, "My friends and I stick together and we're loyal to each other and true till death." Some people like that rigidity as far as identity and it seems like a slightly more upscale version of jock identity in terms of having a moral high ground in regards to straight edge.

J.R. CONNORS (CAVE IN): I had been smoking cigarettes before I got into hardcore, so I felt really alienated at a lot of straight edge shows. I always had the stance of hardcore being more of a brotherhood of misfits, getting together and tolerating each other *because* you were all freaks, drunks, and generally had nowhere else to go. So when the whole straight edge thing popped up, it really put me off from the scene.

GAVIN VAN VLACK (BURN, ABSOLUTION): Straight edge eventually became so homogenous that you had the same kind of reactionary situation as when straight edge originally came about. It stopped growing and it became more about an image or fashion statement than it was a progressive lifestyle. People take things to extremes. I've seen kids getting punched in the mouth for having a beer! You get a few people with a good idea and then all of a sudden these other people start running it and manipulating it. But at the same time, straight edge also spawned a musical style that people could relate to.

JOSH LOUCKA (SHIFT): The anti-drinking thing never appealed to me. I remember a friend of mine and I used to say, "How can you be so adamant about something that you *don't* do?" We felt like we wanted to hear more about what you *did* do.

SONNY KAY (GOLD STANDARD LABORATORIES RECORDS): Straight edge always struck me as a club for either parent-fearing nerds or jocks who liked harder music than Van Halen. In my experience, the label—all it really was, anyway—was just another gimmicky trend… something to grow out of. Truly "straight" persons don't feel the need to justify their decision by turning it into a gang or a badge of honor.

AARON BURGESS (WRITER): I was straight edge inasmuch as I abstained from drinking and drugs and listened to a disproportionate amount of straight edge hardcore from my

BATTERY

late teens to age 22 or so. After that, it's not like I "fell off the wagon" or anything; I simply accepted that period of my life for what it was, and over time accepted the idea that it was okay for me to have the occasional drink in a social situation. I came to straight edge because of its positive aspects: It answered a lot of the questions I'd been having about morals and personal identity, and it provided me with a sort of moral code that made a lot more sense than the stuff I was learning in Catholic school (though in terms of guilt and abstinence, it wasn't far off from what the nuns there were teaching). Still, I think for all its positive aspects, straight edge can be a really damaging ideology for people who aren't emotionally prepared to deal with life outside of or beyond straight edge—I mean, to some of these people, it's like being a Crip or a Blood; if you're into it full-on and you're vocal about your beliefs while you're in it, then you don't leave the scene without a big, public shitstorm coming down on you. This can really fuck a person up—physically and emotionally; it can keep you in a sort of terminal adolescence where you aren't prepared to cope with life outside of this sort of quasi-monastic state of existence the scene has dictated for you; a state of existence that really doesn't apply to the world beyond the scene.

MOE MITCHELL (CIPHER): I was and am drug and alcohol free but never claimed to be straight edge. The biggest problem with the vast majority of straight edge kids was their lack of politics. They felt like they were part of a movement yet there was no platform, direction, ideology or anything outside of "don't smoke, don't drink." It became this badge of honor. They could have made connections to the broader implications of their boycott or the drug, alcohol, and tobacco industries but few did. The reality is once a lot of these kids hit the drinking age they lost their edge. There are very few straight edgers in their mid-twenties and thirties. I'm still drug and alcohol free and I've done it without tattooing X's on my neck.

Although heavily influenced by eighties straight edge bands, nineties straight edge expanded its focus to topics outside the rejection of intoxicants and animal exploitation. While many of the late-eighties straight edge kids moved in other directions with their lives, a slew of new bands came along with both overt and subtle perspectives on straight edge. Some bands focused on positivity and individual progression and many who followed them used the movement as a starting point to dig into broader social and political issues. The variety of perspectives on what defined straight edge continued to exist in the nineties with some viewing it as a political stance against what they perceived as a negative aspect of the culture, and others viewing it as a way to improve their lives along with other varied viewpoints.

JOHN "PORCELL" PORCELLY (SHELTER, YOUTH OF TODAY, JUDGE, PROJECT X): It seemed like once the nineties hit straight edge became uncool. When straight edge crashed for a bit it was almost like all the kids that were once championing straight edge were getting older and looking back on it as something they had grown out of. Almost all my friends weren't straight edge anymore, but for me it wasn't something to just grow out of. Straight edge was something I really believed in; it helped me improve my life personally and I wasn't quite ready to give up on it just because the trend had crashed.

BRENDAN DESMET (GROUNDWORK, ABSINTHE): The "youth crew" idea had become somewhat laughed at, so people wanted to take it in a new direction and have it make

CHOKEHOLD

sense for the current time period. It was important to find ways to make straight edge respectable and keep it as an anti-authoritarian idea, much like it was in the first place. On the flip side, there were people who didn't see a hell of a lot of reasons to get drunk or stoned. They would often identify with straight edge but didn't necessarily want to associate with it due to some of its more ridiculous aspects. There were larger and more grandiose ideas associated with straight edge—people didn't want to support corporations that made alcohol and tobacco available to the public or which might have tested on animals. People were also looking to express themselves as independent and being under the influence of substances was somewhat of a way of being controlled.

DARREN WALTERS (JADE TREE RECORDS): I know it's popular to think straight edge was big in the eighties and maybe in some ways it seemed like it was. But I think straight edge was much bigger in the nineties when it resurged. Now in certain areas like in Connecticut in 1988 there were a lot of kids, but it definitely wasn't a coast-to-coast phenomenon. Maybe things like the internet helped get the word out there more in the nineties. The accessibility made it more visible. There were also more labels and bands, which made is easier to spread the word.

SEVAPRIYA BARRIER (KRSNA GRRRL FANZINE): The eighties era kids had a lot less to live up to. I don't think they were as image conscious or that it really occurred to them that their actions might be scrutinized locally or nationally. At least on the East Coast the squabbles were much smaller and what it took to be part of the scene seemed to be a lot less standardized. By the early nineties the kids realized that their stage performances and words would be immortalized. The look and attitudes were disseminated across the country and the trends were easy to document and debate or follow. The kids became more eager to tell people what to do, to denounce others, because they knew people were listening and what they said had power.

CHRIS LOGAN (CHOKEHOLD, GOODFELLOW RECORDS): You can only write about straight edge so much. I mean, Chokehold was like, "While we are here and together and thinking clear, what the fuck else can we do?" Let's cause some shit, because we broke out of the cloud they wanted us to be in. Personally, I was always very proud to be straight edge and wore my X's with pride at pretty much every show, but most kids just wanted to sing along, buy the t-shirt and the CD, and then it was time to go home. Straight edge's limitations were just the scene in general. There were not many bands that wanted to take it further than the hardcore show. We were not living in a squat with a bag of guns ready to take down the government, but we just got tired of being in the mold and wanted to rage about something besides booze and drugs.

KARL BUECHNER (EARTH CRISIS, PATH OF RESISTANCE): I was hit by a drunk driver when I was with my girlfriend about four blocks from my house and the driver took off. I don't think he even checked to see if we were alive or dead. It was those types of personal experiences in terms of how dangerous drugs and alcohol can be that fueled a lot of our emotions.

BRENT DECKER (RACETRAITOR): To me straight edge without the political edge is like being in a Christian youth group. Straight edge as a fraternity never made sense to me. For me it was always a political choice in terms of the role that alcohol and drugs play in American society, as well as where the drugs actually come from. There is a trail of misery from South America and Afghanistan to bring the drugs here, as well as the lives that get ruined when it arrives in the States. For a lot of people there aren't a lot of other economic opportunities and they fall into that trap of trying to make a quick buck.

JOHN MCKAIG (PHOTOGRAPHER, SHOW PROMOTER): For a lot of us in Syracuse, straight edge was also about social issues… and not just vegetarianism and animal rights but also environmentalism, ecology, child abuse, corporate ties to alcoholism. These were extensions of what we were talking about. It was more than just being drug free. I'm also not going to judge other people and what their lives might be like. We just tried to be a good example and leave it at that.

KEN OLDEN (WORLDS COLLIDE DAMNATION A.D., BATTERY): My biggest problem with the alcohol and tobacco industries is that they represent the most evil and greedy corporations in the world—their products are human self-destruction. When you look at their history and their actions these companies are the lowest of the low. All you have do is turn on an episode of *COPS*—almost every single idiot on there is drunk. How many women or children are getting beat by some drunk asshole? Look at the ads, how they equate drinking beer with getting women. I'd laugh if it weren't so pathetically sad. Anyway, I decided a long time ago I'm not giving those assholes any money.

MANI MOSTOFI: In the nineties there were two distinct straight edge scenes—one of them was more of a mosh oriented, "jock-edge" scene, which was probably more visible. But there was a second straight edge scene which was kind of a dirtier and more political scene that revolved around labels like Ebullition Records and bands like Downcast and Groundwork. In both scenes there were bands and people who were and weren't straight edge, but at the time it seemed like the majority of folks were. That duality was an interesting thing because those two scenes played off of each other. The nineties straight edge scene was broad based intellectually because straight edge wasn't necessarily the main issue being debated. Straight edge was the given issue. The attitude then was if you start by being straight edge then you can clear your mind and be able to focus on all these other things and ideas like veganism and human rights. There were vegan straight edge kids, Riot Grrrl straight edge kids, all sorts of political straight edge kids getting into environmental, class, and race politics. The main issue most of these bands talked about wasn't straight edge, but straight edge was the lynchpin for the whole movement and exchanging of ideas.

ANDY HURLEY (RACETRAITOR, KILLTHESLAVEMASTER, FALL OUT BOY): I became straight edge when I was 16. I'd been into politics since I was younger and exposed to political hip-hop like Public Enemy and Paris. That was the beginning of me being politicized. But bands like Earth Crisis took some of those politics to straight edge, which made it appealing to me. I'm straight edge in response to the political and social fallout of the war on drugs and COINTELPRO and flooding the minority communities in the ghettos with crack and other drugs. It's basically an attack on non-white people, as well as any revolutionary spirit on kids in suburban communities. From a young age I was always into counter culture ideas and politics, and I think straight edge fit right in. While you're doing any sort of positive work you need to be clear minded and in control of your senses.

The nineties straight edge scene often acted as an entry point for broader issues, but as many straight edge kids became more interested in issues pertaining to animal rights, gender, race, spirituality, politics, and the environment, the occasional overzealous and male dominated tendencies that made some cynical about straight edge in the eighties— which were often criticized by straight edgers themselves—appeared again.

RAY CAPPO: I felt straight edge became very gang-ish in the nineties and I lost the taste for that scene. I couldn't relate to the music because it was all metal, and there was a lot of hate involved with it, too. I always came from a more positive perspective. I never wanted to "exterminate" those who were drinking. I didn't think it was bad to tell people about the harmful effects of drinking, but I never felt Youth of Today or Shelter were motivated by hate. When movements get motivated by hate then it sort of defeats the purpose especially if they are in the name of enlightening other people.

SCOTT VOGEL (SLUGFEST, DESPAIR, BURIED ALIVE, TERROR): Straight edge is a wonderful thing. A lot of my friends were and still are straight edge. But I feel bad for the people who really believe in the straight edge lifestyle because nine out of ten people who claim straight edge soon aren't going to be. If I really believed in it, I'd be really pissed off. It's a great thing, but when it becomes an elitist thing it's a bit ridiculous. You know, those kids who wore the "Shoot Your Local Drug Dealer" t-shirts? I'm sure none of those people who wore those shirts actually did that, but I guess they were just trying to get their point across.

MARTIN SORRONDEGUY (LOS CRUDOS, LENGUA ARMADA RECORDS, LIMP WRIST): By the early nineties I definitely noticed that straight edge had changed. I came from a very poor neighborhood and it seemed like most of the straight edge kids came from the wealthy suburbs. Many of them took on this uniformity. They bought lettermen's jackets and wore Swatch watches and I just couldn't understand what that was about. I remained straight edge, but I definitely did not identify with many of the kids.

GAVIN VAN VLACK: The ideas behind straight edge were great, but the problem is when some folks get a certain zealous attitude about it others just follow it blindly. A lot of the people originally got involved in that idea because it was reactionary to what was going on in the scene in that era. You had fights at shows and a lot of violence and people were dying left and right. The overdose rate back then was pretty insane. The drug scene seemed like a deathstyle more than a lifestyle. Straight edge was very reactionary to what punk rock had become. When you have the punk rock attitude of, "Yeah, I'm going to get fucked up and that's what all my friends are doing" then there is no growth in that.

JEFF BECKMAN (CHOKEHOLD): I felt that straight edge was a very political stance in life. I really didn't see it any other way and couldn't understand why you would be straight edge if you didn't have any opinions of the real world topics. Most of the people

CHARLES BRONSON

I knew like that were the first to just fade away. Then you had the religious straight edge parasites. To us, straight edge was anything but religious. I guess you could say were a part of something that we had problems with in the first place, and that made for interesting times.

JUSTIN PEARSON (SWING KIDS, THE LOCUST, STRUGGLE): When some asshole was beating up some crusty punk for being drunk or slashing tires of someone who smoked weed, I'd just see how they were just as fucked up for eating meat or being homophobic or, better yet, supporting corporations that were in conjunction with alcohol companies and tobacco companies. And, shit, even more supporting a government that pushes drugs on people of color and creates social situation where drugs and alcohol are used to keep people of color down or to control the masses. If straight edge was a prominent aspect of combating the U.S. government and the effects that it has on a large scale of what drugs and alcohol do to people, then I'd see it in a different light.

BRENDAN DESMET: We always associated with straight edge very strongly, but we wanted to get away from the clean cut youth crew type aesthetic, where straight edge was the only topic of conversation. We looked at straight edge as a starting point but felt it was more important to talk about liberation on other levels. We didn't like the idea of straight edge being a bunch of jocks coalescing around one idea that could potentially be exclusive; we tried to bring it full circle and discuss how to change the world around us.

RYAN PATTERSON (COLISEUM, BLACK CROSS, THE NATIONAL ACROBAT): I saw a lot of people trying to take control but then taking it too far. I never got into the message of "clenched fists, clean, healthy living"! I remember hearing a Soulside lyric that said, "There's a lot in this world to stand up for and stand against whether it's the cigarette in your hand or the death of the animal in demand." That's the lyric where I was like, "Fuck, yeah!" There are some things to stand up against and I won't participate in those things. But I never really understood the "physically strong, morally straight" type of vibe. There seemed to be a lot of macho-posturing that came along with some of that scene, which smacked of male self-righteousness.

KATE REDDY: Because I was a girl I didn't really get to be political about straight edge, because the majority of the aesthetic was male. So, it had to be personal for me. There weren't many more girls until the early nineties and by that time I was getting older and I didn't have the same passion for it I had when I was a teenager. It was a personal choice and a desire to be a part of the group. The group was supporting what I wanted to do. I was relieved to not have to do drugs and alcohol which scared the crap out of me. [laughs] It also gave me some freedom and my parents let me do almost anything because they knew I wasn't going to drink or do drugs. So I got to sneak into CB's before I was 16. [laughs]

AARON BURGESS: Because of my age, I was able to experience at least the tail end of the post-Minor Threat straight edge scene firsthand; and to be on the sidelines as SSD started becoming the bigger influence and the youth-crew scene exploded and the scene really lost its sense of humor and the '88-style stuff came into vogue; then to feel completely out of it when bands like Earth Crisis and Vegan Reich and the whole hardline movement sprang up a few years later. By then, I was an outsider, even if I could empathize with some of what those bands were preaching. To me, it just seemed like a moral dead end. As for the violent aspects of the scene, thank God I didn't grow up in Utah; that's all I can say. I saw my share of beat-downs and pissing contests and threats and shows cut short because the singer or someone else got jumped, but that's all I can really comment on firsthand. By the time the scene really started getting violent, I was on the outside looking in.

ROB MORAN (UNBROKEN, NARROWS): Radical stances can be good or bad depending on the issue. Honestly, does it matter one iota if everyone is straight edge or not? Or is it more important that healthcare and education are at a critical low in our country? From a political aspect, I think being tough on issues is important, as that is how change happens. Many great changes have happened because of radical thinking in this world. I'm all for it if it helps the world as a whole. As for lesser things like straight edge, who gives a shit? I don't really give a fuck if the rest of the world is or not. I have felt this way for many years.

RYAN DOWNEY (BURN IT DOWN, SUPERHERO FANZINE): At first the straight edge scene of the nineties looked to be much more politically motivated than the earlier scene, very active in progressive causes. Veganism became intrinsically linked and straight edge kids were organizing protests, talking about feminism, all sorts of things. A lot of it turned out to be empty lip service as the activist fad soon faded like all other fads before it, though a few people stayed true as they moved forward in life. Nowadays it has come full circle as lots of jocks and idiots get into straight edge and make it more like the apathetic homogenized youth crews of the late eighties. Hopefully the pendulum will go once again toward meaning and activity.

KURT SCHROEDER (BIRTHRIGHT, CATALYST RECORDS): In one sense straight edge is cliquish. But I also think there are phases that straight edge kids go through just like anyone else. It's a cultural type of thing as far as being in a sub-cultural group, and you get meaning from separating yourself from mainstream culture. For younger people it's like a support group; you're not getting pressure to do stuff you're against.

JESSICA HOPPER: I identified as straight edge for years and not because of anything that had to do with Minor Threat, though I really loved them and they were one of the first bands I got into. Ethically and morally that was just what I was more interested in. I didn't wear X's on my hands or make a big deal out of it; I just identified as straight edge. But I didn't have an interest in things that were incredibly dogmatic. Hardcore was so macho and at the time there were more interesting things happening with punk. That kind of hardcore seemed built on nostalgia. I thought it was pretty ridiculous that 15 years after Minor Threat people were still trying to rigidly follow this prescription of a code that decided what was okay and not okay. It was like this ultra macho boys club where they were adhering to a dogma and had no sense of humor. I just felt like, "Who cares?"

As the differences between die-hard straight edge kids and those skeptical of the movement widened, the level of straight edge militancy increased. As might be expected, the more people that support an issue, the larger the push to legitimize it.

Although many looked back to the eighties for their initial inspiration for becoming straight edge, the number of people who considered themselves straight edge in the nineties was probably larger. During this time, hardcore drew larger audiences due to a variety of punk/hardcore rooted bands—everyone from Nirvana and Green Day to Quicksand and Sick of it All—signing to major labels and getting more mainstream exposure. Some of those who were exposed to punk and hardcore through these bands sought out the roots of their music, which many found in the hardcore scene. Hardcore bands, and in particular certain straight edge bands such as Earth Crisis, Snapcase, and Strife, sold more records and reached more people.

Other straight edge bands like Mouthpiece, Ten Yard Fight, Bane and others also played an important role in maintaining a straight edge presence in the hardcore scene.

However, while many bands in the nineties spoke out about straight edge, there were others that were straight edge, but took a more overtly political and/or philosophical approach to the movement and often did not even address the topic of straight edge specifically in their songs. For example, bands like Policy of Three, None Left Standing, Disembodied, Endeavor, Groundwork, Threadbare, Portraits of Past, Endpoint, and Frail all had straight edge members, though they rarely spoke about straight edge on stage.

Another new factor was the internet straight edge community, which was gaining popularity even as it was still in its early days with straight edge email lists, chat rooms, and message boards. This broader exposure gave all viewpoints on straight edge a forum to discuss the subject.

NORMAN BRANNON: I feel like every single person in the early nineties was trying to one up each other ethically, myself included. Whether it was being hardline and eating air or claiming to know the absolute truth, it seemed like you couldn't get crazy enough to arrive at that point where you were like, "I win! I'm purer than a snowflake!" [laughs]

TAYLOR STEELE (FOUR WALLS FALLING): You can't look at straight edge as bad or good or black and white. It's all the individual and what he or she does with it. Someone like Tim McMahon from Mouthpiece has always been cool about it. When Four Walls Falling used to play in New Jersey, Tim would have us stay at his house and I was the only straight edge person in the band and he never treated anyone in my band any different than he treated me. But then you get other people with guns in the shape of X's on their shirts and say they're going to kick your ass if you're not straight edge and it turns into a macho thing. It should be about something positive like how Youth of Today and Minor Threat took straight edge. But as with anything that is positive it can be turned into something negative.

JUSTIN "GUAV" GUAVIN (CONVICTION RECORDS/FANZINE): We started to hear so many rumors about our town (Syracuse); it was silly. We heard that if you go to a show in Syracuse and aren't straight edge, you'll get beat up. You'd get beaten up for not being vegan. That we brought guns to shows. That we were constantly fighting. None of it was true! Some of our best friends weren't straight edge. I can literally, with no exaggeration, say that between 1991 and 1996, there were four fights at shows. And none of those had anything to do with straight edge; they were just the usual "mosh pit beefs" and were over in five minutes. Syracuse was untouched by the violence that plagued other scenes. Ask any band who ever played there. I would always hear about kids scared to come to Syracuse for shows because they had heard all these horror stories, like shotguns at shows and shit, and I would just crack up. But it was really disheartening at times to have all this said about you that just isn't true—it just sucked to have this rep that was not deserved. At one point I just got tired of having this reputation for all this absurd shit, so I made the "Straight Edge is All About Automatic Weapons" shirts. Totally sarcastically. [laughs] If that's what people wanted to think about us, then we'd give 'em what they wanted. I just took it to the extreme of absurdity and made those shirts in a very tongue-in-cheek way.

GREG BENNICK (TRIAL): In terms of violence, straight edge for the vast majority of the hardcore scenes in the world was never as violent as people perceived it to be. Straight edge itself was never about violence. It was about being positive, in response to negativity so rampant in the early 1980's punk and hardcore scenes, and improving your life through making intelligent choices, thus avoiding intoxicants. For the most part, the scene wasn't violent everywhere. An exception in the nineties was the scene in Salt Lake City: there, we saw an intersection of animal rights, gang violence, and straight edge. That is a difficult combination to navigate for anyone, and the result in Salt Lake was that violence was a huge part of what they experienced in their scene. The press picked up on the term straight edge, and due to the perceived association of violence with hardcore, they assumed that anyone who identified with that term was a violent, gang related, animal rights terrorist. The *New York Times* ran a story on the violent world of "straight edge" and it infuriated me. I remember calling the *Times*, and finally getting through to the correspondent who wrote the story. I talked to her for 30 minutes and re-educated her about what she'd written about so "expertly." She admitted that her knowledge had been limited and that her job was to write what she could, based on what she knew at the time. I made sure to let her know that stories like hers, while they might sell papers, ultimately did more harm than good for the people involved in the music scene.

NATE WILSON (MONSTER X, DAS OATH): I was in a straight edge band called Monster X. We started because at the time (1992) there were no bands that we could relate to that sounded like what we wanted to sound like. We were playing grind type hardcore, and there really were no tolerant straight edge bands that were playing different styles of music. They were all playing metallic mosh-core or later in the nineties rehashed Youth of Today rip-off sounding hardcore. I'm no longer straight edge, haven't been for about eight years. Even when I was I refused to wear an "X" because I think it just alienated me and gave people a preconceived notion of who I was. We wanted to appeal or be an outlet for other people with the same tolerant beliefs.

JAMES SPOONER (AFRO-PUNK): I was never all about being "true till death." I never wanted to do it for the scene or whatever. I remember getting into arguments with 16 year old kids and they'd say, "I've been straight edge my whole life." I'd say, "That doesn't count!" [laughs] I felt like the kids that had gone through some shit and became straight edge were more about it. At 17, I decided I didn't need straight edge to keep me off drugs anymore. I started talking to my friends about it and some couldn't get their head around it. "Oh, so you're gonna start shooting heroin now?" It was really silly to me. I'm 31 now and I drink, but I feel like straight edge is in my heart, but it's my version of straight edge, which is more about temperance. I have never had a problem with excess.

MICKEY NOLAN (WRITER/SHOW PROMOTER): Over time I began to see where straight edge was somewhat unrealistic and somewhat offensive to see bands talking about cleaning up the ghettos and naïve statements about quasi-mystical forces of righteousness that would wipe drugs off the map and everyone would be happy. I respected the energy and conviction but it wasn't until there were some smarter bands that came down the pike that I understood these things were ingrained in our culture and how a lot of lower income communities had become dependent on the things.

RYAN CLARK: Toward the late-nineties much of the scene started spiraling into very hateful, destructive territory. Straight edge went from a personal conviction to outward animosity. Straight edge communities began to form "crews," which in most cases was just a safer term for "gang." When I started hearing about malicious crimes happening in the name of straight edge, I was over it. People bringing weapons into the mosh pit, people hospitalizing homeless alcoholics, people starting fights and trash-talking within the scene itself. It seemed so contrary to the point of straight edge. Why should a personal decision to live without destructive substances mean lashing out on anyone that chooses to do otherwise? That's a surefire way to precipitate rejection. You gain no one's acceptance or understanding with hate.

DAN YEMIN (LIFETIME, KID DYNAMITE, PAINT IT BLACK): Straight edge became a caricature of its original intent. It was originally about not buying into mainstream America's ideas about how to have a good time and rising above all that. It became this militant thing and its own mainstream within hardcore and very intolerant of people not following suit. Living by anything too rigid is dangerous, too. I actually thought it was great drinking music. [laughs]

CHARLES MAGGIO (RORSCHACH, GERN BLANDSTEN RECORDS): In the nineties people got bored with the rules of straight edge as defined by the song. So they expanded it into militant stances on animal rights and really bastardized it all. It really made me want to eat a veal cutlet and drink a 40 ounce of Pabst Blue Ribbon.

DANIEL TRAITOR (RACETRAITOR, ARMA ANGELUS, EVERLAST, HINCKLEY): The thing that was cool about it though was that everybody was edge, and it didn't stop us from having a good time, and being crazy as fuck, and having that support system for a healthy lifestyle—one that promoted building up the internal strength to go against the shittiness of the world. To have a community and music that promoted that was amazing, and to have it not be some cheesy religious, or health class shit? Well, that was even better because it was from this totally revolutionary perspective. We weren't going to be controlled by that shit. We weren't going to conform to society's escapist impulse.

As straight edge in the nineties became more divided, many people on both sides of the issue became turned off by the posturing. Some chastised the kids who smoked or drank for "buying into" the ultimate corporate scam, while non-straight edge kids cynically mocked those who were straight edge for their reliance on staying sober. Many straight edge and non-straight edge kids grew bored of the debate and instead started to focus their ambition on other issues. For instance, many hardcore kids dove headfirst into animal rights, while others became involved in political issues and dedicated themselves by going on to college and taking their activism in other directions.

In the long run, straight edge, and hardcore for that matter, became less important for some. Instead, they viewed straight edge and the hardcore scene as a gateway to a broader focus of improving one's life or making the world a better place. Even though they may or may not have shed the straight edge label, their immersion in straight edge and hardcore at least at one time in their lives forever changed their outlook.

WALTER SCHREIFELS (QUICKSAND, GORILLA BISCUITS, RIVAL SCHOOLS): When I first got into it I thought straight edge was cool. At the time the scene was divided amongst skins, punks, and metal heads, and I thought straight edge was cooler than all those things. I was into the idea of converting people to that idea and eventually it worked and there was this whole gigantic scene of people who were no longer into a mixture of bands, they were only into straight edge bands and it became boring to me. Everyone became the same and wore the same clothes and talked about the same things and I just wasn't interested anymore. I still see it as having a value, though. It will always exist and I think it's really cool, but I didn't have anywhere to move in it.

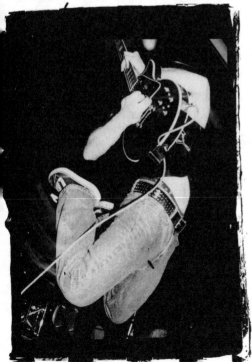

MIKE KIRSCH: It's really easy for something like straight edge to become the crux of your identity. I'm not straight edge—straight edge is a part of who I am and a component of what I am, but it doesn't define me as a person.

CHAKA MALIK: I thought straight edge was great initially but then it became a fashion statement. There was a certain amount of people who really felt something for it at one point, but then when the style became more visible to people who weren't as "hardcore" or "intense" as the people who were really feeling the music then it destroyed the integrity of that movement.

AARON TURNER (ISIS, HYDRAHEAD RECORDS): I personally didn't feel attached to the ideals anymore. I was doing a band and putting out records and I wasn't worried about myself

BY THE GRACE OF GOD

going down the wrong path. I also felt a lot of the music was no longer relevant to me. I guess I grew out of it; a lot of my initial motivations to get into it were reactionary so once that started to fall away I realized I didn't need to adhere to a specific code in order to be counter to the mainstream or to anything else I perceived to be contrary to how I felt in my life.

VIC DICARA (108, BEYOND, BURN): I adore the concept of straight edge and really love the true history of how it became its own entity in 1982 or 83 in D.C. In the later eighties Youth of Today transformed it into a boy's club with a quasi-religious rule book, and even though straight edge did have a renaissance in the early-nineties, the Youth of Today interpretation of it really seemed to stick and dominate over the Minor Threat interpretation. To me now, as a 35 year old father, it seems kind of pointless and dead. But it was a valuable and important thing that I could rally around and focus some of my energy on as a teenager.

JEFF BECKMAN: Straight edge had its time in my life and meant a lot to me. I believe it saved my life and shaped a lot of my thinking to this day. I always struggled with it because I didn't like a lot of straight edge kids we met, and it seemed very trivial and sometimes overly self-righteous. I couldn't justify why a mouthful of beer would make my beliefs any less worthy than if I had a mouthful of Coke. I increasingly would ask myself "why?" to the point where I just didn't get it anymore. That came when I was 33. I couldn't relate to it any more, but it was great when I was younger. I had 13 years of it and I doubt I would have changed a thing.

DEMIAN JOHNSTON: Judge was kind of a joke band that sort of made fun of the over the top mentality. But it eventually became fairly pretentious—"I'm straight edge, but I have a beard, but I also read Nietzsche." We got far enough away from the late eighties tough guy straight edge thing that we went back to it. It seemed like every conversation for a while was like, "Oh my God, Walter's not straight edge anymore?" It kind of died for me after that when that was the most pivotal conversation going on. [laughs]

SEAN INGRAM (COALESCE): I have had my life threatened, and kids who booked our shows health threatened because I sold out and wasn't ashamed of it. I didn't disappear, I said what I felt and moved on. That isn't a trait common with sellouts, let alone be in a band that was gaining credibility. A lot of kids would write me and talk to me in person about how foolish they felt after getting into straight edge so deep, and how alone they felt after they sold out. Coalesce gave them a place to be who they were. A lot of straight edge kids didn't like that. Go on straight edge message boards today, mention my name, and you will still find kids who were five years old when I was touring, testifying what a terrible person I am. It's insane! I'm going to be 80 still trying to live down selling out to little kids.

Although many have stopped being straight edge or simply made it a lower priority, straight edge didn't become any less important to the people who found value in it. People became straight edge for different reasons, but many found a common consciousness or self-awareness that they had not experienced before their interest in the movement. It's likely that nearly everyone involved in nineties hardcore took the ideals they formed from their experience, internalized them, and incorporated them naturally into their lives. Many straight edge kids have gone on to become activists, business owners, full-time artists, lawyers, teachers, professors, chefs, writers, and parents, and if it wasn't for their exposure to straight edge and the hardcore scene, however brief their run might have been, it is possible they wouldn't be the productive people they are today.

Of course, straight edge continues to be an integral part of hardcore as bands like Champion, The Promise, Have Heart, Betrayed, Count Me Out, The First Step, Throwdown, Triple Threat, and others have continued to spread the message from the nineties into the 21st Century. All of these bands were influenced by eighties and nineties straight edge groups, but they have also developed their own unique perspectives on it. While straight edge to some is nothing more than an empty cliché, to many, including people who no longer consider themselves "true till death," straight edge is influential in numerous ways.

SEVAPRIYA BARRIER: Initially, I became straight edge because I was already personally hesitant about taking intoxicants, so the straight edge scene really validated my own beliefs. I think straight edge was pretty funny in the eighties and became ridiculously self involved in the nineties. That said, I loved it! You could be whoever you wanted to be in the scene and you could establish whatever persona you desired. You could gain acceptance if you just followed a few simple rules—that's pretty amazing, really.

MARK HOLCOMB (UNDERTOW): Straight edge opened my mind to things broader than what I was exposed to from my parents or in school. I have to admit it brought about a feeling of moral superiority at times, too. I remember thinking, "Oh, I'm doing the right things that are going to change the world." In retrospect it might have been a little egotistical, but I don't know if I would have thought about those things if it wasn't for hardcore. I probably would have just been an accountant and not gave a shit about anything. [laughs] It influenced me to think a lot more.

MIKE MCTERNAN (DAMNATION A.D.): I'd like to show people that straight edge isn't something just for your teen years or college—it can be something you can hold on to. I've noticed that it is harder to be straight edge when you get older because so many people's social lives are dictated by alcohol. I'm not interested in going out to a bar, so it's hard for me to meet people my age. And how can someone who's never been to a show or never stage-dived to Outspoken or Gorilla Biscuits comprehend straight edge? So, I usually just tell people I prefer Diet Coke. [laughs] Though straight edge has changed for me in its meaning, with every phase I've gone through in my life where I've made big changes I've stuck with it. I remember a few years ago I had a girlfriend who cheated on me and that was really rough. I went to hang out with some people and they were trying to encourage me to drink and they were like, "Don't worry, we won't tell anyone. It'll help you get through the night." I was like, "Why would I take something that has meant so much to me and just throw it away in one night?"

MANI MOSTOFI: What kept me interested in straight edge was the diversity of things that fell under the umbrella of the straight edge scene and part of that was the dynamic going back and forth between these two different straight edge scenes both musically and intellectually. If you listen to the first wave of straight edge bands, some were more aggressive and others more melodic and when you get to the late eighties it gets a little broader. But by the time you get to the mid-nineties hardcore scene you get a ton of divergence. You have bands that sound like Carcass on one end and bands like Lifetime or Ashes who weren't necessarily straight edge bands but they were a major part of the scene.

DARYL TABERSKI (SNAPCASE): There is no one way to think and how we think isn't necessarily right for how you think. Snapcase influenced a lot of people who were doing drugs and drinking because we used to get so many letters from people who had these types of problems and they'd tell us, "You guys were such a huge part of my recovery." We didn't insult them and say things like, "If you drink you suck." [laughs] We would write more about finding the answers within yourself. Being straight edge out of peer pressure is meaningless. Maybe it wasn't the best way to market the band because it was kind of confusing and people had to figure our messages out for themselves, but I think that's a reason why we were able to be a band as long as we were.

ROBERT FISH (108, RESSURECTION): Straight edge, for me, has nothing to do with living a "pure" lifestyle. I know that it would be a dangerous thing for me to drink. I don't do moderation and simply put if I were to start to dabble in those things it would get destructive quick. At the same time straight edge, in terms of what it could mean in a social sense for young kids, is important to me. It is a cool thing filled with a positive sense. Of course people have made it look ridiculous, but in and of itself it can be a very cool thing and a very positive and empowering thing.

BRIAN DINGLEDINE (CATHARSIS, INSIDE FRONT FANZINE): I became straight edge in 1989, at a time when there was no real straight edge scene in North Carolina, when as far as I understood it straight edge was just a word for a punk who didn't smoke or drink. I'm still straight edge today, and the anarchist circles I organize in have become largely sober, in stark contrast to anarchist circles only ten years ago. In that regard, while I now see nineties straight edge as a way to avoid serious political issues while still posing as rebellious, I think sobriety has a lot to offer explicitly revolutionary groups. It's much easier to fight when you don't have any extra challenges, like addiction, inebriation (and the drama that comes with it), or drug raids from the authorities.

EXTINCTION

SCOTTY NIEMET (MORE THAN MUSIC FEST): Straight edge is still the most important aspect of hardcore for me, and this is coming from someone who sold out! It's difficult to explain what motivates a teenager to become straight edge. Sure, there's the pressures of the world and peers and the disgruntled views straight edge kids hold to the drug culture. I abused myself in my head about being queer, about being different, my never diagnosed depression. I just got up and said, "I hate this! I need to figure out how to make my life livable." And that's how I approached it from then on. I surrounded myself with straight edge, with kids who were productive, who had things that meant something to them. It kept me alive, but the shit I let abuse my head was still there. My support system started crumbling, kids were moving out of state, infighting within my scene. Things that were out of my control just put my issues in my head to the forefront again. I was getting eaten up by feeling I was living a double life. I gave up and tried to find out if being queer and not being involved in the gay community had anything to do with my head problems. What I did find out was the gay community left me in bars, after hours parties, and around shit that would let me forget about being too different. Seven years went by and slowly my world was crumbling with addiction and no discipline. I lost touch with the scene almost completely. I woke last fall and felt like I did when I was 16—lost, depressed, and needing to make some changes. I decided that the choices I made as a teenager went further than some youth movement, further than some kind of teen angst. As cheesy as it may seem straight edge has once again impacted how I go about surviving today. I have a lot of new lessons to refer back to. I went seven years doing shit I never dreamt I would be doing. I don't allow myself to beat myself up about it. I have moved on and I'm proud of myself for being able to get myself out of it.

ADAM MCGRATH (CAVE IN): It seemed very natural to me because I had never drank or did drugs and was usually turned off when my peers would get trashed. But I was never comfortable and still not comfortable with telling other people how they should live their lives. So I felt I was carving my own path and straight edge was a personal choice for my own benefit and never had any interest in trying to change other people's lifestyles. Even the Minor Threat song always seemed to me as a complete statement about your own personal being. "I'm a person just like you," and this is how I live my life. Take it or leave it.

D. J. ROSE: Kids start out with youthful ideals and most of them find out they can't meet all the expectations they have for themselves. Now I can't live up to every idea either, but I can be straight edge and vegan. They are ingrained ways of life at this point.

MIKE HARTSFIELD (OUTSPOKEN, NEW AGE RECORDS): My interest in straight edge has never wavered because, simply, it has never failed me. There's really not an outside interest/disinterest that will make me feel differently about the most important personal decision I have ever made.

SCOTT BEIBIN: Straight edge was, for me, spiritual—not in a sense of religion but it allowed me to clearly look inward at who I was and to assess what I was doing and how I was impacting the world around me. I found myself going from being a smart kid to actually being in a community of super-achievers. And being a super achiever wasn't that big of a deal, we were all just positive and making new things. We saw problems and came up with creative solutions for those problems. With music there weren't really venues that hosted our scene, so we had to search out alternative venues. We had to figure out how to do ticketing and how to get the word out about shows. Zines really opened up the channels of communication. We were also among the early users of the internet. Remember the straight edge email list in the early nineties? [laughs] We always adopted new ideas and new ways of communicating.

TAYLOR STEELE: A lot of people get into straight edge when they are young or because it is the cool thing to do. They're young and they are experimenting. To me, it's not about the X's and the fashion because that doesn't mean anything to me anymore. It's a lifestyle that I don't really think about anymore—it's just who I am. My actions are more important than what I call myself.

GREG BENNICK: Whether or not one thinks that straight edge has taken hold depends on your definition of "taken hold." If "taken hold" means that straight edge is *everywhere* and for example when you go visit your grandmother and walk into the nursing home, she and all of her friends have X's on their hands, then no, it hasn't taken hold. If "taken hold" means that every city in the world has straight edge kids in it who are excited about and supportive of their scene, then I would say it most definitely *has* taken hold. We are never going to have a situation where straight edge is common in the mainstream. The influences of drugs and alcohol and the foothold, or rather the stranglehold, they have on the mainstream is far too strong. But the ripples we've established will keep spreading and people will continue to find out about and appreciate alternatives to intoxication.

FIGHT: THE NINETIES HARDCORE REVOLUTION IN ETHICS, POLITICS, AND SO

ANIMAL RIGHTS

Probably the most fervent ideological battles waged within the nineties hardcore scene were issues pertaining to animal rights. These included vegetarianism, veganism, and other related environmental issues. Although many in the hardcore scene incorporated animal rights into their belief systems, these issues divided the scene in some ways. Those who incorporated animal rights into their lives, particularly with respect to their diet, often felt that the choice became an important part of their identity. For those who made these choices, it changed their entire outlook and they even found it to be a catalyst for change in other areas of their lives.

Issues relating to animal rights and vegetarianism in hardcore and punk were introduced in the early eighties. Early U.K. punk bands like Crass, Conflict, and Flux of Pink Indians, among others, spoke out against meat eating and animal experimentation and played an influential role in spreading these ideas around the scene. American political punk and hardcore bands like M.D.C. (though some feel they teetered back and forth on these issues), Crucifix, and, later on, Nausea also advocated for vegetarianism. Many of these bands were highly concerned with the political climate of the time. The Cold War was still playing a role in international politics and threats of nuclear disaster, class polarization, and environmental concerns were topics of major importance in the hardcore and punk scene. Many of these bands saw taking a stance for animal rights issues as one direct way of fighting back against corporate control. Emotional interests in the welfare of animals also played a role. When people learned about animal testing, the often cruel treatment animals receive at slaughterhouses, and the sometimes unsanitary conditions of such places, it made them think twice about their choices. At the least, they felt that not eating meat was a step in the right direction.

Some other notable eighties musical figures also helped spread these messages. Influenced by the ideas of bands like Beefeater, Ian MacKaye and others from the D.C. hardcore scene were rumored or known to be vegetarian and to support animal rights. British post-punk bands like The Smiths also prominently spread a vegetarian message. Their 1985 album *Meat Is Murder* gained international prominence as much for its subject matter as its music. At the time, there was also some congruence between the political concerns voiced in hip-hop and hardcore. Bronx, New York, emcee KRS-One of Boogie Down Productions often spoke about his vegetarianism in interviews and on stage. His political and ethical views were widely shared in both hip-hop and punk/hardcore circles. Although not all of these artists or groups affected the entire scene's outlook on these topics, their impact was noticed and discussed by many and at least had an effect on the members' immediate social circles.

Although many disliked any sort of spiritual affiliation with hardcore, influenced bands like New York's Cro-Mags and Cause for Alarm spoke about vegetarianism and made it a topic of discussion in the New York hardcore scene. A lot of people in the scene considered Krishna consciousness, a spiritual movement rooted in a branch of Hinduism, to be a cult, but several respected people in hardcore investigated and practiced the faith. One of the primary tenets of the group is that every practitioner must be strictly vegetarian. Despite the general disdain for religion that was present in the scene, philosophical discussions about the various reasons for becoming a vegetarian were common. Krishna consciousness had been on the periphery of the New York scene since it started, but its role in hardcore generally grew larger in the late eighties and early nineties (this is covered more thoroughly in Chapter Four: "Spirituality").

By the late eighties, youth crew bands like Youth of Today, Gorilla Biscuits, and others began to link these issues to straight edge. Some were skeptical of this combination because they didn't agree that any sort of moral belief system belonged in hardcore. On the other hand, vegetarianism was one area where both political and non-political hardcore and punk bands had some overlapping views. Youth of Today wrote a song called "No More" on their 1988 album, *We're Not in This Alone*, which was a rallying cry for vegetarianism. Many in the hardcore scene initially scoffed at the notion of vegetarianism being linked to straight edge, but others started to take to the idea. Bands like Gorilla Biscuits and Insted also wrote songs about being vegetarian and they became fairly common in hardcore by the end of the eighties. Youth of Today's vocalist, Ray Cappo, drawn in by its emphasis on the vegetarian diet, soon became more interested in the philosophy of Krishna consciousness. After becoming a Krishna devotee, Cappo quit Youth of Today and started a Krishna conscious band called Shelter that continued to address animal rights issues in the nineties.

Although one could argue that they played a bigger role in the nineties, California's Vegan Reich started in the mid eighties and spread an extreme animal rights message and political philosophy. They were inspired by anarcho-punk and best known for creating hardline, a militant movement in the hardcore scene that combined revolutionary politics, Old Testament style spirituality, and veganism. They were among the first in hardcore to push vegetarians toward accepting the concept of veganism and they also linked with animal rights activists and encouraged people to take direct action against corporations that tested on animals. They were also closely associated with other animal rights activist bands like Statement and Raid. The hardline movement played an important, albeit controversial, role in nineties hardcore due to their stance on animal rights, sexuality, abortion, and other issues.

Although these various influences show that animal rights and vegetarianism had long been a part of hardcore, the cause was taken up in an even more prominent way in the nineties. The debates these aforementioned influences encouraged impacted a lot of participants in nineties hardcore at the beginning of the decade, which is when the issue really came to a head.

Animal rights groups like People for the Ethical Treatment of Animals (P.E.T.A.), which played a role in the animal rights movement in nineties hardcore, also helped spread these messages. Many of these organizations started in the seventies or eighties and gained prominence in underground artistic communities like the hardcore scene, where ideas alternative to the mainstream were typically explored. In the nineties they would often set up tables at hardcore shows, pass out free literature, and pay for ads in zines with the goal of promoting the discussion of these topics and recruiting new members for their causes.

Many activists in the more political spectrum of hardcore felt that human rights needed to be addressed before animal rights. They believed issues such as vegetarianism were personal choices that should be left to one's own conscience. Others, such as Boston's Slapshot, were antagonistic to vegetarianism and felt it didn't belong in hardcore at all. There were also other factions in the scene that echoed mainstream objections: i.e. meat eating is a part of human nature; vegetarians are "wimps," etc. There were also other people who agreed with animal rights on an environmental level, but they did not actually become vegetarians.

By the early nineties the link between straight edge and vegetarianism that was popularized by many of the youth crew bands had arguably become its own sub-scene in hardcore. The two issues became intertwined and it wasn't uncommon to go to a show, meet someone, and have that person immediately ask if you were straight edge and vegetarian or vegan. For some, these were just conversation starters and, because they were so common in the scene by this point, seemed fairly innocent questions. Others, however, felt answering "no" to either of the topics was the first step toward exclusion.

Aside from musical influences, many people from the nineties scene learned about vegetarianism and veganism through animal rights related literature. John Robbins' *Diet for a New America* and Peter Singer's *Animal Liberation* were just a couple of many notable books that circulated in the hardcore scene in the late eighties and early nineties. After reading such sources, bands, fanzine writers, and others spread the information to those around them. Although there were fanzines in the eighties that addressed these topics, a larger number of zines cropped up in the nineties that addressed animal rights, many of which made it their primary focus.

At the same time, the nineties also brought about a broader focus on health issues in mainstream culture. People were more concerned than ever about staying healthy, so natural food stores, organic co-ops, and a new wave of diet fads also became popular. In the process, vegetarian products became more widely available. In the eighties, it was often difficult to find items that vegetarians and vegans now expect any grocery store to carry.

With all of these influences as a backdrop, Syracuse's Earth Crisis arguably made the largest and most widespread impact on the animal rights debate as their mix of metal-influenced hardcore and militant lyrics launched the vegan straight edge movement and their music became one of the most popular sounds in the nineties scene. Through albums on Victory Records and tours with other hardcore bands (and later larger metal bands), they built up a sizable audience. They also received mainstream media exposure from CNN, MTV, and other outlets for their views on straight edge, animal rights, and environmentalism. Earth Crisis were succeeded by other vegan straight edge hardcore bands like Abnegation, Framework, Green Rage, Warcry, Morning Again, Culture, Birthright, and Day of Suffering to name just a few.

While these bands became more prominent in the scene, the level of militancy increased. Many dedicated to these causes felt that just being a vegetarian or vegan wasn't enough. Radical animal rights and environmentalist groups like the Animal Liberation Front (A.L.F.), the Animal Defense League (A.D.L.), Sea Shepherd Conservation Society, and Earth First! became popular, and a number of hardcore kids became members. Some were involved in direct action and even played a role in organizing local, national, and international protests. This deeper focus led to a level of scrutiny that was often extreme. For instance, some vegans began to examine the manufacturing processes of foods and other products and even the sub-components of those items' ingredients to determine whether or not they were truly free of animal products.

Although lots of people dedicated to animal rights saw these developments as a sign that their argument was taking hold, others grew tired of the militancy and often responded in

reactionary ways. Earth Crisis reportedly had meat or dairy products thrown at them during their sets in some cities. Some of the more militant hardline adherents were also verbally confronted by those who didn't share their views. While these responses were somewhat rare, the fact that they were occurring showed that some rejected the tone that had been set.

By the end of the nineties, several of the more militant vegan straight edge bands had folded. Like many of the political issues that were so heavily debated in the nineties, animal rights took a back seat to other topics. A new generation took the reigns and hardcore, as it always does, moved in a different direction. Even so, many of the nineties vegan and vegetarian bands left a strong legacy as bands like Maroon, Purification, Ceremony,

7 Generations, Risen, and others continued to create music that addresses animal rights issues. Those who supported animal rights in the nineties were witness to a movement that evolved to become a broader part of our culture as a whole. Not every person interviewed in *Burning Fight* is vegetarian or vegan, but the majority experimented with these dietary choices in their youth and many remain committed vegetarians or vegans to this day.

DAN YEMIN (LIFETIME, PAINT IT BLACK): The content of hardcore had always addressed human rights issues, so it was only a matter of time before somebody made the connection to animal rights. If we're really against violence and suffering then why wouldn't that branch across species?

BRENDAN DESMET (GROUNDWORK, ABSINTHE): Vegetarianism was a pretty bold statement to make—you couldn't sit down at the dinner table and follow the norm, which is very appealing to the disenfranchised nature that goes along with kids often drawn to hardcore.

RAY CAPPO (SHELTER, YOUTH OF TODAY): I felt vegetarianism was right even as a teenager, but I didn't have the self-control or discipline to do anything about it until I was 18 and I moved out of my parents' house. I thought it just went right along with straight edge and controlling the senses. Youth of Today really liked to rock the boat. A lot of people think everyone loved us, but we took so much abuse. When we were straight edge we were abused until the straight edge scene sprang up again. Then when we started talking about vegetarianism about half the straight edge bands wrote us off as losers. We were mocked and lost some of our fan base. The first time we went to Europe we got beer bottles thrown at us in about 90 percent of the cities we played in.

KARL BUECHNER (EARTH CRISIS, PATH OF RESISTANCE): My grandmother was a vegetarian and her husband worked for a company that had slaughterhouses. She saw the butchering with her own eyes and described it to me. I already valued animals so her influence played a primary role.

CHRIS BOARTS-LARSON (SLUG AND LETTUCE FANZINE): For me personally, [animal rights] is still one of the basic platforms of my being. I generally still assume that people are vegetarian when I meet them, and for so many years it seemed like most people I knew were. I was originally exposed to the subject/topic in the late-eighties through the peace punks. I went vegetarian myself in 1990 and have been ever since. I've had periods of time where I have been vegan, but I have never proclaimed myself vegan. I would definitely give credit to the New York City anarcho-punks like Nausea for being a big influence on my decision to go vegetarian. At that time it was just everywhere—not in a "you must do this" sort of way, but the information was available; there was literature distributed at shows, with bands' records, in fanzines. It made sense to me [then], and it still does.

ANTHONY PAPPALARDO (IN MY EYES): Even though animal rights existed in hardcore before, Ray Cappo really tackled that issue and brought it to the attention of the entire scene. I thought his lyrics were blunt and cool. He put it in people's faces so you had to have a stance on it. A lot of people I know who got into vegetarianism then still are, because it really struck a nerve with them. Your diet is part of your daily life and plays a much larger role than, say, drinking. Cappo struck a nerve with a lot of kids.

VIC DICARA (108, INSIDE OUT, BURN, BEYOND): My friend Tom Capone introduced me to vegetarianism about halfway through high school. He himself got exposed to the idea through Youth of Today, who in turn were exposed to the idea through the Hare Krishnas. The idea seemed extremely appealing to me, and very soon after my initial exposure to it, I stumbled across a huge blue vein in a piece of chicken my mom had cooked and decided on the spot that vegetarianism was the way for me to go.

SCOTTY NIEMET (MORE THAN MUSIC FEST): Going vegetarian at age 16 and eventually vegan was a great way for me to apply some discipline and directly achieve something. I could say, "Here, this is something I have done to put a dent on everything I think is fucked up in this world. Here's something any person can do. There isn't anything keeping people from educating themselves and putting change into practice."

ADRIENNE DROOGAS (SPITBOY): My initial involvement with vegetarianism was highly influenced by political bands who spoke about not eating animals. I always equated it that if you were a punk or hardcore kid then you were probably a vegetarian. I guess I always assumed that we would all be conscious of these types of issues and grapple with racism and homophobia and we'd be conscious of our environmental impact. I thought it was great. Even if those people aren't still vegetarian then at least for a time those same people did analyze their roles in this society and what they consume a bit more seriously.

NORMAN BRANNON (TEXAS IS THE REASON, ANTI-MATTER FANZINE, FOUNTAINHEAD, SHELTER, RESSURECTION): I remember seeing *Faces of Death* when I was pretty young and there was this scene of a chicken slaughterhouse. Watching the chicken slaughterhouse was one thing, but what really affected me was that there was this music in the background that was completely making fun of it. Essentially it was the sounds of chicken clucking to a goofy song. It really bothered me that it was mocking the slaughter and for some reason it made a big impression on me. Somewhere in the late-eighties I started reading books like *Animal Liberation* and that was really when I made the decision, which was kind of big deal in my parents' house as I was only 14 years old and didn't really cook for myself. I remember I felt like I was dissing Jesus by being vegetarian. [laughs] My mom would say, "Jesus eats meat." I'd say, "I don't care, I'm not Jesus." She'd respond, "You think you're better than Jesus?" These were the quality debates that we'd have. [laughs]

KATE REDDY (108, KRSNAGRRRL FANZINE): I was always attracted to vegetarianism as a kid probably because I grew up on a farm and actually had to kill animals. I just thought it was so messed up. My parents raised veal calves. You always felt like you had to shut down part of yourself. My parents would say, "It's only natural" and you'd be feeding this baby calf or sheep or something and they'd kill them. I did eat meat but as soon as I had the independence to stop I stopped. Once I stopped I never looked back. It was a very natural decision to make. You grow up in the country and you see people hunting and the dead animals. I just felt it went against my idea of hardcore, which was about doing the right thing for other people.

JUSTIN "GUAV" GUAVIN (CONVICTION RECORDS): I was raised eating meat, like everyone else. "It's natural" was my excuse. I said it was natural because that's what I was taught. I was told that eating meat is normal, and if you don't eat meat, you'll get sick. When I was 17, someone gave my grandmother a book called *Diet for A New America* by

John Robbins. She wasn't interested in it, so she gave it to me. It sat on my bookshelf for a few months. One day I was bored and picked it up. I wanted to put it down because it was calling into question everything that I was comfortable with. I didn't necessarily want to know all the things I was learning. But I have never been one to shy away from the truth, comfortable or not, so I kept reading. By the time I had finished *Diet for a New America*, I had stopped eating meat. Stopped eating eggs. Stopped drinking milk. I finally gave up cheese three months later, on my 18th birthday. The fact is giving up meat was easy. I started to view meat for what it is. It's not a "Whopper." It's not a "McNugget"—it's a hunk of muscle that has been ripped off of an animal every bit as intelligent and smart as your dog. It's a carcass, like the kind you see at the side of the road. It's simply not appetizing to me anymore.

JIM GRIMES (EXTINCTION, STORMTROOPER FANZINE): I'll be the first to admit that I used to think vegetarianism had nothing to do with straight edge when I was a teenager. I was just kind of ignorant to the issues and the information just wasn't out there as much. But over time you meet people and they tell you to check out a book or something and you learn and progress. Hardcore is such an interesting music forum that you can gain a lot of stuff just by picking up a record and seeing a reference to something like *Lies My Teacher Told Me* or *Diet for a New America*. It's intense. To me, everything in the world is debatable, but eating an animal is just wrong and I'll go to my grave thinking that.

NEERAJ KANE (SUICIDE FILE, HOPE CONSPIRACY, EXTINCTION, HOLY ROMAN EMPIRE): My parents were actually vegetarians before they came to the U.S. They came from India and had never eaten meat in their whole lives before coming here, but they started to eat meat because they wanted to fit in. They also raised me to eat meat because they didn't want me to feel left out. So, I ended up trying pretty much everything when I was a little kid. I had known about vegetarianism pretty much from the culture I grew up in, but it was never forced on me. Eventually, though, I found out more about vegetarianism and the animal rights movement through hardcore and I got into it when I was about 15. The funny thing was when I went vegetarian my parents got back into it, too. [laughs] They were like, "We only started eating meat because of you, so forget it." [laughs]

DUNCAN BARLOW (ENDPOINT, GUILT, BY THE GRACE OF GOD): Animal rights and vegetarianism are important because it brings attention to the fact that we live in a closed system that all of our actions have an impact on the system as a whole. Personally, I love animals and I try to live my life with as little cruelty as possible. Naturally, I slip up here and there and buy a product that I learn later tests on animals. I try to stay informed as much as I can so that I can make educated decisions on which products I purchase.

SCOTT BEIBIN (BLOODLINK RECORDS): I became vegetarian when I was 13 years old. There was a girl in junior high who I liked and she told me she was vegetarian and I said, "Cool, me too!" [laughs] For the next year all I ate was Twizzlers and Strawberry Crush. But I read *Diet for a Small Planet* and *Diet for a New America* and I became vegan right around the same time I became straight edge. I used to go to fur protests before I was really going to shows. I was very interested in animal rights and environmental issues. I got turned on to the radicalized politics from being frustrated at how ridiculously ineffective the mainstream animal rights groups I worked with were. They were more interested in the protests and I was more into direct action. I'd hear things about Earth First and the Animal Liberation Front (A.L.F), and at the time you couldn't find out about these things on the Internet. I found out about most of it from hidden pamphlets at Trash American Style, which was this amazing record store in Connecticut. At that time it was such a clandestine thing to get a hold of something like *The Anarchist Cookbook*. Now you just can Google it. But then you had to really search it out.

JASON ROE (KILL THE ROBOT FANZINE): I went to this concert that P.E.T.A. had in D.C. It really opened my eyes to what went into meat. Later I read an interview with Harley Flanagan from the Cro-Mags which convinced me that eating meat was wrong. Harley said something about the state that cows were in when they were slaughtered and how that stress was in the meat. That left a huge impression on me. I then tried to be a vegetarian without telling my parents. They caught on when we went out for ribs and I wouldn't eat. Things were fine after that.

DENNIS MERRICK (EARTH CRISIS): I went to high school with Tim Redmond of Snapcase and he was a vegetarian. We'd talk about it and he'd explain to me at lunch why he didn't eat meat and what sorts of foods he put in his diet. He'd talk about why it was a good ethical choice and why it was healthy so he put a lot of the ideas in my head first. It was also just a natural extension of being into straight edge and hardcore and trying to make a change through music. I got into issues of human rights through hardcore and animal rights were just an extension of that. If I cared about marginalized people I also cared about the environment and animals. I didn't become fully vegetarian until I was 19 and I moved out of my house and had to take things into my own hands, which made a big difference in terms of choices.

SEAN MUTTAQI (VEGAN REICH, PRESSURE, CAPTIVE NATION RISING, UPRISING RECORDS): The early years of becoming vegetarian for a lot of us had little to do with diet. Looking back diet may have even suffered a bit in the early years. [laughs] As a kid I didn't really know what I was doing. It was just sort of like, "Okay, cut meat out." I didn't have anyone around me to guide me, and there weren't really that many vegetarian products back then. There were a couple of things, but generally speaking there wasn't a lot out there you could get that was vegan. It was basically brown rice and lentils. Everything was tied into political causes. Animal liberation was just a natural extension of that for me and it always took precedence over any dietary concerns. Of course, over years of doing research on how to be healthy with a vegan diet, becoming a professional martial artist, studying Chinese medicine and so on, I learned a lot about diet and health, but that was never the main factor when I first got into it.

NORMAN BRANNON: I don't remember ever eating vegetables at my parents' house, so becoming a vegetarian was kind of intimidating. I knew a kid at the time that was born and raised vegan. I remember hanging out with him and his mom and thought the food was really good and it was vegan. So, I knew I could totally be vegetarian. I was always more attached to vegetarianism than straight edge because it is something that directly affects human beings and the environment. Vegetarianism was probably the smartest trend to come out of straight edge hardcore.

MANI MOSTOFI (RACETRAITOR): I got into vegetarianism through the influence of the *Voice of the Voiceless* compilation put out by Doghouse, as well as the Gorilla Biscuits song, "Cats and Dogs." I thought the lyrics made sense. Those records got me into vegetarianism and I remember when I first became a vegetarian and said to myself, "I'm never going to become vegan; that's just too extreme." [laughs] Then Daisy Rooks did a zine and wrote an article about veganism and there was this one line in there that said something to the effect of, "If you're vegetarian and you care about animals you should probably become vegan because of these reasons." And that really struck a chord with me. This one line in one article that this one girl wrote made me pursue this idea very strongly.

MICHELLE (TODD) GONZALES (SPITBOY, INSTANT GIRL): I was a vegetarian since I was 15, which was way before I was in a band. When I was younger, my mom kind of went through a hippie vegetarian phase, so it was part of my consciousness as I grew up. But as I grew older and started to better understand my place in the world as a Chicana, I made a conscious decision not to be vegan. One of the ways I was able to observe my heritage was through food. You use a lot of cheese in Mexican food, so that was a sticking point for me. I didn't become vegan because I felt I was going to have to give up more of my heritage and I felt like I was holding on to every shred I could in the scene already.

JOSH LOUCKA (SHIFT): You read about factory farming and it's pretty horrifying. The idea of not allowing any animals to be killed is a pretty childish notion because animals kill each other—that's just the way the world works. But the factory farming was taking the idea of man being dominant over animals to absurd levels. Profit was the only driving force behind how you keep and treat animals. If you see how they are treated it just seems wrong. And of course reading about all the chemicals and antibiotics pumped into them didn't help matters either.

RYAN DOWNEY (BURN IT DOWN): When I was 12 my best friend at the time and his family were vegetarians. They also listened to a lot of Bob Dylan and probably smoked a lot of pot. And they were really involved in veterans' rights—a great family. One day I offered my friend some bacon, he turned it down, and when I asked why he said, "I don't believe in killing animals for food." It made sense to me right then and there. And I have been a vegetarian ever since. When I was 16 I got turned on to veganism by the band Vegan Reich around 1990. I became vegan when I was 16 and continued to adhere to a vegan diet for the next 14 years. The inter-connectedness of the animal struggle to the human struggle, from world hunger to pollution, and my natural affinity for animals all coalesced to shape my militant animal rights view. I saw it as the most important issue for a long time. I still feel that it is very important.

KEN OLDEN (WORLDS COLLIDE, DAMNATION A.D., WORLDS COLLIDE): In the late eighties vegetarianism was introduced to the mainstream hardcore scene, and I think what we saw in the early nineties was the result of that new awareness. Vegetarianism is very logical, whether you look at it from an ethical point of view or for health, eating less or no meat makes a lot of sense. But first a person has to be exposed to that idea, because it's very much against the mainstream—especially at that time! I mean, the veggie food in the early nineties sucked! [laughs] It wasn't like it is now, where any big food store stocks a nice selection of mock-meat products, back then you had to put in a lot more effort; it was even more expensive, and the options were limited. So, people really had to want to do it. I've been vegetarian since 1989, which was when I was exposed to the issue, and I immediately knew what was right and gave up cold turkey on all meats.

SCOTT BEIBIN: At the time I felt it was very important to be consistent and part of the political consistency I had with being straight edge was also being vegan. I saw being just vegetarian as wishy-washy and, if anything, it was worse than being a meat eater, because at least if you were a meat eater you were being honest about killing. Vegetarians might think they were doing good, but their actions were still enacting slavery. That was the mindset that I had at the time.

CHRIS LOGAN (CHOKEHOLD, GOODFELLOW RECORDS): We never shoved the topic down anyone's throat. It was all about educating. This was the thing that kind of split us apart from the whole militant animal rights scene. We wanted to educate because burning down people's houses and blowing up factories is not the way to turn people on to your cause.

MIKE HARTSFIELD (OUTSPOKEN, NEW AGE RECORDS): The singer for Against the Wall, Mike Madrid, bet me I couldn't go vegetarian for a month. I tried it and I felt much better physically, it was a noticeable improvement so I stuck with it. As far as our message in Outspoken tying into the vegetarian movement, it was pretty simple, killing animals for food was just something you didn't need to do.

TODD GULLION (TIME IN MALTA, ICE 9): I think it's a natural branching out from the abstention from alcohol and drugs, and it brings a "holistic" dimension to the cause of straight edge. The next natural branching would be some sort of religious practice which I know was true for a lot of people including me. I have been a strict or less strict vegan or vegetarian at various times, over the years of my life. From a purely sociological point of view, group abstention from an agreed product in a community provides group identity and initiation into the group. It says, "We believe in this value so we do this action, if you have this value you should do the same."

BRENDAN DESMET: There is very little in this world in the way of truth. We tend to see things very black and white in our younger years. But one of the things that really rings true to me is the concept of vegetarianism. People can argue all day long whether or not we're supposed to eat meat or whether or not we want to eat meat; what they can't argue is that vegetarianism is beneficial to the world around us. And I wouldn't have it tattooed on my body if I didn't think so. [laughs]

Obviously, animal rights issues impacted a lot of people who played a role in the nineties scene. Whether it was for personal or political reasons, the treatment of animals was of great concern for many. However, because such a focus came about there was bound to be a debate about the steps one should take to help the cause. Direct action against those involved in animal exploitation became a relatively common topic of conversation.

Many disagreed with these forms of protest because they sometimes involved violence and the destruction of property. The aforementioned "hardline" bands were among the most extreme advocates of this type of action.

Sean Muttaqi founded the Hardline Records label and was instrumental in the hardline movement. He was involved in the anarchist punk scene but tired of what he saw as contradictions in that movement. Muttaqi got together with some like-minded friends from the anarchist scene, and promoted radical environmental change, animal rights activism, a strong belief in the rejection of intoxicants (though there is a debate over whether or not hardline really was a part of straight edge), and a belief in the "natural order," a concept that opposed homosexuality and abortion. These topics were extremely controversial and marginalized the hardline movement to a large degree. Bands, hardline offshoots, and zines also sprung up with similar perspectives. Some followed a more militant vein, such as Memphis, Tennessee's Raid, and others chose a slightly less extreme approach.

Many in the scene who weren't a part of hardline also took an interest in direct action. As vegan straight edge bands like Earth Crisis became more popular, the more these messages became palatable to people who may not have taken to them so quickly before this time. Direct action, of course, was a controversial topic, as in many cases it involved breaking a law of some sort. Whether it was vandalism, breaking and entering, or verbally antagonizing people wearing clothing from animals, these measures were viewed even by many vegetarians and vegans as extreme. However, this didn't stop many from becoming involved in these and other forms of protest.

While the more controversial aspects of the animal rights movement often received the most attention, there were just as many who became dedicated to these issues on a more personal level. They applied principles of non-violence to their diets, one of the main ideas that attracted many people to animal rights in the first place, and tried to influence others by example or through one on one conversation. There were also people who supported animal rights issues, but did not actually become vegetarian or vegan.

The more militant segments of the scene often debated with those who took a less radical approach to animal rights. This tension impacted the overall climate of the scene.

SEAN MUTTAQI: During the early eighties I had gotten progressively more into the animal rights stuff. I started reaching out, writing some radical articles, and looking to make contact with Animal Liberation Front (A.L.F.) people. I also got exposed to the ideas of M.O.V.E. [an underground, spiritually-rooted, political group from Philadelphia]. After the [M.O.V.E.] bombing in 1985 a couple of the members came out to the L.A. area and I got exposed to a lot of their ideas and philosophy, which was very influential. I started to make more international contacts, which led up to hardline. We knew people from England, Germany, Canada, and all over the U.S. and we were trying to figure out what the next logical step should be. We started to realize that the approach we were taking was too radical and not accepted in the anarchist scene. We were too radical and too militant, and though we still held a lot of anarcho-syndicalist beliefs, we found ourselves at odds with inconsistencies in the more individualist oriented American anarchist movement, so we broke off and started our own thing.

DANIEL TRAITOR (RACETRAITOR, EVERLAST, HINCKLEY, ARMA ANGELUS): I remember basically my girlfriend at the time got a *Vanguard* [hardline/animal rights fanzine] from someone involved in hardline and showed it to me. I looked it over, and it reminded me a lot of my own beliefs that had been shaped my father's religious beliefs (Bahai), at least the little I knew about either of the movements at the time, the idea of religion being more about the meaning of the words than following the letter of the law, and all the religions teaching an essential truth. The idea of supporting liberation of colonized peoples world-wide was also very attractive to me at the time, because I was really starting to get into the history of the black movement in America, the Black Panthers, Malcolm X, and Latin American Revolutions, Salvadore Allende and Cuba/Castro's whole thing.

MIKE KIRSCH (FUEL, TORCHES TO ROME, BREAD AND CIRCUITS): There was this feeling about veganism and vegetarianism where you felt you could make a personal statement or impact. It sucks when a death squad is murdering a family in El Salvador and it also sucks when these animals that have feelings and relationships and can feel pain and affection and they are getting butchered by the millions just because we're either too busy to think about living another way or because there are these larger structures in place that make a tremendous amount of profit off of that. They also make a profit from creating that disconnect—you know, that stuff doesn't just appear magically in a container in your local grocery store, there is massive violence committed on your behalf to bring this to you. It wasn't like one day I woke up and I was vegan. It took a while to develop and process.

KATE REDDY: I thought it was romantic to do fur bombing, but I just never went in that direction, which I'm glad about now because I thought it was misdirected because it was another kind of violence. Vegetarianism, ultimately, is about non-violence. But I was attracted to the romance of setting the minks free. I didn't know where to do it, but I had the idea. [laughs]

VIC DICARA: It's powerful that people stand up and *do* something, beyond just talking or "educating." I don't condone violence towards one animal in the name of non-violence towards another, but in some cases I could see how a violent action towards an oppressive group might be justified for the sake of greater non-violence. Still, it's not something that I am into, personally.

ADRIENNE DROOGAS: I remember people taking direct action and going outside and spray-painting buildings and liberating animals from various institutions. I think people taking action on whatever they believe in is awesome. A lot of times it's easy to talk about stuff but much harder to actually do something about it. On the other hand, I'm not going to ridicule someone who eats meat or kick someone out of my house if I find out they eat meat. There's a certain line where it goes from supportive and encouraging to fucking ridiculous. I remember going to a vegan potluck that I was all excited about and when I got to the door this woman asked if I was wearing leather and I said I was wearing some leather shoes I'd had for about five years. They're like, "Well you have to take them off and put them in this bin or you can't come in." I just remember thinking she could have invited me into the house and we could have ate great vegan food and had this amazing discussion about leather and veganism but instead you just told me you're not allowing me into your home and it had nothing to do with communication—it was more about you can't come in the door unless you follow our strict guidelines.

SEAN MUTTAQI: Hardline was a loose group of people—some from the anarchist movement, some from the animal rights movement and some from the straight edge scene—who had gotten together and coalesced around the same ideas. We decided that we needed to start something that could actually get something done. The experience

an **animal rights benefit** for Student Action Corps for Animals

shelter
nation of ulysses
$5

born against
desiderata
(all-ages, of course!)

sanctuary theater 6pm march 30

from all of us was that you might know a few other people who might be coming from the same perspective as you but it was always that most people weren't. And there were always too many others who were not only not doing anything but were also screwing things up. We decided we needed to start something that was very disciplined. We also realized that spirituality needed to be intertwined with that, because we knew a lot of people who may have been vegan and out there doing stuff but were treating other people like shit by sleeping around and stuff like that. The whole belief system at the beginning was that you have to act responsible in your personal life if you're telling the world they need to change their actions. You can't say you have to close sweat shops down if you were wearing the clothes that were made there. Of course, nobody is perfect, nor did we expect that, but we wanted to have some basic standards.

STEVE LOVETT (RAID): Essentially, Hardline was a record label in the beginning, not a movement. Shortly after our demo (Raid) was released I saw an ad in *Maximum Rock N' Roll* about Hardline. At that point they had not released any records, but I sent our demo to Hardline Records to hopefully be released. Sean was vegan and inspired me to become vegan as well. Before our seven-inch was released, [all the members of Raid] became vegan. After conversing with Sean about the shortcomings of the straight edge scene, we created the movement. Sean's background was influenced by the punk inspired anarchist and animal rights movements. Hardline as a movement evolved quickly into a force within the straight edge and punk scene. Hardline was a way of taking straight edge into new areas; we were beyond straight edge because we engaged in more social/political struggles.

RYAN DOWNEY: Hardline Records formed and released three seven inches that blew my mind! Talk about taking no shit! Vegan Reich, Statement, and Raid talked about direct action against animal abusers and other radical topics, which connected with me in a major way. It also articulated a stand about violence and overthrow of the social system that spoke to me above and beyond the "street justice" within hardcore. But it was, for a short time, a viable movement I'd say until about 1993 when it disintegrated and most of us became disillusioned with what seemed like unrealistic goals and too rigid of a stance about more than a few issues that did not seem to adequately address reality. I personally had no problem with gay people, ever, but I found myself arguing about hardline's stance on homosexuality with straight edge kids who otherwise agreed with us more often than I was doing much about animal rights. I am still drug-free, I don't eat meat, I don't believe abortion is correct, and it's been 18 years since then. But people grow and change in profound ways throughout your teens and twenties and something like hardline is far too small to encapsulate my—or most thinking people's—worldview. But certainly in 1990 everyone was talking about hardline, though at most, it probably only ever had a few hundred adherents, and I was chief among them.

SCOTT BEIBIN: I was friends with the kids who were involved with hardline. I came down to the "Hardline Gathering" and gave workshops on herbalism—I was very interested in alternative medicine since I was a teenager. When I went down there the way the ideas were being filtered into that scene was so incredibly comical. They were saying the Inca society was vegan or homosexuality doesn't exist in nature. The one thing I never connected with in hardline was the homophobia.

BRENDAN DESMET: Hardline was important for hardcore. It might sound somewhat shocking, but it was a logical extension of taking something too the extreme, which is important for people to do in order to understand the negative side of extremism. There are some people in the world who don't respond to education and they need something to hit them right between the eyes, so there's a place for aggressive tactics—not aggression in terms of violence, but eye-catching tactics are what it takes for some people to understand these ideas.

SCOTTY NIEMET: I had/have this love/hate relationship with groups such as hardline. I took a pretty proactive stance on direct action, but I never felt the need for hardcore kids to turn against other hardcore kids with their variations on how to approach the grey areas of animal rights. I felt this uncomfortable view of hardline, that they were being way too divisive within the hardcore scene. I would even say they were becoming like an outsider group recruiting through hardcore. Just like Christian groups, I feel hardline was coming in stating their rules and making people decide if they were "true" vegans or not. They never took a step back and thought that maybe some kids were taking things in their own hands outside of the scene to take actions on animal exploiters. It was a bit too "look at me I'm more of this and this and this than you... you have the information, make a change now or you will be banished." Also, being a queer, animal rights activist vegan I didn't hold anything lightly that told me that me being queer, I was somehow less of an effort for the "cause."

As stated previously, aside from being known for their animal rights militancy, hardline was also controversial due to the group's stance on abortion and homosexuality. Some agreed with their extreme animal rights and political positions, but their views on reproductive and sexual issues were viewed by many as reactionary and the opposite of what hardcore was about. Both of these topics were fervently debated in the scene at the time as many felt that people should be able to make their own choices about them, especially in a sub-culture that is known for alternative viewpoints. On the other hand, many involved with hardline felt that if one were to truly live a "cruelty free" lifestyle, people should apply these beliefs to all forms of life, including the unborn. Although many supported animal rights in general or even more militant ways, the combination of animal rights, sexuality, politics, and abortion provided fuel for discussion on all sides.

SEAN MUTTAQI: In regards to what some people perceived as "homophobia" was the stand hardline took that said if you were hardline, you could not be gay, that homosexuality was not part of a healthy, natural lifestyle from its perspective. People took that and wanted to jump to conclusions and would say hardliners were homophobic and were out beating gay people up and had an anti-gay agenda. But those things never happened in hardline. It was a case of a sort of reverse P.C. fascism where they were saying, "If you don't believe what we believe then we're going to make demagogues out of you." But with hardline, it was never as outsiders portrayed, and with Vegan Reich, it was never an issue we sang about anyway. We'd do shows and gay people would come out just like anyone else. Violence never erupted between us and anyone over their sexuality. It was quite the opposite as individuals and as a band. Working within the animal rights movement, anti-war movement, and so on, you constantly interact with people who have different lifestyles and moral codes than you do. I always thought it was funny that Hardliners would get flak for simply deciding that homosexuality was a lifestyle they didn't want to engage in or stating they believed it was wrong. In general, I think the P.C. liberal crowd is just as eager as the "Christian Right" to make other people believe in what they believe and to enforce their views. As much as people wanted to criticize hardline for having its belief system, those same people wanted to enforce their beliefs in reverse. I personally think it's valid to hold an ideology or a religious view without having to fear being labeled "fascist," where going in you know that certain things aren't allowed and to expect others who hold that line of thinking to abide by the same rules. For instance, don't become a Buddhist monk and then complain that you're supposed to be celibate. Don't be straight edge and sneak a drink once in awhile. Likewise, if you're born into a tradition where your lifestyle choices conflict with the rules of your church, or temple, mosque and so on, then just leave it behind. Don't call people fascist because they have a different moral code than you adhere to. Hardline had a set of beliefs a lot of which conflicted with more typical liberal or left-wing viewpoints that prevailed in the hardcore scene, so people wanted to dismiss it with broad strokes that weren't necessarily accurate. So even though I can see how hardline's views on homosexuality were controversial and at odds with many people in the hardcore scene, I don't think it's legitimate to make the leap of considering hardline homophobic or that it was trying to oppress people. That said, I should also clarify that I am speaking from a historical perspective regarding my input or participation in a movement, the involvement in which ended over 15 years ago. From my current perspective as a Muslim, I have even less concern with what non-Muslims choose to do or not do, as long as it's not oppressing others. The West as a whole has not chosen to embrace Islam as its guiding principle, nor Christianity for that matter, and the *Quran* is clear that there's no compulsion in religion, so, really, what people want to do in a secular society, they're free to do. They might not make the same choices I make, or believe the same things I do, but I'm not about trying to force my religion down people's throats or be some type of morality police. I live the example I want to give and that's the extent of it.

SCOTT BEIBIN: I kind of agreed with hardline's abortion stance in that I viewed abortion at this time as being the same thing as killing animals, the killing of innocent life. It didn't make sense to be vegan and for abortion, if your reasons for being vegan were against the killing of innocent life. Over time my viewpoint on that changed drastically. My reasons for being vegan became very political and environmental and not just the ethics of killing. When you're vegan you are sometimes killing creatures because when your grain is harvested there are animals killed in the process. When your food is transported from one side of the country for the other, the emission from the trucks is partially causing cancer and killing people and animals along the way.

KIM NOLAN (CHICKS UP FRONT, BARK AND GRASS FANZINE/COOKBOOK): Although I embraced veganism and influenced a lot of hardcore kids to go vegan through the *Bark and Grass* cookbooks, I wasn't into hardline for one specific reason: they were pro-life. I was friends with some hardline kids, but I couldn't get behind it. I also didn't think, and still don't, that animal rights are more valuable than human rights. So hardline, for me, just didn't resonate with my personal values though I did see how it was an extreme offshoot or natural progression of veganism.

SEAN MUTTAQI: At the time, abortion was an issue people were debating a lot within punk rock and hardcore. Pro-choice and pro-life views always existed. Around the time hardline started, the pro-choice viewpoint was more prevalent in hardcore. As hardline and vegan straight edge started to differentiate themselves from each other, eventually vegan straight edge started to include a lot of people who were pro-choice, even to the point where a lot of modern vegan straight edge kids took it to a different level with an actual "anti-life" stance in general, like it's a crime against the environment to reproduce. That wasn't the case back then, but it was headed that way. People can make different arguments in terms of what trimester abortion should be cut off at, if they think there
is a limit at all. I just felt that if you're going to be vegan and say that people and animals have an innate right to exist, then you don't have a right to kill a child any more than a chicken, if you're taking that [vegan] argument. I mean, let's be real—a three-month human fetus has more going on for it developmentally than a fully grown shrimp. That said, that argument is specific to people who consider it wrong to kill animals under any circumstance. What I'm after here is consistency. What I mean is, if you're unwilling to make exceptions for people eating meat in any circumstance, then hold true to that absolutism in your belief in the sanctity of all life. There are plenty of world views that present a different take, with well founded, justifiable arguments from opposing sides. If you are willing to hunt and kill animals, believe in a more survival of the fittest notion, or don't moralize on the notion of taking life, then the abortion issue, that decision, is rooted in a different place. Even from a religious point of view, some of the world's major religions differ as to when the soul enters the body and in accord with those perspectives their views on abortion are reflective of that. For instance, many rulings in Judaism don't believe the soul enters until the baby's head exits the body. Though having partial rights before birth, in Judaism full human status is not accorded until birth. In Islam, the soul is generally considered to enter the body at 40 days, making abortion permissible, albeit frowned upon, up until that point. Christianity has varied its view over the centuries to the soul being present at conception, to entering later. My point is now, as it was then, not to enforce some conservative right-wing Christian agenda, but to encourage people to have a belief on this issue in conjunction with their moral views. Unfortunately, I think most people just pick a side that is the common view of their social scene or peer group and run with it without thinking.

BRENT DECKER (RACETRAITOR): I see the logical connection between being pro-life and vegan. I don't necessarily agree with all of it, but I can see the logic behind it in terms of respect for all life. The majority of the people in that movement were just like anyone else in America in that they were probably raised with some homophobic ideas. But it would be wrong to reduce hardline to the two issues of abortion and homosexuality. I remember Day of Suffering was pro-life but that was just a small issue in regards to their more radical stances on other political issues, which were probably more intriguing than the majority of the people who were trying to call them out for supposedly being "pro-lifers."

STEVE LOVETT: [Raid] practiced what we preached. If you believe that destroying the earth or slaughtering animals is wrong, then you certainly couldn't sit there passively and watch. We did create a fairly large local scene that supported us and shortly after many hardline bands followed including Monkey Wrench, Recoil, Limit, Pure Blood. At that point the scene shifted—punks hated us, but it didn't really matter because nihilistic gutter punks are not who we were reaching out to. In many ways we opposed that lifestyle because we believed in personal accountability. We had many enemies besides the gutter punks, including Nazi skins, rednecks and frat boys. We had to fight to be respected. I think that's why hardline grew big in our city, because we provided youth with a sense of belonging. Although we weren't a gang, the Stomp Crew certainly had that mentality.

JOSE PALAFOX (SWING KIDS, STRUGGLE, BREAD AND CIRCUITS): Direct action is great, but it's also important to look at the broader issues such as why people eat meat so much and how that's connected to our whole capitalistic society. This society we live under is so terrible for all species that until we look at the gross global inequalities and how we're connected to that and the consumer divide between first and third world nations then it will be difficult to really make broad changes.

DAY OF SUFFERING

DENNIS LYXZEN (REFUSED, INTERNATIONAL NOISE CONSPIRACY): If you were serious about political struggle and making a change, then hardline is a weird way to go. I've been vegan since about 1992, but if you think the main problem in the world is that people are eating meat then there is something wrong, because there are social and political structures you need to consider. I came from a leftist working class background and I just felt that there was a fascist strain in hardline that made us uncomfortable.

NATE WILSON (MONSTER X, DAS OATH): I felt that life and the sub-culture of hardcore was built around tolerance, and hardline was just completely intolerant in every way shape and form. People aren't clones of one another—that's something hardcore has always been very much against. Individualism is something that excited and attracted me and turned me on to what was going on in the scene in the early days. Hardline seemed to take on a very narrow minded attitude that seemed very conservative to many of us back then, and seemed to be opposite individualism. The same can be said for the Animal Liberation Movement. People don't need personal choices crammed down their throats. It's not practical, and in the long run just doesn't make people "see the light."

NORMAN BRANNON: I've been vegetarian for ethical reasons over anything else. There's something in my psyche that doesn't want to participate in violence against animals or anything else, really. I never promoted or decried direct action. Everybody's journey is a personal one. I'm pretty darn pacifist on any level so any sort of violent direct action rubs me the wrong way and it makes you no better than a meat eater. I can see why someone can get so upset, but I'm also a little bit realistic in the sense that I feel like most people who are vegetarian are people who are predisposed to thinking for themselves more than the average person. And let's face it, there are a lot of average people in the world who don't make a connection or have the humanity it takes to understand that killing and eating an animal might not be a good idea. But I've never looked down on my friends who eat meat. Judging a person's character is incredibly complex and vegetarianism is only one part of that. Some kids were judging people's entire characters based on that one aspect and I thought that was too incredibly simplified and ridiculous.

MANI MOSTOFI: The main problem with hardline and a lot of people's attitudes about politics is that most people tend to gravitate toward a more authoritarian approach, which is like "We have the answer and everyone will have to succumb to it." I was into the democratic method of discussing and trying to influence people with ideas. It wasn't that I was against militancy as it was the idea of an overemphasis of animal rights. I was really into animal rights, but I always thought if you're going to pursue animal rights you have to pursue human rights almost as a prerequisite. It's hard to get people to go vegan when they don't even have options for what they have to eat. The fact that animal rights got so big was symptomatic of the fact that it's easy to be into that for white middle class kids. It's an easy thing to do because all you really have to do is convince people that Tofutti is an acceptable alternative to ice cream and you've got them. I think direct action can be a good thing, but the problem with the hardline rhetoric was it was too "cult-y" and it was almost more about being tough and puritanical than it was about the real issues. Hardline definitely tried to beat issues into people's heads. But it also forced people to discuss that even though most folks in mainstream society eat meat, we have to figure out a way to interact with that in our own lives. They had an extreme approach that I wasn't necessarily into, but at least the issue was brought up and discussed.

JESSICA HOPPER (HIT IT OR QUIT IT FANZINE): I think vegetarianism was fairly common in hardcore and even if you're sort of a vaguely political person you think about what you put into your body and who you support with your purchases. Bands were singing about it and making it more fashionable. I think things like vegetarianism are kind of easy. White middle class kids are prone to embracing a struggle they may or may not have. I became a vegetarian by the time I was in tenth grade and it's a pretty radical thing for a kid in the Midwest. I guess I found it ironic when there were bands singing about how much shit they get for being straight edge and vegetarian playing to a room full of people who were also straight edge and vegetarian for the most part. I think there is a lot of romance in being the other and positing yourself in a struggle. Being vegetarian is pretty un-radical in and of itself. But when you're younger it's something that sets you apart from your family. What you put in your body is one of the most basic lifestyle choices that you can make.

BRIAN DINGLEDINE (CATHARSIS, INSIDE FRONT FANZINE): For the first couple years, I resented [bands like Earth Crisis] just for their posturing, and then I became vegetarian but still hated the consumer veganism of their part of the hardcore scene. I identified as "freegan" years before it became a common term, because it seemed to be the only approach that made sense in light of my dropout lifestyle—I couldn't afford to eat at the vegan restaurants the straight edge crowd went to! —and my opposition to capitalism in general. It wasn't until 1999 that I became vegan myself, and then only because I'd met anarchist vegans who provided a much better example. I'm still vegan today, which I fear is not the case for some of the people who got into it because it was a popular trend.

SEAN INGRAM (COALESCE): At the time, I thought hardline was very attractive. I had no direction in my life, and it was kind of a religion—a reason to live; to be undeniably righteous for a righteous cause. But as everyone figured out, nothing man builds is righteous. It was all bullshit, and ended up turning very Nazi-like. I don't find any honor in blowing buildings up or intimidating doctors. I know a lot of hardcore vegans find that kind of idea romantic, but I find it [to be] bullshit. It seems like the biggest waste of time in the world. It just seems that there are so many more important things than animal rights. I just don't see violence as any reasonable choice. You can't terrorize and call it righteous. One of my good friends from the day is a very outspoken vegan. We used to talk about the A.L.F. Whereas I sold out and stopped caring, instead of my friend going to jail for unplugging some egg refrigerators or something, he went to law school and is actively using his skills for what he believes in. That, to me, is amazing, and that's why I call bullshit on hardcore animal liberation kids.

SCOTT BEIBIN: I don't think hardline is all that dangerous. With hardline and the radical veganism we were espousing at that time, we pushed the middle. Basically, people looked at hardline and they felt it was so extreme with all its viewpoints; however, people could relate to what was in the middle, which was becoming vegan. That's what really triggered this mass exodus from people eating meat. They were not interested in being hardline, but they were interested in being vegan.

MIKE KIRSCH: There's something to be said about drastic things having to be done to change things. With that said, we can't lose our humanity in that process. If it becomes about simplifying the issue then it has lost its point. When the focus becomes so much about the political line and that "this" is the key issue and if you're with "this" then you're basically good and if you're against it then you're basically our enemy. That can be useful sometimes, but if it's just around one or two points then it misses the whole point of it. For that matter, what about being an American or driving a car? Where does all this shit come from? That doesn't mean that rationalizes abusing animals or eating meat, but people need to have a little humility about their situations and make more connections and not just settle for one issue. A lot of people who got into hardline had sincere intentions and they ended up making connections to broader issues through that scene. It's real easy when it comes to a platform of a couple of issues, though.

RAY CAPPO: I didn't really care if a person was into veganism or not, my main question was who are we, why are we here and what's the goal in life—it was a spiritual movement, so hardline and things like that didn't phase me. I saw it manifest in the way that people were very angry. In Krishna consciousness I thought we were rebels, but blissful rebels. We didn't have to bomb a fur factory to make a statement about wearing fur or animal rights, whereas hardline seemed to be about destroying things. I thought a lot of it was based around hate.

TIM SINGER (DEADGUY, KISS IT GOODBYE, NO ESCAPE, BOILING POINT FANZINE): Extreme animal rights is beyond comprehension to me. On one hand you're a peace loving vegetarian, on the other hand you're into this militia type shit. It's like you've gone so far left that you're right wing. You're taking choices away from people under threat of violence. It's completely like a bad movie. I couldn't believe it had as much legitimacy as it did.

ANTHONY PAPPALARDO: You have to realize that what you're doing is being absorbed by other people. Even though I'm vegetarian, I don't think it's cool for someone to write a song advocating kids to go out and blow up a fur factory. People work there. Some of the stuff was so simplistic. People want to be acknowledged for things but they don't want to be held accountable. You have to realize you're responsible for what you say. If you don't understand that then you have a real problem.

KURT SCHROEDER (BIRTHRIGHT, CATALYST RECORDS): Psychologically there are some individuals who are just attracted to extreme ideologies. A lot of the people who got into hardline got into it for the same reasons they got into militant straight edge—it was kind of this elite, macho group. There were two sides to hardline—one was that side and the other was a more thoughtful side. A lot of the kids I knew were more intelligent about it.

DANIEL TRAITOR: Animal rights is an issue that has to be taken from a compassionate approach. This is a relatively new development in human history. In many cases, there isn't an option for many people to be vegan or vegetarian, and many others haven't been properly educated about it. Human beings take time to change, and it's my opinion that an important part of accelerating that change is a compassionate approach. In a way the people who have done a lot for the animal rights cause are the ones that have started vegetarian groceries like Whole Foods or companies that develop and market vegetarian products—and, of course, all of those dedicated activists who have done sustainable education to people that laid the groundwork for companies to have a consumer market.

STEVE LOVETT: It is interesting how hardline evolved into this sort of straight edge subculture, even 15 years later. Ultimately, I think the movement should have been less centralized and curbed some of its ideology. Hardline taught me a lot of lessons regarding extremism. If you think eating meat is evil, then what does that make the people who eat meat? Keep in mind, from my perspective hardline ended up with "These things are evil and those people who engage in these activities are evil and we will destroy the behavior or lifestyle that we don't approve of." You see the same mentality across the morality spectrum, be it evangelical Christians or fundamentalist Muslims. I fell into that trap and began to act out of hate instead of love. While both emotions are necessary, acting out of hate is self destructive. We did take hardcore and straight edge to the next level. We brought direct action into the hardcore scene both from animal rights and environmental perspectives. From that point of view, I think that it was successful.

GREG BENNICK (TRIAL): I never believed hardline. I didn't take their tough talk of violence seriously. I didn't take their revolution seriously. I didn't take their adherents seriously. And they proved me right. Without exception, every hardliner I ever knew is no longer hardline, and no longer straight edge. It wasn't ever a movement. It was a fad, easy to latch onto because of its promise of immediate violent revolution. Yes, animal abuse and violence towards animals is reprehensible. Yes, sometimes change in any realm requires direct action. And yes, there are committed people everywhere dedicated to bringing about change. But the hardliners weren't those people. As Emma Goldman said, "If I can't dance, I don't want to be part of your revolution." Hardline promised violence and logic and anti-abortion rhetoric. It bored me immediately. Revolution needs to be creative to capture the imagination longer than the fuse lit by fury will burn. Hardline's fuse burned out quickly and it was never attached to any explosive. As for animal liberation, the world does need to continually move towards compassion and appreciation for animal life. This needs to happen not because animals are soft and fuzzy and warm. It needs to happen because the amount of suffering in this world that is self-inflicted is too overwhelming to allow for life to continue on the planet. We need to come to a state of understanding about the ways we create suffering and why, both against animals and against humans, and then work to reverse that process however we can with that increased understanding as a guide. Those who work to oppose suffering are heroes.

KURT SCHROEDER: At some point immediate action needs to be taken. If any of the abuse of non-human animals was taking place in front of people they would stop it. If they saw it happening on the street any average person would stop it. But for some reason it becomes a different attitude because it's done behind closed doors. The whole point of getting involved in the A.L.F. was to stop it because it was happening, even if it was outside the mainstream view. It's not always the most effective tactic and I'm not saying it always needs to be used, but you have an arsenal of tactics to achieve a goal. And it's not for me to tell someone they shouldn't do it.

ANDY HURLEY (RACETRAITOR, KILLTHESLAVEMASTER, FALL OUT BOY): It's really important that people do as much as they can to take apart the system and the shit we live in. It's going to be hard to have a fundamental change in every person to create an organic change in its structure, but I think no matter what we do, civilization will eventually collapse because we simply can't sustain it. Meanwhile a lot of animals are still going extinct. Direct action, little by little, does *something*. Every time you can stop an aspect of unnecessary animal testing then that's a plus.

TIM SINGER: The whole world is not going to stop eating meat; it's just not going to happen. Now that doesn't mean you can't speak out against it or stand up for what you believe in. Sometimes it sucks to be right but that doesn't mean you can take a gun and make others buy into what you believe. I'm a total vegetarian, but I lived next to a guy that went out and fished for his own food and he would freeze it and eat it all winter. He was providing for himself and his family, so how am I going to judge that? My life experience is so much different than his. I can't judge him.

JIM GRIMES: The world can't change purely from music. John Lennon probably influenced more people than anyone else, but the world still sucks. [laughs] People think they can take an ideology they heard off a piece of vinyl and go for it, and those kids probably burn themselves out. Once you go full on and put blinders on yourself, you'll probably be at the bar in six months eating a burger. I bet most of those kids are like that today, and it sucks because there are people out there who have been doing it much longer who don't get as much credit. There are always different people who need to just rage one hundred percent. Those are the people who burn out. If you want to go burn down the McDonald's headquarters then fine, but then do it and just live it. Do it one hundred percent. But I don't know anyone who can commit to anything one hundred percent because we're human beings and we all have our own faults.

To this day, the impact of animal rights on hardcore is felt not only in the scene but also in the broader public consciousness. Militancy, though resisted by many, only served to increase awareness about these topics. Because these issues related to a person's diet, they also had an impact on peoples' lives outside of the scene. Others were turned off by the extreme nature of these debates, saw no value in changing their lifestyle in that way or thought it was more of a sacrifice than they were willing to make. Some rejected vegetarianism because they didn't want to give in to what they saw as social pressure.

However, many who delved into animal rights and vegetarianism made the issue their life's work and subsequently created or joined activist groups that have exposed the mainstream public to the controversies surrounding factory farming, diet choice and related issues. Groups like P.E.T.A. have practically become household names. Animal rights activists like Peter Young and several members of the S.H.A.C. 7 (Stop Huntingdon Animal Cruelty), both of whom have received international media attention, also had roots in hardcore. Young released minks from fur farms in the Midwest in the late nineties, eventually did prison time, and now lectures about animal rights issues. The S.H.A.C. 7 were charged with stalking and "terrorism" against Huntingdon Life Sciences, a company that tests on animals. They were declared guilty in 2006 and were sent to prison.

Although hardcore has addressed a wide spectrum of topics, animal rights is one that has maintained a strong and lasting presence. Attention paid to most topics is cyclical, but like straight edge, animal rights and vegetarianism/veganism particularly have become almost inextricably linked with the scene. Not every person involved with hardcore is drawn to animal rights issues, but it's difficult to find another topic that permeates all of the sometimes territorial and varying sub-scenes within hardcore as thoroughly.

Animal rights impacted people on several levels. The issues made people think and make decisions about how to act. Consequently, animal rights could act as a catalyst and impact other areas of peoples' lives by introducing them to a more complex world and prompting them to consider what actions to take in these new areas.

GREG BENNICK: The amount of suffering in this world seems limitless to me and my life is a mission to help diminish that suffering however I can. In terms of animals, who don't have the mental ability to alter their environment according to their desires, it was obvious to me that in order to live in a way which promoted less suffering for them, and thus for me as well, that I needed to change my lifestyle away from one which embraced eating or wearing animals, or supporting those who make their living killing or torturing animals.

MANI MOSTOFI: It was natural why animal rights became a huge issue in the nineties hardcore scene because most of the kids were white middle class kids and they didn't have to face anything deeper than what their dietary intake was. Now Racetraitor was an all vegan straight edge band but we never had a song about animal rights. We thought the issues of race and class were far more important to make hardcore kids think about. Then again, the animal rights issue was a major stepping-stone for a lot of kids. A lot of those people who were into that stuff are still into it in one way or another. A lot of them stuck to that issue as well as broadened out into other issues. On some level that perspective of engaging the world is still there for a lot of the nineties hardcore kids, even if they aren't a part of the scene or stopped being straight edge or whatever.

STEVE HART (DAY OF SUFFERING): I think most people choose to be straight edge for their health and veganism is also a healthy way of living. It's healthy for our bodies and our environment. It was really just a natural progression. In the nineties, veganism wasn't as easily accessible as it is today. We had a way of living, we had a message, we had a voice, so we used them. I know for a fact that veganism wouldn't have been as well known today if it weren't for bands screaming their message of veganism in hardcore.

ANDY HURLEY: If you're going to have compassion for humans then it's important to think about our home, our planet, and the rest of the life on that planet. Through our way of living we threaten it more and more every day.

AARON TURNER (ISIS, HYDRHEAD RECORDS): Animal rights was a product of a general political consciousness that hardcore has always had in one form or another. At the time I was politically opposed to what was going on environmentally. There's this anti-authoritarian vibe and some really insightful discourse about it through lyrics, but there's also a lot of dogma. Whether people want to believe it or not hardcore is just a scene and people will always come and go and adopt the rituals and appearance for a short time and let it go. Meat eating is a mainstay of the American way of life and punk and hardcore is pretty counter to that. In principle I agree with vegetarianism, but my desire for meat just overcame my ethics after a while. But I don't think it's bad for people to not eat meat or dairy for a while even if it's not for the right reasons. I lived vegan for three years and vegetarian for 10 and I'm not sorry that I did. And I did become genuinely interested in animal rights and I think it's important to know about the effects you have on the outside world. And it didn't hurt there were bands playing music that were promoting that message. Music has been used to convey a message throughout human history and hardcore is just another stage of that occurrence.

VIQUE MARTIN (SIMBA FANZINE, SIMBA RECORDS): Sadly, I think that a lot of the people who cared about animal rights back then seem to have become apathetic about this cause. But for all the people who started eating meat, there are still a ton of people who left the scene but retained their ideas and lifestyles to some extent. I know a lot of ex-hardcore kids who still don't eat meat and have chosen a different path than one of direct involvement in music, but are on a path of academia or social work. Great things come from smart hardcore kids, and although they may not look it anymore, most true hardcore kids will be hardcore till they die.

RYAN DOWNEY: I got really involved in animal rights activism because I felt like a lot of the punk rockers and even the straight edge kids were faking it. They seemed more interested in fashion and creating a social clique within the subculture than in leaving

this world a better place than they found it, and that always concerned me. I feel like God wants all of us to help each other. Martin Luther King spoke a lot about the interconnectedness of all. I have felt that as a "truth" since I was very young. That kind of passion can ignite into hostility and the unfortunate consequence, from about age 16 to about age 20, was that I was consumed with rage that overwhelmed my drive and my compassion toward other people. I believe we should love the oppressors as well as the oppressed and that we have a responsibility to fight oppression. When I was a teenager I focused my passion in some of the wrong directions. Burned out by age 20, I retreated from activism, but by 21 I was full-fledged again working for animal rights. These days I still stay informed and stay involved in various ways.

FREDDY CRICIEN (MADBALL): I respect straight edge and vegan kids. Everyone's diet could probably use a bit less red meat and alcohol, depending on your personality. [laughs] I respect what it's about, but at the same time we're all different. You could miss out on having a friendship with someone if you prejudge them. I can understand wanting to avoid people who can't deal with drinking or eating meat, but you've got to just respect people for who they are.

NICK FORTE (RORSCHACH): I think the most important aspect to come out of the vegan/animal rights/vegetarian movement in hardcore was that it gave many kids a necessary and basic mistrust of what this culture tells us is the "truth." It really lifted the veil on many issues for me and others, both animal rights related and otherwise. I think it taught kids that you need to research things much further than what TV ads told us, or our parents or schools. How the debates impacted me is quite direct; I was a vegetarian for about 15 years and vegan for about five years. These issues still have relevance in my life to this day, but my views have changed over the years to some degree and I am now no longer a vegetarian. What has stuck with me is the inherent mistrust for cultural trends, which is always a good thing.

STEVE LOVETT: I am still following my ideals today. I work at a fairly large environmental nonprofit. I have three kids who have all been raised vegetarian. I think my lifestyle choices of self-sufficiency and bioregionalism were derived from hardcore. I've seen most kids who were young and idealistic abandon their former beliefs, like vegetarianism. My views concerning animal rights have changed a little. There was a time when everything was black and white. All of my friends were vegetarian or vegan, now only a few are strict veg. I used to be opposed to all animal experimentation, now I think there may be a few legitimate reasons for some small controlled experiments. Certainly, I'm not talking about the cosmetic industry, but with revolutionary life-saving medicines or procedures. I am active in my local environmental movement. I work for a fairly large environmental restoration organization. I'm serving on a committee for the city I live in to preserve open space, be it acquiring land for parks, community gardens and agriculture, and sustainable timber harvesting or setting up conservation easements on target parcels. Also, I'm working on fundraising to get a skate park in a neighboring city. Ultimately it is D.I.Y. If you want a better world, think globally and act locally. Do it yourself, don't wait for someone else!

KEN OLDEN: I've been a vegetarian for over 15 years now, and I've always been pro-animal rights. I support just about anything that helps animals because they don't have many advocates in society. I think sometimes a little violence even can help others take your position more seriously — which is unfortunate, but maybe part of human nature. Most great revolutions had two arms, the non-violent peaceful part, and the more aggressive militant part. If you look at history, when you see significant changes in society, you had both. We can look at the American Revolution, the movement to abolish slavery, the civil rights movement in the fifties and sixties. I see the animal rights activists from a similar perspective.

SEAN MUTTAQI: Animal rights continues to be a major part of my life to this day. I'm still vegan and raise my kids vegan. I work for animal welfare issues within the Muslim world. For instance, I made *hajj* and didn't have to compromise my veganism. No sacrifice or meat eating involved. For most people I knew during the hardline period, the key people involved, I'd have to say that although their beliefs and lifestyles may have changed in other areas, the majority have carried with them a respect for animal rights and the environment, and have remained either vegan or vegetarian. That said, in the broader picture of the vegan straight edge scene, it seems like there's not a whole lot of people left who stuck to it. Anytime something reaches a bigger level, when it becomes a trend, it just doesn't have a deep enough impact on those involved to last over the years. That said it's always up to a new generation to press the issues. It's cyclical. You fight for change, make an impact, that impact is felt for a time, starts to fade, and then someone else eventually picks up the torch and carries on where those of us before left off. And for those of us who still hold true to our beliefs, hopefully we help produce a better generation ahead through how we raise our kids. My kids are already all about it. They play music, do martial arts, and are completely into veganism. It's not about making clones of ourselves or forcing children into our lifestyles. I always give them the choice to make their own decisions. But if you show kids a positive way, and are open with them about why you have made the choices you do, in general, I think kids will make the right decisions.

VIC DICARA: To this day, animal rights and vegetarian related philosophy remains vital and important to me. I think the way humanity treats the rest of the world is a dramatic testament to our residual bestial nature, and that would be one of the best things to focus on from an evolutionary angle. In other words, if we really want to evolve out of the jungles, we should work on dealing with the rest of the Earthlings, and the Earth itself, in a non-animalistic, more compassionate manner. I think vegetarianism is a simple and practical step in this direction.

BURNING FIGHT: THE NINETIES HARDCORE REVOLUTION IN ETHICS, POLITICS, AND

SPIRITUALITY

An essential component of hardcore is the spirit invested in the music. Every form of music comes from within, but the passion displayed at a hardcore show can be similar to what is seen at a religious ritual. At nearly every hardcore show, bands play their songs with the utmost intensity, singers testify to an issue that is close to their hearts, and fans struggle to reach the stage in an effort to be a part of the experience. To many, hardcore is a religion—it can have its own values and belief systems (e.g. straight edge, vegetarianism/veganism, D.I.Y.), classic texts (e.g. records, zines) and leaders (e.g. band members, zine writers, show promoters) who speak their minds and sometimes find themselves wrapped in controversy.

During the nineties, something controversial happened in hardcore: a variety of religious ideas, most prominently from the Hare Krishna movement and Christianity, began to have a very visible presence in the scene. The Krishna conscious band Shelter was probably the first primarily religious hardcore band, but others like 108, Focused, Strongarm, Prema, and Zao followed suit and also openly discussed their spiritual beliefs. Although there were bands in the eighties that wrote about such topics, the nineties bands took these messages further. For example, several Hare Krishna influenced bands made their spiritual beliefs the central focus of their music and their lives in general. Members of the bands moved into Krishna temples, had special Krishna haircuts, wore robes and other trappings of the group and followed a strict diet and other ritual behaviors. As with other notable debates in the nineties scene, religious adherents openly advocated for their causes. Most people involved in the scene, however, saw this as intrusive.

Many in hardcore have had fairly strong agnostic/atheistic stances due to disaffection with organized religion, so the presence of anything spiritual in the scene was hotly contested and is still discussed now. Most people feel that hardcore is about rejecting the norms and values of mainstream society. Pioneers like Minor Threat derided organized religion as being "full of shit" (in the song "Filler"), and found the corruption stemming from religion had such a negative impact on the world that they saw no place for it in hardcore. Others felt the need for religion or spirituality in their lives at some level, and first Krishna and then later other religious ideas were brought into the hardcore scene in an attempt to fulfill that need.

DAN YEMIN (LIFETIME, KID DYNAMITE, PAINT IT BLACK): The first rule about hardcore is that there are no rules. But hardcore has always had a healthy distrust of institutions like organized religion, which historically have been about social control and domination, not to mention being the cause of wars and genocide and inquisitions. With a historical pedigree like that how can you embrace it as a part of hardcore?

VIQUE MARTIN (SIMBA FANZINE/RECORDS): I don't believe the term "spirituality" should be thrown about, especially saying that it has a place in hardcore. Not everything has a place in hardcore. That's the point of it. Racism, sexism, homophobia, etc, those things don't have a place in hardcore. Most organized religions have those things in spades, and dressing them up in the guise of "spirituality" doesn't change this. I am not a spiritual person and I am just fine and dandy with this. It doesn't mean that I'm not deep, intense, committed, passionate, and interesting. It means I'm not spiritual or religious. And anyone that tells me that I would be happier or more fulfilled or "whole" if I allowed

God, Jesus, or Krishna into my life is wrong. That's why I detest people preaching or pushing their religion[s] and agenda[s] on me. It's condescending, arrogant, and offensive.

SONNY KAY (GOLD STANDARD LABORATORIES RECORDS): Hardcore should be an interest, an activity, and a form of communication, separate from one's faith—just like church and state are supposed to be. Why must religious zealots infuse everything with religion? Their brains are capable of intellect and reason, but to expect it of them is like asking the impossible.

BRIAN DINGLEDINE (CATHARSIS, INSIDE FRONT): If you ever saw a Catharsis shirt, you know what I'm going to say—No Gods, No Masters! Part of the vitality of the hardcore scene was the constant debates about what should or shouldn't have a place in it. So on one hand, I guess I can't complain about spirituality in hardcore, when I wanted so much for it to be a space for radical organizing and resistance; on the other hand, I feel that hardcore has always been at its best as a place of rejection of the status quo, and fucking religion is part of the status quo.

While some argued spirituality and religion had no place in hardcore, spirituality acted as an important component for several classic hardcore bands including Bad Brains and their Rastafarian message and the Cro-Mags and their dedication to Krishna consciousness. To many, rejecting all spiritual influences would be to disregard the impact of those legendary bands themselves. Furthermore, if hardcore is truly about thinking for yourself then why the need for a complete ban on spirituality?

SEAN INGRAM (COALESCE): Hardcore has always been an open forum. I may not always like what's in it, but it's still an open forum. If bands wanted to focus their energy on their rebellion against sin so be it. It didn't bother me.

SCOTT BEIBIN (BLOODLINK RECORDS): Hardcore is a scene of extremists, so it's not a surprise that religious extremism would enter the equation. Hardcore attracts extreme personalities and those who would be gurus, which is why we've had cults in the hardcore scene. Hardcore kids are looking for answers whether they be spiritual or in the profane world. The hardcore scene is a place where there is information and acceptance and you feel comfortable sharing and exploring your ideas. Spirituality fits into that mold very much so. It can be a good thing for some people because it's a way to get their bearings. I think religion is a crock of shit, but I don't fault people for falling into it, considering their circumstances in life.

MATT FOX (SHAI HULUD): If you have a guitar or banjo or any instrument and you want to sing about what moves you, you do that because that's inside of you. So, I don't think religion should be excluded from hardcore or polka or anything else. There's no exclusivity in any music.

The debate of whether hardcore should allow for or include spirituality caused turmoil in the eighties and the issue was brought to a head in the nineties with a focus on Krishna consciousness, Christianity, and Islam. The aforementioned bands, as well as a number of others, took inspiration from their varying spiritual perspectives (sometimes narrowly fashioned, while in other cases more open-minded) and opened a wide array of discourse about spirituality.

RAY CAPPO (SHELTER, YOUTH OF TODAY): Every question that everyone asked me I had already criticized the [Hare Krishna] devotees for—I had already went through that level of questioning everything. Believe me, before I put on a robe and danced in the street I had thought about it. [laughs] I didn't do it because it was cool; it was probably the most un-cool thing ever. People hated God, but for me I never thought that you had to hate God to be into hardcore or punk. Hardcore is about being against the grain.

SEAN MUTTAQI (VEGAN REICH, CAPTIVE NATION RISING, PRESSURE, UPRISING RECORDS): The point a lot of people on the atheist tip were making was that spirituality had no place in hardcore because spirituality was somehow anti-revolutionary and the antithesis of free-thinking. The problem with this premise is that most historical revolutionary movements and liberation struggles had their impetus in the religious/ spiritual milieu. I'm not saying people involved in the hardcore scene have to be spiritual either because there is clearly that atheist and agnostic influence since the beginning, as well. I just don't think anyone can make the argument to its counter that you have to be an atheist to be into hardcore. And clearly that anti-spiritual perspective did not win out. Spirituality has absolutely been allowed into the modern hardcore scene, with some of today's top hardcore bands being Christian. The absolutist anti-religious perspective was a knee-jerk reaction from people who had a fairly simplistic attitude about the world. That said, I also find a lot of the spirituality practiced in today's hardcore scene to be equally simplistic and very close-minded and conservative, so who knows what the solution is. I ultimately wish people from both sides would broaden their horizons a bit.

BRENDAN DESMET (GROUNDWORK, ABSINTHE): The defeatist attitude that punk and hardcore are often associated with should naturally have the yin to its yang. The negativity in terms of being so anti-everything including God and spirituality was bound to get balanced out at some point by Christians or Krishnas or even Mormons. The more people you have involved the more variance you are going to have. People are also looking for something different, which in some cases meant tapping into spirituality. It's human nature when you're looking for answers to turn to something like religion to hold on to. Hardcore is no different than any other scene of people.

SEAN CAPONE (POSITRON FANZINE): Underground scenes like hardcore are often beacons to a certain type of person who has an extreme need to believe and belong; a tribe of individuals trying to define codes of spiritual or ethical behavior which hardcore, through an ultimate poverty of imagination, or a souring of youthful optimism, is unable to provide. Religion arrives pre-packaged, with a prescribed value system and a lifestyle to support it, seemingly metonymical to the punk ethos but lacking any subversive quality, and personal salvation guaranteed. I think that when hardcore music emptied itself of violence and sexuality—to be replaced by empty style, fear, and middle-class repression—it left the scene vulnerable to the irrational allure of religion.

KYLE NOLTEMEYER (ENDPOINT, GUILT): Whether there is a place for [spirituality] or not it made itself a place in the scene. People in hardcore might say that being into spirituality means you're enslaved; at the same time, people into spirituality might say that being into anything outside of spirituality, such as being into hardcore, is a way of being enslaved. [laughs] Everyone has their core beliefs. Hardcore is even almost a religion in itself. It has its own prophets. Its own shows are like worship experiences.

MOE MITCHELL (CIPHER): All ideologies and tendencies should have a home in a scene that challenges rigidity and conservatism. Christian and Krishna hardcore make a lot of sense to me. What else would a Christian kid scream about other than his love of Christ? Why not? Diversity is what made hardcore so attractive to me. It seems we're losing it as hardcore becomes mainstream and marketers are looking to put their hands around a "hardcore sound."

> **SHELTER-108**
> **FARM RETREAT WEEKEND**
> **JULY 09-11**
> **GITA-NAGARI, PA**
>
> A HARE KRSNA HARDCORE EXPERIENCE
> AT THE KRSNA FARM IN PA
> THIS WILL BE HOSTED BY SHELTER AND
> 108
> THERE WILL BE INFORMAL GROUP TALKS ON
> KRSNA CONSCIOUSNESS,
> CAMPING OUT, HIKING, VEGETARIAN FEAST-
> ING AND LOTS OF OTHER FUN STUFF
> THE RETREAT BEGINS AT NOON ON FRIDAY
> AND WINDS UP SUNDAY NIGHT WITH A
> SHELTER 108 SHOW AT THE NEW UNISOUND
> THE COST OF THE RETREAT WILL BE $25
> PER PERSON WHICH INCLUDES ROOM,
> BOARD AND A REDUCED TICKET PRICE FOR
> THE UNISOUND SHOW
> FOR MORE INFO CALL (215)242-6478
> OR (718)855-6714 KATHLEEN

In the early nineties, there was a contingent within the hardcore scene that focused on Krishna consciousness (also known as Gaudiya Vaisnavism, the name of the orthodox lineage the movement comes from). Often known in the West as the Hare Krishna movement, this new sect was brought to America in the sixties by A.C. Bhaktivedenta Swami Prabhupada. Prabhupada's teachings initially caught on in the Lower East Side of New York City as hippies, bohemians, and other anti-establishment oriented young people were drawn to the philosophy and parts of the group's lifestyle which included vegetarianism, belief in karma and reincarnation, the rejection of all intoxicants, and the idea that the soul was the real self. Many drawn to the movement already felt out of place in mainstream society and ideas such as reincarnation and karma likely appealed to young minds who saw a lack of justice in the world.

STEVE REDDY (EQUAL VISION RECORDS): Once you got below the superficial level you realized it's a pretty hard discipline that asks you to control your senses while you're living in an environment that wants you to indulge your senses at all costs. In the beginning, Prabhupada came here and people from the Lower East Side started to join and he started initiating people and many of them left. People would ask Prabhupada about it and he would say, "Don't be amazed that someone leaves, be amazed that anyone stays."

Over time, the Krishna movement became well-known in the West due to its highly publicized exposure through Beat Generation poet Allen Ginsburg and Beatles guitarist George Harrison. But the movement ran into some high-profile trouble after Prabhupada's death in the late seventies when scandals involving money laundering, drugs, kidnapping, and murder were associated with some of the newly appointed gurus. These incidents brought media scrutiny upon the International Society of Krishna Consciousness (ISKCON), the organization Prabhupada set up to carry on his teachings after his death.

The Krishnas spent much of the eighties attempting to combat the negative stereotypes resulting from the scandals. Meanwhile, several notable figures from eighties hardcore— members of Cro-Mags and Cause for Alarm, for instance—were drawn to the philosophy, which was showcased through lyrics and album artwork.

NORMAN BRANNON (TEXAS IS THE REASON, ANTI-MATTER FANZINE, FOUNTAINHEAD, SHELTER, RESSURECTION): I don't remember a time when Krishnas didn't exist in the hardcore scene. John Joseph [Cro-Mags vocalist] and a lot of other folks had been initiated for years. One thing Krishnas had that poor hardcore kids loved was free food. [laughs] The Krishnas would often have food at Tompkins Square Park, which was four blocks from C.B.G.B.'s. I remember going to a show, going crazy, leaving the matinee, and then running to the park to see if the Krishnas were still there with food. A lot of times the Krishnas there were ex-hardcore kids.

Although some mocked its influence, Krishna consciousness' synchronicity with the tenets of straight edge as well as expressing major differences with other more recognizable mainstream religions gave new anti-establishment adherents a comfortable way to practice spirituality.

While Krishna played a smaller role in the eighties New York hardcore scene, former Youth of Today vocalist Ray Cappo drew new attention to the faith during the nineties by bringing some of its abstract concepts down to earth through his lyrics. His songs were not only about worshipping God but about improving one's lot in life, as well as the world one is surrounded by, through self-reflection, philosophical study and positive action.

NORMAN BRANNON: When Ray Cappo got into Krishna consciousness it was a little controversial because he was really the first person who wanted a complete lifestyle change. The other guys were practicing but if they didn't become monks and disappear then they were still on the outskirts of the hardcore scene. Ray, however, wanted to give it all up and move to India.

Cappo's Krishna conscious band, Shelter, was a synthesis of many of the spiritual and philosophical realizations he had when first becoming interested in the faith. While Shelter's debut record, *Perfection of Desire*, had religious overtones, many of the lyrical concepts were also applicable to others concepts about spirituality or the nature of "reality."

RAY CAPPO: What struck me the most about Vaisnavism was that it wasn't talking about religion. I had sort of thought religion was interesting, but it was exclusive, whereas I felt the *Bhagavad-Gita* was inclusive. It wasn't condemning Jews or Christians or Muslims or Hindus. You can always change your religion, but you can't change the fact that you're a spirit soul. That's what you are. You can change your country and nationality and even lose your body, but you can't change the fact that you're a living entity that inhabits a body. With that as my paradigm, I can then see that all these trees and plants and animals around me are all like me and struggling to survive. That's why vegetarianism has been an important concept in my life, because I don't want to cause harm to any living entity, and when you do you have to suffer some reaction from that, so it's better to tie up all your actions in a spiritual path, because there can't be any peace in this world because things are always stepping on other things just to exist. So, you have to be a little more minimal and simpler and a little more thoughtful.

Cappo, as well as several other hardcore veterans, reached a point where disillusion with society brought about questioning their own place in the world when hardcore no longer provided the answers. By pondering these issues, as well as being influenced by the Krishna-influenced bands like the Cro-Mags, they decided to investigate Krishna philosophy a bit further.

RAY CAPPO: I was at a point in my life when I was open to different things. What I understand about reincarnation is I know that I'm not a body. That's a huge step right there. I know I have a body because I have analyzed it since I was a child and I've seen it change, so therefore I can't be it. So, what am I? Right now when I go home I always wake up in the morning and brush my skin with a thick brush. Every time I do that cells flake off of me and every time I eat nourishing food new cells form. So, what am I, the cells that are flaking off? No, I am the observer of those cells. So molecularly everything is changing in my body and on a subtle level even my mind is changing. I've witnessed my intelligence change. I am an observer; that's all I am—I'm a passenger. So, I've reincarnated in this lifetime. I've got new flesh on me right now that I didn't have when I was seven years old. This isn't a stretched out version of my seven year old body—it's a completely new incarnation. When you start analyzing the soul or self it is a slight leap of faith to say that life which has never died which has observed changes is going to be diminished. Energy can't be destroyed or created, but it goes somewhere. There is some type of energy that is animating this body. I don't think I'm just some machine that's plugged in for a few years and then you unplug it and it dies.

VIC DICARA (108, INSIDE OUT, BURN, BEYOND): Me and all of these dudes I grew up with on Long Island would go into New York City every Sunday to the C.B.G.B.'s matinee. Tom Capone and I would go there and a couple of blocks away from CB's was a really cool record store called Bleecker Bob's. We were looking at the fanzine rack one day, and we were vegetarians already, and there was a zine there called *The Razor's Edge* with this wacky drawing on it of a cow with a human face getting chopped by a guy with a cow's face. We were like, "Holy shit, we have to check this out!" I have to also mention that we were super intrigued by the Cro-Mags. We took a look at the zine and it mentioned something about Krishna, so we were like, "Cool! We want to find out what all the beads and the *Age of Quarrel* and all that crap was about." Tom bought the zine and read it that night. The next day he was like, "Holy shit this stuff is cool." Then I read it. I always thought these dudes were like flower people, but there was some really serious philosophy there.

STEVE REDDY: If you were to ask me what a Hare Krishna was in 1987, I would have said it's a dude with lots of tattoos who beat the crap out of people. [laughs] Dave Stein got me this vegetarian cookbook and in the front was a chapter on reincarnation and karma and I read it and was pretty intrigued. I was pretty religious growing up; I was a Catholic and I got into college and started to feel out of place with it. I got another [Krishna conscious] book and read it and then got another book and read that. I hadn't met anyone else who was a devotee, though. Eventually, I went on tour with Youth of Today. When I went to pick them up I found out Cappo was into Krishna consciousness too, and I didn't even know it. So on tour we would visit temples in every city that had one. We would meet devotees and ask questions and get more books and read more. When we got back from tour, that was it for me. I moved to the temple in Brooklyn and then I found out about the farm in Pennsylvania and moved there. The idea of simple living and high thinking made sense. Living in New York City there is injustice in every direction. You turn down one street and a guy is buying a hundred thousand dollar watch and you turn around and there are a bunch of homeless people. It wasn't what I thought of as to how to be happy in life. To live on a farm with animals that weren't killed was really great. The more you have the less satisfied you are and because the farm was simple it was appealing to me.

KATE REDDY (108, KRSNA GRRRL FANZINE): I was attracted to Indian philosophy as a child. My parents were kind of hippies so I used to go the Ramakrishna Mission and took flute lessons from this woman who was a devotee of Ramakrishna when I was a kid. My mother's friends would go to India and bring me back *Bhagavad-Gita* comic books, so I had an early exposure to the texts. Then I forgot about it for a bit. Now I was already straight edge and vegetarian and I ended up bumping into my future husband Steve [Reddy] at Lollapalooza and I was friends with Porcell and we started to go to the temple. There was so much bad publicity about the Krishnas at the time that I was reluctant to become involved. I remember being attracted to it, but I ended up doing my own thing for a few years. When I came back to it the whole thing seemed very natural. I always was attracted to doing something that was different from the society at large. I was looking for more than just what was existing in the hardcore scene and I felt very fulfilled when I got into Krishna consciousness. Also, there were grown-ups involved who were completely alternative. I remember thinking, "These people didn't grow up and give up their ideas. They have an ideal they stuck to." They didn't get into that "true till college" kind of thing. [laughs]

ROBERT FISH (108, RESSURECTION, THE JUDAS FACTOR): My initial attraction to Krishna consciousness had very little to do with hardcore. It was more of a personal escape as opposed to a social one. Theologically a lot of it attracted me, but a lot of it I couldn't put my thumb on. Even in 108, a lot of it I believed in, but there were certain aspects that I didn't feel comfortable with. At the same time there were other parts that were so attractive to me that made everything else worth it. In 1991 I was extremely depressed and would get headaches for days. I remember right before the Ressurection/ Lifetime tour I destroyed my room on impulse. Eventually, I got married and we had our first child and I realized I couldn't do this anymore. I needed to understand who I was. Was I just chanting because it made me feel better or because it's what I am? I wanted to see Vaisnavism not as a religion but as a fabric of life, where it's a part of what you are and not a religion. When I saw it in that setting, all of a sudden it clicked for me.

JOHN "PORCELL" PORCELLY (SHELTER, YOUTH OF TODAY, JUDGE, PROJECT X): The world typically works on envy and longing for things. Most people spend their lives chasing the carrot on the stick—if I could only buy this house, if I could only be in that band, if I could only get that Mercedes. [laughs] In the early nineties I began to realize I had lived a life that many would be envious of—I played in bands that achieved some degree of notoriety, and had achieved some fame, though it was on a very small scale. I started to realize that a lot of the things that people were after I had and they weren't satisfying me more than anything else. It was around that time that I was drawn to more spiritual matters and checking out Eastern philosophy and reading the *Bhagavad-Gita*.

RAY CAPPO: I went from believing the Krishnas were weird, to the Krishnas are sort of cool, to this is the way I want to live my life. The more time I spent in India the more I realized how I was just prejudiced against other cultures. For example, if I saw somebody in a robe I would think "What a freak." That's how I grew up. I didn't see any men wearing robes or shaving their heads. But in India it's a very common thing. In Indian culture, in any kind of priestly family they shave their heads with a little tuft of hair in the back and most cultured people wear robes. In fact, robes have been worn for thousands of years. Jeans are new. [laughs] If I took the guys from New Found Glory and dropped them in 13th Century India, who would be the freaks? India is one of the few places in the world that has a preserved culture. For example, if I want to find out about what Greece was like I can't go to Greece today. Practically speaking, no one's worshipping Apollo or Zeus there. But they worshipped for many years and the timeline sort of ceased. A lot of these ancient languages and cultures are dead, but Sanskrit is not a dead language. It's used openly by scholars and priests. It's pretty much the same philosophy that has been passed down for thousands of years with some varying degrees. One hundred years ago in Tokyo women wore kimonos and now everything is becoming "strip mall-ized"; K-Mart culture has taken over the Earth. If you go to Louisiana, Maine, or California you are going to find the same Gap and Abercrombie and Fitch. There are no individual cultures that seem to pervade. It's there to some minute degree, but with this whole global industrialization you can go to Starbucks in Tokyo or L.A. or Germany. It's globalization of products and what it's doing is that it's giving quality controlled French fries... what we're doing is losing authentic culture and it's kind of unprecedented. We're actually experiencing it within our lifetime. It's scary.

STEVE REDDY: The Western mentality is that everything comes cheap. I remember thinking that once I moved into the temple it would all be over. Mission accomplished, right? [laughs] I was going to be pure and the effort was over. But you come to the realization that it's not over. You strive to meditate and be humble and serve humanity and God. Those are decisions that you have to make per second for the rest of your life, and it's hard! We have free will, so it's not life on easy street. When I moved to the farm I had $300 and I went into a three bedroom house and they gave me a room and I offered my money and my car to the guy running the place. I thought, "Here, I'm completely surrendered! It's over." He goes, "You probably want to hold on to your money. And that's your car? We don't want it." [laughs] You're looking for something that's easy—like a born again Christian. "I'm going to say this phrase and it doesn't matter what happens afterwards—I said it!" But that's not how it works. Once you commit that's when the real struggle comes in. It's an internal thing. That path is the destination. There's no real destination, only the path. When you come to terms with that you get a little let down. It's not like when you run a race and you only have a mile to go.

Shelter's first album, *Perfection of Desire*, was released in 1990. By the time their second record came out they had toured the country, ignited a lot of debate, and started a new label (Equal Vision) to release the music of like-minded bands. They drew a lot of criticism for that, but also found that others were taking notice of the philosophy. New Krishna conscious bands were forming, a bevy of Krishna related zines started, and people outside the East Coast hardcore scene, where Krishna consciousness had its initial influence, started to notice. In particular, Shelter arose as one of the most popular hardcore bands of the early nineties as they mixed spiritual and philosophical ideas with catchy music. The band 108 also became a highly respected musical force due to their more rebellious nature and notable musicianship.

Cappo's charismatic personality also helped push Krishna to the forefront as fans were attracted to the music while others were curious as why the ex-Youth of Today frontman had joined a "cult" (which is how many viewed the Krishnas). Generalizations, of course, do not quite accurately assess the situation. Although these new devotees had immersed themselves in their new faith, they were also aware of the charges of "brain-washing" that had been linked to the Krishnas for a couple of decades. But what drew them to the movement were the ideas.

ROBERT FISH: When I first started to follow the tenets of Gaudiya Vaisnavism it was very much focused on the specific disciplines, my struggles with aspects of them, and on learning about a culture that was quite different than anything I had ever been privy to. Like any sort of life premise, there is always an awkward stage in the beginning where you over-emphasize externals and you tend to stick to the aspects that are most comfortable and avoid those aspects that one finds difficult. However, at some point the practitioner of any discipline, philosophy, or lifestyle will hit that stage where there is a deep and life-altering moment where you step back, examine life, and find your person within, and at times maybe outside of that given lifestyle.

RAY CAPPO: I was strongly drawn to the idea the Vaisnavas believe in when it comes to humans not just being a "body." You take a birth, you start to get old, you dwindle, and you die, and you try to survive by consuming the bodies of others. We have no romantic visions of this world. Devotees accept that it's a bad bargain and try to make the best of a bad bargain. I understood that you could be a concert pianist and all of a sudden get in a car accident and destroy your fingers. I understand how you can finally meet the one you love but she doesn't love you. Or she dies. Or you die. I understand how you can work your whole life to make money only to have it all taken away from you by force or by the weather. I understand that this is a planet of death and I don't have any romantic ideas of this utopia on Earth. The *Bhagavad-Gita* gives us such information on the material world and one of things it says is to become very regulated, sort of the way straight edge is. Another thing it says is [to go on] pilgrimages to holy places, to be thoughtful, to spend time in the morning meditating. So, there are ways to transcend this planet of death. But this isn't something I understand just from reading a book; it's something I've lived and it's fully realized.

VIC DICARA: I was drawn to Vaisnavism mainly because they had a philosophy. Another real important band in my life was Bad Brains, and they were spiritually oriented with the Rasta stuff. They had so much energy and I wanted to find a way to tap into that. I remember I pulled a Bible out and I was like, "This isn't making any sense at all and it's not even really telling me anything." For me, there wasn't much in the Bible other than some moral stories and history but nothing that was scientific or philosophical.

The deal with the Krishnas was that they dealt with supernatural stuff in a scientifically logical way. It was all about logic and people actually used their brains—not necessarily the people in the present day movement, but the people who wrote the texts and the foundations it's based on. Also, I was interested in spiritual stuff, but I was also a punk, so it was kind of against my grain to be into a mainstream religion. But here was an opportunity for a religion that was taboo, so it was a real mesh. It was a one-two punch that knocked me out.

KATE REDDY: When I was a kid I liked the imagery and the religious sentiment—the fervor of the whole thing. As I got older and started thinking for the very first time about mortality—why do we have to die and grow old? I really liked the idea of a religion where you could just go chant, sing, and dance. And the loving, sharing, and eating together makes up an important aspect of Krishna consciousness and its practices. But in the *Bhagavad-Gita* I also read about the immortality of the soul and it just made so much sense to me because I believed in reincarnation as far back as I can remember without even being taught to. Finding other people with similar ideas and experiences, I just felt at home.

STEVE REDDY: I pretty much read the intro to the *Bhagavad-Gita* and a light went on. It addressed stuff you don't hear most people talking about. What's the point of life? Do I die, do I just lie in the ground and wait for Jesus to come and then I go up? It addressed the deeper points of why to do good. In life you often don't know what to do or the reasons to do anything, which can lead to depression. I bought into what the *Bhagavad-Gita* was explaining and it was a relief to me. Just like people who accept Jesus as their savior. If that creates some shelter for them, that's awesome. I feel like we're eternal. I see old people and they're not like, "Okay, soon it's going to be completely over." [laughs] Christianity had such a powerful hold of the world, so you know that the pendulum would swing against it.

JES STEINEGER (COALESCE): It wasn't until I picked up *Quest for Certainty* that I understood the basic premises of the Krishna stuff. Heidegger claims that truth is disclosive; one "uncovers" her experiences so that truth may be disclosed. Just as the straight edge agenda had been disclosed as true, so too was Prabhupada's Krishna message. Although I was not raised in a strictly religious home I was by no means raised in an atheistic one, so the prospect of religiosity was not hindered by my upbringing. *Quest for Certainty* compelled me to get to my local library and check out every book that I could find with regard to "Krishna consciousness." Within a month I was convinced that the straight edge narrative lacked any ground for its practices. Why not drink-up and clock-out? "Let us eat and drink for tomorrow we die!" Since it lacks any grounding in the transcendent, straight edgers exhibit their inheritance of the Enlightenment attempt to provide a fully immanent account of the world. The straight edge agenda is built on the modern paradigm and as such it struggles like hell to find purpose and value in the world. The Krishnas awakened me to the pre-modern world.

SEVAPRIYA BARRIER (KRSNA GRRRL FANZINE): Krishna consciousness appealed to me because it presented God in really concrete detail and because the means of achieving a relationship with God involved a variety of aspects including asceticism, emotional connection, and personal accountability. It shapes my views of everything and informs my decisions. It structures my days and influences my plans both short and long term. I'm not even sure where to begin or end with what it means to me—it's really just so much of who I am.

NORMAN BRANNON: I've always been into philosophy and transcendental concepts. My family was fundamentalist Christian and I rebelled against that early, but they put a lot of bullshit into my head and created a lot of issues and self-conflict. The thing about Krishna consciousness I appreciated the most was it was a philosophy that encouraged questioning and discouraged speculation. Everyone in the early nineties hardcore scene was questioning everything which was cool, but at the same time I felt like it was a bunch of dudes sitting around and creating truth from a Kinkos copy-card. I appreciated the fact that [Vaisnavism] was ancient. Even if you think it's bullshit it wasn't invented by a kid with an X tattoo. [laughs] I also appreciated the fact that it discouraged speculation which almost every major religion did. When my best friend died my mother used that as an attempt to preach, which I felt was pretty shitty. I told her, "Here's the deal. Chris was 18. If God is fair then how come Chris only had 18 years to accept Jesus? And I don't want you to speculate—I want you to show me biblical passages that prove your point." She couldn't do it; she tried to speculate. I felt it was amazing that the Krishnas frowned on that. You had to back things up with some sort of spiritual passage. It was almost like you were in law school, which appealed to whatever intellectual side I had.

VIC DICARA: I liked the way Eastern philosophies approach religion and spirituality as if it were something logical and scientific. There's not a whole lot of hocus pocus and "faith" and "just believe"—there are lengthy, detailed explanations of just about every aspect of what they talk about. And these explanations are right out in front, not hidden away for debate in some seminary or some "mystical" version of a scripture.

Of course, just as Krishna consciousness was provoking introspection for many, there were those who were skeptical of the movement's intentions. Many saw the influx of Krishna in the scene as a direct method of exploiting hardcore purely in the name of religious preaching, which brought about some heated arguments.

MARK MCCOY (CHARLES BRONSON, DAS OATH): I hated everything about [the Krishnas]. They had nothing to offer me except my immediate dismissal.

DAN YEMIN: I've been to a Krishna wedding and the rhetoric is disturbing. It's very hierarchical in its beliefs and full of people who are searching for something. But using hardcore as a missionary tool is somewhat disturbing. You hit kids at a vulnerable age when they are looking for their identity. I could see how seductive it was for straight edge hardcore kids because a lot of the lifestyle aspects of Krishna consciousness were congruent with many familiar elements from hardcore. There was an abstinence from drugs and alcohol and vegetarianism was very important. But any organized religion sinking its hooks into hardcore is disturbing to me.

VIQUE MARTIN: I had always felt that religion was great if it made people happier and got them through hard times. But ever since I had found feminism I'd detested the "barefoot and pregnant" ideology that seems to run rampant through most organized religions. Raised by Jewish atheists and sent to a Christian elementary school, I knew a fair bit about them. Krishna certainly didn't seem any better with its dogmatic division of labor (keep women in the kitchen) and denial of sexuality. Screw that! "Man, Cow, Woman, Dog" offended a lot of people.

ADAM NATHANSON (BORN AGAINST, YOUNG PIONEERS): Born Against wrote a song called "Eulogy" about Steve Reddy joining the Krishnas. The drama that ensued after we wrote the song was an unfortunate experience. We picked out a specific person to write about in a song and that was nutty and not cool. Honestly, the fact that Sam [McPheeters] and I are still in one piece is testament to the fact that [Steve Reddy] maintained his composure quite a bit. We had known him for years and I guess at the time we were frustrated by his choice of joining the Krishnas. I will say religion is still a load of horse shit, though. I know it's the most pedestrian observation, but religion is not the solution to anything—I mean, look at the world right now and the problems religion has caused. At that time we felt that religion was not going to help matters in the scene. I was into bands like Crucifix and just wondered why religion was a part of our scene. On a personal level, I can't figure out why people need a book that says "Thou shalt not kill." Didn't you grow up in an environment where you shouldn't kill anyway? Do I need a book to see I shouldn't kick a dog? Even though I really don't think in the case of "Eulogy" that we did the right thing on a personal level, I still have the same opinion about religion and I'd venture to say everyone else in the band felt the same.

JOSH GRABELLE (TRUSTKILL RECORDS, TRUSTKILL FANZINE): I started *Trustkill* Fanzine in 1992. I was pretty anti-religion back then. The word "Trustkill" itself was derived from my feelings about people putting too much trust into religion. In issue two of *Trustkill* I did a fake interview with Krishna, where I interviewed Krishna himself and we get into this big argument and I ended up beating him up in the end. It was supposed to be funny, but obviously if you were Krishna you'd probably find it offensive. It stirred up a lot of shit. 108 actually wrote a song called "Scandalous" about me and the article in my zine. Steve Reddy drove four hours from his house and came down to one of the shows I had at my house and basically threatened to beat me up for the article. We're friends now, but he wasn't too psyched back then.

SCOTTY NIEMET: With us trying to find things that we could apply to our lives to get us on paths to better humanity and the world we live in, there was an easy door for spirituality to walk right in. With groups such as Krishna and Christianity, where a large part of their religion lies on recruitment and finding common goals within people, it was quite easy. I was drawn early on to Krishna and what it had to say. It felt really close to the new and growing ideals I was setting for myself. And, wow, Ray, Porcell, and Rob Fish were into it! Over time I realized I was more content on making my own rules and that the confining routine Krishna has set up for its devotees left me not advancing my political goals for veganism and finding a comfort with my homosexuality.

NICK FORTE (RORSCHACH): I was dead set against the encroachment of various religious cults in the hardcore scene. I found this to be a disturbing turn of events in the hardcore scene as it rose in popularity. These groups were using a music scene to indoctrinate people with their brand of mass opiate and it ran against everything I was interested in about hardcore such as thinking for yourself as an individual and deviation from a flock or herd mentality. There were some great run-ins between my band, Rorschach, and the Krishna kids who were in bands like Shelter and 108. We had some pretty "lively" debates both at shows and in fanzines, and even in our lyrical content. We always looked forward to playing shows with the Krishna bands. This, I think, was a really great thing, this kind of lively debate and discourse. I can't imagine that level of debate in music today. In our camp, we all really loved messing with these people, but I think the Krishna bands just found us to be annoying and a thorn in their side. We were raining on their parade and they just couldn't fathom why we would have a problem with them. They had a whole agenda that just used the hardcore scene as a gateway to their belief system. It felt like a scam to me.

TAYLOR STEELE (FOUR WALLS FALLING): When it first started in the late eighties, it was interesting and learning about it was pretty intriguing. And the food was pretty good too. [laughs] But after a while I just saw it as a westernized version of Hinduism. It wasn't as bad as evangelistic Christianity because it wasn't on TV and in your face 24 hours a day. It was a lot easier to blow off, basically. But if someone is into it and it's a positive thing for them, then who am I to say it doesn't belong? You could say the same thing about Buddhism or atheism. As long as it helps you treat others better then fine, but if it turns you into a militant jerk then it's probably not the best thing for you to get involved with. [laughs]

JEFF BECKMAN (CHOKEHOLD): [Krishna was] barely a subject that deserved debate. A cult had infiltrated a music culture for recruiting purposes—out of the airports and into the venues. I think what upset us the most was how it was blindly accepted in so many circles. We laughed at pop culture and the sheep mentality, yet it existed in our own scene where we thought we were so beyond that. The more I found out about it the sillier it got. Then in the middle of being in [Chokehold] it kind of spread like a cancer in the scene, so obviously we were disturbed by this. We addressed it and like any other easily disproved fictional religion the people involved couldn't accept the questioning of it, which put us right in the middle of this battle, at least in New York and the New Jersey area. It seemed to be the only place in American hardcore that bought into that shit—elsewhere it was Christianity, which was a different idea but the same crutch. But we were called racists, schoolyard bullies, insensitive, intolerant, and close minded for taking a stance against it. I think this was a driving force that separated us from a lot of bands and hardcore circles.

DENNIS LYXZEN (REFUSED, INTERNATIONAL NOISE CONSPIRACY): Krishna made sense for a lot of people because they got free vegetarian food and they got you to think about spirituality in a different way. Krishnas came to our city and we hung out with them and they seemed cool, but one day I sat down and started talking politics with them and I never went back to the Krishna restaurant. [laughs] A friend of mine let a Krishna guy check a fax at his parent's house. We found the fax and it was addressed to the guy and said, "Remember you are not to become friends with these straight edge kids. Your mission is to convert as many of them as possible." I got into a discussion with a guy and he said if you were to try and change the world politically then you would be going against Krishna, because what we have now is a manifestation of Krishna's will.

DUNCAN BARLOW (ENDPOINT, GUILT, BY THE GRACE OF GOD): I don't mind religion; however, when people take it upon themselves to go on a crusade, I find that I have little tolerance as it is everyone's right to follow their own spiritual path. Religion, of any fashion, leaves an imprint as it opens people's minds to different ideas. It was probably a really positive thing for some of my friends to experience Eastern religions, but the didactic nature of organized religion has always been imperialistic by nature, and thus allows little room for discourse.

RYAN DOWNEY (BURN IT DOWN, SUPERHERO FANZINE): I had always believed in God from a very young age, and because I had to deal with death very young, I was always very interested in things concerning spirituality, death, the nature of existence, and that sort of thing. Because of those interests I found it very exciting that the Hare Krishnas were introducing those topics into hardcore. My first encounter with it was when Tim Yohannon debated Ray Cappo in *Maximum Rock N' Roll* around the time the first Shelter album was released. I loved that album and its raw passion, its sincerity, its true yearning. At the time, and especially when Vic DiCara joined the band, it was exciting and thought-provoking. I read a lot of Krishna books in high school, but I had some real problems with the role of women in their philosophy. And even bigger to me was that supposedly its founder, A.C. Bhaktivedanta Prabhupada, was "infallible." If he was infallible then why did he make such terrible choices about the eleven people who should also be "infallible" and succeed him after his death? If you read about the history of the ISKCON organization after his passing, it's filled with murder, drugs, guns, rape. It's clear that their group is just a group, a small cult, and not a "clear transmission" of God's will through any sort of spiritual masters. I do think there are a lot of great truths in the teachings, but like most things it is fouled up by many of the practitioners.

Regardless of one's opinion on the debate surrounding Krishna in hardcore, the inclusion of Krishna-core bands, zines, and devotees within the hardcore scene helped individuals develop their own position on issues relating to religion, philosophy, and one's place in the world.

KENT MCCLARD (HEARTATTACK FANZINE, EBULLITION RECORDS): The Krishna movement was people searching for a way to change themselves and a way to affect their world through betterment of themselves. Whether or not you agree with the route they chose, that's primarily what that movement was about. The Krishna thing flourished because everyone was trying to figure out how to make themselves better people. People saw it as a way to do exactly that. Some people were anti-religion and hated it and it worked for some people and not for others, but ultimately it makes sense why it was there. Krishna consciousness is about changing yourself to make the world a better place, maybe for them it was more about pleasing God, but ultimately it was about making a change in your life.

NEERAJ KANE (SUICIDE FILE, HOPE CONSPIRACY, EXTINCTION, HOLY ROMAN EMPIRE): Being from an Indian family, my parents were stoked when I started walking around with Shelter and 108 shirts. [laughs] They were somewhat suspicious of ISKCON, due to its cultish tendencies. However, they found it odd that hardcore kids were singing about principles that stemmed from Vedic traditions which I had known about through my upbringing as part of a Brahmin family. I didn't become a devotee or anything, but I thought the discussion of the ideas that were not from a standard Judeo-Christian standpoint fostered some good dialogue and infused another passionate element into the whole mix of ideas that was present in hardcore.

SEAN MUTTAQI: I had differences with the Krishnas in terms of some of the things they believed in—things on a theological level. I always found the concept of social justice and reincarnation to be a bit at odds with each other, when one can always write off suffering of the poor to some cosmic "punishment," rather than being victims of human greed or political and economic conditions. But at the end of the day, most of the people who got into those ideas were trying to make a positive change in their lives and the world around them. In a lot of ways I think the people involved with things like Krishna or hardline are missed. I don't mean that new people miss them within the scene—to be honest, I don't think most people today care enough to even ponder it—but for those left in the scene from back then, even those who disagreed with Krishna or hardline beliefs, I think they miss the charged atmosphere of debate and expression, and I think the scene as a whole is at a loss now for the withdrawal of these ideas and others. There were just so many people back then trying to do different things in hardcore and expose people to different ideas. That's what is truly missing from today's hardcore scene.

BRIAN LOWIT (LOVITT RECORDS): A lot of people thought it was okay as they promoted vegetarianism and a healthy lifestyle, but as people dug further into the religion they saw there was stuff they found questionable. A lot of people into punk and hardcore stand in opposition to a society where people blindly accept ideas without question, which most religion asks you to do so in the end did not stick around. For some, it was an extension of the straight edge movement but they believed that this was a higher form of faith due to its ties with religiosity and spirituality. I personally never really got into it, but I did read a lot of the flyers and stuff they would pass out promoting it and sort of just accepted it as being there since I got used to seeing them so much.

CHAKA MALIK (BURN, ORANGE 9MM): One of the things about hardcore is if you're willing to throw yourself off a stage fearlessly then your faith element is way different than other people's faith element. Krishna ideology was new to a lot of kids and it potentially opened up a wider avenue for faith. You're this kid from the suburbs or the city and someone that you respect is telling you that this ideology is a great way to go and you grew up reading the Bible or whatever you were raised when you read that you were raised with a certain reverence for it. Now when something is exposed to you and you get into it yourself without your family feeding it to you, which isn't necessarily a negative thing, but when you can find a faith ideology on your own it only increases the idea and vibration of faith in the universe. People I knew that were feeling Krishna, and many of them are feeling it to this day. That shit saved them! It was a faith platform that they were able to be a part of and that is really important.

BRENT DECKER (RACETRAITOR): I appreciated some of the Krishna influenced bands' takes on some of the political issues. They tempered a lot of the nihilist view that happened in the vegan straight edge scene. You had this branch of people who started out being into environmentalism and they ended up in this kind of crazy anti-human category. It was basically nihilism—hating everything. Shelter and a lot of those bands tempered that mindset with spirituality and they inspired people because there songs weren't just about everything being fucked. There was still hope for things.

FREDDY CRICIEN (MADBALL): I was never opposed to Krishna. It's kind of weird when you bring religion into this style of music because any and everything goes, good or bad. But it's a free world and if you have your beliefs and that's what you want to talk about in your music then go for it. Some people were sincere about it and others misused it for their own gain.

MIKE HARTSFIELD (OUTSPOKEN, NEW AGE RECORDS): A Krishna conscious friend of mine years ago and I got in a debate about this very subject. I was telling him that Krishna had no place in hardcore. He asked, "Isn't the hardcore scene a place we come together and share ideas, feelings, beliefs? Who is to say what belongs and what doesn't?" I thought that was a really good point and have since changed my ways of thinking about many issues. I'm sure many years ago when people first heard about this new "straight edge" thing, some were opposed and probably didn't think it belonged.

ROB PENNINGTON (ENDPOINT, BY THE GRACE OF GOD, BLACK CROSS): As a part of my spiritual growth, the Krishna movement was something that was cool for me to experience. It was my introduction to more of an Eastern form of spirituality, and I still to this day take some concepts from that in my overall religious framework. Just like the majority of faiths, I didn't buy into the whole thing, but I was interested in a lot of the aspects of it. I was drawn to the concept of us being more than our bodies and how we are not of this perceptual world and a lot of our frustrations come from that. That gave me more of a blueprint on how to live a peaceful life than some of the forms of Christianity I had been exposed to.

The focus on Krishna waned by the mid-nineties. Whether people grew tired of the debate surrounding it or the Krishnas were better understood as they became a recognized faction in the scene, the discussion provoked a sense of critical thinking about philosophical and spiritual issues outside the usual parameters.

VIC DICARA: It was probably, to date, the hardcore scene at its most active. People really had to have opinions on the issue. You either hated it or you loved it. You couldn't be in between. I remember the first Shelter show at The Anthrax in Connecticut, and there were literally protests. The guys from Born Against showed up and had anti-Krishna flyers. It was awesome. It made you come alive. The stuff that sucked about it was that the charisma cult was also happening. Probably a lot because Ray was involved; he has a lot of charisma and he kind of uses it. People were thinking, "This is going to be the next big thing for straight edge, so you better get into it." The other side, though, was about substance.

ROBERT FISH: In some cases people from ISKCON were basically born again Christians with saffron robes and I couldn't relate to that. I stayed associated with it because there were parts of it that I thought were incredible. There were also things I didn't agree

WAR ON ILLUSION

Issue #1

Prema
108
Straight Edge
Spirit Vs. Matter

with, but not all of this is theology it's just how it plays out. We deviated from the normal ISKCON kinds of answers when people would talk to us. The idea with Gaudiya-Vaisnavism is that your focus is to be a servant of Sri Radha and you want to help facilitate her intimate exchange with Krishna and your joy is through your helping her fulfill her joy. So, how do topics like abortions fit into it? Well, it doesn't really. But the body itself is not our goal, so why get so hung up on it?

MANI MOSTOFI (RACETRAITOR): When I tell people about the nineties hardcore scene and that a huge component of it was the Krishna debate, people who have no exposure to older hardcore get so weirded out by that. [laughs] Like how is that possible? It was kind of like a pseudo-cult and I'm not down with it ultimately, but I think it does have a place in hardcore. It's not surprising that a fringe religion would have a place in hardcore. Hardcore is all about looking within and searching for answers that weren't necessarily conventional. I was wary of it at first but eventually I liked the fact that the bands were talking about anti-materialism issues, which was important for the scene.

KURT SCHROEDER (BIRTHRIGHT, CATALYST RECORDS): Ever since I was young I was pretty much an atheist. But I was intrigued by the mythology of Krishna consciousness. The bands were incredible live, which was attractive and made a lot of people jump into it. But the trend didn't last that long. I agreed with a lot of what they were saying, even though I wasn't a religious person. At the same time I disagreed with serving a higher power and that kind of stuff. Some people in the hardcore scene wanted to have a religious belief but they were disgusted with what they grew up with, so this became something new they could incorporate with their other beliefs.

SEVAPRIYA BARRIER: There were lots of trends in the early nineties scene that gave greater validation to folks' lifestyle choices. Krishna stuff was popular because basic tenets fit easily into straight edge kids' ways of seeing the world. And it of course helped that there were straight edge all-stars involved. But all trends die, right? And most of the folks that were seriously involved in Krishna stuff stepped back from hardcore as they pursued other interests.

GREG BENNICK (TRIAL): My perspectives on Hare Krishna have changed a lot over the last couple years, specifically in the last few months. In the eighties and nineties, I was weirded out by the influx of mindless hardcore Krishna drones in the hardcore scene. In the nineties, I went to India and explored Hare Krishna and realized that I didn't believe in the concept of God, regardless of his/her gender/color. Recently, I have been talking more and more to Krishna people and I have come to understand a bit more of what they are about. I am not moving into a temple anytime soon, but I appreciate what seems to be a gentle belief system. The world is full of aggressive faiths and extremists from numerous faiths. The world needs less fanaticism, more meaning. The Krishnas seem docile enough. Check back with me after they start flying planes into the sides of buildings. Until then, I am more interested than I was before.

Unbeknownst to many in the "traditional" hardcore scene, an entire Christian hardcore scene—which wouldn't really hit its peak until the late nineties and into the decade that followed—had also developed. Some in hardcore and punk have practiced a form of Christianity since the genre's birth, but many ignored anything with a Christian slant due to the often oppressive associations made with the mainstream form of the religion (fundamentalism, patriarchy, etc.).

Nonetheless, in small pockets of the country—California, Florida, Pennsylvania, and Illinois, to name a few—a devoted cadre of Christian kids became loyal to a few bands that played just as extreme a style of music of, say, Snapcase, Integrity, or Earth Crisis, but instead they screamed their hearts out in the name of Jesus.

TIM MANN (FOCUSED): Growing up I was always into punk rock. I wasn't a Christian, but I was always going against the grain. But think about it: you're a Christian and no one, especially in hardcore, accepts you, so by being a Christian you're going even more against the grain. Most kids use hardcore as a soapbox to share their lives on the stage. I loved hardcore, but nobody had done a hardcore band with such an adamant Christian message. I wanted to write lyrics and use our testimony and leave it at that. There are a lot of different theologies and churches, but I'm not going to go out and save the world. That's God's job. All He's doing is using me as a pillar. I was never going to go up on stage and be a preacher—that's not my job. I didn't go to seminary or a Christian college. I used to just share on stage that, "Hey, this is my life and this is what's happened to me. Take it for what it's worth."

CHAD NEPTUNE (STRONGARM): It got pretty complicated—here I am rebelling against the punk idea of doing whatever you like, but the straight edge movement seemed to hate the establishment and organized religion, and here I am a Christian. It's not just a religion; it's more a relationship for me. But you get looked down on in the straight edge movement for being into religion.

the hope that lies within... my blood.

FOCUSED

RYAN CLARK (TRAINING FOR UTOPIA, FOCAL POINT): Faith is a hard concept to swallow. The teachings and stories of the Bible are well backed and accurately passed on. And if you believe the words and accounts to be true, then you'll also need to accept that God the Father came to earth as a human man, Jesus Christ, to ultimately die for the sins of humanity, giving us the opportunity to accept His sacrifice and, through this acceptance, be with Him in Heaven for all eternity after we die here on earth. If you're willing to take the Bible as truth, then this is the decision you will be faced with, and it's a hard one to swallow for some people because it is *purely* faith-based.

DIRK LEMMENES (FOCUSED): I had grown up as a Christian, so for me it made perfect sense to have faith be a major part of the band. In hardcore, Krishna had become a major influence, so it seemed like kids were open to spirituality. It turned out they were much more close-minded when it came to Christianity. We wanted to stand up for what we believed, despite the resistance and sometimes open hostility towards it.

CHAD NEPTUNE: We'd been through all this turmoil as we started getting older. You ask yourself, "Where is your life going?" But at the same time we had this complete passion to tell everyone in the world about God. It was such an overwhelming feeling that I wish everyone could feel it at least once in their lives. It was like a fire consuming us, as cliché as that might sound. [laughs] Hardcore is in your face, down your throat and we believed in that sentiment and applied it to our own music.

As the mid-nineties approached, Tooth and Nail Records assembled a roster of Christian bands that attracted large followings based purely on word of mouth from their local scenes, as well as notable appearances at Cornerstone, an annual Christian music festival held in western Illinois every summer in which tens of thousands of Christians from all over the country gather to check out Christian music of all kinds. Groups such as Focused, Unashamed, Focal Point, Strongarm, Living Sacrifice, Training for Utopia, and Zao hit the stage and expressed their Christian views through their own style of hardcore music.

Often, these Christian hardcore bands stuck to their own scene, which had developed parallel to the "traditional" hardcore scene, although this tendency changed by the end of the nineties. Mimicking the music they saw, the zines they read, and the labels they purchased from, the Christian hardcore scene became its own entity in which there was little crossover, with some exceptions (Focused, for instance, played a lot of California shows with bands like Strife).

Already wary of organized religion taking hold of hardcore with the Krishna-core movement, many hardcore kids were distressed as they found out about this "alternative" Christian-based hardcore scene, which they saw as a recruitment tool at worst or a flaccid imitation of the music they loved at best. Christians in the scene, of course, offered a different perspective.

RYAN PATTERSON (BLACK CROSS, COLISEUM, THE NATIONAL ACROBAT): I just couldn't ever buy into Christianity wholly. I've always been turned off by Christian music because I think there's a lot more to life than being, "Hi, we're a Christian band or hi we're a straight edge band." I prefer my music to be about people and not under the guise of a certain stance.

DAVE MANDEL (INDECISION RECORDS, INDECISION FANZINE): There is nothing safer than Christianity as far as mainstream ideology. I never understood how kids got into it. Later on a lot of kids were only introduced to hardcore through their church, but I never really considered them hardcore kids. There would be these shows going on and it would be all Christian bands, and none of those kids would ever come to hardcore shows. It was like that scene existed side-by-side along the hardcore scene but I would never really call it the "hardcore scene." It was a scene that mimicked the hardcore scene. You had this handful of Christian bands that played regular hardcore shows. But all of a sudden they wanted to bring their church friends to the shows and those kids started bands and eventually their own scene because they didn't want anything to do with our scene, which was fine because we didn't really want them there either. [laughs] It was mutually beneficial for everybody, but that's how those sub-sect scenes develop.

RYAN CLARK: Christianity generates skepticism and persecution in every aspect of society, not just in hardcore. The name Jesus is either the most annoying or most beautiful word in the world, depending on who you're talking to. What makes it even harder for people involved in the hardcore scene is the aspect of submission. This is commonly viewed as weakness. Hardcore and straight edge tend to be very pride-based; submitting your life to a higher power holds very little place in that mentality.

MARK MCCOY: The fact that kids are so afraid of Christian bands is appalling. This is just another display of the social motives weak people employ to construct some sort of mock-up crusade to go on. Everyone knows you can't escape Christianity; it's the fabric of our existence in America. Hardcore isn't some sacred cow that's immune to society's influence. No matter how much of a fucking dinosaur you are with your beliefs, all you can really do is kindly look the other way until something like this disappears. Luckily, it works out nicely since hardcore is such a quick phase for most.

TAYLOR STEELE: Hardcore is not mainstream. In the United States Christianity is mainstream, so I can understand checking out other forms of spirituality such as Krishna consciousness. Krishna consciousness is definitely not mainstream, so you can understand why it might have a place in a music scene like hardcore. But Christianity or Christian hardcore doesn't seem to make sense. Now as far as someone having an individual interpretation of Christianity that he or she might incorporate into hardcore that's one thing. But if it's the same old thing then what's the point? Not all Christians are the same just like anyone else. But if you're going to be Pat Robertson with a guitar with youth crew sounding songs then that's not good. [laughs]

DON CLARK (TRAINING FOR UTOPIA, FOCAL POINT): Hardcore is about unrelenting passion. I was able to see what passion meant to so many people my age. To me, the power of scripture rose above so many political issues and a lot of those issues became contingent on how I viewed scripture. Not that a lot of these issues weren't important, but they took somewhat of a backseat to the greater answer for me. It was a true time of awakening.

KENT MCCLARD: It's one thing to say "Krisha sucks" or "Christians suck." But it creates much more interesting dialogue when they are actually a part of our community. You can have this dialogue about religion and the role it plays in our lives. That dialogue was much more useful because there were people in our scene who actually were Christian or Krishna. There's really no dialogue in our scene with Christians who aren't into hardcore. If we are really going to understand our world then we need to have more experiences with it. As much as I might disagree with religion, it's still good to be able to talk to those people and learn something from them about how they think.

DAN YEMIN: If you need some sort of system to codify and organize your spirituality then fine, but the Christian right is affiliated with a lot of ideas that are pretty messed up—a lot of anti-gay propaganda and a strong desire to limit reproductive freedom, for instance. If you're going to call yourself a Christian hardcore kid then you better make it clear that you're not that kind of Christian and differentiate between the dark side, so to speak.

RYAN CLARK: Christianity, just like every single religion, culture, association, or race has a number of issues that people find difficult to get past. When "secular" culture thinks of Christianity, it thinks of America stolen from the natives, televangelists, close-minded legalists, etc. The Christians that people are used to might be judgmental or self-righteous, but these people do not truly stand for Christ or the teachings of the Bible. They are essentially the "bad apples" of the Christian culture. Christianity is founded in love and sacrifice and there are millions of good examples that rarely get acquainted with Christianity in the eyes of mainstream culture.

MICKEY NOLAN (WRITER, SHOW PROMOTER): The kind of Christianity that pervaded hardcore was more rigid and came from a more well-to-do background. There was a group of wealthy evangelical Christians who were looking for ways to infuse their values in popular culture. It was like, "Here's this Snapcase record—why don't you try to learn to play these kinds of riffs and we'll give you all the money you need to crack the message into this scene."

CHAD NEPTUNE: I always felt the greatest thing about going to a hardcore show was seeing people expressing the way they feel by wearing their hearts, literally, on their sleeves. Like, "If this is what I feel then I'm going to tell you about it." In a lot of the zines back then, there was a lot of negativity toward Strongarm and they gave us a lot of flak. But in a lot of ways they also respected us because we weren't just some Bible-thumping, mindless guys. We came from the same place everyone else came from. We didn't have an agenda. We'd just say, "Hey, this is what we believe. This is our music. I hope you get something out of it, just like you might get something out of any other band." Today it's so accepted to be a Christian in the scene, but I remember people wanting to actually fight us because of what we believed.

DIRK LEMMENES: I definitely felt like some bands were a little pushy about their spirituality, but that was their prerogative. We (Focused) always felt strongly about sharing what we believed, but then leaving it up to kids to decide whether they were interested or not. We weren't into shoving our beliefs down people's throats. We just shared what we believed and welcomed conversation and debate.

RYAN CLARK: Tooth and Nail's only objective in releasing albums for Christian artists was to give these artists a platform and allow them to speak their mind about their faith

and have a quality label back them. What the bands do with their message is their objective. I can't speak on behalf of other labels. Secondly, it is *always* a goal for Christians to help open other people's eyes to the truth and sacrifice of Christ. Words like "conversion" and "recruitment" have a negative, seemingly brainwash-like connotation, but this stigma is not accurate. The truth of Christ is the single most important thing in every Christian's life. It is the reason for which they live each day. Christianity is not subjective. It's absolute. Therefore, Christians view "conversion" as the best thing that could ever happen in anyone's life, and thus, if their goal is to convert, they are essentially loving people enough to offer them the gift of joy on earth and life eternally.

STRONGARM

MANI MOSTOFI: At first I was really accepting of the Christianity in the scene—I was kind of a universalist when it came to religion; I didn't care what the book you read was, I just wanted to know what your approach to things were. I assumed that these were punk rock kids that had their own interpretation of Christianity. I thought some of the kids were really cool. But eventually I realized that most of these kids were from the evangelical wing of Christianity and they were using hardcore to get kids to their church. This definitely was an issue in the scene growing a bit more conservative by the end of the nineties. It was tied to corporate Christian institutions too and it was weird that Bible thumpers from the Midwest somehow co-opted our cultural expression. That wasn't the case with every band as bands like Zao were counter-culture and that's how they felt about Christianity. But those kids were in the minority.

RYAN DOWNEY: I hated the dogmatic, outright dismissal of Christian bands by many in the hardcore scene who preached diversity and yet would not allow any spiritual conversation whatsoever. But I also despised the bands that had nothing thought-provoking or challenging to offer, who chose to play it safe and preach what their parents taught them and what the status quo of the sort of young Republican evangelical thing is all about. Christ is about revolution, equality, and positive change—things that should not be incongruent with punk rock but are incongruent with middle America, the suburbs, and everything else narrow that many so-called Christians represent. At the end of the day most of the bands were just that, bands, for better or worse, and things ended up becoming blurred as apathy set in. Nobody really cares whether a band is Christian these days but that's more symptomatic of the fact that nobody cares, period.

CHRIS COLOHAN (LEFT FOR DEAD, THE SWARM, CURSED): Spirituality is an important part of humanity that religion co-opts. And in hardcore, the puritanical rhetoric that blew up in the nineties got so out of hand that it opened the door to things like Christianity. It got to the absurd point where Christian hardcore somehow made sense to people. I still look at the phrase "Christian hardcore" and I don't want to recognize or validate it. Because "Christian" to my experience represents status-quo thinking, spiritual terrorism, and all the things that hardcore represents the freedom from. But it's there regardless. I wouldn't deny anybody their right to speak their mind, but I do think the unofficial but distinct backbone of hardcore culture was its uncompromising refusal of traditional social and religious systems. But then who makes the rules?

DON CLARK: I thought the ideology of free speech, tolerance and diversity was supposed to include all human beings and belief systems—especially in an underground punk movement. I always believed that parameters, especially in hardcore, were counter-productive to the movement. Granted, there were always kids who had a problem with God entering hardcore, but to be honest most people were really open to it. It was more about quality. If the band was good, they were respected, as well as their beliefs. I think the same is true today.

Aside from Krishna consciousness and Christianity, other forms of spirituality also existed in many of the fringe movements of hardcore such as certain aspects of the politically oriented faction of the scene, as well as

hardline, which espoused a support for the "natural order" and in fact professed to follow a tradition of Abrahamic spirituality, which for many ended up in the framework of an Islamic-leaning perspective (for more information about hardline see Chapter Three: "Animal Rights"). Again, this connection alarmed some, while others didn't pay as much attention.

SEAN MUTTAQI: Even going back to the first *Vanguard* magazine I had quotes and references from The Quran. I spent a lot of years studying Islam. My father had given me Malcolm X's biography when I was a kid. I had contact with M.O.V.E. in the eighties and during the early years of hardline I was heavily into the Old Testament via the Rasta influence and Taoism and Buddhism through my martial arts background. Around 1994 or so, I spent some time in Jamaica exploring Rastafarianism and hung out with Rastas in the hills, but ultimately I just couldn't get with the concept of God being a man, which was the same thing that always turned me off about Christianity. Ultimately, I ended up at a vegetarian Sufi *masjid* in Philadelphia, which inspired me to take my *shahadah* (declaration of faith within the Islamic tradition), which I did with a *shaykh* in Oakland shortly thereafter. It was the culmination of years of study. Some years later when the Vegan Reich reunion happened it was just a natural outlet to incorporate into the music.

MANI MOSTOFI: Some people in Racetraitor got into Islam for a variety of reasons. Part of the attraction to it was that people in Muslim communities were dealing with political issues and we were dealing with political issues in the hardcore scene, so there was some common ground there. We were all really into Malcolm X so we had a positive view of it. But it was funny because we got labeled a "Muslim" band when the only official Muslim in the band actually quit. [laughs] We had Islamic lyrics and imagery but a lot of bands use Christian imagery and metaphors as a stylistic choice. We were definitely influenced by Muslims, but we weren't Shelter. The way I was influenced by Islam was not the standard Islamic thinking; I was more into Sufi-leaning stuff and Islamic mysticism, but I never made that my one thing.

BRENT DECKER: The Islamic perspective on a lot of things is much closer to a lot of the revolutionary ideas that were in the scene, but Islam like any religion also has some bad parts. You don't need to look too far for examples of Muslims doing crazy things. But for every terrorist you also have the example of someone like Malcolm X, which is much more in the true spirit of Islam, and that's what influenced us. We didn't want women to go back to 7th century Arabia. [laughs] I probably didn't do a great job of articulating that at the time, which probably led to some of the fallout. I didn't have answers to a lot of questions but people would push me on a lot of things. I would just be like, "Why are you asking me this? I'm 20 years old and trying to figure all this stuff out myself." [laughs]

STEVE LOVETT (RAID): Originally hardline was an agnostic organization. Most of the hardline founders were agnostic, atheist, or pagan. Overall, hardline took no stance on religion because it was a personal choice. It was natural for a purist ideology like hardline to adopt some religious aspects. As time went on, the all-encompassing ideology fell short of explaining many of the basic questions of life that religion provides. Overall, it was a mistake to incorporate religion with hardline, be it Christianity, atheism, or Islam. I bailed before hardline morphed into an Islamic cult but checked in occasionally from the sidelines over the years. Personally, I think religion is still the opiate of the masses; however, atheism requires the same sort of stubborn faith.

RYAN DOWNEY: I have always been an activist, but I have never identified with much of activist culture, its exclusionary practices, its outright dismissal of spiritual thinking beyond incense and crystals, and its emphasis on aesthetics over genuine change. On the other hand I hated the fact that Christians, Muslims, Baha'is, and other people of faith I encountered for the most part had lost the revolutionary spirit and compassion that drove the prophets and that I feel was the most crucial part of Jesus' message. Christ overturned the money tables, remember? It seemed to me that a lot of people adopted religion and felt like they should neuter themselves and that shutting your mouth and smiling made you "spiritual;" on the other hand, other extremists clearly take it to the opposite and worse extreme of blowing up innocent people. I felt alienated by all of it and with Burn It Down in particular tried to cut through the crap inherent in the young Republican youth group set's take on Christianity and the hardcore scene's knee-jerk reactionary dogma about God and covertly racist dismissal of Islam. I had learned through years of being into extreme animal rights and human rights causes that yelling at people didn't help; so I tried to shape the band's message into something people of all walks of life could get something out of and feel included by. I don't know if we pulled that off. There was always a struggle internally because half the band was always, if not opposed to what I believed, vehemently apolitical, and focused way too much on the straight edge aspect of my life, which oddly enough I never brought onto the stage.

The inclusion of various forms of spirituality (Judaism, Buddhism, Mormonism, and other spiritual beliefs were also expressed and debated) in hardcore instilled an even stronger passion for defining one's place in the world, regardless of one's spiritual beliefs. This debate paralleled the focus on ethics and politics in the scene for much of the decade, as well as individual lifestyle choices such as straight edge and vegetarianism/veganism.

The divide over spirituality was often immense, but the formulation of a position on such issues allowed people to better pursue their own ideas and interests both during and after their involvement with hardcore.

SEAN INGRAM: Spirituality belongs in life, and if you are in a hardcore band, and it plays into your life, it should play into your music. I am not of the line of thinking of those guys that make those "God Free Youth" shirts or whatever. I still stand by the fact that hardcore is an open forum. You may not like what's in it, but it's still an open forum.

JESSICA HOPPER (HIT IT OR QUIT IT FANZINE): People can do whatever the hell they want. I don't think anything "belongs" anywhere. I am a religious person, and I came into that on my own in my adult life. It belongs in hardcore as much as it does anywhere else. First and foremost it's about the person making the art and what they have to say and what it means to them before any allegiance to a formal scene aesthetic is observed. A good enough band can change people's minds about anything.

GAVIN VAN VLACK (ABSOLUTION, BURN): I have a weird thing with organized religion. I've never been a team player because if there is a winning team then there has to be a "losing" team. I would never begrudge someone for their spirituality, but I hate being told you have to believe something or you're going to hell. Was Christ a Christian? He was someone who believed that there was a right and wrong way to go about things. Lord Gautama was the same thing. The problem we deal with is someone takes these beliefs and tries to manipulate the situation. If you are doing the right thing and being of service to your fellow man then my hat's off to you. But if you are using the words of a prophet to manipulate other people and make them bend to your will then you are nothing more than a snake oil salesman. It happens with every religion and that's the reason why I think organized religion doesn't work.

DANIEL TRAITOR (RACETRAITOR, EVERLAST, HINCKLEY, ARMA ANGELUS): I don't think there is a place for recruiting hardcore kids in the scene, and in general I am not a big fan of proselytizing because it misses the point of spirituality. But I believe spirituality is an essential part of our humanity, so I believe it can have a powerful and beautiful effect on people's lives, and it has a role in the world. Unfortunately, that role has been misconstrued, distrusted, and used for the wrong ends by many individuals who want power, who are driven by misknowledge or to feed their own egos. And because people have exposed this hypocrisy which is great, it has further obscured the true meaning and purpose of religion. I wish we wouldn't throw the baby out with the bath water, but I understand and deeply empathize with why that happens.

DARYL TABERSKI (SNAPCASE): People have the right to have their opinion on the messages just like the bands have a right to share their message. So often hardcore is energized by kids desiring to be passionate about something; they're often searching for their place in the world. Just like there are a lot of kids who are into the whole anti-religion thing—it's not so much that they are passionate about being anti-religion, they just are searching for something to be passionate about.

JASON ROE (KILL THE ROBOT FANZINE): For me, coming of age and being gay, life was hard. I came from a religious background and my sister had recently died. Religion for me was great. I was able to suppress my sexuality and deal with mortality at the same time. When I became ready to deal with my total identity I moved away from being deeply religious. Hardcore is about expression and if you want to express your self religiously or take a stance against the bullshit of religion both are equally valid. As long as no one tries to stop anyone else from being who they want to be expression is cool.

BRENT DECKER: On one level I agree with the agnostics, because I understand why this scene, which prided itself on rejecting mainstream ideas, would question a band talking about spiritual matters. People have a lot of life experience to have that visceral reaction to spirituality because most people's experience with religion has been very oppressive, in general. Either they were exposed to a shitty Catholic priest, or shady evangelical pastors, or a crooked imam molesting children—whatever the case, that's what turns people off obviously. But then again spirituality has always been a part of most political and community activism. The most radical people I've ever met are these nuns from Guatemala. So, I never had that dichotomous relationship with spirituality and activism and non-rebellion. In fact, I had it the opposite because when you got deep into true spirituality it can help strengthen the spirit for what you are trying to accomplish. So, there was a different kind of energy and power in that, which I think some other leftist groups don't have to offer. I was less interested in the relevance of spirituality in the hardcore scene. But the community activist realm forced me to think about my calling in terms of spirituality. I converted to Islam during the midst of Racetraitor and it was kind of a crazy time. People would call me up and tell me I was a homophobe, or some bands wouldn't play shows with us. And I understand some of that response. Mainstream fundamentalist Christianity sucks and should be destroyed, but people didn't see a more nuanced understanding of what spirituality was. A lot of people who were politically active in the hardcore scene weren't necessarily active on a community level, so they just didn't understand where the spiritual influence was coming from due to it being so hotly debated in the scene.

TIM SINGER (DEADGUY, KISS IT GOODBYE, NO ESCAPE, BOILING POINT FANZINE): Religion, to me, just boils down to laziness. Someone might say, "Well, what do you believe in?" I just tell them I struggle with that constantly. I've got an inner moral compass and try to listen to it, and it's a constant struggle. It's a hard thing if you actually care to try and think things through. With religion it's like, "Here's a book with all the answers." I suppose I wish I was comfortable enough to buy into something like that, but I just can't.

JOSH GRABELLE: The 20-year-old me would have said fuck religion—it doesn't have any place in hardcore. And I did say that when I was that age in *Trustkill* Fanzine 1, 2, and 3, and I got a lot of shit for it. I'm not going to say I regret what I said, because I don't. But I was 20 years old. I had some things to get off my chest so I did. I'm 32 now and we have 350 million people in this country alone. How many of them are on Xanax or Prozac and are depressed and suicidal? I honestly feel whatever makes you happy then do it. Life's too short to not be happy and not get what you want out of this life. So if God, Jesus, and Muhammad make you happy then go for it. If Krishna saved your life then great. Over the years my mindset has changed.

DIRK LEMMENES: I think people are resistant to any new element introduced into their music and/or scene. Most people felt that religion didn't have anything to do with hardcore or straight edge. But I always felt that hardcore was about expressing what was important to you. It always seemed logical to include spirituality in our music (Focused) because it was important to us. Hardcore was supposed to be about sharing what you were passionate about.

STEVE REDDY: Krishna consciousness added some sublime meaning to my life and gave me some extra security as a person, something a little transcendental that I relished. Before I got into Krishna consciousness I felt a little existential, and basically that comes around to "why the fuck not?" with everything. Because I'm part of a philosophy that has some deeper reason for not doing things, then that helps me out. Hats off to those who do it just for the sake of not doing it—that's hard to do when everyone else around you is doing it. Voluntary austerity without much purpose behind it... that's tough. If you don't have some kind of focal point, which Vedic philosophy has been for me, then your perspectives constantly change.

KATE REDDY: My spiritual life hasn't impacted me negatively at all. It's only been an incredible experience for growth and community and coming to a realization of what is our own internal and eternal nature. It gives me the opportunity to experience happiness regardless of my external situation, and that's what straight edge does too, so it's connected

TRAINING FOR UTOPIA

with that. So you're straight edge and you don't need anything to feel good, that feeling comes from the inside and it's just a deepening of that expression, which comes from such a long line of teachers and learned men and women and great spiritualists. It had led me along this path of my whole life, which has turned out better than I expected. [laughs] It also created a basis for understanding the world in a non-judgmental, non-violent and open-hearted way.

KENT MCCLARD: There is no doubt that spirituality belongs in hardcore. Hardcore is spiritual. I'm an atheist, but I can understand what draws people to the scene and to religion as well. When I started going to shows in the eighties there was this communal energy of these people who were all having fun and were angry and we were defining ourselves by being different. It was almost a religious feeling. The best shows I went to were when there was this sense that everyone in the room had some commonality and it was important. And that's a religious experience.

RAY CAPPO: I had a guy who told me he was inspired by our music and decided to become a Christian monk, and I never felt like, "Oh, man, I lost one!" [laughs] I just appreciated that people were on some kind of spiritual path and that human life was not for self-edification. Straight edge was like that and that's what I liked about straight edge. It's when people think it's an end in and of itself is when it really becomes sad. Human life is all about bringing your consciousness to a higher place. I've always had that as a theme of my existence and it's something I'm proud of that I got into at a young age.

...NG FIGHT: THE NINETIES HARDCORE REVOLUTION IN ETHICS, POLITICS, AND...

SOUND

Although the topical debates within nineties hardcore were among the most interesting aspects of this era, one cannot ignore the fact that people are often drawn to hardcore by the power of the sounds themselves.

This section of *Burning Fight* contains 31 oral history articles about several notable bands from the time period. These bands were chosen either due to their overall impact on one or more of the main debates focused on in this book, or the musical boundaries they crossed in transforming the definition of hardcore music.

There were, of course, dozens of other bands that were just as important for nineties hardcore, but either because I was not able to track down members (Ashes, Bloodlet, Day of Suffering, Econochrist, Falling Forward, Frail, Lincoln, Still Life, and many others), their continued relevance beyond the era lofts them into a broader category than "nineties hardcore band" (Cable, Converge, Drop Dead, Hatebreed, Madball, Sick of it All, Zao, and others), or sheer space within the book, these are the ones I chose to feature. Of course, there are always the inevitable limitations of one person's knowledge about a topic as expansive as hardcore, so the stories of some of the omitted bands would be better served by someone more familiar with them.

I also wrote several other articles on influential bands from the nineties, but I found interviews and retrospectives in other places that were far more complete than what I was able to gather, mostly because I wasn't able to track down many band members. Here are a few recommendations:

H2O: *Alternative Press* Issue #241 (August 2008)
Lifetime: *Alternative Press* Issue #203 (June 2005)
Outspoken: Interview with several members in Norman Brannon's *Anti-Matter Anthology*
Shai Hulud: *Alternative Press* Issue #216 (July 2006)
Snapcase: Interview with several members in Norman Brannon's *Anti-Matter Anthology*

These and other interviews and retrospectives are well worth searching out for the stories behind these groups.

There were also many inspiring nineties hardcore bands from other countries such as Acme, Chokehold, Manliftingbanner, and Refused. But in order to keep the book manageable for readers and myself, I limited the scope to bands based in the United States.

Some chapters that follow feature commentary from one or two members of a group, while others contain reflections from all the members. By no means are these the complete stories of these bands, but the chapters should serve as an overview and shed light on the motivations of the musicians, and through them, provide a window into the socio-political and ethical concerns of the time period.

108

Vocals: Robert Fish (Rasaraja Dasa)
Guitars: Vic DiCara (Vraja Kishor Dasa)
    Kate Reddy
    Norman Brannon
    Daniel Hornecker
Bass: Tim Cohen (Trivikrama Dasa)
    Franklin Rhi
    Tony Valladerez

Drums: Chris Daly
    Tom Hogan
    Matt Cross
    Zach Eller
    Mike Paradise
    Lenny Greenblat
    Alan Cage

108 was among the most visceral bands of the nineties, weaving together a mixture of blistering hardcore, metal, and post-hardcore along with philosophical reflection that made for intellectually stimulating and emotionally cathartic music. Along with Shelter, 108 was a driving force behind the Krishna consciousness movement, a major presence in nineties hardcore. Regardless of one's take on the Krishna philosophy, there's no denying that 108 made a significant impact on the scene.

108 was formed by ex-Inside Out/Beyond member Vic DiCara after he discovered Krishna consciousness. However, DiCara (also known by his Krishna name, Vraja Kishor Dasa), vocalist Robert Fish (a.k.a. Rasaraja Dasa), and their musical comrades set out to communicate ideas rather than promulgate their particular brand of religion. That's not to say that 108 didn't speak about spiritual subjects; they did, but the philosophical ideas that they tackled were largely ubiquitous issues without dogma. Whether analyzing the possibilities of the afterlife ("Deathbed"), the concept of vegetarianism ("Killer of the Soul"), issues of masculine dominance in both the hardcore scene and society at large ("Woman"), or the struggle for survival in daily life ("Curse of Instinct"), each 108 lyric is part of a search for truth. Although many dismissed the band as "Krishna-Core," 108 developed a strong fan base with their full-lengths, *Threefold Misery* and *Songs of Separation*, as well as the searing *Curse of Instinct* EP, all reflecting the band's honest and anguished mood.

Musically, 108 took the ethereal spirit of Bad Brains, doused it with the ferocity of *Age of Quarrel*-era Cro-Mags, and imbued itself with the introspective lyrical and artistic sensibilities that were a big part of nineties hardcore. In turn, 108 created a sound that dared audiences to explore new artistic and philosophical territory.

Not only did 108 push boundaries sonically, but they also pushed them in terms of audience participation by challenging listeners to consider the concepts they spoke of with an open mind. Issues pertaining to karma and the more controversial aspects of Vedic philosophy may not have been every fan's prime concern; however, the band presented these topics in a down-to-earth manner. 108 also played to every facet within hardcore — from the tough-guy realm to the more politically conscious set — without compromise, so their popularity was partly due to that universal appeal.

In 1996, 108 cut its already shaky relationship with the International Society of Krishna Consciousness (ISKCON) after a rugged touring schedule, which spanned several years. The band reunited in 2006 and put out a new record in the summer of 2007. Although a new chapter is currently unfolding for 108, the nineties were the members' formative years.

After a decade long hiatus, 108 is performing again and is still dedicated to the search that got them started in the first place.

DIVING INTO KRISHNA CONSCIOUSNESS

VIC DICARA: I have always had a bent towards the occult, the supernatural, the spiritual, the paranormal. At the same time, I was always very counter-cultural and shying away from mainstream stuff. The Hare Krishnas fit both bills.

ROBERT FISH: I first started reading Krishna books when I was 15 years old. Over the last 18 years my understanding of the philosophy and the various angles, presentation, and nuances developed quite radically. When I first started to follow the tenets of Gaudiya Vaisnavism [traditional term for what is called "Krishna consciousness" in the West] that I was introduced to, it was very much focused on the specific disciplines, my struggles with aspects of them, and on basically learning about a culture that was quite different than anything I had ever been privy to. Like any sort of life premise there is always an awkward stage in the beginning where you over-emphasize externals and tend to stick to the aspects that are most comfortable and avoid those aspects that one finds difficult. However at some point the practitioner of any discipline, philosophy, or lifestyle will hit that stage where there is a deep and life-altering moment where you step back, examine life, and find your person within, and at times maybe outside of, that given lifestyle. For myself I have become attracted to and found interests in elements of the tradition that are outside of the original "backyard" of the ISKCON angle. I wouldn't say that externally I am all that different, but the pieces of the philosophy that initially attracted me have become more natural and the areas that I avoided have come to resolution, to some degree, by having a firmer grip on the texts and on the world outside my initial sight.

VIC DICARA: Another thing about my personality —I'm really into things that are rational, logical, well defined, organized. Up until the point that I had been introduced to Hare Krishna, I had always found that this aspect of my personality was completely at odds with the side of me that was enchanted by the supernatural. But when I checked out an Upanishad it all clicked, because even though it dealt entirely with spiritual subjects, it did so in a very rational, logical way.

COMBINING HARDCORE AND KRISHNA CONSCIOUSNESS

VIC DICARA: Playing music is what drew me to Krishna consciousness, not the other way around. I just continued playing in bands after I joined the Krishnas partly because it was one of the only smart and natural things I ever did in that regard — I mean, not completely throwing away something in order to become "spiritual" — and partly because all the big heads in the temple wanted me to keep doing my bands so that I could expose lots of kids to the ideas of Krishna consciousness.

ROBERT FISH: Music is a natural expression of the self. As I was exploring spirituality in the context of Gaudiya Vaisnavism, it was only natural that such an interest played a part in my music. It started before 108, but 108 was by far the most concentrated of any of the bands I was in.

KATE REDDY: [Combining hardcore and Krishna was] not natural in the traditional sense, but if you take into consideration the principle behind it, which is to dovetail your natural affinities and create a seva, or service, from those affinities, then yes. Why not?

TRIVIKRAMA DASA: Music has always been a big part of spiritual ways of life. There is music and songs sung in the Hare Krishna temples starting at 4:15 a.m. up until when people start going to sleep. I started playing guitar around 15 years old and found music to be an important form of expressing my feelings and trying to gain awareness and understanding of what was going on inside myself and my surroundings. So, while I was already playing a lot of music because of my involvement with Krishna consciousness, I wanted to play more music and make an attempt to do something connected with spirituality and playing instruments.

ROBERT FISH: [Vaisnavism] was the common thread of the members of 108 and was a rather important part of our lives especially in terms of how our initial contacts with the theology had affected our lives. Although Vic was the only one who sought life as a monk and spent any length of time living a monastic life, it was still a rather important part of our lives and how we related to everything around us which naturally found a place in our music.

KATE REDDY: [Hardcore and Krishna consciousness share] vegetarianism, anti-establishment tendencies and the ideal that principles and concepts drive action. Detachment from average goals and a deep sense of community. And P.S., the hardcore scene was, and most likely is, as sexist as any religion ever was. What it has in common with some varieties of religion are good people who are ultimately there to challenge the sexist notions so ingrained in our mind, body, and spirit. We all have *samskaras*, or impressions, on our minds that we carry with us in whatever flavor of life we choose, so the hardcore scene was neck in neck with the Krishnas on women's issues, I can assure you.

ORIGINS OF 108

VIC DICARA: I left Inside Out to join Shelter, and after about a year or so in Shelter it became painfully clear that Ray Cappo and I could not long survive in the same room, let alone the same band. We clashed with each other at every step. So, he orchestrated some hocus pocus bullshit with some guru guy — probably 'cause he knew how into hocus pocus stuff I was — with the end result of kicking me out of Shelter, moving me away from their temple in Philly and down to D.C., and telling me to start my own band with this nice but very goofy guy who lived there. That nice but goofy character was the first singer of 108. In the middle of recording *Holyname*, he was trying to do his vocals and I was like, "This ain't gonna cut it," and gave him a pink slip.

ROBERT FISH: I first encountered Vic around 1989. I received a letter in the mail from him along with a fanzine. He had read an interview where I talked of my interest in Vaisnavism, so he wrote me and sent me a magazine he had written while in Inside Out. A year later I moved into an *ashram* in Philadelphia. After about two months of living there I received a call from Ray Cappo saying that Shelter would move to that temple after their first U.S tour. When they arrived I met Vic in person for the first time. By the time he arrived at the temple it was only a matter of months before I realized that *ashram* life wasn't for me. The day my mother passed away I left the Philadelphia Temple. I had a little contact with Vic after that but nothing significant. Then about a year later my band Ressurection was playing a show in Atlantic City, New Jersey, with Worlds Collide and Lifetime. Vic showed up with his new band, 108. He watched our set and I watched theirs, which was their first show. The next day I got a call from Vic asking if I wanted to join 108. I agreed and went down to D.C. to put down some vocals for the 108 album and then in a few weeks left for a U.S. tour with Ressurection. When I returned I was to join 108 for a tour, but I had so many issues going on in my life I just couldn't do it at that point. 108 then played three shows with Vic singing and playing guitar and then called it quits. A year later I heard they were getting back together, so I called Vic and we reunited. I brought along Chris Daly, who was playing drums in Ressurection. Our first tour started on March 15 and ended September 5 and it was history from then.

VIC DICARA: Writing letters was a big deal in those days, before email and message boards took over. Rob and I used to write letters back and forth — both [of us] being into hardcore, straight edge, and Krishna. He had done some fairly goofy youth crew type straight edge band [Release], but that's how I knew he was a singer. Before 108 he was singing in a band called Ressurection. When I gave the original [vocalist] a pink slip in the studio, I figured I would sing half the songs myself, and the other half I would give to Rob. I figured it would be a good way to get him a bit more into being a Hare Krishna. And that's just what happened. I did half the vocals, he did half the vocals. And he eventually wound up getting awfully into being a Hare Krishna...though not until he first split from the band and gave up on the idea and started Ressurection in the meanwhile.

KATE REDDY: Before I joined the temple I was in a bunch of different bands. I loved playing music, so the summer of ninth grade I joined a band called Last Action. We only played one show, but it was with Underdog and Wolfpack. I looked exactly like a boy, but my future husband, the singer of Wolfpack, said, "Check out Kate Kindlon...whooo, she's hot!" I realize now that he was making fun of me. But I was happy then. And Underdog was one of my favorite bands, so I felt really excited to share the stage with them. Only there wasn't a stage it was just an area in the VFW Hall. After that I was in All Fall Down, Growing Up Skipper, and The Giving Tree. I was a band playing girl, so Vic asked me to join 108. I probably would have blooped if I hadn't been in 108. I wasn't really cut out for the women's *ashram* in the traditional sense, although I did learn a lot of *shastra* (Vedic Book learning) at the temple, which has served me well in countless ways.

TRIVIKRAMA DASA: I started to become friendly with Vic when we met in India and started hanging out a bit. Before coming to India, I played in Shelter for a very brief period. Vic asked me to play bass for 108 when we returned to the States and I said sure.

VIC DICARA: The explicit goal of 108 was to communicate and share my experiences and experiments with Krishna consciousness. That goal really stayed amazingly constant over the entire span of the band.

KATE REDDY: I remember sitting on the lawn of the Philly temple trying to learn to play false harmonics. 108 was basically a metal band and I was definitely a more straightedge and emo D.C. band loving hardcore girl. Although I loved Leeway and did see Celtic Frost play once. But I loved the irony of being a "chaste *Mataji*" and playing bone crunching riffs while my amp was on 11. That really worked for me.

ROBERT FISH: We didn't really have any goals except to address what we were experiencing. 108 wasn't your conventional band. In our entire existence we practiced 15 to 20 times. Literally, Vic would record his songs on an eight-track, we would practice once or twice and then go on the road through the U.S. and Europe and then record. We never really talked about anything nor did we approach the band in any strategic manner. We would simply play when we wanted and just let things happen as they did.

"HOLYNAME"

VIC DICARA: We recorded [Holyname] in a small home-based recording studio somewhere outside Washington D.C. I don't know where the temple idea came from, but I did create the demo versions for *Songs of Separation*, *Threefold Misery*, and others in various temple attics and basements in Dallas, Philadelphia, and New Jersey. I just put together the songs I felt like putting together at the time. I had two people involved with the recording who had no background at all in hardcore, which may have helped some non-traditional instruments and stuff find their way into the songs.

SPEAKING ABOUT KRISHNA

VIC DICARA: We immediately started playing live, long before we had recorded anything more than a boom-box demo. Personally, I despised the word "preaching." I would, of course, tell the Hare Krishna people that I was "preaching" because that's really the only language they consistently understood. But, personally, I was just trying to vent and share my own positive and negative experiences with the way I lived my life. I felt that would be a better way of "preaching" anyway — rather than trying to overtly convince people about something, just familiarize them with it through human, emotional communication. Of course, I can't let myself forget that I always love a good verbal fight and printed up all kinds of controversial flyers, pamphlets, and zines and handed them out at shows and deeply enjoyed the philosophical kung-fu that would ensue.

ROBERT FISH: I was much more interested in preaching to myself than anyone else. The main tenets or aspirations contained within Vaisnavism were something I aspired for. Yet the disciplines and mentality that were considered ideal were simply far from who I was. When I sang songs such as "Thorn," "Liar," or "Woman," I was thinking about myself as lust was an area I struggled with in a major way. At the same time we wanted to share our experience, and for those who are young, enthusiastic, and a bit naïve you couldn't help but to come off as "preachy," but that wasn't the intent. It was a way for me to try to evolve myself into the person I wanted to be.

TRIVIKRAMA DASA: I wouldn't say we preached. I wanted to share a spiritual message. I wanted to practice spiritual meditation like chanting the Hare Krishna mantra, and I wanted to connect with people and share some of the things that were helping me in my life. I believe everybody's common denominator is that we are all spiritual beings, so connecting with people by playing music and talking about the spirit a bit is a good way to harmonize with people in a deep way.

ROBERT FISH: Even though I was "one of them" it was pretty obvious that I wasn't. My demeanor and obvious lack of interest in [ISKCON's] causes gave everyone a sense of that. In some respects I obviously wanted to share the experiences I was having with Krishna consciousness and there was definitely a tinge of righteousness there. However, I tried to encourage kids to look at and think about it. I stayed away from presenting one institution or angle over another. I just tried to use the context of the music and lyrics to create discussion. As far as how I felt about those looking to "use" us? Well, there was resentment because I felt many of them were just fucked-up Christians with robes and a shaved head, which I just didn't care for in the least. At the same time it was no different than being surrounded by straight edge kids who were moronic jocks. I just dealt with it and made it clear that if they wanted a puppet to look elsewhere.

DEBATES

VIC DICARA: We always gave 1008% to every moment of every song at every show. Hardcore people connected with that and liked it. Born Against and kids from that scene — the ones who staged the original anti-Krishna demonstration at The Anthrax on the first show of the Shelter/Quicksand/Inside Out tour — would hang around with us a bit and shoot the breeze and even talk on the same wavelength about social and spiritual things and would tell us they decided to give us a chance because they loved our shows. There weren't too many real debates involving the band. Shelter's early shows already stirred all those debates up and they were over and done with. There may have been one or two similar protest type things against 108, but I've pretty much forgotten them. It was more like I personally would get into debates with people, because that's what was fun for me. I do remember a few bands and people deciding to oppose 108: *Trustkill* Fanzine, Chokehold, and, really slow and missing the boat, Slapshot a few years later. As far as we were concerned, the more the merrier. Bring it on.

ROBERT FISH: Shelter definitely got a much stronger reaction than we ever did, which was interesting as they were much more inviting in terms of lyrics and mood whereas 108 was rather blunt and heavy. I think between the two bands there were some significant subtle aspects that turned the table in terms of hostility. Shelter was an entire package of evangelism. A Shelter show meant *prasadam*, tables of beads and books, *harinama* (chanting) parties, and stories of how there was a "better way," whereas 108 was low key. We came, loaded, had a simple table with CDs, shirts, and maybe a book or zine, we played to exhaustion and that was about it. That, in my opinion, is why Shelter really stirred people up whereas 108 said what we said and made no bones about it, yet we didn't turn a show into a visit to a temple. We were two bands with Vaisnavism at the root, but how we approached it and our interaction with people were worlds different.

KATE REDDY: The funniest [debate] was with Eric Rumpshaker, who I just love. He really knew his stuff, did great interviews, and was not afraid to stir things up. After that interview, Vraja started wearing a *dhoti* at all the shows. Eric had made him feel like a gross materialist during the interview, in such an effective way that we all entered our radical communist period right away. By the end of the interview we thought we should be tying paper bags around our feet because shoes were too decadent. One other funny interview story: I don't know who it was anymore, but the funniest misquote in an interview ever was, "A band in all varieties of religion," instead of the real quote from *Bhagavad Gita*, where Krishna says, "Abandon all varieties of religion, and just surrender unto me." I guess the kid really thought 5,000 years ago God incarnated to get bands going in all religions.

VIC DICARA: Most of our encounters were really great. We left the violence and aggression to the legacy of the Cro-Mags. Most of our encounters were really very positive — always intense and to the point but almost always positive. We would almost always become very friendly with the bands we toured with and have a lot of fun together — even kinda crusty, un-Krishna bands like Bloodlet. We had a great time with them. From time to time there were hecklers, but we would always verbally beat the shit out of them so people gave up trying. I do remember one show in Orange County, California — on the *Songs of Separation* tour — some kids did try to stage an old-style protest with anti-Krishna flyers and shit. It was great; it just gave us a whole pile of really dry fuel to burn to a crisp. I'm not talking about burning the flyers — I mean the energy. We tore the shit out of the place that night. It was one of our best shows ever and did we punish the living hell out of those kids! [laughs] There was once a similar situation in Germany. Basically, I lived for that kind of stuff. If some kids thought they were going to bring their ideological beef to me at a 108 show I was right there like a jaguar to pounce on their jugular veins. I dedicated 24/7/365 to this shit, and I would sooner sit on a hot spear than let some nine-to-five adolescent philosophical toe-wetter try to step up to the plate in my ballpark. I would light up with joy and go for the throat head on. It was my favorite thing in the world. Rob kinda lived for it, too. So, kids gave up trying to do it. Except for the really brave and foolhardy ones. [laughs]

KATE REDDY: We were passionate about Krishna consciousness and being punks we liked to argue and be righteous. We were new to the philosophy, but we did our best. Imagine everyone hammering all of your beliefs all the time. I realize now that religion is deeply personal and doesn't need to be logical to be valid. Is love logical? Is color preference or food preference, or even sexual preference, logical and defendable by argument? It doesn't always have to be to be "valid."

ROBERT FISH: The violence [at shows] didn't really stem from religious beliefs. We played aggressive music and things happened. Besides one particular encounter, I don't think we ever had an encounter that led to violence. The only one I can think of happened on our first tour in Europe with Refused. Basically, some kids decided our beliefs made it appropriate to throw marbles at us on stage. So, in between songs I asked who thought throwing marbles at us was appropriate. No one said anything. After the show the guys from Refused pointed out the person who did it. So, I confronted him and asked him what the problem was. At this point, the kids realized it wasn't the wisest choice in expressing themselves. It ended with me illustrating to the leader what it felt like to be treated like an animal by dumping a pitcher of water over his head in front of the majority of the audience. The other situations generally happened with our music simply

as background music. Two times it was rather bad. The first was in Washington D.C. A group of drunk skinheads always hung out at the club and would start with anyone they felt they could handle. So, during a show Vic and our bass player at the time, Franklin [Rhi], went outside for a walk. The group decided it was a good idea to mock Vic and called him a "fag" and other "intelligent" remarks. The bassist from another band playing the show, Crown of Thornz, grew up within a gang type of environment and was rather aggressive. So, he confronted the group. Face to face they didn't say anything and when Vic and Franklin started to walk away they hit Franklin in the back of the head with a beer bottle. Franklin went in the club, cleaned off, told the rest of us and our friends, which included some older D.C. guys who were tied with the Cro-Mags. We went outside and the group had attacked a guy and girl so everyone got involved. It was utter chaos! When all was said and done the group of antagonists didn't fare too well. On subsequent trips to D.C. they never showed again.

KATE REDDY: Now when I think back, I am startled by the lack of tolerance in the scene in general. How P.C. would it have been to be against a Jewish movement in the scene? Yet we accepted the hatred many had toward us because of our spiritual beliefs without feeling like we had any rights. We weren't clear thinking enough at the time to realize the irony of a scene which was supposedly so radical that had such a strict set of unwritten rules.

"SONGS OF SEPARATION"

VIC DICARA: I never had any important motivations for writing any of my records except for the simple feeling of having emotions inside that wanted to get out and be understood by other human beings. Almost all of the 108 writing, right up until just about the very end of the band, was done exclusively by me. I would hole up somewhere by myself with a boom-box (later, an eight-track cassette recorder, and at the end, a digital eight-track) and a drum machine and write the beats, the bass lines, the guitar parts, the lyrics, and the vocals. Then we would go into practice mode; I'd show everyone the demo, explain the parts and we would practice them maybe a dozen times at most before heading into a studio to record them and then on the road to play them for people. With *Songs of Separation*, I remember the damp basement room in the dirty old basement of the Philadelphia Hare Krishna temple where I did almost all of the writing. I also remember living in the Hare Krishna storefront in New York, with no shower or kitchen, for a few months, during which time we would head a few blocks south into the really old part of Manhattan and go down into Don Fury's basement to record. I actually played the bass and both guitar parts, which was partly a symptom of a control freak, partly out of practicality since our schedule as a band was so tight and the rest of the people hardly had a chance to get familiar with the songs before it was already time to record them. I remember Don Fury telling me I had "quite a set of lungs" or something producer-ish like that after I finished the vocals for "Deathbed." I remember the fun of de-tuning my strings while playing and recording "Opposition." I remember a few Hare Krishnas showing up with food for us, one of whom would much later become my wife and another of whom soon after married Rob. A lot of good memories, although being absolutely penniless and living in a storefront in Manhattan was a bit more stress than I would probably like to have again.

ROBERT FISH: We recorded this record after our first tour, which lasted five straight months. We went through a lot together and we really wanted to define ourselves, especially in relation to Shelter and how people lumped us together, while at the same time we were finding ourselves in terms of the theology and the dynamic of what we were and who/what we aspired to be.

KATE REDDY: We practiced for a short time and then we split [for] tour. I have good memories of playing with Into Another at City Gardens. Someone threw a bra at me. I got really pissed about that. I loved playing with Snapcase — those guys were fun, amazing, and open-hearted people. When everyone jumped on the stage, they kind of protected me from either getting crushed by a bunch of boys going ape-shit on stage or by my stack falling down on top of me. I also really remember playing the Whiskey with the worst sunburn of my life. I actually hobbled off the stage and splayed myself out on the sticky hot naugahyde seats of the van. After that show, 108 and Shelter and our whole crew spent three days camping in Grass Valley. It was so beautiful and we had a blast. We did skits and cooked potatoes on a bonfire. One amazing man named Rtadvaja Swami came with us and took care of us. He is probably the reason we survived that tour. I also have fond memories of going on tour in Europe with Refused. They were the best bunch of boys ever! We went to Venice for the day with them and it was beautiful. They really tolerated our crazy Krishna shenanigans with no judgment — hats off to them for that.

STRAIGHT EDGE AND KRISHNA?

VIC DICARA: I became straight edge in 1987 because my friends in high school introduced the idea to me, exposed me to a lot of hardcore and "straight edge" music and the whole thing seemed to fit me perfectly at the time, which it did. Less than a year later, the same friends (Tom Capone, among others) introduced me to the idea of vegetarianism, which also just seemed to be a simple and perfect concept for me. And it was and still is. Less than a year after that, the same friends and some new ones started sharing some of their interest in Krishna consciousness with me through the Cro-Mags and through this fanzine that had popped up at the time called *The Razor's Edge*. My interest in Krishna consciousness built at a steady and gradual pace until I became friends with Ray Cappo and Steve Reddy, who were the first guys since the Cro-Mags to go completely over the top with Hare Krishna, moving into temples, shaving their heads, chanting on prayer beads, et cetera. At that point my interest went pretty ballistic. So, yeah, for me at least, the two "religions" — I meant to say that — go hand in hand. But Krishna consciousness is obviously a huge step beyond straight edge, in both positive and negative ways, as both a governing religion and a liberating philosophy. It is way too much of a leap for most people, but for me some kind of smooth ramp connected everything and I rode up it at full speed.

ROBERT FISH: I was always drug-free. I witnessed enough reasons to be drug-free by the age of eight to never have an attraction towards alcohol or drugs. Straight edge became a social aspect of my life right before I turned 14. Within six months of that time, I became a vegetarian. Aspects such as karma were a reason behind the turn to vegetarianism, but it wasn't specifically due to a religious context. Even as I started to get into Vaisnavism, I never saw straight edge as an extension as one is a discipline and the other a spiritual experience and theology. One may indeed lead to another, but I never saw it as connected.

VIC DICARA: There are positives and negatives to every way of life. On the negative side, it is true that both Krishna consciousness and straight edge are elitist, exclusionary, conservative, and repressive. But both straight edge and Krishna consciousness have positive aspects, as well. Both can be extremely productive, liberating, progressive, and genuinely enlightening. What a human being needs to try to do in life is to identify and separate the positive effects of their way(s) of life from the negative and recognize each. You can actually benefit from both, but not if you can't recognize them.

ROBERT FISH: In some respects, I would agree that straight edge is a belief, but it also gives a social environment and identity. Krishna consciousness, of course, is the same. However, when one is confined to it purely in a social environment, identity, and context it will be short lived. The hardcore/punk movements themselves create this same dynamic. Just as with straight edge or Krishna consciousness how many from the punk/hardcore scene actually retained that sense of purpose, belief, and lifestyle after the music and social scene no longer met their fancy? That is why most fall away from such beliefs and others maintain the beliefs or evolve within those beliefs without necessarily living within those social environments. So, in that respect I believe such an argument is true, but it applies in the majority of social contexts.

TRIVIKRAMA DASA: Everyone has to choose what is necessary for themselves. My involvement with the Krishna consciousness movement has strongly encouraged me to be more free-thinking, by challenging "normal," "materialistic" attitudes, beliefs, and behaviors, and by directing me towards the exploration of the inner self and the spirit of the universe. We are all going to die; we are in a temporary situation; we are all in the same boat so how can we best help each other and see each other's spirits? How can we find our lives' missions and develop divine love? I don't think these ideas are exclusionary.

SCENE FASCINATION WITH KRISHNA

VIC DICARA: Nobody would have cared for [Krishna consciousness] if it wasn't for musicians making it a part of their art. If it wasn't for the Bad Brains and their amazing mixture of Rastafarianism, metal, and punk none of this would have ever happened. The Cro-Mags would have never been the band they were, would have never sounded the way they did, and would have never been into Krishna consciousness the way that they were. And if it wasn't for the Cro-Mags and the mind-boggling, concrete-tough expressions of Krishna conscious strength and power that they delivered in their LP *Age of Quarrel* then Ray Cappo would never have become interested in Krishna and Shelter would never have formed. Shelter dropped a huge steroid into the whole mix that previously existed with the Bad Brains and the Cro-Mags. Suddenly, the whole spiritual hardcore thing became a V-8 engine. People like me started to dive passionately into spiritual thoughts and our bands — like Inside Out, Amenity, Forced Down — started to express those passions almost exclusively. So, it was the art, the pure music that fascinated and attracted people to Krishna consciousness and similar ways of thought. People would hear this amazing, intense music and would need to connect with the people who created it. And that connection was tied pretty closely in with straightedge and spirituality, and even the cult of the Hare Krishnas.

ROBERT FISH: Hardcore has a certain evolutionary cycle and part of that cycle encompasses periods where beliefs and causes take certain precedence. Today, most kids and bands don't express political/social beliefs or moral related issues. I believe that period will re-emerge and that after a scene gets saturated with particular moods you simply see a recession and rebirth. This isn't to say that there will be a rebirth in popularity in leftist politics, vegetarianism, etcetera, but I believe that more "cause" based influence will eventually re-emerge from time to time.

VIC DICARA: Obviously, in retrospect, Hare Krishna was a fad in the hardcore scene… in that it came, was huge, died out, and is now all but gone. Why did it fade away? I think it simply burned itself out. At a certain point almost every single kid into hardcore music had either visited a Hare Krishna temple or had a very close friend who did. Ten or 15% of them decided that it was great. The rest decided that the negatives outweighed the positives and wanted something different. The next thing to crop up in hardcore was hardline, which honestly was just all the negative aspects of Krishna consciousness — the elitism, the repression, et cetera — without any of the religious trappings. It attracted all the kids who wanted to be just as "holier than thou" as we Krishnas were but didn't want to have to be Hare Krishnas to do it. After a while, that scene took over from Hare Krishna, but both finally faded away when enough kids got fed up with all this emphasis on how you eat, breathe, sleep, and fuck. That's why the late-nineties music is, by and large, such a pile of useless shit. People were completely burnt out with messages, movements, meanings and needed some time to just have stupid music again.

TRIVIKRAMA DASA: There really were a tremendous amount of people who listened to hardcore that got very involved in Krishna consciousness and many of them are still seriously practicing. Maybe a lot of these people kind of expanded their horizons and lost touch with or grew out of listening to hardcore, going to shows, and making music. Actually, I still have friends who are active in Krishna consciousness and hardcore. Perhaps people are sharing less of themselves spiritually and hardcore may be being infiltrated more by materialistic mentalities.

"THREEFOLD MISERY"

VIC DICARA: [Threefold Misery is] the record I'm personally the most proud of. It just happened naturally, progressing from one stage of music-consciousness to the next and just doing whatever came naturally.

ROBERT FISH: There really was no difference except that as a band we were at our peak. As individuals our lives were more intense, we had that camaraderie that really drove an intensity, which was especially driven as we were all at personal crossroads. Vic continued to write the songs, but the dynamic of the group really bled into the songs and execution of the songs.

TRIVIKRAMA DASA: There was a lot of creativity making the record: burning candles, making guitar feedback for long periods of time, getting out feelings and solving problems in the music itself. There is a lot of richness in that music. You can hear it when listening to that record, which by the way was completed in its entirety in a few days for very little money.

"CURSE OF INSTINCT"

ROBERT FISH: The only songs not written by Vic were "Curse of Instinct" and "Pyro Stoke," which appeared on the *Curse of Instinct* EP, which was recorded at the same time as the *Threefold* record. Both of those songs were musically just jams that we captured with the tapes running. The lyrics from "Curse of Instinct" were written by me and really expressed the intensity of my life at the time. In that year, I really disintegrated into a deep depression and had a serious experience with suicide. Subsequently, counseling went terribly and I was very desperate to find myself. It was a very dark period for me, and the song was my initial attempt to articulate where I was.

VIC DICARA: Personally, since that was the one song I didn't write the lyrics for, I just connected to the song on a purely abstract, musical level. It is a chaotic, disturbed emotion that somehow tries to solve itself by blasting the fuck out of itself.

END OF 108

VIC DICARA: I got involved with Hare Krishna for a number of reasons, but within a year or two I quickly got the main feeling that I should try to go balls-to-the-wall and really try to do the standard *sadhu* thing and renounce the world and become liberated and enlightened and all that. A good deal of the time I was in 108 I had a nagging feeling that in some ways it was preventing me from doing that. It was a growing tension that, after about four or five years, made me want to finally stop doing the band and try my hand at the full-bore *sadhu* thing. It only took a year or so of the full-bore *sadhu* thing for me to realize that this wasn't really the right way for me to be trying to live my life in the first place.

ROBERT FISH: [It was] the same crossroads that made *Threefold Misery* and *Curse of Instinct* such intense records. It was time. Vic was experiencing his last grasp at being what he aspired to be. I was a mess and needed to find myself, which just couldn't happen in that dynamic.

VIC DICARA: After 108, I tried to delve really deeply into studies and stuff. Trying to stay longer in India… almost dying there of brain malaria and a train wreck, among other things. I wound up the "president" of one of the Hare Krishna temples (Towaco, New Jersey) and kind of the "headmaster" of a live-in school we started for people who wanted to really seriously learn about Krishna and not just move into a Hare Krishna temple and wind up selling books in an airport or something. It was a very positive experience overall, and the fact that it helped clarify to myself — even through what I was learning from studying those ancient scriptures — that doing the "monk" thing was really not what I should be doing, so that too was a positive effect.

LEAVING ISKCON

ROBERT FISH: ISKCON is like any other institution in the world. There are great individuals, there are questionable ones, and there are evil ones. I think the institution is positive in that it offers a social circle in which one can discover different aspects of the philosophy that can't be learned by reading a book, and you can be exposed to fantastic individuals. Still, there is an obvious tension anytime any spiritually based philosophy has an institution built around it. In some respects the two are diametrically opposed. My whole life I over-thought things and I just decided to be what I was and not worry about it. The last time I went to India I took *diksha* initiation, which is the first step in Vaisnavism. All these things that bothered me about Krishna consciousness didn't play a role in Vaisnavism. Take abortion, for instance. We're vegetarians and believe in sanctity of the soul, but it's not about politics. Anything in the west has to be categorized. Do I believe in abortion? Of course. I don't live in a fantasy world. Do I think it's always a good thing? Not necessarily. But I have to worry about how I'm a part of that. If I want to stop abortion then I should believe in sex education and trying to empower young single mothers and help get them through school. When you look at Vaisnavism outside of ISKCON it doesn't take on that political slant or Judeo-Christian slant of Vaisnavism. There were a lot of theological things that made more sense to me, but also the nature of institutions and by partaking in an institution that means you have to sacrifice.

VIC DICARA: I left the lifestyle of that particular social group behind. I did not leave my soul behind. I have basically the same thoughts in my head and aspirations in my heart now as I did then. The only difference is that now I don't feel like that specific social-religious sect or group of people is something that would be a positive part of my life right at this point, or right at this conception of how I know how to interact with them. But religion is the most interesting thing in my life. Now religion as a social entity? I see it as just a different form of government —in fact, a far more insidious form of government, since it pretends to be something different. Spirituality and awareness of "God" and the hugeness of the universe and shit like that...well, that's just the most inspiring thing in my life right now. Personally, I experience that type of spirituality in the kiss of my wife, in the sound of my kids' voices, in the smell of the air, and in astronomy equally as much as I experience it in a sacred mantra, a scripture, or what have you.

KATE REDDY: Whenever people institutionalize a religion, I believe it's with good intention to educate and create a community. However, there are always unscrupulous people who will use religion for their own political gain or to push through personal desires. For instance, did Henry the 8th really ponder whether or not God could be approached directly by average people, without the aid of a priest? Or did he push for the Church of England to separate from Rome because he really wanted to marry another woman? The Catholic Church was completely power hungry and corrupt. Men like Martin Luther had both a political and philosophical desire for change. But the change happened largely because one man really couldn't stand not sleeping with one woman. So, yes, I think that like anything in this world, when personal desire mixes with anything, even something as pure as the path of Bhakti Yoga, it can be a mess. I live outside of the community, but I really love and respect so many people on the inside. If a person's desire and intentions are true, who am I to judge?

ROBERT FISH: As for where I am today, I am still very much involved with Gaudiya Vaisnavism although I am somewhat distanced from ISKCON, especially in terms practice and the overall theology. After 108, I began reading deeper into Gaudiya theology and found more balance and comfort in the more traditional and orthodox teachings of Gaudiya Vaisnavism, which looks and feels very different from what was presented in 108 and in ISKCON. Gaudiya Vaisnavism has evolved from a belief to a very fabric of my life and being. It isn't something I have to practice but something in which is a part of who I am, what I do, what I think about and what I aspire for.

TRIVIKRAMA DASA: Religion means linking up with God or the universal spirit so it is something I really want to strive for. Krishna says, "Abandon all varieties of religion and just surrender unto me," so I hope to understand that more and more as I get older. I hope I can internalize more and more spiritual philosophy and eventually live it more and more. I have obstacles that I need to overcome though, mostly internal enemies.

SELECT DISCOGRAPHY:

Holyname (CD/LP, Equal Vision, 1994)
    Fish, DiCara, Eller

Songs of Separation (CD/LP, Equal Vision, 1995)
    Fish, DiCara, Reddy, Daly

Threefold Misery (CD, Lost and Found, 1996)
    Fish, DiCara, Cohen, Cross

Curse of Instinct (MCD, Lost and Found, 1996)
    Fish, DiCara, Cohen, Cross

Creation. Sustenance. Destruction. (CD Discography, Equal Vision, 2006)

A New Beat from a Dead Heart (CD/LP, Deathwish, 2007)
    Fish, DiCara, Cohen, Hogan

AVAIL

Vocals: Tim Barry
Guitars: Joe Banks
Bass: Justin "Gwomper" Burdick
　　　Charles McCauley
　　　Rob Kelshian

Cheerleader/Roadie: Beau Beau
Drums: Erik Larson
　　　Ed Trask

Avail's unforgettable choruses and engaging performances took nineties hardcore and punk by storm. Formed in Northern Virginia, Avail created melodic hardcore that was as steeped in classic hardcore ala Minor Threat and Bad Brains as it was in the emotionally fueled post-hardcore of Rites of Spring, the Bay Area melodic hardcore of bands like Crimpshine and Fuel, and posi-core anthems of Gorilla Biscuits. Because they had a variety of influences, it wasn't uncommon to find X'ed up straight edge kids singing along next to crusty punks and indie-rockers at any given show during Avail's never-ending tours.

Avail formed when its members bonded over a love of music in high school. Tim Barry was the drummer in the early days, but he soon transitioned to the role of frontman. The band's first full-length, *Satiate*, was completed soon thereafter. Band friend Adam Thompson mailed a copy of the record to California's Lookout Records — home of Green Day, Operation Ivy, and Screeching Weasel — and the label decided to give the band a shot due to a combination of their impressive songs and a reputation for having a stunning live set.

The band lived together and worked jobs for a few months before writing a new record and hitting the road yet again. They toured with everyone from Endpoint and Snapcase to Rancid and Lagwagon, which only increased the diversity of their fan base. The group also played the notable Dayton Hardcore Fest several times in the early-nineties, which drew audiences from all around the country. The group's energetic performances at the fests impressed those traveling to be there. Those folks then went back home and told their friends and the positive feedback spread.

With each new record the band's songwriting talent grew. Both *Dixie* and *4 A.M. Friday* took the group's sound to another level both musically and in popularity. Barry penned songs from the heart and was proud that he never wrote a tune he didn't believe in. Instead of writing songs about standard topics, Barry tended to focus on issues that pertained to his home state. By the time *Over the James* came out (1998), Avail reached what many saw as a songwriting pinnacle.

As the late-nineties came about, the years of touring took a toll and members missed their adopted hometown of Richmond while on the road. Though traveling the world provided innumerable memories, the lack of stability was too much of a downside to continue touring the way they had been. As of 2008, the band members have set down roots; they continue to release records periodically and even tour on occasion. Though they don't perform as often as they used to, Avail is one of the most respected bands of the era crossing the invisible but often stifling lines separating the worlds of hardcore, punk, and indie rock.

EARLY DAYS/"SATIATE"

TIM BARRY: We were all in bands in high school. I was in a band called Learning Disabled Kids. Eventually I wound up in rehab and when I got out I became the drummer of Avail. We were still in high school, so we were playing in garages. About 14 of us took over [and lived in] a house on Grace Street in Richmond, Virginia. Eventually I started singing. *Satiate* came out of all those experiences. We took the songs we wrote in that house and re-recorded the ones we thought were the best and made a record. We went into a studio up in Maryland, which was our first true recording experience. We worked with an aging metal head we dubbed Rob "Rock." He had a studio in his basement and he wanted us to play electronic drums otherwise his neighbors would get upset with the noise. [laughs] That's why the recording came out so crisp and odd unlike most punk bands at the time. It was a 100 percent learning experience. Back then having vinyl out was a really big achievement. We didn't have the Internet to get the word out. We had to network with folks and hope to hook up with distros throughout the country to get the word out.

BEAU BEAU: We all grew up in the same town and were all in different bands. Tim and I had been good friends forever. I used to travel with them and sit on the side of the drum-kit and help him out, and then it slowly progressed to me being a not-knowing-how-to-do-anything roadie. I'd help pack and unpack the van, and they'd pay me five bucks for these services at every show. I was broke and didn't have any money. Eventually, they took a vote and said, "Hey, who says Beau should be an official member of the band?" They all voted me in and decided if they weren't getting any money then I wouldn't either. [laughs]

TIM BARRY: Take yourself back to high school. Every band in high school has one dude who pretends to be the manager or roadie. There's that one dude always hanging around the band and Beau was that guy [for us]. We grew up together. I was originally the drummer and I had this piece of shit drum set that would always fall apart during shows. When it would start going to hell he'd always be there to run up and set it up again. At some point our singer quit and I ended up at the front of the stage. The funny thing was that Beau always sort of made his way on the stage. Originally he'd do sign language to the things I was saying to the crowd and jump around on stage to get the dance-floor going. It got to the point where we played a show once where he wasn't there and it just didn't seem right. [laughs] So, we just made him a part of the band.

BEAU BEAU: It started with me sitting next to Tim and helping him when he was the drummer. When he became the vocalist, I started to hang out off to the side toward the front of the bass rig. Eventually, I just started to become part of the on-stage show. I don't know how it happened because it was never planned. [laughs] The music just overtook me and the rest is history. I go to all the practices and have a say in everything. I'm a full-fledged member of the band. I couldn't necessarily write the music, but I'd help put it together. "Okay, start with the Bad Brains part and move into the Born Against part, followed by that little bunny-hop thing." [laughs]

TIM BARRY: We set up our first tour by pay phone. We used a sound duplicator that made it sound like you were dropping a quarter into the phone so we were able to get some free minutes. This was way before the age of commonplace cell phones. [laughs]

BEAU BEAU: *Satiate* was neat, but it was a long, drawn-out process. My most vivid memory is sitting down for about eight hours for days and days and stuffing the records into the sleeves. God, it was horrible. [laughs]

INFLUENCES

TIM BARRY: If you get in our van and hear the music we listen to it's really a blend of southern rock, bluegrass, country, and hardcore in the vein of, say, Snapcase or Cro-Mags. On top of that we also play a mixture of Soulside and Dag Nasty. So, basically all of that is what we've been trying to imitate all these years. [laughs] At the same time, we're all just working-class guys. If John Cougar and Bruce Springsteen don't speak to you then you're not working-class. [laughs] That's our roots music. So, why not incorporate our influences into our own sound?

LOOKOUT RECORDS

TIM BARRY: Our friend Adam Thompson sent *Satiate* to Lookout, and somehow Larry Livermore decided he liked it and he put it out. It was all an experiment. When people seemed to receive the record well we were confused. We didn't understand anything. We came from the suburbs and at that point we lived in the city. Everything was new to us

LYRICS/POLITICS

TIM BARRY: Joe [Banks] and I have always written the lyrics. I've always been active politically and that is naturally reflected in a lot of our songs. There was no one angle we tried to shove down people's throats, though. We just wanted people to be aware of their surroundings, if we had any sort of agenda. The more political stuff that influenced some of our songs reflected things that troubled us in Richmond, typically. Monroe Park, for instance, is a place where we all hung out and the city closed it and tried to "clean it up" for Virginia Commonwealth University.

BEAU BEAU: We tried to make a conscious decision not to be an overtly political band. We wrote about some politics, but we mostly stuck to local issues. If you wave your flag out there for what you stand for then people will assume a lot of things about you. We have such crazy political and social differences within our band that we can't fly a banner.

TIM BARRY: My lyrics were kind of like journal entries. A song will pop up and it will strike a chord with me and inspire me to write about something. I think it was Woody Guthrie who said you can only write songs you've actually experienced first hand. That's true as I can't write about things I don't feel. Sometimes I'm dissatisfied when I hear bands singing about things that are so cliché. I'd rather hear something honest. If you got your heart broken, sing about it poetically and do it with some emotion. Don't just make it up for the hell of it.

"DIXIE"

TIM BARRY: We recorded *Dixie* with Larry Packer up in Maryland. I don't know how it happened. It was built on journal entries and improvised songs. We didn't have any demos. Everything on the record we only played live before—I don't think the guys in the band even knew the lyrics. None of us really had lives. I don't even know that we have lives now. [laughs] We all worked shitty jobs and quit them to go on tour.

BEAU BEAU: There was no bullshit about the way the record looked or sounded. It was just us. We weren't worried about budgets and release dates.

ENTHUSIASTIC LIVE RESPONSE

TIM BARRY: That's when we realized people actually liked us. We'd play consistently at The Wetlands in New York City. We opened for Rancid one night and I remember feeling a vibe between us and the people coming to see us and singing along. It felt like the whole place was all one big band—not just us entertaining people. It was the first time in my life when I could sing without a microphone and hear the words just as loud because so many others would be right there with me. I was blown away by the intimacy of the experience. Louisville was our home away from home. Endpoint made us popular there. We played with Billingsgate on our first tour down in Florida and we also played with Endpoint. The guys from Endpoint were like, "Man, this show is crazy. There are people pulling guns out at the show and calling you guys 'fags' while you're playing. You've got to come up and play with us in Louisville!" [laughs] So, we went there and played and I swear to God there were 800 people there to see Endpoint and they put us on right before them and the next time we came back there were 300 people and the next time there were about 1,000 and suddenly we were even more popular in Louisville than we were in Richmond. That's all because of Endpoint. They really helped us get to the level that we achieved during our prime.

BEAU BEAU: The live show is what hardcore is all about. I'm not knocking our records, but they are nothing like being at an Avail show.

TIM BARRY: A lot of people say they would just listen to the records to find out the time changes and how the lyrics went so they could sing along at shows. [laughs] Music is to be shared, right? Shows are where it all comes together and that should be the way it is for any band. If they can't do it live then they shouldn't do it.

"4 A.M. FRIDAY"

TIM BARRY: It was about the time [of *4 A.M. Friday*] that we fell into a rhythm. People were coming to our shows. Instead of me calling people and begging to let us play a show, people were calling us. Our lives became regimented. We stopped working for a while and we moved into another house. We all paid about 80 bucks a month for rent. People ask us, "How are you able to pay rent off a band?" Well, you live communally and in a poor neighborhood.

BEAU BEAU: For the first records I would go to the studio and sleep, and then I would wake up and sing or yell my lines and then go back to sleep. I didn't care about production value. By the time *4 A.M.* came around I got more involved, though. I did the collages for the front and back cover and I started moaning and bitching because it would take nine hours to set up the microphones and stuff. [laughs]

TIM BARRY: I remember laying down tracks with the band and then pounding down forties at night and writing lyrics and singing them into a microphone on my own. We also toured nine months a year. We started to go overseas pretty consistently and that's when I began writing songs more focused on Richmond because I was never there. The writing process was no different than any other record except now it was a bit more of a routine. We'd go home, write a record, wait three months for the record to come out, leave, don't come home for a year.

"OVER THE JAMES"

TIM BARRY: There's an energy to *Over the James* that perfectly captured those moments in our lives at the time. When I listen to songs on that record I think of certain colors. They all just shoot out when each track comes on. If the songs don't do that then I think records don't work. That record was so much fun to write. This is when Gwomper was in the band. He was a roommate of ours. We made him leave for a while before because we had a no drugs policy in the house — there were people in the house who had a problem with that in the past and we didn't want them to have to deal with that in the house. He ended up hitchhiking across the country for a while. A couple years later I was walking down the street one morning and here's Gwomper sitting in the laundromat by himself with a trash bag that contained all his clothes. He said he had just come back into town and he told me about his journey on the road. We'd known each other since we were 12 so of course I invited him back to live at the house. I asked him if he'd take care of the place for five weeks while we were on tour. When we came back we needed a bass player. We've always been more about playing with friends than finding any sort of amazing musicians, so we taught him how to play bass. He started writing riffs right away. His first show in his whole life was in front of 800 people. He was pale white and shaking. [laughs] It was such a good experience writing the record though because we were all friends writing songs together like in the old days. We spent hours writing that record and having a good time. Joe constantly came in with other ideas for harmonies, which really pushed us in different ways. It was also so nice to be home for a bit and have the chance to soak it in because we had been on the road for so long.

DIVERSE CROWDS

TIM BARRY: To this day I can't figure it out. [laughs] All those groups of people are notorious for fighting with each other at shows. There were some fights we had at our shows, but they were so few compared to what you would think would have happened in an environment like that. So, here I am looking out at a crowd with crusty punks standing right next to dudes with Xs on their necks and they're all dancing and having a good time. We just got real lucky. We'd play shows and straight edge hardcore kids would be singing along with crusty punks next to the "normal" girl who came to the show from high school with pretty blonde hair. Our audience was unique at the time because there were typically punk and hardcore shows and they often wouldn't intersect. We would bring people from both sides of the fence and it was a nice feeling to see that happen.

SINCERITY

TIM BARRY: Any show you go to you will know in a second if the band is faking it. If they mean it, you'll also know it in a second. I mean it when I sing every night. I've sang these songs so many times, yet every time I get up on stage and sing those lyrics I'm taken back to the time they were written, and I think about where I am now and it all makes sense. If it ain't truth, it ain't worth it.

"ONE WRENCH"

TIM BARRY: Avail is basically just a way to vent. *One Wrench* was a record that a lot of people didn't like, but it was one of our most honest. It really represents a time period for us — over the course of one dark, cold winter — where all of us were in complete hell emotionally and we wrote this completely dark and depressing record. I guess when we write we don't really care whether people are going to be into the record or not — it's how we feel and we can only write what we feel. The lyrics on that record mean more to me than any lyrics I've sung. That was one of those spots in my life when I was thankful that I had a band and a voice and a pen and paper to write with. I sang songs on that record where I was so blacked-out drunk I don't even remember singing them. And nobody stopped me. It's like a big journal entry of that time period.

NO REGRETS

TIM BARRY: As soon as something becomes popular then people slander it. That's how it's always been with Avail. It happens with anything anyone does with a creative output. The very first thing you can't do is get an ego about it or have a fragile ego because everyone isn't going to like what you do. We've always just tried to write music we felt and enjoyed and we're happy to share it with others.

BEAU BEAU: I've never given a flying rat-shit about what people think of us. I'm performing and having a good time and if you're into it then awesome. If not, I don't care. [laughs]

SELECT DISCOGRAPHY:

Satiate (CD/LP, Lookout, 1992)
        Barry, Banks, McCauley, Larson, Beau Beau

Attempt to Regress (7", Catheter Assembly, 1993)
        Barry, Banks, McCauley, Larson, Beau Beau

Dixie (CD/LP, Lookout, 1994)
        Barry, Banks, McCauley, Larson, Beau Beau

4 A.M. Friday (CD/LP, Lookout, 1996)
        Barry, Banks, Kelshian, Larson, Beau Beau

The Fall of Richmond split with Young Pioneers (7", Lookout, 1997)
        Barry, Banks, Burdick, Larson, Beau Beau

Over the James (CD/LP, Lookout, 1998)
        Barry, Banks, Burdick, Larson, Beau Beau

One Wrench (CD/LP, Fat Wreck Chords, 2000)
        Barry, Banks, Burdick, Trask, Beau Beau

Front Porch Stories (CD/LP, Fat Wreck Chords, 2002)
        Barry, Banks, Burdick, Trask, Beau Beau

BURN

Vocals: Chaka Malik

Guitars: Gavin Van Vlack
      Vic DiCara
      Ian Love

Drums: Alan Cage

Bass: Alex Napack
      Manny Carrero

For a time, during the transition between the eighties and nineties, hardcore fell into a chasm where the progression of the genre stalled. Carbon copies of trendsetters like Youth of Today and Uniform Choice seemed to appear everywhere hardcore thrived. Although some of these bands were dedicated and enthusiastic, others grew tired of the same formula. Along with Quicksand, Inside Out, and other experimental outfits, Burn brought a different take on hardcore to the scene and their impact is still felt today.

After ending a run with New York hardcore group Absolution, guitarist Gavin Van Vlack felt the urge to rip through the stagnancy that he felt gripped the genre. Many groups were still playing a typical hardcore sound with passion, but aside from a few groundbreaking outfits the tendency toward mimicry was prevalent. A lover of all forms of music, Van Vlack vowed to put a stop to that trend. Burn was his testament to holding true to his word.

After rounding out the lineup with vocalist and longtime New York hardcore veteran Chaka Malik, bassist Alex Napack, and drummer Alan Cage (formerly of Beyond), Burn set forth to bring a new sound to the scene. The group's first show was with Sick of it All and they impressed hardcore musicians and fans with drop-of-a-dime time changes, fluid songwriting, and heartfelt lyrics. Burn's self-titled seven-inch released in 1990 added to the group's reputation. The record showcased Burn's hardcore roots and also demonstrated their interest in mixing sounds — the manic expressionism of jazz artists like John Coltrane, for instance, which affected the way the band utilized time signatures — into the musical recipe. To top it off, the lyrics and vocal stylings of Malik were revelatory — each song coming off as a charged philosophical discussion in and of itself.

As Burn continued to awe those at their shows with their mammoth presence and progressive songwriting, the group captured the attention of major labels, which were looking for the next big thing in the post-Nirvana bidding frenzy. But Burn found itself unsettled to be in such a situation, and Cage left the band to become a full-time member of Quicksand, which had already signed to Polydor. Consequently, Burn never found a replacement for Cage's unique drumming style and the band soon ended, although they would briefly reunite to assemble a final record in 2001 (*Cleanse*).

Over time, Burn's sound has become embedded in the tenor of countless bands. Although many attempted to conjure up Burn's brazen aura, no one could replicate it. Still, since they set the bar high, the groups that came afterwards naturally had to aim for the same trajectory. Although Burn had a short run in their initial incarnation, they were a daring, uncompromisingly honest force that became part of the foundation of nineties hardcore.

ORIGINS OF BURN

GAVIN VAN VLACK: Prior to Burn I was in Absolution. I'm not sure what happened with that band —there were a lot of lineup changes really quickly and it started to turn into a jam band. I've never been big into instrumentals. [That kind of music] has its place, but I don't find that in my repertoire of what I want to do as a musician. I wanted to branch off and try different things, and I wanted to get with people who wanted to do something more progressive.

CHAKA MALIK: I was just a crazy dancer in the hardcore scene and Gavin Van Vlack was this great, invaluable person on the planet and he said, "Hey, man, I'll start a band for you, but I can't be in it because I'm going to do something else." He went away and Alex came up with the musical structure for "Drown" and "Out of Time." We tried to interview guitar players, but then Gavin came back. Sick of it All asked us to play a few songs before one of their shows at CBGB's and it was sold out and off the hook.

GAVIN VAN VLACK: At the time of Burn I had become so fed up with music, and I was desperately searching for other avenues of sound. I really loved the old jazz guys like John Coltrane and Miles Davis, and I considered them to be forerunners of progressive music. I started to incorporate jazz into what I was doing and somehow it worked. I was looking to get beyond what the hardcore scene was doing at the time because it was kind of limiting.

IMPACT OF ENVIRONMENT

GAVIN VAN VLACK: We hung out in Manhattan, which is where a lot of cool stuff was happening, but we were really a Williamsburg band. We were living on the south side of that area and it wasn't the posh neighborhood it is today. It was industrial and totally screwed up. The atmosphere of Williamsburg really set into our music because it was so bleak and desolate. You basically had a bunch of kids who were hanging out in a warehouse district; you had the projects on one side, a Hasidic neighborhood on the other side, and it was this industrial wasteland.

CHAKA MALIK: We were into the softest music. People would travel with us and we'd be listening to The Smiths and Sade and Cassandra Wilson. We didn't listen to any hardcore around each other. I was a huge fan of hardcore, but that was something I did on my own time. Hardcore was for me in my room by myself working my life out. We were huge fans of music and all relatively similar in social ideals. Like Chris Rock said, "If you're a crackhead your wife better be a crackhead too otherwise your relationship is not going anywhere."

ALONE IN A CROWD

GAVIN VAN VLACK: The music came out of a certain amount of isolation we felt. We didn't really belong to a particular scene. Alan Cage had been in Beyond, which was a band that wasn't about a scene. Alex was in Pressure Release, which was kind of a straight edge band. Chaka had never done music before really, but he was eager to be in a band. The thing Chaka brought to Burn was that he had a certain passion in his anger. He was a really volatile person and I don't mean volatile in the way of, "He's going to kick your ass." He was brought up in a very politically aware atmosphere and he was much more aware of politics than most kids our age.

CHAKA MALIK: I didn't even know what a goal was or maybe I had some intangible version of a goal in my heart or mind, but it wasn't like I wrote anything down. I wasn't interested in selling records or being big. I was a crazy dancer and just wanted to have fun. It was a lot of fun, especially early on. When I would see Absolution play I thought they were an amazing band — they had soul, spirituality, and all these amazing elements. But Burn was my chance to express myself. It wasn't to get recognition or some kind of fame, but if someone is able to express themselves artistically it can change your whole perspective on how you view yourself.

GAVIN VAN VLACK: For me it has to come down to my own behaviorisms. I'm a person who is constantly trying to get out of my own head. I do that through my music and my art; for a time I did it by way of doing a shit-load of drugs. It was never about me; it was about getting outside my head. When you get on stage all eyes are on you, so what it

is was something that came over us when we played the music, because we really felt that shit.

REPUTATION

GAVIN VAN VLACK: We had a lot of things thrust upon us as far as what we were about. I heard all sorts of wacky quasi-religious things about us; I heard people call us a straight edge band, which was never really the truth. At one time we were all vegetarians. I'd have to say we were kind of nuts. [laughs] We did a lot of stuff that most bands didn't do. I learned from Alan not to kiss any asses. Promoters would tell us to go on stage and we'd say, "No, the people haven't even shown up yet." There was one situation that I will totally credit to Alan that was amazing! We played a show in Pennsylvania and showed up late. The promoter said he wasn't going to pay us what we asked for because we showed up late, even though we had shown up on time to play, we just weren't there for soundcheck. The promoter tried to pull this crap where he went on stage and said, "Burn's trying to rip us off. They're not our friends." So, Alan walks out on the other side of the stage and says, "Give the kids all their money back; we'll play for free."

CONFRONTATIONAL SHOWS

GAVIN VAN VLACK: Allentown is an old steel mill down and the mills got shut down. The Klan came in there and starting telling the kids, "This is why the plant got shut down" and started to use the Klan rhetoric to get kids infuriated. I mean, when I meet a kid who is 16-years-old and is a Grand Dragon? Jeez! That scene as well as parts of New Jersey were Nazi strongholds at the time. Some of the kids weren't up front about it, but they were sure wearing the colors. We were like, "Okay, you're Nazis, I'm half-Mexican, Chaka is obviously black, let's roll." [laughs]

SELF-TITLED 7"

GAVIN VAN VLACK: That record was recorded so fast. The way we wrote those songs originally in a couple of days just hanging around our house in Williamsburg. When we got in the studio it was cool because the songs were given just enough live performance to get the intensity across. There was a sense of urgency behind it and everything is so desperate sounding.

DON FURY

GAVIN VAN VLACK: Don Fury's studio created so many amazing records. His studio was the size of a shoebox. If you've never met Don Fury, he's one of the most flamboyant characters ever. You never really knew which Don you were going to get when you showed up. It could be Don Quixote, it could be Don Fury, it could be Donna Summer. [laughs]

LYRICS

GAVIN VAN VLACK: Chaka and I have two different ways of writing lyrics. I'm a little more tongue-in-cheek and cynical about things; Chaka is a little more prophetic. He writes very deeply from inside his head. He was writing about the wars between the Superego and the Id. He was trying to understand who he was and what he was about. Just like any kid he was trying to figure out, "Who am I? Why am I here? What the fuck does all this mean? Are we a science experiment in a Petri dish?" Chaka wrote about things such as "Tales of Shatou," where you have two people — one who is blessed and one who is cursed — and what dictates this? One of the hardest questions in physics is why there is something instead of nothing. That's where Chaka was coming from; he wrote from a very deep place. "New Morality" was originally an Absolution riff but the guys said it was too political. I was like, "Left wing? What the hell, we're not a skinhead band why are we worried about that?" [laughs] But it ended up not fitting the dynamic of the first record.

"LAST GREAT SEA"

GAVIN VAN VLACK: *Last Great Sea* was basically a demo that we had done for Roadrunner toward the end of the band. I honestly think I blew that deal — me and my big mouth. I think I pissed off somebody at the label. I said something to someone's face who worked in A&R and I screwed up any kind of deal. I believe a lot of A&R people don't really understand music. I liked the guys who worked there, but I didn't want to be a metal band. We were approached by a couple of labels, but we were kind of unapproachable at the same time. We were pretty volatile people — mostly Chaka and myself. We had gone into Nazi strongholds and played shows and raised riots. We also didn't have pop sensibility. We were writing bombastic, aggressive riffs. We weren't writing verse/chorus/verse — that's what made Burn indigestible to the mainstream. After that there was some talk of, "Hey, why don't we do this or that?" But that just wasn't what the band was all about.

END OF THE ROAD

GAVIN VAN VLACK: When you stop believing in what you are doing and when you start faking the moves that's when it's best to step away from it. I kind of feel like that's what it was like with Burn when we broke up. I felt like it didn't have the same energy and purpose [at the end]. It was going in a direction I didn't see myself going musically. What made Burn great was about us doing what we did and bringing it as hard and fast and furious as possible. It kind of started to be about looking at other sounds that were getting big. I have nothing against musical success, but I want to believe in what I'm doing. That may keep me broke for a long time, but to compromise myself to that degree… I just can't do it. Alan was also really in Quicksand, so we were pretty much without a drummer. Alex had also left. We played with another drummer and bass player, but it started to deviate from what I wanted to do with the band musically.

MEMORIES

GAVIN VAN VLACK: I'm nowhere near the same person. Looking back is kind of like looking across a lake at a house you used to live in a long time ago. You have good memories of it but you know there is no reason to go back there. But it was an amazing time.

VIC DICARA: Burn was the absolute pinnacle of New York hardcore! They were philosophical and sophisticated, yet tough and heavy and scary—kind of like the Cro-Mags in that sense. But their music was way more complex. One of the few bands I still enjoy listening to today, and I'm just happy I got the chance to play with those guys later on.

SELECT DISCOGRAPHY:

Self-Titled (7"/CD, Revelation, 1990)
 Malik, Van Vlack, Napack, Cage

Cleanse (CD/12" EP, Equal Vision, 2001)
 Malik, Van Vlack, Napack, Cage

Last Great Sea (7"/CD, Revelation, 2002)
 Malik, Van Vlack, DiCara, Carrero, Cage

CAVE IN

Vocals/Guitar: Stephen Brodsky
Vocals: Dave Scrod
　　　　 Jay Frechette
Guitar: Adam McGrath

Bass/Vocals: Caleb Scofield
Bass: Justin Matthes
　　　 Andy Kyte
Drums: J.R. Conners
　　　　 Ben Koller

Cave In was among the most sonically progressive nineties hardcore bands. Beginning as a metal-core group, but eventually broadening their scope with hints of Brit-Pop, space-rock, and prog-rock, Cave In constantly refreshed their sound. They realized early on that though tradition often anchors one's passion for a particular genre, the process of internalizing that format and filtering it through one's own creative lens is where the greatest intrinsic rewards occur.

Inspired by a variety of music — from the ambitious hardcore meets post-hardcore of bands like Minnesota's Threadbare to the layered rock of groups like Failure — Cave In's peppered their sound with extreme noise, speed metal, and heavy hardcore.

While their early records were memorable for their sheer power, it wasn't until the band's first full-length, *Until Your Heart Stops*, that people understood what they were attempting to achieve. A mixture of noise-laden hardcore, death metal, and space rock, *Until Your Heart Stops* (1998) is merciless in its complexity, precision, and spirit.

Jupiter (2000) pushed the band's metal-laden assault toward denser, fuzzed-out riffs and harmonious vocals. The group's sound matured, which prompted cries of "sell-out" from some. Yet while rooted in hardcore, Cave In never remained entrenched in any musical patterns.

Major labels became interested in the band after *Jupiter* and a decision had to be made— would the band remain firmly in the parameters of the hardcore scene, or would they venture into the world of ethical quagmires that major labels offered? Ultimately, Cave In chose to go with RCA Records because the label offered the opportunity to record with a larger budget, which brought about *Antenna*, an effectively crafted melodic rock meets prog rock record. They were scorned by some for signing to RCA, but as the nineties ended the ethical implications that once surrounded such a move didn't seem as important a battle to fight.

After touring on *Antenna* for over a year, Cave In noticed RCA wasn't as willing to stay committed to a long term investment in the band. Like any sort of big business enterprise, major labels want quick results. *Antenna* was met with rave reviews and the band was able to tour the U.S. and Europe, but even with Cave In's dedicated fans in support — many were leftovers from the early days, with the addition of a large following of new rock-minded folks along for the ride — the band struggled with some of RCA's limitations. In the end, Cave In parted ways with RCA and ended up on a somewhat permanent hiatus, interspersed with occasional recording sessions and small tours.

Cave In's evolution is impressive considering the expanse of its sound. They torched all expectations, proving the sound of hardcore is limitless.

ROOTS OF CAVE IN

STEPHEN BRODSKY: I wanted to experiment with heavy music like Converge was doing, and it was Adam [McGrath] who turned me onto their music. We had a class together our sophomore year of high school, and prior to that we spent time with separate crowds. But he always had his Walkman with him, and I got to hear stuff like Chokehold and Frail for the first time. I remember hearing a copy of *Halo in a Haystack* for the second time — the first time was almost a year earlier, but I couldn't get into the vocals then — and I didn't want to give the headphones back. In fact, I wanted to skip the rest of my classes to go home and write an album just like it, right there and then. I turned Adam onto Sunny Day Real Estate, and when we decided to form a band together, I thought it'd be cool to play heavy like Converge did but to also to mix in what I loved about the *Diary* album as well. That's where my faux-English accent comes from on some of those early, early recordings. Me and Jay Frechette, our first singer, loved Failure's *Magnified* album and I tried to incorporate some of their obtuse and unpredictable melodic sense into the mix, as well.

ADAM MCGRATH: I loved the angst of your typical American "townie" heavy-metal and early-nineties alternative rock. We were all at the perfect age to have that era of music make a profound impact. As many hardcore folks say, my friends and I were not the most popular kids in school. We were outcasts because we didn't pay any attention to being a jock in a very sports focused school system. We got off on being freaks and mutants. Nirvana was sort of the gateway into underground music or hardcore for me. I learned from their music, influences, and attitude that something existed entirely free from MTV — my suburban window to what I knew and viewed as music. I learned about the Melvins, The Wipers, and from there I could only dig deeper. It's funny to think that at this time the Internet was not present in our world. I did not learn how to "log on" until I was a freshman in college in 1997. So, all my learning and exposure was purely word-of-mouth, zines, and older hardcore kids in my town. I remember looking at Fugazi's *Repeater* record mesmerized by the sweaty and energetic photos, making it clear to me there was some vital and exciting music taking place somewhere to which I must seek out and absorb. I was also fortunate enough to grow up in an area known to us as the Merrimac Valley consisting of five neighboring towns all with their own local bands, style, and scenes. Many of the early shows we went to totally had the "grunge" vibe turned up to 10. Although there was one place in North Andover, Massachusetts, called the Red Barn where hardcore was the main presence. This is where I can first say I was exposed to abrasive and confrontational energy and passion of hardcore.

RAMBUNCTIOUS BEGINNINGS

STEPHEN BRODSKY: Aside from Travis Shettel in Piebald, I didn't really hear very many bands in the local hardcore scene trying to make a mix out of loud noise and melodic vocals. I think this sense of alchemy maybe gave us a sense of humor about what we did, as well. We always got a laugh out of bands who took themselves way too seriously, and I remember having band practices where we couldn't get half way through a song without someone pulling their pants down and chasing the rest of us around the room. I mean, we were still sophomores in high school when we recorded our first demo on my cassette four-track machine with the missing tape deck lid.

ADAM MCGRATH: We were naïve townies in our parents' basements writing our poor man's versions of Converge and Cable songs. We pulled it together just by sticking with it — working at it as much as we could while still being in high school and living with our parents.

J.R. CONNERS: We were just a bunch of kids wanting to play music because it was fun. We started to take it a little more seriously when we went out on our first week long tour. We got to see different places, meet some cool people, and I guess we just caught the bug.

STEPHEN BRODSKY: We were a mess, but a passionate one, nonetheless. We were always scrounging for rides to shows, then borrowing gear to play whenever we could if our own stuff was too busted or inadequate. We shifted from one basement to the next. Our parents were very supportive but always to a certain point, and we managed to surpass that point with all of them at different times. But we were young--sophomores in high school! It was a big deal when we finally had gotten driver's licenses! Then we could at least bug our folks for their vehicles instead of constantly asking our friends. The band didn't really feel fluid like a real "band" usually does until we went from being a five-piece to a four-piece, shortly after Caleb joined.

EXPERIMENTATION

STEPHEN BRODSKY: [We experimented musically] simply for identity's sake. There were a lot of bands doing what we did, so the best way for anyone to be left with an impression of us was to scramble our music a bit. It was also our way of announcing our own listening tastes...and to rip off something was always in the spirit of tribute of some kind. Our early, early songs were very...thankful.

ADAM MCGRATH: I never thought about [experimenting] in terms of confidence until I got a bit older. Because we all had such very broad and adventurous tastes in music we have had the tendency to stretch out. Most of our favorite artists in and outside of hardcore had the bravery to look outside their envelopes. The more rules you put on your creative output the more your music will ultimately suffer. It seemed natural to try and always push your own boundaries to be better than yourself. That's what all our favorite artists did.

J.R. CONNERS: I wouldn't say we intentionally challenged any notions of what we should sound like. We just did what we did, and screw anyone who didn't like it. The spirit of punk rock gave me that confidence.

STEPHEN BRODSKY: It wasn't until we became a four-piece band that attempting the music we were going to try and make felt truly inviting. Once we got over feeling secretive for having a strong affection for late-eighties/early-nineties punk-grunge-alternative-whatever, I think our songwriting shaped up a bit. We backed off on the Converge rip-off's to let a Failure rip-off or an Unwound rip-off creep in every now and then. It was both weird and friendly to hear the results of that when it happened.

ADAM MCGRATH: We always just had confidence in each other to always stretch and pull influences from all genres. So many people have different ideas of what hardcore is or what it should be. Therefore, they just put rules upon themselves because trying new sounds ideas would go against what hardcore is to them. Rules are just bullshit, really. [laughs]

"UNTIL YOUR HEART STOPS"

STEPHEN BRODSKY: I felt pretty ambitious about making heavy music at the time. Aside from the four of us sharing that same ambition with one another, it really helped me to play music with Converge for the time that I did. I learned loads from all of those guys, and I dissected all of it in their rehearsal space and later I could apply it to some of the stuff I was working on for Cave In. We made lots of demos--from scratchy guitar-plugged-direct-into-the-four-track style ones to studio recordings with different vocalists. The music felt just prepared enough for when it came time to make the album.

CALEB SCOFIELD: I was asked to try out for the band while they were writing *Until...* Talk about a trial by fire! I thought I was a competent bass player until Steve started teaching me the songs. I had to completely change my approach to playing. I had played in bands before but only as a singer. I definitely showed up to the recording without any bass gear. But at least by that point I knew how to play the songs, or most of them anyway.

ADAM MCGRATH: Our inspirations were Deadguy, Rorschach, Threadbare, Quicksand, Cable, Lincoln, Neurosis, but most of all Converge. The only things I can recall about the writing of *Until...* was that there were tons of riffs to remember, and we had kicked out our second and final singer days before we were to go into the Piebald house basement and record with Kurt. We were now a four-piece and Steve had to quickly write lyrics and be ready to sing on an entire full-length. We were excited, inspired and hungry to get out there a see at least what the U.S. had to offer. We just wanted to be a real band and play with our favorite "real" bands.

STEPHEN BRODSKY: We wrote this [record] in the basement of a house that all of Piebald was living in. The sound would travel through the heating ducts into each bedroom, so we had to be fairly reasonable with our work schedule. I remember taking mixes out to Kurt [Ballou's] old Volvo and playing them in his cassette deck. Kurt was way into drum triggers, and I had just bought my first Boss delay pedal.

J.R. CONNERS: It was a little hard on me. I was a lazy kid. But the writing and recording of that record was great, even though it was stressful for me half the time. I had a lot of trouble getting certain things down when we wrote the music. It turned into a great experience once we went into record it, though. It was a lot of fun hanging out with Kurt in his dingy basement studio. The walls were all painted red, and the drums were shoved into a corner sideways--it was great!

ATMOSPHERICS

ADAM MCGRATH: Maybe it was the day we saw Pink Floyd's *Live at Pompeii*, and we all had one of those pinnacle music moments where our minds got completely blown! We were not even getting stoned in those days! [laughs] All of a sudden this stony/atmospheric vibe naturally started to set in to our music. I can't say exactly what influence it was for us, but I think there is a good start.

J.R. CONNERS: A lot of it most likely came from trying to emulate bands like Failure and Pink Floyd. Mostly Failure, though; we were heavily into that band and they were a huge influence on Cave In.

STEPHEN BRODSKY: Back then I didn't see many bands using effects pedals. I learned quickly that they're great to have for covering up mistakes and guitar flubs. The aesthetic was nice, too. It looked cool to see a bunch of gadgetry in front of a guitar player's feet, and then to see their LED lights when the house lights went off during a performance.

CALEB SCOFIELD: I remember trying to think of different ways to have less musical downtime in between songs for our live sets. As we started to become more interested in different effects and pedals, we realized with the right combinations we could do off-the-cuff sampling and endless delays. It was exciting for us to do this live, because it broke up the routine of playing the same songs over and over. We would create these soundscapes with our pedals that were impossible to ever duplicate. It was something different every night.

LYRICS

STEPHEN BRODSKY: I like a lot of the *Until* lyrics. They were assembled very quickly, and I took much of them from college writing assignments I had completed. I had an excellent English teacher in the later part of my high school experience who helped me find great appreciation for poetry, and some of the *Until* songs began as lines pulled from my own poems that mutated into songs I could scream. But I had to assemble a bunch of lyrical stuff sort of last minute, mostly during the week of vocal tracking, because we had just parted ways with our then-vocalist. So, what you have is sort of the Kurt Cobain approach, with various lines from different pieces of writing and poetry dropped into songs. But each Cave In song has a little story that gets bent or distorted, by one or perhaps a few different visuals within the lines. Some of our earlier songs do have more a lyrically political slant to them. But this was never a full-throttle thing in our writing style. We were never a united group of vegans or straight edge kids, although things like that did apply to some of us as individuals at different points in time.

MID TO LATE-NINETIES CREATIVE FRENZY/SONGWRITING

STEPHEN BRODSKY: There was simply the collective attitude that we were all locked into the moment of sharing perceptions of what heavy music could be played like. We were all very conscious about who was doing what, and how bands were progressing and in what ways, and we'd discuss it. Like when Converge did *Unloved and Weeded Out* and their songs had gotten longer and more involved, or when Coalesce hit a songwriting peak on *Functioning on Impatience* and really stretched their format. These kinds of things spawned much material for conversation.

ADAM MCGRATH: Technical ability seems to just be the trend for the past few years--everyone trying to out-wank each other with no concept of actually writing a song that people may remember. What happened to the song? I don't care how fast you can play some jack-off scale. I don't care how many time signatures you can fit into one riff! Where is the song? Not like a pop song, but an actual point the movement of music is trying to convey. Why are Minor Threat, Black Flag, Misfits, and Bad Brains so legendary and monumental? Not 'cause they play as fast as some hair metal dude in guitar video, but because they wrote songs!

"JUPITER"

J.R. CONNERS: We simply wanted to play rock and roll. We weren't trying to make a statement or anything like that. We listened to much more than hardcore music, so it just came out naturally for us.

ADAM MCGRATH: We had tried to write more crazy metal songs of the *Until...* ilk, but it seemed the creative batteries for hardcore were dead. We had taken that style as far as the four of us could. We needed try something new and we already had the feeling that Steve wasn't feeling the screaming his face off every night. He could actually sing! Why would we have him deliberately shred his voice? So, we just tried some new ideas, new sounds, and new effects pedals. We were always confident enough in each other to always try new things and move our music forward.

CALEB SCOFIELD: By the time we started writing for *Jupiter*, there were a lot of bands doing the more metal based sound and doing it a hell of a lot better than we could. We were playing shows with bands like Dillinger Escape Plan and Botch and just being blown away. Not that it was a competition, but I just remember feeling like we couldn't hold our own against these guys. We wanted to step outside of our realm and see if we had something different to offer ourselves and the people who enjoyed our band; something that still complimented our abilities but might also help us to stand out in a different way. I think *Jupiter* was a very important step towards us figuring out just what we wanted from the music.

STEPHEN BRODSKY: We ate loads of Morning Star foods at this point. I remember Hot Pockets being the particular treat of choice. The Outpost is the studio we recorded in — it's very removed from Boston, so we didn't have much to do other than play our instruments, really. The drum room there was a big deal; every drummer wanted to play their drums in that room. I remember the owner of the studio had come in after our first night of tracking to listen back to what we had done. At that point, all of us had gone home, and when we came back the next day to begin working, everything sounded a little tampered with, and we couldn't figure out why.

CRITICISM

J.R. CONNERS: When *Jupiter* came out, we got so much shit from people because we weren't playing metal or hardcore. We heard everything from "sell-outs" to tough guys yelling out at shows that we're "gay"...pretty ridiculous.

ADAM MCGRATH: We had bottles thrown at us. We were called "faggot" over and over again. Yep, hardcore kids can be creative. We never second guessed ourselves though and we wanted nothing to do with the steak-head [portion of the] hardcore movement anyway.

STEPHEN BRODSKY: Oh yeah, sure, there were critics. But some of the more obvious reactions — like having chewing gum thrown at us on-stage or being tagged with really homophobic remarks — were in conjunction with us changing our live sets altogether. Some people were simply upset that they weren't hearing the songs they came to see us play. We didn't perform the *Until You Heart Stops* songs live for very long after the album had been released--maybe a year or so, tops. My voice couldn't take it. We'd try combining some of the newer stuff we were working on together with older material in our sets, and I hardly felt like I delivered a strong mix of the two from my end of things.

CALEB SCOFIELD: I think any negative criticism we were met with only helped fuel us to continue to do things a little differently. If some dude throws a bottle at me for not playing "Crossbearer," well, then guess what? Now we're never going to play the song again, asshole. To some degree it left a bad taste our mouths. We sort of developed this us against them attitude. It's tough when you realize fatal flaws in a culture you grew up in. We just hoped that for every person that swore us off after *Jupiter*, there were two more that swore us in.

MAJOR LABELS

STEPHEN BRODSKY: Bigger labels were looking at what we had established for ourselves as a bunch of work they didn't have to try and do themselves. But once we were in, and then had a manager who we put our trust into, we became less involved with our business transactions. This was strange for us, because we'd always worked with our friends on most levels. The social dynamic of having business relationships just got kind of weird, and basically we felt like we ended up feeling like certain people were trying to make a bigger deal out of Cave In than we thought we were. It's just the typical music business attitude to act that way, really.

CALEB SCOFIELD: Major labels are kind of like strippers. They're really good at making you think they like you. But in reality they're just all over you because they think you might have some money left deep down in your pocket somewhere. And like an asshole, you keep throwing ones at them until you're broke. Then you leave the strip club and feel kind of dirty for having ever gone. I hope I haven't offended any strippers.

"ANTENNA"

ADAM MCGRATH: By then hard-line hardcore had written us off, so it really had no influence. It was an opportunity that at the time seemed like a good thing for the band. Our background certainly gave us a good perspective of reality to keep our feet on the ground going into the dysfunctional corporate world.

J.R. CONNERS: We signed to see how far we could take it. It was foreign territory for us and we wanted to explore.

STEPHEN BRODSKY: I remember lots of video gaming [during the recording of *Antenna*], *Grand Theft Auto 3* to be exact. We set up drums in a small room at Cello Studio, and they sounded too trashy, so we then spent two weeks tracking them in the big room. I remember being about 80% into finishing guitar overdubs, and then Rich Costey got a hold of one of those Dietzal amps, which is a German amp that costs about $4,000. After that, he was gung-ho about re-doing almost everything with that amp. Also, I was using the bathroom one day, when I literally bumped into Slash as he was exiting. I was too star-struck and my bladder was pinching from needing to pee, so all I was able to mumble was, "Excuse me." And we were really hoping to get him to play the guitar solo on "Penny Racer."

WINDING DOWN

STEPHEN BRODSKY: We were burned out. There was so much time that we had spent around one another in such a short growth spurt, that it felt almost natural to sort of gravitate away from the band when we were finally able to do that. And we were a little jaded by the experiences we had working in the major label world, of which we didn't cut ourselves off from overnight. It took months, really, which was draining. But it's nice to have come out of it all, feeling on top, with our dignity still intact, and most importantly, as friends.

LOOKING BACK

ADAM MCGRATH: I feel like all of our records have been [an artistic] search! Our fans have been able to listen to all the different planets in our collaborative creative mind's galaxy.

STEPHEN BRODSKY: Being a fan of music in all shapes and forms prior to ever going to a hardcore show was a good perspective for me to have. I knew of many people who kept hardcore so precious to them that when it failed to meet their expectations on a musical or ethical level they were crushed by it.

J.R. CONNERS: I learned to be honest to yourself and the people around you, and never back down from your beliefs. Don't let anyone fuck with you.

CALEB SCOFIELD: Cave In was one of the biggest learning experiences of my life. There were some questionable moments, but all-in-all I remain very proud of everything we have accomplished as a band. I try and imagine what my life would be like had I not made that trip down to Methuen to try and become a member of one of my favorite hardcore bands, but I just reach a wall. A big fucking sonic death wall!

SELECT DISCOGRAPHY:

Beyond Hypothermia (CD, Hydrahead, 1997)
    Brodsky, McGrath, Conners, Frechette, Kyte, Matthes, Scrod

Until Your Heart Stops (CD/LP, Hydrahead, 1998)
    Brodsky, McGrath, Scofield, Conners

Creative Eclipses (MCD, Hydrahead, 1999)
    Brodsky, McGrath, Scofield, Conners

Jupiter (CD/LP, Hydrahead, 2000)
    Brodsky, McGrath, Scofield, Conners

Tides of Tomorrow (CD, Hydrahead, 2002)
    Brodsky, McGrath, Scofield, Conners

Antenna (CD, RCA, 2003)
    Brodsky, McGrath, Scofield, Conners

Perfect Pitch Black (CD, Hydrahead, 2005)
    Brodsky, McGrath, Scofield, Conners

COALESCE

Vocals: Sean Ingram
Bass: Stacy Hilt
      Nathan Ellis

Guitars: Jes Steineger
        Cory White
Drums: James DeWees
       Nathan "Jr." Richardson
       Jim Redd

Coalesce made their mark on the mid-nineties hardcore scene with instrumental virtuosity and guttural vocals that delivered abundantly cynical and spiteful lyrics. Along with acts such as Deadguy and Converge, this Kansas City-based four-piece was as influenced by experimental groups such as Today is the Day and Neurosis as they were by hardcore pioneers. While some purists disdain bands like Coalesce for deviating too far from traditional hardcore, these Midwesterners took pride in stretching their sound as far as possible.

Formed in 1994, Coalesce started after the break-up of two groups, Bind and Restrain, both of which struggled to find their own niche in the Midwest hardcore scene. When ex-Restrain vocalist Sean Ingram hooked up with Bind and Amara guitarist Jes Steineger, bassist Stacy Hilt, and drummer Jim Redd, the new foursome harnessed the energy of a traditional hardcore band with the addition of chaotic metal/noise influenced guitars and razor-sharp, off-beat time signatures.

Their debut seven-inch released on Chapter Records featured the somewhat controversial "Harvest of Maturity," a song some interpreted as Ingram cynically looking back at his time being straight edge. The seven-inch captured the attention of both hardcore kids and heavy music aficionados, and after a flurry of small tours, Earache Records — a long established and highly influential label in hardcore, metal, and underground music — took note. Coalesce's powerful Earache debut, *002*, along with their follow-up split EP with metal/grind giant Napalm Death, increased the band's notoriety, as did their tours with Bloodlet and 108.

In the midst of Coalesce's early success, the group also encountered its share of troubles. Ingram, Steineger, and new bassist Nathan Ellis didn't always see eye-to-eye on artistic direction. Steineger found himself immersed in Krishna consciousness, and the religion became his priority for a time. Ingram, on the other hand, fueled a substantial amount of rumors as some felt his lyrics were veiled attacks on different factions in hardcore. Consequently, Coalesce found themselves on the ropes numerous times, and just when the group seemed ready to take on the world they would disappear... and reappear... and then vanish once again.

In 1996, Coalesce reassembled with multi-talented drummer James DeWees (also of Reggie and the Full Effect) and created what many feel is their most complex hardcore/noise epic — *Give Them Rope* (Edison Records). While many hardcore bands of this era were espousing political musings, Coalesce plumbed the inner depths of their tenuous personal and musical experience and transferred it into their own wicked plate of remorseless and more skeptical social commentary and dynamic songwriting.

As Coalesce weathered their share of personal, musical, and emotional challenges, they continued to put out quality records that were restless in nature. *Functioning on Impatience* (Second Nature), *012: Revolution in Just Listening* (Relapse), and even a reworking of Led Zeppelin classics known as *There is Nothing New Under the Sun* (Hydrahead), brought acclaim, which started to reach further into the metal and extreme noise scenes. But as their audience widened, so did the hardcore scene's critical eye. Still, the band never complied with notions that applied to most hardcore bands; instead, they undermined those expectations, even if this very attitude played a role in the band's continual problems.

Eventually all the bursts and breaks took their toll on the band, leading to a temporary halt in 1999. They reappeared briefly a couple of times in the years following but were never able to return to their earlier levels of activity. In the summer of 2007, however, the members reunited to go on a brief tour and announced the writing and recording of an album to be released in 2009.

Coalesce won many over with their ambition, talent, and ability to push hardcore's sometimes staid musical tendencies into new and challenging directions.

ORIGINS OF THE BAND

SEAN INGRAM: Coalesce got together in 1994 as the brain-child of Jes Steineger, Jim Redd, and Stacy Hilt. They were more into experimental type of music, but when they asked me to sing, and they realized I was a screamer, we went a more hardcore direction. They still used the same ideas they were working with, but they applied them to fit my style. We first started to play for the reasons other bands start, I guess; we were young, full of energy, [so] it was natural to want to start a hardcore band.

JES STEINEGER: By spring 1993 I made contact with the local straight edge clique in the far suburbs [of Kansas City]. I was absorbed into the community via everyone's "younger brothers" (i.e., my first band was constituted of the scrubs who weren't able to make the cut in the band that would come to be known as Restrain). After nearly a year in that scene of being denied any corporate advancement into the big guys' band, as well as my favoring the Krishnas over the vegans, I bailed. Stacy Hilt, whom I was in high school with, joined my first band Bind right as it was morphing into Amara, a pathetic attempt at a Krishna-core band that lasted about two months as the perpetual basement-show opener for Restrain. He came with me as we more or less separated ourselves from the suburban vegans. After numerous attempts to find a drummer for a new project, and my increasing exhaustion with trying to get a band off the ground, Stacy told me about a "kid he just met at a show." He told me he had set up the following Saturday morning with this new guy to rock out in his — the new guy's — basement. That Saturday morning, five minutes before I left my home, Stacy called and told me he couldn't make it: "Sorry, dude. Don't sweat it, though. This guy's cool and he knows you're coming." And that's how I met Jim Redd; cold turkey. After we brought in and set up my equipment, it was on. I was just standing there in front of Jim, as he warmed up on beats I had never even heard a live drummer play. I was so scared and just kept thinking to myself, "Man, now's the time to deliver if you're going to impress and snag this guy." I let go and out came the off-time chorus riff to the song that would become "Harvest of Maturity." Jim looked back at me for a bit while I kept working it out. "How are you counting that?" His ability to a feel out a rhythm to something like that solidified the bond. That was the birth of Coalesce; that one riff contained so much of what we would continue to flesh out over the years. Jim's critical and demanding demeanor influenced my personality deeply and set the tone for how I would construct Coalesce songs clear until the end. By the time we had three or four songs and spent significant weekends going to shows to find a singer, a leak to the old straight edge scene took place. The old bassist of Restrain had spoken with Stacy and was curious to hear what the new project sounded like. Once he heard it, the word spread and we were able to make contact with Sean, who had at some point after his graduation moved to Syracuse. He came back to Kansas City around Easter 1994 and we gave him a demo of the songs. When Jim and I heard what he had done to what would become "Harvest of Maturity," we nearly pooped our pants! [laughs] "Again, again, again, again…!" We were sold. Sean was sold. Sean definitely codified the hardcore element of the sound that I wanted to preserve — to a large extent, at the expense of where I think Jim wanted to go creatively. He moved back that summer and by the fall we were in the studio recording our first seven-inch for Chapter.

EARLY SHOWS

JES STEINEGER: Between fall of 1994 and the record-release party sometime between January and March of 1995, our live show came into its own. I remember vividly one night after a show in Wichita, wandering into the living room of the house we were staying to find everyone frantically trying to hook up a video of the show. Once it came up, the first scene was my face, screaming at the top of my lungs with my eyes clinched tight, as I sprang backward across the stage right into Sean. I'll never forget the hush that fell on the room and then Sean's voice: "Dude. I am so proud to be in a band with Jes." In those days, Sean and I were tight — real tight — and the fact that I was so proud to be in a band with Sean contributed to the familial bond I had always imagined in "my band." All of us were teenagers; tasting what is was like to be above the law if only for a half-hour every month or two. Even our rehearsals became more and more intense — as long as they didn't follow band meetings at the local Indian all-you-can-eat buffet. By the record release party in 1995 I had totally abandoned any concern for physicality during a show; riffs became blurred, the most banal noises were embraced, and I became exhilarated at seeing my own blood. Years later, I would discover a profound, even prophetic, statement of what I considered the "Coalesce event" to be in Nietzsche's *Birth of Tragedy*. To this day, that text expresses much of my analysis of Coalesce in particular and of the hardcore scene in some general respects: fascination of the "folk" music of disillusioned latter-20th century bourgeois youth on a cultic level, loss of self in the violent upheaval of cultural mores, and exhilaration of one's own disintegration into the whole, an attempted communal identity in backlash to the idolized individuality of modernity — succinctly put, the rite of the hardcore show.

SEAN INGRAM: One of my favorite memories was our first trip to New York. The guys at Earache showed us around the city. We literally showed up in New York in a van, no shirts on, and straw hats on. We were total bumpkins comparatively. It was when everything was totally new... new smells, tastes, sounds, people. After that, it was old hat and not as exciting. We broke up many, many times, and it usually revolved around religion, or what Jes was working on in his life, or someone not liking me. Big surprise.

UNIQUE SOUND

JES STEINEGER: It seems feasible that for some of us embedded in the sub-cultural particularities of the Western underground hardcore scene, our sound was different enough. Enough so that when I first heard the Deadguy E.P. I thought, "Damn, those pesky Rorschach people decided to build on something that we are trying to build on." In other words, at some sub-psychological level I felt we were doing something different or I wouldn't have felt defensive or protective of what we were developing. Yet, I refused to ever let that be something primary or conscious. What was primary was the event itself, whether it was in the studio, at practice, or at a show: I lived for Coalesce to take me beyond the discursive, to a realm that for all intents and purposes the Krishnas had nurtured within me. And the fact that it did it so well provides me the historical and autobiographical evidence for its being just as powerful as Krishna consciousness, Nietzschean Dionysianism, Tantric left-handed-ness, or some offshoot-sectarian Christian theology in bringing forth that which my soul was seeking beyond the rational and mundane.

SEAN INGRAM: I usually assume it was because we didn't come from a hardcore scene. We played with indie and emo bands — that was who we were friends with. We were into more that than whatever was big at the time. Tool was an influence; Rage Against the Machine was an influence, and Metallica, of course, Jes's old stand-by for new ideas and direction. We took those influences and put them in the Coalesce blender and whatever came out we went with.

NATHAN ELLIS: The unique sound was all Jes. In the early days he played all the Coalesce songs with one finger. I've never seen anyone do that, but it made the Coalesce sound that much different. His ideas and songwriting process were what made the band stand out. He would be influenced by something Metallica wrote five years prior and play me something that he thought was a rip off of a certain riff, and I couldn't even tell what the hell he was talking about. I've never played with anyone else who played music that way, but in those years of playing and writing with him, he really screwed me up. I can't play music like I used to. It's like I took the red pill. [laughs] The "brutal" side of things came from Sean's voice and James' drums — Sean, for obvious reasons, and James because he played drums like a guitar player. He was not concerned in the slightest with his drums being in tune, or having fresh heads. He just hit everything as hard as he could and focused on the dynamic of the riff instead. The sound changed a bit when I got involved. More of a groove came out, and I don't know why. Maybe because that's where Jes was going and I saw what he was doing and contributed more of the same on top of it. The only other influence I can remember ever being prevalent was the desire to do something different. Maybe throw in a wah pedal, maybe play a distorted bluegrass riff, or maybe start a song with just vocals.

JES STEINEGER: "Experimentation" and "technicality" doesn't quite fit the vibe I remember. It all had a peculiar form of intentionality; we would put together what gave itself to be put together. When we were done with a song, a record, or even a cover, everything just fit. By no means did I ever consider it experimental or technical. Personally, I rejoiced when a band that considered technicality to be central witnessed a Coalesce show for the first time; their utter shock that we sounded like a disharmonious car without a muffler was pure delight (I remember this happening in particular the first time we opened for Converge, Disembodied, and Embodiment). I wanted so badly to emphasize that care of any traditional sort was something I totally lacked. That it wasn't about the rehashed tone of distortion that no one has improved upon since James Hetfield. That it wasn't about a presentation of some kind of entertainment. That a show's purpose wasn't about recapitulating in a perfect representational manner what was captured on a record. No. For me to try and relay what I consider "it" to have been "all about" would require that I go on negating every positive criterion one might muster. It was, if anything, the pursuit of the trace left by that which eludes us. And ultimately, Coalesce could only go so far in contributing to that pursuit.

SEAN INGRAM: Jes is a monster for progression. He would always want to reinvent Coalesce each record and take it further. I specifically remember him saying, "We need to give this bitch a haircut and buy her a new dress" on several occasions referring to Coalesce as a whole. In that respect, Jes was amazing to work with. The dude was never happy with not outdoing himself and taking things further.

VOCAL TONES

SEAN INGRAM: It always bums me out when people call it my "growl." I learned to use my diaphragm and control my vocal chords instead of shredding them and squeaking out. I never think of it as a growl, because I'm pushing as much air if not more than when we first started. I don't know if it's lost in the recordings or not. But it wasn't a conscious change. Whatever I sounded like, that's what we did; I did consciously try to strengthen my vocal chords because touring was hard on them, but I didn't change the tone to fit anything. I always say my balls dropped after the first seven-inch.

LYRICS/MOTIVATIONS

SEAN INGRAM: The two songs that meant the most to me were "A Safe Place," which was about my wife, and "Grain of Salt," which was about my relationship with my father. I love those songs mainly because they wrote themselves with no edits or changes. Luckily I've been able to patch everything with my father; I'm having a great time with him in his later years. I never thought I would; I've always hated him, but I had to let that hatred go, and it's been worth it. I just always wanted to write something I was feeling passionate about, something that bothered me, something that threatened me, whatever I felt was real. I always hated to read lyrics that were just pretty words with no meaning other than to sound pretty, or disturbed, or "evil," the four letter word when it came to Coalesce.

JES STEINEGER: Sean was going to write what he was going to write, I was going to play what I was going to play, and we were going to sound how we would sound. Coalesce came into being simultaneously with Sean's disillusionment with the vegan straight edge scene that he had been so involved with. Hence, I always considered his position on the straight edge thing as his deal which he was free to work out as he saw fit. Certainly much of what he wrote about had nothing to even do with petty ideological squabbles, but rather, the recapitulation of our immediacy. I knew how to find myself in much of what he said; but lyrics were always secondary for me — the vocal icing on the cake of the chaos. I, too, was perpetually trying to work out some issue or other of my own. Regardless, for me to ask myself whether or not we as a unified band unit had a different take on the scene, life, or music than others in the hardcore scene is paradoxical. I never cared. Once Coalesce had lift off, it was the sole dimension of the event that mattered and nothing else. It was my own Frankenstein. However, the fact that it always had a beginning and an end which gave way to the rest of my life provided the condition for my ongoing questioning of the ultimacy and totality constituting the horizon of that event. In other words, Coalesce could never become the totality of life, and hence, there was always a space for the meta-position of a theological or metaphysical critique. And I felt the pangs of that critique throughout the lifespan of Coalesce, which I take to be something that really drove the other guys nuts. Because Coalesce was the pinnacle of self-absorption for me, though, despite its communal constitution and perhaps even at the expense of any concern for a "fan-base," it was essentially at odds with any spiritual message I could try to infuse it with. I had an ambiguous vision of what it was and what it was supposed to be, and that, for better or worse, never included how other people appropriated it.

SEAN INGRAM: My opinion on lyrics is that if you don't feel strongly about it, don't write it. I've never supported political bands that use their bands to do nothing more than recite P.E.T.A. pamphlets or rewrite straight edge songs for the 100th time. I see more now how music can be extremely powerful as a political tool, but when you are just slapping a band together to push some tired politic in hardcore, isn't that the same thing people accuse Christian hardcore bands of? If a band is serious, they should realize that the lyrics and thought put into them are just as important as how off-time the riff is or how fast they can play it. I like sarcastic commentary as much as the next guy, but joke lyrics take away from a powerful song.

"GIVE THEM ROPE"/DEFYING EXPECTATIONS

SEAN INGRAM: That period was all about the angst tied up in Jes. He was in the Krishna temple, left, and wanted to do it all. It was the most amazing time. From *Give Them Rope* to *Functioning on Impatience* is when I have the best memories. When Jes and I got along is when we made the records I like the best. We seriously didn't try to write anything to fit into any scene. We actually considered it a compliment when people didn't know what to call us. That was the highest compliment you could give us.

CONTROVERSY

SEAN INGRAM: I personally think it had a lot to do with being from Kansas City where there was no hardcore scene. We hung out with punks and emo kids. A lot of my attitude came from living in Syracuse for a bit, too. Maybe some guilt for not caring about straight edge and veganism anymore, and then anger at myself for how I treated people when I was vegan and straight edge and then seeing it in others. We never were a part of a scene. When we hung out, we didn't go to shows and then see the other hardcore kids at the pizza shop. We drove 40 minutes to each other's houses and practiced, and then we played shows with indie bands to no one. There wasn't that scene to rub off on us; we were still just our own people. We didn't dress the style, we didn't have all the tattoos, we didn't talk the talk; we just played what we wanted to hear.

JES STEINEGER: There was a disconnect sometimes between some of the themes that Sean chose to develop lyrically and what I was doing in Coalesce. For instance, when you ask about "controversies" or the strange animosity that Coalesce received from a certain contingent in the hardcore scene because of their appropriation of Sean's lyrics, such things couldn't have been further from my life-world. I don't remember ever being "anti" anything — veganism, straight edge, Vaisnavism, whatever — so as to say, "Hey Sean, write a song against these people" (nor did Sean ever think that way, in my estimation); I simply came to lack any concern for those cliques. I thought they were all adhering to failed attempts at ultimate concern, not just for me, but objectively. If any of the backlash from some in the hardcore scene was legitimated by lyrics that Sean was writing, it simply adds evidence to my claim that the discursive element of Coalesce was never primary for me. For instance, I think the most incredible thing Coalesce ever recorded was the enhancement to *Simulcast* on the re-recording of *002*. This is one of the first recordings that Nathan contributed to, it represents a time when Ed Rose was really coming into his own in developing the texture of our recorded sound, and it is that take in particular that captures the ideal non-discursivity of the ensuing Functioning years. There are no words, mind you, in Sean's contribution to that take — no logos; just the bare depth of the soul's power in the human voice. It is a single live take giving expression to the Coalesce I had envisioned. All this to say: petty controversies concerning counter-culture ideologies that surrounded the scene's appropriation of Sean's lyrics were never a concern of the Coalesce I participated in, no matter how much one argues that Sean's lyrics necessitated such a concern.

STOPS AND STARTS

SEAN INGRAM: Jes was really searching for God, and that's such a huge life issue. Compared to that, the band just wasn't important to him. It wasn't until later that we just decided to go for it and take out another guitarist. We understood Jes didn't want to be in it, but he had to understand that we had an investment too and wanted to finish what we started, even if it was just one tour, so all the fans who missed us could see us for once and we could put some closure on this monster. It was unfair for one person to decide that for us, so we took a chance and went for it. Cory was an amazing guitarist. I wish we could have had more time to write more with him.

NATHAN ELLIS: During the first Coalesce break up, after the first tour with Bloodlet, I was in a short-lived band with Sean called Anasazi. We were a band for a week and half, wrote three songs, and played them all at the Kansas City Hardcore Festival in 1996. We are lucky nobody saw it. It was bad. So bad, in fact, I am pretty sure it was the event that got Sean to call Jes again. After they re-kindled the flame and started playing again on a regular basis I jumped in the van as a roadie and toured the country with them. It was a great experience for me — a high school kid touring with one of my favorite bands. In the summer of 1997 Stacy got tired of music. I don't know what happened, but as soon as he decided he wanted out, I got to jump in. Previously I had never played bass before. I was a guitar player. But when I was asked to give it a shot I, without hesitation, got my tuition money back from community college and bought bass equipment. A week later we re-recorded *002*, and shortly after that we did the Get Up Kids split, the Bush League compilation song, and other releases just started snowballing. Pretty quickly we started writing *Functioning on Impatience*. That was the first time that I started bringing ideas to the table, and sure enough, Jes thought they were good. So we wrote that record as fast as we could and had a great time doing it.

EMOTIONAL FUEL

SEAN INGRAM: I think my work ethic and Jes' flakiness were always at odds. There were times I had to convince him to be in the band. But then again I've never worked with anyone sense that just made me blast out 10 songs from the heart before. Those were really new times, learning to be in a band relationship.

JES STEINEGER: Although I have never considered my relationship with Sean to have been as intense as to call it "volatile," I will say that it continued some of the complexities that manifested in his relationship with Jim Redd. Jim had the most incredibly critical attitude I had ever met in a person. Despite all of its flaws, it pushed me to bring forth things that I never could have otherwise. In some less abrasive form, I continued the friction that existed between Sean and Jim in the first years by taking on the role of Jim's hyper-criticism. For Sean, though, I think such criticism was always damaging somehow. If he invested himself in an idea, in something that he wanted to see manifest in Coalesce and Jim or I criticized it, or worse, rejected it, such criticism or rejection always felt like a harsh blow to Sean. I feel like something in Sean's disposition was always affected in this sort of cut-throat, sometimes sarcastic, atmosphere and perhaps he became a bit hardened in these exchanges, rather than "pushed forward." And it was this sort of complexity that taught me a lot about how communal decisions are made; no matter how wonderful one thought his riff, his drum beat, his bass line, his packaging idea, or his lyric, such things were always fit for the chopping block if someone else in the band couldn't find something in it. And that's tough, man. If you really like something and want to nurture its maturation, it is so difficult to set it aside for the "common good," especially when the commonwealth is defined by a harsh critical attitude. There was much in my attitude that contributed to the sporadic friction between Sean and I, and if I could go back, I'd try to find a way to be less abrasive in my criticism. There were those times, however, when we would have to high-tail-it out of town when the adherents to some boob-like ideology were looking to beat us up for our ostensible stance against it — that, obviously, would bring such controversies into my world quite rapidly. Today I am more content to see an anti-scene-politics banner in Coalesce than I was then, even to the point of wishing I could have absorbed some of the crap that Sean took from those imbeciles. Their platforms were/are ridiculous and juvenile, and their music was/ is hollow at best. There is so much more that could be said so as to help inform the dynamic between Sean and I, but in the end, my only hope is that he (as well as all the other participants in Coalesce) recognizes in my decisions and pursuits the better, even if self-motivated and naïve, elements of those decisions' intentionality. They were never meant to "replace" him (them) or entail a rejection of his (their) person, even if they necessarily entailed a significant transformation in the nature of our relationship. And today I feel like our relationships, having been brought together again with the intention of giving closure to what I initially never felt was a necessity for Coalesce but which was seemingly demanded, are expressive of that.

NATHAN ELLIS: I was the young kid who tended to keep things pretty light. I had rent money to collect, but no wife to answer to. I know that Sean was thrown into the "dad" role in the band and he played the part. He took care of all the responsibilities of booking, dealing with contracts and record labels, and buying vans. There was tension, but it was all the frustrations of being in a band and crammed into a van together that brought out that tension. There were no fist-fights or overdoses or missing band member dramas, but there were plenty of uncomfortable silences on long drives. There were accusations of who needed the band more and who didn't care about the band or its members. But, in retrospect, there were some awesome times, and valuable lessons learned. Like, never trust anyone from the East Coast.

BUMPY ROADS

SEAN INGRAM: I think it was the time we did the Boy Sets Fire split and Zeppelin that shit was going downhill fast. I had to find Jes somewhere in the U.S., get him back home and make him fulfill his obligations to the record labels we agreed to record for. By the time 012 came around, we weren't even a band, we just made the record to help Relapse recoup what they could from our advance they gave us, and salvage what we could of

our band. I'm happy with the record now, but it was one of those records that you take the last take, and don't listen to again until it comes out.

JES STEINEGER: I can't give any causal explanations for "why Coalesce broke up when it did." I claim Hume when it comes to such requests. Life is complex and multifaceted and so Coalesce was complex, dysfunctional, and multifaceted. Originally, I wanted to live in a Krishna temple, the first of many failed religious pursuits to come. Jim never really loved hardcore, wanted to go to school, and was at odds with Sean pretty much the entire time he was in the band. Some of the stuff he did to Sean in the end was pretty unforgivable. Sean felt the pressures of an oncoming marriage and its complexities in terms of time, as well as some animosity for having more or less bankrolled the '95 tour with his mom, despite the lack of loot. Stacy and I were stuck in the middle of the Sean and Jim divide, and in the end, chose a side we regretted. We were all scared to commit to Earache for the length of time they wanted us to sign. And I, at least, couldn't imagine sustaining myself over any lengthy period of time with the physical demands of the Coalesce live show. The 1996 hiatus worked as a kind of germination period for Coalesce within the hardcore scene: in some unexpected way, a few more people came around. My failure at the Krishna thing, disillusionment with a brief and failed marriage, desire for the antinomianism of the Coalesce show, and heightened sexual appetite all led to my desire for the continuation of Coalesce. Those are at least some of the elements at play in any explanation for why I wanted to keep doing Coalesce after the '96 hiatus. I guess it's fair to consider the post-96 Coalesce to be its "second phase." DeWees' arrival made Coalesce a much more free event; less rigid than the years with Redd. James knew what Coalesce was doing from a musical standpoint since he was majoring in music theory and, despite his essential goofiness and playful heart, such knowledge informed his drumming that made Coalesce what it was. I really wish I could have played with James during those final shows in 2005. For me at least, despite James' lack of pessimism and light-heartedness, strong disillusionment, and bleak nihilism founded *Give Them Rope*. Indeed, nihilism is the absence of aesthetic content — it "is" ugly, the lack of beauty and being. I don't think any amount of re-mixing or re-mastering could rid that record of its muddy and dark underbelly. Since I can't remember how to play 80% of that record, it allows me access to aspects of the recording that I never planned on accessing. I consider it an overt and disturbing Dionysian incarnation wrought with a truck-load of sad reminiscence.

NATHAN ELLIS: Coalesce ended simply due to life taking its toll. Sean got married and kids started happening. Jes wanted to give school and studies a go, and James had other music ventures so he didn't care too much initially about the demise of the band. I was the one who was young and ready for more touring and more record writing. But at the same time I could see that at that time it was better to leave it alone. Sleeping dogs, you know? It was time for a break. I didn't really realize how long the break would be, or if it would be permanent so I started up a "side-project" (The Casket Lottery) that turned full time as soon as I figured out that Coalesce was really in no hurry to come back.

LOOKING BACK

SEAN INGRAM: I think I should have stood up to Jes more and not let him fall into so many crazy tangents. I was always so scared to lose Coalesce. I wish I would have not been so competitive with our contemporaries. I was a dick to a lot of people, and that was uncalled for. I am nobody, and Coalesce is just some band; it's nothing to be rude to someone over. The thing I think I'm most proud of is when some guy came up to me at a show and handed me a hand written lyric of mine. I couldn't read what it was, but the dude apparently had issues and had this lyric in his wallet and snuck into the show; he walked straight up to me, thanked me for him not feeling alone, had me sign it, then just left. I only wish I would have been more spiritually mature to do something more.

JES STEINEGER: I'm proud of the way in which Coalesce contributed to my understanding of the world. Perhaps "proud" isn't even the correct caricature of such a comportment, but it is close enough. There's a conflict in my appraisal, though, and perhaps it's this conflict that originally compelled me to quit in '99. Coalesce helped me make sense of the world by instantiating something concrete with which I could think about my life. Yet, what gives itself in my reflections on Coalesce's music (in particular, the concrete expression of the various periods of my life in that era as pollutions of the deeper titanic essence) are quite regrettable experiences that unavoidably, and certainly unfortunately, provided the condition for Coalesce's very possibility. And it is these experiences that I wish I could change. Hence, again paradoxically, the things I'm most proud of in Coalesce are inextricably tied to conditions that I would do anything to change. But then again, what would life be if we could change the mistakes of the past?

SELECT DISCOGRAPHY:

A Safe Place (7", Chapter, 1994)
   Ingram, Steineger, Hilt, Redd

002 (CD, Earache, 1995)
   Ingram, Steineger, Hilt, Redd

Napalm Death Split (MCD, Earache, 1995)
   Ingram, Steineger, Hilt, Redd

Give Them Rope (CD/LP, Edison, 1996)
   Ingram, Steineger, Hilt, DeWees

Functioning on Impatience (CD/LP, Second Nature, 1998)
   Ingram, Steineger, Ellis, DeWees

012: Revolution in Just Listening (CD, Relapse, 1999)
   Ingram, Steineger, Ellis, DeWees

There is Nothing New Under the Sun (CD, Hydrahead, 1999)
   Ingram, Steineger, Ellis, DeWees

Ox (CD, Relapse, 2009)
   Ingram, Steineger, Ellis, Richardson

FIGHT: THE NINETIES HARDCORE REVOLUTION IN ETHICS, POLITICS, AND SOU

DAMNATION A.D.

Vocals: Mike McTernan
Bass: Alex Merchlinsky
Guitars: Ken Olden
        Hillel Halloway

Drums: Dave Ward
       Dave Bryson
       Colin Keroz

Washington D.C.'s Damnation A.D. carried on hardcore's longstanding tradition of probing the darker side. Like Integrity, they played hardcore that was influenced as much by the somber outlook of British post-punk bands like The Cure and Joy Division as much as it was by metal, noise, and hardcore itself. With a combination of down-tuned, sludgy metal riffs, depression-laced lyrics, and experimentation, their records were unique sonically and also stood in contrast to much of the politically motivated hardcore of the nineties. While the members were willing to discuss political or scene related issues one-on-one, they chose to use their music to express their emotions. Their songs were unflinchingly heavy and their lyrics were thematic and philosophical, which allowed a variety of fans to relate to their sound.

Damnation A.D. began as a studio project for former Worlds Collide guitarist Ken Olden and roadie Mike McTernan. Both were straight edge, longtime hardcore fans, and had known each other for years. Worlds Collide had toured and developed a following with their blend of hardcore, metal, and rock, but disagreements about their musical direction brought the band to a close. Meanwhile, Olden and McTernan talked about starting a hardcore band that was heavy and experimental while also containing a straight edge message. Many straight edge bands had traditionally played a more traditional fast hardcore sound, and though they liked that approach, they felt that hardcore and straight edge needed something new. Olden soon put together some demos and played all the instruments while he and McTernan co-wrote lyrics. However, as they were attempting to assemble a full band, they found it difficult to find the right mix of members who were both straight edge and capable of playing the technically challenging songs they were writing. In turn, the band became more about exorcizing personal demons and venting about life's frustrations as opposed to being solely about straight edge. Soon the group expanded their lineup to include ex-Worlds Collide vet guitarist Hillel Halloway, as well as D.C. area musicians Alex Merchlinsky on bass and Dave Ward on drums.

After tinkering with their sound, they impressed many with their 1995 Jade Tree Records full-length, *No More Dreams of Happy Endings*. Lyrically, the album delves into emotional subject matter as many of the songs deal with recognizing and grappling with the darker side of life. Songs like "The Hanged Man" and "No More Dreams" became anthems for many of their fans who were attracted to the band's willingness to explore depression and personal frustration. Musically, the album conjures up a stark atmosphere that mixes thick metal-core riffs, pissed-off screams, disturbing sound samples, and delicate instrumental touches that allow for a contrast in mood.

Soon they followed up with an E.P., *Misericordia*, which touched on the same feelings but was not quite as progressive, though songs like "Addiction" became popular staples at their shows. Drummer Dave Bryson replaced Ward after the release of the E.P, and the band also parted ways with Jade Tree and signed with Revelation Records for the 1998 release of *Kingdom of Lost Souls*. This record was an ambitious blend of their now patented dark and experimental hardcore sound with even more technical song structures and diverse songwriting influences. After the release of the album, Bryson quit the band. This loss brought the band to standstill as they struggled to find a replacement. They tried to get the band going a few times, but Olden became busier with other musical projects like Better Than a Thousand and his music production work, while the other members became more committed to other aspects of their lives. They re-grouped after nearly a decade for a couple of reunion shows and in 2007 they returned with a highly anticipated full-length, *In This Life or the Next*, on Victory Records.

While it's obvious that Olden and McTernan's longtime friendship has helped steer Damnation A.D.'s creative process, their desire to explore their innermost feelings remains of the utmost importance in their friendship and their musical journey. Along with bands like Unbroken, Coalesce, Converge, and Disembodied, Damnation A.D. helped push musical and lyrical boundaries in nineties hardcore in uncharted directions.

ORIGINS

MIKE MCTERNAN: Ken originally came up with the idea [for Damnation A.D.] while he was still in Worlds Collide. He had always wanted to play really heavy stuff, but Worlds Collide was going in more of a grunge-rock direction. Some of our original riffs were ones that were too heavy for Worlds Collide.

KEN OLDEN: Mike was one of my best friends. We were both straight edge and had a lot in common. It looked like Worlds Collide was going to end, and I've always been the type of person who wants to continue doing music no matter what, so I started to ask myself what the next sound I wanted to do would be like. And I knew I wanted Mike to be involved with it. The thing that was so cool about Mike was that he was so dedicated to hardcore and if anyone deserved to be in a band and be able to sing he sure did. He didn't necessarily have aspirations to be in a band and he didn't feel like he was naturally comfortable with a mic in his hand... he was kind of reluctant. But it was cool because he was really down to earth and humble about it. I've always had a goal of doing music with friends so it wasn't hard to get Damnation going with Mike on board, as well as Hillel and Alex from Worlds Collide, too. I'd been hanging out with these guys for years, so it made it a really comfortable situation.

MIKE MCTERNAN: Ken recorded the music for the first four or five songs that we had by himself. He was playing so much with Worlds Collide that there was not time for anything else. After their summer tour in 1993, they were all headed in such different directions that they decided to do their own things. So along with Hillel and Alex, we really got Damnation off the ground. Ken even played drums for our first shows. But after a while he realized that you can't play many leads from behind the drum set, so we picked up Dave on drums.

INSPIRATIONS

KEN OLDEN: I guess I've always come from a heavy perspective in terms of sound, whether it was the roots of Worlds Collide or what we ended up doing with Damnation. It's funny, though, because although today many consider hardcore to be this extremely "metal" style, when we were doing Worlds Collide we would get flak for sounding too metal. People would say things  to us like, "Hey, Worlds Collide — Metallica is playing across the street!" [laughs] I just really wanted to create a new sound. Worlds Collide was one of the early metallic sounding hardcore bands in the early-nineties when things were still pretty old-school sounding. With Damnation I realized that if I just tuned my guitar down then we would automatically be heavier than every other band out there. It's funny how changing the tone of your guitar brings a totally different perspective across.

SOUND

MIKE MCTERNAN: The feeling I got from Ken when I first met him was that he loved the message in hardcore, but the music was not heavy enough.

KEN OLDEN: I was into a lot of heavy stuff, but I also just wanted to do something that was totally new and innovative. And I wanted it to be dark... really dark. Part of why I did this was because it fit well with Mike's voice. He wasn't going to be singing a melody; he was going to be screaming his lungs out, so the music had to match the intensity of his voice. On the music end I was definitely the "band Nazi" in terms of deciding what direction we were headed. [laughs] I wanted to be entertaining to listen to, but I also wanted to, as musicians, be entertained. If you're a tennis player you want to play against someone at your level. Whether or not you win or lose you're going to enjoy the fact that your opponent made you work. On stage, I wanted to be breaking a sweat! [laughs] I wanted to play songs that were challenging on guitar and writing parts that had some musical depth to them. The goal of Damnation was to have a lot of fun but to also do something we thought was original and really musical. We definitely got a bit self-indulgent in writing long intros and five or six minute long songs. We had samples going and brought lights with us to try and capture some kind of mood on stage. We were also known to be a band that came in with a lot of equipment and a lot of volume. [laughs] We just tried to do things musicians would also appreciate, as well. Plus, I felt like we could have lyrics that kids could relate to, because everybody has their down days. I remember when I would listen to the Damnation albums when I was driving. Suddenly I'd look down and be going 30 miles-per-hour over the speed limit! I couldn't help it — the music just got my adrenaline pumping. At the shows it seemed to do the same to the kids.

METAL "CORRUPTING" HARDCORE?

KEN OLDEN: Hardcore in the mid-nineties was cool because there were so many styles to listen to. Maybe some people don't like that but diversity in almost any situation is a plus since it exposed you to new ideas and people. Some people have blamed me personally for bringing metal into hardcore, which is funny to me. [laughs] When I look and see how many bands today play more metal-core I feel pretty good, since that style was obviously enjoyed by many. Bands like Cro-Mags (*Best Wishes*) and Judge (*Bringin' it Down*) brought metal into hardcore, but with them it was more hardcore riffs and metal production. My generation put the metal riffs in with the metal production. But we can go back to the late-eighties to see how it started. One more thing I will add is that everything goes in cycles. The old-school style of hardcore, which I also enjoyed, sounds fresher and more original after a few years of metal-core dominance goes by.

ATMOSPHERE OF "NO MORE DREAMS OF HAPPY ENDINGS"

KEN OLDEN: At the time I lived in a house that me and most of the members of the band lived in. We recorded that whole album there on a 16-track, which is not going to give you an overall great sound, in my opinion. But because we all lived in this house we'd have band practice and spend a fair amount of time recording. It was a three level house and we'd put the drum kit up in the attic which was all wood, but we'd have the studio in the basement so there's this snake going out of the window of the basement and up three levels into the attic. So, I'm in the basement playing guitar and I'm talking to the drummer through a mic. [laughs] The whole house got turned into a studio and I think every room got used at one time. It was definitely not some controlled experience so that allowed us to experiment, which added to the flavor of the record. With the combination of the sound, the lyrics, and the artwork, it all just somehow came together.

MIKE MCTERNAN: Ken wrote most of the lyrics for *No More Dreams*... I felt comfortable singing the lyrics that Ken wrote because I think he knew me — and probably still does — better than I knew myself. I have always had problems with depression, anxiety, self-loathing, and confusion. I have never been able to realize my full potential because I always bring myself down. That would probably be the underlying theme of all of my lyrics — past, present and future.

KEN OLDEN: Mike and I are pretty similar in our feelings. We're both pretty upbeat and positive people, but yet everything's also not a bed of roses, so it's not hard for either of us to write some dark lyrics. [laughs] This might seem kind of odd but in the eighties I was really into Bauhaus and The Cure and a lot of goth music, and as I decided I wanted to be a musician that's the stuff I was listening to. We realized you can look at things either from the glass is half empty or half full perspective, so we tried to tap into both sides of that. It's also kind of reassuring to find out that everyone has their own dark days and I think that's why people were able to relate to some of the songs on *No More Dreams*.

STRAIGHT EDGE INFLUENCE

KEN OLDEN: I never really "became straight edge." I was already living that way, and then I started getting into punk/hardcore music and discovered that how I was living had a label. I've never smoked a cigarette or been drunk in my life. I never liked the taste of alcohol, and my father is a doctor heavily involved in cancer research. When I was young I worked with my dad during the summers in his hospital, and I saw the lung cancer patients every day. After that there was no chance I'd ever pick up a cigarette. Being straight edge was really easy for me, because that was me; it's how I naturally was. That's why I'm still straight edge to this day, even if I hadn't found a name for it, I'd be this way.

MIKE MCTERNAN: I don't think Ken or I were ever the type to get down on others for having different beliefs. So unless it got in the way of the band, it was not an issue. We both have always had respect for others and their beliefs.

KEN OLDEN: [Mike and I] are both still straight edge, actually. It was just one more thing we had in common. We have similar goals in terms of what makes us happy. What Mike and I would consider fun might be boring to other people. We're pretty easily entertained by things other people might be bored by. [laughs] So, that's probably why we've always hung out. I've been in bands with guys who aren't straight edge and they are still friends of mine, but when we're not playing I'm not socializing with them because we have different ideas in terms of interests. So, that's why Mike and I bonded because we were hanging out all the time. You want to have a band where you can get along, which comes in pretty handy on tours. [laughs] But the issue was more in the background for us as a band. My original concept was to do Damnation as a straight edge band because I thought it would be a nice paradox, as a lot of straight edge bands were considered to be pretty upbeat and clean-cut while we were coming from a much darker perspective, so it might have created a more complicated version of straight edge. But we ended up deciding that musicianship was more important than straight edge as we really wanted to push boundaries and we just wanted to play with people we liked who could also help challenge us and push us further, regardless of whether or not they were straight edge.

"MISERICORDIA"

MIKE MCTERNAN: I had been listening to *Wish* by the Cure a lot while I was writing lyrics. I know that they had a huge influence for me on a couple of the songs.

KEN OLDEN: [*Misericordia*] was the beginning of our riffs getting a bit more rock-y. It was more of a transitional record. I feel like I didn't really define a sound for the record and it was a bit all over the place. The arrangements were a bit jumbled and I would clean them up now and change things around, make them crisper. That's also the only record we did on ADAT and I hated those things. [laughs] There was a whole bunch of issues with that. It was a decent in-between record, I suppose. [laughs]

MIKE MCTERNAN: Recording those songs was weird because for *No More Dreams* we had a ton of time and we could work on making it sound exactly as we wanted. But in the middle of *Misericordia* our time was cut short and it had an effect on the way it ended up sounding.

LEAVING JADE TREE

MIKE MCTERNAN: We felt that we were headed in the opposite direction of Jade Tree. We needed to be on a label that was more in touch with the crowd we were playing to. We were the only heavy band on the label and the bands they were signing were getting further and further away from what we were doing. I don't think they knew what to do with us.

KEN OLDEN: It's always tough when you're working with friends and Tim Owen and Darren Walters (co-owners of Jade Tree) are great friends of ours. The thing that was sort of weird about being on Jade Tree was that we were kind of the odd band out in terms of sound. We'd often be on tour with Walleye or Lifetime and we were friends with all those guys, but we didn't feel we were playing to an audience that was most receptive to our sound. On the other hand, there were definitely some cool things coming out from Jade Tree. Of course, some people who were into Jade Tree stuff, who never would have given us a chance if we were on another label, gave us a shot and checked us out because Jade Tree was an "arty" label. So, we got taken a bit more seriously because we were on Jade Tree, and we also had a bit of an arty, underground credibility. Also, at the time Jade Tree was a smaller indie label so the recording budgets weren't as big and right at this time it seemed like the production got stepped up even in hardcore. You started hearing other bands were spending $10,000 dollars on their records. In the early-nineties that was unheard of! I started to realize we needed a lot of time in studio. Now, Battery — an old-school straight edge sounding band I was also in at the time — could record a whole record in a few hours. But Damnation might need a day just to get drum sounds. After doing *Misericordia* I felt like we needed a bigger budget than Jade Tree might be able to afford. I also felt like we wanted to be on a label where there were more bands from the same genre. But I can't take anything away from Jade Tree as they were always totally supportive of us and they are still a great label to this day!

SIGNING WITH REVELATION

KEN OLDEN: At the time I had done a Better Than a Thousand and Battery records with Revelation and their A&R guy at the time, who went on to leave right after we signed, was super cool and it seemed like an easy move. There were a bunch of labels looking at us at the time and were willing to give us decent budgets and Revelation was trying to make a commitment to signing more bands like us. They did a pretty good job, overall. First and foremost we got to record the album we really wanted to make. I was really happy with *Kingdom of Lost Souls* and they were a big part of us being able to make that record. At the same time, they weren't necessarily the right label for metal hardcore as that's not how their network was set up. They were known for old school hardcore and some of the Southern California pop-punk and then they got more into the old school thing again, with a few bands here and there like Shai Hulud and The Judas Factor that made a pretty good run. But the bottom line is what's the meat and potatoes of the label. You'd think Youth of Today, Gorilla Biscuits, and those kinds of bands. We also lost our drummer at the time, so we lost a lot of momentum as a band, too.

"KINGDOM OF LOST SOULS"

MIKE MCTERNAN: I feel that *Kingdom* was our best album in terms of what we put into it. I am so proud of that record! As with anything Ken does, he has a vision of what he wants. He would not settle until he knew I had done my absolute best.

KEN OLDEN: That's really the one record out of all my experiences as a musician that I am really satisfied with to this day. It's pretty damn close to the way we wanted it to be. Part of the reason it didn't get much exposure or hype was our fault. I can't say Revelation dropped the ball as labels are counting on bands to get out there and tour and we didn't really do the promotion on our end. The thing that's cool for me to see is that the sales for that record have stayed steady and even picked up over time by word-of-mouth. More people gave it a chance over time, which is cool. That record is part of why people care about Damnation to this day.

SONIC TRANSITIONS

KEN OLDEN: Other musicians can appreciate that often times the budget of your record really controls how things turn out. *Kingdom of Lost Souls* came out the way I always heard our records in my head, but we just finally had the budget to do it the way we wanted to. I like everything else we did too, but those records had some technical limitations in terms of the type of studio we recorded in and how many hours we had to set up guitar or drum sounds. If I had the time to do that on the other records then maybe the others would have turned out the same.

MIKE MCTERNAN: We were never able to really judge the reaction to *Kingdom* because we only played a couple of shows after it came out. I have always gotten mixed reviews from people who liked the other records. As with anything, it is hard to live up to people's expectations.

WINDING DOWN

MIKE MCTERNAN: I can only really answer from my point of view. I never had the vision that the rest of the guys had. They pictured a band that could go beyond the hardcore scene and do something big. On the other hand, I was content playing to a few kids in a basement. We just were on different levels. For me, a lot of it was my lack of confidence. In general, I was just not happy and that affected my attitude toward the band. When I should have been really motivated to get things going, I just sat back and let things fall apart.

KEN OLDEN: I was doing Battery, Better Than a Thousand and Damnation all at the same time and all of those bands operated as full-time bands, which was pretty intense to say the least. Battery and Better Than a Thousand were easier to do because the songs weren't as complicated, but Damnation took much more time just due to the complexities we were trying to achieve. Mike and I both worked really hard on the songs and lyrics, and it was pretty time consuming. Past all of that there were also some personality factors in the band that happened. Mike and I were still good friends and some of the other guys were more into doing their own thing. We lost our drummer who was pretty unique and to replace him wasn't going to be easy. I guess I didn't want to play these songs with a drummer who couldn't cut it. All of this stuff just kind of burned me out. [laughs] It was hard to find a reason to keep going. Damnation was the band I put the most effort into, but at the end it became its undoing because I was kind of tired of it all. But we never officially broke up; we lost our drummer and then just sort of stopped playing.

There were never any issues between us; we're all still friends.

AUDIENCE RECEPTION

MIKE MCTERNAN: At the time, people had a hard time figuring us out. We were trying something that was not being done at the time. We brought our own [stage] lights and had samples running through our set. Of course, they were a lot more primitive than what bands have now. It is amazing that bands have the ability to tour and make a living off what they are doing. If we had something to do with that and bringing heavier music into the hardcore scene, I am proud of that.

KEN OLDEN: I always thought we were a solid band and loved what we were doing, so from a personal standpoint I think we were doing some cool things; I think we were pretty unique at the time. It seemed like when the band stopped we got way more popular, which is true with a lot of groups for some reason. [laughs] I can think of tons of bands — like The Smiths, for instance — that gained a much larger following after they broke up. I haven't really been playing music in a full-on manner for a few years and it's been cool to bump into some of the newer bands out there and they say really positive things about us, which is humbling. I'm happy some of those songs finally got their due.

LEGACY

MIKE MCTERNAN: Being in a band that had the opportunities that we had was so great. I was able to travel and meet new people. That is what I miss the most. Most of the kids who are around today have no idea who Damnation is. So, even if I tell someone that I used to be in a band, it won't matter. But it's cool. I preferred being a roadie anyway.

KEN OLDEN: It took up most of my time for several years, but I loved it and it was a major priority for me at that point in my life. I cared about it and it was a rewarding experience. It impacted my life in a positive way because as a musician I get a natural high from creating and playing music. It's amazing to see this little thing that started in my head and there are thousands of kids who know the lyrics and love the songs. I was just happy to share so many adventures with my friend Mike. I'm proud we got to make music with the other guys and had the chance to see the world. We never took that for granted, each day on tour was like a dream; we were just happy that most nights there was somebody there to hear us and support us.

SELECT DISCOGRAPHY:

No More Dreams of Happy Endings (CD/LP, Jade Tree, 1995)
McTernan, Olden, Halloway, Merchlinsky, Ward

Misericordia (CD/LP, Jade Tree, 1996)
McTernan, Olden, Halloway, Merchlinsky, Ward

Kingdom of Lost Souls (CD/LP, Revelation, 1998)
McTernan, Olden, Halloway, Merchlinsky, Bryson

In This Life or the Next (CD, Victory, 2007)
McTernan, Olden, Merchlinsky, Keroz

DEADGUY

Vocals: Tim Singer
Vocals/Bass: Tim "Pops" Naumann
Bass: Jim Baglino
Drums: Dave Rosenberg

Guitar: Chris Pierce
Tom Yak
Chris "Crispy" Corvino
Keith Huckins

New Jersey's Deadguy formed in 1993 when ex-Lifetime members Chris Corvino and Dave Rosenberg were jamming in their basement. Both were longtime hardcore fans, but they were also inspired by the sometimes abrasive rock of Amphetamine Reptile Records (aka: Am-Rep) bands of the early nineties. Eventually the two brought in good friend "Pops" (Tim Naumann) and formed what would become a much imitated sound that mixed metal, the caustic noise rock of groups like Today is the Day and Unsane, the experimental punk of bands like The Cows, and the innovative hardcore of Black Flag. They became a four-piece when ex-No Escape vocalist Tim Singer stepped in on vocals. They weren't sure how well their sound that combined hardcore, metal, noise, and rock would be received, but ultimately they didn't care — what mattered was that they were making the music they wanted to play.

After playing shows up and down the East Coast, Deadguy recorded *White Meat* and then later *Work Ethic*. These seven-inches were notable for their dissonant brand of hardcore as well as their dark, twisted humor on the cover artwork. Singer, who created those visual images, was also known for extremely personal lyrics that matched the darkness of the artwork.

As Deadguy moved closer to what many view as their finest creative hour, they also added ex-Rorschach guitarist Keith Huckins on second guitar (just before the *Work Ethic* seven-inch was recorded). With Huckins, Deadguy recorded the *Fixation on a Co-Worker* LP, which brought the band more attention than they had before. While Singer screamed his lungs out in frustration with the world, the others did their best to unleash hell on their instruments, as the songs were dark and insightful as well as brutal and precise.

Toward the end of a U.S. tour in support of *Fixation…*, some of the members became frustrated with the direction of their lives. Unhappy with his job as a graphic designer for a large company, Singer was also tired of living on the East Coast and wanted to move to Seattle, while Rosenberg wanted to keep the band going at their current pace. The group parted ways in a somewhat disgruntled manner, with Rosenberg, Corvino, and Naumann deciding to keep Deadguy running and Singer and Huckins choosing to move west, which led to the creation of the band Kiss It Goodbye.

After the departure of Singer and Huckins, Deadguy moved Naumann over to vocals and brought in guitarist Tom Yak and bassist Jim Baglino, which resulted in the *Screamin' With the Deadguy Quintet* ten-inch. After heading out on the road with Bloodlet, Deadguy came to an end.

Although the lifespan of Deadguy might appear to have been cut short, especially in the wake of the split after *Fixation…*, their creative ambition was anything but short. *Fixation…* stands among the influential hardcore records of the nineties because of the group's unique sound, lyrics, artwork, and propensity for flushing anger straight out of the larynx.

ORIGINS

DAVE ROSENBERG: Crispy (Chris Corvino) and I played together in Lifetime briefly. We both split that band pretty early on and became friends and roommates. We lived in a house in New Brunswick with about 12 people. We used to do shows in our basement and Deadguy even played our first show there. I played in a bunch of bands, but I wanted to try something else musically. Crispy and I used to go in the basement and play jazz type stuff. One night we went to an "AmRep Night" at CBGB's and saw The Cows and Unsane. We thought Unsane was the heaviest band we'd ever heard! Around the same time I picked up the first Today is the Day record. Basically, we studied a bunch of records we liked by these amazingly heavy bands and added a bit of Black Sabbath and started to make up parts [for songs]. We then taught Pops (Tim Naumann) to play bass. Crispy was always a bass player previously, but he wanted to try playing guitar, so he taught Pops how to play bass. We had been playing as this power trio and Tim came in with his vocal style and we all just fit together.

CHRIS CORVINO: I went away to college, came back to Jersey and Dave and I moved together with a bunch of other knuckleheads and we, at one point in time, which is funny now, were like, "Well, we are all too old for this bullshit." [laughs] He and I were in that position and Tim was in a project he was just finishing and we were just standing around looking at each other with nothing else to amuse ourselves so we were like, "All right, let's go." At first it just wasn't happening. It was hard to get something that we were enthusiastic about. It was kind of getting away from a dirtier Sub-Pop thing and getting into more of a something that was more of what we were into. We thought we could always throw in some heavier things like the band Unsane. We were confident rip-off artists. [laughs] We would just throw together as much stuff as possible and not worry about, "Oh, this part doesn't go next to this part." We didn't give a damn.

TIM SINGER: I was in No Escape and I went back to college at Rutgers. No Escape was kind of fizzling out. I ran into Dave at a show and we started hanging out. He and Crispy had been trying to write songs. I started hanging out with them and we started practicing. Our first show we played we had one original song and a Black Flag cover and an instrumental where I made up words while we played it. We actually had t-shirts for the show, which was pretty funny. We were called Deadguy by that point, but we surely hadn't developed into a real band yet. [laughs] We kept writing and got some other people involved and we started to put together some songs. Originally it was Dave and Crispy's vision. They were really into The Cows and Jesus Lizard and were into a whole new approach to playing heavy music since so many bands were doing things the same old way. We weren't interested in 10th generation Judge bands. We were more into Unsane and some of the stuff from AmRep. At the same time, the scene a lot of those noisy bands were from was kind of lame with 21 and over shows and we weren't really part of the hipster art crowd. We were still a part of the hardcore scene, but we thought it needed a jolt — it had become formulaic and manufactured. Our music wasn't going to have a predictable mosh part that everyone stands around and waits for. We were listening to different shit and thought we might as well incorporate it into what we wanted to do. I still considered us a hardcore band though, so we worked in the same channels and had the same ethics. We just wanted to try something new.

DAVE ROSENBERG: We always wanted to be heavy. We knew we didn't sound like any of the mainstream hardcore that was out there. To us, we were playing metal, but it was metal filtered through our own ideas and abilities. Half of our songs are in 6/8 and weird time signatures; this was just how Crispy and I wrote songs.

TIM SINGER: When we first started we tried it the old fashioned way. Our bass player had never played bass before. Our guitar player was a bass player who switched to guitar. That helped us be a little noisier and looser when we first started. Keith we called the six-fingered man. He's super tight and rock solid when he plays. Eventually through playing we got tighter. Things got more complex and we tried to throw curveballs in there. We had a sense of adventure. Anyone has the right to put a guitar around their neck and experiment. I've always liked the left field approach to things. The way I structure my lyrics is very different from typical pop or rock. I liked finding our own voice and not being classically trained at our instruments. A lot of it was us playing stuff in the basement and us being like, "Well, do you guys like it?" We weren't sure if it was any good. [laughs]

CHRIS CORVINO: When I was a kid I knew how to play bass pretty well, but we didn't have a guitar player so I had to move to guitar. It was one of those situations where I had an extremely limited vocabulary on guitar, so to speak, but an unlimited desire to do things. We were more interested in what sounds we could make. We would worry about the musicality of it later. We just found sounds. Nothing was off limits so it was super easy to make music. If I made a sound and could repeat it every time we played it, it didn't matter. I could play bar chords and power chords and stuff like that. We did a lot by numbers. Dave and I listened to a lot of different music and would always talk about numbers. Whether it be like this part is seven times or this part is a seven tune or this is three/four as opposed as a four/four. So we did a lot of things structurally. It wasn't until later until we got a second guitar player and I got my feet under me with guitar we were able to go into more of a metal direction. I learned some different chords and there we went.

"WHITE MEAT"

DAVE ROSENBERG: Crispy and I came up with *White Meat* in our basement. We had about eight songs and were trying to figure out what worked for us at the time. The band was never terrible because we always thought we might suck. [laughs] But that was the thing that Tim and Keith brought to the band. We were worried we sucked and those guys would just say, "We're great! Everything's perfect." Until we recorded that first record we had only played live so that was our first experience of finding out what we really sounded like. Those songs were very organic and sort of a testing of the waters to see where to go.

TIM SINGER: *White Meat* was a self-released thing, but we did it along with a label to put it in his catalogue. As for the cover [of the record], I was in a design class and our teacher gave us a stack of pictures and said, "Make something," and that's how I came up with the cover. I actually turned that in as a school project at the same time. [laughs]

ENTER KEITH HUCKINS

TIM SINGER: When we started playing out we thought kids weren't going to know what to do. We didn't really have mosh parts and I didn't repeat myself in the choruses. I was writing more like a diary and trying to be truthful as opposed to having an agenda. We already really liked the direction we were going and then we got Keith Huckins in the band and he's an amazing musician. I thought Rorschach could have taken over the world, so it was great that he got involved.

DAVE ROSENBERG: Crispy was not a guitar player, so when he played he created a lot of organic, noisy, off-time stuff. Keith brought the chugga-chugga heavy side out of us. In some ways he made us truly metal. [laughs]

KEITH HUCKINS: After Rorschach I was in another band [Die 116], which was me being in a very bad place in my life at that time and thinking it was the way to go. I quit the band abruptly and I tried to get Andrew [Gormley] to quit with me and start another band. But it was a combination of me being a fuckin' mess and him believing in the band, so he didn't quit. So, I was left floundering. This was the first time in a long time I didn't have Andrew working with me, so I didn't know what to do. I had always wanted to work with Tim [Singer]. Tim and I tried to start a side-project back in like 1991 or '92 and it just never got off the ground. I went to see some band in John Hiltz's basement and Tim showed up. I hadn't seen him in a while. I was like, "Dude, the timing is right. We need to play!" He was like, "I just started this band Deadguy, and I'm loving it." I was like, "Fuck!" [laughs] I was thinking once again we'd missed paths. So I semi-kiddingly said, "Well, you guys only have one guitarist, right? Obviously, you need a second guitarist." [laughs] At some point, though, Tim came back to me with the demo and I thought it was really fun. I talked to the guys and tried out. We hit it off great. Once again, here was a bunch of suburban New Jersey nimrods together — we had the same mannerisms and sense of humor.

"WORK ETHIC"

DAVE ROSENBERG: *Work Ethic* was more calculated. We sat down and hashed out more cohesive songs. I don't like the way it was recorded, but I think the songs were pretty decent.

TIM SINGER: I had a real job by the time of *Work Ethic*. I think I stole that image from my job and I credited myself as I.B. Stolen. That was where Huckins finally played on a record with us. Getting Keith in the band was a jolt of electricity.

KEITH HUCKINS: I was thrilled with *Work Ethic*! The songs were great and really fun to play. At that point it was the best production I'd ever had. It sounded really heavy. Now it sounds a bit muddy, but at the time I was really into it and it really felt like we were going to do something. We were also the cockiest sons-of-bitches at that time. [laughs] We'd finish a song and make a tape of it and go listen to it in the car. Steve Evetts told us to listen to our recordings in a car stereo because you'll always get a sense of how it's going to sound. The five of us were sitting in the car listening to the tape in the car and were like, "We're the baddest motherfuckers on earth! We're going to kill everybody!" [laughs] We had these shirts that we made up that said "Global Domination" on the back. [laughs] We were totally believing our own hype.

AUDIENCE PERCEPTIONS

TIM SINGER: We played every single show we could up and down the East Coast. You couldn't really dance to us the way you could our contemporaries like Mouthpiece or Lifetime, so people were into it but they weren't moshing to it. We didn't know if people liked it, but they bought our shirts like crazy. [laughs]

LYRICS

TIM SINGER: I had quite the interesting youth and was exposed to a variety of different situations. When you go to college you see a lot of fucked up shit. You see date rape happening around you at a party. When I started working at a real place I noticed the big-wigs were now wearing 500 dollar suits but judging by the way they talked to each other in the bathroom they are still cocksuckers. Everywhere you turn you make these little observations. That's the kind of shit that draws me to music and it's what drives me to do music. Johnny Cash sings songs about violent situations, now obviously he didn't do all these things but something about these emotions draws him to exploring them. If something good happens to me it probably won't end up in a song. Artistically, emotion is what drives me.

DAVE ROSENBERG: We had lyrics with some substance. Most of the lyrics were personal, though. Tim had some real issues in regards to working for "the man." But it wasn't a goal to be political. We rarely spoke at all, let alone about anything of substance.

CHRIS CORVINO: We weren't really a political band. We were really a "one trick pony" on the stance of our policies. We knew we were just pissed... about everything. [laughs]

ARTWORK/AESTHETICS

TIM SINGER: We were kids from New Jersey who were angst ridden in our own right, but we weren't from the streets. We weren't macho people; I guess we were more intellectual in our approach. We were tongue-in-cheek and tried to go for a retro pulp fiction type of feel with our art. I grew up loving the Dead Kennedys and Black Flag artwork, so those were my biggest influences graphically in terms of my approach. I tried to see us as part of a bigger picture where hardcore came from Black Flag and Minor Threat and they all came up with their own thing, which is exactly the approach we were trying to take. We weren't trying to be "New Brunswick" hardcore or New York hardcore; we were just trying to be an original hardcore band that was trying something different.

DAVE ROSENBERG: Part of our aesthetic was that we never wanted to do a record cover with 50 guys holding the microphone and singing along. We wanted to be a bit mysterious. I don't know what else we could have done with music like that. The art was kind of dark and weird, which is what we sounded like. [laughs]

KEITH HUCKINS: We were all angry suburban kids, not sure of what we were even pissed off about, and didn't know how to release those feelings in any other way but in the form of music. Tim has quite a bit of emotional shit he's been working through with his various bands throughout the years. But as far as the rest of the guys, it came down to the fact we all just liked playing heavy, extreme music.

CHRIS CORVINO: Tim said he wanted to be the "car wreck" of all bands; we wanted to take everything that was aggressive and put everything we had into one band. That feeling never stopped. Even if we weren't practicing, I would spend hours over Tim's shoulder as he designed. He would look for pictures of old tools and old hammers and weird clip art. The titles of some of the songs just came from old encyclopedias. We would flip through pages and look for stuff that differentiated us from something like one of those bands with a cool graphic but you can't really tell what it says, but it looks kind of cool and thorny and satanic. We wanted to be more subversive. But we also didn't want the lyrics to be like faux torture mythology that other metal bands linked to. Playing live meant a lot to us. We didn't want to be theatrical; we wanted it to be as nuts as it could be but still be able to play.

"FIXATION ON A CO-WORKER"

DAVE ROSENBERG: We were constantly playing every weekend, so we were having a hard time writing songs because we had no practice time. We could have written more songs for that record if we had more time. We had been playing together for a while by the time *Fixation* was recorded. We could now finally sit down and really analyze parts and see where they took us. Knowing that we were trying to do a full-length record, we had 10 songs and we knew we wanted to be diverse. There were a lot of influences from other music we were listening to at the time such as Dazzling Killmen and Today is the Day. We also were listening to a lot of Black Sabbath and jazz, too.

TIM SINGER: I'm not sure how the record came together. [laughs] But we liked it. We worked with Steve Evetts and he got it. Once the singer starts coughing up a lung a lot of studio folks were pretty baffled, but Steve understood what we were going for. We had played so many shows and we had gotten a lot tighter as a band. There was confidence in succeeding at doing something that was not a guarantee. We had this really good energy when we recorded. It was a total experiment and we had this freedom and confidence in our songwriting. I found my voice in my lyrics. Every singer in their first band has lyrics they had written for the previous ten years just waiting to come out. But some of the songs are kind of stupid and small minded because you just don't know what you're doing yet. With the Deadguy lyrics I was just like, "Whatever comes to my mind I'm going to explore." I remember Henry Rollins once said something to the effect of every song is an idea. You will be talking to your friends and an idea will hit you like people are lazy and that's why they smoke in their cars with their kids. I can write a song about that because it speaks to something I have a feeling about, not just some preachy anti-smoking anthem. It's a real, palpable thing that happens, and it angers me. I wanted to write about things from my own perspective. The band also hit a stride musically. No territory was forbidden.

KEITH HUCKINS: Recording *Fixation* was kind of like recording *Work Ethic*. We'd go into the studio and bang some shit out. It was also really weird to record because at the time all the guys other than myself lived in Hoboken. I would get out of work at five, drive down to the studio and if I was lucky I'd get there by seven. They usually tracked the drums before I got there and it always sounded great. It was a total feeling of giddiness, for lack of a better term. We'd finish a track and be like, "Fuck, yeah! You fuckin' guys!" [laughs] Crispy was hysterical with that stuff.

CHRIS CORVINO: It's funny that record is more popular now than it was when it first came out. What happened was we got better as a band. We were going to be a punk band and play way over our heads and play as loud as we can. We didn't want to sound like Pantera or Metallica taken to a ridiculous hyperbole. We wanted to get whatever we wanted to get across and we wanted it all to be at once in every song. The downside of it was that we kind of got overly fascinated at the fact that we could make neat sounds. For a band of our budget playing our kind of music, it was rare that you got that sound. We were lucky enough to have a good enough engineer. We played a mix of Marshalls and Dual Rectifiers, which were kind of just coming into popularity with that kind of mid-range metal kind of sound. It tightened us up a little bit. Had we have stayed with that lineup, I would be very anxious to hear what our next record would have sounded like.

DAVE ROSENBERG: *Fixation* was very representative of the lurching, dark, antagonistic stuff that we wanted to play. We had just graduated college. Tim was working with an hour commute so that's where a lot of his lyrics came from. The rest of us were working shit jobs and trying to get by and we just hoped the band would be able to get us through to the next day. Overall, that record was a huge catharsis for us. I know it was for Tim because he had a lot of pain built up inside of him at the time, which he was able to channel into his lyrics and his vocals.

TIM SINGER: With lyrics it's hard to be really introspective and honest, but I really tried to do that. I always tried to weave lyrics in a way to where they could be left open and interpreted. I tried never to be self-righteous; I always tried to find my culpability in the situation for which I might be writing a song about. I always drew from personal experience, so when writing things would often come naturally to me from my own life — my own feelings would well up and want to explode out. When I first started No Escape I always carried around my lyric book and would write my songs about all the different typical hardcore topics. But I got into things like the Rollins Band and I was like, "Here's my fucked up journal, and I bet if I share things from there then there will be other people out there that say, 'Hey, that's my fucked up journal' and be able to identify with it." That's what I love about everything from Johnny Cash to Rollins. To this day, when I hear well written shit I just love it. I don't care if it's P.J. Harvey — writing deeply about honest topics is as good as it gets. Eventually, I got better at it. "The Extremist" was about this girl I knew who tried to kill herself for attention. I think everyone knows someone like her and it's almost a cliché. Certain things would just hit me. One girl I knew had her dad tell her how fat and ugly she was. That's all I needed to hear — I had to write about it. Shit like that is so foul and so everywhere and so honest and this is the kind of stuff that moves me. It moves me more than writing about Saddam Hussein or about being vegetarian. Now if I saw some animal get brutally killed or something maybe I'd write a song about that. But I just wanted to come from an honest experience.

DISASTROUS TOUR

DAVE ROSENBERG: Our first U.S. tour was a nightmare! Crispy, Pops, and I got into a fight with Tim and Keith out in California. We got to Seattle and had no shows on the way back so we just drove straight back in 50 hours. We were in slightly different places in our lives. I had just graduated from college while Tim already had a day job. At that time, Crispy, Pops and I had literally zero dollars and Tim and Keith had been working so it wasn't as hard for them to be out on the road for that long. On the other hand, we did play some cool places and met lots of cool people. We went out and killed it every night and we'd move on to the next place.

KEITH HUCKINS: We had a booking agent who put together a slip-shod tour. It was a disaster from the get-go. Egos definitely came into play, too. It became very hard to deal with each other. Tim and I ended up kind of forming one side, while Pops, Dave, and Crispy went the other way. Tim had made up his mind that he wanted to move to Seattle. He put it out there that if anyone wanted to come that they could. It was kind of shitty in a way on our part because it was kind of like the "it's not you, it's me" thing with a girl. We didn't come out and say we were done, which is what should have happened. I've got a pretty strong feeling that I'm held pretty responsible because it was almost like I came in and stole Tim, which wasn't the case. But the situation just didn't work for us.

TIM SINGER: We went on tour and it fell apart by the time we got to Seattle. Keith and I formed one camp and everyone else formed another. Dave has a very strong personality and Crispy and Pops just wanted to keep the band going so they stayed with him. We didn't break up in Seattle, but we got there and the tour was falling apart. I wanted to stay an extra day or two. We had a great show there and the other guys wanted to go straight home. We had one of those melodramatic band meetings and I was like, "If you guys want to come out there with me then awesome. If not, best of luck."

CHRIS CORVINO: We had pockets of places around the country where we were extremely popular. For some reason, someone would be at a show and get a tape of us and we would be on some college radio station. We'd show up to this town where we had never been and didn't know a soul and there would be hundreds and hundreds of kids at our show. That happened to us in Virginia, for instance. Then we'd go to the next town and they'd be like, "Who the hell are you guys?" There was really no one for us to tour with. We weren't really known well enough to the big bands that we might have been able to tour with. I mean we had played some shows with Neurosis and we did play shows with grind bands, but we were coming from hardcore. It was at a time where people didn't really veer off to make all these tours. There was no such thing as Hellfest or those tours… this was eleven years before that. It was pretty uniformly shitty.

DAVE ROSENBERG: Tim said he was going to move to Seattle meanwhile we were still practicing and planning on doing the band. We thought about changing the name but just decided to keep it. We were very fortunate in that people liked what we were doing. But what made the sound what it was is that we all came from different perspectives and a lot of post-teen angst was exuded in our sound. We were starting to get into some stuff that was a bit more epic than we had done previously. We had started to hit a wall. Then we went on tour and it was a big debacle. There is an unanswered question of what would have happened had we stayed together with that original lineup.

CHRIS CORVINO: We had a lot of friction on that tour and we did this band 24/7 with a lot of intensity and a lot of ego collectively and individually. It was good for a while, but then it was kind of toxic for the band staying together. We'd all had enough of each other and Tim wanted to split and then we talked about trying to keep it together. It just didn't work. We were so far away from being able to approach the band like, "We aren't as close anymore. We aren't like brothers anymore, but let's stay together for the kids." It just wasn't possible. So they went their way. We did nothing for a while. [We stayed] kind of inside of ourselves, but we kept it together and made another record.

LIFE AFTER "FIXATION"

DAVE ROSENBERG: We asked Tom Yak who was our roadie to come play with us and he was in this strange life transition so it worked out. We had all these people who wanted to sing and they all wanted to sound like Tim. It was kind of like when Judas Priest brought in Ripper Owens. [laughs] We couldn't find a bass player to save our lives. Jim from Human Remains said he wanted to do it, which made us excited because he was really good, but we didn't want to interrupt what Human Remains was doing. We started playing with Jim and we all clicked right away and we were playing shows within a few weeks. Jim and Tom both understood what we were going for with our whole aesthetic so the transition was easy.

TIM SINGER: Singers are replaceable so if they wanted to keep going with it I was fine with that. I just didn't want them to sing a few of the more personal songs I wrote. "Nine Stitches" is about no other human being on Earth than me. How can anyone else sing that and have it mean anything? That was my only real problem with them going on. I suppose I was happy with what I was doing with Keith in Kiss it Goodbye too, though.

"SCREAMIN' WITH THE DEADGUY QUINTET"

DAVE ROSENBERG: The record was shorter because we wanted to do a ten-inch, not because we didn't have enough songs to record. Victory was just starting to understand distribution and college radio. Previously, they didn't really look into that type of thing in regards to promotion. We had about two weeks to get the recording done for Victory to get the record to radios before a big college radio time. We went to this really expensive studio and it was a total disaster. We recorded one song and left. Later on we heard the recording and it sounded great, ironically enough. [laughs] We ended up having Steve Austin from Today is the Day come up and help us record and it ended up being a really fun experience. Sometimes people aren't into the vocals, but I still like it. The music is kind of a mess and there is a ton of really heavy, weird shit coming at you from every angle.

CHRIS CORVINO: For whatever reason, we got back to it and it was clearly a different band. Well, it was and it wasn't. Up to that point, each record was completely different. If we kept the same lineup, we very well might have come up with the exact same record, just with different personnel. Who knows? We were always very adamant about thinking, "We already did something like that. Let's do something else." We were really conscious about that because that was a big problem with hardcore bands. They could only play a certain way. We never wanted that, so that is kind of how we allowed ourselves to do another record with different personnel. We went back to something a little more noise sounding, a little more obscure. We worked with Steve Austin who I had done my best to rip off a decent amount of times. [laughs] It was a chance to continue to do something that was still kind of like the band's next step. Some people think that was our best record, some people think it was our worst.

WINDING DOWN

DAVE ROSENBERG: The week after we finished *Screamin'* we went on tour with Bloodlet. We all got along really well and life was a bit easier in terms of having a booking agent.

But we also broke down the first weekend, and we got into fights with people all over the place. We played a lot of shows on that tour — I think like 50 or so with only a few nights off where we drove huge distances. Tom decided he didn't want to tour anymore and we had some other people fill in on guitar for us, but it just wasn't the same. Our last show was with Strife in New Jersey. Jim took it the hardest. I was at a point where I had to get a real job. Crispy also just got a job as a teacher. Since we didn't have a firm lineup anymore we just decided to stop it.

CHRIS CORVINO: For me at least and maybe Dave too, we were exhausted trying to go uphill with this thing. We were into it for ourselves, but we had gone through so many misadventures with the band that we were so tired. Our guy Tom, who was the roadie then guitarist and resident tattoo artist, couldn't tour anymore and we couldn't find anyone else. People who were into that kind of music were able to do their own band. At that time the heavy thing hit a high mark and then was gone. That's when the kind of underground punk hardcore scene went sort of retro. Oddly enough, ten years later it is back.

LOOKING BACK

DAVE ROSENBERG: It was a great experience despite the pains we went through. We got to do things that 99 percent of the population will never get to do. We traveled the country and played to thousands of people all over the place. I'm just glad that some people were psyched that we were around.

KEITH HUCKINS: Before and during the album the whole process was just so much fun. It sucks that things soured the way they did, because we would get together to practice and we wouldn't even practice. We'd just sit on the couch and watch T.V., hang out, and have so much fun.

CHRIS CORVINO: I definitely have a feeling of unfinished business with that band. I wish we were able to put out the next two, three, and four records and stick it out in the decade when nobody gave a shit to now when there are now whole tours and labels and legitimacy to a type of music that was formerly played in V.F.W. Halls. I have always felt that way. I don't have enough ego to say that we started this [type of sound] because obviously there were bands playing really heavy music at that time in different parts of the country in different scenes. But we were able to put it together and take it to kids who necessarily didn't see that at the local V.F.W. or local 600 capacity club and get to play bigger and bigger crowds.

TIM SINGER: It's like when you study art history. The stuff that really matters is the stuff that propels things forward. There could have been 50 artists like Van Gogh, but who did the next thing? I like the idea that we played a part in leading music to the next thing. It sure wasn't intentional. We just wanted to play honest music we were happy with.

SELECT DISCOGRAPHY:

White Meat (7", Popgun, 1994)
   Singer, Naumann, Corvino, Rosenberg

Work Ethic (7"/MCD, Blackout, 1994)
   Singer, Naumann, Corvino, Huckins, Rosenberg

Fixation on a Co-Worker (CD/LP, Victory, 1995)
   Singer, Naumann, Corvino, Huckins, Rosenberg

Screamin' With the Deadguy Quintet (CD/10", Victory, 1996)
   Naumann, Corvino, Balgino, Rosenberg

DISEMBODIED

Vocals: Aaron Mussett
            Jody Minnoch
Guitars/Drums: Joel Johnson
Guitars: Mark Wilcox
         Mario Diaz de Leon
         Tony Byron

Bass: Tara Johnson (Anderson)
Drums/Vocals: Justin Kane
Drums: Joel Anderson

Like many nineties hardcore bands that incorporated metal elements like pick squeals, double bass, and apocalyptic lyrical imagery into their songwriting, Minnesota's Disembodied created a sound that was heavy, technical, and emotional. Some accused them of attempting to use hardcore as a stepping-stone for the potentially more lucrative metal market, but they stuck with hardcore labels for their releases and only played D.I.Y. tours and shows.

Disembodied formed when guitarist/drummer Joel Johnson, bassist Tara Anderson (now married to Johnson), and vocalist Aaron Mussett, all ex-members of a little known hardcore group called Crawlspace, joined with former Rain drummer Justin Kane. They had been huge hardcore fans for years but felt a need to create music that was even more ominous and heavy. A metalhead since his childhood, Johnson set the tone for their sound as he quickly came up with several song ideas that excited the rest of the members. Soon, the band had a batch of songs which rapidly became favorites at their early shows. Some of those songs ended up on the group's debut EP, *Existence in Suicide*. The title's foreboding tone would become a staple for them throughout their existence. They were also critical of organized religion and used dark imagery the way a lot of metal bands did to push this point.

After the release of the EP, they played shows all over the Midwest. Unlike many hardcore bands of the time, they played with powerful, high wattage amps and had more of a "professional" set up. Some saw this as a bit out of place at V.F.W. Halls or basement shows, but they, along with bands like Damnation A.D., won over fans as the volume emanating from the speakers felt relentless.

In the beginning, Disembodied's sound was a dense, down-tuned blend of Black Sabbath style riffs, the somber tone of Unbroken, and the sheer volume of noise outfits like Today is the Day. As they grew into their own sound a bit more, they utilized the more off-time rhythms of avant-garde metal bands like Meshuggah. Their first full-length, *Diablerie*, exhibited all these characteristics and helped them gain a national audience, allowing them to play in more places than they had previously.

Just as the band started to gain momentum, they went through a series of lineup changes. Mussett left or was asked to leave the band on more than one occasion, which left Kane shifting from drums to vocals and Johnson moving from guitars to drums each time. Chicago native Jody Minnoch became the singer for a short time, but ultimately they ended up going back to Mussett after a long U.S. tour in 1996.

Despite the stops and starts, Disembodied continued to write new music with some added experimental sounds. Using wah pedals and other effects, fast build-ups, and a layer of Neurosis style noise, *If God Only Knew the Rest Were Dead* built upon the intricate and complex songwriting style they had already established. Mussett also increasingly used his signature whisper-into-scream verses to express his inner frustration. Struggling through a variety of personal problems throughout the existence of the band, Mussett sounded desperate, pained, and lonely. Many were drawn to their music because they identified with his lyrics and were moved by the way he delivered them.

After going out on the road with Brother's Keeper, both bands recorded for a split release on Trustkill Records. Around the same time, Disembodied assembled their final songs, which were released on their last record, *Heretic*. The band then broke up with some of the members going on to form the metalcore group Martyr A.D.

Disembodied's combination of metal and hardcore is a primary influence for many bands of the past decade. While some felt they never quite reached their full potential, their music and legacy stands behind as a testament to their power as a band.

ORIGINS

TARA JOHNSON: Joel, Aaron, and myself were all friends from high school. Joel and I had also been dating for a few years. We were all in a band previous to Disembodied called Crawlspace, but we had decided that we wanted to start a new band, so we started Disembodied. We knew Justin from going to shows and his band, Rain, had broken up, so that's how Disembodied started. We all clicked from the moment we met.

JUSTIN KANE: Rain started by playing smaller shows in our area, but then as we drew more kids we started to play the Twin Cities, which is where I met Joel and Tara. We ended up playing shows with them in Fairbault. Rain ended up stopping, so I just got together with Tara and Joel because we all hit it off so well. I remember when Joel was in Crawlspace he played drums. As we played all these shows together and started hanging out more, the next thing I knew he was playing guitar! [laughs] He's an insane musician and amazingly talented. He wanted me to play drums for a new band because he wanted to play guitar, and I was totally into the idea. They wanted to play a heavier style of hardcore than what most people were doing at the time. I grew up with a metal background so that worked for me. [laughs]

AARON MUSSETT: Tara and I were friends in high school. She later introduced me to Joel, who introduced me to punk and hardcore music. He was already messing around in a pop-punk project playing drums that never really took off because of his interest in hardcore. The pop-punk band then morphed into more of a hardcore band and that's when I joined. We had two vocalists for a while then we decided maybe it would be best if we just had one. That's when Joel moved to guitar with a whole slew of songs he had already written and we nabbed Justin who we had met at different hardcore shows we had been frequenting. That's when we decided we wanted to be the heaviest hardcore band ever. Joel tuned his guitar down about two steps down from standard E tuning and started listening to a lot of metal. This was when Earth Crisis had just dropped "Firestorm" and the hardcore music scene started really started to go in a heavier direction as opposed to the old school.

MINNESOTA HARDCORE IN THE EARLY-NINETIES

TARA JOHNSON: [The area scene] was small but fucking awesome! That was the best time that I can remember going to shows. There were basement shows almost every weekend and there were some pretty amazing bands. There wasn't a really heavy scene as much as there was a punk scene. Back then, both the punk and hardcore scenes were really unified and all types of bands could play together and there would be no problems. But we really wanted to do something different, so we tuned really low to C-sharp, A-sharp, and G-sharp, which no bands were doing then. We used these fucking bass speakers for the guitars that made it sound really fucking heavy. They were a pain in the ass to tour with, though. We just wanted to go out and make an impact on a scene that we loved.

JUSTIN KANE: Hardcore was different in the early-nineties. I remember I was questioning everything and waking up every morning wanting to save the world. When I think about it, that early-nineties era of hardcore woke so many people up to so many different issues. It was really an amazing time! Early on, coming from the Midwest it's a little tough because if we wanted to see a big show we'd drive six hours to Chicago. But the scene in Minneapolis was cool with great local bands like Bloodline and Threadbare. I remember playing at the University of Minnesota at The Hole and some of those shows were amazing. Also, Fairbault had a really big straight edge scene and we'd book Groundwork and Snapcase for 300 kids, half of which were straight edge kids in a town of 12,000 people. So it helped to have the Fairbault scene involved. The next thing you knew Minnesota was on the map and even more bands came through and they all had something interesting to say and it really made an impact on us. We were able to question more things by checking out bands like 108 and Endeavor. It was so inspiring to see our scene grow!

INSPIRATION FOR SOUND

TARA JOHNSON: We all loved hardcore bands like Earth Crisis, Coalesce, Deadguy, and we wanted to push the envelope and be as heavy as we could be. It was a great way to release a lot of anger and frustration. It was a really exciting time for hardcore. As for being dark and evil, Aaron's lyrics were always dark and depressing. I think all of us besides Justin came from broken homes, had fucked up families, and we had a lot to be pissed off about. And pentagrams were just fucking cool to put on everything. As far as bands that I was influenced by, Unbroken was and is the best fucking hardcore band ever! I was blown away when I heard *Life.Love.Regret.* I think I listened to that record at least two times a day for months when that came out. That was at a time when my family had just fallen apart — both my grandpa and grandma had died within months of each other and I was fucking depressed. That record was very therapeutic for me because it came out at a time where I was feeling lost and abandoned, and I felt like it was talking to me. As far as [Disembodied's] sound, Joel wrote all of the music and he has been a metal-head since he was in fifth grade. He's got pictures of him when he was barely in middle school with metal shirts on. He grew up on bands like Iron Maiden, Testament, and Slayer. I think those were his biggest influences and he obviously incorporated those into our sound.

AARON MUSSETT: With metal and some hardcore the dark elements just come along with the sound. Of course, I can only speak for myself, but this kind of music was a heavy outlet for me — a way to purge all of my teenage angst and frustration I was feeling about the world I was living in. When we first started, we were highly influenced by bands like Earth Crisis, Unbroken, and Snapcase. They had that heavy, metallic sound we were drawn to. As we progressed we started to open our ears to more metal bands like early Sepultura, Pantera, Machine Head, Fear Factory, and especially toward the end, Meshuggah. We wanted our drum sound to sound as deep and heavy as the drums off of Sepultura's Roots album and our guitar tone to sound like Machine Head. I, on the other hand, wasn't even really listening to metal at that time, although it still had a special place for me.

JUSTIN KANE: One thing I loved about Disembodied was that we had good heads on our shoulders. We knew we wanted to stand out a bit. Being a band from the Midwest was tough enough, but we wanted to try something new in playing something so dark. We also wanted to be able to play to different audiences. We'd play to crusty punks and a bunch of straight edge kids and emo kids all together and they'd all be into what we were doing. In Minneapolis you had to take what you could get and some of our best shows were playing in a basement with a band like Spitboy. We could play within all the factions in the scene and people seemed to respect us for trying to do something different. Of course, one time we played with Youth Brigade and that was a rough! The next thing you know there were people heckling us off the stage. But aside from incidents like that, we just had fun and I think people respected us for it, for the most part.

"EXISTENCE IN SUICIDE"

TARA JOHNSON: We had written those songs and we knew nothing about recording. We just looked in the yellow pages for a studio and happened to find this studio that was in an abandoned beer brewery. It was like a fucking castle. It was super creepy inside, but the atmosphere was really great to record in. We recorded everything live and only did it in a few takes. We really didn't have a lot of money. I think it was like $200 or something like that. We were just happy to be recording. We thought it was pretty fucking cool that we actually had put something on tape. Our friend Fang had started this label Furface, named after his kitty, and wanted to put it out. I remember going to his house after he had the CDs made putting them together. I was so stoked that we had actually recorded something. Joel wrote all of the songs for Disembodied; he was just a fucking guitar genius. He always had riffs going. He would come with another song and we hadn't even finished the song we were working on. It's funny, when I go back and listen to the first EP I think we sound so young and inexperienced, but I think that's also what's so brilliant about it. It was really innocent and authentic. We weren't trying to be anyone else.

JUSTIN KANE: A lot of the songs on that record were more political than we were known to be later. Aaron questioned things and wanted to be educated about so many issues in the world. We had songs about Native Americans and the loss of their land, for instance. But it got to a point where we wanted to play with all genres. If you get to be real political you tend to play for one group and we didn't want to alienate anybody. I've talked to people about Disembodied before and they ask us what we were about and what it comes down to was, "They're heavy!" [laughs] That said, we all were passionate about a variety of issues on a personal level, and we always felt we could make more of an impact on people by talking to them after a show and sharing perspectives than by just railing about something from the stage. Aaron wanted to make the lyrics more personal so the listener could really identify with them in a personal way. A lot of the lyrics were very touching, because of the way he deeply wove his feelings into them. We started to see that others could relate to them, too.

AARON MUSSETT: Joel had already written the material. I had the lyrics from my journals and we threw the songs together and got them tight in a matter of weeks and headed to the studio. We wanted to record a record before we even had our first show, so we each threw in a hundred bucks and tried to find a place that had good sound and could record us for cheap. Looking back, I like the songs, but the subject matter was a little naïve and trite. I think that record was our only real "hardcore" record in my opinion. [laughs]

EARLY RESPONSE/EARLY SHOWS

TARA JOHNSON: The Midwest was a hidden gem. All of the "big" bands were from one of the coasts, but we had some fucking amazing bands here. We had Bloodline, Downside, Threadbare, Libido Boyz, Destroy. And the great thing about the Midwest is that shows were so much more personal here. They were smaller and at much smaller venues, so there was a lot of interaction with bands that others in bigger cities didn't get. We played a ton of basement shows. Seriously, we would play anywhere, and we did. I remember booking that first tour. I have no idea how I did it, but it was pretty good. We either slept in the van or crashed at some kid's house. We made enough for gas money. We didn't even get any money to live on from the band, so it was whatever you brought you needed to ration out to last the whole tour. We really only ate one meal a day and just hoped that some kid would make us spaghetti. Plus, most of us were either vegetarian or vegan, and our options were very limited back then. We lived on gas station food for the most part. We got a good response right from the beginning. It didn't matter if we were hardcore kids playing a crust punk show, or playing with bands that didn't sound like us — somehow it caught on in more than just the hardcore scene.

JUSTIN KANE: Sometimes people were like, "Who do they think they are?" because we were playing down tuned music, which was different. We didn't say a lot between songs because we wanted all of our energy focused while we were playing, kind of like Coalesce. When they played you couldn't take your eyes off them and that's the kind of vibe we wanted. It wasn't that we didn't care about issues, but we felt people could make their own judgment through reading our words and they could come and talk to us one on one. We wanted to make personal connections more than ram things down people's throats. People have to choose for themselves what they believe… that applies to politics or straight edge or anything in between. But we always felt that whether you're friends or family we're still going to be there no matter what you decide. At the time, people would act like you were going to hell if you sold out straight edge or whatever, but I guess we tried to take a more inclusive approach.

TARA JOHNSON: We played the Goleta Fest and somehow they thought we should play last. We were so nervous; I couldn't believe that they were making us play last. We had never been to the West Coast before. I thought it was going to be a disaster, but it was fucking amazing. I couldn't believe that people had actually heard of us. I will never forget that show because we slept outside. Justin got his dick pierced in front of a ton of people, someone in the band shit their pants, and we played an amazing fucking show. I was so nervous to play in front of so many people, so of course something had to go wrong. When we were playing, the stage was kind of wobbly and Joel's [guitar] head fell off and landed on my cord and busted my cord. That kind of shit always happened to us.

JUSTIN KANE: When we pulled up to the Goleta Fest we ended up playing at night to a ton of kids and it was just crazy. It was so different than what we were used to. We had been playing basements and then here's this grip-load of kids and a stage and people totally stoked about us playing and it was just amazing the response we got. We met so many friends there and it was just an amazing experience. We discussed our views with everyone it was just such a cool fest with people hanging out who loved hardcore.

LYRICS

JUSTIN KANE: The lyrics were personal and attached to Aaron's life. He would explain them to us and we always thought they were really interesting. Whether they were about relationships or families, we felt everyone could relate to them.

AARON MUSSETT: When I wrote lyrics I was coming from the only place I could come from — my own personal feelings and experiences. I was married at an early age. My parents had just gotten divorced and my wife and I just had a child. You could say I had a lot to be pissed off about. I didn't see a bright future for myself except in Disembodied. That band was my solace...a way to escape and vent my anger on the world. My catharsis, if you will. When I wrote then and when I write today it's not necessarily about exactly *what* I wrote, it's about the feeling that come across when you read the lyrics. I always wanted people to delve into themselves and find their own interpretation about what I was writing about. I think that way it becomes more personal. The words then transcend just my feelings and become your feelings as well. Then the feelings and the words evolve and become something much greater, inter-personal. I always hated when kids would come up to me and ask, "What are you writing about in this song or that song or what does 'If God Only Knew...' mean?" I always wanted people to draw their own conclusions, so I would just ask them "What does it mean to you?"

TARA JOHNSON: Aaron had issues just like all of us, and it was a huge release to be able to sing about it. He was amazing in the studio. I loved his voice. When we would be recording and we would get to the vocals and it would all come together, I remember getting chills. I know that he got into the whole Krishna thing, and so I know he was influenced by that at some point. He wrote all of the lyrics so all of the recordings reflected what was going on in his life at that time. Aaron had been through some personal shit, and even though life sucks at times, it makes for good music.

ANTI-RELIGION STANCE AND DARK ARTWORK

JUSTIN KANE: Overall, we pretty much had an anti-religious stance. People in our band were spiritual, but we were definitely cynical about organized religion. It wasn't that we wanted to be satanic or whatever, you know? [laughs] We just felt people shouldn't just bow down to everything they were told. They should question their beliefs and come to their own conclusions. Also, later in the nineties you'd have bands playing "real" metal and we were also listening to a lot of death metal, so I suppose the vibe of those records came out in our music a bit. It was dark music, so why not make dark artwork for a whole aesthetic approach? I've struggled with religion a lot in my life because I don't know what to believe. You see all this terrible shit happen in Christianity alone... this is right, this is wrong... it's confusing. I wanted to seek something, but I felt like I was getting mind-raped.

AARON MUSSETT: I guess you could say that most forms of Christianity and I have beef. [laughs] Not so much my exposure to the religion per se, but what I've witnessed through history. The atrocities that have been committed in the name of God and religion in general are staggering. Most organized religion of all kinds is just as guilty. I think blind faith and rampant fundamentalism are major contributors to this. I just see so many contradictions in religion, like pro-lifers supporting the war in Iraq, preaching peace and love but then being condemned to a life of eternal torment and agony in hell if you don't follow "their" rules. I find it so ironic that most religions are saying the same general things just in different ways but still manage to fight about whose God is the "one" God. Don't get me wrong, I'm not an atheist. I consider myself a very spiritual person, but I just don't prescribe to one said religion. In fact, I was raised partly in the Hindu traditions...one of my favorite bands back in the day was 108! I just prefer to take the wisdoms of all the great teachings and create my own philosophy. I think religion can shut a person down to all the many different possibilities out there and inevitably only limit your understandings of the world around you. In fact, I'm convinced that most of what is written in the almighty Holy Bible is in fact just pagan mythologies passed down through the ages. I'm also not judging people because that do have faith in a certain religion...it's just not for me.

TARA JOHNSON: Most of the people in the band were totally anti-religion and that reflected in our lyrics and artwork. I didn't really care. I just wanted to play fucking music. The religion thing is a difficult question. I grew up going to church, my mom worked at the church, it was all around me. I always questioned everything and that got me into a lot of trouble. So when I got into hardcore, I was rebelling against society telling me what and how I should be. To see Christian hardcore bands pissed me off. Not because they believed in God, but because they were fucking pushy and always tried to force their beliefs on others. I was rebelling against that and now it was in my scene. I was pissed. In Christianity, you either believe in God or you're going to hell. It's that simple. Black or white. With Krishna, I didn't feel threatened by it. They were very spiritual, but they did also believe in vegetarianism, which was a big part of hardcore. I also think that just for the simple fact that it wasn't Christianity it was more accepted.

PERSPECTIVES ON "MESSAGES"

TARA JOHNSON: I was both straight edge and vegetarian/vegan. The band as a whole was neither. We didn't want to label ourselves as anything other than a fucking heavy band. There were enough bands that were promoting those issues. We didn't want to close ourselves off to anyone. I would X up when we would play shows because I was definitely proud of the fact that I was straight edge, but it was nothing that we ever talked about. We were proud of the fact that we were just a heavy fucking hardcore band that didn't exclude anyone from listening to us. Hardcore was a much different

scene back then compared to today. The scene was more unified. So many different styles of bands could play together and we all got along for the most part. I think we fit in because we didn't try to be anything other than what we were — four or five kids trying to figure out who we were and who we wanted to become, experiencing many things for the first time, playing music just for the love of it, not to become big fucking rock stars. We never thought or expected to make a lot of money and we didn't care. If we cared, we wouldn't have lasted even five years with all of the shit that we went through.

AARON MUSSETT: We definitely listened to straight edge bands when we were younger. Hell, I was straight edge too before I smoked my first cigarette. We just didn't want to segregate ourselves from people who would like our music in spite of our message. So, I tried to steer clear of those messages and keep it more personal. "Nicotine" was about these exact feelings — being judged by others, the scene, et cetera, for *not* being straight edge. I remember seriously thinking I was going to get my ass beat for smoking cigarettes in Salt Lake City by some youth crew out there! Although we believed in these causes such as animal rights and the straight edge movement, Joel, Tara, and I all being vegetarians and/or vegan, we didn't want to ostracize ourselves from folks who would dig our music without feeling like they're being judged. We never labeled ourselves a straight edge band, although I think a lot people thought we were. The politics in the scene were really beginning to bug me to the extent I even stopped going to shows. There were other bands on the same wave-length as us in that respect...the first ones that comes to mind are Coalesce and Converge.

RESPECT FROM VARIOUS ASPECTS OF THE SCENE

AARON MUSSETT: We didn't want to divide ourselves. The main way most bands do this is by labeling themselves a certain way. We wanted the metal kids and punk kids to like us just as much as the hardcore kids, you know?

JUSTIN KANE: We wanted to keep our doors open to everyone and not settle for anything. Mark from Impetus Inter who played guitar for us for a bit would get us on shows with bands like Disrupt and then the next day we're playing with a melodic hardcore band. We played with anyone and for anyone. We just loved playing wherever. You know your heart is in the right spot for hardcore if you're saving money from a job just to go on tour. I remember us having conversations about how much money we were bringing to eat on tour to budget for at least five bucks a day. [laughs] But we just loved playing so much that these things were always on our minds.

LINEUP CHANGES

JUSTIN KANE: The lineup changes were hard for all of us. I was a head case and didn't know what I wanted to do with my life and that caused conflict with everyone. Other people in the band were struggling with things, too. But the core of the band was Joel and Tara. They just kept it going no matter what. I struggled with a lot of things growing up and it would bring me in and out, but then I'd realize how much I missed that "family" and we'd always work it out and I'd come and play again.

TARA JOHNSON: We never had one stable second guitar player. I don't know why that was. That didn't really affect us, though. We either had one guitar player or two. If we only had one, we used more cabinets. We didn't really care either way. Of course, two guitar players are better than one, but there wasn't much to choose from. As far as Aaron goes, he was way in and out of the band. He missed a lot of practices, which made it difficult. He ended up getting a girlfriend, having a kid, and just kind of disappeared. It was hard to get together for practice week after week with no singer. It definitely took a toll on us.

"DIABLERIE"

TARA JOHNSON: We were really excited to have what we considered a good amount of money to record [Diablerie] at the time, which really wasn't much compared to what bands get now. We spent a few days in the studio and I was really proud of how that record came out. We went into the studio really prepared and I think it came out great for our first real record. Of course, the levels on that record are not the best, but at the time it was great. It was a great learning experience for all of us. That record definitely showed how much we had progressed from our first EP, which was really a demo. We were just trying to put out a record that we were proud of and I think we accomplished that.

JUSTIN KANE: The first time we recorded, we had a lump sum of money and there was a guy named Paul Bush sitting there in the studio and he threw some insane price at us and we turned around to leave, but then he said, "How much do you have?" And we told him we didn't have much, but he said he'd do it. On Diablerie, Carl Severson from Ferret Records, who put it out, went to college in Minneapolis for a while and he gave us a bit more support. He was putting out some great records and suddenly we had a budget and we went in with Paul again. We had the songs already, so we laid them down, and Carl got involved and helped us with artwork and everything came out great. We were young and didn't know the process very well and we were flying by the seat of our pants. [laughs] All we wanted to do was play. The records just helped us keep reaching that.

AARON MUSSETT: When I wrote the lyrics to Diablerie I was in a very dark place in my life. The theme of the record to me was my total displacement of my life. "Anvil Chandelier" was about how from the moment we are born death is inevitably hanging over our head, following us wherever we go. When you have a child it kind of puts things in perspective. Being forced to not just fend for the life of yourself but having a responsibility for the ones you love as well. "Forget Me" was a song of self loathing and self-righteousness. Kind of a poor me, "emo" song about losing yourself in your emotions and ultimately letting them control you. "Devils Grin" was rather similar, about losing everything you love most and blaming it on the outside world as opposed to taking responsibility for your actions. You can use the stigma of "the devil" to mark anything inherently "bad" that happens to us and for most people "the devil" just becomes another scapegoat for taking responsibility for our lives.

MUSICAL PROGRESSIONS

JUSTIN KANE: That just came with experience. The timing got better with playing more and more. The song structures got more complex. Joel is insane. [laughs] He always had two new songs fully written every time we'd practice. He'd plug in his guitar and just rip them out. [laughs] He's probably the best guitar player I've ever played with!

TARA JOHNSON: Well, Joel was/is an awesome song writer. He just progressed over time just like we all did. He really pushed us to be better musicians. He would come up with shit that we were like, "Yeah, how the fuck are we gonna do that?" and somehow we would pull it off. With every recording we just tried to push ourselves to do stuff that we couldn't do before or had not heard before.

TOUR STORIES

JUSTIN KANE: On our first tour we ran into Groundwork in Arizona and Brendan DeSmet talked to me and I was telling him how we were getting our each other's nerves after being in the van together for so long. He told me every band on tour hits a wall because you're broke and frustrated. But it's all about whether you decide to break through that wall and keep going or just stop. So, we were on each other's nerves and the van broke down and that wall really hit. [laughs] It worked out in the end, but these are the learning experiences that really change you. When you're hot and sweaty and broke and don't know how you're getting to the next show… it's pretty intense.

TARA JOHNSON: Orange County was like our second home. Every time we played The Showcase it would be sold out and so many kids knew the words from the first time we played there. And there was this time we played Philly at Stalag 13. There was this fight with some punks and someone smashed a bottle over a dog's head and eventually like 10 cop cars came and surrounded us, shut the show down, and treated it as if it was a fucking riot. There was another time when we were on tour and Jody Minnoch was singing for us. We ended up leaving him [after some disagreements] in Boston and Justin sang for the rest of the shows.

JUSTIN KANE: I took a blow up doll that I named Twila into a coffee shop in Cleveland during the Cleveland Hardcore Fest in 1996 and bought her coffee and I was talking to her and it was hilarious. People looked at me like I was crazy. [laughs] Tara or Joel took a picture and developed it. My mom put it on her fridge and I think she still has it there.

"IF GOD ONLY KNEW"

TARA JOHNSON: That was my favorite Disembodied record. We had more time to record this time than the last record. We recorded at the same place with the same person, so we felt really comfortable. The songs were amazing, the lyrics were amazing, and it sounded really good. That was the first record that I was really happy with the overall sound of the record.

JUSTIN KANE: We had a handle on things by this point in terms of writing and recording. I think that record sounds really great and it's what we were shooting for in terms of a sound. Everything really came together for us by this point. We could play a show and I'd get chills through my whole body because you'd see a kid singing every lyric and that's just an amazing feeling. Or you'd get a letter from Belguim saying, "You's guys very heavy!" [laughs] I know it sounds like I'm making fun of that, but I was sincerely touched that someone on the other side of the world, who spoke another native language, took the time to write us in our own language and attempt to convey that our music meant something to him. It really blows my mind!

AARON MUSSETT: I was in a totally different place in my life [by the time of this record]. We had gotten a rather enthusiastic response from *Diablerie* and touring and we just wanted to make a record we could really be proud of. Joel had most of the songs already written while on tour and we recorded them almost immediately after we had returned. I had already decided to give my child up for adoption. I don't want to delve into the matter in too much detail here, but I knew he would be raised in a much healthier environment than I could ever provide for him; suffice to say it was the hardest decision I've ever had to make in my life. Much of this pain and inner turmoil can be felt on *Diablerie* and *If God Only Knew*... "Heroin Fingers" was not about heroin, as many thought; it was a metaphor for addiction to love or sex or attention or whatever you hold dear. I was asking, "Can all these things outside myself, mostly the love of my wife, save me from my own suffering?" "Gone" is simply a song about isolation, a song about the estrangement of my own ego, being away from my friends and wife on tour and being completely displaced from my environment... which also rather ties in with "Dislocation," which was about being completely disassociated with yourself. "When you can't even stand the sight of yourself how can you look me in the eye and tell me everything is all right?" "Bloodshed Rain" was a more socially aware song about how the human race will inevitably create its own undoing and how what we consider "advancement" may be hidden behind a guise of death. As much good as we create, we can create just as much bad; it is the universal law of balance.

"HERETIC"

TARA JOHNSON: I think that Aaron mentally was over it at that point. I don't think that he put as much thought and effort into that record actually. I definitely don't think it was our best record. Aaron was going through some personal shit and it definitely showed on that record. I think the rest of us were still into it, but we were frustrated with Aaron not giving 100%.

AARON MUSSETT: I think this record was just the natural evolution of the band, but we rushed a few of the songs. I think it is our best record, if not at least my favorite... it sounds the most mature. It was also when my writing was at its peak. There are a few songs on the record that were more blatant. Although most of the songs were metaphorical, if you want to write a song that basically says "fuck you" what better way than to say...well "fuck you"! I think this record comes off that way more because of the subject matter. A lot of the songs dealt with religion. What can I say? I'm tired of people's lives being dictated by a 2,000 year old religion. People need to start thinking for themselves and taking personal responsibility for their own lives!

COMING TO AN END

TARA JOHNSON: No matter what, I always considered Disembodied to be the four of us: Joel, Justin, Aaron, and myself. When Aaron wasn't in the band for a while it was still kind of in its beginning stages, so it was only natural when he ended up back with us, but when Justin left it was different. I think that the biggest change was when Justin left. He was going through some shit and just having a hard time playing. That was really hard for me. The beginning of the end was when Aaron just stopped showing up for practice. We really wanted him to be a part of the band, but we just couldn't get him to show up for practice. We would have our "interventions" with him, he would say he was into it, but it would start all over again in a month or two. It was too hard and we didn't want to get another singer. So, we just decided it was over and he seemed to be shocked about it.

JUSTIN KANE: I stopped playing for a while because I was going through some major life issues. When I was in Disembodied I struggled with depression and anxiety. It wasn't Disembodied's fault that I quit a few times, it was my fault. It wasn't working out for me and I left. But then I realized how much I missed Joel and Tara and we ended up doing Martyr A.D.

TARA JOHNSON: We just decided [to end the band] after a while of trying to get in touch with Aaron. One day we just called him and told him it was over. I think that he was surprised because it was just normal at that point for him to show up every three months, but it wasn't fair to us who were putting that much time and effort into something and he didn't seem to care. I regret that we didn't end it by playing a last show, but what can you do? We played a really shitty last show, so I don't like that that's my last memory of the band. If we could have just taken some time off maybe it would have lasted a little longer. Who knows?

LOOKING BACK

TARA JOHNSON: That was an amazing time of my life. I have so many good memories of Disembodied. I think it ended prematurely, but I went on to be in another amazing band (Martyr A.D.), so I don't have any regrets. I wish we could have gone to Europe. That was something that I always wanted to do with that band. I definitely think that Joel's songwriting influenced a lot of people because I can hear his riffs in bands even today. We weren't the first heavy band, but I think that we were one of the only bands that sounded like that and we were able to cross over into different scenes and were accepted. I do also wish that we would have done our last record with Ferret. Carl Severson was such a good friend and I think that we made some bad business decisions, but we didn't

know anything about that side of it. We made some mistakes, but I think in the end we made more friends than enemies, so it was worth it.

JUSTIN KANE: It's funny because I know there were bad times where I just wanted to blow my head off, but when I think about things now it's great because I've come to terms with everything from that time in my life. I only really remember the good things. And that's true with everything in life otherwise if you focused on the negative all the time you'd be a basket case. There were so many good times, whether it was Joel and I driving the van for a show and talking for six hours and being like, "Oh we're here and no time has passed" or meeting so many different people in so many different places, it was really amazing. I'm super thankful I was in Disembodied and that some people feel we made a difference in the scene or their lives. We were just playing music from our hearts. The memories may fade a bit, but I'll never forget all the great times. In the nineties, there were a lot of hardcore kids who were 16 through 24 and in those times you're trying to seek yourself out and figure out who you are. You're going through personal changes and growing up, and I know I struggled a lot with that stuff. You'd come home after the summer of touring and your good friend has a girlfriend. You'd go on another tour and someone else started a job or bought a house, and you'd feel a bit like you missed out. I'd question all the time whether or not I was doing the right thing. But then again I was able to do some things with my life that most couldn't, and I'm grateful to have such patient and understanding friends like Joel, Tara, and Aaron, who really were always there for me and had such a great impact on my life. I still get that feeling burning inside when I hear one of our old records, or records of other bands of the time. It brings back so many memories.

AARON MUSSETT: All in all I don't regret a thing about Disembodied. In fact, I think if we would've stuck it through and got past our differences, and our egos, Disembodied could have been something great. I think we probably could have made a living out of it if we really wanted it. Obviously we didn't. I'm still amazed by the fact we had such an impact on so many people and bands. I still get e-mails from random people saying how much we "changed their lives," and all we were really doing was being authentic. I tell you, it means more to me now, not being in a band when you run into that one random person and they're like, "Aaron from Disembodied?" You have no idea how Disembodied got me through some of the worst times in my life...and that in the end made it all worth it.

SELECT DISCOGRAPHY:

Existence in Suicide (MCD, Furface, 1996)
    Mussett, Johnson, Johnson, Kane

The Confession (7", Moo Cow, 1996)
    Mussett, Johnson, Johnson, Kane

Diablerie (CD/LP, Ferret, 1997)
    Mussett, Johnson, Johnson, Kane

If God Only Knew the Rest Were Dead (CD/LP, Ferret, 1998)
    Mussett, Johnson, Johnson, Kane

Oxymoron split with Brother's Keeper (MCD, Trustkill, 1999)
    Mussett, Johnson, Johnson, Anderson

Heretic (CD, Edison, 2000)
    Mussett, Johnson, Johnson, Byron, Anderson

FIGHT: THE NINETIES HARDCORE REVOLUTION IN ETHICS, POLITICS, AND SO

DOWNCAST

Vocals: Kevin Doss   Drums: Shawn Sellers
Guitars: Brent Stephens   Chris Hervey
Bass: Dave McClure   Javier Vasquez

California's Downcast established a reputation that extended beyond merely making records and playing shows. They created dialogue about social issues with broad personal, philosophical, and political implications, which helped put the Santa Barbara/Ebullition Records scene on the hardcore map nationally, and influenced the political outlook of a variety of nineties hardcore bands.

Huge fans of hardcore and punk since grade school, vocalist Kevin Doss and bassist Dave McClure desired to become active participants in the scene. Wowed by The Minutemen, Black Flag, X, and many others, the longtime friends became involved within a music community that opened their eyes to a host of injustices going on in the world. Although they tried to form a band in high school, they had more luck getting involved in community activism. Seeing the hardships many had to endure on a daily basis led these middle-class suburbanites to become even more committed to making a difference. Eventually, some members attended the University of California at Santa Barbara (U.C.S.B.) where they also met like-minded individuals such as future Ebullition Records owner Kent McClard and Exedra fanzine editor Sonia Skindrud. Along with other newfound friends, this group of people injected fresh political ideas into the local scene.

Around this time, Doss hooked up with guitarist Brent Stephens, who also shared similar beliefs and had a love for hardcore and Metallica. Doss and Stephens then started a band and McClure joined the fold. Soon, the group put together some songs culled from their varied influences: classic California hardcore a la Black Flag, sludgy Black Sabbath riffs, and the noise from the experimental D.C. post-hardcore scene.

Downcast started out playing shows throughout Southern California, sharing the stage with straight edge hardcore bands as well as the more political leaning punk groups. Although all of the members of Downcast were drug/alcohol-free and vegetarian or vegan, they felt there were enough bands flying the straight edge flag, so they kept these particular issues in the background while focusing on dilemmas they felt were glossed over in the scene such as sexism, white privilege, and maintaining a D.I.Y. ethic.

Their vinyl debut was the first release on McClard's Ebullition label and came inside an issue of the *No Answers* fanzine he published. A year later saw the release of their well-received full-length. The most notable aspect of the LP was the large booklet of essays included in the packaging, which showcased thoughts from each member about a host of political and personal issues.

Word soon spread about Downcast and their various causes, one of the most hotly debated being Doss's direct approach to violence at shows. Downcast strongly felt that although hardcore shows should be energetic and fun, people shouldn't have to worry about getting hurt. They also felt that some of the machismo in the pit prevented females from enjoying shows as much as some males. Doss, large in stature himself, was never bashful about insisting on audience members respecting the physical boundaries of others. This attitude caused something of a backlash from those who felt physical interaction was an innate part of a hardcore show.

The band toured with Born Against and Rorschach in 1992. A year later, McClard helped Downcast set up a European tour, which found the band scheduled to play 58 shows in 60 days. After some initial shows fell through, morale suffered, which led to a lack of communication just as the band was, arguably, writing their best material. The members weathered the rest of the tour, which found crowds responding enthusiastically to their sets, but by the end of the trek the band was finished.

After the members got back to California, Doss taught himself guitar and formed Not for the Lack of Trying with McClure and now longtime friend, Sonia Skindrud. After Not for the Lack of Trying split up, Doss and McClure worked together again in the band Jara.

Downcast was extremely important to the socio-political discussion present in nineties hardcore. Similar to groups such as Iconoclast, Fuel, Spitboy, and Econochrist, Downcast created passionate music, provoked dialogue, and helped set the tone for many of the debates that were present in the nineties scene.

EARLY PUNK/HARDCORE DAYS AND THE FORMATION OF DOWNCAST

DAVE MCCLURE: Kevin and I have known each other forever, probably since second grade. We both got into punk pretty early and I felt very fortunate that I was exposed to it early in life. It sounds kind of crazy, but I was listening to punk in the third grade. [laughs] I just got really lucky where friends of friends of friends exposed me to it. So, it's about 1979 and I was listening to The Ramones and The Clash. And then I got exposed to the L.A. punk scene very early, so The Minutemen, X, and Black Flag were huge inspirations for me. I turned Kevin on to them and we both got hooked on the sound and the culture of it all. We lived far from L.A. in terms of us being so young to drive and the area had virtually no public transportation, but we knew this scene of bands existed somewhere. It was all happening right around us. We were able to see some of the bands from the era, but unfortunately we weren't able to see as many as we would have liked. Eventually, we started a band in high school and when college came around Kevin went to U.C. Santa Barbara and that was where he met Brent [Stephens] and equally important people like Kent McClard and others from the whole Ebullition and Santa Barbara scene.

KEVIN DOSS: Dave was basically my link to hardcore. We lived right behind each other and I could jump over a wall behind my house and be at his place. So, we hung out all the time, and he knew a guy who got him into punk and hardcore and then he passed it on to me. So, we're hooked on this stuff, this crazy intense hardcore and punk happening in the eighties, but we didn't know anyone who was from the actual scene where we were at. I'm sure there were people around, but we just didn't know them or know how to find them. This is long before the Internet. [laughs] So one day Dave says to me, "Ask your parents if you can go see Black Flag, Minutemen and the Ramones with me." I was stoked beyond belief! [laughs] But I knew my parents would never go for it, so I lied to them and told them we were going to the movies. Dave's dad was into some alternative types of things and he supported us going to the show, so he drove us to the Hollywood Palladium and dropped us off and was like, "All right, see you guys in a few hours." Here we were, these young kids on our own, and we walk into the Palladium and it's insane! There were people jumping off the second story balcony for The Ramones and Henry Rollins was beating people who tried to jump on stage, many of them seemingly wanting to attack him, during Black Flag. It was so just intense and we were hooked! Eventually, we started this horrible band in high school as we felt like we wanted to become part of the actual scene, but it didn't amount to much. Then, I went to U.C. Santa Barbara for college and that's where I met Brent [Stephens] and Kent McClard, and we started hanging out and going to shows a lot. Soon, I dropped out of college and went back home and started a band with Mike Hartsfield and Dan Adair, who went on to play in Outspoken. We had all known each other for a while, so we started this band called Stomping Ground. It was going good and then Mike got asked to be in Against the Wall so he went and did that. Then Brent saw us play and he liked us and we asked him to play. But then we wanted to do something different with our band, so that's when we talked about doing Downcast. None of us drank or did drugs but we didn't want to be another Southern California straight edge band. That's not a slam on those bands as they served a huge purpose and I appreciate everything they did, but it was getting to a point when you'd go to shows and there'd be six bands on the bill that were all friends with each and all they did was talk about how important it was to be straight edge. Granted, that area is a big party scene and that was important to have some solidarity with others in terms of not drinking and what not, but there were also other issues in addition to that we wanted to address. We wanted to talk about more politically active things.

DAVE MCCLURE: Kevin and Brent talked about forming a band. They needed a bass player and Kevin asked me to play seeing that we were friends for so long and had similar ideas. It's kind of funny that we were known as a Santa Barbara band, but only half of the band lived there. We had more drummers than Spinal Tap and most of the drummers and I lived in L.A. But we were seen as a Santa Barbara band due to our affiliation with Kent McClard's Ebullition records and being more active in the scene there than in Los Angeles. The affiliation was completely valid. As Brent and Kevin were putting the band together, Kent was starting to do a record label, which was Ebullition. He almost did the first Inside Out record as his first release, but Zack [de la Rocha] backed out at the last minute and it was released on Revelation Records. So, instead there was an issue of *No Answers* fanzine that Kent was publishing that came out as a package with the Downcast seven-inch. I always felt Kent was an extended member of Downcast because he helped us tremendously and our vision of what we wanted to do and address in the straight edge hardcore scene was very similar. Kent and many other people in the general Santa Barbara area like him were doing fanzines, making pamphlets, organizing benefit shows, sharing ideas... there were all these people around doing thoughtful things around us. To me, it felt like an extended community and we were all growing and learning from each other. We were discussing Marxist Leninism and anarchism, not just t-shirt sizes and alcohol consumption. We were probably over our heads a bit, but we were taking all of these things on and it was a special moment for all of us.

FORMULATING POLITICAL IDEAS

KEVIN DOSS: Part of the reason we became politically motivated and active was because we grew up in a conservative area. We grew up in suburbs of L.A. that were somewhat affluent and we were surrounded by a lot of Republicans and white people who all seemed to think the same way about everything and it was all very consumeristic and materialistic. We knew there was more to the world out there and we wanted to explore other ideas and make some kind of a difference. We aspired to be more than nine-to-five people. Experiencing punk rock and hardcore and finding out about what was going on in the world really impacted us and opened our eyes. Dave and I started working for homeless food program called Frontline and it was started by this guy who wanted to feed people in need, so he bought a pot of coffee and made a 100 peanut butter and jelly sandwiches for some homeless folks and just went and gave them to the people directly. Soon, this turned into feeding a couple thousand people on a regular basis. We were isolated from this whole other world in our area, so we signed up to help out homeless people with Frontline and that was huge for us! To be white, suburban middle class kids and see this stuff, it just changed our outlook on the world entirely. We recognized we had some privilege, so therefore we should try and give back. So, we'd go to a show on a Friday night, stay up late and hang out and eat something, and then go make sandwiches at two or three in the morning and then stay up through the morning and help feed the people. It gave us a perspective on how to directly help others and we felt like as long as we were doing something we were headed in the right direction.

DAVE MCCLURE: The early L.A. punk scene and many other politicized bands educated me. There's no doubt in my mind bands like The Clash and The Minutemen and X gave me a politicized world view and a sense of political ideology at an early age. It was raw and undeveloped, but it was at least starting. [laughs] But when you're in grade school and junior high and learning about Latin American solidarity groups and labor movements and United States imperialism it's quite amazing and eye opening. That's a testimony to what punk had to offer. In fact, I feel like I learned more from punk and hardcore than in I did in college and that's no exaggeration! At the time we all felt other scenes were preparing to up the ante in terms of what a politically active scene was like. Dischord, the Northern California Bay Area scenes, and ABC No Rio, for example, inspired us to up the ante ourselves and force us to ask what does it mean

to be politicized or what does it meant to be straight edge, especially as white men of privilege? We couldn't relate to a lot of bands near us. In Santa Barbara a lot of other people felt the same way as us — that more could be brought to the table in terms of ideological framework. The stereotypical Orange County straight edge scene was too limited and conservative for us. We loved many of those bands, but we were more interested in seeing relevant politics rather than irrelevant slogans. Seeing what other locations and scenes were doing in Berkeley, D.C., and New York, we knew that even though they were far away from us, we felt like we had a strong connection with them. And that's why we decided to be more overtly political with Downcast.

SOUND AND RECORDED OUTPUT

KEVIN DOSS: We were all really into hardcore and punk, but Brent was also into Metallica. He loved their music so much. I loved the energy of them too and I thought it added some intensity to our sound. The first record I ever got was Black Sabbath's Paranoid and that influenced every band I've ever been in. I love that heavy, thick sound that bands like Black Sabbath, The Melvins, and Tool use, so we mixed that raw, heavy sound with Drive Like Jehu or Black Flag. It was more aggressive and that was mixed with the metal, which then got mixed with a bit of Swiz and Verbal Assault and bands were listening to like crazy. At the time we wanted to emulate everything that was blowing our minds, like Verbal Assault songs — how could we not think this was the best record ever written at the time? [laughs] Dave has the most unique musical taste of anyone in the band, as he was also into a really wide mix of things, but overall Brent and I were into the metal thing and I think that really comes through on our records, even though it started to change by the end of the band.

DAVE MCCLURE: Brent wrote the music because he was the only real musician in the band. [laughs] I was just happy to be in a band and participate. Musically, it was Brent's formulation of being influenced by early straight edge hardcore bands and adding a bit more metal to it, and Kevin and I added a few things from there. The one thing I kind of regret is the metal sort of thing wasn't my favorite style of hardcore to be honest, but as the band went on we were writing music going in a different direction. We were really influenced by the sound Swiz obtained and that's the direction we wanted to move toward musically to some extent, but at the time we were going in that direction things ended. I thought the music got better as we went along, though, because we all were getting better musically just by the nature of playing together. Because of the sound we developed it got us pigeonholed as us being a typical straight edge band to some extent, and I felt we didn't have much to do with that scene due to our politics, but our sound probably pigeonholed us. I think it just took us a long time to develop what we wanted in terms of sound. We wanted urgency and aggressiveness but my feeling was we were only starting to develop our potential at the end of the band. We never made a good record. We were much more about the live experience. Then again, we also didn't go to locations that knew how to properly record a hardcore band, nor did we have a clue how to get a good recording sound. It's embarrassing that there are two version of the LP out there. The second version is a different mix, which was ridiculous because people liked the first one better. I can't even remember why we did that. But our records were just dog dirt. [laughs] There was never a push for any of our stuff to be on CD. There were some good live recordings from our European tour, and there was talk to release them on CD with the studio recordings, but it failed to materialize.

KEVIN DOSS: I like the records. I think they were indicative of what we wanted to write at the time. As I got older I wasn't necessarily into the same sound, but I'd never done anything like that before so making the seven-inch was a new experience to me, and that's what made it special. We put a lot of effort into the records, but I agree with Dave in that the live experience of Downcast was way more fulfilling for us and people who saw us. Sometimes we'd connect with people by way of the records, but I think if we had any lasting impact it was more because of the live show. There was so much more energy and I think that's true for hardcore in general. You can listen to a Judge record but that's nothing compared to the fright you feel seeing Mike Judge on stage in front of your face! [laughs] I'd talk about whatever I was feeling at the time between songs and the band would play quietly and then it would build in intensity.

DAVE MCCLURE: I liked the direction we were going toward the end, but the band ended up breaking up. We were just so much better live. In my opinion, anything on vinyl wasn't interesting other than the packaging. With the LP our attempt was to put out a record that had a politicized fanzine to go along with it. We liked the idea of packaging the seven-inch with *No Answers*, so we took it one step further and turned the LP into more of an experience about reading essays about our perspectives in addition to listening to the record. It was good in that maybe that was the first time we set ourselves apart from the stereotypical straight edge bands in Southern California. It was a bit more intellectual and had a bit more depth to it ideologically. Bands like Judge and Chain of Strength were fine and I didn't want to necessarily disassociate with bands like that, but we felt more in line with bands like Los Crudos, Fuel, Born Against, Rorschach, Spitboy, and Econochrist. I was learning so much from all these amazing bands and people. That's what I cherish the most about that era — having friendships with people like Martin from Los Crudos and Adrienne and Karin from Spitboy, Sam and Adam from Born Against, the Econochrist people, and Mike Kirsch. These people honestly helped change my life and gave me a shared vision of how to keep some of the ethics and values that we were attempting to express in the hardcore scene sustainable in our own personal daily lives.

POLITICS/ETHICS/VIOLENCE AT SHOWS

DAVE MCCLURE: In the early nineties, the hardcore movement existed when there wasn't much happening on a grassroots level politically. It wasn't like the anti-globalization movement in Seattle, for example, that was very organized that occurred later on. We were actively outspoken against dilemmas like the Gulf War, and especially for me living in Los Angeles, the social and economic polarization that led to the rebellion of 1992, but I think that was also a strange time for hardcore. There certainly wasn't a communist party we felt we could align ourselves with as there were so many contradictions in those groups. There was this void politically and hardcore didn't fill that totally, but it did fill a void in terms of being able to have a place to spread information and take part as an activist. The hardcore scene, at the time, filled a need for a lot of people who wanted to make a difference in some way. All these bands that spoke out and became politically active can feel proud of what they tried to do. Some bands felt like they were failures, but what a brilliant way to inspire people, have conversations, and bring issues to the table!

KEVIN DOSS: One of the core beliefs of hardcore for me was when growing up listening to bands like The Clash and X their big message was you don't need to be like anyone else. And that's a big deal to have that idea validated for you! We're socialized so heavily from day one in our country to be a certain way that to be yourself and have integrity and express what you want, it's a difficult thing to have the confidence to do that. We started to meet people as the band got going and we'd realize, "Hey, these people are into some of the stuff we're thinking, reading, and talking about." And that made us feel like we weren't quite so alone. We were trying to be a non-capitalist band, which a lot of people probably laughed at us for. We never made a cent off Downcast. We're selling shirts for five bucks each and they cost us four bucks to make. We were really into the whole D.I.Y. thing that extended into stuff we were learning about like imperialism, women's rights, and vivisection. We wanted to strive for an egalitarian society and what better stuff to sing about in a band than what you're thinking about? We were trying to express the way we were thinking in the hardcore world that wasn't always so concerned with doing that.

DAVE MCCLURE: Downcast tends to get associated strongly sometimes with trying to address issues like sexism. Whether we were naïve to take that subject on the way in which we did, I don't know, but it was at least a reaction to the male chauvinism and violence that happened around us, as well as the subjugation of women in underground culture. We were trying to address those issues because of what we saw at some Southern California hardcore shows, which weren't fun or inclusive at the time. I don't know how comfortable women were in being active in participating, but I'm sure a lot of them felt like coat racks and justifiably resented that. Part of that might have been the aggressiveness of the music, but the male ritualism taking place played a role, too. We were influenced by the D.C. scene and the ways in which they were trying to combat sexism and violence, such as how Fugazi was pretty bold in addressing those things. Looking back, we probably took it too far at times, but at the same time being confrontational about it and having the discussion about it was good. We were experimenting and we were young and stupid and didn't know any better in terms of how to handle these sorts of things. We just wanted to see how it worked. It's a fair criticism for someone to say that we over-reacted, but we also saw a void in participation and we wanted the scene to be more inclusive for women and also for those that just were not interested in putting up with all the stereotypical hardcore rituals that were really growing tired within the scene.

KEVIN DOSS: We started playing in a really supportive place in Santa Barbara. We played free shows in a little red barn with Sawhorse, Spitboy, Fuel, Econochrist, Born Against, and Rorschach. We were all trying to do something a little different. People would print out these informational pamphlets and zines and bring free vegan food. It was mix of the hippie Woodstock vibe with the anger of hardcore. I remember Kent McClard got arrested one time because the cops showed up and said the decibels were too high at the venue. Kent said, "Fuck you, we have a decibel meter right here and the sound is within the law." So, that stuff would happen in Santa Barbara, and then we'd then go play with a band like Judge somewhere else and we just didn't feel we had as much in common with them. We'd play hard and talk about the same stuff whether it was for four people or 2,000. I remember playing for three people for a club in North Carolina and we set up and played anyway as hard as possible and we went crazy for those three people who took the time to come see us. There were some days in San Diego, at a co-op they used to have shows at, where there were some confrontational things that occurred. If there were skins at shows bullying people in the pit or people dancing to aggressively we'd say something about it. We didn't want to be a soundtrack for violence. I'd put the mic down and stop people from beating the crap out of each other. I'm not the smallest guy, so I never had a problem with bullies as I wouldn't be someone who would let that stuff happen to people. I never got into knock-down, drag-out fights, but there were some close calls. We just wanted people to feel safe dancing how they wanted as long as they weren't infringing on other people's personal space too much. So, I took every opportunity between every song and never let a chance slip by to stop violence from happening. If it was just people dancing then that's fine, but we'd be at shows and there would be 250 pound guys punching people in the back of the head when they weren't looking. People wouldn't come up front because they were afraid of getting the shit beat out of them. I was like, "Fuck you, that's not going to happen or we're not going to play. Period!" We wanted people to dance their asses off as long as it was a group thing that was pure energy, not a football game or a hockey match. Here we were up there talking about sexism and there are 10 women who have to leave because they were afraid of getting hit by idiots. I'm sure people thought we were a bummer and they thought we wanted people to stand there and watch us with no energy, but we never wanted that. We just didn't want things to get out of hand.

DAVE MCCLURE: Looking back, we didn't necessarily have movements of social and political organization going on at time that we felt we could place ourselves in comfortably. So, we were angry about Bush Sr. wanting to invade a sovereign nation and we felt this sense of not knowing how to express a voice of dissent in any way other than through hardcore, which felt valid at the time. Whether it was writing fanzines or doing interviews, we loved it because we didn't care about promoting Downcast. [laughs] We always pushed the interviewer and the audience to get really involved in a discussion and spreading information. It wasn't so much that we were right or wrong, but that the discussion itself about these topics existed in print and expressed at a show. It was a chance to communicate with people and find communities that felt similar. We weren't political organizers, but I felt like our band was a form of activism to some degree.

STRAIGHT EDGE/ANIMAL RIGHTS

KEVIN DOSS: We essentially were a straight edge band, but we never wore Xs or anything like that. At the time, we felt like there was enough of that going on and we didn't need to be additional spokespeople for that movement. We also had friends who were hitting the bong and drinking, but that wasn't our thing. We were trying to put the personal and political together as much as we could. People might call me a sell-out now because I'm only vegetarian and not a vegan anymore, or that I might drink a beer once in a while, but at the time we felt like if we weren't living the life we were talking about we were being hypocritical. We pushed ourselves and became vegetarians and vegans and tried to find some balance with a regular life. There were people even more extreme than us. There were people like fruitarians who might call us out then for not going far enough, but that's what was so great about the time. The hard part was that it was judgmental, but there was also some accountability. People would call each other out at shows and write articles about each other, but it gave kids at the time an opportunity to live an alternative lifestyle if they chose to. Living in Southern California is one thing, but say you're talking to kids at shows in Iowa, Nebraska, or Indiana and talking about the drug trade and its impact on Mexico and these topics people may not have heard about and then it gives them options to think about. Maybe they would think, "Hey, funding the tobacco industry is totally disgusting, so maybe I can start there by not smoking, or maybe I can eat less meat." We'd share ideas with kids and it was way to communicate. You can talk about women's rights and they might think, "What's the big deal about me and my buddies watching porn or treating our girlfriends like shit?" But maybe they would re-think these things, and that's the best thing about the whole experience of the scene. We were sharing things with each other that helped us grow into our own skin and enabled us to choose our own path in life. It's not easy to do that and you're only exposed to certain things via traditional American culture, so how do you know there are other options unless you find out about them? Hardcore changed so many people's lives.

DAVE MCCLURE: We were all vegetarian and that had to do with hardcore. I'm vegetarian to this day and I absolutely can point to punk/hardcore in terms of inspiring me to do that. What we liked about straight edge was that it was a really ethical way to live one's life. It never felt like an exclusive litmus test to judge others for me ever. It felt very ethical to not smoke cigarettes and not exploit animals, even in terms of just diet. It felt like a really sustainable way to live, which is what a lot of us were looking for. We didn't want to isolate people who ate meat or smoked or whatever, but we addressed these issues because we thought they were important.

EMOTIONAL STRUGGLES

KEVIN DOSS: Hardcore was the right place for us because we had all this energy and anger but didn't know how to utilize any of those feelings when we were young. It's like you wanted to go out and fight these idiots who did or said offensive things, but you knew physical violence wasn't necessarily a good thing. [laughs] So, we'd plug in to different protests around Santa Barbara and L.A. We went to march with laborers in Sacramento. But for us in general, hardcore was also a great outlet. I've had a lot of anger stored up whether it was about stuff with my parents or stuff going on internationally or in my community. One of the immediate attractions to me about punk/hardcore was the energy that could come out of it. It felt a little like therapy. [laughs] You play 50 shows in two months and you come home purged. When you don't have that anymore, you need to figure out what to do with all that anger. I went from that lifestyle to being a dad. There was no transition and that's why I stopped playing in bands. I needed to focus on my family. I had already mellowed out a bit by the time I was around 26. I was working construction and meeting all sorts of people who didn't necessarily share the same viewpoints, but they were good people who did the best they could with what they knew. But these realizations never sunk in until the baby came out of my wife's body. The doctor let me catch her and I was crying and it was like, "Wow, there really was a baby inside there!" [laughs] It was such a mind-blowing, life-changing experience. I'm a fireman now and when we go to house fires they are intense situations. We're witnesses to gunshot wounds, stabbings, family violence, but with a structure fire you've got to be really aggressive and intense but stay cool. It's a license to go ballistic to get the people out before the house burns out. And I can honestly stay it's a similar feeling to the insanity of a show. You have a license to go a little crazy. I need that in my life and hardcore was like that for me and now it's being a fireman. If I don't have some intensity then I feel a little empty.

BORN AGAINST/RORSCHACH TOUR

DAVE MCCLURE: It was the greatest month ever! [laughs] I don't know how the arrangements were made but Born Against and Rorschach were doing this U.S. tour. We became part of it for a month, and I'm not sure if we forced ourselves on the tour dates or if we were invited. [laughs] We met with Born Against in L.A. and they weren't excited we were coming along as that meant three touring bands instead of two playing for small shows with no people. We didn't know if we'd have gas money for any of us after a show, let alone all three bands. But we did a month with them and we all got along well. It was an amazing experience! A lot of it was just having conversations every night after shows with people and that's what I remember the most. I remember Sam McPheeters dragging a few of us to Jeffrey Dahmer's house in Milwaukee where those murders had taken place. The police tape was still wrapped around the place. We thought about breaking into the house to see everything inside, but we were too chicken shit for that and of course we left. [laughs] Rorschach blew out my bass speakers one night and that was an honor! Chicago was also wonderful. We were on the bill with Screeching Weasel and Ben Weasel kicked Downcast off the lineup. [laughs] We were ready to play and we were informed we were no longer on the bill. It might have been there were too many bands, but I'm also sure it was because he hated us. [laughs] And of course Screeching Weasel was just amazing that night and blew me away.

EUROPEAN TOUR/END OF THE BAND

KEVIN DOSS: Kent McClard actually financed the tour and came with us. Europe was a totally different experience in more ways than one. There was a bit of a language barrier, but people were so interested in what we were doing, and they'd feed you at every show. I think I went there with 20 bucks and we were supposed to play 58 shows in 60 days. We played every day and that's what got us around. We'd eat the meal given to us and we'd play at hostels, clubs, and basements and all the kids were really stoked. It was this really indescribable experience. We went to Prague and played there and there were probably 600 people there, which was a huge crowd for us. We started our first song and everyone was jumping up and down and people were bouncing in unison and the singing from the crowd was louder than what was coming through the PA! I just threw the mic in the audience and let them sing the first half of the song. I stood there in awe thinking this was the weirdest thing. I wrote the song in my parents' garage two years before that night and here we are half way around the world and they know every song word for word. It was just one of those jaw-dropping experiences. Most of the tour was like that and people were so into what we were doing. The personal upheaval in the band was superseded by what was going on at the shows. Brent played really hard and we were all feeding off each other. But aside from the shows, we were having a tough time interpersonally. We spent the first couple days of the tour in an airport sitting around as the first couple shows fell through. Brent was iffy about going in the first place as he was dating this woman pretty seriously, but he decided to go in the end. He ended up getting really depressed right from the get go and he alienated himself from everyone else in the band. I'm sure we weren't the most supportive people either. So we all stopped talking to each other. We all took it personally and we didn't talk about it for 10 years. The band basically imploded.

DAVE MCCLURE: The tour was amazing. Just to a have the opportunity to go over to Europe was incredible in and of itself. But we had a guitarist who hated touring, and partly as a result of that, people's communication skills were at an all-time low. There was a lot of ridiculous passive-aggressive communication between us all. The first half went well, but Brent stopped participating with the rest of us at some point, and it just spiraled out of control and we all stopped talking to each other. It was ugly and I regret it. I felt really embarrassed and sorry for Kent since he worked so hard organizing that tour. The last show was in England. But it's ironic because we actually played our best live shows at the same time, so that was an interesting contradiction. [laughs] Kevin announced to me that he was quitting with a week left of the tour. He made a phone call to Sonia Skindrud to see if she wanted to start a band when he got back. Kevin never played guitar before ever and he went back and formed a band with her and he learned how to play very good, very fast. So, the drummer, Shawn, and I ended up in that band, too.

KEVIN DOSS: Near the end of the tour Brent talked to Dave who talked to me about wanting to keep things going and I just said I was done. That was a mistake on my part. I figured if we couldn't get it together on a tour then we couldn't keep it going at all. That was the wrong way to look at it, looking back. I'm glad that I was able to play with other people and I ended up learning guitar, but we never recorded those last songs, which was some of the best stuff Downcast had written. But I was too much of an asshole to allow it to happen. There's always been a bit of regret on my part for letting it happen that way and not figure out a way to make it work. It's a supreme irony in that we couldn't express ourselves interpersonally in a conflict with each other, yet we had no problem with conflict and taking about ideas on stage to complete strangers.

DEATH OF CHRIS HERVEY

DAVE MCCLURE: Everyone I know that knew Chris Hervey loved him [Hervey was murdered in 1996]. If Downcast ever sounded good, Chris was the anchor. The last time I saw Chris was October 1994 at the historical march of over 700,000 people in Los Angeles against a California initiative, Proposition 187, that would deny social services, health care, and public education to immigrants. It's a meaningful memory that I have of him. Amongst a lot of things we talked about was how much the punk scene helped shape his world view and how inspired we were at the march. To say his death was tragic is an understatement. It is no exaggeration to say that 13 years later people that I run into that knew him or even just met him briefly on tour still talk about him with me. It's not surprising considering the impression he left on everyone.

LOOKING BACK/LEGACY OF THE BAND

KEVIN DOSS: If we affected ten people then we reached our goal. Downcast was a short-lived band and I think we did some things other people weren't doing at the time. If there are people out there who took something positive from their experience with us, whether it was seeing us or reading an interview or checking out a record, then that's great. We were so in the moment, four kids doing our thing and totally into it. We felt like we were doing the right thing at the time and Dave and I tried to continue it with other bands, but it wasn't the same. Downcast served a purpose for the time. Brent had a lot to do with the appeal of Downcast with his talent and energy. The way we fed off each other, I think, was what made it memorable for us.

DAVE MCCLURE: We've done nothing to preserve any legacy of Downcast at all. [laughs] We're not known that much today like Los Crudos or Econochrist as they've done things to keep their name out there whether they've wanted it to be out there still or not. [laughs] I don't think we have any legacy except for those people from the time who might remember us. But I think we contributed to that era of hardcore in ways that were productive. I think we helped bring up subject matter that wasn't necessarily being taken up by others. Anti-imperialism and addressing issues of privilege in regards to racism weren't the typical straight edge band topics. There were many others who did that too and probably much better than us, but I felt like we at least had a voice in the conversation. And if we have any sort of legacy that's where it would be.

KEVIN DOSS: My perspective on life is different these days. I go to work and see death all around me as a fireman. People are dying from gunshots, accidents, and fires. I come out of that and feel that most people are doing the best they can with what they know. Being as judgmental as I was at the time, I wish I had a better perspective, but you're young and you feel so passionate about these ideas and don't know what to do with them and you're like, "Fuck everything! I need to express this!" Now I still feel mostly the same about all those things I talked about in Downcast. For instance, I have two daughters, so not being into women's rights would be idiocy for me now. [laughs] It's extremely important for me in terms of raising healthy kids. Now I'm trying to take on the system while also raising healthy human beings who feel good about themselves. But I think I've softened as far as personal accountability. We never were about forcing ideas on people, but we did want people to think, so we'd come across strong. Now being 37 it's interesting to see how these things have become so ingrained in my life.

SELECT DISCOGRAPHY:

Downcast (7", Ebullition, 1991)
    Doss, Stephens, McClure, Vasquez

Downcast (LP, Ebullition, 1992)
    Doss, Stephens, McClure, Hervey

EARTH CRISIS

Vocals: Karl Buechner

Guitars: Scott Crouse
Erick Edwards
Kris Wiechmann
Ben Read

Bass: Ian Edwards

Drums: Dennis Merrick
Mike Ricardi

Vegetarianism, veganism, animal rights, and straight edge were all addressed in one form or another by many nineties hardcore groups, but Earth Crisis made one of the biggest impacts on all of these topics. With their combination of militant lyrics and metal-style riffs and vocals, their sound influenced much of the metal sound that many hardcore bands played in the nineties.

Formed in 1989, Earth Crisis was assembled by Syracuse residents Karl Buechner and D.J. Rose to become a new voice for straight edge and animal rights. Although several notable bands helped pioneer the focus on these topics in the eighties, Buechner and Rose (the original vocalist) felt the issues needed a push. After playing some shows and then going through some lineup changes, Buechner became the frontman, while Rose — busy setting up Syracuse hardcore shows — decided to bow out in 1991 before the band had recorded anything. The group solidified with Scott Crouse and Ben Read on guitar, Ian "Bulldog" Edwards on bass, and Mike Ricardi on drums. After Earth Crisis released their debut seven-inch, *All Out War*, Ricardi left the band and drummer Dennis Merrick came aboard.

Their famously intense live shows often provoked so-called "hard" style dancing and on-stage pile-ups with kids clambering to reach the microphone to sing along. Earth Crisis played at the 1993 More Than Music Fest in Ohio, which brought in people from around the country. Their set at the fest was energetic and aggressive and helped raise their profile within the hardcore scene.

Firestorm (1994), their second seven-inch, elicited debate about Earth Crisis and their politics. The self-titled opening track on the record — famous for its "open E chord" chugging and controversial lyrics — became an anthem for vegan straight edge hardcore kids. However, some questions arose about their lyrics, which advocated "violence against violence" in defending neighborhoods from drugs.

Destroy the Machines (1995), their first full-length, found the band combining their hardcore/metal sound with more technical musicianship. Some criticized the outfit's delving into metal, but the members insisted they were just following their musical interests. Around this time Earth Crisis also achieved some mainstream notoriety, appearing on environmental television specials on CBS, CNN, and MTV.

Earth Crisis became one of the best selling hardcore bands of their time and toured the U.S. several times, often with other popular hardcore bands like Snapcase, Strife, and Madball. They also toured Europe and Japan. Their next album, *Gomorrah's Season Ends* (1996), was possibly their most diverse record in terms of music and lyrics. Guitarist Erick Edwards — brother of bassist Ian Edwards — also became a full-time member of the band at that point.

In 1998 Earth Crisis signed with Roadrunner Records and released *Breed the Killers*. However, the record didn't reach an acceptable level of sales for the larger record company, so the label and the band parted ways. In the meantime, the group continued to tour the world, including having a spot on the Ozzfest tour, and continued to spread their messages of straight edge and animal rights. After a couple of final releases, Earth Crisis played their last show at Hellfest in 2001 (until a 2008 reunion tour brought them back to the stage).

Although some questioned their intentions and the motives behind some of their lyrics, Earth Crisis was one of the most popular nineties hardcore bands. A good portion of nineties hardcore was about raising awareness and sparking revolution of the mind, body, and spirit. Earth Crisis is rightly considered an important force in that regard as they changed attitudes and motivated many fans to action.

ORIGINS OF THE BAND

KARL BUECHNER: All of us had been in garage style hardcore bands, and we'd get together and play for friends or skaters or whatever. So, we cut our teeth with music in that way and by the time we were all about 19 or so we could recognize the other people who were living true to straight edge and who were decent enough musicians to start a serious band with. [laughs] We all gravitated toward each other because of our similar ideals and our somewhat different taste in music than the average hardcore kids back then. We were definitely into Slayer and D.R.I. and early Metallica records, as well as Killing Time, Agnostic Front and Sick of it All. That's kind of what our sound was — it was a combination of what we thought were the best elements of those two styles of the spectrum.

DENNIS MERRICK: The initial start [of Earth Crisis] was a bunch of guys Karl hung with who were all straight edge dudes. Karl was playing bass and D.J. Rose was singing. They had a few songs and played a couple shows and nothing really happened. Karl always had a vision for Earth Crisis, though. He was relentless about making the band succeed. The four guys he was involved with originally, other than D.J., all stopped being straight edge. He really wanted it to be a vegan straight edge band with a powerful message, so he did everything he could to find people with similar beliefs. He met up with Scott Crouse, Ben Read, Mike Ricardi, and Ian Edwards who were all in a band called Framework. They did it as a side thing along with Framework, but after Earth Crisis played its first show they got really excited and wanted to keep it going. The guys came up to me at a show and they knew I was vegetarian and straight edge, so they asked me if I'd be into playing for them. They said Mike didn't want to go on tour because he wanted to stay home with his dog. [laughs] They said I needed to be vegan to be in the band, which I had been trying to do for a while, so it was probably the kick in the ass I needed to become vegan. I joined the band and we played the More Than Music Festival in Dayton, Ohio about two weeks later and that was sort of the first show we played for a lot of people outside Syracuse.

INFLUENCES/OUTLOOK

KARL BUECHNER: At first because we were combining elements of metal with hardcore a lot of the scene was put off by that because we did sound different. That was the biggest problem we had at first, but obviously people began to understand what we were trying to do musically. We were doing what was true to our taste. After a while we were rewarded for that because it set our sound apart. And there were bands like Conviction and Merauder that had that metallic style; we just took it further and added in some technical aspects and always tried to re-invent ourselves sound-wise to keep ourselves motivated. At the same time, we retained the purity of our message. Once we started to grow, straight edge went from being one of the smallest factions in the overall hardcore scene to one of the most dominant. If you look at record collections from the early to mid-nineties you'll realize there were a lot of straight edge bands from this era... not just here in but in Europe, Australia, and other places. There was also some opposition to that as far as why we were against drugs and alcohol and the reason why we were against it wasn't because we were uptight — we wanted to be the best athletes and musicians as possible and that's why we are against drugs and alcohol. Once we took the straight edge vow and we gained clarity of thought by abstaining from those poisons, and it enables us to be more effective animal rights activists and environmentalists. When you try to explore those things they are a lot easier to understand if you're not a drug addict or an alcoholic. I look at my own life and by being straight edge I am more effective in the things that I care about.

DENNIS MERRICK: I was the only guy in that band who didn't like metal when I joined. We'd go on tour and the rest of the guys would be listening to C.O.C. and Slayer and I always wanted to listen to Turning Point and Judge. [laughs] I actually grew to really like metal over time, though. As we continued we got more proficient and we were able to play more technical stuff, which probably made us sound a little more metal. We ended up loving that marriage of metal and hardcore. Back then metal didn't have much of a groove to it and hardcore did. We mixed that metal sound and added that hardcore groove and made our own sound. You can play a lot of different types of music and still be a hardcore band. Look at the variety of sounds that came about in the nineties.

AMBITION

KARL BUECHNER: Our goal was to be the best vegan straight edge band possible. We wanted to take our time to craft our music and lyrics and forward a message to people. Over time, it began to work. Earth Crisis played at least 800 shows and we stayed together for over ten years as a band. We were on CNN and *48 Hours*. Every time the media came to do a documentary on hardcore or vegan straight edge and we were a part of it, our message came across crystal clear. It helped get more people into things and motivate them, so we're really proud of what we did. At first the band was more about venting our own feelings of rage or frustration — later on when we realized that people were listening to what we said and took it to heart we tried to put more of an emphasis on attempting to come up with some solutions to these problems.

D.J. ROSE: The band really broke out at the 1993 Dayton Hardcore Fest. This was pre-Internet and these rumors spread and people would say, "Have you heard what happens when this band plays? People go insane and the band goes berserk, the singer screams his ears out and there are like 50 dudes in ninja masks beating the crap out of each other." [laughs] So, they had the opening slot of the heavy bands at the fest, which was kind of a crappy slot but it ended up working out for the band because the afternoon set was the emo set and the first hard band of the day brought about 50 people with them, as well as people from Chicago and Albany and places where the band was going over really well. So, there was all this anticipation to watch them play, which was partially based on all the crazy rumors. [laughs] When they played the lights went out and all you could hear was the chug-chug of "Firestorm" and you could just forget about it. The place exploded! We watched a video and tried to count the amount of flash bulbs going off during "Firestorm" and there were over 300. People went nuts! A lot of people weren't sure how to take the band so they  were antagonistic, but once they met the guys and talked to them they found they were actually pretty down to earth. But I think that show is what made Earth Crisis.

"ALL OUT WAR"

KARL BUECHNER: We had finally established a real lineup and while we were composing the songs, I was working with a woman who ran a wildlife rehabilitation center. On weekly basis I would see animals that had been beaten with pipes or had been doused with gasoline and burned or even intentionally stomped on. A lot of hatred was building up inside of me from seeing all these vicious acts of cruelty and people not really being punished for it. I have a deep reverence for animals. I think their intentions are very pure, so to see an animal brutalized and then see in the paper that the person who committed the act would get a few months and that was it. That really got me riled up and that is reflected in the tone and lyrics of the record.

VEGAN STRAIGHT EDGE

KARL BUECHNER: Earth Crisis was and the members will always be vegan straight edge. The more interviews we did, the more we toured, the more records we put out, people began to see that our goal was to be a band that went out and distributed animal rights literature and tried to write positive lyrics and educate people and not force things. We were more into trying to teach people something and we didn't want to exclude anyone.

ABORTION

KARL BUECHNER: For most of the band, we were and are in 200 percent agreement that most abortions are the outright murder of a defenseless human life. Ultimately it's no different than what happens to an animal in a slaughterhouse. Both beings are victims for either someone's convenience or profit. Obviously these are not things that people want to hear because they are in direct contrast to what the powers that be deluge our minds with such as, "A fetus doesn't feel pain; animals exist for us to slaughter and devour." These lies lead to death, misery, and regret. In the actual procedure, the unborn are basically vacuumed out and dropped alive into a container of chemicals where they die in agony. So, the parallel between issues of abortion and animal rights is a line I tried to connect in a paragraph I wrote in *All Out War*. "Pro-life" is the title of a religious anti-abortion movement that also protests the execution of prisoners who are guilty of heinous crimes. So, we basically approached the whole thing from a different angle — respect for all innocent life across the board. Realistic reproductive education entails showing people an unborn child in their mother's womb... responding to her voice by moving about, growing, sleeping, and so on in order to teach the reality of their situation. Basically between that and promoting the idea of free distribution of birth control in schools and colleges, we tried to show the truth and offer some of the solutions. The music industry and Hollywood relentlessly promote the lie of free promiscuous sex. Obviously a lot of people try to live this fantasy and end up having to deal with an unwanted and unplanned child who they are pregnant with. It may take 10 or 20 more years before that child knows their first true day of happiness. If they are allowed to live and are adopted or raised in an orphanage at least they have that chance. If a pregnancy occurs after a woman has been raped or if incest or if the unborn has been so wounded in an accident or sickness that all they would do is suffer then I can see how abortion might be necessary or even merciful. Sometimes from what I understand it can also be necessary to save a woman's life if there are complications. Overall, most abortions aren't for any of these reasons, though. They are done to terminate an unwanted pregnancy that resulted from irresponsible sex. In 1991, our friend Shane from Framework sang in Earth Crisis for a few months before I took over vocals and gave Bulldog my bass. Shane wrote a song called "Stand By" that we kept. I wrote a paragraph in the lyric sheet of *All Out War* to define what we meant with one of his lines in the song. I basically stated we wanted to attack the problem of abortion with education, peaceful protest, and compassion. At its essence, Earth Crisis was about treating all innocent life — both human and animal — with respect. It would not be truthful to overlook this issue. So even though we raised the issue in an awkward manner, I think the essay in that record has done a lot of good.

"FIRESTORM"

KARL BUECHNER: I lost my friend Jason, which was directly related to drugs and alcohol. When Scott's younger brother was born he walked through a part of the hospital where these babies were born that were addicted to crack, which was a pretty big epidemic still at the time. It was sickening to all of us that someone had no problem with walking over to a pregnant woman and selling her something that was not only killing her but also her unborn child. A lot of incidents and observations like these influenced the lyrics and intensity of our music. It was the ultimate injustice that there were all these bands and artists out there promoting drugs and gang culture. They were getting huge record contracts from major labels and million-dollar prime time MTV video pushes. We really came out against all these things, and that's where *Firestorm* came from.

DENNIS MERRICK: *Firestorm* was a great experience for me. I grew up straight edge and vegetarian in the hardcore scene. I'd never really been in a real straight edge band before, though. The first song we wrote was "Unseen Holocaust" and then we did "Eden's Demise." We were writing obviously vegan straight edge songs. I felt there was a rebirth of straight edge when we started to play those songs live. It felt great to be a part of that. I grew up listening to Minor Threat and Uniform Choice and they sparked something in me. It felt cool to be involved in a band that was sparking something else. *Firestorm* came out when I was studying in Africa for a college class and I got a letter from Tim Redmond from Snapcase about the show and he said it was amazing. The guys got Mike to fill in for me and the crowd was singing so loud that you didn't even need a microphone. I got so excited, but I was halfway around the world. I was having an incredible experience in Zimbabwe, but I couldn't wait to start playing some shows with the band because the record was being received so well.

KARL BUECHNER: "Firestorm" is about fighting back against the ruin brought by the drug epidemic. Hard drug use has become so normalized over the past 30 years that we are at the point where we've devolved into a strung out society. Everyone is affected across the socio-economic and racial spectrum. Whether a family member is an addict or a victim of a street crime for drug money, the overall health and safety of entire nations is being jeopardized. Parts of Mexico, Panama, and Columbia have been destabilized through shootings and even car bombs. The cartels terrorize the politicians, police, and citizens and they can't control the corruption. The Mexican Army basically shut down and disarmed. The police in Tijuana face things so out of control. The song "Firestorm" is an account of the vigilantes who have burned down crack houses and shot dealers in an attempt to take back their neighborhoods. These things happened in Central Florida and West Texas. For some reason they only received a minimal amount of news coverage.

DENNIS MERRICK: Some people said "Firestorm" was a racist song because their argument was the majority of drug dealers are people of color, so they thought we were talking about harming people of color. That in itself is a racist thought though because they are assuming most drug dealers are African-American or Hispanic. If a person's doing something evil they shouldn't be allowed to continue doing that, regardless of their skin color. The controversy used to piss me off, but it actually was healthy because it meant people were thinking. As far as "Firestorm" went, that song is about people in a drug dealer infested neighborhood and taking their neighborhood back. It was controversial because it talks about killing drug dealers, basically. If a neighborhood does take itself back and in the process of doing that they take out somebody who is doing something bad then that's what has to happen. One thing I didn't like about the controversy was that "Firestorm" became an anthem in a negative way for a lot of idiot kids in some places. If some of these kids wanted to fight someone who wasn't straight edge at a show they'd say they were going to "Firestorm" them, which I thought was idiotic. Those aren't the people who need to be put in place.

RUMORS/CONTROVERSY

KARL BUECHNER: Some people prejudged us for supposedly being fascist straight edge thugs. [laughs] But most people realized after a while that *Maximum Rock N'Roll* wasn't the most reliable source of information. Especially after we'd go and play all over, people began to see what kind of people we are. We were never out there to judge people or hurt anyone; we wanted to share knowledge people and motivate them to try and do their best and help alleviate some of the suffering in the world. Earth Crisis always toured and played with all types of hardcore, metal and even hip-hop bands... we played with Warzone, Biohazard, Madball, Strife, Skarhead, Downset, Vision of Disorder, Candiria — some of which don't have a single straight edge member — and we got along fine with them. They respected us and we respected them and they are making some incredible music.

DENNIS MERRICK: There was a show in New Jersey and some kids were throwing yogurt at us while we were playing. At one point a kid with a fur coat ran across the stage to make fun of us for being into animal rights. We didn't do anything but our fans beat the kid down. He was being disrespectful and he probably deserved it. [laughs] There were a lot of misconceptions about us being a violent band, but the only time we ever had any physical altercations is when people were outright disrespectful.

D. J. ROSE: People would say, "Someone from Earth Crisis beat my friend up." Oh really? You mean your friend at the show wearing the fur coat and throwing cheese and yogurt at them? I fail to see why that happened. [laughs] But everyone wants to see things from their own viewpoint and they don't want to take a step back and look at these things from both sides.

"DESTROY THE MACHINES"

KARL BUECHNER: Every time we were in the practice room we were stoked and encouraging each other. We were brimming with energy. Going to practice was something we'd look forward to all day. We were hyped on the energy and the fun of the band. All we were doing was writing songs for our tastes. There were so many people out there who were interested in what we put together.

DENNIS MERRICK: It was interesting because it was a transitional phase for us. Ben Read was still with us for the first part of the writing for that record. He wrote a lot of the music for *All Out War* and *Firestorm* and his writing started to get phased out due to his leaving for Scott's writing. Scott really took responsibility for writing most of it. It was definitely a metal record. We recorded it with the guys from Believer so the production on it was pretty metal. I was in college so I'd travel every weekend to Syracuse to practice. We recorded in Pennsylvania in weekends, so I'd blow off my homework every weekend and work on the record. It was a continuation of the message we were trying to get across with *Firestorm*.

MEDIA ATTENTION

D. J. ROSE: We had been asked to do some of these media things for a while, but we realized people could twist your words around. There was this guy from Atlanta who worked for a show called Network Earth and he said no matter what he wouldn't make us look like idiots. We realized if he gave us a fair portrayal then this could get some good attention for the issues we cared about. Karl and I were also media savvy enough to not answer any negative questions because they often cut out the questions and just use your answers, and they are often taken out of context. A person might have a three-minute answer and they use the five seconds where you might get angry so we were careful of that. We then got asked to do MTV *Smashed* and *20/20* and this Brazilian TV show and though the shows might not have directly appealed to hardcore kids it did reach people who probably didn't even know what hardcore was.

"GOMORRAH'S SEASON ENDS"

DENNIS MERRICK: We always believed the struggles of any marginalized groups are always interconnected. You can't believe in animal rights without believing in human rights or vice versa. Both struggles go right along with each other. For example, forests are cleared in South America for the production of beef for U.S. companies like McDonalds. Those forests are where a lot of indigenous people used to live in South America. Basically, this deforestation is displacing indigenous people. That's an obvious place where human and animal rights are connected. I don't think a person can fight for one cause without fighting for other causes. Exploring more human rights issues on *Gomorrah's Season Ends* was just a natural extension of what we always felt. We believed in fighting for those who couldn't fight for themselves. We've always addressed human rights issues but this record had more of a focus on that perspective. I wanted to make it obvious that all the issues we touched on in the essay within the record were addressed. We wanted to show all these issues — homophobia, animal rights, racism — were all interconnected. You have to struggle against all these evils for the world to become a better place.

BROADENING MUSICAL HORIZONS

KARL BUECHNER: Most of us were classically trained. Some of us played in orchestra and jazz band in school. We were more open-minded in terms of sounds than many other bands at the time. We were very experimental with our sound. We liked the aggression and power that metal had and we loved the energy and ideas that hardcore was promoting, so we melded the two together for what in our view was perfect. We loved Judge and the early Slayer albums; we loved *Ride the Lightning* and *Master of Puppets*. When we started to play our version of metallic hardcore in the straight edge scene a lot of kids weren't into it because it wasn't a sound they were used to. That was one of our biggest obstacles because we sounded so different than the traditional old-school sound.

DENNIS MERRICK: We were becoming more about exploring new musical boundaries. We were listening to Meshuggah a lot and that inspired us. The record definitely had more of a metal feel and we were getting more creative, which in some ways might have been to our detriment. We had a lot of cool parts but in some cases the songs didn't always blend together. We started to figure it out on *Breed the Killers* and *Slither*; we wanted to keep our creativity intact but keep the songs listenable. Our musicianship was getting better and we were trying to do cooler stuff musically. It got to the point where we had to back it up a little bit and make the songs more actual songs as opposed to just throwing interesting parts together.

END OF THE ROAD

KARL BUECHNER: We reached the point where some of us were married and starting families. It just didn't seem to be right to be on the road all the time and we were a full-force touring band. We agreed it was the right decision. We were at our peak and that was the time to shut it down and do other things.

DENNIS MERRICK: When we did the band full time we didn't have time for anything else. Earth Crisis was our life, but once people started having families we had to re-evaluate what was more important. So, when Ian, Erick and Karl came to us about doing the band part time, we just felt like if we weren't going to do it full time then why do it? There wasn't any bad blood; we all still hang out. There were just changes in our lives that made it tougher to do the band. So, we decided to bring The Path of Resistance back and work on that band when we could.

LONGEVITY/ACCOMPLISHMENTS

KARL BUECHNER: It's incredible how much we accomplished without a dime of tour support or without a video on MTV. Earth Crisis lasted 10 years and we had 10 CDs while bands on major labels in the same time span that had hundreds of thousands of dollars worth of hype machine behind them came and went. That's why people began to see that we were sincere after lasting for so long and continuing our message. From the beginning the goal was to promote veganism and straight edge. We had all seen people we cared about destroyed by addiction and hated the dealers who were to blame. I spent some time at the Syracuse Wildlife Rehabilitation Center [where I saw animals that had survived] cruelty... so sickening that it filled me with hate. So Earth Crisis was how I boiled it down and vented out that rage. Every release had a specific theme both musically and message wise, so we had songs about everything — the threat of nuclear war, ghosts of Native Americans, vigilantes, cloning, everything. Overall, though, the focus always stayed on vegan straight edge.

SELECT DISCOGRAPHY:

All Out War (7", Conviction, 1992)
    Buechner, Crouse, Read, Edwards, Ricardi

Firestorm (7"/MCD, Victory, 1994)
    Buechner, Crouse, Read, Edwards, Merrick

Destroy the Machines (CD/LP, Victory, 1996)
    Buechner, Crouse, Wiechmann, Edwards, Merrick

Gomorrah's Season Ends (CD/LP, Victory, 1997)
    Buechner, Crouse, Wiechmann, Edwards, Merrick

Breed the Killers (CD/LP, Roadrunner, 1998)
    Buechner, Crouse, Edwards, Edwards, Merrick

Slither (CD/LP, Victory, 2000)
    Buechner, Crouse, Edwards, Edwards, Merrick

Last of the Sane (CD/LP, Victory, 2001)
    Buechner, Crouse, Edwards, Edwards, Merrick

ENDPOINT

Vocals: Rob Pennington
Bass: Kyle Noltemeyer
     Pat McClimans
     Jason Graff
     Jason Hayden

Guitars: Duncan Barlow
     Chad Castetter
Drums: Lee Fetzer
     Rusty Sohms
     Kyle Crabtree

Formed in 1987, Louisville's Endpoint was the musical conception of founding members Duncan Barlow (guitarist), Rob Pennington (vocalist), and Chad Castetter (guitarist). Their music took hardcore in unique directions as they utilized melody, introspective and sometimes depressed lyrics, and progressive, indie-rock leaning song structures that were a counter-point to some of the anti-intellectual and macho elements of the scene. Along with bands like Falling Forward, Lincoln, Hoover, Split Lip, and Ashes, they helped lead a movement of like-minded melodic nineties hardcore bands that felt hardcore need not rely on metal riffs or mosh parts to be intense and emotional.

Endpoint began with as a mish-mash of influences, which accounts for what some felt was an all-over-the-map sound on their debut, *If the Spirits Are Willing* (Slamdek/Doghouse). They followed up Spirits with more streamlined hardcore on their second record, I*n a Time of Hate* (Conversion), as well as an appearance on the *Voice of the Voiceless* (Smorgasbord) animal rights compilation. In the midst of these early recordings and performances, they fine-tuned their sound while embarking on probing and self-revealing journeys. While writing some of their best material, they — along with several other notable "emotional" hardcore bands — created a trend in hardcore that called for one's deepest and most personal emotions to be present and exorcised while playing, prompting equally turbulent responses from audiences. It wasn't uncommon to find the band totally losing it on stage while many in the crowd sang along with tears in their eyes.

The emotional release from these shows was embodied on their next album, the aptly named *Catharsis* (Doghouse Records). This was arguably the group's landmark record, particularly in terms of lyrical content. Pennington wrote several songs condemning sexual violence and prejudice. Songs like "Days After," "Iceberg," and "Caste" became anthems for many nineties hardcore kids. Going to an Endpoint show was an ethereal experience for their fans, which put an immense amount of pressure on the band. They followed up *Catharsis* with the more somber and melodic *After Taste* (Doghouse) in 1993. *After Taste* contained several memorable tunes that became staples at their performances. With the stress of fans — some of them on the verge of suicide — contacting members of the band in a search for answers, the experience began to take its toll.

After seven years, band leaders Barlow and Pennington decided to bring Endpoint to a halt, but not before recording a final EP (*Last Record*) that brought forth an entirely new sound that combined elements of the melodic, emotional hardcore they were already known for with post-hardcore, rock, and feedback drenched noise.

While Endpoint was criticized for their unflinching honesty by the "tough guy" set, as well as from the slate of hardcore purists who rejected their deviation from traditional hardcore formulas, the band connected with a lot of people emotionally at a time in their lives when they needed it the most. In reciprocity, Barlow and Pennington received just as much from fans, which forced these guys to mature from rambunctious hardcore kids into adults: Pennington has been a special education teacher for several years; Barlow an author and university professor. Although these men both became teachers as adults, even in their younger years they were able to inspire and lead by example, proving it was okay to focus one's deepest and darkest feelings in a positive way by bravely standing up and voicing their own fears and painful self-realizations.

ORIGINS

ROB PENNINGTON: At that point [when we started Endpoint] I thought being in a band was the best way to participate in the punk rock scene, which at that time exuded a feeling of mysticism of, "I'm doing something different" and I really belonged. My full participation in punk by playing in a band was very important to me at that age. You were either a really good skateboarder or in a band or you were one of those "tough" punk kids. Basically, I wasn't tough and I wasn't very good at skateboarding, so I wanted to be in a band. [laughs] When I was about 16 I was in a band that was called Fist and then later changed its name to Foodfight, and Duncan was in a band called Crisis. We knew each other but this mutual friend of ours inspired us all to come together and form Death Watch.

DUNCAN BARLOW: Endpoint started in 1987 under the name Death Watch. Less than a year after forming, we decided that the band needed to stand for something more than simply playing rock, not to mention the name was terrible. Rob and I mulled over several names and finally settled on a geometrical term. It seemed funny at the time, the paradox of searching for change and selecting a name that represented the end. I suppose if we had ever really thought about it, we would have realized the signifying qualities of the name and the search for change. Rob was the best person for me to be around, as we both constantly challenged each other's morality and decisions. We kept each other in check and as time progressed and other members moved on in other directions — marriage, drugs, careers — Rob and I continued following our ideals and attempted new things. We weren't the most progressive band; however, I feel we had a special intensity that really allowed the audience to cross that boundary of band/audience relations and actually become a part of everything. The actual ideals of the band changed with time, and as we moved on to new ideologies to discuss we never abandoned our earlier convictions.

ROB PENNINGTON: We were teenagers from Kentucky in a time very different from now. [laughs] Now there about twelve million bands on tour all over the country with their own vans; when we got going we just wanted to play some shows. I remember playing in Indiana was a big deal for us. [laughs]

ROB PENNINGTON: Louisville folks were supportive of us. The scene was pretty small at the time — between all of us we had a large peer group that identified with what we were doing. We had some good shows with other amazing local bands like Kinghorse and very quickly we amassed a large group of peers that came to see our band play. Going from Death Watch playing to 50 people to Endpoint playing for a couple hundred people — and within a couple years there were several hundred people coming out to shows — it was somewhat surprising and very inspiring.

INFLUENCES

DUNCAN BARLOW: Where we started was much different from where we ended. We were incredibly influenced by a local band called Malignant Growth that used to play shows with Minor Threat and Black Flag. They had incredible intensity and emotion. After a few years passed Dag Nasty, Rites of Spring, Verbal Assault, and Neurosis really had an impact on what I was trying to do with my songwriting. We seemed to levitate towards bands that had strong political lyrics and driving melodies.

"IF THE SPIRITS ARE WILLING"

ROB PENNINGTON: We recorded [If the Spirits...] at Juniper Hill Studios with this guy named Cubby Cleaver, who still has a label in Louisville. The cool thing back then was to have a tape and Scott Ritcher was putting out tapes of Louisville bands on his label, Slamdek. Scott made several pressings of it and it was eventually re-released by Doghouse. Some of the songs are so terrible, and there are so many of them on there! [laughs] There is such a difference between what 16 and 17-year-old kids are playing now compared to what we accomplished back then. Kids are much more sophisticated and have more access to different tools to make music now.

DUNCAN BARLOW: Our drummer borrowed some money from his friend and we did 17 songs for under 400 dollars. We recorded at some studios before and the sound was so poor that we never did anything with the songs; however, the studio in which we recorded *Spirits* was quite nice and spent time working with us. I think we did the entire record in three days. We went on hiatus for about a year after we recorded that, got a new drummer and second guitar player, and came back to a large audience we never anticipated. So many things influenced that record, as you can tell it runs the gamut musically; some songs sound like Metallica, some sound like the Youth of Today. We were 16 to 17 years old and, looking back, we were musical sponges, auditioning new styles and sounds. Rob and I were also developing our political ideas around that time.

ROB PENNINGTON: During that time there were definitely different elements of punk: there was the angry, pissed-off kind of thing and there were those that came from a more artistic approach and dealt with feelings. There were also those from a more political perspective and this had quite the impact on us, not to mention the things our eyes were opening up to in our community. I remember the police officers were so terrible to us at that time. We all used to converge on several parking lots on Bardstown Road and every six months we'd get booted off. We'd play kick-ball or hang out. I remember one time the police came up there and almost ran everybody over; they got out and started yelling at someone and grabbed a friend of ours who had been drinking and slammed his head into a police car. He didn't react at all other than to say, "I'm sorry." They threw him down and started kicking him and another friend of ours ran across the street to call the police station to tell them what was happening and then a car came by and picked him up, too! It was constant harassment! I was born in the suburbs and definitely had a sheltered life until that point. But it made me so angry. I remember also being very angry at the social class system that is set up at schools. Of course, now being an educator I understand the whole shifting and sorting process of public education, but back then I had a sense that it was wrong. I always felt out of place back then and it came through in those early lyrics.

"IN A TIME OF HATE"

ROB PENNINGTON: Louisville was more of a punk community and everyone came to every show regardless if bands were hardcore or punk or whatever. As we started traveling and playing out of town we started to realize there was this segregation in other cities between punk and hardcore kids. The more we traveled we became more affiliated with the "hardcore" scene and we made more connections in that circuit. One of the people we met was Dennis Remsing from Outspoken and Conversion Records. He and Tony Erba from Face Value helped us get on a compilation called *Voice of Thousands*, which was kind of our first release. I remember we played in Middlesex, New Jersey and it was one of our first big shows. People didn't know our stuff and didn't really react until we played the song from that compilation and the whole crowd jumped on top of everybody. It was chaos. I couldn't even see; it was a sea of kids crawling on the stage. Someone hit Chad Castetter in the groin and he's kind of an intense fellow. He picked up his guitar

over his head and was using it like an ax. He went berserk and split two kids' heads open, which got us all in some hot water. [laughs] Eventually, we went to Cleveland, Ohio and we knew Integrity recorded there, who we were friends with at the time. It was kind of a lame process. It was our first out of town recording experience.

DUNCAN BARLOW: I was never a big fan of *In a Time of Hate*. We recorded with this producer who hated us and made terrible racist jokes. We recorded for two days and drove home. It sounds horrible and you can tell when you listen to it that there was a desire not to be there. We didn't do the artwork, Conversion records did, and it came off a bit more "straight edge" than we really were as a band. Also, the LP came out about a year after we recorded it, so by that time we were working on the songs for the next record, which were more developed.

MIDWEST VS. "COAST" HARDCORE?

ROB PENNINGTON: I remember showing up to shows in flannels and jeans and we looked like Kentucky hillbillies. [laughs] We'd roll out in front of this place in, say, New Jersey with hundreds of kids with their hair styled and in windbreakers and full-on athletic gear. It was way different then back home where everyone just wanted to fly their freak flag. [laughs] People would dance hard in Louisville, but I had never seen kickboxing until we played out of town. There was definitely this hardcore camaraderie in other places, which was cool in a way, but it was also less diverse. But it definitely influenced us; sometimes not for the better. You can tell *In a Time of Hate* is definitely influenced by our exposure to the broader hardcore scene as it's a much more "hardcore" record than the stuff we did later.

DUNCAN BARLOW: The Midwest was awkward and seemed really believable. The bands really tried to live by example and simply have fun. We supported each other in every way possible. The coasts sometimes seemed like they had a "sound" or something. There were some great bands mind you, but when we played on the coasts we always felt like outcasts. On the East Coast there was this obsession with The Smiths and The Gap that I never fully understood. The Midwest seemed less concerned with the fashion or marketability of the music. This, of course, did not lead to very good record sales toward the end of the era. The last Endpoint record really confused people. I should say though that it's problematic to view things in terms of geography because there were so many great movements and bands from every area. Perhaps geographic seclusion can lead to something authentic in one area of musical development, but it is important to know that all the Midwest bands were listening to the bands on the coasts and when we all broke out the coasts began listening to our music, too.

STRAIGHT EDGE BAND?

DUNCAN BARLOW: We never were [as a full band]. There was a time some of us were interested in that idea, but since Louisville was a small town, it was impossible to find a band of people who were all drug-free. Not to mention, in hindsight, straight edge was a very limited phase for many people. If you were to take a survey of people who were drug free in the nineties today, only a few of us would be left. It matters less to me now than when I was seventeen and really needed something to support me in my battle against peer pressure.

ROB PENNINGTON: I guess we weren't a "straight edge" band because all of us weren't straight edge. We also went through a lot of members over the years and several of the members weren't. During that time, though, straight edge was a really important part of my life. In Kentucky there was a lot of alcohol abuse and a lot of peer pressure to consume it. Straight edge really helped me stay clear of making more wrong choices than I probably already did. I hope we never alienated anybody because of straight edge because we would talk about it on stage as Duncan and I were both straight edge. But many of my friends weren't straight edge. You look at that as a singer later in life and hope you made the best choices possible and hope you didn't make anybody in the crowd feel bad about themselves. When you're playing and there are hundreds of people there and you make a statement that goes to the extreme in one way or another you're going to alienate people. Our intention was to do a band that could give something back to everybody because we related to lots of people and to this day my peer group is so diverse.

MUSICAL PROGRESSION

DUNCAN BARLOW: We grew as musicians — not much, mind you. [laughs] By 1993 we weren't listening to much hardcore, we were really into the Touch and Go bands and Sub Pop bands so our influences were really changing. This is not to say that we didn't listen to hardcore at all, but that it was much harder to impress some of us with the standard fare.

ROB PENNINGTON: Lyrically, I became exposed to a lot more people and a sense of responsibility set in. Back then people wrote us letters all the time and it really made me feel like I had some sense of responsibility, which influenced the kind of songs I wanted to write. Across the U.S. I also met a lot of strong vocal women who made a major impact on me. Somehow we attracted this group of caring, socially responsible folks to our shows and I was meeting them and learning a lot from them. I've learned a lot about who I am as a person through meeting people from all over the place in the scene and staying up all night and having these great conversations. These experiences really shaped who I am now.

DUNCAN BARLOW: Endpoint occurred at a very influential moment in our lives, as it began when we were all sixteen years old. As we played shows and interacted with other people in the scene, we realized that the people who claimed to be progressive thinkers were actually quite backwards and proved to be borderline racist or sexist. I'm talking outside of the context of their private jokes, but outward actions that signified their masked opinions.

FORERUNNERS OF EMO?

DUNCAN BARLOW: I suppose looking back I would agree with [us being considered "emo"]. However, what we think of "emo" now is so different than what it meant at that time. "Emo" was about emotion, which was a messy thing; now it seems quite homogenized and sterile, not very emotional at all. When I hear "emo" bands these days I think of high end compression. When I think of "emo" in the eighties and nineties I think of dynamics.

ROB PENNINGTON: When I think of the early "emo" bands I think of Rites of Spring and a lot of those D.C. bands and early punk music and how emotionally charged it was. I'm flattered that people would put us in the same company as bands like those; to me that's the beauty of this type of music — the emotional outlet. To this day I can go see a band that may not be that great musically, but if they are really charged with emotion and I feel what they are sending out there then I'll love them as opposed to a band that is super polished and sterile. We really wanted to be ruled by emotion. I'll never forget this show we played in an art gallery in Chicago. It was the weirdest thing. There weren't a whole lot of people there and the stage was kind of odd, but I remember we played some *Catharsis* songs that we had just written and we lost our minds. I mean, physically hurting ourselves! We were all going through relationship break-ups at the time and something snapped in us. Before that we were always super positive and cared about people and we put out a lot of love, but that show we really tapped into the pain we were feeling. After that, Endpoint really became what it was; that's where that "emo" tag may have come from. You'll see a lot of hardcore bands that are like coaches, "All right, kids! Let's do it!!" They are really positive, but you can't necessarily connect with it emotionally and that's probably kind of how we were up until that show. It wasn't until we told ourselves it was okay to lose your mind when playing music and to tap into those energies that we really began to become the band we became known to be. We realized that's the most important message we could share. To accept people for who they are, they had to be willing to not hide what was going on inside of them, and be able to express themselves and let it out. And that's where it changed for us; one night at some weird art gallery in Chicago. [laughs]

DUNCAN BARLOW: It was a strange time where most of us were experiencing growing pains; more specifically we experienced this strange phenomenon where several of us were suffering with severe depressive episodes that lead to erratic behavior and emotional outbursts. We all pulled in different directions and I would argue that this pulling generated a stress that formed the music and lyrics. We were a group of kids from Kentucky. I think there is something in the water in Kentucky that drives people a little crazy. Someone once told me it was the barometric pressure of living in the Ohio Valley, but I never gave that much credit. [laughs] But I can say that, as a group, we were a very depressed and volatile group of kids. We didn't express our depression through elaborate stage antics or costumes like many groups of the era did, we simply wrote punk songs and played them. I think anything that is sincere and not performed for the sake of performance will have an effect on people. I don't fully understand the conditions of that period, and I may never fully understand or appreciate playing a show and having the band and the crowd cry together — the very idea of it seems laughable and absurd at times — but I know I was there in the middle and I know my life will never be the same.

SCENE RESISTANCE TO EMOTION OF THE BAND

DUNCAN BARLOW: Any time a person or group takes a stand someone is going to comment on it. It's the point of taking a stand. If everyone agreed with the rhetoric then there would be no reason to say a thing. When other bands were singing about drugs and meat eating, we tried to think about other ideas. Not that we were the most original band, but we wanted to talk about things that were relevant to us.

ROB PENNINGTON: Part of it just boils down to the whole aspect of competition — so many people like to make themselves feel better by putting somebody else down. I wish I could say I've never done it before. It touches people deeply, either positively or negatively, to see someone exposing themselves on stage and discussing what's happening on the inside. We probably made some people feel like, "What's wrong with them?" And I understand that. I remember a band saying we brought "lunchboxes and crying" to hardcore. [laughs] And I think the quote also mentioned us bringing "faggoty-ness" to hardcore, as well. [laughs] Sometimes it's easy to line yourself up as a tough guy as opposed to being so-called "emo."

MASCULINITY/GENDER THEME IN ENDPOINT'S MUSIC

DUNCAN BARLOW: Masculinity was an odd problem for us. We were young men coming out of adolescence in the south. There were social codes that seemed very peculiar to us and we noticed tendencies within ourselves and inside our scene that we wanted to address. At the later part of our teens, we were forging these ideas and trying to challenge people around us to do the same.

ROB PENNINGTON: We were working through a lot of our own emotions and feelings on insecurity — part of that had to do with not being the jock or as masculine as many of the other kids we knew were, as well as questioning the typical societal view of the qualities that encompass being a man. We rejected the idea of hardcore being some kind of boys' club and I think that spoke to a lot of women in the scene, who had probably been pushed to the back so many times. Generically speaking our next record, *Catharsis*, was about not having a stereotypical format or caste that makes you a person. Because we were bullied as kids it kind of came out as a lash against masculinity, but really it was about being okay with who you were.

"CATHARSIS"

DUNCAN BARLOW: We were looking for a name for [*Catharsis*] long before we began recorded. Chad actually suggested the title. We had a list of about 20 possible names and his suggestion was the best. The writing of *Catharsis* was a wonderful time; the band seemed to really hit its stride around this time. We were the best of friends and at times the worst of enemies, but that volatile situation seemed to really work musically and lyrically.

ROB PENNINGTON: We just let go with *Catharsis*. Early on I don't think people connected with us, but after that Chicago show I mentioned and we decided to get let it all hang out I think people could really latch on to what we were trying to convey. All the songs were about ourselves and there were times that I would caution myself slightly because I knew people were starting to listen to us and I didn't want to make anyone feel like an outsider. All the lyrics were extremely personal. There is nobody out there who has never been emotionally hurt somehow and I think people could identify with a song like "Remember." We were just saying out loud that this hurt. The song "Iceberg" was about me going into my head and retreating and getting caught in depression. All those songs were just direct incarnations of what was going on inside of us.

"DAYS AFTER"

DUNCAN BARLOW: There were so many of our friends who suffered from sexual violence. It was always an issue that concerned us, especially Rob. He wanted to write a song that really embraced his feelings at the time.

ROB PENNINGTON: I started getting a lot of letters from women for some reason or another at this time. "Days After" was written about a woman who had shared an experience of sexual violence with me. Sometimes I felt like, "Hey, I'm a guy writing about these songs. What can I really say about it?" But I guess I felt like I had to say something in response to these types of situations that were actually happening within the music scene. I got so many letters from women telling me about these horrible events, and I didn't know how to deal with it other than to write about it. I was just a kid still, really, and I didn't know how to respond. I thought it was beautiful that people felt comfortable enough to share these things with me, but I look back now and just hope I always said the right things. We had a large contingency of women that came to our shows that really helped diversify audiences at shows. The scene was segregated at the time. In the early nineties I noticed a lot more women putting out zines and going to shows. I would say that was a very important era for us. It was cool to see more women putting on shows and getting really involved, which I don't see as much anymore touring.

"AFTER TASTE"

ROB PENNINGTON: We were all growing and changing and listening to a lot of different things. We also had some new band members — we had Kyle Crabtree come into the band, for instance, and he was just a great guy. We also added Pat McClimans who was a great bass player. Because we were listening to different things we had moved farther away from the influences on our earlier records, which definitely affected our sound. I don't think the lyrics changed a whole lot; they were still very personal. I just remember it being a really fun time and I think we were at our prime at that point.

DUNCAN BARLOW: I feel [*After Taste*] was the least cohesive record we ever did and the recording value drives me crazy! Most of this record developed out of confusion. Because of the popularity of *Catharsis* we started thinking about expectations of the scene and that really caused a problem in my song writing. We were still wrestling with depression and at times fooling ourselves that we had passed through it, but looking back it seems pretty obvious that we had not. I plan to remix the record one day and perhaps then I'll enjoy listening to it again.

AUDIENCE BREAKING DOWN

DUNCAN BARLOW: Oddly enough, yes, the stories are true. It was a fascinating experience. We really believed in what we were saying and we never looked at the crowd as fans but as a part of what we were doing. Most of the times that people in the crowd were crying we were crying as well.

ROB PENNINGTON: I guess I would just let myself become overcome with emotion and didn't pay so much attention to it in the heat of the moment. There were a lot of dark places for me to attack. When that happened I felt like I connected with people so deeply. Some people were uncomfortable with it, but I guess it was just a passionate experience that happened for some reason. I don't know, maybe people could relate to us? I think they felt okay at the shows to release themselves in that way.

"THE LAST RECORD"

ROB PENNINGTON: The *Last Record* was awesome, but at that time I was a mess. Here I was in this semi-popular band and everything seemed messed up. "Mather's Point" was about me being at the Grand Canyon and wishing I had the strength to jump off. It was a pretty dark time, needless to say. But the music is beautiful and it's my favorite record that we ever did.

DUNCAN BARLOW: They were the songs that happened to come out of us. We weren't really trying to generate a particular sound. I just sat down and began writing the songs on that record. Personally, I think that *Catharsis* and the *Last Record* were the best records we ever did. More specifically, *Last Record* was the best sounding record Endpoint ever released. It really seemed to finally capture the angst and depression we felt. However, it was a bit of a departure, so I understood that most of the people that liked the band wouldn't care too much for it.

ROB PENNINGTON: We felt we were as good as we could ever be. You get a sense of how far a band can go and whether or not it can be pushed to a different level. We all felt it was just time to stop. It started falling apart; it was taking a lot of unnatural work to keep it together. I was actually relieved after playing our last show. I remember going out back and cried a little bit and afterwards I was so relieved. It had become a big responsibility and it felt good to let it go.

LIFELONG FRIENDS

DUNCAN BARLOW: I consider Rob more family than friend. We challenge each other, argue, and support each other. He's been there for me through most of my life and I know that he will continue to be there for me. We have grown apart musically, but that doesn't mean that we'll never collaborate again. Our journey has been amazing. We have hurt each other and healed each other. We have seen so much of the world together and managed to touch people's lives. Neither of us would be the same if we hadn't have met in 1987 while skating with Bill Danforth in Louisville. By the way, Danforth didn't like us too much and ditched us! [laughs]

ROB PENNINGTON: I love Duncan like a brother. Growing up we kind of complemented one another — we each had strengths and we affected each other quite a bit. I'm an only child and Duncan is the closest thing to a brother I've had.

MEMORIES

ROB PENNINGTON: All those experiences made me who I am. Without traveling and meeting so many people and being exposed to their ideas I probably wouldn't be the person I am today. Endpoint was a good lesson in intimacy with other people and bearing it all.

DUNCAN BARLOW: My favorite memories are the summer before we recorded *Catharsis*. We played so many fun shows, we were all in love and happy, and we began a strange and beautiful love affair with Split Lip from Indiana. We would travel back and forth having bottle rocket wars in the middle of the night, playing pranks on friends, and eating vegan junk food. It was the moment of youthful naivety of which I will always remember fondly.

SELECT DISCGRAPHY:

If the Spirits Are Willing (CD, Slamdek/Doghouse, 1989)
    Pennington, Barlow, Graff, Sohms

In a Time of Hate (CD/LP, Conversion, 1991)
    Pennington, Barlow, Castetter, Hayden, Fetzer

Catharsis (CD/LP, Doghouse, 1992)
    Pennington, Barlow, Castetter, Noltemeyer, Fetzer

After Taste (CD/LP, Doghouse, 1993)
    Pennington, Barlow, Castetter, Crabtree, McClimans, Noltemeyer

Last Record (MCD/EP, Doghouse, 1995)
    Pennington, Barlow, McClimans, Crabtree

GROUNDWORK

Vocals: Brendan DeSmet
Guitars: Dave Jackson
Guitars/Bass: Jerid Francom

Bass: Jim Kuehl
      Britt Hallett
Drums: Thayer Johnson

In a scene where heaviness, noise, and politics were common attributes, Arizona's Groundwork was among the heaviest, noisiest, and most politically outspoken early-nineties hardcore bands. Their music was chaotic, but they also weren't afraid to add sparse, somber melodies as a counterpoint. Their politically conscious lyrics were thought provoking and informative — terms that also describe their overall direction.

The members of Groundwork met during high school in their hometown of Tucson, Arizona. After being exposed to hardcore in the late eighties, they each joined a band and took an active role in the scene. As much as they liked the hardcore they had heard, they felt something was missing. To them, hardcore was about investigating ideas and developing a social and political outlook. All of the members, who were straight edge and vegetarian or vegan at the time, wanted to form an artistic outlet that spoke to their personal and political passions. To that end they decided to form a band as a side project, and the first time they jammed they found that the bond among them was already strong. It only took one practice for the group to come up with a song. Soon enough, they were playing local shows.

At first, Groundwork had to scrap for any attention. Although Tucson had a hardcore scene, the city was not a regular stop for touring hardcore bands. Consequently, the members of Groundwork (and other close friends) made it a mission to put their scene on the map by playing as many shows in the area as possible. They also traded shows with bands from out of town in the hopes that a bigger scene could be established.

Musically, Groundwork was a mixture of the sludgy intensity of Rorschach, the complex riffing of Burn, and the heavy/quiet/heavy experimentation of Fugazi. One can see the band's musical development by tracing the path of their early seven-inches to their LP, *Today We Will Not Be Invisible Nor Silent*. Every emotion within their songs — from the quiet and introspective to the catastrophically frayed and frustrated — is reflective of many personal and political issues the members and many others in the scene were wrestling with at the time.

Groundwork was respected for their topical lyrics and outspoken nature. They probed themselves and their audiences for answers to tough questions about activism, one's place in the world, racism, personal ethics, animal rights, and a host of other topics. Although there is no easy answer to any of these issues, Groundwork's struggles with them had a contagious effect on audiences and prompted self-reflection.

Just as Groundwork was hitting their stride, the band crumbled amidst myriad personal issues. Even after the group's break-up, their legacy became more relevant as many bands continued exploring similar ground both musically and lyrically. Their efforts locally also helped the Tucson scene become larger, which was also one of the group's main goals from the outset. Over the years, their influence took hold in bands as wide-ranging as Cave In, Racetraitor, Disembodied, Prevail, and The Hope Conspiracy. Some of Groundwork's members went on to form the bands Absinthe and 400 Years. Although their later projects were just as respected and influential, what they accomplished with Groundwork has left an indelible stamp on hardcore's political and musical fronts.

ORIGINS

BRENDAN DESMET: Groundwork was a group of friends who knew each other from school and the hardcore and punk scene in Tucson, Arizona. Everyone in the original lineup of Groundwork was in other bands at the time. We all decided to get together as a joke outside of our regular bands — we wanted to play some classic hardcore covers for fun at house shows. There weren't any totally vegan straight edge bands in Tucson at the time either, and the four of us were. We decided the four of us would get together and pick some classic straight edge songs to cover. We got together in a friend's garage one afternoon and we decided we were going to learn an Insted song and a Judge song. It went so well that Dave showed us some songs he had been writing that weren't going to fit for his other band, Suspended Animation, and we all liked it so much. Before we knew it we had a song written and that was really the birth of the band. We named the band Groundwork and started writing more songs. We didn't have any intention of doing a lot with it, but the ball started rolling really fast. Plus, there was some sense of dissatisfaction on our parts with the bands we were in at the time. We wanted to get more involved and have a more direct message. So, we never made it as a cover band. [laughs] We ended up writing a song in our first practice and it just became obvious that we needed to write our own music.

INFLUENCES

BRENDAN DESMET: Being young, we were all really driven. There was a sense of idealism that comes from being young and feeling you can really make a difference. You get really energized by this small world that you exist within and you feel like you can conquer what's going around you. The four of us were driven in different ways. There was a bond especially between Thayer, Britt, and myself because the three of us had a history of not being straight edge in our younger years. Having gone through some experimentation with drugs and alcohol, straight edge was really powerful for the three of us, whereas Dave had always been straight and felt like being away from all that had kept him on the right path. That's how the four of us came together to begin with. I think I was the first person among my friends to go vegan, but shortly thereafter Dave and Thayer both did, as well. We tried to influence the community of people around us. At that time the vegan straight edge ethic was starting to push forward and it hadn't evolved into too much militancy by that point. The two ideas of veganism and straight edge had a lot in common and worked well together and a lot of bands were starting to come forward with those ideas, and we felt that it just rang true to us. However, we strayed away from where some of those other bands went in terms of some of the genericism and militancy, although we were spoken to and recruited by some people from the hardline movement. But we also had the influence of a lot of the other punk and hardcore coming up at the time whether they were more musically unique like Burn or more politically outspoken like Downcast and Born Against.

POLITICS AND HARDCORE

BRENDAN DESMET: It's hard for me to imagine when punk and hardcore didn't speak to me on a political level. Even from when I was young kid first getting into it through my cousin, it wasn't very long until I started picking up on my feelings about the way the world works and the idea of being disenfranchised. An alternative ideal and outlook was being expressed in hardcore and that really resonated with me. There was a sense of camaraderie and belonging in hardcore, and some broad and simplistic ideas I had against general rules and government and racism stuck with me, so it just made sense to us to discuss political ideas. We developed our political ideas as we grew up and met more people and bands. Politics played a big part with our band because we were all so attracted to the ideas.

AUDIENCE PERCEPTIONS

BRENDAN DESMET: We received both positive and negative responses from audiences in regards to our ideas. Locally, kids followed each others' bands just based on friendship and scene community. It started with lots of house parties on our side of the town, which eventually grew into the broader Tucson scene. The years went by and things became more developed into regular shows and tabling and bringing bands from out of town. Ideas were made very concrete and tangible. Some kids fell by the wayside and new kids came along who were attracted to the ideas. Once we toured, people started to know what we were about… for the most part. [laughs] We became a bit of a thorn in the side of the basic straight edge hardcore concept. Things started to get very wide and diverse and even divided to some degree in the early nineties. Some bands kept some core ideas like straight edge with them, but they didn't necessarily follow the path that had been set for them by others or broke free of that to some degree. We certainly didn't go the more commercially viable route of the sound. A lot of bands and people stuck to the classic lyrics associated with straight edge such as getting "stabbed in the back" and friendship and positivity, and at the shows these people would show up with their girlfriends who stood to the side while they got macho in the pit. We were friends with a lot of people from this part of the scene and we didn't want to be completely removed from it, but we also weren't particularly interested in the ways that some of these things were developed into traditions that weren't being questioned, which we found to be very detrimental, such as the violence in the scene, the over-hyped commercialism, and the lack of integrity that came along with some of these things. When we would speak out against people killing each other in the pit or when we'd go off a little bit about various political ideas that weren't necessarily easy to digest we didn't always get the best reception. There were a lot of kids who just weren't having it and wanted to resist any sort of change in dialogue in the scene. But then again after playing with and listening to bands like Chokehold and Four Walls Falling it reminded me that there were other bands out there that took an approach more like ours, so we didn't always feel totally isolated.

TOURING

BRENDAN DESMET: When we toured the U.S. there were several people in the band who had not been out of Arizona very much at the time. So, it was a learning experience for all of us. We really enjoyed it. Whether it was shooting fireworks at one another or coming into scenarios where you almost die every so often when you nearly run the van off the road to meeting people who became a friend for life that you didn't even know 24 hours earlier — it was quite the experience. Playing with bands like Chokehold, Iconoclast, Rorschach, Merel, Struggle, and Unbroken was such an amazing thing to experience, as well. On other occasions we would get to meet these well known people from the hardcore scene who we'd always looked up to who we'd get to play with, which was often pretty eye-opening. [laughs]. You idolize these people and you have these expectations of them that are never realistic. In fact, very often they shatter your expectations completely. [laughs] But these things helped us grow. We came out of the shadows of things other people said and we realized they weren't necessarily smarter or better then we were. Overall, we met some really cool people and we never would have succeeded on any level if it wasn't for those people who helped us along the way.

DYNAMIC SOUND

BRENDAN DESMET: I was really lucky to play with people who were just fantastic musicians. Thayer used to beat the shit out of his drums. He and Dave were both weaned on the metal scene and that came through in their playing to some degree and how they wanted things to sound in terms of taking a more punishing approach. For us, it was very important that the music be emotionally driven. We just tried to channel every ounce of our beings into those songs. We took a long time to write our songs and we used to beat ourselves over the head about them and how they sounded and whether or not they were good enough for us. Dave and Jared had completely different approaches in terms of music, but somehow it turned into fantastic music. Had we continued on past the LP, I think there would have been a lot of really good music to come. We all liked a variety of music, but there was something about playing music that was really heavy and crushing one moment but then sort of quiet and introspective. We felt that reflected the rollercoaster of emotions and ideas that came along with the lyrics and what we wanted to get across to people. It was stark and we wanted it that way. By the time we did the *Living With Fear* seven-inch we grew into the idea that the music could be really harsh and heavy while maintaining some sense of melody.

EMOTIONAL FUEL FOR MUSIC

BRENDAN DESMET: There was a bond of friendship among all of us. We loved each other, fought with each other, were driven mad by one another. It was like a family and we certainly operated that way. But most families are dysfunctional in one way or another. [laughs] We channeled some of our feelings about each other and where we lived into our music. We had to kill ourselves to get people to pay attention to us and our city, as hardcore is often so regional. Politics and ideas also fueled our emotions, as well. You can't get involved in some of these ideas without being passionate. We were involved in animal rights groups and political activist groups. Having the world at large resist you and tell you you're wrong makes you take an even stronger stance in some ways. We drew a lot from our personal emotions and experiences from these things and our personal lives and poured it all into the band and used it as a vehicle to express those ideas.

BLOODLINK RECORDS

BRENDAN DESMET: Scott [Beibin] was out on the West Coast for one reason or another. Somehow he ended up in Tucson and saw us play and that was pretty much it. He offered to do a record with us and we were so excited to get people to pay attention to what we were doing. We wanted to get a record out and not have it go poorly. We did a seven-inch with Scott and it could have been a better or worse experience depending on how you look at it, but he did get it out for us and it did find its way into some magazines and got reviewed. We scored really big when we got a good review in *Maximum Rock N'Roll*, and Scott was very personable and friendly and was really supportive of what we were doing. He wasn't always the most organized in terms of running the label which led to some problems later, but we kept working with him because he did come through on some level. After the first few records he put out the label skyrocketed forward. He worked with a lot of bands that were hugely influential in the early to mid-nineties from Chokehold and Unbroken to Frail and Ordination of Aaron. We were excited to be a part of all of that.

"TODAY WE WILL NOT BE INVISIBLE NOR SILENT"

BRENDAN DESMET: There is no one particular meaning behind the name of the album. We just found it to be a really powerful phrasing that encompassed a lot of the ideas and feelings the band had over time. It was very hard for us to make and get that record out. We were writing it at a very tumultuous period in the band's existence. We were trying really hard to get an opportunity to have people pay attention to what we were doing. As the writing and recording of that record closed, the band fell apart, so the title of the record just seemed to fit our existence in many ways.

END OF THE BAND

BRENDAN DESMET: There were so many rumors why Groundwork broke up. My favorite was that I started doing heroin, quit the band, and went on to roadie for Stone Temple Pilots. [laughs] But I'll say this: the band had really become a dysfunctional family. We still cared about each other and were excited about what we were doing, but there was some in-fighting and some troubles among us. We didn't always get along as well as we should. Things started to fall apart during the writing of the LP. What really, truly broke the band up was kind of a personal matter, but basically a lot of the trust among some of the members started to dissolve. The woman I was romantically involved with at the time and a couple members of Groundwork had some relations during the time she and I were together. As a result of that infidelity there was a huge blow-up. I was unable to contain my sense of frustration and anger that something that betrayed my trust like that would occur. There is a sense of jealousy and rage involved in that sort of thing when there are romantic ties. The members who were involved with that were not particularly well-prepared to deal with what happened. It was tough for them to face up to the poor decision making they'd been involved with. But it was a testament that the trust and support we'd built together over the years had faltered. Once that came to the forefront, we talked about it and I made my decision that once everything was admitted and out in the open that I didn't think I could continue on, so I quit. There was some hope that once some time passed that the wounds would begin to heal, but it was quite amazing how things dissolved. It was almost like a giant sense of relief for some of the members. We wanted the LP to succeed and we wanted to tour Europe, which was a big dream for us. To have all of that fall apart was really tough. At the same time, there was this extreme sense of tension in our last months of existence because of those secrets being held. When everything came out in the open and the burden was lifted, the responsibility for keeping everything together for the sake of the band was also lifted. Everyone was really upset on a personal level, but I got the impression that everything was finally over and we could move on. From there a couple of the members of the band ceased to be straight edge and vegan right after that, and people went on to do things completely removed from hardcore, and some of us just moved forward in different ways in hardcore. It sort of divided the local scene as some people sided with my side of the issue and some sided with the people who were on the other side of it. It was really just very tough for everyone, but it was a learning experience, nonetheless.

LOOKING BACK/LEGACY

BRENDAN DESMET: To this day people will suggest that Groundwork was important. Whether it was because they liked our records or they saw us live or they became friends with us, it's amazing that 15 years later people say that to you. There aren't a lot of opportunities in life where you can have that kind of impact on people in some way. Some people say that Groundwork influenced other bands later on either musically or politically and I don't know if that's true or not, but it's flattering that people mention us. We tried hard to have a positive influence on people — we wanted people to question things and engage with us in conversation. We were trying to also learn about ourselves in the process. We tried to have an impact on our scene in terms of putting it on the map, which is what I think everyone should try and do for their own scene. We brought books and literature to shows and had benefit shows — we tried to get people to think. It was a big era of growth for the Tucson scene, and not just because of us, though I'd like to think that we worked pretty hard to make those positive changes. Hardcore is much bigger than Groundwork or any other band or movement or scene. All the members of Groundwork were happy to have the opportunity to have fun and meet people and get out there and experience life.

SELECT DISCOGRAPHY:

Lay Down (7", Break Even Point, 1992)
   DeSmet, Jackson, Hallett, Johnson

Living in Fear (7", Bloodlink, 1993)
   DeSmet, Jackson, Hallett, Johnson

Groundwork/Unbroken Split (7", Bloodlink, 1993)
   DeSmet, Jackson, Kuehl, Johnson

Today We Will Not Be Invisible Nor Silent (CD/LP, Bloodlink, 1994)
   DeSmet, Jackson, Francom, Kuehl, Johnson

GUILT

Vocals/Guitars: Duncan Barlow   Bass: Ashli State
Guitars: Kyle Noltemeyer   Christian McCoy
Lee Fetzer   Drums: Jon Smith

Led by vocalist/guitarist Duncan Barlow, guitarist Kyle Noltemeyer, bassist Ashli State, and drummer Jon Smith, Louisville, Kentucky's, Guilt played a form of hardcore that pushed emotional boundaries as well as genre constrictions. Guilt drew influence from eclectic sources — from Neurosis to Kerosene 454 — and they nurtured their more metallic early approach into an amalgam of sounds that became noisier, melodic, darker, and more dynamic with each record.

Guilt first formed in 1991 under the name Step Down as a somewhat traditional sounding hardcore band. After some early lineup changes and deciding to experiment outside of hardcore's norms, the members re-shaped the project—this time re-naming the band Guilt and focusing on the emotional scars with which the members were wrestling. Their first release, *Empty*, was more of a straightforward hardcore/metal E.P., which drew positive responses but was actually just a first step for the band. Subsequent releases would become increasingly complex musically.

Their *Synesthesia* ten-inch, which was released in 1994, was a combination of the band's hardcore roots and the emotionally-laced aggro-metal from *Empty*, but their songwriting had evolved and incorporated noise, rock, metal, and more melody. This mixture would eventually become their trademark sound.

Barlow struggled with depression throughout Guilt's existence and his lyrics reflect his often troubled state of mind. They were well written, metaphorical and often extremely dark. Many connected with the feelings expressed in those lyrics, which sometimes brought about violent reactions from audiences.

Bardstown Ugly Box (1995), Guilt's only full-length, was an ambitious post-hardcore record. Recorded with indie-rock legend Bob Weston, the album was a leap forward sonically and thematically as the band found themselves experimenting with song structures, time signatures, and more complex rhythms and riffs. Although rooted in hardcore and punk, the record incorporates elements of Shellac, Nirvana, and Neurosis. Barlow's lyrics grew more abstract, yet one could still grasp the feelings of pain, regret, and fear that he was trying to communicate.

Guilt's final release during their original run, *Further*, was just as dynamic as *Bardstown* and the record found the group again experimenting musically and lyrically with songs that followed a more frantic pace. All the emotions conjured up in the music seemed heightened, as if the band was playing for their very lives. The record's opener, a showcase of tribal drumming and complex guitar riffs, would stun audiences when they played it live. The rest of the songs, all of them untitled, were agitated blasts of metal and melody, somewhat akin to the songs of Kerosene 454.

After a well-received tour with Earth Crisis in 1995 and a headlining tour in 1996, Guilt called it quits. A year later the group reformed for a Halloween show in Louisville that approximately 1,000 people attended. They also released their final record, *Bittersweet Blue*, at this reunion performance. They may not have sold the most records, but sales weren't the band's main concern; rather, it was the relationship developed among the members through their music and psychological self-exploration that satisfied them. Some felt that Guilt didn't represent the hardcore sound of their time, but they took the revolutionary spirit of the era and defined the sound for themselves.

THE BEGINNING

DUNCAN BARLOW: Guilt was an attempt to reconcile all of the anger and hostility in my life. Endpoint, at its height in popularity, became sluggish and I felt as if we were putting on a show and not being true to the depression we felt inside ourselves. Guilt was an attempt to embrace the negative inside myself, to step away from what people expected me to be. I started writing the first Guilt songs in my head during the 1992 Endpoint tour. We released a seven-inch later that year but those songs were actually from our band Step Down. We just released the record under the new name because we didn't much care for the old one. The ten-inch was actually the first real Guilt recording. I asked the guys in Step Down if they wanted to play in Guilt and all but one wanted to do it.

KYLE NOLTEMEYER: I played in Endpoint for a time and we practiced in the basement of my house. We started another band called Step Down around the same time, which was pretty straight ahead hardcore. Duncan started to sing for us. We did that for a while and we got a pretty decent following. Eventually we morphed into Guilt and became a lot more metal.

DUNCAN BARLOW: [Guilt] was the beginning of my disenchantment with hardcore. After touring with with Endpoint, I felt people were focusing on all of the wrong things. They were good looking, clean-cut, Smiths loving kids, which isn't necessarily a bad thing, but it felt to me as if they were following some lifestyle that was counter revolutionary (I use that term very loosely). The thing that bothered me the most is I could feel the sway of it infecting me, so I quit Endpoint and focused on creating something I felt was beautiful in its ugliness. I wanted to write songs that had shapely sounds within a storm of volume and anger.

INFLUENCES

DUNCAN BARLOW: Kyle and I had an eclectic music library and we wanted to write heavy music that reflected our musical tastes as well as generate an alternative for people who felt heavy music didn't have to be a mindless macho anthem, which in hindsight seems like an impossible thing to market. To be honest, none of us really listened to much hardcore at that time. We were really into the Touch and Go bands of that era. We were trying to find new ways to play and augment the limited scope of the notes we knew.

KYLE NOLTEMEYER: I remember Duncan playing me a Neurosis album and that really influenced what we wanted to do. Jon was an amazing drummer and Ashli was a really good bass player and that made a lot of difference in terms of how we were able to push ourselves and our sound constantly forward.

DUNCAN BARLOW: We wanted people to think about things. We wanted to express the notion that playing into genre, while successful, was very damaging to the political potential of punk music. In terms of lyrics, I grew up Catholic, a religion I dumped at a young age, but that ingrained strange types of guilt and self-doubt in me as a young adult. I was fascinated by the tug-of-war between the world we live in and the supposed spirit world we were to enter after death. I should say that I was very atheist at the time, but always wished that I could believe. Kyle and I had such heated and long debates over the Bible. He always believed and has in fact started a church in Louisville with some of his friends. I never really found salvation in a Deity, but I came to better understand my position apropos religion. I remember reading Steppenwolf and thinking that Herman Hesse's book captured the spiritual dilemma perfectly, so on *Bardstown Ugly Box* I wrote a song based on the novel.

AESTHETICS

DUNCAN BARLOW: With Endpoint I was trying to suppress all my negative emotions and get beyond them. With Guilt I understood that I had to look these things in the eye and reconcile with the problems that generated the animosity. Sometimes it worked, and sometimes it simply made matters worse. I was always trying to find a way to fix what felt wrong inside of me. It had never occurred to me that some of the things that felt wrong were actually things that were quite normal for people. I think I made it very difficult for people to relate to me and because of this it became equally as hard for me to relate to them. I had this unrealized urge to alienate myself. I couldn't have understood it then, but it seems quite clear to me now.

KYLE NOLTEMEYER: Duncan was definitely the band leader musically. A lot of the feelings that permeate our sound really stemmed from him, too. The band was an outlet for his anger. That's not to say the rest of us didn't think these thoughts from time to time, but Duncan really channeled his emotions into the sound, which helped define what we were.

DUNCAN BARLOW: I wanted to write lyrics that dealt with the problems between the spirit and the corporeal world. I always found it to be a highly complex and problematic relationship. The name actually reflects this idea--the self and the ever impending threat of non-being. I read this book called the *Courage to Be* and there was a section where Paul Tillich wrote about guilt. It's been years since I've returned to that book, but I seem to remember him writing that guilt is generated by the fear of non-being. As a young man, I struggled with depression and this fear of non-being was always surrounding me. I thought, at the time, that it might be best to face these feelings directly. It was semi-successful, but sometimes it was no better than poking an open wound.

SHATTERING EXPECTATIONS

DUNCAN BARLOW: I think some people expected something more positive. However, lyrically Guilt was about dealing with the abstracts of depression. Slowly over time I began finding ways to manifest the ideas, but the first ten-inch was pretty vague lyrically. I would be lying if I said we did not want to shatter people's expectations. We always wanted people to think about what they were listening to, not to simply accept the band because we were ex-members of other bands. Most of the popular hardcore bands were breaking up and people wanted to try new things. It was a strange and exciting time because you never knew what to expect of people. I was always let down when people started bands that sounded exactly like their previous bands. We were always looking for new and exciting sounds.

"SYNESTHESIA"

DUNCAN BARLOW: That record was actually recorded in a day. We didn't think we were going to continue as a band so we recorded just to document the songs. However, when we recorded, it really brought the band together. We were really happy with the record at the time because we didn't really know what the songs would sound like recorded. When you record something on the fly, it feels so fresh. However, over time we wished we had spent a bit more time on it and really produced it. There are quite a few mistakes in the songs, but it's good for what it is, a document of a certain band during a certain period of their lives.

KYLE NOLTEMEYER: *Synesthesia* was really the core beginning of Guilt. We had ideas about creating a lot of hype around a band before it even existed. We talked about using colors and symbols for song titles. We weren't trying to get big or anything; we just thought it would be fun to add an element of mystique to the music. It was also kind of a backhand slap to everyone that used gimmicks to get big, actually. The music really took off after we put the band together. When you have the attitude of "Let's enjoy ourselves and do what we want to do" then it makes the whole experience that much more freeing. There was no formula for us. We didn't care. We would write metal songs, noise songs, whatever.

DUNCAN BARLOW: Kyle and I were always interested in writing songs that we would like to hear--heavy music with interlaced melodies. We didn't really think about what was happening around us; we wrote what came through our hands.

VIOLENCE AT SHOWS

DUNCAN BARLOW: When we started, a violent group of people came to the shows because the music was slow and "heavy"; however, as soon as the violence and fighting seemed to become a trend we made a choice. Whenever a fight broke out, we would end our set. Eventually the violent element stopped coming to our shows. At one show, we stopped, packed up, left, and the fight was still going on. I was told it reached a riot status. It was really disheartening.

KYLE NOLTEMEYER: Louisville hardcore was fantastic back then. There were always a couple hundred kids that came out and it was a diverse crowd. It was a bit aggressive at times, though. There were guys that showed up looking to fight. There were times when we wouldn't care, but sometimes it would get pretty bad and we'd stop playing. Our music was heavy and some of the kids fed off of that, which was good and bad. Hardcore is about passion and pure emotion. We were all letting our anger out at shows in a variety of ways.

VICTORY RECORDS

DUNCAN BARLOW: We wanted to find a label with broader distribution than Initial Records, but there weren't many labels at the time that sounded promising. Snapcase convinced us that Victory was a decent label, so we talked to Tony [Brummell] and he asked us to put out some records with him. I don't think the controversy came until a bit later when he signed a band that had questionable lyrical content. He was very respectful of our opinions regarding the matter and eventually stopped putting out records with the band.

"BARDSTOWN UGLY BOX"

DUNCAN BARLOW: *Bardstown Ugly Box* was a way of looking at myself. Bardstown Road is the strip in Louisville where we all grew up. I really liked the way it sounded more than anything. It came to me one day when I was visiting my mother in the hospital shortly before her death. We also wanted to mix our influence of indie-rock and metal. I think it is a very good record, but because it had an indie sounding mix and wasn't over produced and slick some people didn't seem to take to it too well.

KYLE NOLTEMEYER: That was the next step for us. I've never really found a category for it. It was heavy but it wasn't metal. At the same time, it wasn't exactly hardcore either. We were trying to bridge the gap between genres. That record was the essence of what we wanted to do musically. We had long songs, lots of time signature changes—we went all over the place.

DUNCAN BARLOW: Our listing song titles like chapters was an attempt to do something different with the way people look at records. To think about the lyrics as chapters of something greater, a whole or a unit. I was really into Herman Hesse at the time and thought about how he might have arranged a record listing.

WORKING WITH BOB WESTON

DUNCAN BARLOW: Bob is a great guy; one of the friendliest people I've ever met. We had a great time recording with him at Steve Albini's old home studio. The drums, vocals, and bass sound phenomenal; however, we were a bit unhappy with the guitar sounds — they sounded flat — but he asked us what mics we wanted, and not knowing much about mics at the time, we said to use whatever Nirvana used while recording with him, so it's partially our fault. Now that I listen to the record, it's really something special, very different sounding than all of the other bands that came out in the nineties.

"FURTHER"

DUNCAN BARLOW: I was trying to add more melody into the music. I became friends with some of the people in Kerosene 454, and really liked the melodies on their first CD, and wanted to see if I could add pop type melodies in our aggressive music. I'm quite pleased with how that record came out. It's one of the few records of mine I still listen to from time to time. One of our major influences on that record was Neurosis. I was a huge fan of their music and I saw them do this drum piece live once, about a year before they actually released *Enemy of the Sun*. We used it for a while, and it just ended up on that record a few years later. We weren't really a band at the time, so I knew we needed to fill up the space. Jon and I recorded it and it turned out pretty nicely. We had Kyle come in and put a guitar track on all of the songs because we felt that he deserved to be part of the record since he started the band with us.

ABRASIVE TONE ON "FURTHER"

DUNCAN BARLOW: I was very frustrated at the time. My depression had put me in a position where I was standing at odds with the world, my friends, my girlfriend and ex-girlfriend, my band mates, and myself. When I look back, I must have been a real nightmare to be around. The record was a direct manifestation of these problems.

END OF GUILT

DUNCAN BARLOW: Kyle had left the band to get on with his life — a job, marriage, home, children — which for him was a good choice as he is a very stable guy and living in a punk house and touring with a band wasn't making him happy any longer. We asked Matt [Wieder] from Mouthpiece to play with us, since I had known him for a few years and quite liked him. We had a huge falling out over the summer that would haunt the both of us for years. We wanted different things. I was on the high and mighty D.I.Y. indie kick and he was into the idea of pop bands and pop culture. It's funny now to think that there really isn't much difference between the two these days. Ashli just vanished. We found out later she joined Ink and Dagger. Jon and I were pretty burned out on playing loud music. We both wanted to take a break and that's when we started the Aasee Lake. That 1996 tour with Guilt aged me, and it broke several of my friendships with people in the band and people with which we toured.

AUDIENCE RECEPTION

DUNCAN BARLOW: Guilt was fun, but it didn't go over very well. We didn't really play into the genre. We didn't use pentagrams or claim to be a metal hardcore band. The critics seemed to like us quite a bit, but that doesn't mean much. We really believed in what we were doing and didn't want to seem ironic like so many of the metal bands of the time. In fact, many people just wanted to hear another Endpoint and completely rejected us. We were jinxed from the beginning and we navigated through the problems. It was interesting to watch the hardcore scene, a few years later, sort of adapt the same aesthetic as Guilt, and yet still completely ignore the band. After a while, we knew that the band was not going to make it. We had all grown apart and I wanted to experiment with country music and electronics, which I did in two separate groups a year or so later.

KYLE NOLTEMEYER: We went on tour with Earth Crisis in 1995 and we finally started to get some attention, but then we broke up. [laughs] About two years later later we played a Halloween reunion show in Louisville and there were about 1,000 people there. It was the most fantastic show I ever played. Sometimes I wonder what would have happened if we had kept going.

ISSUES RESOLVED?

DUNCAN BARLOW: Yes and no. At times it seemed as if I was rubbing a wound raw. It helped me realize that I needed to refigure myself, my life, and how I treated others. Naturally, this took several years longer to see any progress, but it was a type of awakening. We attracted depressives because it seems they could relate to this problem. I always hoped that Guilt could be a resting point for people like me, but never a place to stay.

SELECT DISCOGRAPHY:

Empty (MCD/7", Initial, 1992)
    Barlow, Noltemeyer, Smith, Fetzer, McCoy

Synesthesia (CD/10", Initial, 1994)
    Barlow, Noltemeyer, McCoy, Smith

Bardstown Ugly Box (CD/LP, Victory, 1995)
    Barlow, Noltemeyer, State, Smith

Further (CD/10", Victory, 1996)
    Barlow, Noltemeyer, Smith

Bittersweet Blue (7", Nerd Rock/Initial, 1997)
    Barlow, Noltemeyer, State, Smith

A Comprehensive Guide to Anger Composed in Drop D
(CD Discography, Nerd Rock, 1999)

INSIDE OUT

Vocals: Zack de la Rocha

Guitar: Vic DiCara

Bass: Sterling Wilson

Bass/Guitar: Mark Haworth

Drums: Alex Barreto

Chris Bratton

Some bands slowly build a legacy with gradual amounts of recording and touring, while others capture something special with just a handful of shows. With only a short lifespan, Inside Out helped change the face of hardcore with diverse musicianship, angry, existential lyrics, and a charismatic stage presence that captivated those fortunate enough to see them perform.

Inside Out formed from the members of Southern California's Hard Stance and Chain of Strength and New York's Beyond, three late-eighties hardcore bands that all reached impressive goals in their own right. Hard Stance guitarist and California native Zack de la Rocha wanted to put together a project where he could express both his emotional anger and political frustration. The group had a couple of early stops and starts but finally solidified when guitarist Vic DiCara moved out from New York to fill in the missing piece.

Musically, Inside Out channeled the intensity of old school hardcore giants like Minor Threat while developing their own mixture of metal influenced hardcore and punk, screamed melodies, and post-hardcore. Along with Burn, Quicksand, Shelter and several other ground-breaking units of the era, Inside Out pushed their artistic vision forward and created a sound that people try to emulate to this day.

Although their recorded output is what pulls in listeners year after year, it was Inside Out's emotional live show that made them one of the most exciting bands of their era. They didn't play a lot of shows — their 1990 tour with Shelter and Quicksand being their only jaunt outside of their West Coast home base — but the gigs they did play were legendary. They went berserk from the first note of feedback and they never let up until every ounce of energy was expended.

Inside Out songs such as "Burning Fight" and "No Spiritual Surrender" epitomized a feeling many shared at the time — utter frustration with nine-to-five American life and the idea that western civilization was built upon the bloodshed of indigenous cultures, which still carries repercussions. To this day, "No Spiritual Surrender" still has the power to jolt the listener back to those angry sentiments and frayed nerves.

Although the future appeared bright for Inside Out, a lengthy run was not in the cards. Not too long after the release of their highly influential *No Spiritual Surrender* seven-inch, DiCara became enthralled with Krishna consciousness and left the band to focus on forming a more Krishna oriented group (which eventually became 108, another important nineties hardcore group). Around the same time, de la Rocha also started Rage Against the Machine, a musically innovative and overtly political hard rock meets hip-hop hybrid.

Inside Out only existed for a brief time, but their impact was strong enough to leave a lasting legacy. People still clamor for bootleg videotapes as well as stories from those lucky enough to have caught a performance. Of course, the fact that de la Rocha went on to start one of the most popular rock acts of the nineties doesn't hurt in prompting curiosity.

ORIGINS OF INSIDE OUT

ALEX BARRETO: Zack befriended me after he saw me play drums for Against the Wall. He was quick to ask if I was interested in replacing the drummer for his band Hard Stance, and after playing a couple of Chain of Strength and Hard Stance shows, I agreed to join. Right from the start at my first Hard Stance practice I saw that he was the band leader musically and lyrically. Every once in a while he would get on the mic to coach the phrasing for the singer and I just remember really digging the sound of Zack's voice a lot. Zack would usually be the one to give me a ride home and I would be pretty blunt and say, "Dude, I really think you should consider being a singer. Your guitar playing is awesome, but I really like it when you get on the mic. Even when you're just goofing around it sounds really cool." Keep in mind I was the new guy in mix and these guys were like brothers to him and I felt like a jerk for stating the obvious. God help us, but that raw talent that guy had needed to be provoked! Zack was working construction in the area I lived at the time. Inside Out was writing and practicing at my parents' home in Moreno Valley. He would come over after work, take a shower, eat some tacos, pick up my best friend Vito and do some street skating until dark. We'd maybe jam a few riffs and spend the night instead of driving back an hour to Orange County. The next day he would come back after work and do the same exact thing all over again. We wrote a lot of songs in that bedroom. Fucking magical hardcore bedroom!

VIC DICARA: I moved out to California after recording the Beyond record. In the meantime, Beyond played a show with Chain of Strength and gave their drummer, Chris Bratton, my phone number. When they got back he called me. I wound up hitting it off with Alex Barreto, who came up with a brilliant idea: Zack de la Rocha had recently given up on his band, Inside Out. Alex's idea was to get him to start it up again with the original bassist, Sterling Wilson, but with Alex on drums and me on guitar. We tried it out as a rehearsal in Alex's bedroom in Riverside, California, and it was an amazing chemistry and clicked right from the start.

ALEX BARRETO: The original lineup played a short set opening for a Chain of Strength show at Fairmont Park in Riverside, California. It seemed like the crowd overlooked them, but it came off as a one time performance/side project. I was drumming in Hard Stance with Zack and Rob Haworth both on guitar and had no idea that they were even up to any Inside Out business. Let me just say that I was front and center pretty focused on Zack and was feeling what he was throwing down... the look in his eye, the tone of his voice, he unleashed a fierce yet vulnerable sensitive vibe and to this day I'm shocked because it seemed that I was the only one at this show who noticed his potential. Even though Zack had been reluctant to break up Hard Stance, I encouraged him to pursue Inside Out with me on drums while he was giving me a ride home one night after a Hard Stance practice. Finally, after I helped out with some gas money and springing for Little Caesar's Crazy Bread, he agreed to give Inside Out a go! I feel bad in hindsight for the other members in Hard Stance, but I strongly felt Zack needed to keep paving this new road and that I would compliment this journey. Since Rob was not showing interest I had been jamming with Vic DiCara, thanks to Tom Capone for referring him to the Chain of Strength crew. It was pretty obvious that Vic was a great guitar player with his own style and was a great asset to any band that would have him. After introducing Zack and Vic we got right down to business with Sterling Wilson on bass and me on drums. It seemed like an explosion of chemistry was unleashed in my bedroom right off the bat!

IMPACT OF PREVIOUS PROJECTS

VIC DICARA: Aside from my high school experiments with learning how to be in bands and create songs and music, I had really only been in one band before — Beyond, which was the most fun I ever had in a band before. So, I was coming from a real high, but I was headed towards taking music a lot more seriously, which became a good thing for Inside Out and had good results, but lost a bit of the fun.

ALEX BARRETO: I think Sterling had more of a D.C. vibe and was never one to try and fit in with the trends at all. I admired him a lot for that. He played in one of my favorite bands called Reason to Believe. Vic ruled in Beyond, which I think had a tasteful rock/

metal riffage sound and brought that East Coast groove. Zack wrote all Hard Stance words and music, which also had a darker tone and riff attack and I had a blast playing drums to it. I was getting a little more into a heavy Sabbath groove, Dischord noise, and melody. Zack was experimenting with the same blue prints for a less youth crew vibe.

MOTIVATIONS

VIC DICARA: From the get-go we wanted to have a D.C. approach to hardcore rather than a New York City approach. In other words, more intellectual and feminine, less macho and violent. We did manage to break a lot of ground in that regard and introduce a lot of positive directions regarding spirituality, social awareness, and non-violence.

ALEX BARRETO: I never recall talking much about musical intent. It all was naturally falling into place. The lyrics seemed to be the significant focus more than anything. The evolution of the sound was really more about the urgency at first, then we mastered the art of the "No Spiritual Surrender" mantra build up and that trick continued onto many Rage Against the Machine — the "fuck you, I won't do what you tell me" — songs and so on.

EARLY NINETIES ERA OF EXPERIMENTATION

VIC DICARA: To me, this was the golden age of hardcore. I feel hardcore has receded into conservative trends since then with the fact that anyone who meanders too far from the conservative checklist of "what hardcore is and what it is not" winds up being cast into one of the 1,051 sub-genres and "post-whatever-core" labels and not really counted as a part of hardcore anymore. Ultimately, I believe it was actually the lyrical concepts that fueled the musical openness and growth of the era. We started dealing with more sophisticated concepts than just friendships, betrayals, and scene unity, which opened our hearts and minds to more sophisticated musical ways to express those thoughts and emotions.

ALEX BARRETO: People were learning how to play beyond power chords and felt obligations to explore their musical chops. Some bands changed it up and it was a refreshing compliment to making art, while many failed to deliver the goods in those modern times of the nineties.

DRIVE TO PUSH BOUNDARIES

VIC DICARA: It came naturally. I am an incurable non-conformist. Actually, I think none of the good records from this era have become dated. Burn's EP is just as relevant musically and lyrically today, Quicksand's EP, ours too. I think this era produced music that transcends generations to some degree simply because it is good music. Look at Zeppelin or The Beatles. People get into that stuff today just as much as ever. Look at Pink Floyd. Bands that pushed the boundaries are less likely to be pigeonholed into those very same boundaries. Also, a person comes to a point in his or her conscious awareness of life at which he or she feels the dichotomy between the wants and desires of her soul and the contrast of the realities of material existence and begins to climb the wall that is the question, "Why?" I consider my impulse to be an extremely positive instinct cultivated over thousands of lifetimes. To truly "escape" from illusion is to become more "grounded." Music creates an escape from the trivial and superficial neurons firing in the brain and grounds me into emotional foundations with roots that drink almost directly from the true self.

ALEX BARRETO: We saw a deficiency and lack of impact in the bands emerging from our contemporaries in the underground. We wanted to take soulful elements from different styles without concerning ourselves with current trends. It was an opportunity to expand our interpretation of hardcore as it became evident to me that the value of hardcore became a blur. My aim was just to keep my heart in the right place and luckily the rest of the band was there to provide mutual inspiration and support.

EMOTIONS BUBBLING BENEATH THE SURFACE

VIC DICARA: Zack had a background of family pain that he was grappling with, as well as the common social pressures of any high school kid, and he instinctually understood how to express those emotions and pain and hope with his vocal chords. That's what makes him an excellent vocalist. As for me? I wanted to crack the code and escape the "Matrix." And I wanted it really badly. Anyone's music emanates from their essence, their being, their "soul." It might be that my "soul" is closer to the "surface" or more "on my sleeve" than most. In any case, for me the whole point of music is to open a channel between the soul and the world around me. The pain in the music came from different individuals in the band, from different sources. It is more desperation than a pain, to my ears. The recording and playing of music, I think, is not so much "cathartic" as it is "nurturing." In other words, pain and desperation are realities of existence that cannot just be cleaned away by blowing a musical load. Instead, when you really play music, you nurture those feelings; you connect and funnel them in positive pathways.

ALEX BARRETO: Inside Out was very emotional yet rockin', hence the name of the band. We did celebrate and explore our frustrations from "inside" to show what we felt was important to protect. At all costs stand up for yourself and your identity. I was really young, like 15 or 16, while everyone else was 19-20. Regardless of our personal issues in our own lives, outside the band it was really cool that there was volcano of emotion that erupted every time we got together in my bedroom to practice. It was like a live show going on with those dudes going off, amps cranked, walls shaking, Zack screaming, Sterling headbanging, Vic throwing his B.C. Rich around and breaking lamps while my nice family, God bless them, let us terrorize them while they watched Telemundo down the hall in the living room. The nature of hardcore that I loved was always cutting to the chase and speaking out, reaching and protesting, even towards yourself, in a self-help kind of way. To a mainstream person our band probably came off angry and negative. I hope at the end of the day that any band I'm in has no emotional filter. We had no reservations. We were young, temperamental guys letting out all our anger, love, frustration, disappointment, and resentments out in the open.

INSIDE OUT/QUICKSAND/SHELTER TOUR

VIC DICARA: It was controversial internally as well because I was in Inside Out yet I traveled with Shelter on their Hare Krishna caravan. This wound up causing me to leave the band while still on tour in Chicago at a place called The Vic Theatre, ironically.

"NO SPIRITUAL SURRENDER"

VIC DICARA: At our first rehearsal in Alex's bedroom, Zack told me he had considered naming the band No Spiritual Surrender and suggested we use it as a title for a song. I went home and wrote the song and came back the next rehearsal and showed to everyone. We all tweaked the chorus a bit and it was finished in about 20 minutes. It just manifested itself out of a John Bonham drum loop ("When the Levee Breaks"). The lyrics just came straight out of my pen in about 15 minutes flat.

ALEX BARRETO: I'm bummed on that EP. It could have been produced better studio-wise, and I just feel that Sterling and I had a special quality and it's a shame we both played a big role in the conception of the band and weren't on the record. Our personality and style as a rhythm section complemented the fierceness of team Zack and Vic. I wish we would have recorded a live album instead. We had like 20 songs that I wish we could have recorded. I have practice tapes that got passed around throughout the years and in between songs there is a lot of light joking and laughter, despite the serious dark vibe of the band. Those guys are comedians and were really fun to hang with. We were all addicted to Little Caesar's Crazy Bread and dipping sauce and after every writing/jam session we couldn't wait to get our Crazy Bread on! Those were fun innocent times, man. In respect to the EP, I know they did their best at the time with a modest budget. Studio time was always expensive and I know how it is to feel rushed and to settle for whatever you can afford to pay for. I like putting on the vinyl seven-inch once in a while, but I wish there were more tracks to rock out to.

RECORDING

VIC DICARA: It was tremendously fun. We did it at a place called Pendragon, which we heard had done something with Dag Nasty, so we were very excited. I came in, literally, with charts drawn up about all the guitar tracks and overdubs I would be doing, and with a bunch of different amps. Zack came in with a similar notebook of how he wanted to do all his stuff. It was great! We all did everything in just about one take. I remember best that Zack made the engineer shut off the lights in the room during his recording of "No Spiritual Surrender" so he wouldn't feel self-conscious that people were looking at him through the control-room window.

ENERGY OF THE LIVE SHOW

VIC DICARA: We were "inside out." Our hearts were on our sleeves. It's just the personality of who we were and are. Look at the rest of the bands we have done. They are all known for going nuts live. What's the point of playing live if you don't hurt yourself at least a little bit?

ZACK'S VOCAL CHARISMA

ALEX BARRETO: I think Zack grew up not having the luxury that the majority of his friends did growing up in rich, white, conservative Orange County. Also, being a minority in that high society built a lot of resentment over the years. I'm a Latino dude and I know how it feels to be judged and how it fucks with you and makes you second guess your self-worth. I'm not ashamed of my race and I won't speak for Zack, but I assume he's not either. I think we both found ways to generate self-esteem by being the best surfers, the best skaters, the best guitar players, the best drummers, the best basketball players, the best break dancers, and the foosball champs! We both came from lower class homes to being in a more Caucasian realm and as teenagers we sought our way to fit in. I think that was our common up-bringing. When we got into punk/hardcore it felt like it was the first scene where all races were welcome and I think that influenced Zack to pull out the cork of his suppressed rage and let everyone know he had enough and at all costs express his disgust of this soulless environment. Kind of like a perfect storm, Zack was a time bomb, and it was an honor for me to encourage this explosion. Regardless of the criticism Rage Against the Machine received for the hypocrisy of being on a major label, it was a necessity for them to become one of the most important bands of the nineties. The charisma that it took to deliver those thought provoking messages that started brewing even as early in the lyrics he wrote in Hard Stance then Inside Out, well, it's pretty obvious that Zack had the courage and personality to inspire the underground and now the entire globe!

VIC DICARA: He was so fulfilled to finally be in a band that worked, that people listened to, and that we had the right chemistry to create powerful sonic art. It just jazzed the fuck out of him and he reciprocated by giving every ounce of himself to it. I feel really bad to this day for leaving the band and sort of breaking his heart. That doesn't sound so cheesy if you realize how much he really loved Inside Out. Even when Inside Out fell apart as a result of my decision, he went on to create something even bigger and stronger.

CHEMISTRY

VIC DICARA: The most important lesson that hovers over my head to this day from Inside Out is this: chemistry. A band is not about a single person — even about four or five people — it's about how all those people involved work together. As for Inside Out, it's fairly indescribable. It's just each individual supplied an element that the other was lacking and the entire whole fit together like a jigsaw puzzle.

ALEX BARRETO: The first batch of songs came together really fast, and it was really exciting to be in a powerhouse band that was just a fucking wrecking ball of chemistry.

Everything was fine until out of the blue Sterling called me to let me know everyone decided to kick me out, for no reason at all. To make matters worse, one of my best friends, Chris Bratton, was gonna take over my gig....great, thanks a lot friends! I was really upset and hurt about it. It just seemed that most of that decision was immature and out of convenience—I couldn't drive a van and Chris did. The growing pains of the band entered at this time. The song writing chemistry was unfocused. After recording the EP Zack and Vic realized 50% of the original lineup was gone and at this time I was already moving on with Chain and Statue. Instead of holding a grudge I co-wrote songs with Vic for a project and also was hanging with Zack for some Hard Stance farewell shows that I agreed to do. I think they both missed the chemistry we had in Inside Out, so they asked me to rejoin and I thought it wouldn't hurt to give it another go. It was nice to be invited back, but I must say it wasn't the same special band from my magical hardcore bedroom, and with Sterling gone I was just going through the motions.

END OF THE BAND

VIC DICARA: It's simple — a little blue guy named Krishna made me do it. I was starting to come to a few impasses with Zack on the subject of Krishna, but that was really minor and not the reason for splitting from the group. I simply wanted to be a monk and leaving Inside Out to join the band Shelter just afforded me the perfect escape route into that style of life and I jumped on it and rode that train for the next decade.

ALEX BARRETO: Remember I was the kid who encouraged Zack to sing and brought Vic into the picture. As a founding member to resurface to promote and tour the record I didn't play on was kinda of a bummer. The writing was on the wall. We played a couple warm up shows locally before the Shelter/Quicksand tour. From day one Vic was pretty distant to us especially Zack,Vic couldn't wait to dive into Krishna land. Shelter had a crew of devotees traveling along in a bus and Winnebago and I only saw Vic on stage for our set. Zack and Mark Haworth traveled in a van with Sammy and Porcell and I was gladly hanging with the Quicksand dudes in the van of suffering (Tom Capone's van with no AC). In mid-tour Tom's van broke down so I did get to travel with Ray Cappo and the Krishna crew. I got to stay in many Temples and be a fly on the wall in this controversial religious cult. The Krishna's were very nice; they fed us and were like our guardians for this adventure. I was the only guy besides Vic and Ray to be really social with the devotees while everyone else was like keeping their guards up. Despite the lack of band camaraderie we did deliver action packed live sets and at least we did our job in that sense. The last show was in Chicago. Zack came to ask if I know any good guitar players back home. Let's just say I knew why he was asking this question. We lost Vic on my welcome back to the band tour. It was a quiet, tense, and depressing plane ride back to Cali knowing that it would be imposable to replace Vic. We recruited our friend Mike D from San Diego to take on the gig and played a few small shows, but I was over it and threw in my towel. It just wasn't the same band at all and my heart was in Statue and Chain. Goes to show a lesson that you can't mess with a group of souls blending--that perfect energy makes undeniable chemistry.

MEMORIES

VIC DICARA: Inside Out was a peak for me in terms of chemistry and collective energy. I never could match that again in a subsequent band. I really enjoyed all the shows we played. The people who listened to us were so rad. They got so into the shows! It was a very interesting time for me intellectually and spiritually as I still had a foot in "both worlds" before I dove into the Hare Krishna swimming pool for eight or nine years. I am disappointed that I left the band for Shelter. That was certainly the wrong thing to do. But that's what happened. And things turned out pretty awesome for all concerned in the long run. I'm happy that kids love the music to this day.

SELECT DISCOGRAPHY:

No Spiritual Surrender (7"/MCD, Revelation, 1990)
    De la Rocha, DiCara, Haworth, Bratton

FIGHT: THE NINETIES HARDCORE REVOLUTION IN ETHICS, POLITICS, AND SOU

INTEGRITY

Vocals: Dwid Hellion   Drums: Tony Pines

Bass: Tom Brose   Dave Araca

       Leon Melnick   Mark Konopka

       Steve Rauckhorst   Chris Dora

                               Brandon Abate

                               Nate Jochum

Guitars: Aaron Melnick

          Christopher Hawthorne Smith

          Frank "3-Gun" Novinec

          Frank Cavanaugh

          Blaze Tishko

          Dave Felton

          Vee Price

          Michael Mario Jochum

          Robert Orr

Emerging from the Midwest industrial metropolis of Cleveland, Ohio, Integrity was one of the most popular and notorious hardcore bands of the nineties. The group's ultra-dark imagery, violent reputation, and metal-influenced music helped push the genre in new sonic directions. Although many nineties hardcore bands were known for spreading a message or furthering an agenda, Integrity was assembled for one purpose only — to achieve a pure and almost sadistically dark artistic expression.

Integrity's founder and vocalist Dwid Hellion was originally from Louisville, Kentucky, but he moved with his family to Cleveland in his late teens. Growing up a fan of the foreboding imagery of bands like Samhain and Septic Death, as well as the melancholy atmosphere of groups such as Bauhaus and Joy Division, Dwid loved the aggression of hardcore but wanted to take that sound and mix it with some of the most uncomfortable subject matter that humanity had to offer. Through befriending guitarist Aaron Melnick, Dwid found someone able to comprehend the vision he was working toward and the two, in addition to a rotating cast of supporting members, set out to create a presence unlike any other.

Early on, Integrity put out the *In Contrast of Sin* (1990) seven-inch on then fledgling Victory Records, which drew praise and helped the band capture some early attention. They soon released the *Those Who Fear Tomorrow* LP, which was among the most compelling hardcore records of the nineties. The album's first song, "Micha: Those Who Fear Tomorrow," set the record off with a menacing intensity and metallic groove that never lets up at any point on the album. At times *Those Who Fear Tomorrow* recalls the hardcore/metal synthesis of the Cro-Mags and Judge, but Integrity's style and lack of concern for convention shift the record in a more twisted direction. Dwid's disturbing lyrics worked in unison with the caustic music combining apocalyptic imagery, fictional accounts of serial killers, and a general feeling of isolation and anger.

Integrity was known for their volatile live shows, as well as a trail of violence that seemed to follow the band wherever they played. Some insisted the trouble was the result of fans misinterpreting Dwid's lyrics and on-stage banter, while others claimed that Dwid himself, as well as various members of the band, were also instigators. Whatever the case, it is safe to say that wherever Integrity played there was bound to be mayhem.

But as rumors spread about Integrity, so did expectations. Many saw the group as the antithesis of the politically-conscious aspects of the hardcore scene; others felt the band represented the true spirit of hardcore: making one's own rules and determining one's own artistic expression. While people debated their relevance, Integrity was busy creating a follow up full-length, *Systems Overload* (1995), a record that combined the dark metallic sounds featured on *Those Who Fear Tomorrow* with a bit more of a streamlined traditional hardcore approach.

Less than a year later, Integrity wrote an interesting concept album, *Humanity is the Devil*, a ten-inch record complete with a booklet describing a new "religion" that Dwid created called the Church of Holy Terror. As usual, Dwid's perspective connected with the group's core following while those who didn't "get it" shrugged their shoulders.

Over time, Integrity shuffled through a variety of members with the exception of Dwid and Aaron Melnick. Dwid was arguably the driving force of the band and as his interests drifted toward the more philosophical some members just couldn't go along for the ride. After a couple of even more experimental records — *Seasons in the Size of Days* and a few seven-inch recordings — Melnick also parted ways with the band. Integrity soldiered on, but it seemed some of their ominous aura had dissipated.

Though they were popular with many and disliked by just as many others, Integrity profoundly influenced hardcore in the nineties and years beyond in terms of their musical approach and their penchant for causing controversy. While some of the more aggressive

aspects of the group drew more attention, it is important to note Dwid maintained his goals and outlook throughout the existence of the band despite the rumors and innuendos surrounding his group. Dwid was one of the most enigmatic figures in nineties hardcore and Integrity's legacy continues to build with each passing year.

MUSICAL/ARTISTIC ROOTS

DWID HELLION: The first bands I got into were Bauhaus, Motley Crue, The Smiths, The Cure, The Sex Pistols, Siouxsie and the Banshees, and Samhain. I was living in Louisville, Kentucky in 1984. I was 13. Samhain played at a church recreation hall on the street behind my house with a local band named Maurice, of which some of its members later formed Slint and Kinghorse. I was always attracted to the darker elements of art and culture, when I was a very young I was enamored by Sammy Terry, a late night horror host who played classic horror movies late Saturday nights, so it was a natural transition from that into bands like Samhain. A couple years later I acquired a copy of the Peace compilation, which was a double album with hardcore/punk bands from all over the world. Lots of incredible bands were on that — that's where I first discovered Septic Death and Japan's notorious G.I.S.M. Looking back now it is obvious that I was initially drawn to their strong aesthetic. Obviously Pushead's art is legendary. And Sakevi of G.I.S.M. is still a tremendous inspiration. As far as why I gravitated toward music subcultures, I suppose it has to do with my personality. A lot has changed with the adoption of conformity within the genre — originally it wasn't accepted by many. Even metal fans hated punk and hardcore enthusiasts, and in turn a lot of punks hated hardcore, as well. Eventually that all changed and it became an established genre.

FRANK "3-GUN" NOVINEC: I first met Dwid when Die Hard was going on around 1989. In 1990 they started Integrity and that's when my best friend and I started Ringworm. I met them when I was in a band called Force of Habit, which was kind of a joke hardcore band. Some of the guys from Integrity came to watch us practice and we became fast friends.

ARTISTIC MOTIVATIONS

DWID HELLION: I wanted to make music that I wanted to listen to. There weren't any bands doing what I wanted so I started a band. I was friends with Aaron Melnick, who is a very worldly and talented musician and artist. He and I got together and made Integrity. Aaron and I had very similar interests in music and we blended all the elements we preferred in our favorite music together, and the outcome was Integrity. We were despised by our peers for being different, and that was a very rewarding feeling at the time.

FRANK "3 GUN" NOVINEC: I thought they were really cool because they were doing the Cro-Mags/Slayer hybrid thing. I found the hardcore scene through the thrash metal scene. They were one of the originators of combining metal into hardcore — that was before it was cool to like Slayer. Nobody cared before then and that's what turned me on to them. That was a time when hardcore was really stale. Everything had already been done and most of the post-hardcore stuff just didn't do it for me. Integrity was really a refreshing thing.

ENVIRONMENTAL IMPACT

DWID HELLION: As with anything, people are naturally influenced by their surroundings, their culture and their peers. Cleveland was a heavily industrial city, lots of factories and little hope. Very little to do, and as a young person involved with this type of music, you could be assured to be extremely isolated, alienated, and above all… severely hated. It's no wonder why there's a consistent thread of similarity within 90% of the bands that came out of Cleveland. Even the mainstream bands all carry certain attributes that clearly show where they were from. Cleveland is a desolate and hopeless place. Pollution and factories are abundant. Most young people realize this early in life and resent the fact that they are cursed to reside in a wasteland. This frustration often escalates into a lawless and aggressive behavior pattern.

FRANK "3-GUN" NOVINEC: Cleveland is what it is. It's a blue-collar town and people that live there love it and people who aren't from there think it's a shithole. Integrity really wanted to create something that was hardcore but from more of a dark side. They weren't singing about burning churches — more so just the darker side of life. They were from a dark industrial town, kind of like Black Sabbath was, and that's just what was reflected in their music. Integrity probably tried to promote some of the violence more than anyone at the time. Dwid kind of played the pied piper sometimes.

MUSICAL ATMOSPHERE

DWID HELLION: We didn't fit in with the rest of the hardcore scene, and that was a great thing. The band had a mood, had a character, a personality all its own. It was an attempt to set out to be different, more an expression of Aaron's and my interests. I think in mood we can relate Integrity with Joy Division. There is something unsaid and unseen by our inspiration of their music, but it has a pulse within our music. I have a very distinct personality and flavor of interests and this tends to show. Again it wasn't an attempt at originality, or distinction, merely expression of who I am and what interests me. To be perfectly honest, I paid little attention to the bands of the nineties with few exceptions. We were more a result of my personal influences as well as the influences of Aaron Melnick. Aaron lived in England when he was in his early teen years and was exposed to bands like Joy Division and Bauhaus. He actually first introduced me to the music of Joy Division, which still remains one of my all time favorite bands.

THE COMBINING OF METAL AND HARDCORE

DWID HELLION: I agree when some say that metal may have corrupted hardcore. But it was like shooting bullet holes in an already sinking ship. Hardcore was destined to be corrupted. All musical genres eventually become exploited and used up by the mainstream, until it dies, then years later is revived as a nostalgia marketing scheme. You also must keep in mind hardcore was a blend of punk and metal. We were condemned as "too metal," and the lyrics were not straightforward, and most people were upset by that. The punks hated us, the metal kids hated us, and the hardcore community hated us. I love that.

DARK LYRICS/APOCALYPTIC IMAGERY

DWID HELLION: I suppose it is my nature, my interests, and possibly my upbringing to some degree. There was not one single event that made me the way I am. I have always been this way. Since a child I have always had an interest in the arcane, and I will always gravitate toward that direction. All the lyrics have always been personal accounts or attacks on aspects of my interaction with the world. I write about what I see. Take it as you wish.

FRANK "3-GUN" NOVINEC: [Integrity was] just like, "We don't give a fuck." They didn't care about what was going on in the scene at the time. They had already been around for so long and they wanted to do their own thing. At that point everyone was so about the scene and Integrity just didn't care. They had the mentality of older style bands. They didn't care who was straight edge or who was vegan. At that time a lot of kids were all about who they knew and what kind of status they had in the scene. Integrity didn't pay any attention to any of that stuff. I think Dwid's lyrics were great. Everyone was singing about the same bullshit at the time. His songs were refreshing and not the same old rehashed, preached messages over and over again.

"THOSE WHO FEAR TOMORROW"

DWID HELLION: The album was written about my vision of the world at that time in my life. The imagery was as important as the music or lyrics, always has been. The influence was self-manifesting, each aspect influenced and inspired other aspects to make the album the way it ended up.

INFLUENCE OF AARON MELNICK

DWID HELLION: Our relationship was volatile. He always wanted the band to go in a different direction entirely, and he was staunchly opposed to most of the imagery, lyrics, concepts, and vision that defined Integrity. He later quit to form his own band.

FRANK "3 GUN" NOVINEC: Aaron had one of the most generic rigs we'd ever seen. [laughs]. He had this junk guitar but it had this EMG pick-up in it and that's what made it sound so unique. Not for nothing, but that's a sound you come up with on on your own. Aaron and Lenny were such good musicians and that's what helped set Integrity apart because there were a lot of bands back then that couldn't play for shit. Mixing Cro-Mags and Slayer was pretty ingenious and Aaron was the one that really pioneered that kind of sound.

"SYSTEMS OVERLOAD"

DWID HELLION: I see no real change in vision. The songs were a bit more hardcore, but that was mainly due to the fact that *Those Who Fear Tomorrow* was condemned as "too metal" a few years earlier by the hardcore scene, and at the time of *Systems*, *Those Who Fear Tomorrow* was heralded as "innovative" and "revolutionary." In a great part, *Systems* was more "hardcore" to try to shake the trend followers from our backs. The album served its purpose. It was angry and jaded and vindictive, and most people hated it at first.

"HUMANITY IS THE DEVIL"

DWID HELLION: I wrote that little book that we put inside the album. I wanted to make a concept album that was also interactive. When I was asked to do interviews at the time, I would allude to a religion called Holy Terror. This was never a real religion; it was something I dreamed up. I even went so far as to do interviews as "Jack Abernathy" (founder of the Holy Terror Church of Final Judgment). It was a successful study in human behavior, and many people still believe to this day. It was simply the way the album was meant to be created. Now the record label has censored the lyrics by removing them and in their place, leaving a blank white sheet in corporate defiance.

FRANK "3-GUN" NOVINEC: Dwid definitely had his own thing going on when it came to stuff like that. That was his thing and no one really questioned it. He was the leader of the band and he had a vision. We didn't question anything and let the train keep rolling. I'm not dissing it at all; it was just his thing. That was part of the mystique of the band.

VICTORY RECORDS

DWID HELLION: I think the label helped get our music out to a worldwide audience, and that was a great help for us. But the label is the antithesis of generous or fair.

CONFLICT

DWID HELLION: Most of the band had hoped to become a typical "hardcore" band and fought with me to give in. As the band released more albums, some of the members decided it was their chance to make their own band and their own albums so they departed Integrity in pursuit of their dreams. A band that generates more contempt than income and is still existing for nearly two decades generally tends to lose members over the years.

VARYING LINE-UPS

DWID HELLION: It really is difficult to say which lineup is the definitive one; every incarnation of the band has brought something special and unique to Integrity. Most bands in this genre do not last more than five years; eventually members move on and line-ups change. I enjoyed playing with Frank "3-Gun"; he is a true entertainer on and off stage. Mike and Blaze are amazing guitarists and were a great songwriting team. Aaron and Leon Melnick's contributions really added a different level to the albums they played on. Dave Araca was my favorite Integrity drummer. His playing was always flawless and inspiring.

MISCONCEPTIONS?

DWID HELLION: People generally project what they long for or fear onto others. We are simply a reflection of those fears and desires. I am not responsible for other [people's] interpretation of my work.

LEGACY/IMPACT

DWID HELLION: I simply wanted to make the music I had always heard playing inside my head. It was not my intention to necessarily defy the standard musical blueprint at the time. And I never anticipated how offended people would become simply by us making music that was a bit off the beaten path. Personally, I do not see why making original music is considered so controversial.

SELECT DISCOGRAPHY:

In Contrast of Sin (7", Victory, 1990)
    Hellion, Melnick

Grace of the Unholy (Cassingle, Progression, 1990)
    Hellion, Melnick

Those Who Fear Tomorrow (CD/LP, Overkill, 1991)
    Hellion, Melnick, Smith

Den of Iniquity (CD/LP, Dark Empire, 1993)
    Hellion, Melnick

Systems Overload (CD/LP, Victory, 1995)
    Hellion, Melnick

Humanity is the Devil (CD/10", Victory, 1996)
    Hellion, Melnick, Novinec

Seasons in the Size of Days (CD/LP, Victory, 1997)
    Hellion, Melnick, Novinec

Integrity 2000 (CD/LP, Victory, 1999)
    Hellion, Felton

Closure (CD/LP, Victory Records, 2001)
    Hellion, Price, Abate

To Die For (CD/LP, Deathwish, Inc., 2003)
    Hellion, Tishko, Jochum, Rauckhorst

The Blackest Curse (CD, Deathwish, Inc., 2008)
    Hellion, Jochum, Rauckhorst

LOS CRUDOS

Vocals/Drums: Martin Sorrondeguy   Drums: Ebro Virumbrales
Guitars: Jose Casas   Joel Martinez
Bass/Drums: Juan Jimenez
Bass: Lenin Montes de Oca
        Oscar Chavez

Chicago's Los Crudos was one of the most politically active and adamantly D.I.Y. bands in nineties hardcore. Although many groups from the nineties conveyed a political point of view, few had the same dedication that Los Crudos did, which earned them much esteem.

Coming from Chicago's primarily Latino working-class Pilsen neighborhood, Los Crudos had a different approach to music than many of their contemporaries. While many nineties hardcore kids came from the (largely white) suburbs, Los Crudos reflected Latino heritage, most obviously in the choice of singing all of their lyrics in Spanish. Most of their songs analyzed social dilemmas that affected their neighborhood, including issues of immigration, discrimination, and economic empowerment. Each Los Crudos performance or record was a mixture of ethics and education delivered with a hardcore sound that echoed the genre's iconoclastic pioneers like Minor Threat and M.D.C., as well as contemporary fast hardcore bands from around the world.

As powerful as Los Crudos was musically, it was vocalist Martin Sorrondeguy's political lyrics, and especially his between-songs banter, that drew a cross section of audiences to their message. In turn, their depiction of the reality of the immigrant experience in the United States became an educational tool and inspired many who had the good fortune of seeing the band perform. Sorrondeguy, always confident on the mic, had a knack for captivating an audience. While some people preferred that the band just "rock out," Sorrondeguy insisted on explaining the songs (often in English when playing to predominantly non-Spanish speaking audiences) in the hopes that listeners would understand each issue better.

For Los Crudos, hardcore was about immersing oneself in the human experience, not just being a passive viewer; taking life by the horns and no matter what your perspective, speaking your mind, sharing your feelings, and taking an active role in your community. They were primarily concerned with issues of immigration, oppression, and racism worldwide and consequently inspired many others to understand these dilemmas better.

As with any outspoken band, Los Crudos encountered their share of criticism from those who felt that hardcore bands should simply "shut up and play." But what many didn't acknowledge was that in addition to hearing a political message at a Los Crudos show, the indefinable sparks of emotion that make hardcore the cathartic experience it is were also present. At the least, Los Crudos forced people to think about tough issues; at the most, the band was the epitome of the revolutionary spirit that hardcore represents.

Ultimately, Los Crudos accomplished everything a hardcore band could ever hope to: they put out loads of records (most of them self-funded and *always* with D.I.Y. record labels), they toured the U.S. as well as Europe, South America, Mexico, and Japan, they inspired legions of fans around the world to be more politically active, and they sweated their emotions out at every show. Most importantly, Los Crudos claimed their own space in a scene that acts as a refuge for many who feel marginalized, yet ironically sometimes mimics society at large by marginalizing those who come from a minority background.

ROOTS OF THE BAND

MARTIN SORRONDEGUY: Los Crudos started in 1991. I was coming from a very different place from a lot of the kids I met at shows. Many of the kids were coming from suburban areas while I was coming from the city in more of an urban place, and I felt like I couldn't relate anymore to a lot of what the suburban bands were singing about. I felt I needed to take more of an open position on my take of hardcore. I ended up coming together with a couple people and we started Los Crudos. We wanted to show people where we were coming from, which were the Chicago area barrios. It was really bizarre because many people, even old friends of mine, rejected it. They were like, "Why are you guys singing about this stuff?" It was bizarre because people I thought would have been really receptive to it, but more than anything maybe it was too real for them. There was this huge divide that happened between the old scene of people I knew and the new people I was doing the band with, and I was okay with that.

ORIGINS OF THE NAME

MARTIN SORRONDEGUY: The word "raw" came up. It stuck. In Spanish crudos literally means raw, but a slang version of it means to be hung over. We talked about what that word really meant and why we would use it. In regards to all the things we sang about we thought it was like comparing it to being hung over and not being able to see clearly — the rawness of the situation around us. At first, some people were like, "Yeah, party!" The band wasn't a straight edge band. Some of us were and some weren't. But we were clear on why we chose the name for the band and it wasn't about partying. [laughs]

FIRST SHOWS

MARTIN SORRONDEGUY: Our first shows were in our neighborhood and we thought we wouldn't be anything more than a neighborhood band. I had it in my mind that no one would be interested in releasing our music so I already decided that it would be self-released and we'd do it on our own entirely. We were playing the city a lot and then we started playing in northern Chicago so we started to get out of the city and the next thing you know we're being invited to play Milwaukee and Minneapolis and it spread out. We first released our demo tape in our neighborhood and it did fine but when we put out our first record we pressed 1,000 of them and we got rid of about 400 really quickly but I was sitting on the rest. But then the reviews in *Maximum Rock N'Roll* came out and they vanished really fast. People overseas started to mail order and the next thing you know we found out this wasn't going to be a neighborhood band anymore.

EBRO VIRUMBRALES: I had been going to see Los Crudos play since about 1992 and knew Martin from shows and from buying records from him. In late 1995, their original drummer wasn't sure that he wanted to be in the band anymore, so I told Martin that I would play drums for them if they wanted and I ended up joining. As far as initial impressions, I thought that they were a great hardcore band and I also thought it was cool that they were singing in Spanish. Coming from a Spanish speaking background, I could understand what they were saying and could relate to the anger. They definitely stood out from most of the local bands at the time. My impressions of the band didn't really change when I joined; it just felt good to be part of a band that I had admired for a while and whose music I liked.

COMMUNICATION

MARTIN SORRONDEGUY: It was really about communicating. I felt there was a lot to explain with the songs we were singing. If we played in, say, Idaho and none of the kids knew Spanish we felt we should share what our songs were about. Sure, we could have just played our set and walked away and they may have said that band sounded really good or they sounded like shit. [laughs] We just felt we had an opportunity. We're in this room with all these people and they are here to listen to us. That's where a lot of the impact of wanting to tell stories about immigrant workers in our neighborhood or about our friends and families really came to the forefront. You can get a show anywhere, anytime. We wanted to do something a little different and have kids walking away saying, "That was intense. I wasn't expecting that."

THE SOUND

MARTIN SORRONDEGUY: A lot of our influences were classic hardcore. We loved old hardcore punk. We were influenced by foreign bands as equally as American bands, though. We loved what Italy did with American hardcore and the way they ran with it. We also liked the early Brazilian stuff. I had been listening to punk from all over the world so our influences were from all over the place. At the time a lot of people were moving away from the classic hardcore style and emo was starting to get big and the more metal sounding stuff was also gaining steam. We just really wanted to be short, fast, powerful and to the point. Also, a lot of really good old hardcore stuff has a certain melody. There were certain bands that had catchy melodic parts but they just played really accelerated. We wanted that as well. We wanted to have songs that rang in your head. Our goal wasn't to grow as artists. That's not what we were doing. A lot of bands start out playing fast, aggressive hardcore and they end up eventually going for an indie-alternative sound. That wasn't what we were after. I wasn't interested in growing as a vocalist or whatever. We were on a different trip.

EBRO VIRUMBRALES: The sound of the band was in place before I joined, but it just reflected what the guys in the band liked to listen to — stuff like old foreign hardcore punk, especially old Italian stuff. The sound was a good way to express the anger and frustration that we all felt.

CLAIMING THEIR OWN SPACE

MARTIN SORRONDEGUY: We claimed our space in hardcore. It's not like we waited around to see if people wanted to include us. We were like, "Fuck you if you don't dig this." That was our stance. It's not like I was waiting for approval of what we were doing. We just did it. We just said this is what we're about. As we went city to city we got very different reactions. Some people were overwhelmingly supportive and of course you'd get a few hecklers here and there, but for the most part people were pretty much embracing what we were doing. I guess I was surprised it didn't happen sooner as it took some time, but it did happen. We took a stand on a lot of things locally. We refused to play almost every club that played the typical hardcore and punk venues because there wasn't anything organic or real about most of these places. It was like somebody was making money off the scene and we rejected that. We sought out alternative places from people's houses to laundromats to cultural spaces — everything that was outside the grip of club owners.

CRITICISM

MARTIN SORRONDEGUY: We were criticized by people, but I don't know where they were coming from. We wrote a song called "That's Right, We're That Spic Band." There was some old Chicago people talking about us and they were like, "Los Crudos? Oh, they're that spic band, right?" It was really weird. [laughs] We just decided that's the title of our song right there. It was our anthem for the later part of the band.

EBRO VIRUMBRALES: There were times that we got heckled; usually, Martin did a good job of shutting people down that were trying to talk shit and it didn't escalate into something else. The band got to a point towards the end where we had been around long enough that most people knew what they were getting when they came to see us, but there were times when someone would say something stupid like "Yo quiero Taco Bell" while Martin was speaking in Spanish. I guess it just showed that we weren't always "preaching to the converted."

TOURING MEXICO

MARTIN SORRONDEGUY: Playing Mexico was totally insane. I still watch the footage from the shows and I get chills in regards to that kind of response we got. It was so crazy. That's when I realized our songs weren't really our songs anymore; they became other people's songs. The first tour we did of Mexico was really insane. I had heard there were large scenes but you don't know what it is until you experience it. Going to Mexico City was like time-warping back to 1982. In the States people were pretty mellow at shows and we realized how tame the shows here had become. When you went down there it was so raw and crazy. People had such energy and people made their own punk clothes, which was so amazing to see. We played shows in the streets while it was raining and punk kids were ripping their jackets and clothes off and laying them on the ground so we wouldn't get shocked. It was a side of punk we had not been exposed to.

EBRO VIRUMBRALES: I had been to Mexico before, but really only the touristy areas of Mexico City and some smaller towns around there, so I got to go to some places that I probably would have never gone to normally. We were there for about two or three weeks and traveled from town to town by bus, because we didn't want to get pulled over by corrupt police looking for a bribe, which happened the last time the band was in Mexico. Most of the shows were cool and there are a lot of stories that I could tell, but the first show that we played in Mexico City really sticks out: it was in a huge warehouse type of place with a gigantic metal gate at one end of the building and the stage at the other end. There was a good number of people inside, but there were even more people outside. These kids couldn't afford to pay and at one point during the show, they started beating on the metal gate, making a huge, thunderous sound. Then they started throwing rocks and bottles at the building and turning over cars outside....it was pretty crazy and seemed like it was going to turn into a riot. The owner eventually let them all in and the place was completely packed, then when we played the entire room went crazy. If you watch Martin's documentary *Mas Alla De Los Gritos* you can see a small part of the show at the beginning and you'll see what I mean. The last show that we played in Mexico City, some kids tried to do the same thing and the owners of the club stood on the roof with machine guns and threatened to shoot all of them. We didn't hear about this until the show was over but luckily no one was hurt.

END OF THE BAND

MARTIN SORRONDEGUY: I felt we did what we had to do at that time and it just got really exhausting after a while. Basically I finally asked myself, "What can do we that we haven't done before?" We had already toured the states, been to Europe and Japan. Were we going to go a different direction creatively? No, we weren't, and it was time to stop.

EBRO VIRUMBRALES: On the last tour, it was starting to feel like it was the right time to call it a day. The band had been around for seven years and had accomplished much more than anyone had ever expected and we didn't want to turn into some band that was stagnant and going through the motions. When we discussed it, I basically left it up to Martin and Jose since they had started the band and their decision was to end it.

RESPONSE FROM NEIGHBORHOOD

MARTIN SORRONDEGUY: In the context of our neighborhood it was so important that we did the band. I remember people from our neighborhood asking us for our autographs, which was kind of disturbing to me but this is just what people thought was going to happen. I think it showed other kids in our neighborhood that you can do this. You don't have to wait around for someone else to come around and release your record. You can make shit happen on your own. That example was good for the young kids to see because I think many of them realized they could be a part of it. Hardcore is not just about music or style; it's about kids being creative and political and they are channeling energy into different shit and not falling into those stereotypes and becoming gang-bangers. They're being punk and that makes me really proud. I remember a kid coming up to us in our neighborhood and wanted to take a photo with us because he said when we got famous he wanted to remember how we originally started as. I just said, "We're not going to be famous like that." For us, retaining the D.I.Y. attitude allowed us to keep that relationship with people in our neighborhood. We wanted to convey a message to people of you don't need to have someone else do this for you, you can do it on your own. We wanted to show that example and have everyone come out and do it. People were seeing us organize our own shows and making our own shirts and eventually other kids followed suit. Now when you go back there is a whole scene there, which is really amazing.

LASTING IMPACT

EBRO VIRUMBRALES: Speaking as someone who was a fan of the band before I joined and without trying to sound too corny, I feel that Crudos was a band that people could see was "real." The lyrics were talking about things that a lot of people could relate to, and at the same time the band wasn't trying to exclude people that didn't have these same life experiences. Martin did a great job of expressing what the band was about when we would play and because of that I think we were able to reach a lot of people, even those who might not have normally checked out a band like us.

MARTIN SORRONDEGUY: We were looked at as a little different in our neighborhood when we started, and some people thought we were crazy. But other people really embraced us. I had kids come up to me and say, "My grandfather saw your lyric sheet and he loved your lyrics but he hated your music." [laughs] We were really working with our community so I think there was a mutual respect between us. We were all helping each other out, which was going beyond the duty of just being a band.

SELECT DISCOGRAPHY:

La Rabia Nubla Nuestros Ojos (7", Lengua Armada, 1991)
    Sorrondeguy, Casas, Chavez, Martinez

Split with Huasipungo (7", Lengua Armada, 1992)
    Sorrondeguy, Casas, Chavez, Martinez

Las Injusticias Caen Como Pesadillas (7", Lengua Armada, 1993)
    Sorrondeguy, Casas, Martinez

Los Crudos/Spitboy Split (LP, Ebullition, 1995)
    Sorrondeguy, Casas, Montes de Oca, Sorrondeguy

Canciones Para Liberar Nuestras Fronteras (LP, Lengua Armada, 1996)
    Sorrondeguy, Casas, Motes de Oca, Virumbrales

FIGHT: THE NINETIES HARDCORE REVOLUTION IN ETHICS, POLITICS, AND SC

MOUTHPIECE

Vocals: Tim McMahon
Guitars: Matt Wieder
         Chris Schuster
         Pat Baker
         Pete Mattson
         Pete Reilly

Bass: Sean McGrath
      Dave Rosenberg
Drums: Jason Jammer

New Jersey's Mouthpiece carried on the straight edge hardcore tradition of eighties bands like Chain of Strength, Uniform Choice, and Insted. At first, they felt that many of the "youth crew" anthems spoke for them so well that emulation seemed to be the best tribute, but as time passed they built upon the foundation of those earlier bands and became a group that voiced their own concerns with their own angry yet slightly melodic songs.

Although paying tribute to the past was important for them in the beginning, Mouthpiece also realized that hardcore was about adding one's own unique thoughts and concerns to the scene. After playing some shows in New Jersey, New York, and Pennsylvania, they established more connections around the East Coast. At this point, McMahon sent their demo to New Age Records and owner Mike Hartsfield (also guitarist for straight edge outfit Outspoken) liked it. Hartsfield asked the band to appear on a compilation and then record some songs for a seven-inch of their own soon after.

As that first record came out in 1991, the straight edge hardcore scene was still going through a transition. In the previous year or so, many who were once part of the popular late-eighties "youth crew" straight edge movement started to cast the straight edge label aside. At the same time, this was still a couple of years before the straight edge revival popularized by bands like Earth Crisis and Strife ushered hundreds of new kids into the scene across the country. Mouthpiece, along with bands like Outspoken and others, helped bridge the gap between the two eras.

Some criticized Mouthpiece for their lyrical focus on personal perspectives — straight edge, friends, life — as typical hardcore topics. At the time, there was a burgeoning movement of bands becoming more political. But McMahon felt that though he cared about such issues (he's a longtime vegetarian, for instance), he didn't feel the need to add his voice to those debates. Instead, he thought it would be more honest to speak about issues that were directly impacting his personal life.

Mouthpiece's only full-length, *What Was Said*, continued the aforementioned lyrical themes with a sound steeped in the band's straightforward hardcore meets melodic punk influences without coming off as derivative. Their songs had varied tempos, structure change-ups, and a melodic edge, and though their music wasn't as progressive as some of the more experimental outfits of the time, it sounded natural and mature.

Many felt their most accomplished release was their *Face Tomorrow* EP (1995), which was even more reflective and musically diverse than their LP. They didn't stray too far from the sound they were known for, but *Face Tomorrow* found the band heightening all of its attributes, particularly in terms of merging an even more melodic backdrop to their primarily hardcore sound.

Six years after the band's creation, Mouthpiece ended their run the same way they started — still displaying a contagious enthusiasm for hardcore. Along the way, they carved their own niche in straight edge with records and performances that were passionate, heartfelt, and reflected the band's pure love for the scene.

ORIGINS

TIM MCMAHON: A couple of us were in high school and we got into hardcore and punk around the same time. So, we were all going to shows together and experiencing some really good times. We saw Judge, Gorilla Biscuits, Bold, Turning Point and so many great bands of the late-eighties. We were blown away by [hardcore] and we just wanted to be a part of it. A lot of us also did zines at the time, too. We wanted to leave our mark on the scene somehow. The next step from doing a zine was to do a band and get up there on stage and share what was in our hearts and minds. Jason, our drummer, and I got some guys from our high school to put something together. Jason and I were straight edge and I would write these totally ridiculous straight edge lyrics. [laughs] And we'd have these non-straight edge guys in the band. We didn't know what the hell we were doing at first. [laughs] That was about 1989 when we started messing around trying to start a band. Finally, we got together with this kid Chris, who was about two years older than us. He was a skater that we all knew and he had this half-pipe in his back yard that seemed bigger than his house. [laughs] Everyone knew who Chris was — he was straight edge and was into bands like Youth of Today. He played bass and Jason got together with him and started talking about playing together. And then they started talking to this guy Pete who lived in Princeton, New Jersey and he played guitar, so they all got together to mess around. They eventually asked me to sing. Things started to come together — we made stickers and t-shirts, flyers, everything. We stuck stickers all over the place. We called ourselves Control at first. I remember seeing Judge at a show at City Gardens and I remember talking to Sammy from Judge and we told him we were a local straight edge band and he was like, "Hey, we're doing a show at The Anthrax in about two weeks and we need an opening band. You guys should do it!" We were like, "WHAT?! WHAT?!" [laughs] We basically froze. He gave Jason his phone number and he said to call him about the show. He had never heard us or anything like that; maybe he just liked our sticker. [laughs] Then like idiots, we didn't call him. We were like too nervous to do it. Eventually, we had a show at our guitar player's house in his basement and had some kids watch us and I remember that show was such a great experience. Everything just started growing from there. We started to meet people and play out in places like Pennsylvania. We went from being a little band just screwing around in a basement to playing all around the area. In 1990 there were almost no straight edge bands around. We thought all the people into the late-eighties straight edge bands would really get into us because we were trying to keep it alive, but a lot of people from that era seemed to be dropping out of that scene. I guess we were trying to create a new crowd. There were a lot of kids who started coming out and for a lot of them their first show was a Mouthpiece show.

EARLY NAME CHANGE

TIM MCMAHON: We thought Mouthpiece was a little bit more interesting name than Control. It had nothing to do with that thing that you put in your mouth when you're playing sports or whatever, which a lot of people seem to think it meant. [laughs] To us, Mouthpiece meant a spokesperson for a group. We sort of saw ourselves as a voice for the straight edge scene, which seemed to be crumbling at the time we started. We wanted to get up there and talk about these issues that we felt were so important.

INFLUENCES

TIM MCMAHON: We played a few shows as Control, but quickly changed our name to Mouthpiece by early 1990. Throughout 1989 and 1990, the straight edge hardcore scene was still pretty strong and vibrant. There were a fair amount of bigger straight edge bands still around and playing. Bands like Judge, Chain of Strength, Gorilla Biscuits, Insted, Turning Point and Release were all still playing and many of those bands we actually played with in our very early days as Mouthpiece. So, when Mouthpiece started, we weren't trying to bring anything back because the scene was still pretty much happening. Before we knew it, late 1990 really started bringing on major changes. Virtually every substantial band was breaking up, venues were closing, shows were thinning out, and kids were dropping out. Because we were all still so fired up about straight edge and hardcore in general, we couldn't understand why people were moving on. We just kept pushing on, playing the style of music that we loved and delivering the same messages that inspired us. Musically, Mouthpiece leaned towards a Southern California hardcore sound. Chain of Strength was without question our biggest influence. We loved their sound, which in a way seemed to put a slightly new spin on the old Boston and D.C. sound, but it turned into its own thing. Chain of Strength did not sound like New York hardcore and it wasn't that we didn't love New York hardcore, but we just adopted more of a Southern California sound instead. Another aspect about Chain of Strength was that their lyrics really struck a chord with me. Songs about being let down and disappointed in hardcore bands and kids that moved on and abandoned hardcore was something that I felt. It wasn't just songs about being straight edge and unity. They took a different angle and I could appreciate that.

EARLY RECORDINGS

TIM MCMAHON: We met this kid who asked us to be on a compilation record. This guy sent us into a studio and we recorded a song called "Hold Back," which was the first song we ever recorded. He paid for us to record this song and the comp ended up never coming out. So, we decided to just send the song out to some labels to see if anyone was interested in doing something with us. We always really wanted to do a record on New Age Records. Turning Point had done records with them, so had Outspoken and some other bands we really liked. At the time, New Age was the shit! They were about the only label really putting out classic sounding straight edge hardcore at the time. So, we sent a tape to Mike Hartsfield, who ran New Age. He ended up liking it and immediately responded to it and said he was putting out a compilation record called *Words to Live By*, which was going to have songs from bands like Turning Point, Drift Again, and Undertow. He asked us to be on it. We couldn't believe it! We were like, "This is incredible!" He ended up using "Hold Back." Within a few more days he asked us to do a seven-inch as well. We were so psyched!

WHY ME? RECORDING STUDIO

TIM MCMAHON: Mouthpiece recorded all of our records at a studio in south Jersey called Why Me? It's the same studio where Turning Point recorded their LP. Actually a ton of bands recorded there: 4 Walls Falling, Edgewise, No Escape, Flagman, Shadow Season, Godspeed, Worlds Collide; it was one of the more prominent studios recording hardcore in the early nineties. The engineer and owner of Why Me? was Joe DeLuca, who looked very much like Howard Stern. Total eighties long hair rocker guy, never wore shoes, always seemed to be barefoot. Good guy with the exception of his smoking, which he did right there in the control room at all times. He also kept copies of the more popular bands' records and put them out like magazines for people to look through. Every time we were in there we looked at the Turning Point LP over and over again. Joe also had a room that was designated as the band hangout room. It had a fridge, a table to eat at and a nice big sofa (which Mouthpiece would shoot our "What Was Said" promo photo on). What was interesting about this room was that Joe stored all the reels for the bands that he had previously recorded. The wall was just packed tight with reels. Thinking back, if we were dishonest thieves we could have walked out of there with some valuable reels and sold them on eBay many years later. [laughs]

"WHAT WAS SAID" LP

TIM MCMAHON: I remember Dave Mandel from *Indecision Fanzine* [and later Indecision Records] had been staying with me for a month or so right around the time that we were recording. Dave would go to the studio with us while we recorded the LP. While the band was recording the music, Dave and I would be generally bored out of our minds, so we'd leave the studio and walk a few miles to some Chinese restaurant. We'd usually bring food back for everyone, but the walk seemed like it took forever. When it was time for me to record the vocals, there was one particular song called "Gauge" that I had envisioned someone yelling the word "gauge" in. Since Dave was there we thought we'd give him a shot. Now one thing that I need to mention is that we had a nickname for Dave — Manface. It really meant nothing more than being a play on his last name, Mandel. Anyway, day in and day out we would be there at

the studio calling Dave "Manface." After Dave had hopped into the room to record the vocals and had done his level checks and gotten comfortable, Joe, the engineer said, "Take it away, Manface!" to which every single one of us laughed our asses off. [laughs] Up until that point I don't think Joe had even acknowledged Dave's presence, so it was just hilarious to come out of left field with the nickname like he did. We ended up using that on the matrix of the LP.

"WHAT REMAINS"

TIM MCMAHON: "What Remains," the opening song on the LP, had a great deal of meaning to me. I was sent a small flyer-like fanzine at one point. There was no return address on the envelope, which was a nicely, strategically folded up Xerox copy of the photo from the cover of Youth Of Today's *Break Down The Walls* LP, only the name of the fanzine was *Fuck You*. At first glance, just from seeing the cool *Break Down The Walls* envelope, I was thinking the zine might be pretty. As I started reading it over, I realized that the zine was really one big shot taken at various people in bands. I happened to be one of those people the editor chose to rip on. I don't remember exactly what was written, but I do recall him slagging me pretty hard and saying that I would be off to college in a year or two, drinking and becoming a frat boy. Apparently the editor, who went only by the name of Chuck U Farley, a reference from the 1990 movie *Pump Up the Volume*, decided I wasn't a person to be taken seriously and that I would soon be eating my words on straight edge. I was furious. This guy obviously didn't know me and had only judged me from afar. What was really pathetic was that he went by a fake name and didn't have the courage to let his true identity be known, yet he went out of his way to send me a copy of the zine. I immediately wrote the editor back. I remember the first line from my follow up letter, "You wanna fuck me, well I'd rather fuck you," which was a direct quote from an Ice Cube song. I went on to really give this guy a piece of my mind, tell him that he had no idea who I really was and that I would back up anything I said. His return letter was a little toned down and the apologies started coming. We went back and forth for a few weeks and by the end we were virtually friends. At the very start of this whole ordeal, because of this fanzine and nameless critic who chose to question me and falsely judge me, I wrote the lyrics to "What Remains" as a response. Eventually, I met the editor, Ron Little. Many years later, Ron went on to sing for the late-nineties band, Rain on the Parade. By the time Rain on the Parade started, Mouthpiece was broken up or on the verge of breaking up and Ronny and I were totally cool with each other and talked on a regular basis. We would even joke about how his fanzine brought about some of my best lyrics and one of the best Mouthpiece songs.

LIVING/BREATHING STRAIGHT EDGE HARDCORE

TIM MCMAHON: One of the main differences between Mouthpiece and a lot of the other straight edge bands of the time was that we really ate, slept, breathed, and lived straight edge hardcore. We were not some sort of fly-by-night group of guys who popped into the scene two months before we started the band. We all had been going to shows for years before Mouthpiece started and we all took hardcore seriously. We read a ton of zines, a couple of us did our own zines, we talked hardcore with dudes who came before us, we went above and beyond to learn the history. In terms of how Mouthpiece looked at straight edge slightly different than some of the other bands of our time, we went out of our way to avoid being cheesy. I specifically tried to give Mouthpiece a darker image. I didn't write lyrics using the words straight edge or drug-free or anything over the top or cliché. Other than the Dave Smalley inspired fist logo that we would adapt as our own, we didn't cover our shirts, stickers, and records with a ton of X's. The second pressing of our first seven-inch had three big X's on the back cover, but I kind of looked at that a little differently. It was more of a nod to the old D.C. straight edge than anything. We just tried to keep things very traditional and classic. A lot of other bands at the time were going out of their way to talk about the so called "sacred mark" or "straight edge pride" and we just let our actions do the talking for us.

FLUCTUATING BAND MEMBERS

TIM MCMAHON: I think Mouthpiece's main problem was guitar players. [laughs] And I have no idea why. From the day we started we had this core of myself, Jason on drums, and Chris on bass. Our original guitar player was into playing music and was kind of into hardcore but not really into it at the same time. He was a cool kid, but he just didn't fit in with the band that well. We started the band during high school and obviously when you're making that transition from high school into college sometimes bands fall by the wayside. For myself, Jason, and Chris, it was probably the most important thing to us. We loved doing the band and were really dedicated to it, but a lot of the guitar players that came and went seemed to have other priorities. Finally, toward the end of the band we had one of our more solid line-ups. Chris eventually went on from playing bass to playing guitar. Matt also joined us and played second guitar and that lineup lasted a few years. It could have continued on but the only thing was Chris had a problem with touring. He hated it! He would play within our area no problem, but he was just one of those people who doesn't like being on the road. He always seemed to have bad luck. I remember one time we played in Connecticut and we had some friends of ours come up with us to the show. They did a project band that was basically a bunch of noise. [laughs] Anyway, the guy who sang for the band made some comment about some of the kids at the show who were just standing there while his band played. I think he said something like, "Fuck all you guys from Connecticut" or something like that. This was probably not the wisest thing to do. [laughs] It was all pretty silly, but a few of these Connecticut guys walked outside enraged and looked for the closest car that had New Jersey license plates and just started destroying it. It turned out to be Chris's car, even though he had absolutely nothing to do with the incident. He had this Jeep and they ripped up the roof and smashed the front window and did stuff to the side-view mirrors. It was just horrible. At that point he was like, "I am never playing in Connecticut again." He always seemed to have strange stuff like that happen to him, which made him hate being on the road. Experiences like that seemed to traumatize him [laughs]. The first time we went to California he kind of flipped out and wanted to fly home. Luckily, we had two guitar players with us at the time, but we had this huge show at The Roxy with Outspoken, Strife, and Chorus of Disapproval. There were about 1,000 kids there! Our record had just come out and it was our first trip out there and it was the first chance for kids to check us out live. We were so psyched to play the show and Chris just couldn't handle it for some reason. I think he was supposed to fill in on bass for Ressurrection; their music is really noisy and they told him to basically play anything. But he got all worked up about it and wanted to play the stuff right. They convinced him to do it, got him on stage, and they did a couple of songs and then they wanted to do songs he didn't know and he pretty much flipped out. He dropped his bass and walked out of the place and walked the streets of Hollywood and found a phone and called his family and told them he had to get home. We went out there another time with him and he had the hardest time sleeping. He had something happen, like an air mattress busted on him one night and he couldn't sleep, so he left for the airport at like 4 a.m. and paid like $1,000 to change his flight around to go back home. He didn't tell us so we woke up and he was gone. We had no idea where he was! Of course, this was in like 1996 when most people didn't have cell phones, so we were frantic in that we had no way to get a hold of him. Finally, we called his parents and we eventually figured out what happened. And after that tour, our other guitar player, Matt, had been living in New York and hated it and got an opportunity to move to Louisville to play with Guilt. Though he didn't want to leave Mouthpiece, that situation just seemed to be the best thing for him to do with his life. At that point, we decided to break the band up and just play a couple of last shows, which ended up turning into about five last shows. [laughs] I guess that was an annoying aspect of Mouthpiece, but that is just part of what we were. In the end, everything turned out fine.

MOTIVATION

TIM MCMAHON: The fire that kept us going was that we simply loved doing the band. Even though we occasionally lost some members, there was never a time when we were like, "Oh, man, we've gotta end this." We would always just look for somebody else. We never thought twice about breaking up, at least until the very end. By that point, the band had been together for six years. We had done a full-length, a couple of seven-inches, a U.S. tour; we played all over both coasts. The only thing we didn't get to do that we wanted to was to play Europe. By the end we felt like we accomplished much and even more than we had set out to do. And by that time I was ready to do another band. But the reason we kept it together for so long was that we had the drive for it.

ACCOMPLISHMENTS

TIM MCMAHON: Mouthpiece generally accomplished everything we set out to with our records. We wrote the best songs we could at the time and I definitely wrote some very honest and heartfelt lyrics. I never tried to force anything lyrically; I wrote about whatever motivated me enough to write about. Just about every single Mouthpiece song has to do with one specific person or at least one specific incident. In a way, many of those lyrics were therapeutic for me and served as a genuine release for some heavy thoughts, feelings, and emotions. I never wanted to write lyrics that were too simple, so I tried to put a twist on words that might leave people wondering what I meant exactly. I didn't try to hide anything and if you looked into it with a little bit of thought, you could piece things together and understand what I was saying. We were also generally satisfied with the sound of our records. They weren't too polished, but they also weren't overly raw and hard on the ears.

MESSAGE

TIM MCMAHON: The main thing that I wanted to get across about Mouthpiece was that you can start and end a straight edge hardcore band as a straight edge hardcore band. A lot of bands have not been able to do that and have not been able to mean the things they said when they were playing in their prime. Mouthpiece started in 1990. All the core members of Mouthpiece are all still straight edge and are still into hardcore. Everything we said then still means the same to us today. Unfortunately, recently Sean McGrath, who was our last bass player, passed away. He had cancer and up until then he was still straight edge. This was a guy who was dying of cancer and his doctors told him the best thing he could do for his chemotherapy was to smoke medicinal marijuana. He was adamantly against this, as he was straight edge and vegan. Finally, after a while he listened to the doctors and he did it, but he was really concerned about it and wanted to know if we still considered him straight edge or if we were disappointed in him. I just remember telling him, "Jesus, man, the most important thing is for you to live!" He was in an incredible amount of pain due to his chemo and this was one thing that helped him get through it, so who am I to say he wasn't straight edge? It really touched me, though, that the last months he was alive he was still concerned of what we thought of him doing this stuff. I just told him if I was in his shoes, I'd probably do the same thing. Straight edge is about living your life and staying alive. You don't want to drink and do drugs that damage your body, but if your body is already damaged and this is something that can help you, you've gotta do what you've gotta do. The bottom line is that the last lineup we had, including Sean, was all completely still straight edge. That's one thing I want people to know or remember about Mouthpiece. There were so many bands that created the slogans, like "True till death!" We stuck to those words to the end and still have to this day.

LEGACY

TIM MCMAHON: We've stayed in people's minds over the years because we started during a time when there wasn't really anyone else doing what we were doing. At the end of the eighties and beginning of the nineties it seemed the straight edge hardcore scene had been falling apart and we came out of that. As time went on, straight edge came back. I guess we pretty much stayed the same over our six years of existence. We managed to maintain our ideals. We weren't a band that started as a total straight edge band and then ended up leaving it behind. We were straight edge the entire time and we sort of bridged the gap by playing with some of the older bands when we started like Insted and Turning Point and Release to playing with bands like Earth Crisis and Floorpunch when we broke up.

SELECT DISCGRAPHY:

Self-Titled (7", New Age, 1991)
McMahon, Schuster, Mattson, Baker, Jammer

What Was Said (CD/LP, New Age, 1993)
McMahon, Schuster, Reilly, Rosenberg, Jammer

Face Tomorrow (7"/MCD, New Age, 1995)
McMahon, Schuster, Wieder, McGrath, Jammer

FIGHT: THE NINETIES HARDCORE REVOLUTION IN ETHICS, POLITICS, AND SO

RACETRAITOR

Vocals: Mani Mostofi
Guitar: Daniel Traitor
Bass/Guitar: Brent Decker
Bass/Guitar/Drums: Karl Hlavinka
Guitars: Eric Bartholomae

Bass: Pete Wentz
      Rich Miles
      "Survivor"
Drums: Andy Hurley

Chicago's Racetraitor had a direct political approach in mind when they started in 1996. Every member of the band was fed up with what they considered to be mere lip service paid to topics surrounding race, ethics, and politics in the hardcore scene at the time. Bands had addressed these topics for years, but the members of Racetraitor wondered how many were willing to integrate activism into their lives on a daily basis. Racetraitor formed as an attempt to provoke discussion by asking such questions and forcing people to take a stand on divisive issues. Although some might debate Racetraitor's success in delivering their message, the band captured the scene's attention.

Comprised of ex-members of Midwest hardcore acts like the vegan-straight edge Everlast and the noise/grind outfit Hinckley, Racetraitor quickly made a name for themselves by playing shows throughout the Midwest and conjuring up debate before, during, and after shows. The group provoked audiences with their confrontational stage presence, explaining all of their songs in detail while pointing an accusatory finger at those who, in their view, benefited from "white privilege." This concept is based on an idea that people of European descent benefit economically, politically, and socially from living in a society that was built upon the slave labor of people of color. The band caused an uproar at the 1997 North Carolina Hardcore Fest as their set prompted such heated arguments about race and class with members of others bands and audience members that the entire show came to a halt. Soon after, Racetraitor achieved added notoriety with cover stories in *HeartattaCk* and *Maximum Rock N'Roll*.

Some accused Racetraitor of utilizing extreme politics and stage antics as a gimmick or leveled criticism that since the members were from the suburbs what right did they have to speak to issues of race and class in America? The band responded by stating that half of the group was of Middle Eastern descent; therefore, they weren't a completely white band. However, they conceded that every hardcore kid, including members of Racetraitor, were benefiting from white privilege. They felt to merely acknowledge this fact and shrug it off would be to ignore the problem. As they saw it, the only path toward social justice in America was to fight for radical change.

Though Racetraitor was known primarily for their stage banter, they also had an interesting musical progression. Originally, they created short power-violence blasts that lasted from 30 seconds to two minutes. As the group fine-tuned their approach — especially after the arrival of drummer Andy Hurley — their sound became more metallic and technical. Racetraitor's only full-length, *Burn the Idol of the White Messiah*, was a blend of Deicide-style death metal with chugging vegan straight edge hardcore. The record is strewn with fuming vocals and tribal-influenced drumming, which punctuate their political lyrics. *Burn the Idol...* also contains a lengthy essay in which the band explained their political, personal, and spiritual outlook.

Just as *Burn the Idol...* was released, bassist Brent Decker, an Islamic convert, left the group to pursue social activism. The group scurried for a replacement, which ended in a musical chairs-like rotation. After putting out a split record with Burn it Down on Trustkill Records in 1999, Racetraitor disbanded.

Over the years Racetraitor's legacy has continued to draw quite a divisive line. Some feel that the group was the last bastion of political dialogue in nineties hardcore. Others insist the band's approach might have been an impetus for the "anti-P.C. backlash" present in hardcore of the later nineties. Regardless, the band members have become involved with the issues they were passionate about over the years, which lends credence to the argument that the band was sincere.

THE IMPETUS FOR RACETRAITOR

DANIEL TRAITOR: I was just coming out of being in a vegan straight edge band called Everlast and we were all slowly getting into more politically conscious hardcore, which is the direction the scene as a whole was gravitating toward at that time. Everlast had some social commentary but a lot of that revolved around straight edge, which isn't bad but it's just one aspect of things. Everlast ended up sounding more like Downcast or Struggle by the end and when that broke up we did this grind band called Hinckley for a while. Brent and I then went on to form Racetraitor. For me, activism became a priority. My band became an extension of my activism, as opposed to my activism being an extension of being into punk or hardcore. That was a good and a bad thing, but what really drove with Racetraitor was that all of these issues were prevalent in hardcore at the time, the consciousness was there and I felt like I wanted to be doing something more direct. We can't just espouse ideas without some kind of action or tangible way of being involved in these issues that might somehow affect the world.

KARL HLAVINKA: When I was first getting into hardcore in my early teens, I saw that it was a vehicle for radical ideas. It was very attractive since it was a place where dialogue could be brought up and acted upon. I had gone to a Disembodied show here in Milwaukee with one of my friends and was expecting to see the new ex-Everlast band. The band was called Hinckley and featured most of the members of Everlast... gone insane! Me and my friend were blown away 'cause they just set up, would say something intelligent, and shred the audience over a mess of feedback while busting into chaos. The singer, Jody Minnoch, was going ape-shit, convulsion-like, and the energy was something I don't think I've seen since from a band. Eventually I started writing Dan and met up with them to play in Hinckley. Soon, we broke up like most bands and we already had ideas for Racetraitor going with me, Dan, and Brent. We asked Mani to sing and that was that. Me and Dan would put together songs in my parents' basement or in some crazy building with empty rooms where Mani went to school. The goal from the start was to be as in your face as possible on issues recognizing our role in historic and present colonial relationships with non-white and indigenous people around the world.

BRENT DECKER: In high school I got involved in various activist ideas and for me Racetraitor was just a natural extension. I didn't necessarily learn a lot from Clash records, but music has always been a reinforcement to find the strength to question things. Our early songs were about 27 seconds long so we also had to explain what the songs were about. We were reacting against the thing going on in the hardcore scene where bands would have, say, Zapatista pictures on their shirts, but it didn't seem like many people were involved in these types of struggles on a day-to-day basis. A number of us were involved in various political movements and organizations. When we first started playing and we talked about white privilege I didn't expect there to be that much of a backlash; I thought that American History 101. I know some people reacted to how we came across and who we were, but it did strike a nerve that people weren't comfortable talking about white privilege. A lot of people in the scene thought they were these awesome anarchists living, by choice, in collectives and they thought they were super radical and then you bring up white privilege and there seemed to be a problem with that for some reason. We were over the top and I don't think it was totally productive or even a great analysis of the situation in America and it was kind of reductionist of other people's struggles from whatever background they might be. A lot of times people would agree with Los Crudos or Instant Girl, but when it was one of us talking about white privilege then people didn't seem to react to it very positively.

MANI MOSTOFI: There was kind of a shift away from hard politics in hardcore at the time, like the politics associated with Ebullition and Bloodlink Records and those labels. People started to gravitate to more nuanced personal issues like how people relate to each other, which I thought was interesting. But there were some bands that were trying to reprioritize what had traditionally been seen as political hardcore and talk less about that and more about personal issues. Right about then you also saw the first wave which became bigger in more recent years of apolitical hardcore. All that stuff started to kick in around the same time. When I got into hardcore I felt like I found a place I belonged — I could be myself and share my ideas and hear other people's ideas, which was a really cool thing. But the shifts I saw in the scene were moving in the opposite direction of my personal growth. I got more into radical race politics and also came to terms with my Iranian background. I had the perspective of, "What does it mean to not be a part of the dominant American culture?" I was coming to terms with that at the same time, so I felt more alienated by hardcore which is obviously a very "white" thing for the most part. All those things together made us want to do a more extreme political band. I wanted to reassert myself in that scene and to make my feelings heard loud and clear, and I think Dan, Brent, and Karl had similar things going on.

CHOOSING THE NAME "RACETRAITOR"

DANIEL TRAITOR: I had gotten really heavily into race and identity politics and looking at the question of the privilege that comes with race and the history of race and its construction. A big issue in my life was that half of my family was from the south and they were fundamentalist Christians and I felt like I could never tell them what I believed in or what I was learning about because I would be labeled as — what so often happens on The Jerry Springer show when they had white supremacists on — a "race traitor." I thought, "Wait a minute, that's awesome. I am a race traitor. I'm totally on the side of humanity. I'm not on the side of one race."

MANI MOSTOFI: We were really getting into radical politics and there was sort of subtle systematic idea of "whiteness." There is this white power institution—not in the way a Nazi skinhead would see white power, but a far less obvious and more destructive white power, which is how our system operates whether it's the government or the media. It constantly reinforces values of people from white backgrounds. We were also studying third world revolutions and getting into the Black Panthers and Latin American revolutionary movements. When you want to destroy every institutional privilege that is associated with being a white American then I suppose some people might call you a "race traitor." I didn't necessarily identify myself as white, but at the same time we realized no matter what category of race you're put into or identify with, all these things are sort of false. Race is more of an idea. In hardcore not a lot of people were talking about that. People were talking about being anti-racist, like don't use the term "spic" or something like that. What we wanted to say was what's important about race is power. What we're against is that power relationship and we wanted to destroy that power relationship, which is what we might be considered a "traitor" to. I am from an immigrant family, but we were upper middle class. I realized what advantages I had. Our whole idea was what advantages do you have that you can turn around to bite the hand that feeds? A lot of people who hated us or didn't get us for whatever reason, years later

eventually something would happen in their lives, maybe they witnessed something or traveled to a different country, and they would tell me "I didn't get you guys at the time, but I get what you are saying now."

ANDY HURLEY: The whole point was that we were looking for the cause of the problems. The analysis of Racetraitor was that imperialism and colonialism were the problems. As Europe rose up it became an imperialist country that would displace indigenous populations around the world, which was the beginning of capitalism and the start of most political ideologies, pro or con, since. We felt imperialism was the problem, and a big part of that was the slave trade and the displacement of the indigenous population on this continent.

EARLY STAGES OF THE BAND

DANIEL TRAITOR: When you are younger and waking up to the reality of the world it's a very painful experience. Racetraitor was our outlet for that, and a very real outlet for the emotions we were experiencing that were related to the knowledge we were encountering. It's a hard thing to know if we took the right approach looking back. This scene in a lot of ways is a reaction to people lashing out against us for being different, and so to try to pressure people through making them feel uncomfortable may not have been the best approach. We wanted to make a statement that the message was more important than the music. I think the audience was ready for it on a certain level because the consciousness level was up in hardcore back then and we were trying to agitate people and push them to the next level. I had a notion in my mind of people in the world who aren't comfortable right now; kids in Africa dying of A.I.D.S. aren't comfortable; kids in the ghetto having to deal with gang and police violence aren't comfortable; so you shouldn't be able to come to a hardcore show to relax — you're going to come here and be agitated. That was definitely a type of negative reinforcement. [laughs] We were also involved with this Black Nationalist organization at the time (U.H.U.R.U.) in which this type of reinforcement was effective on me in jarring my reality. We'd go listen to people speak for an hour and they were basically just slamming white culture, calling white people crackers, and their style was very confrontational. This group was founded by these post-Black Panther activists who had this style of not sugarcoating things, which is somewhat appropriate for punk rock.

BRENT DECKER: A lot of us had gotten over the traditional hardcore style and we had become disillusioned with that scene in terms of what those bands were talking about. We just decided to play these short twenty second songs as kind of a reaction against the typical hardcore song structure. We all had kind of chaotic emotions we were trying to vent and these emotions fed directly into the sound. Also, Dan was starting to listen to Deicide all the time where a lot of grind bands were doing the whole punk/grind sound, so we started to develop into a more metal/grind sound and tried to take our instrumentation to another level.

MANI MOSTOFI: The sound reflected the attitude. We were into that extreme sound, but it also reflected how we wanted to come across. We were pretty angry young men. [laughs] I don't know if I had the right to be as pissed off as I was, but that's what punk rock is about, right? We just tried to play the angriest kind of music we could and portray it in the angriest manner we could. But as angry as I was I wasn't necessarily as irate as I was while we were playing. There was somewhat of a calculated decision to take everything — the sound, the name, the way we presented ourselves on stage — one step more confrontational. The only problem is that eventually the persona becomes a part of you and the negativity of the stage personality creeps into your own personality.

BRENT DECKER: Race is an uneasy subject and we thought we knew more about issues of race than we actually did. That being said it's a very kind of intense, personal subject that is rarely discussed openly and honestly. I don't remember many other bands talking about that.

EARLY DEBATES

KARL HLAVINKA: One of the earlier shows was a fest in Greenville, North Carolina, that caused a ton of hype. Not necessarily our set in general, but after the fact a lot of bands would say shit during their sets and Mani would go barging in from the merch table raging full on. 400 Years' set was delayed by at least 45 minutes or more and Seein' Red's might have been, too. It's hard to remember every detail because it was the most surreal fest I ever participated in. Going on no sleep after driving straight there made everything more surreal. Even the next day discussions continued into other bands' sets. I think anyone who was there probably remembers that fest as very intense whether they hated us or not.

ANDY HURLEY: If Mani's up there screaming and calling everyone crackers it was getting people talking about the issues. It shook people up. Did they really go home and think about it? Maybe not, but maybe they did, too.

MANI MOSTOFI: An important thing that stuck with me was when 108 played in Chicago. During the height of the Krishna movement in hardcore there were primarily two major bands — Shelter and 108 — and they were like good cop, bad cop. Shelter was good cop and said you should be into Krishna because it's this peaceful, happy lifestyle. Bad cop was 108, who were like, "Fuck the world, be Krishna." Regardless of your opinion of Krishna, Shelter and 108 were phenomenal bands. Anyway, when 108 played this show in Chicago, the show turned into a big debate afterwards and part of it was because Rob Fish was a total prick on stage in the way he displayed the Krishna message. It wasn't peace, flowers, drum circles, it was, "Fuck you, this is a valid idea. This is the true nature of the universe and you guys are assholes if you don't get it." People were like, "What the hell?" and there was this big debate about it. His response really stuck with me the entire time we were doing Racetraitor. He said, "Look, I've played hundreds of shows and I've tried to express what's on my mind in a productive, fair way and tried to be nice about it. But when I'm a dick or confrontational everyone pays attention and talks about what I'm trying so say." That's exactly what Racetraitor wanted to do and that's what was effective about the early days of the band. We'd get up on stage and call everybody a bunch of crackers and we'd say they were the guys who were forcing the slaves to build the pyramids and it didn't matter if they wore choker necklaces. Somebody had to be offended and once someone is offended then people pay attention. For all the stupidity that people saw that was behind our approach, I've never been more successful at something in my life in terms of setting a goal and reaching it. We wanted the crowd to be angry in a way that is provocative and they'd have to think and debate. And it worked! So, for all the criticism we got we really had an artistic goal and we executed it almost perfectly, and I think when we tried to broaden the artistic goal is when it got sloppy. At least the shows we were at, people were talking about things I hadn't heard them talking about before.

ANDY HURLEY: The thing we'd say is you can cut off the branches, but the tree is still there. Until you cut out the roots, which we believed were white imperialism, you couldn't change much.

KARL HLAVINKA: The aggressive tactics were used to basically call hardcore kids out as being isolated, hidden nerds inside this rotting tomb of alternative consumerism. That there was a relationship of domination going on outside of it that kept punk rock encapsulated and that if punk and hardcore were really about autonomy deep down, some fundamental contradictions would have to be examined. The response to it was a mixed bag. I was eighteen, so at first I still had a moderately romantic view of the imagery of what this network, or scene of bands, zines and pseudo-celebrities had to offer. I was expecting a little more proactive response, but after our first tour I saw that the reactions were very uncomfortable and mostly passive.

DANIEL TRAITOR: I do have to give respect to some of the older people in our scene who were trying to reach out to us in understanding what we were going through — people like the guys in Los Crudos, Torches to Rome, and some more activist people that were involved in the scene — and they tried to help us get to the next stage in our own development and political sophistication. Unfortunately, we were kind of arrogant on one level, so we weren't ready to take that step. Those criticisms were valid and those people I mentioned were engaging us in some serious, productive dialogue. Then there was another group who criticized us because we were attacking their idea of what they wanted hardcore and punk to be, which was more of a place for them not be accountable for anything other than their basic responsibilities. There were also a lot of people who came from lower income white backgrounds and from working class backgrounds who were genuinely and legitimately upset with what we were saying because they did have to struggle. One of our problems with our approach, which stemmed from our involvement with U.H.U.R.U., was that it de-legitimized that side of the debate, which was wrong of us to buy into.

BRENT DECKER: We weren't trying to define anyone else's struggle or define how they should react to oppression. It's much more about talking about race and class from the point of privilege. That was the whole point of this band in a white majority scene.

MANI MOSTOFI: We made mistakes like everyone else, but we also had success. Conversely, I only remember a handful of our critics trying to find common ground with us. But we weren't speaking from any other perspective than our own in regards to our personal class and race backgrounds. If anything I underplayed my own "brown" background and rarely wielded it in our defense. What we were talking about was our power and how it relates to everyone. We talked about migrant workers and those kinds of issues because these aren't just black or brown issues, they are everyone's issues, but we made sure to talk about them from our perspective. And in the end we made sure to point the finger at ourselves, too. We were saying that you as a middle class kid have to pay attention. Los Crudos was hugely influential on Racetraitor. I remember Martin [Sorrondeguy] talking about gentrification at a show and white kids moving to his Latino neighborhood and he was saying it wasn't a problem that white people were moving into the neighborhood; rather, the problem was they weren't becoming a part of the community. Our thing was not that we're talking about these issues; it's the way we're talking about them.

SHIFT IN SOUND AND APPROACH

KARL HLAVINKA: I pushed a lot of the more metal and technical stuff at first. Everyone was pretty familiar with metal already from their past and present. Also, bands like Abnegation were starting to push the envelope on "metalcore" with way more riffs and double-bass. That showed other kids they could finally take hardcore to a more crossover route. Once I had become friends with Andy and could shift to guitar it seemed like the best way to branch out to more audiences. We could present more elaborate song structures that weren't too popular in hardcore yet and at the same time bring an elaborate message to crossover into all the genres and scenes we could. I don't think it ever really materialized to what we were thinking, but it was decent enough.

DANIEL TRAITOR: One thing I'm proud of that we did is that we kind of threw everything out the window. Musically, I would say we became more complex because we are musicians. I love music of all kinds and enjoy it as an art form and I always want bands I do to be interesting; I never like to do just one thing and never change or explore new avenues.

BRENT DECKER: I stopped seeing the band as any kind of vehicle for change not too long before I quit, as it started turning into more of a spectacle. Beyond hardcore, and beyond music, the things we were talking about in the band were things I was committed to beyond the musical realm. I remember we were playing this Indiana Fest and there was all this controversy and there were all these people there and I remember that it felt really empty to me. I felt my commitment to that kind of work was being compromised by putting on such a spectacle and we were talking like such crazy revolutionaries, but we had so much more to learn about all this stuff. I met some really cool people and it was fun at some points, but at that time I was also going through a lot of changes spiritually. I converted to Islam before I quit the band and I got pretty involved in some pretty crazy shit and started to think that music wasn't really that cool anymore. So, I was less satisfied with the band making an impact and at the same time converting to Islam made me look at other aspects of my life and cutting them out and trying to focus on my own spiritual growth and maintaining the activist work I was doing. I guess I didn't care about arguing with five hardcore kids for six hours after a show at that point. [laughs] I think Mani, Dan, and Andy also wanted to make the band less confrontational and wanted to follow more in the footsteps of, say, Gandhi and wanted to be more compassionate in their approach, which I respected, but I just had my fill of the band by that time.

MANI MOSTOFI: The reason for our shift in focus was that was had been interested in the U.H.U.R.U. group. We were drawn into it because we were young and we wanted concrete solutions. We thought you could actually reach these utopian kinds of visions, but the problem is that utopian visions never totally come to fruition. When we started talking about spirituality we were admitting that there is more to the picture. We were trying to look at the inner essence of all human beings as valuable. So, if we're not white and not black and not essentially master or servant then where does our humanity and our sense of justice come from? A lot of the stuff we were into — many of the third-world anti-colonial movements — had this spiritual philosophy that went alongside their political analysis. So, it wasn't that shocking that we were influenced by these things. We used to give the examples of Gandhi or Martin Luther King or Malcolm X. These people represented the exact political analysis that we thought was right and they all incorporated spirituality into their outlook. So, we were trying to tell hardcore kids who were really anti-spirituality in a very strong way that you can actually find common ground with other people with different ideas. You don't just have to find common ground within a system of oppression. You can find common ground in a system of values and justice as well.

SPIRITUAL INFLUENCES

DANIEL TRAITOR: On one level if you're investigating identity politics you are going to get to some deeper questions about the nature of humanity, that nature of our identity, which led me back to spiritual questions that have always been a component of my life. I've always been looking for deeper truths that are out there, and that is where the race politics lead right back to the humanity of the issue. Spirituality is very important to me, but I've always had notions of spirituality that were not the "mainstream" notions of spirituality. This was one place where there was a misunderstanding with the band because some people thought we were just trying to bring "religion" into hardcore. We were just trying to understand the spiritual nature of life.

BRENT DECKER: Outside of the anarchist circles that a lot of people in punk tend to gravitate toward, I can't think of anyone I've worked with over the last ten years who was involved with political work, public health work, or social work who is not spiritual to some degree. So, there didn't seem to be any sort of line between spirituality and activism to me, but where I did see more of a line drawn was in music where a lot of the more political bands were coming from more of an anarchist or socialist perspective. For example, if you look at a lot of Latin American political change it is often sparked by revolutionary Catholic movements, which are not necessarily sanctioned by the pope, but nonetheless these groups have spiritual roots. I remember there were bands that wouldn't play shows with us because we were supposedly "religious" now. Their whole definition of religion was so simplistic. To them, religion meant their fundamentalist grandmother. [laughs] If you go down the list of all people who have changed things for good throughout history, most of them come from some kind of faith background. I guess the part of it that makes sense is a lot of people drawn to hardcore are rebelling against that middle-of-the-road, shitty repressive Christianity or Islam or Judaism or whatever, but that's only one side of the coin when it comes to spirituality.

KARL HLAVINKA: My take on the spirituality within the band was one of "victim" for being against exclusionary, ideological thought. I was kicked out of the band off and on during that time period and it's pretty funny looking back on it. The band members were predominantly subscribing to common, "civilized" spirituality that originated historically out of desert fringe pastoral/agricultural societies. [Being the] furthest thing from egalitarian, its contradictions and origins were taken as givens to find a more cohesive group of ideology. Us against them. That stuff really began to tear the band up as people started going their different ways based on ideology or lack thereof. The influence of spirituality is important, but it's always going to be varied and subjective to habitat, economy, and material conditions.

"BURN THE IDOL OF THE WHITE MESSIAH"

BRENT DECKER: What that album title was talking about was the whole iconic image of Jesus being "white" and how messed up that is on so many levels. When religion is a part of an oppressive system you see a lot of imagery of the oppressor. That title was specifically about Christianity in the Americas, but it could easily be about any other oppressive form of religion in any other part of the world.

DANIEL TRAITOR: We were trying to understand the spiritual nature of life and how that can affect social change. That title, in a way, sums it all up. An idol is what? Something that distracts you from the true nature of spirituality; an idol can be considered different forms of religion that are about making money or control. The "white messiah" we were talking about in this case is in our culture and coming from a punk perspective the "white Jesus" is the ultimate symbol that is used to oppress or used to justify slavery or to oppress women. So, *Burn the Idol of the White Messiah* means to burn this false notion of religion that we've been fed and bringing up the essence of spiritual reality. We're destroying the false notion of religion, but we're not throwing out the whole notion of spirit existing. By completely rejecting religion you are basically saying you accept the oppressor's definition of religion. What's more empowering is to say that you don't accept that narrow definition; you are going to define religion and spirituality for yourself from your own investigation of life and truth.

MANI MOSTOFI: To me the "Idol of the White Messiah" was threefold: one was this idea of the "white Jesus" or that God is "white" and what the implications of that are;

we wanted to destroy that idea. The other aspect of it from a more spiritual bent was this mystical message of what we have is not reality; what we see is not reality — these are idols. If we destroy these things we find out what and who we truly are. The other white messiah was also America or the western neo-liberal system and that was always a big part of it for me. Whatever problems the U.S. has there have been good things that have happened here. There are a lot of great things about our system that the rest of the world can learn from, but I don't think all these things were necessarily invented here or we have ownership over them. Free speech might be a novel thing for some people, but throughout history people have been demanding just that. But it hasn't been the most successful system in promoting socio-economic justice or implementing the right to, say, adequate health care. So, the white messiah, to me, was also about all these things we'd been brought up to think are the answers, but just because the U.S. system has benefited us doesn't mean that there isn't something better we can come up with.

TRANSITIONS

ANDY HURLEY: Mani was still into U.H.U.R.U. and Dan and Decker were more into activism from a spiritual perspective. Decker kind of disappeared. He had to pursue Islam in his life. There was a time when we were going to change the name to War of Armageddon. There was a lack of communication between some of us. After Decker left, it was Mani, Dan, myself, and a rolling cast of members. [laughs] I considered the spiritual path, but I ended up being into things more like Ishmael and the anti-civilization sort of perspective. We were all basically going in different directions.

DANIEL TRAITOR: Brent left the band and we were also having some ideological conflicts among the rest of us. We were trying to get through it and we took off a couple of months completely and we eventually found some people to fill in and get it going again. We had to figure out what we were going to say at that point because we were not doing the same thing anymore. We were also trying to figure out what we were going to pursue in our own lives, as well. And I wasn't sure the band could exist amidst all this uncertainty. Looking back now I can see it totally could have worked.

MANI MOSTOFI: There was also a big delay of the record coming out, which is always a curse. In order for a band to remain important on any level they always have to be visible. Plus, we weren't such a super confrontational band anymore and our shows weren't as big of a spectacle. And because our sound shifted away from power-violence and more towards metal-hardcore, the people who ended up following what we were doing changed a bit. Now we had to be more of a band because we had a record. We also never had an official permanent bass player after Brent left. We had at least four different bass players after he left and when I look at today's bands that is actually not too bad. [laughs] Dan, Andy, and myself were the band for pretty much the band for the rest of its history. Brent and Karl were highly influential people in the band, too. Eric eventually became a permanent second guitarist. But it took us about another year to gain momentum again and we started to tour and play more shows again.

FINAL ERA OF THE BAND

DANIEL TRAITOR: I don't know if I was in a place personally to know what the hell we were doing at that time. I had gone through a lot of hard stuff. I was taking my entire world view and throwing it out the window and completely re-investigating reality from my most fundamental beliefs. It caused me to be angry a lot and I wanted to externalize it and blame other people; I was miserable at most of the shows we played. I wanted perfection and wanted to be this revolutionary unit and I felt like we were these jag-off punk rockers just playing shows and I never wanted the band to be that. I thought I'd rather not do that band at all than have it be like that. I just quit at some point. We had this last U.S. tour that was actually really fun and we had some awesome shows on it. But then when we came back Andy quit and then we didn't know what we were going to do and then Brent came back and we were going to do it full-on again and then I just kind of flipped out and left. We all went our own different ways. Racetraitor was what it was. It served its purpose and I don't think it could have existed in a different era.

MANI MOSTOFI: I played a big role in the band eventually breaking up in that I became really driven and pushy about trying to cross over. I wanted to become more of a professional band and to fashion ourselves more along the lines of like a Rage Against the Machine, where we didn't compromise our message one iota. We never wanted to go into the mainstream, but we wanted to be a larger band within the hardcore scene itself. But the problem was a lot of people were into us because our music was heavy and we were a good band to mosh to and not necessarily for the reasons we used to get attention. So, that caused a big problem with Dan because he was trying to figure out how to be productive with his time in terms of being a productive human being. I was really pushy about keeping it going and that also affected Andy and pushed Dan away. Eric eventually quit our tour and he told Andy to quit, too.

RACETRAITOR'S ROLE IN "P.C. BACKLASH"?

MANI MOSTOFI: To blame Racetraitor is kind of silly because we were never that big. I think what happened was that some people got burned out by all the discussion and debate. We realized you could start the conversation by being controversial, but controversy alone couldn't sustain it. We could get people talking and we still believed the hardcore scene was an important place for dialogue in the world. While the nineties was a wonderful time for debate and discussion in hardcore, and it may have burnt some people out by the end, there were just as many people who were into hardcore for the stage diving and to buy records and many never paid attention to discussion in the first place. So, maybe Racetraitor might have been one of the final breaths, but we were reacting to that wave of anti-politics that had already started.

KARL HLAVINKA: Politically correct should probably be redefined as "what hardcore is right now and always was" — following the status quo while labels cash in on alternative consumer markets. That's "politically correct" in civilized life. To blame bands like Racetraitor and others is completely ahistorical and shortsighted. Just head back to

"Chickenshit Comformist" by the Dead Kennedys and watch Jello [Biafra] shred up the same exact situation as the present but 20 years before. Word for word, it sums it all up and applies today. I think people stopped the dialogue because North American hardcore felt powerless as a whole as aesthetics, fashion, and buffoonery shifted back into dominance. Trade in your hardline tattoo for a faux-hawk… one brutal decision after another.

DANIEL TRAITOR: A lot people who actually were discussing and debating just seemed to become less interested in hardcore and delved more into the issues they were actually debating from that time. The people who weren't into the issues just stayed into hardcore and a lot of the folks that were into the issues went out in the world and tried to make a change from outside the boundaries of the scene. It's unfortunate because I wish it could have held together for longer, but maybe that's just part of the cycle.

FINAL REFLECTIONS

DANIEL TRAITOR: It could have been cool if we could have kept it together for longer, but I feel like that had its own purpose in our own lives and maybe it had its own purpose in what the hardcore scene has become.

BRENT DECKER: I'm a little surprised at how much the band still comes up and I've actually had more positive feedback than negative. I regret how I left the band and some of the disrespectful tone the band had at times. We thought so many of these issues were so clear-cut at the time and very black and white and that analysis wasn't very deep in terms of race in America. But it was a good start — I mean we were about 20 years old at the time.

KARL HLAVINKA: The most memorable things are Hurley and I driving to and from Chicago about twenty million times together, reaching my house at 5 a.m. while he still had another half hour to go. All the excursions and tours were amazing; especially all the friends we made who opened their homes to us as a place to hang out, sleep, and eat. That's the most important lesson of hardcore and the real part of the "community." What we accomplished? Speaking for myself, I think it just was a big part of a continual process of learning and maturing. An ironic story, the last Killtheslavemaster show was in Tucson with Bury Me Standing in 2002, which had Brendan from Groundwork on vocals. He had no idea who we were and during our set I gave him a short shout out, disclaimered that we weren't kissing ass, that getting into Groundwork in 1994 was a massive influence in so many ways. That bands like that helped influence a process of thinking and that somewhere, 2,000 miles away, over eight years ago, there were some young kids who took their effort to heart and carried it on. He wasn't expecting it at all. It was pretty spontaneous on my part and he seemed pretty touched. So, if some kids got the same feeling or experience I did with Groundwork out of the bands I did, then it has been worthwhile.

MANI MOSTOFI: I remember this story a friend of mine told me about being in Europe and going through this kid's hardcore record collection. The kid had pretty much every good nineties straight edge hardcore release like Outspoken or Mean Season, but he also had almost every KRS-One record. And my friend asked the kid what got him into KRS-One and he pulled out the Racetraitor record and pointed to our essay where we quoted KRS-One. The fact I got one kid to get into KRS-One, who is a far more important artist than us or most hardcore bands for that matter, is amazing. The reason I got into straight edge is because I thought it was more punk than punk rock itself; it was even more rebellious and undermining of our system and culture. Racetraitor was trying to do to punk and hardcore what punk and hardcore does to the mainstream. I feel that was pretty ambitious, and I still stand by a lot of the things we were trying to draw attention to. I also think it helped me eventually channel my anger better. I used to say something on-stage to the effect of: "The reason why I scream in this scary, ugly voice is because the world is a scary, ugly place." Eventually, anyone who wants to stay an activist for more than seven years needs to come to terms with the fact that all around us there are small instances of human beings acting in compassionate and just ways.

BRENT DECKER: All of us are still involved in activism in some way. But Racetraitor was part of a learning process for all of us. A key thing for us is that we were and still are involved with these issues. I've contributed with public health work in Latin America and have been working with a gang violence prevention program the past few years and trying to help people get into drug treatment centers instead of incarceration. Mani has been involved with issues regarding Palestine and some anti-war stuff. Dan has worked with the ONE campaign. So, when we have these people all these years later still criticizing us and telling us we were going to sell out, it's ironic that all these people are just running thrash labels and that's their counter-cultural thing and that's the extent of it. [laughs] Not that every moment of your life has to be political, but I spend the majority of my week doing things trying to make this world a better place.

SELECT DISCOGRAPHY:

Burn the Idol of the White Messiah (LP/CD, Uprising, 1998)
    Mostofi, Traitor, Decker, Hurley

Make Them Talk (Split release with Burn it Down) (MCD, Trustkill, 1999)
    Mostofi, Traitor, Hurley

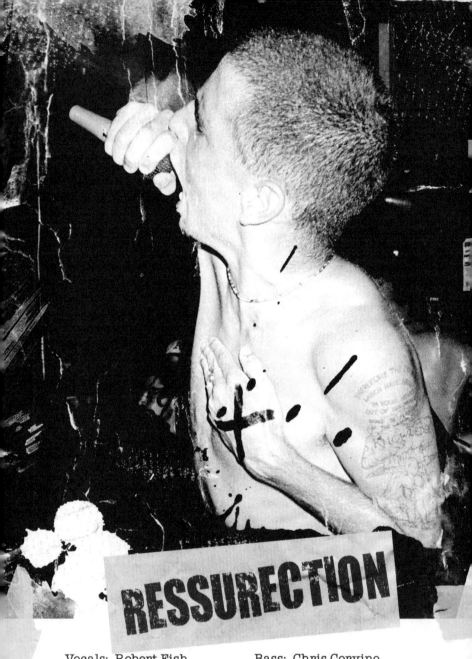

RESSURECTION

Vocals: Robert Fish
Guitars: Chris Zusi
          Dan Yemin
          Norman Brannon
          Bryan Maryansky
Bass/Guitars: Dan Hoernecker

Bass: Chris Corvino
      Dan Cavalleri
      Little Dave
Drums: Chris Daly
       Ari Katz

"I refuse!"

Although this chorus to Ressurection's song and album of the same name might sound like a typical cry of young rebellion on the surface, the lyric, much like everything else the group represented, stood for much more. In fact, one might say the phrase encapsulated the sentiment that was felt by many in nineties hardcore — a rejection of all aspects of the status quo. Ressurection, along with bands like Downcast, Struggle, Rorschach, and Policy of Three, stood as an embodiment of the hungry spirit that motivated many of the era's debates, movements, ideas, and attitudes while being wrapped up in a torrent of jagged chords, off-kilter rhythms, and frustrated screams. Some called Ressurection a "nineties Black Flag" because of their intensity, heaviness, and the chaos that seemed to erupt wherever they played, but their sound also utilized hints of D.C. post-hardcore, speed metal, and noise. This combination would influence numerous bands that delved into the metal and noise fueled sounds that became popular in the scene by the late-nineties.

Ressurection formed in 1991 primarily as an outlet for vocalist Robert Fish, who had been involved in hardcore since the mid-eighties. Fish experienced an unsettling adolescence and often times felt alone even in a scene that gave him the confidence to speak his mind. Inspired by longtime friends Dan Yemin and Ari Katz (both of whom later went on to form New Jersey's Lifetime), Fish wished to vent his disappointment with the world in a band that was noisier and more chaotic than his previous band, Release (a more straightforward straight edge hardcore band).

During their first practice, Yemin, Katz, and guitarist Chris Zusi yielded "Melting Away," a song which allowed Fish to exorcize some of his personal demons. Not too long after, Zusi left the project and guitarist Dan Hoernecker replacing him and helped Yemin and Katz write the music for their first seven-inch. As Yemin and Katz grew busier with Lifetime, Fish sought the help of others — beginning with drummer Chris Daly and bassist Chris Corvino, as well as Zusi again who returned to the fold to replace Hoernecker, and several others — to bring his vision to life. Eventually the core lineup featured Fish, Daly and Zusi, with the addition of bassist Little Dave, Norman Brannon who played second guitar on their 1992 tour, and Bryan Maryansky, who also joined the fold briefly.

Ressurection hooked up with New Age Records in 1991 and put out their first seven-inch in 1992, followed by another seven-inch for Redemption Records in 1993. In between these two records, they went on their only full coast-to-coast U.S tour in 1992. Although they barely made enough to scrape by for gas money and peanut butter and jelly sandwiches, they were ecstatic to be sharing their music and ideas with kids who were eager to scream along in unified desperation. On stage, Fish was a charismatic spokesman for a new wave of hardcore that was politically conscious, accepting of more philosophical forms of spirituality, and personally self-revealing.

I Refuse, Ressurection's only full-length, was highly anticipated, but when it became available by mail-order in 1994 fans were left shrugging their shoulders due to the muddy-sounding production. Listening with a careful ear, one can get a hint of the band's power in songs such as "Culture," "Sympathy," and "I Refuse"; however, the recording results just did not do the band justice. This, in part, resulted in Ressurection joining the ranks of many bands that were perhaps best represented in a live setting and whose records were left to tide one over until the next time the band came through town.

As Ressurection continued to build their reputation, ever-shifting group dynamics began to take their toll. In addition, Fish also became the full-time vocalist for 108, while Daly went on to form Texas Is The Reason with Brannon. Consequently, Ressurection fell by the wayside.

Although many felt the group ended before they had a chance to create their best music, Ressurection captured the uncorked rage that was a key undercurrent in nineties hardcore.

ROBERT FISH: I had just moved out of the Philadelphia Hare Krishna *ashram* in January 1991 and Ari Katz, who was my best friend at the time, was playing in Lifetime. One day we were sitting around with Dan Yemin from Lifetime [and later Kid Dynamite and Paint it Black] and Ari put on a record I had done and suggested we do something together. So, we called a friend, Chris Zusi, and wrote a song called "Melting Away." A few weeks later Ari, Dan, and I recorded the song and we then got Dan Hoernecker to play bass and we played our first show. At that point, Dan moved to guitar and we got our friend Chris Corvino on bass. We recorded our first seven-inch and then Ari and Dan Yemin left the band to concentrate on Lifetime. We then added Chris Daly on drums, another friend of Dan's replaced Chris on bass for a few weeks and Chris Zusi joined the band full-time. Then, in December we went on a two week West Coast tour. Upon returning home Chris and Dan left the band and we added Little Dave on bass.

CHRIS DALY: Rob formed Ressurection with Ari Katz and Dan Yemin from Lifetime. I originally played drums for Lifetime and was kicked out before they recorded the seven-inch for New Age. Ari was immediately replaced on drums in Ressurection by me, and everyone was happy after that. Ressurection was a much better fit for me.

NORMAN BRANNON: I was living in the Krishna temple from 1991 until the middle of 1992 and I was miserable. I hated living like a monk. I met Rob at the Philadelphia Govinda's Restaurant and we became really fast friends. When I would feel miserable at the temple I would call him on a calling card and complain to him for hours. [laughs] I was into being a devotee but being a monk was a whole different lifestyle. I was 16 years old when I moved into the temple and I hadn't really lived, so for me to renounce all things I hadn't done, I knew my stay was going to be short-lived. My biggest problem was that I had nowhere to go. Rob was incredibly supportive and cool and finally one day he said, "You should just live with me." I asked, "Well, don't you live with your dad?" He was like, "My dad's cool, he won't care." And that was that. [laughs] So, I moved from the temple to Rob's house, which was kind of the epicenter of what was happening for hardcore in New Jersey at that time in the early nineties. I met all the Ressurection, Lifetime, and Mouthpiece people and everyone who did shows. I got along great with everyone in the band. Dan Hoernecker was a great guitar player and responsible for a lot of Ressurection's sound at the time, which was some pretty fucked-up, dissonant, heavy shit. Everyone in Ressurection wanted the music to sound disgusting, so that was the objective. [laughs] My parents had sold everything I left behind at their house including my first guitar, which was a beautiful Gibson SG that I miss dearly. So, I did not have a guitar at the time and I was kind of jonesing to play one. The band practiced in Rob's garage so I asked Dan if I could play his guitar when he wasn't there and he was really cool about it. So, I maybe picked it up once or twice and that was it. One day Dan comes to the house and opens up his guitar case and the headstock is literally snapped. Immediately he looks at me and thinks I did it. And I didn't do it. He goes ape-shit and rightfully so; I'd be bummed out if my guitar was broken. But I didn't do it, so don't blame me. [laughs] He made it a political issue in the band and was very upset and wanted me to own up to it even though I wasn't responsible for it. Rob had only known me for three or four months and he was put in the middle. I was really surprised when he told Dan that, "If Norm says he didn't break it then I believe him." Dan basically quit the band and that was that. They were in the process of booking a tour for that summer for Ressurection and Lifetime, which was a pretty big deal because at the time

hardcore bands didn't really go on full U.S. tours. They could have done the tour as a four piece, but Rob turned around and asked me to play guitar, which initially made me uncomfortable for obvious reasons. [laughs]

ROBERT FISH: The summer of 1992 we went on a five week U.S. tour with Lifetime and Norman Brannon played second guitar just for the tour. This was then the lineup for the next few years before we added Brian Maryansky, who later went on to be in Jets to Brazil. As far as the name... I was rather obsessed with anything anti-Christian so I chose the name to be both symbolic towards my dislike of Christianity as well as a way to emphasize the band's determination to reignite the straight edge scene, which had died down at that point. Something about the environment... flag-waving, God-loving and beer-drinking... it just felt right. I remember when I came up with the name I was, for whatever reason, sensitive that people not mistake me as a religious type although I had just moved out of a Hare Krishna temple. I loved the name, but the idea that someone may take it as some religious connotation, led me to put the "ss" [in the name]. I remember when I made the logo I drew the two ss' like the Nazi era "ss". I guess it was my way to draw a parallel between religion and the horrors of the Nazis; plus, I thought it funny as everyone in the band at the time, Ari, Yemin, and myself, were Jews. However, by the time we started to play I had dropped that logo idea.

INFLUENCES

ROBERT FISH: We were highly influenced by Black Flag, Void, Bl'ast, Corrosion of Conformity, and the Dead Kennedys. We had a raw idea as to what we wanted to sound like. It came off live but recording it never seemed to work. [laughs] Lyrically, it was just me. I don't think there was any real influence besides whatever came in my head.

CHRIS DALY: We had the obligatory New York hardcore influence, but definitely leaned toward noisier, chaotic, power-core groups such as Black Flag, Half Off, and Negative Approach. We also listened to a lot of metal growing up — mix that with those other influences and there you go.

EARLY SHOWS

ROBERT FISH: The first shows were at first rather small but enthusiastic. We developed a large circle of friends and literally that whole straight edge scene revolved around my house. Lifetime, Ressurection, and Mouthpiece all seemed to feed off one another in playing shows and just trying to make it work. Within a year the shows were just amazing. All of us were involved in putting on shows, putting out zines, and getting as many out of town bands to play the area as possible. By the time we all put out our seven-inches the scene had really become rather large.

ADVENTURES ON THE ROAD

ROBERT FISH: We wanted to play as much as possible and in as many places as possible. We went to California in the winter of 1991/92 for 10 days of shows and then we did a U.S. tour with Lifetime in the summer of 1992. It was so awesome! We were lucky to get $100 a night between both bands. We had a tiny cargo van with no windows crammed with 10 men, equipment, clothes, and merchandise. You could barely fit in the thing. We had a loft that you needed to be lifted onto and slid into like an easy bake oven. Sometimes we would wake up and the roof would be caved in slightly and would be touching your nose. Four more people would be stuffed onto the floor between the loft and front seats and one person sitting between the front seats. We had no money, no promoter, no label support, and pretty consistent nine to thirteen hour drives each day and it was fucking amazing! [laughs] A few of the guys had money their parents gave them or a credit card, but Little Dave and I were flat broke. We ate peanut butter sandwiches every day. We would share our money to buy bread and peanut butter and that is all we ate unless we stole something. It was rough but so amazing! After that we did one tour with Shelter. We took all our money and bought a van. This thing was a monster. It had a three foot hole in the fucking floor, which we put wood over so we wouldn't fall in. We built a loft and left one morning. A few hours into the drive the engine blew and we were fucked. We did the next few shows in a U-Haul. U-Haul will tell you not to ride in the back of their trucks due to exhaust; that it will kill you. We lived to tell about it, barely. [laughs] I remember falling to the ground at the first show because my head hurt so badly from the fumes. It was crazy. Of course, U-Haul charges by the mile so we disconnected the speedometer. After a few days we met some kid in Detroit who had a van and he drove us the rest of the way. Of course when we returned the truck we ran because they were going to ask how we managed to drive 80 miles between Pennsylvania and Detroit. [laughs]

NORMAN BRANNON: I had never been outside the East Coast, so the idea of going to Los Angeles was amazing! But when I look back at that time now I could not believe the squalor we were living in. [laughs] We were touring in a cargo van with no windows in the summer. We built a loft for two bands' equipment but that takes up a lot of space, so literally there were points where we were lying on top of each other because that's the only way we could fit in the van with all our stuff. If there would have been an accident we would have died. At the same time it was really fun until we ran out of money. Chris Daly came down with chicken pox in Las Vegas. I remember him throwing up in the middle of the street. We ended up making it to L.A. and played two shows with him fully in the midst of chicken pox and then he just said, "Look, I've got to go home." So we cancelled whatever was left of the tour and drove straight back to New Jersey, where I ended up coming down with chicken pox. [laughs] So, it was harsh but in one of those youthfully naïve kind of ways.

CAUSTIC SOUNDS/AREA INFLUENCES

ROBERT FISH: Well, we were all huge Black Flag fans who were straight edge. So, we put the two together to some degree. From a personal perspective, I was in a very depressed and desperate time in my life which came through in the lyrics. When the local punk/hardcore scene started to emerge again we found ourselves as sort of outsiders from what was going on. There was a great club in New York City called ABC No Rio, which was focused on promoting a more social and political perspective. It was a perspective that many of us were attracted to and in some respects wanted to replicate in New Jersey. However, as things grew it seemed to shift in focus to a more external and superficial feel. That resulted in songs like "I Am Not Youth Culture." It was my way of saying that although the dress and music may sound the same but the content and drive differed greatly and was actually adversarial in spirit. At times I was overwhelmed and just felt like a stranger in my own skin and my discomfort with other people and social situations also came out in my lyrics.

NORMAN BRANNON: I loved the fact we never had tuners. We pretty much tuned our guitars as low as they would go and then tuned to each other and that was it. [laughs] So on one level we had this trashy, guttural sound coming out. But then you have Rob who at that point was coming of age in a lot of different ways. Ressurection came about after his mom died of lupus and that was something that was pretty fresh on his brain, for example with "Sympathy." Rob is actually an incredibly calm and normal person, but when you give him a chance to say something with a microphone he goes crazy, which is great. [laughs] It's cliché to say people "get it all out" through the music, but for Rob I think that was a pretty legitimate assessment.

"CULTURE"

ROBERT FISH: At that time many of the externals of the punk scene started showing up in MTV and gained media attention such as stage-diving, dancing, et cetera. Also, the shift of more mainstream acceptance was starting. Initially, it was kids who just years earlier would have targeted punk kids as a punching bag and now they were starting to look like us and listen to heavier music... so "Culture" was a reaction to that also. The song was making the point that what we were a part of couldn't, and would never, be defined by pop-culture or those outside of the scene. It wasn't about a particular look, style of dance, or heavy music, but an experience and attitude

"I REFUSE" LP

ROBERT FISH: I think we recorded and mixed in 10-12 hours because that was all we could afford. We were dirt poor and recording just wasn't all that important to us. We were a live band and we knew it. I think the songs are good, but the recording is terrible. We just wanted to get it out to go back on tour. We were broke and had no resources and to be honest I don't think we gave a damn as we never really thought of the big picture. So, we recorded as quickly and cheaply as our budget afforded us and played as often as possible.

CHRIS DALY: The recording, obviously, is quite disappointing. The music was written very naturally and, unfortunately, both us and the "engineer" who recorded it had very little experience in the studio. It would be fantastic to one day try and remix it and see its true sonic potential.

NORMAN BRANNON: The band was in debt and New Age gave them some money and they spent almost all of it getting out of debt and they only ended up having about $1,000 to make the record. They recorded and mixed it in a weekend and it's not the kind of music you can churn out in a weekend in the studio. Unfortunately there was no money to do it right. The songs were great but the recording just didn't do it justice, which I think was actually fairly common for bands from that time. At the time you were really confined by the analog studio.

PERSPECTIVES ON STRAIGHT EDGE

ROBERT FISH: We were friends with most of the bands at the time, but we were also a bit older and had been a part of the whole straight edge thing for a longer period so it had already branched out for us. Most young kids don't think of anything outside of their own experience. At first we were rather outspoken about straight edge as it wasn't a popular subject when we first started. The whole straight edge scene from the eighties had disappeared. There was no straight edge scene in New Jersey, Pennsylvania, or New York at the time other than the bands that hung out at my house (i.e. Ressurection, Mouthpiece, and Lifetime). However, as soon as straight edge started to get a bit bigger, which was after the first year of the band, we sort of didn't care about talking about the whole thing although it was still central in terms of the individual members.

CHRIS DALY: Ressurection definitely existed as a straight edge band. We wanted people to think outside the box and see there was more that just sing alongs and Champion sweatshirts — as great as both of these were — involved in the genre. We definitely got respect from people who normally would be turned off by the gang mentality of straight edge hardcore, which made it fun being able to play very diverse D.I.Y. shows.

NORMAN BRANNON: Ressurection was a straight edge band, but I always looked at it as more of a punk rock band. It's all semantics. Hardcore and punk rock are interchangeable. But at the same time there was something very pure about what Ressurection was doing that I enjoyed. Their approach to straight edge wasn't about positivity, which was pretty universal at the time. The fact that Ressurection would come on the stage and it was very aggressive and even negative in some ways appealed to me because it was a more realistic picture of straight edge.

POLITICS

ROBERT FISH: At that time there was also an impetus for substantive lyrics with the Gulf War in full-effect, which forced many of us to look at broader issues. There was

a sense of politics in Ressurection although I wouldn't label us as a political band. We wrote about political topics, such as the Desert Storm war, a woman's right to choose, and the dynamics of the punk scene becoming more mainstream, but all in all the band was about whatever was in my head when we wrote a song. We never sat down to map out an agenda. I wanted [to speak to] people who were straight edge and vegetarian, as well as people who held similar beliefs (pro choice, anti war, etc.), but I didn't want to be a band defined by a certain ideology. There was already so much of that. So although we touched on different things that were politically and socially oriented I also wanted to speak to the things that were going on in my head and my heart which didn't fit that spectrum.

VAISNAVISM

ROBERT FISH: The only song that Vaisnavism ever influenced me in writing, whether in 108 or Ressurection, was "Why?" I lived in a temple before Ressurection was a band. I lasted about seven months. It was clear pretty quickly that I was way too much of a maverick emotionally, psychologically, philosophically, you name it, and when I moved out of the temple I was treated rather indifferently. Essentially, if I didn't want to live as they had envisioned, I wasn't worth much. "Why?" was the second Ressurection song and I wrote it after my first trip back to the temple after I had moved out based off a conversation I had with a "friend" who tried to convince me to put my maverick mind to rest and just have faith in what I didn't feel comfortable with. Outside of that I don't think Vaisnavism ever really influenced my lyrics. "I Refuse," for instance, certainly fits into the idea of a soul and such, but it wasn't something I would say was influenced by Vaisnavism as it is a thought process that came to me well before I had ever heard of Vaisnavism.

PERSONAL STRUGGLES

ROBERT FISH: I really was a rather fucked-up person and struggled to keep myself together so it all had to come out somewhere. With each band I became more comfortable in understanding myself and more specific in how I would articulate my life. It was just a dark time in my life. I certainly couldn't articulate any of it at that time, but I think it came out in ways. I do remember before a show we were all gathering at my house and I just freaked out, went into my room and destroyed everything in it and fell to the ground in tears. A few of my friends came in after hearing things smashing and me yelling and they just asked if I was okay. I think everyone knew I was not doing well, but we were young and no one knew what to make of it or how to help so we all shook it off and that was that.

IMPETUS FOR CATHARSIS VIA LIVE SETS

ROBERT FISH: I would start by saying that I never would have expected Ressurection to be characterized as one of the more angry bands of that era. I mean we had members of Lifetime (Ari Katz and Dan Yemin), Texas Is The Reason (Chris Daly and Norman Brannon) and Jets to Brazil (Chris Daly and Brian Maryansky) in the various line ups of the band! [laughs] At the same time it was a very dark period of my life. Since I was the singer, wrote all of the lyrics, and was essentially the mouthpiece of the band, the anger probably mostly comes from what I was going through. I had just gone through the death of my mother when the band started and was trying to figure out who I was so I think there was a tension and desperation to the music and to our appearance. Part of it was also the scene at the time. I remember at one point we had five shows in a row end with full blown riots! So, the energy at the shows was a bit strange. I don't really have a clear answer to it as I think it was a combination of things.

END POINTS

CHRIS DALY: It was a great time and it definitely was an important part of my musical upbringing. I just wish we had a better sounding record to leave behind....

ROBERT FISH: Chris Daly and I were in 108, which became a very active band in terms of recording and touring. It was just time [for the band to end], really. Ressurection was really a moment in time and it never occurred to us that we should get our act together and worry about recording or doing things in an organized way. It was also around this time that Chris started Texas Is The Reason. I never set out to achieve anything other than to play, travel, and get some shit off my chest. So, I really liked what we were doing at the end of the Ressurection. We had become more musical with Brian joining, a bit more influenced by the Dischord feel without losing our personal ethics. However, between 108, Texas Is The Reason, Zusi going to Notre Dame, the constant fights at shows, and other factors, it was time to stop. I remember our last show. During the last song a fight broke out and when that ended our drummer and bass player were being held back from one another. We were all going in different directions and we imploded. I don't think I articulated much of what I was going through in the band, but at the same time it was a good outlet just in terms of playing and keeping myself busy and staying alive. It was more of the survival process than a healing one but important to me nonetheless.

SELECT DISCOGRAPHY:

Self-titled (7", New Age, 1992)
      Fish, Hoernecker, Cavalleri, Daly

Culture/Pretty Love (7", Redemption, 1993)
      Fish, Zusi, "Little Dave," Daly

I Refuse (CD/LP, New Age, 1994)
      Fish, Zusi, "Little Dave," Daly

FIGHT: THE NINETIES HARDCORE REVOLUTION IN ETHICS, POLITICS, AND SOU

RORSCHACH

Vocals: Charles Maggio　　　　Bass: Thomas Rusnak
Guitars: Keith Huckins　　　　　　　Chris Laucella
　　　　Nick Forte　　　　Drums: Andrew Gormley

With a combination of blast-beats, metal riffs, and cacophonous vocals, Rorschach was among the most intense, creative, and influential early-nineties hardcore bands. They had a staunch D.I.Y. ethic and were one of most consistently touring hardcore bands of the era. Whether the group played a show for 10 kids in a basement in the Midwest or headlined an ABC No Rio matinee, Rorschach was determined to get their music out there. In the process, the outfit displayed an enthralling though sometimes painful-to-witness mixture of hardcore, grind, metal, and noise and created a small, but dedicated, following during their existence, which actually increased in the years immediately following their break-up.

Rorschach officially began in 1989 when guitarist Keith Huckins, bassist Charles Maggio, and guitarist Nick Forte decided to start up a band that was serious about bulldozing any perceived notions of formula that so often gripped hardcore groups. Of course, many hardcore and metal bands of the past had attempted such ambitions — Black Flag, Corrosion of Conformity, and Bl'ast, to name a few — and also had success. Yet the members of Rorschach felt strongly that their musical instincts were about to tap into a sound that hadn't quite been reached. Soon, drummer Andrew Gormley and bassist Chris Laucella joined the fold, Maggio switched over to vocals, and behind an early batch of powerful demos, Rorschach slowly fought their way into the sometimes insulated New York hardcore scene.

By the time Rorschach recorded and started to get their name out there, with the support of the ABC No Rio scene, word started to spread about this band that pulled no punches in terms of intensity and power. Partially as a reaction to the bevy of "youth crew" clones that peppered the country at the time, Rorschach searched for other explosive avenues in which to express its frustration with life in America. Also, feeling somewhat isolated from the perceived "jock" oriented factions within hardcore during this era, the band was looking to create a sound and a scene that allowed the musicians to be themselves and to simply create sounds that best exemplified their feelings.

After testing the waters with local shows, some extensive tours, and the release of a full-length album, *Remain Sedate*, Rorschach quickly became one of the hardest working bands in hardcore, touring America nearly non-stop the next few years. They booked their own shows and tours and utilized independent record labels like Vermiform and Maggio's own Gern Blandsten to release their music. Although Rorschach would sometimes end up playing to nearly empty rooms on their summer jaunts across the country, those who showed up were riveted by the band's live-set and became instant fans. The impact the group had wasn't fully felt until more and more bands attempted to emulate Rorschach's sound.

Eventually bassist Thomas Rusnak replaced Laucella as Rorschach kept writing and touring even in the midst of the members' college and work schedules. Also, as word spread about the band, more people showed up to support the group, especially in their home base of ABC No Rio. Along with outfits like Born Against and Citizens Arrest, Rorschach helped establish this politically-fueled scene and became something of a legend across the country due to word-of-mouth and by way of zines.

By 1992, Rorschach had weathered a variety of personal storms. For instance, Maggio was diagnosed with Hodgkin's disease, while tensions arose about the group's direction. However, in the midst of this turmoil Rorschach produced what is considered by many to be their best record, *Protestant*. The album wasn't necessarily a radical departure for the band; however, it showcases the group at the height of its powers. Maggio's voice, banshee-like and desperate, cuts like glass as the rest of the band bursts back and forth between sludgy verses, pounding build-ups, and scientific time-signature changes. All the years of constant playing and refining brought the band to a point of confidence, which was visible at every gig.

Not too long after *Protestant* appeared, Rorschach crumbled under the increasing tension. By this point, some members wanted to take the group in different directions, while others were becoming more serious about personal or work endeavors, so Rorschach called it quits.

Rorschach's story isn't much different from many other bands, as every musical relationship always goes through its ups and downs. Yet when it comes to the legacy of the band, their unforgettable live intensity, and the diverse array of influences, Rorschach is definitely among the most influential and memorable.

ORIGINS

NICK FORTE: I was a 15-year-old full on hardcore/metal kid living in suburban New Jersey when I saw the drummer who was to be in Rorschach, Andrew, play drums in a thrash metal band [Torment] at a battle of the bands at the high school we both were attending. I was shocked that anybody at our high school could play drums so damn well. This guy sounded like a real drummer at a young age. I had it in mind to form a band with him, though I figured realistically this would never happen. He was a couple of years older than me and we weren't friends or anything and honestly, I can't remember how I convinced him to play music with me, since I could barely play bass guitar at the time. But he had a vague interest in punk rock and his metal band was breaking up. So we started an admittedly pretty bad hardcore band around 1987. We did a few originals, some 7 Seconds songs, Minor Threat, Agnostic Front, etc. Though it was great playing with Andrew, the band couldn't sustain a steady lineup, and we disbanded without much fanfare after about a year.

ANDREW GORMLEY: In mid-1989 Nick gave me a call to let me know that he was starting a new hardcore band with some people that he met at shows. He mentioned that the drummer they were practicing with wasn't working out and then Nick said goodbye. I thought he was trying to get me warmed up to the idea of playing with him again, but he said that wasn't the purpose of the call. A week later, he called me back and asked me to play in the band. I wasn't the biggest fan of hardcore, so I agreed to play in the band as a temporary drummer. I don't think I ever mentioned the "temporary" thing again.

CHARLES MAGGIO: Two members of Rorschach were in one stupid, dumb band in Northern Jersey, and two members were in another dumb band in Northern Jersey, and we knew each other from going to shows, so when both of our dumb bands broke up we decided to give it a shot as a new band and added a bass player.

NICK FORTE: Eventually at a Sunday metal matinee show at some dive bar in Nyack, New York, I think this was in the spring of 1989, I got to talking to Charles and Keith [Huckins] who immediately seemed like guys who were more serious about having a band than anyone I had met and we had the exact same taste in music, which was a lot of New York hardcore and straight edge stuff and a healthy respect for old punk and hardcore bands as well as an ample amount of metal. I hadn't met anybody who liked hardcore and metal and who lived anywhere near me, so these guys seemed like the ones to try to have a band with. Plus, they also had a hardcore band that was breaking up. It's hard to remember some of our earliest get-togethers to work on music, but since Charles was a really good bass player, they wanted to have a band with two guitar players and Charles on bass. I pointed out that I had no clue how to play guitar so basically Keith, who was an insanely good metal guitar player, taught me a few basic things on guitar, enough to get started, and I learned the rest as we progressed. But I had never played guitar until Rorschach started. At this point I had lost touch with Andrew as he had gone on to college. So, for a while, this early version of Rorschach had a glam metal friend of Charles and Keith filling in on drums while we looked for a singer. At this point, we were aping the sounds of New York hardcore primarily, straight edge type "spirit of 88" stuff. We auditioned a bunch of singers but nobody was any good. Charles would show them the lyrics that we had and he would demonstrate how to sing them. Finally one day, Keith and I were like, "Why doesn't Charles sing? He's better then everybody we've tried out." At this point, Charles was still pretty undeveloped as a vocalist and was miles away from the shrieking howl he is most known for. So we had Charles on vocals now and we had a friend of Charles, Chris, who was a very good bass player, to be the bass player. The big key score was me convincing Andrew to play with us, and I remember telling him that these guys could really play. He decided to give it a try. I think the first "official" Rorschach practice was maybe the summer of 1989. It wasn't long before we very consciously decided to make a huge shift and try to make our music darker, more fucked up, more pissed off and not like what everybody else was doing and now we had the personnel to pull it off. We chose the name Rorschach to reflect our intentions. It was a weird name that was hard to pronounce and the meaning was unclear, so we liked it.

KEITH HUCKINS: We were a bunch of suburban kids without a clue, basically. [laughs] We went to a bunch of shows, but we didn't have any ins with anyone, so it was really hard to hook up shows. If ABC No Rio hadn't come along, we would have struggled really hard, because no one else really gave us any breaks early on.

THOMAS RUSNAK: I joined Rorschach about half way through its lifespan. I was playing in a band called Evil Dean at the time. We played a show at ABC No Rio that my close friend Chris [Boarts] of *Slug and Lettuce* set up. Chris and I grew up about two blocks from each other. We used to listen to punk and hardcore records together as kids. She introduced me to a lot of people around the New York scene. I called her about contact info for Rorschach, as I wanted to book them in my home town of State College, Pennsylvania. *Remain Sedate* was a favorite record of mine at the time. Chris told me that Rorschach and Born Against were both looking for a bassist. I called them both and, getting an answering machine in each case, left two messages. Rorschach called me back first and it wasn't long after that I was touring the East Coast with them.

INFLUENCES

CHARLES MAGGIO: We all came from different places which totally helped us find a nice somewhat unique sound. A short list of definite influences includes Slayer, Voivod, Corrosion of Conformity, Die Kreuzen, Bl'ast, and Black Flag.

THOMAS RUSNAK: Really, Huckins wrote all the music. With that said, he pretty much let me play what I wanted to his songs and parts. At the time I think my big influences affecting what I was playing in Rorschach were Corrosion of Conformity's *Animosity* LP and Scratch Acid's two EPs.

KEITH HUCKINS: I grew up a total, complete metal-head. I cut my hair maybe a year before Rorschach started. Rorschach's sound ended up developing because I wanted to write more of a mosh-core thing, but I couldn't do it. The songs just never came out the way I wanted them to. They always ended up sounding more quirky and metallic.

NICK FORTE: Collectively, we were mainly influenced by tons of eighties metal, punk, and hardcore. Negative Approach, D.R.I., Black Flag, Bad Brains, Corrosion of Conformity, Youth of Today, S.S.D., The Misfits, Metallica, Slayer, Sepultura and a million others that we learned a lot from back then. We were all soaking in tons of fast, loud music--the heavier, the better. The fact that we liked metal as much as punk and hardcore, but were more into the ethos of D.I.Y. hardcore made our perspective unique from other bands in that we mixed some things together that, up until then, weren't mixed together in quite that way. A lot of hardcore people hated metal and metal people thought hardcore was too simple or something. We didn't make these distinctions in the music we listened to and played for each other or got excited about. Keith and I were huge fans of Voivod and we definitely owe them something in the odd guitar chord structure department. For me, the first Die Kreuzen album was pretty crucial in what I thought was an interesting and different interpretation of hardcore and it definitely influenced how some of us thought about Rorschach. I know a lot of people think we were huge Black Flag heads, and we were, but in some ways we were equally into Bl'ast, who were very much a Black Flag rip-off band, but they were a band we could go see live (Black Flag was long gone) and they were doing the kinds of weird song structures and a had a certain dark, fucked up vibe that we were really drawn to. Also, the Neurosis album *The Word Is Law* was a record that really blew us away at a crucial formative point for the band, and seeing them perform that material live really raised the bar of what could be done with heavy hardcore. I feel like we worked extra hard after Neurosis blew through town in 1990. For me, that was a big moment. Back then, they were a really fucked up hardcore band. We wanted to be as good live as they were. By the time we got really rolling, our sound and style was pretty well formed.

REACTION TO PERCEIVED STAGNANCY IN LATE-EIGHTIES HARDCORE SCENE

CHARLES MAGGIO: We started out as that "youth crew" scene died down, and we were all fans of the genre but didn't want to be part of it. We liked what bands like Life's Blood, Collapse, and Absolution were doing in New York, and we made a conscious decision to write music we liked as opposed to writing music we thought other people would like.

NICK FORTE: Well, me, Keith, and Charles were fully into the whole "youth crew" straight edge hardcore thing when it was peaking, but we got tired of it pretty fast. There were some good bands, but it was winding down by the time Rorschach started and we felt like it became a real jock movement or a Gap ad or something. Our sound was a reaction to the stagnant sounds of hardcore. We didn't talk about it much, but looking back, we were pissed off kids. We didn't really fit in or look good or cool or anything and the straight edge scene seemed like it was for people with lots of "cool" friends and I just couldn't relate to any of it nor were we included in this scene. A lot of the hardcore from the straight edge movement just wasn't angry and pissed off enough for what I was feeling at that time. I wanted to see and hear serious freak music and it was becoming hard to find. I didn't really want to hear lyrics about "the scene" or "unity" when I felt like, on a personal level, I was battling extreme depression and feeling pissed off and frustrated with just being alive. So, yeah, I lost the Champion sweatshirt, grew a big beard and grew my hair long and listened to Godflesh with the shades drawn quite a lot towards the end of high school. But the goals we had in mind for the sound of Rorschach when we started were to try and be as original, weird, and heavy as possible but still hold onto the pure energy of the hardcore thing. Another point we never really discussed but it was definitely an imperative, was the desire to be just totally fucking devastating live. We wanted to rip people's heads off and just crush an audience. By the time we were touring steadily we had achieved this.

KEITH HUCKINS: I don't think we were a reaction to anything, really. We wanted to sound like a band we wanted to go see, but it wasn't in reaction to anything. I've always just wanted to be in a band that I'd go see. I didn't want to be the most technical, the fastest, the heaviest… I just wanted to be intense and be like the bands that rocked my world, like when I first saw The Accused. After I saw them I was like, "Fuck, I want to do that!"

D.I.Y. ETHICS

CHARLES MAGGIO: We were definitely driven by a D.I.Y. ethic, and we tried our best to keep that ethic intact, but we really didn't try not to get more recognized, it was just the nature of the music world then. We couldn't get more popular if we tried. We were not commercially viable, but at the same time we didn't care. That was not a priority.

KEITH HUCKINS: The D.I.Y. thing came from coming out of the ABC No Rio scene and being friends with people like Born Against. If I had ended up being friends with some other band, I could have just as easily got into something else, too. That's not to say that the politics like that are wrong, but I just wanted to play guitar and go on tour. I believe wholeheartedly in the D.I.Y. thing at the beginning, but toward the end of Rorschach when things weren't so rosy, I was like, "I don't want to make a million dollars, but I also don't want to have to worry about blowing my five bucks per diem to eat."

NICK FORTE: I don't think, for a long time, it ever crossed our minds to do anything but be D.I.Y. I mean, we were D.I.Y., but so was everybody we knew. It was just the way things were done in the world we knew. We never had any big label come to us or anything, so there wasn't much temptation to or desire to do anything other than what we were doing. From the beginning, we always had a record label and felt supported and our music was getting out there in way that satisfied us, so there wasn't a problem. Nobody, at first, in the band ever thought about making a living off of this or making money, maybe because we were all pretty young. I think towards the end of the band, as we became older and more successful as a band, some of us were feeling the need to try and go to "another level" in some way and others felt it was a bad idea. It was a hard thing to figure out and to negotiate within the band and, ultimately, it had something to do with our demise. I'm not so sure we really felt it was important to keep our music within the hardcore and punk community. Hardcore was where we started and it was great for us, but it was only where we ended because we broke up. I think we clearly could have gone a lot further with it had the band remained intact, so who knows how that would have played out and on what scale. I always had a basic mistrust of serious art and business mixing together — you just end up having to compromise things and water it down or be misrepresented in some way.

THOMAS RUSNAK: A little known fact about Rorschach is that not everyone was on board with the militant D.I.Y. approach. A big point of stress within Rorschach near the end was that Charles took it upon himself to not inform the band of offers we were getting, such as an offer to play C.B.G.B.'s. There were several offers that came to light after the fact, making it apparent that Charles hadn't allowed the band to make a democratic decision, because of his fear about what we would want to do. That had a lot to do with Keith's ultimate decision to quit. I love Charles, but to this day I think that was the wrong way to handle those situations. I'm sure he has his own take on what went down then, and I don't think he was ever doing anything he thought was wrong. In the end I love and respect Charles as much as anyone in this world, so please don't take this the wrong way.

PENCHANT FOR EXTENSIVE TOURING

CHARLES MAGGIO: I booked our first tour, a 76 day tour, with Adam [Nathanson] from Born Against, and we took the Black Flag approach of play, play, play anywhere that would have us. Play Little Rock, play Nashville, play Tulsa, play six shows in Florida. We thought people would come if we played. It didn't exactly work out that way, but we tried. We knew getting our record in stores was going to be tough, so we took the traveling salesperson approach. It worked to an extent.

KEITH HUCKINS: The first U.S. tour was brilliant on paper, but the reality wasn't the same. [laughs] Adam from Born Against and Charles had this great idea that we were going to play all the places that nobody else played. We were going to play in Ft. Collins, Colorado, and Tulsa, Oklahoma, and Little Rock, Arkansas. Their logic was that since no one plays there then kids would come out to see us. The reality was that nobody plays there because no one goes to see you. [laughs] We played some really memorable and cool shows, though.

NICK FORTE: I think we were young and a little naïve and just feeling like everybody needs to hear this thing we're doing. We didn't give it much thought, really. It felt pretty punk rock. Everybody had a three month break from school or whatever, so okay, let's tour for three months. On our first tour, we didn't think it was that strange to pile into a van and tour America and Canada for three months straight with nobody in the audience really knowing who we were, if there even was an audience at all. The idea was to play as many places as possible and see what happens. So, we played to nobody in Memphis or three people in Oklahoma City, but we blew the minds of those three people. It was a lot of really small shows on the first tour. I think touring was what made Rorschach as big as it was, and also we played every day and got a lot better as band. When it comes down to it, Rorschach was a live band, really. We loved playing live, and people responded. I think it was that simple. We wanted to play as much as possible. Once we had gotten around some, the crowds got bigger, which made touring easier towards the end. But, the amount of touring we did also did a number on our personal relationships within the band. It was just hard spending months on end with a bunch of people in a van. So, touring built Rorschach but also tore us down.

TOUR STORIES

CHARLES MAGGIO: There are way too many stories to talk about, but a typical tour could be summed up as smelly, broke, and hot. We toured in the summers exclusively due to members' school schedules, hence the smelly and hot. The broke part came from the lack of attendance. I guess what held us together the most was the fact that we were doing what we loved every night. It was something we needed to do at night and if that meant driving all day and loading equipment in and out of clubs to do it then that is what we did.

ANDREW GORMLEY: I couldn't imagine doing the tour with Born Against at any other point in my life. We didn't know better, but we made the best of it anyways. One night a couple of weeks into the tour, Chris Laucella decided that he wanted to go home. He started walking down the street towards New Jersey. I think we were in the south at the time, maybe South Carolina or Florida. He figured that he could follow the beach-line and get home eventually. We followed him in the van and picked him up a couple of blocks down the road. Chris didn't try to walk home to New Jersey again.

KEITH HUCKINS: Because we never put our pictures on anything, whatever scene people were from, they thought we were like them. On our first tour we played the Profane Existence house. We pulled up and loading our stuff out and I had my Youth of Today shirt on, Chris looks like a guy from the Jersey shore with his jams on. This guy's like, "What band are you?" And we say, "We're Rorschach." He's like, "That's fuckin' funny." And we say, "Uh, we're Rorschach." So, he's like, "Bullshit, man!" And we're like, "Bullshit, man, you." [laughs] He said, "Man, this isn't what I expected. I thought you guys would be more crusty." We're like, "Nope, we're just five guys from Jersey." The same thing would happen with straight edge kids. But, again, we'd just have to say: "We're Rorschach. What you see is what you get."

NICK FORTE: Well, being on any tour, you usually come back with many funny and weird stories. So, I don't think there was anything that different about a Rorschach tour from any other band in that regard. But here's a couple of things: there was the time the customs guards searched my stuff in Canada and thought a plastic bag of recently cut off dread locks was marijuana. That gave us a good laugh. When I told the guy it was a bag of my hair, he was thoroughly grossed out. In Poland, I remember we were mildly extorted by the border guards for t-shirts and records in order to pass through without being hassled. That was pretty weird. I guess just playing in Poland in the early nineties was a pretty odd experience. I remember we showed up to one show there and it was at a youth rec center at like 5 p.m. on a Tuesday and it was just a handful of like 13-year-olds in their socks bopping around to kind a local punk/oi band. They were having so much fun that we didn't want to wreck it by playing, so we didn't even play. It would have seemed mean. I don't think Rorschach held together very well during the long tours. We had a hard time getting along and didn't really know how to cope with being on the road so much. When you tour you play music for maybe 45 minutes and the rest of the time, another 23 hours of the day, is spent trying to fill time until you get to that next 45 minutes, so it's a pretty frustrating undertaking to begin with. We probably needed a group therapist with us on the road. That might have helped. The music always got better on the road, as relations between various band members got colder. I remember some people in the band barely being on speaking terms for like an entire two month tour, so it was tough. But, still it was fun, overall.

KEITH HUCKINS: When we were in Europe there were these three guys, and I'm not kidding you, all named Oliver. Out of the two months we were there they must have seen half of the shows. They had the summer off and told us they were going to follow us all over. We didn't believe them, but then they kept showing up. [laughs] We called them the Oliver triplets.

INVOLVEMENT WITH ABC NO RIO SCENE

CHARLES MAGGIO: It was nice to be part of the beginning and growing phase of ABC No Rio. The thing that first attracted us to the club was their liberal booking policy — they let us play there — then it was the people. Some great, creative minds were able to show their respective colors in that scene. Some great seeds were planted by some very talented people. Ted Leo, Chris Boarts, Sam McPheeters, amongst many others really cut their teeth there and were allowed to do it with tons of support and without fear of rejection. Rorschach played the same role as any local band plays in its respective scene. We had fun, played with a lot of out of town bands, and got a lot of support from a lot of locals.

THOMAS RUSNAK: I loved playing ABC. There was no place that even approached it in the U.S. for sheer hardcore energy. Just hanging out with Chris Boarts and Al from Nausea are some of my favorite memories. It was a great scene too, because a band like Rorschach, comprised of people who were so nerdy and uncool that even punk rock kids had more fashion sense than us, could still get a chance to be heard. It was amazing!

NICK FORTE: ABC No Rio had a lot to do with Rorschach's development and it was also just a really great place to hang out and see tons of great bands from all over the world. We got involved in ABC No Rio mainly because we couldn't get a show anywhere in New York City when we started. The Sunday matinees at C.B.G.B.'s had just stopped and we gave our demo tape to them and a few other places, but no one ever called. So we heard about this new place that was doing hardcore matinees on Saturdays in the Lower East Side of Manhattan in 1990. We went and checked it out with demo tape in hand, and it was great, a dingy basement with cool people, a great vibe, cool bands, very punk feeling and gritty but kind of arty, too. So we gave our demo tape to the guy who was basically running the hardcore shows there, Mike Bullshit. I remember, we handed it to him and we started walking away, and he was like, "Do you want to play next Saturday?" We were like, "Yeah!" So we played with Citizens Arrest to about nine people in zero degree weather in a freezing cold basement and it felt like what I thought hardcore was supposed to be about. I felt like we had arrived, even though it was so small and maybe didn't seem like a big deal. We went on to play at ABC No Rio many times and got quite a following in New York City this way. We also made a lot of friends through the hardcore scene at

ABC and it just really clicked for all of us. We would go there every Saturday almost, no matter who was playing, just to hang out, but often a great band would be playing too, tons of great touring bands played there in the early nineties. After a time, Rorschach got too "big" to play there and an audience couldn't really fit inside and it kind of became a drag. I remember the audience changing too. I guess it got a lot more "crust core," squatter punk kind of thing, whereas it was a more equal mix before of hardcore kids, punks, crusties and general weirdoes. The last time we played there I remember tons of people passed out in the middle of the street drunk and I was like, "Where am I?" That was the end of our connection with ABC No Rio, as a band, really.

LYRICS

CHARLES MAGGIO: Nick and I wrote most of the lyrics. For my part, I just wrote what I knew. I was a cynical, pissed-off kid. Anything that I wanted to scream about, I wrote about. Some of the stuff was personal, but I tried to make it about a broader subject when I wrote about it.

NICK FORTE: Charles and I wrote all the lyrics in Rorschach, pretty much splitting it 50/50. I was always drawn to dark and difficult subject matter, so this is what I wanted to convey. Also, the words had to go with the music, which was by itself pretty challenging and painful. I also just really like words and had a lot of fun trying to put abstract images together that really convey something, for example "Asphalt Head Rush" a line from the song "Mandible." It's three words but packed with serious imagery. So I went for that kind of thing. Charles had throat cancer during our time in Rorschach, so he wrote a lot about what was happening to him. I think it probably helped him deal with this horrible thing that had happened to him.

KEITH HUCKINS: I tended to like the more oblique lyrics like "Mandible." I liked Nick's use of English. Charles had a tendency to be more to the point, and I liked his messages more, because he was no bullshit.

"REMAIN SEDATE" LP

CHARLES MAGGIO: We were a struggling band with an album's worth of material, playing and hanging out in a burgeoning ABC No Rio scene, and there were two labels that had started up: Vermiform and Wardance. Sam [McPheeters] from Vermiform was really into our band and offered to do our record. We just really wanted to make a solid record. We were all 19 years old and had no clue how to make a record or how the recording process even worked, so we employed Alan Speers who had a basement studio in Suffern, New York. He had recorded our drummer's metal band, and he came cheap. Unfortunately, he was a glam metal guy and didn't really get it. He told our guitar player after one recording session, "Man, you should work on your chops." We were like, "Chops?! What the hell is he talking about?!" In the first three minutes of recording vocals, the guy's dad came running down the stairs thinking someone needed help and couldn't believe someone was actually purposefully making those noises.

KEITH HUCKINS: We had a lot of bad ideas that ended up making the record sound a little weird. We decided our amps sounded weird, so we went out and rented some amps but it didn't sound like we wanted it to. The producer, who was running his studio out of his parents' basement, would be getting yelled at by his mom. [laughs] But it was fun because we were learning. We just wanted to put out a record and go on tour. We loved and really believed in what we were doing, but beyond that we just wanted to play.

NICK FORTE: *Remain Sedate* was sort of an early blueprint for what we were eventually to accomplish. I like the record, but ultimately it catches us in transition from a more normal hardcore sound to a stranger, heavier sound and what was to come later with the *Protestant* record. We recorded *Remain Sedate* the summer after I finished high school, and I remember working on it quite a bit that summer, at a home studio of a guy who recorded Andrew's metal band a couple of years back. The engineer didn't really have any understanding of what we were trying to accomplish. I remember we were having a hard time getting a heavy guitar sound, and he dialed up what he called a real "Clapton" tone. Yuck! Back in those days, it was harder to get heavy guitar tones. The guitars aren't heavy enough on *Remain Sedate*, but they do sound kind of interesting. There are some tracks that I feel are very creative on that record. "Pavlov's Dogs" is a song that never left our set list, as well as "Oppress" where we were trying to incorporate an industrial music vibe, something like The Swans. "No One Dies Alone" was a also a track that stands out to me, and one that only got better in the live set in years to come. The vocals came out totally strange sounding because Charles was battling throat cancer. A lot of people think there are weird effects on his vocals on *Remain Sedate*, but it's just the sound of his ravaged larynx. Overall, we were trying to present something very grim, stark, weird, and dark with *Remain Sedate*. Personally, I think we only nailed it half way, but considering how far we had come from starting the band to *Remain Sedate*, I would view it as a strong debut effort. I knew immediately after it was finished that we could do a better record in the future. It was mainly good to record all that material and get it out of our heads, because once the *Remain Sedate* recording sessions were done, we immediately started writing stuff that was just way crazier.

ANDREW GORMLEY: For me, Rorschach became a band when Keith presented us with the song "Clenching." That was the first Rorschach song that wasn't a typical hardcore song. The musical direction of the band was then set in motion, and a lot of the material before "Clenching" had to get reworked for *Remain Sedate*. I recently listened to a demo/ practice tape of early material which had some of the songs before they were rewritten. It didn't sound like the same band.

SHIFT IN VOCAL STYLE

CHARLES MAGGIO: The vocal style just progressed. While I was on our first U.S. tour — 58 shows in 76 days — I think my body and throat had gone through this adjustment period of making itself able to sing like that every night for 11 weeks. It was not conscious or anything deeper. My lyrical contributions got a bit darker because of the [Hodgkin's disease] battle. "Bone Marrow Biopsy," "Recurring Nightmare #105," and some others really had a therapeutic effect on me and what I was going through.

NICK FORTE: I can tell you this, Rorschach played very loud and usually we could barely hear the vocals. So, I think over time the high pitched screech that Charles developed came out of struggling to be heard at shows over the music. I remember us all being pretty surprised when we went into the studio to record *Protestant* and his vocals sounded like that. I think we had barely heard him in two years of playing live! The music was just too loud. It may have been a combination of that and just a natural stylist progression. I know some of the vocalists Charles really liked were Laughing Hyenas era John Brannon and the singer from Die Kreuzen on their first album, so he may have been going for that, too. Whatever it was, it fit the music perfectly that went with it.

MUSICAL PROGRESSION

THOMAS RUSNAK: I know Huckins was heavily influenced by the new sound that Neurosis was developing at that time. Also, bands like Voivod, Godflesh and Sepultura were in his Walkman a lot. The coolest thing for me was that Huckins was writing parts on tour and we were developing the songs in sound checks before shows. To a large extent that is how *Protestant* was created. Also, I probably don't give Andrew enough writing credit. He really helped Huckins piece together the songs from the myriad of parts that were coming out if his guitar.

KEITH HUCKINS: I just wanted to write shit that was a bit weird and fun to play. "Raw Nerve" was our half-hearted attempt at a grind song, and it was basically just me saying, "Andrew play faster! Andrew play faster!" By grind standards it's not a fast song, but for us it was blazing. [laughs]

NICK FORTE: I think the sound progressed as we got better and better as musicians and also as a band playing together live so much. We had a very good chemistry as songwriters. Keith wrote the majority of the guitar parts for our music, but the songs were constructed collectively. I would get very involved in this aspect of writing Rorschach songs, as did our drummer, Andrew. So Keith would often play me tons of riffs he had on cassette tapes and I would say, "Oh yeah, that one and that one." Every second of every song had to be really engaging, no filler, so it was sometimes hard to get a song to that place. We would piece the different riffs together in ways that made sense from Keith's tapes or things he played at practice. I remember doing this on our European tour as we wrote songs for *Protestant*, combing through tons of tapes of Keith just playing guitar for hours, basically improvising riffs. So then we would try different things, like instead of playing a part four times, let's play it two and a half times and add this other riff for a second and then play this really slow part and then this really fast thing, and just really try to turn a song upside down. I think we did this largely because we had gotten good enough where we could. Writing the song was my favorite part of the band and something that I was willing to spend a lot of time doing and thinking about. It was a very creative environment and everybody's ideas about the music were taken seriously, which also helped.

CHARLES MAGGIO: As we went on in the band, we all kept an open mind and were voraciously ingesting music from all genres. I think the second record had fewer constraints on it as we were not so concerned about making fans and much more concerned about making good music. We really got focused on making music we liked and music we wanted to hear. Every member of Rorschach, myself excluded, was an amazing musician, and they wanted to play at that level. They were really focused on just playing what sounded good to them regardless of whether or not it was conventional. I just fit the lyrics in around what they did.

"PROTESTANT" LP

CHARLES MAGGIO: We went on an eight week European tour in the summer of 1993, flew home, and went right up to Boston to record for a week. We wrote most of the record in Europe during sound checks. We had a new bass player on this record and he made it all come together. We had solidified the lineup and gelled. I wanted people to listen to *Protestant*, and when the needle picked up off the record player I wanted them to suddenly realize that their fists were clenched. That was what the great hardcore records in my world made happen to me. I wanted to invoke emotion, not just from the actual lyrics, but from the guitars, bass, drums, and vocals. I wanted people to feel exhausted after listening to the record.

NICK FORTE: For me, *Protestant* was the record I wanted to make when Rorschach started, but we had no idea how to do it when we first started playing together. It took us many years to build up to it slowly. Over time, we were able to get the sound and intensity that we had envisioned. *Protestant* was written over a long period, maybe two years. Some of this material, we were already playing on our first tour, some we were putting the finishing touches on a couple of days before going into the studio to record it. We wrote a good chunk of *Protestant* on tour in Europe where we would practice during sound checks at clubs, and then try the material out on a crowd right after. I remember we rented a rehearsal space in Amsterdam at the end of our European tour to practice for the recording session we had scheduled in Boston the following week. It was tough to record the album. Again, it was hard to get good sounds and this kind of thing, but it went pretty well. We had to remix the album a couple of times because we couldn't get it right. In the end, we weren't exactly thrilled by the mix that was released — the guitars were too quiet — but the songs were all killer and I think we knew we had made something substantial. As far as *Protestant* being a landmark hardcore record of the nineties, I guess all I can say is it was definitely a personal landmark. It was the culmination of years of hard work and a collective vision of the band. I'm surprised as to how this record still really holds up for me. It's been so long since we made it now that I feel like I have some subjectivity and when I listen to it, I'm like, "Wow, we did that? Crazy."

ANDREW GORMLEY: I don't think we really thought as much about this LP as a whole as much. The focus was on the songs. A couple of the songs were written on the road just a few weeks before we recorded. For the recording of the LP, the person we had engineer the record was Peter Nusbaum. He told us that his hobby was making shitty drums sound great. Judging from the previous recording he did for Rorschach, I would say that was a gross understatement. After the tracking was done, Peter took off to L.A. before we could mix the record. We were left to our own, with the help of the house engineer who didn't know heavy music, to mix the record. Being an arrogant kid with a strong opinion of what we should sound like, I sat at the mixing console trying to make the record sound like *South of Heaven*. But I'm no Rick Rubin! I'm glad the record got remixed by Chris Pierce.

THOMAS RUSNAK: I've heard people talk about that record, but I've never felt like we had that much of an impact on the direction of hardcore. The production of the record itself is a let down for me. I still have an old cassette of an entirely different mix where the guitars are louder and the vocals are stripped down. It sounds ten times heavier than the version that was released.

POLITICAL PERSPECTIVES

NICK FORTE: For the most part, I would say Rorschach was uninterested in politics as a band. Charles was the singer in the band and definitely had some views that he made known through the band and that was fine by us. So, this may have given us the appearance of being really political or something and I don't feel comfortable speaking for the band here, but I got the impression the rest of us didn't care so much about anything other than the music. That may be surprising, but it's really the truth. Then again, in comparison to other kinds of music that has no message at all, Rorschach was pretty message heavy, I suppose. I always found overtly political music boring, and I always got annoyed when people get too preachy or obvious about things in hardcore. We definitely took a stand in a few areas, but overall I'd say we were presenting a very raw, base level kind of thing, and for me, personally, it was all about the music and the overall presentation, more as an artistic statement than a political one.

CHARLES MAGGIO: My lyrics had some political leanings, if you will, but neither Nick nor I ever wanted people to read our lyrics and feel like there was an expectation on them to feel a certain way. We were always writing from a personal place, not a general place. We didn't have an "anti-war" song or an "anti-vivisection" song...we hardly said anything between songs. In fact, we had arranged our songs so that they could be played one into the next and there would be no stopping. We wanted to relentlessly pound music at the audience. We wanted them to go home wanting more and clutching our record under their arm anxious to go home and listen to it.

THOMAS RUSNAK: Unlike a lot of bands from that time period we had five people who all had very different views and approaches to life — two straight edge vegan kids, a kid who belonged to a fraternity, a kid who refused to eat anywhere other than McDonalds and Dunkin Donuts, and then there was me who was eternally high on a myriad of different drugs and alcohol. In the end, I think the tolerance that had to be exhibited to make the band work was what made it so magical and what sealed its fate.

ANDREW GORMLEY: The band was definitely perceived as a political band, and that helped us fit into the political music scenes wherever we toured. What Fugazi was doing at the time was a direct model for Rorschach. All age shows for five dollars were the only shows we would willingly accept. There were some exceptions. Unfortunately, the exceptions were great shows.

END OF THE BAND

CHARLES MAGGIO: Pressure [brought about the end of Rorschach]!!!! Plain and simple. We played our hearts out for every one of the 250 shows we played and never gave less than 100%. But being in a van, and living with your band mates on the road, caused a pressure cooker effect. It all blew up one night in St. Louis four days before the end of the tour. We just blew up. All the steam went out, and we were left deflated and feeling bad about the band. I don't think we ever sat down and said, "The band is over." We got back from tour and we all just kind of understood it.

KEITH HUCKINS: After we recorded *Protestant*, I was very frustrated. It was harder for us to get shit done, but it also felt like things were going to start happening for us. Tom mentioned to me one day that he thought if we got a bigger indie type of label to put out a record — something like Amphetamine Reptile or Alternative Tentacles — maybe it would help get our name out there and we could get more shows. That idea clicked with me. At that point I realized that this is what I wanted to do. But I got really frustrated and quit the band after a show in Massachusetts. They talked me into sticking around and doing a last blast summer tour type of thing and just have fun. I did it and what ended up happening was that everything started to get really bitter. At the time of the beginning of this tour, Nick, Charles, and I were straight edge. Andrew never was and Tom liked his natural friend the weed. But that ended up coming into play on the tour. The guys would give Tom a hard time, and I was just getting over the end of long relationship, so I was like "fuck everybody" and was angry with the world. During the tour I lost my edge, and the guys got really mad at me. Basically, in hindsight, when I quit the band I should have stayed quit because it brought about a lot of tension among us for a long time. Now whenever I run into someone it's great to see them. But it took a while for that to happen.

NICK FORTE: We started the band as teenagers and as you progress into your twenties, you become different people. I think we had a hard time making these transitions as a band. Personally, I was getting burned out on hardcore. I loved Rorschach but didn't like almost any other bands I was seeing and I really wanted to move on musically at the time. I just needed a change. We had a lot of personal problems within the band and it seemed these things were never going to be resolved and were only getting worse. We had differences of opinion about a range of issues, some about the future of the band, other just personal dynamics stuff. It's interesting that when the band broke up, nobody in the band suggested we stick it out. I think everyone had enough of it. Touring really took its toll on the band. We were all pretty different people but had this amazing thing we could come together on, which was Rorschach. But I guess you need more then that to continue a band for many, many years. Had we been a bit older and more mature, we may have tried to continue on, but had we been a bit older and more mature, it wouldn't have been Rorschach. The final nail in the coffin really came when I think the day after we got back from our last U.S. tour, Keith and Andrew had another band. So, we never even discussed anything. It was just over. Looking back, I guess I wish someone had fought for it. It deserved more careful consideration than it got, but Rorschach ended rather unceremoniously and abruptly. I don't remember feeling too bad about it at the time. I was excited to try something new. But it's a tough thing to look back on, because obviously it was a special band, but I think even if we knew that then, sadly, there wasn't really any way to keep it going.

ANDREW GORMLEY: The major reason [we ended] seemed to be the divide/conflict within the band over a few issues. It was as if half the band was concerned with scenes and politics, and the other with the music. Which shows we were playing and not playing seemed to play a big part in the end. We were too stubborn to make a compromise on these issues. Over what I would describe as a difference in moral values, Tom left/ was asked to leave the band at the end of the last tour. Again, no one was willing to compromise.

IMPACT OF BAND ON LIVES OF MEMBERS

THOMAS RUSNAK: Rorschach was the catalyst for the rest of my life. Rorschach created my connection to Ambush in Germany, which I played with for three years, and obviously Kiss it Goodbye caused me to meet Tim Singer who is one of my all time heroes and favorite singers ever, and to move out to Seattle where I met the love of my life who I am married to now. Also, I really learned how to play with honest intensity while I was in Rorschach.

CHARLES MAGGIO: Here I am 15 years later still taking about it. Still best friends with people I met during that time. It will never not be a part of who I am in some small way.

NICK FORTE: I never stopped making music after Rorschach and music is my main focus in my life to this day. I would say this has a lot to do with my experiences in Rorschach. It helped me realize my main passion in life, which is making music. Rorschach may have tripped me up a bit too; we had a fair amount of success in a short period of time, and by success I don't mean crowds or money, I mean something more to do with the power of the music and the connection with an audience we had. I found it hard, for many years, to live up to the musical standard Rorschach created. In other words, it was a fucking tough act to follow. As the years go on, I find that Rorschach comes up more regularly in conversation with people I meet, which seems strange to me. After meeting someone for a bit, it is not uncommon for them to say, with a grin, "Is it true you were in Rorschach?" People are pretty curious about it. Of course, it's nice to get some props for this thing we did so long ago, but it feels weird at the same time. I guess I'm surprised people care as much as they do and that the interest in the group continues. But, it's great that the band is appreciated all these years later.

LEGACY OF RORSCHACH

CHARLES MAGGIO: It blows me away that I have in the past six months turned on the radio to hear a band playing and I had to listen for a good five seconds before I was able to determine that it was not a Rorschach song. We had some rabid fans at the time. Some people would still tell you that we were their favorite band. Overall, the reaction was good. We didn't play shows or venues that allowed for some unknowing person to stumble upon us. Most of the people at the shows had established themselves as fans. It blows me away that people look at us in high esteem, but then I think of the bands I held in high esteem and realize that it is an amazing cycle. A Rorschach fan does not say anything different to me than I would to a member of Die Kreuzen or Corrosion of Conformity or the Big Boys. So, I assume it is a natural cycle, and it feels good.

THOMAS RUSNAK: I hope that if there is anything about Rorschach that gets imitated or influences modern hardcore, it is the band's tolerance of each other's different visions and our willingness to make music we loved, regardless of what hardcore was supposed to sound like. When I started playing with Rorschach I was trying to play hardcore music. By the time I was done I had realized that hardcore music was, by default, whatever I played.

KEITH HUCKINS: I'm really proud of what we did. I wish we were a bit savvier, had recorded some of the albums a bit better, and had better friends and connections. [laughs]

It's a little bittersweet to be honest. You hear about these bands that are supposedly Rorschach influenced and they are doing far better than what we did. At times some of the tours were just miserable. We did well on the coasts, but it would have been nice to be able to fund the band in a way that we could have done it for longer. Overall, though, I have a lot of great memories.

ANDREW GORMLEY: I'm still meeting young kids today who love Rorschach. They were too young to know the band when we were around. If they ask me any questions about the band, I usually just tell them that I was just the drummer. I followed Keith's lead. Nick and Charles wrote the lyrics. I can't take too much credit for it.

NICK FORTE: Rorschach played tons of really small shows to practically no one, but as time went on, and the crowds grew a bit, I could tell that people were getting what we were doing and really feeling it. I mostly remember an audience would stare at us kind of intently and not move much. I didn't have a lot of time to look at the audience though. I mainly looked at the guitar — those songs were a bitch to play. I'm not sure what the legacy Rorschach left behind is. If someone hears our music today and gets something out of it, then that's cool. Maybe we made it okay to like hardcore and Slayer at the same time, or at least admit to it. I haven't followed hardcore that closely in the last 15 years, so I think I have missed hearing a lot of the bands that sound like Rorschach or claim us as an influence. I have heard a few things in the last several years and some of it I do like a lot. If something is done well, it's nice to hear the influence in bands that followed us.

SELECT DISCOGRAPHY:

Remain Sedate (LP, Vermiform/Gern Blandsten 1990)
        Maggio, Huckins, Forte, Laucella, Gormley

Rorschach/Neanderthal Split (7", Vermiform, 1990)
        Maggio, Huckins, Forte, Laucella, Gormley

Needlepack (7", Wardance, 1991)
        Maggio, Huckins, Forte, Rusnak, Gormley

Protestant (LP, Gern Blandsten, 1992)
        Maggio, Huckins, Forte, Rusnak, Gormley

Autopsy (CD Discography, Gern Blandsten, 1995)

Rorschach Live in Italy 1992 (CD/LP, Gern Blandsten, 2002)
        Maggio, Huckins, Forte, Rusnak, Gormley

FIGHT: THE NINETIES HARDCORE REVOLUTION IN ETHICS, POLITICS, AND SO

SHELTER

Vocals: Ray/Raghunath Cappo
Guitars: John "Porcell" Porcelly
        Vic DiCara
        Graham Land
        Tom Capone
        Norman Brannon
        Kim Shopav (Sri Kesava)
        Daniel Johannson ("Supergrass")
Guitars/Bass: Ken Olden
Bass: Franklin Rhi

Bass: Chris Interrante
      Adam Blake
      Dave Ware
Drums: Dave DiCenso
        Eric Dailey (Ekendra Das)
        Trey Files
        Sam Siegler
        Mackie Jayson
        Bill Knapp

The arrival of Shelter prompted a controversial period in hardcore. When Youth of Today's vocalist Ray Cappo delved into the philosophy of Vaisnavism (Krishna consciousness) and abandoned his popular straight edge band for a musical project dedicated to spreading a spiritual message, many in the scene were puzzled. Many longtime hardcore vets disdained organized religion and distrusted Cappo's new project based on its affiliation with the teachings of A.C. Bhaktivedanta Swami Prabhupada, which brought forth cries of Cappo being "brainwashed," not to mention boycotts and even picketing at Shelter's early performances. The peak of this debate centered on a controversial *Maximum Rock N'Roll* article about Cappo and his "conversion." Others, however, felt Cappo deserved a chance to express his ideas. After all, if hardcore is grounded in thinking for yourself, why couldn't a person share what was on his or her mind, even if it pertained to spirituality? Consequently, both sides clashed, which helped Shelter draw more attention to its Krishna conscious message.

Shelter toured in 1990 with Quicksand and Inside Out and around the same time they released *Perfection of Desire*. Lyrically, Cappo expanded on the positive foundation he assembled in his straight edge anthems for Youth of Today, tackling issues of karma, reincarnation, identity, philosophy, and vegetarianism. Packaged along with infectious melodies and energetic and somewhat experimental hardcore, *Perfection* was unique for its time.

As Shelter's popularity increased so did criticism of the group's intentions. Many openly asked, "Were they out to recruit kids for Hare Krishnas?" Always up for a debate, Cappo answered cynics with new songs that were more direct in addressing spiritual and philosophical issues, such as "In Defense of Reality" and "Quest for Certainty." It was during this era that ex-Inside Out guitarist Vic DiCara joined the band, pumping up the already intense experience of a Shelter gig. However, after only a few months, DiCara left the band deciding to form his own Krishna conscious musical outlet, 108. John "Porcell" Porcelly (ex-Youth of Today guitarist), who became a Hare Krishna convert around that time, stepped in to take his place.

After taking a few months off, the group returned with, arguably, their most developed collection of songs. Always searching for a permanent rhythm section, Shelter hooked up with a couple of classically trained musicians through the Hare Krishnas: bassist Chris Interrante and drummer Eric Dailey. With these members in place, the band crafted *Attaining the Supreme*. Advertised by Equal Vision Records as the album that would really make one love or hate the band, *Attaining* found Shelter at its most introspective. Tracks such as "Consumer," "Better Way," and "Busy Doing Nothing" addressed materialism and forced listeners to ask themselves questions about their place in the world. While it is fair to say Shelter encouraged people to check out Vedic philosophy, many who abstained from religion also appreciated the group's points.

Shelter's next record, *Mantra*, was released by the major-label funded Roadrunner Records. Critics saw the band's move as a push toward mainstream success, while the group insisted it only wanted to make the best record possible. Whatever the case, *Mantra* contained all of the band's signatures: thought-provoking lyrics, catchy harmonies, and lots of hardcore riffs. Although some complained of the "slick" production, *Mantra* pleased many of Shelter's longtime followers, winning them new fans along the way.

Beyond Planet Earth, the follow-up to *Mantra*, was a critical and commercial flop. The record was all over the map in terms of scope — ranging from punk songs to ska and even industrial — and lacked the cohesive focus of their previous work.

Shelter parted ways with Roadrunner and did some soul-searching, which prompted the reflective, back-to-roots flavor of *When 20 Summers Pass*. After touring the U.S. and other parts of the world, Porcelly decided to leave the group to focus on his family life. Around this time Cappo entered the world of spoken word, dietary advice, and yoga instruction.

While Shelter's spiritual message was controversial, the band helped usher in a trend present throughout nineties hardcore: debate over a variety of spiritual and ethical topics. Shelter not only challenged people's ethical and spiritual notions, but also urged people to take a stand on whatever they believed in, which was one of Cappo's primary goals dating back to the early days of Youth of Today.

ON THE ROAD TO FIND OUT

RAY CAPPO: At a young age I had what most people wanted but never got: a certain amount of fame and independence and a lot of my desires fulfilled. But I still found myself grasping for something. I knew a lot of musicians who wanted to become popular and I looked at myself and said, "I've already got what they want and I'm still not happy." The more people tend to get money or success they become frustrated when they realize that just enjoying their senses or inflating their ego doesn't satisfy yourself, so I started to wonder, "What will satisfy the self?" At that time I was a vegetarian and I was practicing yoga and my yoga teacher gave me a *Bhagavad Gita*. I knew some people who were into Krishna in the hardcore scene like The Cro-Mags and people like that, but I didn't really trust any of those people as spiritual authorities. And then my yoga teacher said, "Hey, these Krishna guys are pretty cool." So, I thought to myself, "Huh, interesting." The more people I met living in New York continued to help me pursue my spiritual life, but I didn't really fully get into it until I exhausted myself visiting various yoga centers and *ashrams*. Then I had some what I consider to be "magical meetings" in my life with people who really walked the talk in Krishna consciousness. I fell in love with the people and fell in love with Indian culture. The last Youth of Today tour was super frustrating — it was fun in one way, but I was searching for something more. None of the guys in the band at the time had any interest in spiritual life. So, Steve Reddy from Equal Vision, who was our roadie, was asking me what Krishna consciousness was about and we both started to get into it. When we'd go to some town and play we started to stay in various temples. By the end of the tour we were all ready to become devotees. You don't know if it's a few years in progress or a few lifetimes in progress, but I was convinced that regular material life couldn't satisfy my soul anymore.

TAKING THE PLUNGE

RAY CAPPO: I remember one time in particular Youth of Today was in San Francisco, and the night before in Seattle we had gotten into this big fight with some people in the audience. The whole scene was becoming this huge mess. We met this Swami who was also an author and monk; he had a really nice temple in Berkeley and Steve Reddy and I wanted to go visit him in his small *ashram*. Little did I know that this guru was one of the early foundational leaders of the Krishna movement in America. So, we met him and he invited us in to talk to him and he asked us, "So, what are you guys doing?" I was a little arrogant and at that time I had some Krishna books I was selling on tour. I said, "We're just traveling around and playing music and selling books and that's our way to serve Krishna." Then he looked and nodded at us… in the meantime I remember my hair had bits and pieces of it coming out as I used to take a buzzer and put it to my head so parts of it were coming out and it looked like I had some kind of disease. [laughs] And Steve had some crazy haircut, too. The guy looks at us and he's like, "So, you're just traveling around distributing some books for Prabhupada… that's really interesting. I think you two are the biggest fools I've met in a long time." We're like, "What?" His response: "You heard what I said—you're a couple of fools. You think you're surrendering your heart to Krishna? But you're just traveling around, getting into brawls... taking your life half seriously. The fact is that there is a God and you just don't want to surrender to Him. You two are a couple of fools." So, we both started laughing so hard and we looked at each and said, "You know what, you're absolutely right." [laughs] Steve says, "Hey Ray, tell the rest of the guys I'm sick of everything. I'm quitting this tour right now and I'm moving into this temple right now." And I said that I would too after the tour. The rest of the guys were freaking out when I told them Steve wasn't coming back. They're like, "But he's the only guy that knows how to fix the van!" So, they all came to the temple and begged him to wait until after the tour, so he ended up waiting.

GOING TO INDIA/END OF YOUTH OF TODAY

RAY CAPPO: I went on a pilgrimage to India, and I started studying some courses there in *Bhagavad Gita* and some other scriptures. I met with a man who later became my teacher and I traveled a little on my own. I had an open ended ticket and I got this package in the mail from Porcell. I was all set to be a monk and this package showed up and Porcell writes this letter and says Youth of Today is about to be asked to be on a major label, on MCA Records. All my material desires had already been fulfilled but then all of a sudden a whole new slew of material desires came up. If you thought you were famous you could be really famous. [laughs] I wasn't sure what to do, but then I'd meet some other devotee in the India and he'd be like, "Oh yeah I was a millionaire but gave it all up to be here." I kept running into people who were PhDs or had been very successful and they gave it all up. I was very impressed by that. So, I got this other letter from Porcell about Youth of Today possibly going on tour to Europe and at that time no other hardcore bands other than maybe Black Flag and the Dead Kennedys had toured Europe extensively. So, I came back to the U.S. and stayed with my mother for a few months and decided that I wanted to write one more record, and I ended up writing the first Shelter record in about 30 days and we recorded it in two days. Then Youth of Today went to Europe. After living in India I had so many realizations on that tour--I began to understand that no matter how big I get with music it's not really going to satisfy me. Even though Europe was cool, I saw it as another culture that was getting taken over by Americanism. We were playing at these big punk bars and getting things whipped at us and getting into fights. After that tour Steve and I moved to a farm for a year. After living a year as a celibate monk I chose to start up Shelter as a touring band.

JOHN "PORCELL" PORCELLY: We knew Youth of Today was going to break up in 1989. Ray was really into the monk lifestyle and Walter [Schreifels] was more into Gorilla Biscuits; Sammy [Siegler] and I were more into Judge. We didn't think Ray was going to do any more music, because he was so into the monastic lifestyle. But when we got back he did that Shelter record. I didn't think he was going to tour or anything as he wrote it just to share some ideas about some realizations he'd had. He got this tour set up with Quicksand and Inside Out and he recorded the first record with Tom Capone and the guys from 76% Uncertain. He tried to get Krishna musicians but living in a temple you don't always have the most variety to choose from. [laughs] So, he called up Sammy and I and this older guy named Yasso, as well as Graham Land. What I didn't realize was that the tour was like this Krishna conscious circus coming to town. [laughs] Ray lined up a whole bus and he had this *sanyasi* monk and a bunch of young *bramacharis* and it was like this official Krishna preaching thing. But the tour ended up being really

amazing. They did everything—it was like a traveling temple! They would pull over at 3:00 a.m. and chant and burn incense and they would eat together. They wouldn't eat in restaurants and they had cooks on the bus who would make *prasadam*.

QUICKSAND/INSIDE OUT TOUR

JOHN "PORCELL" PORCELLY: I went on the first Shelter tour before I was a devotee and Sammy and I played with Ray as a favor. I really liked a lot of the kids who came with on the tour. The amount of people who came out and boycotted the shows actually showed a lot of prejudice. People were prejudging what Shelter and the Krishnas were about without understanding anything. Many people had these ideas as to what Krishna Consciousness was about but if you asked them what they knew about the philosophy contained within the *Bhagavad Gita* they wouldn't be able to tell you anything. As Shelter went on people became much more respectful because they took the time to read the lyrics and have more of a perspective on where we were coming from. When Shelter first started I don't think kids knew what to make of it, but over time the fear and controversy died down and people were really cool to us.

RAY CAPPO: I remember the biggest controversy centered from an article in *Maximum Rock N'Roll* on one kid who got interested in Krishna but then got "de-programmed." This was interesting because at our first show ever at The Anthrax in Connecticut there were so many people there anti-Krishna that were passing out flyers, but there were also so many kids into Krishna there and they all debated all night. People were screaming stuff at us and we were screaming stuff back. We weren't going to back down about anything. There was one guy who pulled me aside and he had all these tattoos on his arms and he started trying to find these little points of our philosophy that were off and they were little things that most people wouldn't know like some minor detail about the philosophy; for instance, he'd say none of Prabhupada's [Guru of the Hare Krishna movement] god-brothers thought he was even bona fide. I said, "That's not true," and he said, "There are so many leaders who have fallen down from the philosophy, so why would you want to surrender to a bunch of people that aren't perfect?" I said, "Well, you just use your brain and you're going to find teachers in whatever you are into that you look up to and if they turn out to be bad then you reject those teachers." Then he named some former devotees who were involved in some scandalous behavior and so I simply said those are scandalous people—so, what does that have to do with the philosophy? Finally, I said, "Wait a second. You obviously know something about Krishna consciousness because you know stuff about it." I looked him in the eye and I started to realize that he was the guy who got deprogrammed in that article. I asked him if he had ever read the *Srimad Bhagavatam* which is a beautiful work that was only translated by Prabhupada, and asked him to look me in the eye and said, "Do you wish that book was never translated into

English?" And he looked me in the eye and said, "No, I love that book. I didn't write that article my girlfriend wrote that article... I just don't know what to believe anymore." In that time I realized the deprogrammers did more "brainwashing" than "organized religion" does.

NORMAN BRANNON: I remember being at the Shelter/Quicksand/Inside Out show at The Anthrax and thinking that it was the first significant show of the nineties. I remember Quicksand just killed it. Inside Out blew my mind. No one had heard Shelter yet and they were playing some crazy shit and it was inspiring. There were kids at the shows with flyers and fanzines. I thought those things were healthy and it's cool to have a discussion. I wasn't involved with it yet. It was very civil, actually. It was like in here we're going to have a show and outside you can pass out the flyers.

PORCELL JOINS THE MIX

JOHN "PORCELL" PORCELLY: I became a devotee and Vic had just left Shelter to form 108, so Ray was in a mad search for a guitar player for Shelter. They couldn't find anyone and they didn't know I was living at this farm in PA. Some kid was telling them, "I don't know why you don't just go get Porcell; he's living on this devotee farm." They didn't even know I had become a devotee. So Ray called me up and was all excited and asked me to play and I was like, "Ray I don't know how to tell you this but there is no way in hell I'm going to play in Shelter." [laughs] I felt like I was going to jump right back into the fire. He kept calling me and wanting me to do it. It was funny because the reason I decided to eventually do it is because I was reading the *Bhagavad Gita* at the time and the whole story takes place around a war and there's this person Arjuna who doesn't want to fight in this war because he has friends on the other side and he just wanted to live a spiritual life and be non-violent and move away. The book is about Krishna trying to talk Arjuna into fighting—it's an extreme example but it proves the point of it's not what you do but it's the consciousness you do it in. Arjuna was a big guy and had been trained in fighting. It's not that it's a bad thing but you should use your talents for a good cause. Here was this war in which these dishonest people were trying to usurp power from the righteous leaders of society and they wanted to run society for their own sense gratification. For Arjuna to fight in a war against people like that was actually a righteous thing. Even though it might look violent, that was his talent, and for him that would be leading a spiritual life. For me it was a big lesson. I had to ask myself am I naturally a farmer? [laughs] How long am I going to last on the farm with no one to talk to? Some people like that, but I was a punk rock guitar player. The whole lesson from the *Bhagavad Gita* was that I could use my talents in a spiritual way. That's when I decided that maybe I should give Shelter a shot.

EXPERIMENTAL SOUNDS

RAY CAPPO: I was always a fan of a whole range of music and I wanted to experiment with stuff outside the hardcore stuff that we had always done. The first record was just a really fun experiment to do—kind of a challenge to make other kinds of music. As long as Shelter existed there has never been a specific sound. People might say, "I don't really like the new Shelter record because it doesn't sound like the old one." There was never a Shelter sound. It was a mish-mash of different ideas. Even *Mantra*, our most popular record, is a mixed bag.

NORMAN BRANNON: The thing about Ray I really appreciate is that he had a very early conception of the idea that he was songwriting. A lot of people in hardcore were just riffing. There is a huge difference between coming into practice with a riff and actually crafting a song. Ray had a great grasp on writing songs. Everything you heard on a Shelter record was very deliberate and I appreciated that a lot on a musical level.

"PERFECTION OF DESIRE"

JOHN "PORCELL" PORCELLY: When we made *Perfection*, Ray stayed at my apartment and he was burning so much incense that I was like, "Ray, you're killing me with all this incense, man!" [laughs] One day we were walking down the street and having this heavy conversation about the meaning of life and right in front of us this little scuffle broke out. One guy pulls a knife out and stabs the other guy in the stomach and runs away and this other guy falls to the ground and blood is gushing out of him. All these people were freaking out and called the ambulance. We were really tripped out because we just were having this conversation about the meaning of life and how life is temporary and then this guy gets stabbed right in front of us.

LYRICS

RAY CAPPO: Lyrically, I was always inspired by Eastern philosophy and great thinkers. It was my calling to God, really. My father had just passed away and I decided to become a monk. I wanted to write a final record that I thought would be the last record I'd ever write. At the same time, even though I was into Vaisnavism I tried not to write to be a mouthpiece for Western Krishna consciousness. I wanted it to be for thoughtful people who wanted to figure out their connection to the universe. I never tried to make the songs for Krishna consciousness even though that was my path. I just tried to present ideas in a way for everyone to relate to.

JOHN "PORCELL" PORCELLY: I always liked Ray's lyrics. I thought the lyrics on the first record were especially great. One of the best things about Ray is that he can take these really heady subjects and be able to write about them in a way people could relate.

"QUEST FOR CERTAINTY"

RAY CAPPO: At that time of the band all the people in the band were somewhat evangelical monks of Vaisnavism. At the same time I wanted to keep some integrity with the lyrics and make them open for all. "In Defense of Reality" was an attack against people who were atheists. For them reality is here and now and what we see with our eyes, but if we actually analyze it what we see with our eyes is not actually reality. Our eyes are not appropriate enough to give us actual vision. A table appears solid but a table isn't solid. Subatomic particles can fly through a table. What we see with our eyes is not reality. It comes from these empiricists who say, "We live in the real world and these people who believe in spiritual things live in a fantasy world." So, it was an attack against that attitude which was really prevalent in the punk scene which strives to be anti-authority. I agree that we should have a natural rebellion, but a lot of time our rebellion can degrade us. For instance, a person might get sick of school so he or she drops out and becomes a drug addict. I've lost so many friends to drugs and what kind of rebellion is that? I always felt a rebellion should be uplifting.

CRITICISM

RAY CAPPO: If I preached Krishna consciousness too heavy people would just say, "Oh, you guys are just a dogmatic religious band." If I don't preach about it enough and just talk about the ethics that are important to all people then people would say, "You've watered it down."

"ATTAINING THE SUPREME"

RAY CAPPO: *Attaining the Supreme* was when everyone called us sell-outs. [laughs] I remember Steve from Equal Vision took out an ad that said: *"Attaining the Supreme—the record that will either make you love this band or hate it."* People just felt like, "Oh, Ray Cappo is selling out. He makes so much money that they have game rooms set up at these temples that only he is allowed to go in with his exclusive friends." A lot of people are crazy, so it's best to ignore them. [laughs] If I worried what people said my whole life then I wouldn't have done anything. *Attaining* actually had a pretty big grassroots following. We never intentionally tried to make anything more accessible; we just wrote what came from our hearts.

JOHN "PORCELL" PORCELLY: The people we had in the band (drummer and bassist) were people living in the temple. They had no idea what hardcore was—they were these really well trained classic rock dudes. The bass player was amazing and he could sing really great. They were more into melodic music that was in key. They would listen to Black Flag and be like, "I don't get it." [laughs] But music is also a reflection of who the people in the band are. At that time we weren't these angry kids full of rebellion against

the world anymore. Now to this day there are parts of me that are very angry about the state of things, but back then I think we were happier people. And that came out in the music and it made it more melodic.

ROADRUNNER RECORDS

JOHN "PORCELL" PORCELLY: That was the weirdest time in my life. [laughs] After *Attaining the Supreme*, the bassist and drummer loved being in Shelter, but because they weren't from the hardcore scene it wasn't really their thing. They were just devotees who wanted to lead a regular life. So, they quit the band; they just couldn't do it anymore. So, it was down to Ray and I and we weren't sure what to do. I went to India for three months and then went to Philly. Ray was living in the Brooklyn temple and called me up one day and told me to come and we'd get the band going again. Right around the time Green Day and The Offspring had just put out their big records and they exploded. It was a weird time because every major label was trying to sign every punk band out there. Quicksand, Into Another, Rage Against the Machine and Orange 9mm all signed. Roadrunner really wanted to sign us because this guy Howie was their A&R guy and he was from the hardcore scene and was a huge fan of Shelter. At the time Roadrunner was a really metal label and we were more melodic so we weren't sure if that would work out. But Roadrunner was pretty big. They had Type O Negative gold records and had these huge offices downtown. These other big labels were trying to sign us as well, and it was kind of fun because they would take Ray and I out to dinner at these expensive vegetarian restaurants and we'd run up the tabs on these guys. [laughs] Most of these guys were so phony. There'd be some 50 year old record executive with a tie on and he'd be telling you, "You guys are hot; you're the next big thing!" We just looked at the guy and we're like, "What the fuck does this guy know about modern music?" [laughs] He's in his fifties and probably still listens to James Taylor. Sometimes they'd hire the young A&R guy and they're almost worse because they're trying to be hip and swearing and wearing their Sonic Youth t-shirt.

RAY CAPPO: I wasn't opposed to getting bigger. If you were big and it got to you, you can be just as arrogant and proud of your crappy little band that never plays out. There are a lot of people that are big that are very humble. I don't think how big you are has anything to do with your consciousness. I also know a lot of poor people who are humble and others who are arrogant and attached.

JOHN "PORCELL" PORCELLY: We decided to go with Roadrunner because we knew and trusted Howie. We didn't want to be sensationalized because we were like "the Krishna band." We didn't want to be the Stryper of the Krishna scene. [laughs] Howie seemed to understand the band so ultimately we went with Roadrunner. They were a great label—they took a band that sold a few thousand records to *Mantra* which sold about 160,000 copies in the first year. It was really exciting and we actually started to get pretty big.

"MANTRA"

RAY CAPPO: The biggest songs "Here We Go" and "Civilized Man" were literally written at the last minute. It wasn't like some master-plan to write an edgy song or a hit single. I'm not that good of a musician. [laughs] We played what came out and by the grace of God some things worked and others stunk.

JOHN "PORCELL" PORCELLY: We recorded at Normandy Sound, the same place Judge recorded *Bringin' it Down*. It was this huge place and super expensive. The first day we get there the drummer from 76% Uncertain wasn't used to being in a big studio and the producer Tom Soars was really hard on all of us. He'd say, "You guys don't understand. You have to play the songs correctly and in time." He kept making us do it over again until we got it right. He was a punk drummer and he wasn't used to playing under those circumstances. In the end, it taught us how to be real musicians. I learned so much from recording that record.

INCREASING POPULARITY

JOHN "PORCELL" PORCELLY: The last tour we played before *Beyond Planet Earth* was this huge stadium tour opening for No Doubt. I think that went to our heads a little bit and we were thinking, "Hey, here we are opening this tour in an arena for No Doubt. Maybe the next record we'll have our own stadium tour." [laughs] It seemed like there was no limit to how big the band got. We sold about 200,000 records with *Mantra* so we figured it would just get bigger.

"BEYOND PLANET EARTH"

JOHN "PORCELL" PORCELLY: We went into the next record thinking, "We need to write a hit song." We really lost our place, though. I think there are some good songs on the record, but we tried too hard. There's like a rap song, a ska song, a Nirvana-type song on the record. With *Mantra* we wrote the songs because we thought they were good. With this record we were writing songs thinking they were songs other people would like. Once you get into that mindset then you don't write an honest record. I still laugh and think, "Man, we really thought Krishna-core-ska-techno was going to be the next big thing." [laughs] As a spiritual experience it was a good thing because you realize how things like fame are so temporary. We went from playing these big shows to being nobody.

LOSING STEAM

JOHN "PORCELL" PORCELLY: The Krishna focus was losing some steam as well, which was affecting the dynamic of the band as well. Before we had a focus and now we didn't know who we were anymore. We were between two worlds. We got dropped by Roadrunner because we didn't sell as many records as *Mantra*. Roadrunner was having huge success with bands selling a couple hundred thousand or more records. When we sold 80,000 records it just wasn't good enough. We ended up getting in a serious van accident and we took some time off. Ray moved to California. After the van accident my back was still not in the best shape so I was sitting around a lot and I really got into writing a bunch of songs. I wrote a whole record and I called up Ray and told him the songs were more like what Shelter was really like. *Beyond Planet Earth* left a bad taste in my mouth; let's try and write one more record. He said he had a bunch of lyrics written. It was pretty much just him and I and some of our friends and he came to New York and we put it out on Victory.

RAY CAPPO: I've always been a person with a message. I believe the intention behind something is more important than the actual delivery of it. That's why Shelter left a lasting effect. I'm not saying that to boost my ego, it's just what happened. I met people

all over the world who came up to me and said they were inspired by one of our songs or something. It wasn't because I was a great musician; it was because there was a link to the truth. And there's not just truth in one religion or another—you'll find truth in Shakespeare, you'll find truth in *The Quran*, or even something Benjamin Franklin might have said. When truth hits ears it rings.

JOHN "PORCELL" PORCELLY: I look back on the experience and it was really amazing for me. Some people go to college, I lived in a temple and I don't think my experience was any less significant than anyone who went to college. I was completely renounced and didn't have a dime in my pocket for several years. I totally unplugged myself from consumer America and it felt really good. It made me realize how running your life by way of materialism is completely ridiculous. It makes you realize you can live without money. Spiritual life and cultivating who you are and what your principles are what's really important in life—not how much money you make. You can be a person who doesn't make a lot of money and that person is successful and not the person who, say, runs ENRON and makes billions of dollars at the expense of the environment and people.

SELECT DISCOGRAPHY:

Perfection of Desire (CD/LP, Revelation, 1990)
    Cappo, Capone, Knapp, Ware, Knapp

Quest for Certainty (CD/LP, Revelation, 1992)
    Cappo, DiCara, Land, Interrante, Dailey, Sieglar

Attaining the Supreme (CD/LP, Equal Vision, 1993)
    Cappo, Porcelly, Interrante, Dailey

Mantra (CD/LP, Roadrunner, 1995)
    Cappo, Porcelly, Blake, DiCenso

Beyond Planet Earth (CD/LP, Roadrunner, 1996)
    Cappo, Porcelly, Rhi, DiCenso

When 20 Summers Pass (CD/LP, Victory, 1998)
    Cappo, Porcelly, Files

The Purpose, The Passion (CD, Supersoul, 2000)
    Cappo, Shopav, Johansson, DiCenso

Eternal (CD: GoodLife, LP: Reality Records, 2006)
    Cappo, Olden, DiCenso

SPITBOY

Vocals: Adrienne Droogas   Bass: Dominique Davison
Guitars: Karin Gembus   Drums: Michelle (Todd) Gonzales
Bass: Paula Hibbs-Rines

Hardcore is largely populated by males. There are a multitude of social and cultural theories one could consider as to why this happens, but the numbers tell the truth. Yet one of the reasons hardcore exists is to shatter norms, and with bands like California's Spitboy around, nineties hardcore continued the genre's tradition of bringing gender and political issues into question alongside powerful music that carried these messages.

Spitboy started in 1990 after vocalist Adrienne Droogas, drummer Michelle (Todd) Gonzales, guitarist Karin Gembus, and bassist Paula Hibbs-Rines met each other through various mutual friends. Already longtime members of their area hardcore/punk scene, they were exposed to many great groups and took inspiration from hardcore's rebellious and socially aware spirit. They became fast friends and bonded over their past experiences and their love for music of all kinds. As motivated as they were by their favorite bands, they wanted to make their own musical statement from their own unique perspective. They began to write songs and their band chemistry clicked — primarily because of their unified desire to present their music in the most direct and engaging manner possible.

Spitboy's political and artistic approach to hardcore was influenced by the political lyrics of classic punk bands like The Clash, the D.I.Y. hardcore punk sound of the Gilman Street scene, and experimental hardcore and post-hardcore bands like Fugazi. Their sound was a mixture of dissonant yet melodic punk rock, the emotional post-hardcore of Rites of Spring, and the politically laced hardcore of groups like Born Against.

Although their seven-inch releases and various compilation appearances were often met with positive responses, many cite their split LP with Los Crudos on Ebullition Records as a landmark record for the band, as well as for the nineties D.I.Y. hardcore scene on the whole. It was not a surprise when both bands, already close friends and co-conspirators in helping to create more political awareness in hardcore, agreed to create the split release after an invite from the California based label Ebullition Records. The end result was a record that exemplified the diverse ranges of raw emotion and political insight that poured from both bands throughout the duration of their existences.

Although their records were widely acclaimed, Spitboy achieved their reputation from their constant touring, which took the band from coast to coast several times and to other parts of the world. Live, Spitboy connected with audiences, much of the engagement due to the band's perceptive statements about sexism, politics, and personal ethics that occurred between songs and in conversations with others before and after shows.

Never afraid of a debate, Spitboy was also known for their sometimes confrontational approach when discussing personal and political issues on stage. Despite their frank disposition, the members never chastised specific individuals. Instead, they simply wanted everyone — men and women alike — to understand where they were coming from in the most inclusive manner possible.

Spitboy ended their run in 1996. Despite stopping when many felt they still had uncharted territory to explore, the members never faltered in their friendship and love for music. The group only met with one lineup change over the course of their existence (Hibbs-Rines came down with early stages of carpal tunnel syndrome and was replaced on bass by Dominique Davison).

Never wavering in their commitment to political and gender issues, Spitboy played emotional and abrasive hardcore that inspired many to examine their own feelings and ideas. Their intense music and strong friendship set an example for others to address personal and political issues in an open artistic forum. Despite the genre's male dominance, Spitboy claimed their own space in the scene through sheer force of will. If that isn't the very essence of hardcore then what is?

ORIGINS

ADRIENNE DROOGAS: I was living with this guy Doug and he put some guitar tracks down and just being really goofy I sang over it. I was also friends with Todd, who later became our drummer. She heard that tape and said, "We have to start a band and you have to sing." I just laughed and said, "Okay." Todd knew Paula and Paula knew Karin and we all came together and met at this record store and talked about doing the band. We set up a practice space and before we knew it we were a band. It was cool that all of these strangers came together and it just happened to work perfectly.

MICHELLE (TODD) GONZALES: I had been in two all female bands previous to Spitboy. Then it was about a year after Kamala and the Carnivores when I got the itch to do another band. I met Adrienne through some friends at the warehouse I was living at. I actually heard her singing on a tape and thought she had a great voice. When I first met her she was shy and standoffish. [laughs] I asked her about the tape and told her I played drums and wanted to start an all female band. I was already friends with Paula so she was already in. Adrienne was game to do it right away, so we three started hanging out more. We didn't know each other that well, so we wanted to get to know each other a bit more. Plus, we didn't have a guitar player yet so we were still searching. Paula told us there was this woman in San Francisco who played guitar and it turned out to be Karin. Sure enough, Karin came over one night and we started playing. I had written a song on guitar and we showed it to her. We started playing it, and we all just clicked. After that, we were a band.

NAME

(Taken from the Spitboy/Los Crudos LP: *She is alone, isolated, with no companions and no one to talk to on an island she has taken as her home. Her feelings of aloneness and loneliness are overwhelming and she begins to cry. Out of her comes tears, saliva, snot, mucus, sweats natural body fluids. Ashamed by what her body has produced and by her state of helplessness, she tries to hide these elements by burying them.*

She looks imploringly to her gods, who tell her not to be disgusted by the natural secretions of the body. They explain to her the innate beauty of her body's workings and that these fluids are part of her body and part of her existence. With the newfound power that comes out of a belief in her body's creations, she is no longer ashamed by what she alone has made. She proudly saves these elements and out of them life is created in the form of a boy. The boy that is formed is the Spitboy.)

ADRIENNE DROOGAS: Paula, Todd, and I were doing the Maximum Rock N' Roll Radio Show. Between songs we were asking people to call in with band names. My best friend Wendy-O-Matik was there and she told me that her partner Noah kept calling us Spitboy. We asked her why and she briefly told us about the Native Alaskan tale called Spitboy and once we heard the story that was it — done deal. We were at the radio show and frantically trying to get in touch with Karin to run the band name past her. Of course, cell phones weren't invented then so we left her around 20 messages at her house, but when she heard the name and the story she agreed that it was the best name ever.

MICHELLE (TODD) GONZALES: We either decided [on our band name] on the air or right before. We were killing ourselves to come up with a creative name, and we couldn't for the life of us. Wendy told us about this Eskimo/Native legend and we really liked it. Plus, it had this additional catch to the name. [laughs] We weren't really spitting on boys of course, but it just had a feeling to it. My goal to start a band was to be a real hardcore band. I wanted it to sound like the bands I wanted to hear. I didn't want to be poppy or girly in the traditional sense — there was just something missing and we just wanted to fill that void.

FOCUS ON GENDER

ADRIENNE DROOGAS: I had been doing a zine called *Too Far* for a few years, which was all about gender politics and issues, which were very important for all of us way before the band started. We never sat down and said, "Hey, let's only write about gender politics." It was just one of those things that was so important and vital to each of us, so whenever we'd write music and lyrics that seemed to be a recurring theme we continued to revisit. We also wrote about interpersonal relationships and other issues too, but gender politics were really close to our heart. We wanted to utilize the band as a form of expression and it wasn't that we were trying to say that we're right, but we just felt that if people agreed then great and if they didn't then so be it.

MICHELLE (TODD) GONZALES: Adrienne had been doing *Too Far*, and she was writing about all the things we were thinking about as individuals. We just started writing songs and they became very female empowering lyrics. We didn't only write about women's issues, but that was a big component of it. In the early nineties, the hardcore scene was very male dominated. Most of the girls you'd see were there hanging out with their boyfriends. We wanted that to change and hoped to be a catalyst for that change.

CONFIDENCE

ADRIENNE DROOGAS: My ability to get up on stage and speak and sing in front of people goes back to that feeling of family and comfort that I found in the punk scene. I felt so supported that it was like an open arena for me to walk into and say whatever I needed to say. I was also influenced by political punk bands and saw the punk scene as a purely political movement, so it felt comfortable to express my beliefs very openly and honestly. Of course, when Spitboy played our first show I was terrified and shaking from head to toe. I don't think I opened my eyes once. We played at the 61st Street Warehouse in Oakland, and I had my mom come to the show. I never really got over feeling stage fright and before each show I would have this nauseous little pit in my stomach, but once we started playing it always went away and I was consumed with the words, the emotions, the music, everything.

MICHELLE (TODD) GONZALES: When you believe in something that makes you confident. I had been performing since the third grade. I had confidence in my ideas and being in a band comes with a performance element to it, no matter how D.I.Y. you are. I was also raised by only women who were also very outspoken, so I learned a lot about speaking out and injustice because I didn't grow up privileged and comfortable like a lot of people.

BAND CHEMISTRY

MICHELLE (TODD) GONZALES: When something works, it works. We had the right chemistry. We were all very different in a lot of ways, but we had the same ideas about the D.I.Y. ethic and how we wanted the hardcore scene to be more inclusive for women. When you come together and play a song and everything clicks into place, like it did for us the first time we practiced together, that was it. We knew we were a band. We all loved to laugh an awful lot. We would act crazy together and make each other laugh. I remember listening to Liz Phair's *Exile in Guyville* album on tour and we'd all sing along with it for miles!

ADRIENNE DROOGAS: It was just blind luck. For whatever reason we all came together at this particular time and we all had the same political ideals and our personalities meshed. The entire time we were together we never fought or got freaked out or upset with each other. Our relationship was always very loving and supportive. When Paula developed carpal tunnel syndrome and had to quit, we got really nervous and weren't sure if we should do the band any more. I was working at this health food store and Billie Joe Armstrong from Green Day used to come in and I was dating his roommate. I was telling him how we needed a bass player, so he told me to come to a show that night where this band was playing that had an amazing bass player named Dominique. So, we went to the show and she was amazing and I grabbed her and was like, "Please join our band!" Again, we got lucky and she fell right into place just perfectly.

INFLUENCES/SONGWRITING

MICHELLE (TODD) GONZALES: While we were a really hardcore band, we didn't try to sound exactly like anything else. I attribute that to us coming from a different place as women. There was something about who we were as women and playing this typically male music. We weren't going to rehash what everyone else was playing. So, it did get a little melodic at times. Sometimes we might harmonize or do things a lot of hardcore bands don't do. Overall, it was just a reflection of us.

ADRIENNE DROOGAS: A typical practice was Karin would show up and say, "I wrote a song." We'd have her play it for us and then Paula would start playing a bass line and Todd would come up with a drum beat and we'd tape it and I'd take it home and write lyrics to it. At first, whatever music Karin was into would be kind of what we sounded like. [laughs] She was really into Fugazi and Born Against and Fuel at the time and that definitely came out in the sound. Once Dominique started playing in the band — she was an architecture major and a music minor — she was able to come up with songs and her abilities were tremendous, which really mixed with Karin. Once they both started writing together we were all excited because it pushed us in different directions. It was a natural progression. We all wrote lyrics so it was basically when someone in the band had something to say we'd just sit down and fit the lyrics to the music.

SHOWS

ADRIENNE DROOGAS: I always looked at our shows as having a conversation. When we were on stage then I was just having a conversation with a couple hundred people in the audience. It was the same feel as if I'm talking to someone one-on-one. I feel like if I'm open with people then that gives someone else the opportunity to be open also. They may not take that opportunity, but at least they have the option. It makes me feel less isolated when people come to me and say they lived through that too, or that something I said was important for them to hear. It was an incredible opportunity to feel less alone in terms of the issues I was struggling with as a human, regardless of gender. It's really easy to build up walls and be isolated, so I'd rather break down those walls and be open.

MICHELLE (TODD) GONZALES: I remember conversations, but what I remember more is antagonistic comments that we'd have to respond to by guys who were threatened by what we were doing. There were a couple of times that we were totally humiliated. But for the most part we would confront the person without running off the stage. I remember one time this guy kept heckling us and we tried to ignore him but he just kept on going and going. Finally, Karin just said, "Why don't you go home and read a book!" The whole audience cracked up and the guy had to leave and stood outside while we finished playing. [laughs] It was pretty hilarious.

EMOTIONAL OUTLET

ADRIENNE DROOGAS: Spitboy was never impacted or influenced by any of the debates over how people should express themselves. Spitboy was this incredible outlet for us to express our emotions or our thoughts or to relay an experience in the hopes that someone might connect and understand. My personal approach was to not say, "This is what I think and I'm right and everyone should agree with me," but to say, "This is what I think and this is what works for me and if it works for you, cool." I didn't want to dictate terms to anyone, but to simply follow my own terms and if folks agreed or felt an affinity, then that was great. And if nobody could relate that was cool too because my ultimate goal was to express myself.

MICHELLE (TODD) GONZALES: In your early twenties you're really coming into who you're going to be. I formed some of my core beliefs via Spitboy. I was able to put into words about what was going on in the world. In the nineties, there was a definite awareness about sexual harassment and date rape. There was a statistic at the time we did the band that one out of every four women was either sexually assaulted or molested as a child, and that was true for our band. Most people don't work through these things in public. [laughs] But it was the cheapest therapy ever.

AUDIENCE SUPPORT

MICHELLE (TODD) GONZALES: We always handed out lyric sheets. It rotated — for every show someone different would do the lyric sheet. We'd decide ahead of time which songs we were going to play and we'd take turns designing them. We'd hand them out because we wanted people to know what we were singing about. There were always people coming up afterward who appreciated the lyrics or felt like they could identify with what our songs were about. Many women just said they were happy they saw us because they said we had the courage to say the things they didn't have the courage to say. There were a lot of supportive guys, too. Sometimes they would complain in a good natured way about how we said things, which was better than some kind of reactionary response. We'd talk to them and sometimes they'd understand where we were coming from. But regardless we had the exchange and there was a good conversation about the issues.

ADRIENNE DROOGAS: Most people were so incredibly supportive of us. The instances where people yelled at us were few and far between. Of course you remember them because they stand out, but the reaction we had was empowering. I would confront them face to face and say, "What the fuck did you say to me? Why don't you say it to my face?" Everyone's reaction was supportive — people were right there with us. Of course there was racism and sexism in punk and hardcore because you get all kinds of people drawn to the music for a variety of reasons, some of which aren't necessarily the healthiest.

PERSPECTIVES ON RIOT GRRRL

ADRIENNE DROOGAS: I'm all for people finding a source of empowerment, but the Riot Grrrl movement never sat comfortably with me. I didn't want to take part in a movement that told my male friends to stand in the back of the show. I remember that we were on tour and playing a show in D.C. and I was in some pretty big debates with a couple of women about the Riot Grrrl movement. During our set Todd said something like, "We are not a fox-core band, we are not a chick band, we are not a Riot Grrrl band. We are simply a group of women who are playing music." I'm really, really paraphrasing that quote, but that started a whole shit storm. We were told that Riot Grrrls had decided to boycott Spitboy records and shows. Rumors were started that there were problems between Bikini Kill and Spitboy. It got ridiculous pretty fast. Granted, we didn't help the situation at all because in each interview that we did this question would inevitably come up and we would state emphatically that we were not part of the Riot Grrrl movement. It was frustrating that just because we were a group of women, we had to get lumped into a movement that we had nothing to do with. Nobody was asking Fugazi if they were Riot Grrrls. Nobody was asking Born Against or Econochrist. But the fact that we were all women addressing issues of gender meant that we must be a part of the Riot Grrrl thing and, no, we were most definitely not. For me, anyone who points fingers and says, "Those people over there are the problem — white suburban males are the problem — and they are going to have to pay more to come in to the show and stand in the back..." I have friends who happen to be male and are pretty right-on people and they shouldn't be punished because of a systematic problem, because I'm part of that same problem and so are you. Once you start pointing fingers and start saying someone else is the problem then you are scapegoating and not addressing those issues within yourself, and that's never okay.

MICHELLE (TODD) GONZALES: I didn't want to create any kind of rift between female hardcore and punk bands because that doesn't help anything. Unfortunately, I think I achieved that, though. [laughs] Riot Grrrl was about one thing politically, but it was also about something musically that we were not. We were purposefully not using our sexuality as part of our performance. Now we weren't repressed in any way, but we did not understand the blurring of the lines between exploitation of women and using that kind of exploitation as performance. That just didn't make us comfortable. I loved Bikini Kill and I thought they were sexy, but I just wasn't going to do that on stage. I was willing to get up there and perform, but for me that was too vulnerable of a position to be in. It was a little too close to using women to sell products and we just didn't want to cross that line. I also had the sense that as soon as Riot Grrrl was over, we'd be over if we got too closely associated with it. Once the media has had its field day with it and people are over it, no one would be interested in what we were doing.

LINEUP CHANGES

MICHELLE (TODD) GONZALES: Dominique was a little younger than we were, so she brought a different kind of energy. She was also this amazing renaissance woman. We liked her right away because she was so interesting. She offered a different perspective on the world and she was also a great musician, too.

LOS CRUDOS SPLIT/WORKING WITH STEVE ALBINI

MICHELLE (TODD) GONZALES: All of us in Spitboy were crazy about Los Crudos. They were really sincere, political, and super nice guys. They had these amazing stories, and none of them grew up in privilege. They came out to California and we met them and all got along so great. We played some shows together and developed this bond. Eventually it just became this natural idea that, hey, we should do a record together. [laughs] So, we just did it. We had a lot of correspondence via snail mail with pictures, graphics, and cover ideas. We were in contact back and forth on the phone and it was just really fun. It was great to have a brotherhood/sisterhood thing with a band that was singing about things they felt as passionately about as we did.

ADRIENNE DROOGAS: I still get really excited about the Spitboy/Los Crudos split. By that point we were so on with each other internally and so connected. We recorded with Steve Albini, which was amazing! I remember when we were trying to figure out where to record Karin just up and said, "I think I'm going to call Steve Albini." We just laughed and said, "You don't know Steve Albini." But she had his number and decided to call him and he said that he had one weekend free to record us and he'd love to do it. Karin said we can't pay you very much and he said that was fine because he had been recording Nirvana and P.J. Harvey and bigger bands at the time, which helped fund his other projects. We flew to Chicago and went to his house and we were in his living room and we said, "Okay, are we recording here or do we go to the studio?" He then proceeds to walk up to this painting on the wall which was a 1950s style woman in a negligee with her nipples lit up and he presses one of the nipples and his bookcase goes up into the ceiling and there were stairs that go upstairs and he'd rigged a car garage door opener to do this and all his recording stuff was in the attic. We're just standing there in awe of it all. [laughs] He just made the bookcase disappear!

MICHELLE (TODD) GONZALES: This was the first time we recorded with someone who was really well-known. He was also known for getting a drum sound like the way the drummer played live, which was really exciting for me. That record represents the more mature Spitboy. I know people get really funny when you talk about bands that way, but no matter who you are, when you play music with people for many years everyone is going to get better. That's all that word "mature" means. We were just more comfortable with our voices and instruments. We were pushing ourselves to play things a little more complicated. That was definitely a stepping stone for the Instant Girl project, which was what the band morphed into after Adrienne left.

CONFRONTATIONAL?

MICHELLE (TODD) GONZALES: I remember one time in Albuquerque, we were talking about one of our songs before we were about to play it and some guy said, "Shut the fuck up and spread your legs or play." I was totally humiliated and pissed. I got up and was ready to chase the guy, but someone stopped me and said, and I don't know if this was true or not, "That guy was on *America's Most Wanted*, he's a really dangerous guy." We just stopped playing. Women were coming up to us crying and apologizing. People gave us money to get to our next show. It's kind of weird to think of people giving us money, but in the moment it wasn't strange. People didn't know what else to do and they just wanted to show us support.

ADRIENNE DROOGAS: Mostly, [shows were] a very emotional experience. We would play a show and I would be up on stage and I'd start asking that every third woman raise her hand in the air and keep it up until I'd worked my way through the entire crowd. Then, I'd raise my hand also and I'd say that one out of three women will be raped in their lifetime and that this show of hands was the statistics come to life. Or one time on tour in Wisconsin, Todd was relaying an experience of a woman who had passed out drunk at a party and woke up being raped. A guy in the audience yelled out, "Yeah! That was my girlfriend!" and started laughing. Todd grabbed the microphone and said, "Fuck you, that girl was me!" I remember walking to the edge of the stage, handing the microphone to someone, and then slowly walking through the crowd as people parted in front of me. I had this wave of grief come over me because the guy was mocking her. The room had grown deadly quiet with this tension that was palpable. I reached the guy who had yelled at Todd and I leaned forward and in his ear I softly said, "You know what you just did? You just publicly humiliated her. Fuck you." And then I walked back to the stage, picked up the microphone, and we instantly started playing a song. We were all crying these tears of fury and rage and frustration. Women in the audience were holding each other and crying. The guy got dragged out of the show. We went into the next song, which was about rape, and we just lost it. I could hardly sing because I was sobbing. Here was this woman who opened herself up and was vulnerable and then there was this person who just couldn't handle it. It was devastating, but empowering. It was painful, but we were strong enough to take that kind of pain and turn it around and use it as a way to release our anger. I don't see that as confrontational as much as it is emotional and raw and real.

MICHELLE (TODD) GONZALES: If someone confronted us, we were going to confront them back. We weren't going to just stand there in front of a group of people and let anyone humiliate us. We had microphones and at that moment we had the power. If they were going to try and be uncomfortable and threatened because the attention wasn't focused on them, then we were going to let them have it. On the other hand, did we go around beating people over the head with ideas about sexism? Absolutely not. One of the things I remember more than anything else was that people would say, "You guys are so nice." [laughs] They would say it over and over. We couldn't figure out why they were saying it, but we realized there was this impression of us before people would see us. When bands talk about the president or politics about general ideas people would be all rah-rah-rah, but when it came to something personal sometimes they couldn't handle it and they thought we were confrontational. We made them think about something within themselves they maybe didn't even realize existed, and they would then just label us as "confrontational."

WINDING DOWN

ADRIENNE DROOGAS: I pulled aside the Spitwomen when we got back from Japan and basically said, "I need to deal with my shit, and I need to do it in a way that's not public." At that point everything was getting filtered through Spitboy and there were some lifelong issues that I needed to grapple with, and I couldn't do it publicly anymore. I was singing for Spitboy and writing for *Maximum Rock N'Roll* and *Profane Existence* and I was visibly present in the punk scene. I needed to step back and spend time with myself and work on things internally rather than getting up on stage and throw things out in front of 600 people. But it did help me come to terms with so many things inside myself. We all encouraged each other to grow and we supported each other and it was just an amazing experience.

MICHELLE (TODD) GONZALES: We went to New Zealand, Australia, and Japan and shortly after that Adrienne left the band. But we had an amazing time. There was a sense of things winding down. Karin was talking more and more about going to South America. We knew Dominique was going go to graduate school. And we all knew we weren't getting any younger — our lives were naturally moving in different directions. I was getting more interested in doing my own writing and having my own ideas. It wasn't a rebellion against the band or anything, but I was the only person of color in the band and at times that was very difficult for me, not necessarily because of anything anyone in the band did or said but my perceptions of things were just different. It was very hard for me to talk to them about that because being part of the hardcore or punk scene was what had united us all for so long. When I started to feel kind of hemmed in because of my ethnic identity in the hardcore scene, it wasn't a comfortable conversation to have. But everyone seemed ready to move on, and it was good that things ended when they did.

LOOKING BACK

MICHELLE (TODD) GONZALES: There is no way I'd be who I am without playing in Spitboy. Those women and experiences helped me transform into the person I am. I grew up in a really small town on welfare and never thought I'd go to Europe or even travel the United States with a bunch of women and have a blast! We made it happen together, and that was the beauty of what Spitboy did. We were four big ol' brains and a lot of energy and we harnessed it and did a lot of great stuff because we did it together. I gained a hell of a lot of self-confidence because we did it all by ourselves. It was a totally amazing experience and I probably wouldn't have discovered these ideas that I could express articulately, which I eventually channeled into getting a degree in English and becoming a teacher.

ADRIENNE DROOGAS: I'm incredibly proud of Karin, Todd, Paula, and Dominique. I am so appreciative of people like Kent McClard, Lawrence Livermore, and John Yates for being so supportive of Spitboy and putting out the records on their labels. I am thankful to every person who set up a show, did an interview, wrote a review, or came to see us play. I am in awe of the impact that Spitboy had and so grateful that people have felt comfortable enough to share their thoughts and feelings with me. There isn't any one single moment that stands out as the shining example of what made singing in Spitboy such a life altering experience for me, but the entire experience is kind of the shining example — the whole five years! I am proud of all of the good things that we did, all of the difficult situations that we faced and conquered, the boring moments of being trapped in a recording studio listening to them play a song over and over and over again, driving on some highway with Liz Phair cranking and all of us singing along at the top of our lungs. I'm proud of all of it. I feel lucky that I had such an amazing experience with such a beautiful group of women.

SELECT DISCOGRAPHY:

"The Threat Sexism Impressed" b/w "Ultimate Violations" (7", Lookout, 1991)
Droogas, Gembus, Hibbs-Rines, Gonzales

True Self Revealed (LP, Ebullition, 1993)
Droogas, Gembus, Hibbs-Rines, Gonzales

Mi Cuerpo Es Mio (7", Allied, 1994)
Droogas, Gembus, Hibbs-Rines, Gonzales

Rasana (7", Ebullition, 1995)
Droogas, Gembus, Davison, Gonzales

Spitboy/Los Crudos Split (LP, Ebullition, 1995)
Droogas, Gembus, Davison, Gonzales

EIGHT: THE NINETIES HARDCORE REVOLUTION IN ETHICS, POLITICS, AND SOU

SPLIT LIP/CHAMBERLAIN

Vocals: David Moore
Guitars: Adam Rubenstein
Clayton Snyder

Bass: Curtis Mead
Seth Greathouse
Drums: Charlie Walker
Wade Parish

Some might say the progression of the Indiana-based Split Lip resembled the overall musical and personal maturation process exhibited by many nineties hardcore bands. Along with bands like Endpoint, Shift, Lincoln, Samuel, and None Left Standing, they proved that hardcore could have its softer, poetic side right alongside its more innate rebellious and political nature. While they started as a more traditional sounding three-chord hardcore band, over time they crafted a sound that incorporated elements of melodic rock, emotional hardcore, metal, country, and singer/songwriter material. These influences were controversial for hardcore purists but others felt the band simply created powerful music that fell outside the ranks of genre classification. Their willingness to experiment got listeners to pay attention whether or not they liked the direction the band was headed.

Split Lip formed in the winter of 1990 when high schoolers Curtis Mead (bass), Clayton Snyder (guitar), and Charlie Walker (drums) started looking for a new vocalist as well as someone to help out with songwriting duties. Enter singer David Moore and second guitarist Adam Rubenstein to fill these roles. The band's early material was a mixture of mid-tempo and slightly metal Midwestern hardcore influences of the time such as Integrity with touches of the post-hardcore of bands like Quicksand. They eventually caught the ear of the then-upstart label Doghouse Records, resulting in their first release, *Soul Kill*.

As the members headed towards high school graduation, they began to tinker with their sound. A variety of eclectic musical interests seeped into the material, making the band progress from straightforward hardcore into a more complex sound that included melodic rock, punk, post-hardcore, and alt-country. For example, they played with the hardcore spirit of bands like Avail, wrote extremely personal and reflective lyrics in a manner reminiscent of Embrace, and experimented with poetry and atmospherics a la The Cure. While Split Lip didn't sound exactly like one of these bands, they felt sonic exploration was the only way to satisfy their artistic muse.

Their next move was writing *For the Love of the Wounded*, a record that attracted considerable attention due to its integration of raw emotion and musical ambition. They knew they were onto something special as the record drew acclaim from emotional hardcore fans and from some outside of the hardcore scene. In response, the band attempted to top that record with even more dynamic songwriting, and that's exactly what they did with *Fate's Got a Driver*. Arguably their most popular record, *Fate's Got a Driver* was the magnification of every quality Split Lip had already exhibited: head-nodding rock rhythms and riffs, bursts of melody, and equally mournful and hopeful lyrics.

At this point the band was clearly headed in more rock-centered directions, which was bringing a much different type of audience to their shows. Around the same time, the group changed their name to Chamberlain because they felt that a violent sounding name had nothing to do with their personalities or the band. The name change prompted cries of "sell-out" but the band trusted their own insight and focused their sound even more toward alternative rock and alt-country, which was eventually demonstrated on the album *The Moon My Saddle* in 1999. Some of the members were conflicted with the direction their sound was headed. Eventually, Mead, Snyder, and Walker left the band and Chamberlain dissolved after some notable final recordings with new members Seth Greathouse (bass) and Wade Parish (drums), which were released after their breakup.

Despite a somewhat early end, Split Lip/Chamberlain progressed miles beyond what many thought was possible by expanding a healthy musical appetite and nurturing it with passion and emotion. Consequently Split Lip, along with peers like Endpoint, Hoover, Still Life, and Lifetime, helped prove that hardcore was just as much a state of mind as it was a specific pattern of sounds.

ORIGINS OF SPLIT LIP

CURTIS MEAD: The first incarnation [of Split Lip] was Clay and I and another singer who went on to run the one underground punk venue in Indianapolis. We didn't know how to play music. Clay played guitar and I got a bass and just started playing. Clay stole a microphone from a place he played hockey at, so since we had a mic we could have a band. [laughs] We met Chuck through a mutual friend and eventually Adam got involved with it. The average age of the band was about 15. The approach we were taking didn't work out for the original singer. So, we asked Dave to play with us. He was in a punk/funk type band, which didn't really make sense. Once he joined up that was it for about nine or ten years.

CHARLIE WALKER: What was weird about me getting into hardcore was that I just turned fourteen when I met Curtis and Clay and I was told I was a metal-head. I grew up with Slayer and Zeppelin as my favorite bands and my dad was a drummer as well, so I grew up around the old good rock and I met these guys through this girl who went to my high school in my freshman year. She said, "These guys are in my boyfriend's band." It was Clay's girlfriend and they said that they needed a drummer and I remember looking at them and they had "X's" on their hands and I was like, "What's that about?" She said, "Oh they're straight edge." I said, "What's that?" I had no clue. [laughs] So, I said, "Okay, cool. I would like to be in a band with people who can play." So, they came over and we started playing and next thing you know it was hardcore — it was a whole new world to me and I went over to their house and they had all the seven-inches and everything and it intrigued me.

INFLUENCES/DIRECTION

ADAM RUBENSTEIN: We all came from different places musically. David's affinity towards softer alternative stuff like The Smiths or The Ocean Blue, and Curtis' obsession with The Cure mixed well with the rest of our metal and hardcore influences. All of our tastes combined to produce a highly-melodic yet heavy sound. We were so young then. I was only 15 when we recorded the *Soulkill 7"*, so I can't say I was musically developed enough to have any real goals. What came out was simply a surprise to all of us.

CURTIS MEAD: There were five of us who were all into different things. David and I shared a love for bands like 7 Seconds and Soulside, especially in the inflection of David's voice. When I met Adam he was in a three-piece punk band and he wore a lot of metal shirts. He was 13 when I met him and he was already in a Metallica cover band. He got into a variety of contemporary music and took those influences in a very mature way with his songwriting. We were all from different musical interests, but we all came from Indiana. We grew up listening to records from the coasts, but you also had to go see someone play. We were going to local shows and there was a decent punk scene in Indianapolis. I look back at all my favorite records and they all have some kind of melody. That didn't mean it couldn't be hard. Even bands like Inside Out — it was heavy but Zack [De La Rocha] wrote in a melodic way. The Quicksand seven-inch was the same way. That record didn't leave my house till it was worn out! In retrospect it was a great way to mash up New York hardcore and Jane's Addiction, but it was also melodic and heavy. I liked David's singing because he could be aggressive but also very melodic.

DAVID MOORE: I don't recall any conversations amongst the five of us regarding what "sound" we were striving for — not at first anyway. Again, because the music scene was really just beginning to coalesce, there was no real blueprint to follow — not with the way things were changing. Early on it was predominantly emulation and thievery; but I have to say, even in our earliest songwriting attempts, we were stealing from the right places. Adam had a very diverse and comprehensive musical influence — most of which came from beyond the bounds of the punk scene. I grew up on a lot of seventies singer songwriter stuff — Cat Stevens, Bob Dylan, John Denver, James Taylor, etc. so I was coming from a more subtle, dare I say "softer" side of music. U2 was a big influence for us; *The Joshua Tree* created a new medium and pointed us toward the exploration of more melodic songs and lyrics that mined the interior worlds of the soul. Personally, I was always primarily interested in writing and in words. The music was secondary to me. It was a vehicle only, a conduit to carry the meaning...and whatever tune or melody line would serve to further the meaning of the words, that was the one I went with. Our initial "sound" if we had one came from our lack of experience and limited ability if anything — but we had the courage to put it all out there, to expose ourselves creatively and if nothing else, that is a great achievement.

CHARLIE WALKER: I remember in the beginning we all loved Operation Ivy. We all loved Integrity, too. All that stuff is kind of what we went for early. The five of us just got together and it just happened. We never really said, "Let's be just like this band or let's just be like that band." But Adam was a total metal guitar player. He was a total shredder. [laughs] Curtis was the punk one and it kind of just created its own thing in the beginning. Because we were all into hardcore, it just seeped into our music, but we never set out to sound like a certain band.

EARLY DAYS

DAVID MOORE: We developed an early following in Indiana and the surrounding states. We did the right thing by going out on the road very early on. I was the only one with a license when we started touring...in those days that was the only way to connect with your audience or potential fans. We always had a sort of "us-against-the-world" mentality...a very brash and confident air about us collectively. That usually served to do one of two things, either make people hate us, or make people endear themselves to us and want to be a part of our growing following. We fully believed we could change the world. It was beautiful, really; that kind of idealism and self confidence. But things really changed for us in 1992 when the Seattle scene became fodder for the masses. The next thing we knew every high school kid in Indiana wanted to go to shows and be able to jump off the stage like the kids in the Nirvana video. Everything exploded. All the major labels were digging deep into the underground to sign every punk band they could find. We went from playing for 20 to 30 people, to playing for 1,500. It just exploded so fast — a right place, right time sort of thing.

CURTIS MEAD: We played Chicago, St. Louis, Dayton, and Louisville quite a bit. David was 16 and he was the oldest in the band when we got out there. The first recording we did was for the *Voice of the Voiceless* compilation. We got about $400 to record the song and we thought it was the greatest thing in the world! [laughs] We couldn't believe someone was actually paying us to record our music. That's when it hit us that we were really doing the band for real... and we were only 15! It was an animal rights comp. We were all vegetarian, but our approach was pretty personal on those issues and appeared very rarely in songs.

CHARLIE WALKER: The early shows were great! Those were some of my favorite times of my life! We played at the V.F.W. Hall in Indianapolis, or we would play at the Lion's Club, which was the place in town where the old men have their meetings. We would rent it out and there would be 80 kids at a show. It felt really special. We felt like we really had something going on. It felt like music was changing itself. In a way some people call it a revolution; some people just call it rock-and-roll.

CHEMISTRY

DAVID MOORE: Adam and I were usually steering the ship creatively speaking, although early on it was much more collaborative than it would eventually become. Toward the latter part of [the band], Adam and I would write everything exclusively and then take it to everyone else to flesh out. Experience taught us that a multiplicity of creative voices usually makes for a compromised vision — not always a popular opinion, but a true one nevertheless.

ADAM RUBENSTEIN: Typically I would bring a bunch of guitar parts into practice and we would mathematically and somewhat haphazardly piece them together. We'd spend weeks sometimes just playing the same riffs over and over again. Eventually David would come with lyrics and we'd move on to the next thing. We never bothered David too much with the vocals, probably because he wasn't much of a singer in the early days.

CHARLIE WALKER: When you have a certain genre of music, the formula gets so predictable. It's like, "Okay, here's the mosh part. Here's the pickup thrash part." And it was totally predictable. A lot of bands wanted to do something new; something that has never been done before. Out of that freedom came hardcore.

"SOUL KILL"/POLITICAL LEANINGS

DAVID MOORE: [*Soul Kill*] was a cause — one that challenged previous accepted paradigms. I never really delved into socio-political issues in my lyrics, so I had to take my stands elsewhere. It didn't take long for me to realize that, in trying to break out of those inherited "boxes" of thought, you just end up creating another box all together. That's why all movements eventually fail and become corrupted. Shared beliefs become group-thought; group-thought becomes exclusivity; exclusivity puts up walls, and walls keep people from coming together to exact real change. Then you're right back where you started.

ADAM RUBENSTEIN: I'm not really sure what sparked [the politics on this record]. We also used to play a song called "Crimes of Our Own," which dealt with these issues. Perhaps the anti-racism ideals that go along with being straight edge just got us interested in certain issues like the plight of the American Indians.

CHARLIE WALKER: David's lyrics were really his political views and his religious views. Everything was written in such a cool way — almost like poetry. It wasn't completely obvious, though. It didn't come at you; he just told a really cool story and you would get a lot out of it.

"VOICE OF THE VOICELESS"

DAVID MOORE: What I remember most about that compilation is that we were the only band on there with a song that had nothing to do with animal rights. I had to write up a short paragraph to accompany the lyrics in an attempt to connect the dots between the song and the cause the record was promoting. It was yet another cause; it started out with all the right intentions and probably has contributed to a lot of positive change.

SPLIT LIP/ENDPOINT CONNECTION

DAVID MOORE: For a while there it was like we were understudies to Endpoint. Those guys taught us a lot. They were a little older than us and had been at the center of a thriving music scene in Louisville and they kind of took us under their wing. Louisville became our second home. We played together, toured together, slept on the same floors. Eventually I remember it became more and more competitive — or maybe that was just me? I always wanted to outdo those around me, always wanted to write the best line, the best song. They taught us that melody can work in punk music, sensitivity is noble, and that there is power in being emotionally vulnerable, but eventually I wanted to eclipse them. Not a very punk rock way of thinking, I know, but that was the way it was. My first show ever was in Louisville with Endpoint. I was scared to death. They were great guys, every one of them.

ADAM RUBENSTEIN: Split Lip and Endpoint sort of became synonymous for while as we played 90% of our shows together. Those guys were a little older than us, so we naturally looked up to them. We really longed to have that same participatory hardcore atmosphere at Split Lip shows. For a year or so we really wanted to be them, we wrote a lot of songs that somewhat imitated the "Endpoint sound." "Unsolid Ground" or "Evolution" come to mind as inadvertent imitations.

CHARLIE WALKER: [Endpoint] taught us how to do it in the beginning. I was fourteen. Adam was thirteen. We couldn't even drive to a show. And with Endpoint we saw them and were like, "Whoa! Who are these guys?" They had a shit-load of fans and it was raw. I felt like I was watching Iggy and The Stooges. It was so beautiful because every single person at that show was there for that music. Those shows were out of hand. There were people hanging from rafters. It was nuts! We used to play this skate-park on the one pyramid thing with the box in the middle and we would play for kids on the half pipe, jumping off the half pipe and on to the drums and the drums would get knocked over, amps would get knocked over and there would be blood. [laughs]

"FOR THE LOVE OF THE WOUNDED"

DAVID MOORE: I'm humbled and honored if that record has garnered recognition after all these years. That record was me in the throes of the most turbulent years of my youth. I was trying to synthesize and process my world. I had begun a relationship, as fiery and dramatic as all young relationships are (later she would become my wife), and I was attempting to become the artist I felt I could be, the writer I aspired to become. Everything was assimilated through the lens of art and creativity. That was paramount to me and all I cared about. So when I think back on that record and making that record, I think of me trying to make sense of all of that youthful turbulence, trying to make something creative and purposeful. Lyrically, I was exploring themes that involved some major female influences in my life at the time, hence the name of the record.

CURTIS MEAD: *For The Love of the Wounded* has a lot of growing pains. It was an in-between time of figuring out what our talents were and what we really wanted to sound like. That was a great time for us. Doghouse Records approached us at a show in Louisville and asked us to put out a seven-inch and maybe even make a CD if the record did well. It's so funny to think about but it's so true: all he had to say is he'd put anything out and we'd be ecstatic! [laughs] We never thought putting out a CD was something that was attainable for a small band. I still wanted to put out vinyl, but you didn't really see a lot of hardcore bands putting out CDs at that time.

ADAM RUBENSTEIN: We just played so much back then. Every song was crafted with a probably needless scrutiny. Even though we were recording a modest hardcore record, in our minds we were recording *Led Zeppelin II*.

CHARLIE WALKER: We were so excited and also so naïve. [laughs] We had no clue what we were doing in the studio. They said do this and do that and we were like, "No, we want to do this!" So they said, "You guys really don't know what you're doing, do you?" But it was a super special moment because we were so young and we knew we were making a record.

CURTIS MEAD: We had success early on, which made it harder for things later. When you get used to exceeding your expectations, it made us question ourselves a lot down the road.

EMOTIONAL UNDERCURRENTS

ADAM RUBENSTEIN: David always wrote such poetic lyrics and his talents were far beyond his years. He was reading Ezra Pound and Dylan Thomas when most of us were reading *Catcher in the Rye* for the very first time. In order to capture what was going on lyrically we really tried to create the right musical backdrop. Perhaps it's just that drama is often exaggerated in our youth. However, if I had to point to anything, I'd say coming from small towns may have been the reason we came off that way. The Midwestern scene was so insular; it took us a while to become a part of a larger scene. All of us longed to break beyond the boundaries of Indiana.

NEW SONIC AVENUES

ADAM RUBENSTEIN: We pretty much made a conscious decision to leave the hardcore scene. We pushed its boundaries as far as we could take them musically. Also our tastes were expanding dramatically as we got older. We were getting into things like Bob Dylan, Tom Waits, or Elvis Costello. At the time these sorts of things didn't vibe well within our group of friends in the hardcore scene.

NAME CHANGE

CHARLIE WALKER: The first time Clay and Curtis and I got together was at my house and I had a trampoline in my backyard, and we went out there and I busted my lip open! [laughs] My sister came home and was like, "What the hell happened?" She gave me medicine for it and I was kind of like medicine-headed and I looked over at Curtis and said, "Dude, we should call this band Split Lip." So it stuck. Later, we did *Fate's Got a Driver*. It was the stupidest time to change a name, right as we released it. We all didn't want to come across as a Hardline band, and that is what people thought we were based on our name. It sounded like, "We are here to kick your ass." It didn't represent where we were spiritually and musically at the time.

CURTIS MEAD: We probably should have just ridden it out and just gone with it. But we felt like we were adults and felt silly saying our own band name. [laughs] Most people didn't seem to care about it, but we felt like it was a name a bunch of 14-year-olds would pick. It was a tough move to make. We felt like Chamberlain was just a name and didn't have any connotation to it. We thought about it for a couple years, but we felt like we couldn't do it because we kept putting out records. Chamberlain was the name of one of our songs and didn't have a particular meaning, but it also sounded more adult.

DAVID MOORE: It's funny because we had talked about changing the name when I first started with the band in 1990, but we decided against it because the guys felt it would compromise their following at the time. Eventually the name became too much of a burden and it had no kinship with the music. We chose something much more ambiguous. Shakespeare had his "Chamberlain Players" which was a theater troupe — I always liked the sound of the word.

ROCK INFLUENCES

ADAM RUBENSTEIN: I blame our Indiana upbringing. We became very interested in Americana and classic rock. I suddenly found myself more interested in listening to The Band or Tom Petty than the latest offering from Revelation. We just were getting older.

"FATE'S GOT A DRIVER"

ADAM RUBENSTEIN: *Fate's Got a Driver* was written very slowly and in spurts. I was living in a college dorm, while the other guys were scattered around Bloomington, Indiana, mulling scholastic pursuits. We didn't hang out much then outside of sporadic touring. Despite our disjointedness, Chamberlain was still our first love. We were still developing as musicians, but we pushed our talents to the absolute limit on that [*Fate's*]. What's funny is somehow *Fate's* pigeonholed us as an "emo" band or whatever you want to call it, but it came along at a point where internally we couldn't have been more confused about our identity. I think *The Moon My Saddle* has better songs, but what I like about *Fate's* is that we had no idea what we were doing. We just got in there and played without really thinking about the recording process. It's remarkably diverse considering how underdeveloped we were as musicians.

DAVID MOORE: *Fate's* was definitely our most acclaimed and lucrative record in terms of its reception. That was a very tough album to record for me. It was like trying to pull those songs from the depths of my being. They just didn't come easily, most of them anyway. I remember driving home from Detroit where we had recorded the record and listening back to the songs. Honestly, my initial response was disappointment. I didn't feel like the songs had come across on recording. I was in a lot of emotional anguish about it for days after the sessions. It's interesting though, because in the last song — "The Simple Life" — you can hear the beginnings of *The Moon My Saddle* in terms of theme, imagery, and delivery. I am proud of *Fate's Got a Driver*, though it was a bit like my problem child.

CURTIS MEAD: *Fate's Got a Driver* was pretty well thought out. Every step we took we felt was another step in the direction we felt was best to go. A lot of people questioned the sound changing so much from *For the Love* to *Fate's*, but it was just what we were listening to and where we were at. We wanted to challenge our listeners and didn't want to make the same record. Plus, being so young we were still learning how to play our instruments and how to write a song in a different key. We were still figuring out what choruses were and how to get from the verse to the chorus. The whole thing was a learning process. When you're 17 you're a mess anyway and of course the music reflects that. I feel like it's our most representative record. We were really proud of that music and though there was some controversy about us, we liked it because it was making people think.

CHARLIE WALKER: *Fate's Got a Driver* is the real pinnacle of the band. I definitely think it's where we were at our best and when we were all on the same page. We wrote the music in our friend Matt Reece's house. With that record the reason it came out that way was because everyone expected it to be on the same page and we felt like on the first one we were young. I love how you push play and *Fate's* is just kind of in your face. And I think that is where we started consciously writing song to song. It was kind of our first attempt at a real record we thought and we all really did try to work together and keep together musically.

"THE MOON MY SADDLE"

ADAM RUBENSTEIN: Outside of the band's beginnings, it wasn't until after *The Moon My Saddle* that we changed members. It was an uphill battle trying to find our voice again after that. Towards the end we finally started to develop a unique sound, but we had had enough by then. Again, it was just a product of living in the Midwest. We really began to identify ourselves with our homeland, so to speak. Even a couple guys from John Mellencamp's band played on that record. We were quite consciously burying our hardcore past.

DAVID MOORE: *The Moon My Saddle*, for me, was the culmination of many years of struggling to find my voice creatively and musically speaking. The concerted marriage of words and music delivered in a simple, straightforward format with nothing blurring or blocking the flow of meaning in the songs, nothing compromising the overall vision toward which all the songs pointed. It was the first record I could listen to, as if I had finally struck on the thing I had been orbiting around all along. In a word, I chose to be honest. These were the songs I had always wanted to write and I felt a kinship to them, as if they had been here before I found them. I remember listening to the play back of the record from front to back in the studio in Manhattan where we were mastering it. We just sat in the dark and listened to the whole thing. I don't think I've ever felt more proud of myself. We all knew we had accomplished something special. I believed in that record. I still do.

CHARLIE WALKER: David and Adam kind of took the majority of the songwriting and would just come to us with the songs. At that time, David was really into Bob Dylan and listening to a lot of country like Hank Williams and stuff and it just kind of came out. It turned out that way, the whole John Mellencamp, Midwest roots rock. I dug it for what it was but later we got even more country and it just way wasn't my thing.

CURTIS MEAD: Everyone feels like we missed a record somewhere in between. We were writing other songs that didn't end up making sense for *The Moon My Saddle*, so there could have been another record so it didn't seem like such a dramatic jump. *The Moon My Saddle* came along at a point when we thought we were going to be doing this for a living. Some of the record came off as contrived. We got caught up in trying to do what we thought people wanted to hear, and we never thought like that before. Labels were getting interested and we were playing showcases. When that happens to 20-year-olds you're not really sure how to react.

FAN REACTION TO SONIC PROGRESSION

ADAM RUBENSTEIN: The reaction was always highly unaccepting at first, but our listeners always eventually came around. I remember a lot of hecklers. They'd yell out names of John Mellencamp songs or tell David to button up his shirt.

DAVID MOORE: Overall the reaction was bad, particularly when we started touring for *The Moon My Saddle*. I remember literally getting booed throughout our set in a couple of towns. We hadn't been out on the road in a long time, and when we finally came out we weren't playing many older songs, which in hindsight was a pretty stupid thing to do. There was a very strong backlash to that record and I don't think it translated for a lot of people. When you're raised in the underground music scene and you start to experiment with other sounds, influences that hearken toward anything mainstream, people immediately put up a wall. They feel cheated or betrayed. Whatever it was, we took a lot of heat for that record, but we didn't care much about it and, knowing me, I was probably loving the response. I wanted to distance myself from the hardcore scene. I didn't see much value in it anymore. Everyone thought the same, expressed themselves the same, and rested on their collective laurels. At least that's what I believed. I wanted out and I suppose that record was my ticket. I should take this opportunity to acknowledge those individuals who were accepting of our growth and change, because there were a lot of people who felt a kindred connection with those songs. These people embraced us for what we were and what we were trying to do. I can't thank that core group of people enough.

CHARLIE WALKER: We never wanted to be a certain type of band. We never wanted to say, "Oh, dude, let's write this music. Let's be a rock-and-roll band instead of a punk band." It was a natural transition. When you really look at the grand scheme of it, we started out and we were all kids. Your musical tastes change; your ideals change a little bit, and people get into different music. Dave got into Bob Dylan. Adam got into The Police. Curtis loved every punk band on the planet. You get older and you just change. We never wanted to stick to a formula. So, it just naturally came about that we started to sound like Bruce Springsteen. At first the fans hated it. They thought we were totally abandoning everything we believed in. They thought we were selling out. We got booed off the stage. I remember this one show if Philly. This one kid smashed his hand on the stage and was like, "Fuck! Play this song! Don't you guys play anything fast anymore? This is slow!" We got a lot of flak for it, but then again it was some of those same people who would come around about six months later and say, "Man, I really hated this shit at first but I really dig it now." It was a weird give and take.

END OF THE ROAD

ADAM RUBENSTEIN: Those final releases were released by our business management. We had nothing to do with putting them out. Eventually I wanted to come to New York, explore something else. We were all pretty tired of spending our weekends in Midwestern sports bars.

DAVID MOORE: I can't give any concrete reason for it, other than the fact that everything had run its course. There was no magic in it anymore. Somehow, in the years following *The Moon My Saddle*, we had slowly lost that shared love for the simple act of making music. Everything got increasingly more complicated. We took our collective gaze off of what mattered and lost a lot along the way. One day as we were driving home in the van from one of our innumerable Midwestern shows, I turned to the guys and told them that I thought when we got home we should end it. I think I was secretly hoping for someone to object, but no one did. A few days later I went and pawned everything I had — guitars, mics, amps, the van.

CURTIS MEAD: The last two years I was in Chamberlain I took more of a backseat. I didn't miss the hardcore scene of shows because the whole fest thing got out of hand. But I missed the aggressive nature we had in our music before that. We lost the angst we had because we were writing rock songs. I thought that was our key. We were melodic but had an edge and weren't afraid to experiment, but once you start playing what you know you can play then it starts to get too safe. We also weren't all rock players, which is why we ended up going separate ways.

CHARLIE WALKER: David and Adam came to me and said they wanted to go to kind of a different direction. Curtis and Clay weren't doing what they want to do and they were split right down the middle style-wise. It just got to the point where they obviously thought something had to change and when they were asked to leave the band, I stayed for six more months and then I left, too. They got two new guys and it just wasn't the same band and it wasn't the same mission. I felt that it was not the same intent that it originally was. It wasn't the same soul.

LOOKING BACK

ADAM RUBENSTEIN: People think I'm bothered that certain bands we influenced went on to be better remembered. But people still buy our records, and somehow listeners still care about us. That's more than 99% of bands have accomplished. I'm just happy we were part of the tapestry of hardcore and indie history. I have no regrets.

DAVID MOORE: If there is any lasting legacy that might remain — and I'm humbled at the thought that perhaps there is — I would only hope that it would offer others some sort of consolation or solace in desperate times and be a persistent reminder that we all share in the same experience; that there is a thread that connects us. I would hope that it would encourage people to see the majesty in their own experiences and the interconnectedness of all things.

CHARLIE WALKER: I hold the band so close to my heart. It meant the world to me. That was my escape. That was everything. Everything else, I was like, "Screw it, I've got these four guys and we're a band." My parents got divorced and I was like, "Whatever, I've got the band." It was in the most developmental part of my life, age 14 to 24. Me and these other guys were a part of something that we, in all honesty, just created. We didn't know what we were doing, but it just happened and we got taken for a ride for ten years.

SELECT DISCOGRAPHY:

Soul Kill (7", Doghouse, 1992)
> Moore, Rubenstein, Snyder, Mead, Walker

For the Love of the Wounded (CD/LP, Doghouse, 1994)
> Moore, Rubenstein, Snyder, Mead, Walker

Fate's Got a Driver (CD/LP, Doghouse, 1995)
> Moore, Rubenstein, Snyder, Mead, Walker

Split with Old Pike (7"/MCD, Doghouse, 1996)
> Moore, Rubenstein, Snyder, Mead, Walker

The Moon My Saddle (CD/LP, Doghouse, 1999)
> Moore, Rubenstein, Greathouse, Walker

Exit 263 (CD/LP, Doghouse, 2001)
> Moore, Rubenstein, Greathouse, Parish

Five-Year Diary (CD/LP, Engineer, 2002)
> Moore, Rubenstein, Greathouse, Parish

STRIFE

Vocals: Rick Rodney   Guitars: Andrew Kline
Bass: Chad Peterson   Todd Turnham
Drums: Sid Niesen   Mike Hartsfield
                                   Mike Machin

Strife was one of the most popular straight edge hardcore bands of the nineties. The Southern California band gained a widespread following due to their live show and mix of classic hardcore in the style of Uniform Choice or Sick of it All with a heavier hardcore/metal influence that recalled Judge and Cro-Mags. Along with Victory Records label-mates Snapcase and Earth Crisis, Strife became one of the highest selling hardcore bands of the time as their music broke into metal, punk, and hard rock markets due in large part to a long touring schedule and a major push from their record company. Some accused the band of trying to abandon hardcore as they opened for metal and alternative rock bands later on in the nineties, but they remained with Victory throughout their run and continued to play their patented brand of hardcore which grew slightly more technical and even more metal sounding with each release.

Strife formed in 1991 after vocalist Rick Rodney, drummer Sid Niesen, and guitarist Andrew Kline jammed together a few times. Eventually the trio extended an offer to friend and bassist Chad Peterson to join on the low end. Aside from Niesen everyone else was new to their instruments, so it wasn't easy to for them to progress to writing songs but they were among the many who lived for hardcore, which inspired them to play and write continually. Strife's formative songs were fast and raw with high-speed verses and explosive sing along choruses. Their live shows also forced people to take notice. On the mic, Rodney became more of an on-stage conductor for the audience as people clamored for the microphone. It also wasn't uncommon for Kline or Peterson to stage-dive, complete with instruments, at several points each show. The crowd couldn't help but be taken with the band's energy and were often just as much a part of each show as the band.

They put out a seven-inch on New Age Records in 1992 and also made an appearance on the popular *Only the Strong* compilation on Victory Records the same year. Along with two other notable straight edge groups, Snapcase and Earth Crisis, Strife signed with Victory Records and helped the label become one of the largest in hardcore. Strife's first Victory full-length, *One Truth*, came out in 1994 and along with Earth Crisis' *Firestorm* EP and Snapcase's *Lookinglasself* full-length, became one of the best selling hardcore records of the mid-nineties. The band also stepped up its touring schedule and went back and forth across the country on multiple occasions.

Some controversy surrounding Strife arose as some non-straight edgers felt the band was trying to "push" a straight edge agenda on the scene. For instance, some felt their album's title, *One Truth*, was a reference to straight edge being "the truth." However, the title of the record was a line taken from the first song on the album, "Through and Through," which was actually about love. As Strife began to hit various scenes around the country, people began to understand that although the band members were straight edge, the group's message was more about self-empowerment. Strife felt hardcore should be shared by all people and though straight edge was important it was not meant to be some sort of elite club.

Eventually, Strife went back to the studio to record what many consider to be the group's best record, *In This Defiance*. With better production than their previous records and featuring a variety of guests such as Chino Moreno of The Deftones and Igor Cavalera of Sepultura, *In This Defiance* combined their love for classic New York hardcore with faster paced and more intense hardcore and speed metal. Rodney's vocals, much like the music on that record, felt angrier and more powerful sounding than anything he'd done previously. The lyrics again touched on straight edge but also addressed issues like personal failure and remaining positive during times of adversity.

In 1996 and 1997, Strife toured with bands outside of hardcore like Voodoo Glow Skulls and Sepultura. Although some in the hardcore scene saw this as a ploy to step up to a major label, Strife remained with Victory and also regularly headlined hardcore bills. However, there were some intra-band disagreements about their direction. There was also turmoil as Rodney broke away from straight edge, which had been an important foundation for the band. To top it off, the members were more involved with jobs and interests outside of hardcore. Rodney, for instance, flirted with the world of acting and starred in an independent film called *Godmoney*. All these factors forced the band to a temporary halt in 1998.

They re-assembled in 2000 as a more metal influenced group known as Angermeans. After playing some shows and demoing new songs, there was pressure from audiences to play Strife songs. Ultimately, the band decided to once again call themselves Strife and recorded their final full-length, *Angermeans*. The album — which owed more of a debt to the speed metal riffs, anger, and aura of bands like Slayer or Fear Factory than to hardcore — received mixed reviews, and even the band was dissatisfied with the rushed production. After touring in support of *Angermeans*, Strife began to wind down.

Although they never officially broke up, Strife was pretty much finished as the 21st century arrived. The band still plays shows on occasion, but they never again began touring or recording regularly. When they do play, there are those who decry the band for playing straight edge songs with band members who are no longer straight edge. On the other hand, their message of positivity and their powerful music made a strong impact on nineties hardcore. They were a catalyst for introducing hardcore to a whole new era of fans and bands, and their records, especially *In This Defiance*, remain staples of nineties straight edge hardcore.

ORIGINS

SID NIESEN: The band started with Andrew and I. I had been playing drums all my life, so I was always into music. Andrew was really into music, but he hadn't really learned how to play an instrument yet. We started jamming in my bedroom and it was god-awful. [laughs] We originally called ourselves Stand As One and just did three-chord progressions. So, where Strife really started was in my bedroom.

ANDREW KLINE: We were all friends to some degree and we were all into hardcore. We wanted to start a band that sounded like some of our favorite bands like Judge, Sick of it All, Gorilla Biscuits, or Killing Time. At the time we were definitely really into that New York hardcore sound, which wasn't quite as prevalent on the West Coast. We started writing songs and basically learned to play our instruments in our band. All of us, aside from Sid, learned to play by writing these songs. I was 14 years old and was psyched to start a band! We never envisioned it lasting as long as it did or getting as big as it did. We really just wanted to form a band to play a show. Once we did that we wanted to play more shows. It just grew from there.

SID NIESEN: Andrew and I wrote a few songs that were horrendous, but we thought were pretty amazing at the time. [laughs] But it got us to the point where we wanted to do the band for real. We were straight edge and we just wanted to find other straight edge kids to play with. We didn't necessarily care if you knew how to play an instrument or not, because we looked at the band as a family in which there would be a growth process. We heard rumors of a guy who lived in a town near us named Rick who sang for a punk rock band who happened to be straight edge. We literally just called around town trying to find out who this guy was. That's how we found Rick. Rick also knew how to play guitar a bit too, so he helped us write some stuff as well. Chad joined us after that, and he couldn't really play bass. He had his mom buy him a bass and he figured out how to play and that's how we started. At the time we started as a band, the only thing that was really happening hardcore wise was here was in Orange County, and because we weren't from Orange County we had a terrible time getting shows. That's actually where the name Strife came from for the band. We were in such "strife" to get anywhere and out of our frustration sprang the sound of our band.

RICK RODNEY: I sang because I could play guitar but not very well. I was a frontman in two other bands, and I could scream so it seemed like a natural fit. [laughs] We had no intentions of getting signed or even touring. We just were bored and loved the music. After school we'd meet up at our friend Tony's house and just jam in his garage that was relatively sound proof. We'd even jam in his living room and somehow no one complained about this racket, which is surprising because we were terrible! [laughs] Sid ripped at drums from day one, but he was the only person in the band who had any skill at first. Everyone else was just learning.

CHAD PETERSON: We all would meet up after school on most days and skateboard at the same spot. At the time Sid, Andrew, and Rick were into hardcore, and I was into punk. They were already going out to shows on the weekend to see bands like End to End and Outspoken. They took me to my first show ever which was Gorilla Biscuits and Insted at the Country Club in Reseda. This is how I got in to hardcore and what brought me to being straight edge. Watching what was going on at these shows changed me. It was amazing watching the amount of energy in the music. It was so different than anything I have ever experienced. At the time they had a kid from Simi Valley playing bass for them named Scotty Colin. They played one show at Rick's high school and then Scotty left the band. I was sitting at home one afternoon and Sid gave me a call asking if I had a bass and wanted to come down and practice with them. I had never played bass before and had to borrow one from a friend. After going to so many hardcore shows by this point we wanted to help expand the scene in our area. We were influenced by so many bands at the time and brought a lot of background influence to the band as well. When we started as a band it was just to establish a scene in our local area and bring that same positivity we saw at so many shows and on videos to our town. We never really thought it would grow to be like it was for us. We honestly just wanted to play music and have fun doing it.

AUDIENCE PARTICIPATION

ANDREW KLINE: Our favorite part of going to a hardcore show was doing a stage dive or grabbing for the microphone to sing along. We wanted that element and in order to get that you have to put on a great live show. We'd all jump in the crowd and could care less about doing solos. From day one we really wanted people to be able to respond to the energy we put out there when we played live.

RICK RODNEY: I always felt like hardcore was for everybody. One of our main messages was that everyone should be accepted. At my first hardcore show I was wearing a Subhumans t-shirt with cut up jeans, Doc Martens, and colored hair. I remember Bl'ast was playing with Inside Out and Amenity. It was mostly hardcore kids at the show and the kids were cool. I got on stage to stage dive for Bl'ast and dancing with all these kids who were obviously different looking than me, but we were all connected in some way at this little gymnasium rocking out together. That always stuck with me. If I had gone to that show and had been ostracized because of the way I looked or given attitude because of how I was dressed I would have been like "fuck you" and walked away. Everyone has their first show. You're nervous and scared and unsure of how people are going to perceive you. You're unsure of yourself as a human being let alone at this specific environment. You're not accepted at high school, so if you come to a show and you're not accepted by your peers who are also on the outside looking in then you're screwed. So, I always felt like if there was a kid coming to see our band for the first time then I was them right up front with everyone else and a part of it. This experience is what helped me become the person I am today, so I always wanted to turn people on and not turn people off.

SID NIESEN: I was used to going to punk and metal shows where the crowd was barricaded and so distant from the band. We never wanted that. Seeing Chain of Strength we were right up front and singing along with the band itself. We decided from that point that that's what music should be. It just meant so much that we were allowed to be a part of the band for that night. So, when Strife got rolling we decided if there was going to be a barricade we didn't want to play. If the shows weren't all ages we didn't want to play. We want everyone to have fun with us. We felt that if you came to a Strife show then you were a member of the band that night. Our opinion was if kids weren't going nuts then we were doing something wrong.

RICK RODNEY: Andrew would flip into the crowd with his guitar, but people would catch him. It was important for us to give this energy off that it was okay to be on top of each other or on us. We might sound like shit, but it didn't matter. We were trying to facilitate an escape from your everyday crazy life. This was the one place you could come and shed all that shit out of your system and have fun. We'd all go through crap—family life, school, whatever. There's bullshit in everyone's life every day, and some people's shit is crazier than others'. But this was the one place where we could all come together and say, "Fuck it, man. Just let it out." It was aggression but in a positive way. We were just as hyped to play as anyone who was seeing one of our shows.

"MANDEL CAN SUCK IT"

SID NIESEN: Dave Mandel was a really good friend of ours pretty much from the very first minute. Before he did records he was doing *Indecision* Fanzine. He really helped us break out of our area because he started putting a lot of pictures of us in his fanzine. People would see these crazy pictures of us going nuts while we were playing and they started to try and find out who we were. We couldn't get a record deal at the time. Dave offered to put out a record as a joke initially, but we ended up doing it with him. It ended up being one of the funnest recording experiences we ever had. We didn't know what we were doing. We were in this home studio in the town we lived in. The Judge reference in the title happened because it came out sounding like such shit. [laughs] We wanted to re-record it, but we just didn't have the money. The first Judge LP sounded like shit and then they re-recorded it, so we just used their *Chung King Can Suck It* reference in our title in reference to their record. But we didn't have the money to re-record ours. [laughs]

NEW AGE SEVEN-INCH

RICK RODNEY: It was really difficult for us to play shows when we started because the area scene was supremely dominated by Orange County. I remember calling up places and asking if we could play a show. They ask, "What's your phone number?" I'd give them my area code and they'd be like, "All right, we'll get back to you." [laughs] It seemed like if you weren't from Orange County then you weren't shit. We really had to push hard to get down with anyone. But Mike Hartsfield and the guys from Outspoken really helped us out. Mike was doing New Age Records at the time. We had gone through a series of bad shows. I remember we played this show for Kent McClard in Santa Barbara opening for Undertow. Andrew had bought this booty-ass Les Paul thing, and it was the biggest piece of shit ever. It turned out it had already been broken and was glued back together, but he didn't know it. Every time he hit a chord the whole thing would go out of tune. This happened during every song and it was just godawful! We were so embarrassed. We decided to change our name from Stand as One to Strife because that show was so terrible! [laughs] A year or so passed and we started to get our shit together. We played more shows and then Hartsfield wanted to do a record and then everything from there was a blur.

SID NIESEN: We were really big Outspoken fans and they really helped us out in the early days by putting us on their bills. I became good friends with Mike Hartsfield. He was running New Age out of Big Bear. Rick and I would go on weekend trips to Big Bear and hang out with him. Mike was working with a screen-printer as his day job, and the guy would let him use all the stuff for free at night. That's why New Age had such dope merchandise back then. So, we were helping him screen some shirts and he let us make a t-shirt. Rick was on the computer designing the first Strife shirt and when we started printing them up the next day Mike puts a New Age screen-print on the sleeve. Rick and I looked at each other and said, "Why are you putting the New Age logo on there?" And Mike says, "Because I want you guys to be on the label." It was the raddest thing. I remember jumping around like little kids. At the time, New Age Records was it. We were so excited.

"ONLY THE STRONG"

ANDREW KLINE: We did our first real East Coast tour with Mouthpiece and after that Tony from Victory asked us to record a song for his *Only the Strong* compilation in 1993. We recorded "What Will Remain," and that changed things for the band. That compilation got a lot of exposure and pretty much helped us spread our name through our first tours.

SID NIESEN: Tony Brummell and I started building a phone relationship. He contacted me about the West Coast scene and wanted to find out what was going on out here. He asked us to be on the comp and it was a big deal for us. We worked so hard on that one song to make it sound good. It ended up being the song he got the most response to on that comp, and that's how we ended up on Victory.

TOURING

ANDREW KLINE: A Strife tour was the best and the worst thing in the world. [laughs] We were all super close friends. We'd get a van and not only have all five of us in it, but five of our other best friends. We'd have fun all over the country and the world. But being away from home for that long in close quarters gets tough. We'd fight like brothers. But I wouldn't exchange that experience for anything.

SID NIESEN: I'll never forget the second night of our European tour with Sick of it All. Our bus driver fell asleep at the wheel and our bus flipped three times on the Autobahn. I remember my eyes opening and staring at Andrew while we were flipping around. How all of us lived through this we had no idea. We looked at the mangled mess and we like, "How are we alive?" It was like we had angels watching us, not to be religious and weird, but it was like we had someone watching over us because we had so many crazy things happen. People like to think that Strife was so wealthy, but every tour was a struggle for us. I remember getting shit for having an extra tom on my drum set. [laughs] We were in Atlanta and four or five kids wanted to fight me because I had an extra tom. That's how ridiculous it got at a certain point.

"ONE TRUTH"

SID NIESEN: The *One Truth* time period was amazing because it was the time we were starting to break a little bit. We just got off a tour with Earth Crisis and Snapcase who had releases that just came out, and we were the only band on the tour that didn't have a new release. It was hard because we thought we were doing good every night, but we had no reaction every night. Every time we'd play "What Will Remain" the place would go bonkers because that's all people knew of us, but that was it. I remember when we got in the studio we spent six months recording that thing. This old-school metal guy produced it for us and showed us all kinds of cool studio tricks. Andrew and I spent a lot of time in the studio, and I remember we'd go in at like two o'clock one day and wouldn't come out until four o'clock the next day. There were no windows in the studio so we didn't even know how much time was passing. I loved recording that record, even though it took forever. [laughs]

ANDREW KLINE: When it came to writing *One Truth*, we had been playing together for a few years and we had an idea of what we wanted to do. We wanted a lot of sing alongs and dance parts — things that made hardcore fun. We wanted to write songs where the crowd could have huge levels of participation. Everything we loved to do at a hardcore show — grab the mic, stage dive, go crazy — there were so many parts where people could do that in our songs, which was our goal. The title *One Truth* comes from a song on the album called "Through and Through." "Through and Through" is not a song about straight edge—it's a love song, actually. [laughs] If you really examine the lyrics it's pretty obvious that it's a love song, but because it has really heavy music and screamed vocals then I guess you could make it out to be whatever you want. [laughs] We recorded our album and came up with the title by going through lyrics through the songs and we just thought *One Truth* was a cool line.

RICK RODNEY: I felt like I'd write stuff because it sounded good to me. I would never sit down and approach a song by topic. Like I'd never sit down and say, "Okay, now I've got to write our song about racism." Instead, I would approach subjects that I wanted to touch on, but I wouldn't specifically sit down and write about, say, sexism. Karl from Earth Crisis is an amazing writer and can convey his points on paper exactly how he wants them to be. For me, I was always a bit more ambiguous. After I'd write a song, the meaning would often come out of it after I sang it a couple of times. Sometimes it would even take on another meaning after a while. "Through and Through" was for my girlfriend and friends of mine at the time. It was about love, for lack of a better word, or appreciation for people you care about whether it be hardcore kids or other people you're really close to. We were an overtly straight edge band aesthetically, but lyrically we were often a bit more ambiguous, but because of our aesthetic people would just assume that all the songs were only about straight edge. Truth be told, we probably only have four or five songs specifically about straight edge in all of our records. I've always been a bit more in my head or emotional than a lot of people around me, so that always had a role in my lyrics too. I was definitely influenced by straight edge anthems, but I always felt like I was trying to give my own version.

SID NIESEN: The awesome thing about Rick was that he was such a great lyricist and he would write songs in a way that people could interpret what it meant to them. Rick wrote it as a personal song—it was definitely a love song about things that were going on with him and his girlfriend at the time. But he left the lyrics open so people could perceive it to mean whatever they wanted it to at the time. Whether "one truth" meant religion, straight edge, being in love... to Rick, it was about whatever *your* "one truth" was. We knew it was meant to be a love song, but Rick always said it was meant to be whatever you took it as. We had no idea that these words would be something that stuck with Strife for life. It kind of became a slogan at the time.

MESSAGES

RICK RODNEY: Our overall message was have a good time and don't get fucked up. This is an alternative way for myself, you, the person next to you, everyone in the crowd to come together and have a good time and hopefully get something positive out of it. I always wanted a really positive environment around us. We touched on some social issues, but first and foremost we felt like we should just try and have a good time and we'll figure out these issues together. I remember listening to bands that were really hardcore on one subject, and I remember being a bit turned off by that. I always thought of myself as a human being just like anyone else and in no way should I tell someone else how to live their life. I can explain my life through my lyrics and you could get something positive out of it, but I can't tell you how to live your life. At the time I always felt like I could be doing more or could change different things about myself so therefore I didn't feel like it was my duty or my right to tell someone else how to live their life.

CHAD PETERSON: Straight edge was a movement that gave people of our generation a place to feel accepted without the pressures of everyday society. We felt these pressures and knew other people did as well. By spreading this message it gave kids a new place to call home where they didn't have to worry about fitting in.

SID NIESEN: All those [ethical and political] issues that were big debates at the time we had within our own band. We all had different opinions amongst ourselves about all of these things. For us to take some sort of hard stance on one particular issue never made much sense since we all felt differently about these things. I just wasn't about to turn

vegan—it just wasn't for me. I understood the philosophy and why people were into it, but I didn't want to just go along with it because everyone else did. Rick was vegan almost the whole time we were a band and I was never about to do it just for music. Strife was always about doing what we wanted to do and doing it the best we could. We always welcomed everyone open-handedly whether you were straight edge or not or vegan or not. We always felt that telling people the way you do things is right and the way other people do things is wrong was never a way to bring new people into what we do. We just wanted people to have a good time with us. We never wanted to segregate ourselves from anyone.

ANDREW KLINE: We were the band that was friends with all the bands with the various messages. [laughs] We played with Christian bands, Krishna bands—we were friends with vegan bands, tough guy bands, P.C. bands. We didn't give a fuck what beliefs you had. We just wanted to have fun and let people live their lives. We were always open-minded. Although we were a straight edge band, we didn't pigeonhole ourselves into just playing with only straight edge bands. We crossed over into different genres. We'd have punk, metal, and hardcore kids into our music, which helped take us to the next level. We'd play live and pour our hearts into it. People would leave the show and tell their friends, "Man, you've gotta see this live band. It's the craziest thing I've seen." And then there would be 20 more people at our shows the next time.

BREAKING STEREOTYPES

ANDREW KLINE: If you're a straight edge band you get a built in audience, but at the same time you get a lot of flak from people who aren't straight edge. We tried to break the stereotypes of a typical straight edge band. We were very open-minded and accepting of other people. We also wouldn't try and pigeonhole ourselves by only playing with other straight edge bands. We toured with Sepultura and the Voodoo Glow Skulls and played shows with Dancehall Crashers. We tried not to limit ourselves to playing to one audience or one style of band. When you play to people who are already familiar with hardcore or straight edge then you aren't going to reach anybody new. When you play a show with Guttermouth, though, you might be opening people's eyes to music and ideas they have never seen.

RICK RODNEY: People would criticize us and say we were this straight edge band—nothing more, nothing less. I always took that to heart, because I was always heavy. I was never this shallow individual. When you're 15 or 16 or 25, people are still growing and maybe they didn't get the underlying message that was there in the lyrics. Admittedly, I didn't always know exactly what I was trying to say at first, but once it all came out of my pen and we played the songs a few times I felt like the songs had a bit more meaning to them. We were a straight edge band and popular, but we weren't popular because we were talking about a holy war or fucking people up because they weren't like us. Bands like Chokehold would call us rich kids without a message. I'd be like, "Fuck you. You don't even know us." But then again I didn't really hold that against them. I mean, I was 23 years old. I didn't know what I was doing in the world. How can I take what you're saying to heart because you don't know what you're doing either. [laughs] It would be a bummer to hear people talk shit, but that was par for the course.

CHAD PETERSON: Our message has always been very clear—unity and acceptance. This is why we always mixed up the bands we played with so much. We toured with AFI, Voodoo Glow Skulls, Far, Incubus, Rise Against, The Business, as well as shows with Pennywise, and we were always the odd band out on these bills, but as we got up there and started talking about coming together beyond the style of music we were playing and focusing more on letting it out and just enjoying yourself the crowd would always come around. The funny thing about when we would tour with these bands is they always invited us out. These are bands that were familiar with us and respected what we did in the hardcore scene and wanted their audience to experience that. I think it's an amazing thing when bigger bands are willing to expose themselves like that. It was very risky back in those days for a band like Voodoo Glow Skulls to take out this hardcore band and have them play to an all ska audience. They truly believed in what it was that we were doing and it excited us to be able to branch out to a bunch of new kids and spread the message.

RICK RODNEY: I've always lived in my head. I'm a pretty social person which helped me sing for a band. I like being around people, but I've always felt alone in a crowd. I've always been more a voyeur, which is kind of ironic being the singer of a band. [laughs] I felt like I had so much inside and I didn't know how to get it out, which is probably what drew me to singing so I could just get up there and explode once in a while. I always felt disconnected from people around me and I still feel that way. Now I'm a photographer and I shoot and do all this stuff, but I still feel that way. I spend a lot of time alone. I've got my girlfriend and a few close friends I'm tight with, but aside from that I spend a lot of time alone. I mean, the world sucks, you know? [laughs] That's always had an influence on whatever I've done. Maybe I'm just a sensitive guy. [laughs]

ANDREW KLINE: There came a time when I preferred playing with bands that were different than us. When you only play for hardcore crowds you know what to expect.

Every kid is going to know your songs and go crazy. But then we'd play with a band like Sepultura and you'd have to try twice as hard to win that crowd over. It was so fulfilling because their crowd wouldn't know us and maybe have never even seen a hardcore band, so we were exposing them to a whole new genre of music. I felt that was more rewarding—opening people's eyes and ears to something new and different.

"IN THIS DEFIANCE"

RICK RODNEY: The difference between *In This Defiance* and *One Truth* was experience. There were two years between those records and we toured the whole time between and it built our confidence up as a band. We had become more popular and we looked at these bands like Judge and Integrity and Earth Crisis that were a bit heavier, and even some metal bands like Slayer, and we realized our musical tastes had evolved to be a bit heavier. Lyrically *In this Defiance* is more in your face and aggressive, too. But I didn't want it to be too aggressive. I was more confident as a frontman and because the first record was well-received I felt a bit more confident writing more straightforward lyrics.

ANDREW KLINE: *In This Defiance* definitely had more of a metal influence and the production value is much better, too. We had just finished a tour with Sepultura so we were hugely influenced by them. We also wanted to take the heavier elements of bands like The Deftones and inject them in our music. Of course, we were also definitely still into bands like Judge and Cro-Mags, which had a metal influence. We just wanted to make the record as aggressive and in-your-face as possible. We were focused on what we wanted to do, which was to be heavier and angrier. We invited friends from bigger bands to play with us on various songs and it was a lot of fun. It helped expose us to their bands and it exposed a bunch of hardcore kids to their stuff. Igor from Sepultura helped us write and record "Overthrow" with us. Chino Moreno from The Deftones sang on "Will to Die." We had Dino from Fear Factory play on "Grey." Something that was prevalent in rap music was having special guests on songs, and that's where we got the idea from. We wanted to bridge the gap between all of these audiences and bands and incorporate it all into our sound.

SID NIESEN: *In This Defiance* was the first chance we had to spend a little money recording. We got to the point where we knew we had to put out something really good to get to the next step. We worked really hard on the record and we had so many influences because we played with so many bands on tours—Sick of it All, Sepultura, Earth Crisis. That record was where we found ourselves in that we were really playing what Strife wanted to play. *One Truth* definitely had songs we wanted to play, but I think we had our minds set on making that kind of a record instead of just writing what came more naturally. We were really lucky to have met a lot of people who wanted to be involved with it. I'll never forget the day Chino Moreno came up to do vocals on our record and Andrew and I were smiling so big that we hid behind the mixing board because we were so happy with what he was doing. [laughs] Everything just came together on that record. We were so excited to tour on that record because we were so proud of it.

"ANGERMEANS"

RICK RODNEY: The more we became a band and the more we made a living, which was kind of a joke because we were always broke and sleeping on couches, it seemed like the less fun we had. We didn't make any money from our records. We've never seen any royalties from Victory. There was once three months where they gave us about $1,000 each for three months because we were so pissed that they weren't paying us. At that time we all really wanted to be in a band and tour—we weren't about getting a job at Starbuck's or whatever. As we tried to facilitate the band as a career more and more people would get pissed. Our guarantees were about $1,200 and people would find out and protest outside about it. But it cost $1,500 a week to rent a van, and it cost $1,000 to pay for gas. The more we wanted to take it serious, the more people were turned off. Our shows might have been eight bucks as opposed to five and there would be kids standing outside protesting about it. To me, if Fugazi was playing for five bucks I was ecstatic, but I would certainly pay ten dollars to see them. We weren't trying to buy a house or fancy car by touring. We just wanted to survive so we could come home and then go on tour again. Some people didn't get that. I'd get bummed when kids would get upset at us. Everyone else was having a great time, but if there were two kids who were bummed I would get bummed. I'd be like, "Why can't we reach them? What did we do wrong for these kids?" On the flipside, because we were taking the band more seriously, it also became more like a job. There were things we were expected to do. You didn't have to do it, but if you wanted to move forward these were things you "should" do, and most of them just weren't any fun. Being on the road so much and away from our girlfriends and our regular lives took their toll after a while, too. I've always looked at my band members as my brothers. I love them to the end, but I hated them sometimes, and they hated me. By default you're stuck with each other all the time. It was like, "Rick, stop playing that stupid song on the stereo. Rick, stop being a bummer." These things wore on me and on the band. We got into a fight one time at a show in Vegas and that was it. We stopped.

SID NIESEN: I quit the band after a show in Las Vegas. It just wasn't me anymore. I don't know what happened, I just couldn't do it. It felt like everything was becoming repetitive. We played this amazing, sold out show in Vegas and I remember thinking that it just wasn't me anymore. I drove home from Vegas and we had a whole tour to do. They ended up touring with someone else for a while, but everything sort of fell apart after a while. Eventually, Andrew and I started talking again. Both of us were still straight edge and we started hearing rumors that Rick wasn't straight edge and it kind of bummed us out because Rick was always the most vocal one about straight edge during the band. After some time went by, Andrew and I started jamming together again. The stuff we were writing was just amazing. We were bolting out the most brutal metal ever and it felt so good to let the anger out. It was never intended to be a band; it was just an outlet to let our anger out. That's where the *Angermeans* title came from, and that's what we wanted to call the new project. So, we made a three song demo, but we didn't have a singer. Andrew and I both tried to sing, but it was the most ridiculous thing ever. [laughs] We tried out a couple other people and it just didn't work. No one was doing what we wanted to do. I don't know where the turning point came, but we cracked and called Rick to come out. All of a sudden we weren't mad at Rick anymore. We're always going to love Rick, so I think just enough time had passed that we all got over it. He came out and did the most amazing shit we'd ever heard him do. And that's how Angermeans started. We just wanted to do this new brutal band—we didn't want to play Strife songs. But we started playing shows and people wanted to hear Strife songs. We were almost hated for not playing Strife songs.

ANDREW KLINE: We didn't want to just play straightforward hardcore. We'd progressed as musicians and wanted to make a more metallic record. We decided to do what we wanted to do, so we did exactly that. The recording didn't come out how we wanted it, but when it came down to it we didn't have enough money to remix it. There are some really good songs on it, but I don't think it stands up to the first two records.

CHAD PETERSON: I remember writing this record thinking it was going to be the best record we have done. In the sessions leading up to this record the music was sounding great and the writing process seemed the easiest it had ever been. It just flowed. Recording this album was also the loosest I have felt in the studio. I loved this record and musically think it is one of our best. I know the other guys will argue it, but this record really showed how we progressed as musicians by this point. Not to mention I think Rick's lyrics and his thought process in writing them was amazing. But the production left a lot to be desired and unfortunately after so many years of being with Victory they would rather put out something that sounds like shit than a quality product. Victory lost what was truly important and we had to suffer because of it. I wonder how different that record would have been received if it came out how we truly wanted it to and we had the support to do that?

SID NIESEN: We got some flak for playing Strife songs again and Rick not being straight edge, but it wasn't to the level that we expected. At the time we did some A.F.I. shows and they asked us to play with them. We did some Warped Tour shows. The only flak we really got was for not playing enough Strife songs, so we started to add a few that weren't about straight edge. And then here it was all over again. For a minute, it felt right again. Then about six months or so later one of our roadies from day one got killed by a drunk driver. That's when Strife officially reappeared to do a couple of benefit shows for his family. That's when the name went from Angermeans to Strife, and then it didn't last too long. Everyone wanted to tour again except for me. I was okay with doing weekends and mini-tours here and there, but I did not want to tour. They started to get some tour offers and I was holding them back, and that's when they brought in Aaron Rossi to be the touring drummer, and then did a couple of tours with him. Now we just play together once or twice every couple of years and it's mostly just to get us all back in a room together, and it's a good feeling.

FRUSTRATIONS/WINDING DOWN

RICK RODNEY: When the band ended the first time after the Vegas show I remember I wanted total autonomy. I wanted to be out of a band. I didn't want anyone to know who I was. I moved in with this friend of mine to a place where I didn't know anybody. I didn't want to be part of the scene anymore because I had become so disheartened by it. I remember consciously telling myself that I shouldn't be a part of all this fighting at shows with kids getting beating up. All this bullshit just sucked. I was so over it. I was like, "Where did it all go? Where did the fun go? Why are these kids acting like gang members?" That's not shit I want in my life. If I wanted that in my life I would actually go join a real gang that actually means something and not just be with some suburban white kids who are pissed off and acting like hard motherfuckers. That's not to say that's what everyone was doing, but how a lot of kids were acting at the time. So, I didn't want to be a part of it anymore. I didn't want to be straight edge, so I started smoking cigarettes. I was like, "Fuck it. I don't give a shit." I lived my own life by myself for about a year before the guys started talking about doing AngerMeans. By then I missed being in a band, so I felt like giving it another shot. Maybe it was an irresponsible choice, but I didn't want to be a part of it anymore. I wanted to cut my ties, and what better way to do that then to just stop being straight edge? I felt the straight edge scene had turned into something that I didn't believe in. When I first became straight edge there was this overall consciousness about it that I agreed with, but toward the end of it I felt like I had two heads. I couldn't identify with 90 percent of what was going on. There were other factors that played into it, but the violence and overall attitudes I saw straight edge kids having played a big role.

ANDREW KLINE: A lot of kids expected bands to come to their town and play for free, but they didn't understand that you have to rent a trailer or a van to haul your equipment, pay for gas, and try to cover some of your rent while you were gone. We toured so much people were getting stressed out. We were just getting ready to do about two months with Earth Crisis and Hatebreed and Warped Tour right after that. Just having so much touring ahead of us kind of freaked us out. If it were up to me we would never have broken up. The wheels were in motion and we let it slip by. The band could have gone a lot further than it did. Then again, others in the band were ready to settle down. It gets hard being on the road for half the year and being away from home so much.

CHAD PETERSON: Strife grew into something bigger than any of us would have imagined. Becoming an adult and still doing this band meant some of us had to supplement our incomes to be on the road all of the time rather then work a job and do a tour here and there. At this point there were agents and managers telling us when we had to do things and a few of us needed to back away. I wish it didn't come to that because there would be no better job in the world than spending your life traveling with your friends. We still do a couple shows a year and I love it. I'm never happier then when I am up on that stage with my friends and singing along with the kids. There is no greater feeling then looking out and seeing a kid sing your band's lyrics and then that kid sees you looking at him while you're singing along, too.

LOOKING BACK

RICK RODNEY: The impact this time of my life had on me is not something you can get without experiencing it. You can't go to school and get it, or read about it in a book, or buy a record and magically have it. All those things can influence you, but you actually have to go out and live it. This time changed my life forever, and I'm definitely a better person today as a result of these experiences. I'm not straight edge anymore, but I'm still a huge fan of what straight edge hardcore was to me. I would advocate that approach to it to anyone I know to this day—living your life in a positive way, trying to take care of yourself and those around you, being conscious of your environment and the people who live around you regardless of race, gender, or sexual preference, or political views. You give off an energy and if your energy is positive then I think you can make a difference in the world. If you give off a negative energy and you're malicious and hurtful then that's what you're going to get back in life. You have the potential to set this ripple effect. People just need to be good to each other. The world certainly needs it more than ever.

ANDREW KLINE: We recorded some great music and I think it still stands up today. We were the first straight edge band to tour Japan. We toured Europe. We were a tiny band practicing in our friend's garage—we never planned on doing a fraction of what we actually accomplished, and I think we left a legacy behind.

CHAD PETERSON: To this day people are still coming up to us and telling us what a great influence our band had on their lives and got them through a hard time in their life. Kids

will tell us we are the band that got them in to hardcore or we are the first band they saw. It's very humbling because we were just average guys doing what we love and trying to bring people together. I am just glad for whatever reason people liked us. It's because of them that we got to get out and do what we love.

SID NIESEN: I'll never forget how many kids came up to me and said our lyrics or music really helped or changed their lives. It is those things to this day that make me realize that we actually had an impact on some people. I would like to think we had a positive impact, and to me that's the most important thing.

SELECT DISCOGRAPHY:

Mandel Can Suck it (7", Indecision, 1992)
Rodney, Kline, Peterson, Niesen

Self-titled (7", New Age, 1992)
Rodney, Kline, Peterson, Niesen

One Truth (CD/LP, Victory, 1994)
Rodney, Kline, Machin, Peterson, Niesen

In This Defiance (CD/LP, Victory, 1997)
Rodney, Kline, Turnham, Peterson, Niesen

Angermeans (CD/LP, Victory, 2001)
Rodney, Kline, Peterson, Niesen

FIGHT: THE NINETIES HARDCORE REVOLUTION IN ETHICS, POLITICS, AND S

SWING KIDS

Vocals: Justin Pearson
Guitars: Eric Allen
           Jimmy Lavelle

Bass: John Brady
Drums: Jose Palafox

There was a debate in nineties hardcore about the synthesis of art and politics. Many felt having an overt message was more important than advancing a specific sound, while others insisted that an aesthetic had to be articulated properly before advocating a philosophical or political stance. While many from this era tended to come down strongly on the issue one way or another, it is possible to see the merits of either perspective. San Diego's Swing Kids offered a nuanced blend of both takes on the debate. Their sound was peppered with abstract, politically inspired lyrics, noisy yet catchy San Diego style punk riffs reminiscent of Antioch Arrow and Heroin, and the cataclysmic roar of jazz giants like John Coltrane and Cecil Taylor. Their sound, sense of fashion (some of the members wore tight fitting clothes and dyed their hair black), and artistic ambition birthed a slew of imitators that increase with each passing year.

Formed by some ex-members of San Diego political hardcore band Struggle, Swing Kids began as a reaction to what they felt was an element of predictability in hardcore at the time. While much hardcore in the nineties brought about changes in the genre's sound, the era also had its share of bands that followed whatever trend was popular. Swing Kids founding members, guitarist Eric Allen, vocalist Justin Pearson, drummer Jose Palafox, and bassist John Brady, were among those who wanted to create something new. The combination of Palafox's jazz inspired drumming with influence from hardcore often associated with Ebullition Records and the artistically progressive punk of the aforementioned San Diego bands had turned the band's sound into a progressive yet rocking form of hardcore.

Swing Kids quickly built up a fan base in the hardcore/punk scene by word-of-mouth, reviews of their chaotic shows, and the release of a debut self-titled seven-inch (courtesy of Pearson's own Three One G Records). Remarkably, the group had primarily only played benefit shows in their native San Diego and Southern California area by the time the record came out, but news of their inspiring sets traveled fast. They eventually toured parts of the U.S. and their reputation grew.

As popular and sought after as their records were at the time, many political activists in the scene were critical of Swing Kids' more subtle approach to politics, which was a shift from their more directly outspoken precursor Struggle. These critics accused them of putting style before substance. However, the members felt a more textured and metaphorical lyrical approach would provide a more inclusive look at these same ideas. At the same time, they were never afraid to speak their minds on stage when the opportunity presented itself. Palafox, for instance, was (and still is) an immigration rights activist and he often spoke of his personal experiences on stage, as well as in columns in *HeartattaCk* and *Maximum Rock N' Roll*.

After a somewhat disastrous 1996 European tour in which several of their shows fell through, Swing Kids called it quits. Palafox decided to focus on his Latino studies program at U.C. Berkeley and later Stanford University. Pearson went on to form the grind/noise/thrash outfit, The Locust. Sticking to his passion for musical exploration, Brady moved to Chicago to pursue broader musical endeavors outside the realm of hardcore. Sadly, Allen passed away not too long after the demise of Swing Kids.

Although Swing Kids only put out two records (both of which were later combined into a discography release) and appeared on one compilation, the group's brief existence was an inspiration to many. They threw convention out the window and influenced many bands with their passionate performances and their talent for encapsulating politics, fashion, history, and emotion all at once with their captivating sound.

FROM THE ASHES OF STRUGGLE

JUSTIN PEARSON: Struggle ended because we were all getting out of high school. Our singer, Dylan, was also moving away for a while, so Jose, Eric and I just decided to do a new band. Struggle was very political, but we didn't want to start a band that was the same thing. The style also changed and I ended up singing. All the stuff I ended up singing about had political undertones. To me personal songs are political songs as you are writing about issues from your own perspective. I just didn't want to talk about hating cops or how to make abortion safe and legal as that had all been done before. I wanted to be more obscure and take it a different direction. We were in Struggle and there was a big presence in the political community within hardcore, which centered around the Ebullition Records scene. It was kind of becoming stale though as it was all the same rhetoric over and over again. We were really into bands like Nation of Ulysses and Antioch Arrow that were doing something a bit more unique with their art. Eric and I were also really into the idea of the personal being the political—basically our personal lives and how we lived them, even how we dealt with our friends, is political. We wanted to do something more personal with our sound. Unfortunately, it was part of the precursor to what people call "emo" or "screamo," which ended up becoming bastardized and shitty. If you want to talk about some prevalent issues in society then it still does need to be sung about and that is important. At the same time, we were really intrigued by other facets of art. We decided to do things differently, but we were also still just as political. We were doing tons of benefits and we really had an appeal on another level. Our music was also much better than Struggle.

JOSE PALAFOX: Justin and I did Struggle together in high school. We were all really good friends and we wanted to continue playing after Struggle ended up breaking up. At that point there were bands like Heroin and Pitchfork going on and we wanted to break away from the more metal hardcore sound we did with Struggle. Eric was a friend of our too and he had been playing in Unbroken and he also played with us at times during Struggle.

JOHN BRADY: I was the only member of Swing Kids who had not played in Struggle, but Struggle was a huge influence on me and part of the reason I joined Swing Kids. Sometime between my fifteenth and sixteenth birthdays, I had an awakening of sorts. I hate to describe it that way, but ultimately I discovered that punk rock could encompass so much more than getting wasted or high all the time, playing faster, dyeing your hair strange colors and looking tough, cool, or just simply having a nihilistic view toward life. A good friend's girlfriend opened my eyes to political bands like Crass, Conflict, Chumbawamba, and The Ex who showed me that the world extended beyond the ghetto I called home. Through their voices/words, I came to realize that I didn't have to feel threatened by, or scared of, all the things that confused me: black, white, Mexican, and Asian immigrant conflicts in my neighborhood; living on a family income of less than $12,000 a year; living with a single mother who was in and out of mental hospitals leaving my siblings and I with abusive boyfriends; the uncertainty of my future; and the fact that I had very few friends due to the fact that I had moved so much in the decade before that time. The aforementioned bands gave me an ideology, but they were so far away geographically. As a result of the geospatial distance, Struggle became part of my local support network for the new ideas I had come upon. Unlike the bands I discovered from across the Atlantic, they were guys who were from the neighborhood or at least close enough that I could hang out with them regularly. While the guys in Struggle were not immediately great friends of mine, they came to be so as my political awareness and involvement in hardcore developed. In many ways, I looked up to Justin, Eric, and Jose (and of course, Dylan and Toby). When the three of them went on to form Swing Kids after the demise of Struggle and asked me to play, I was ecstatic.

MOTIVATIONS

JUSTIN PEARSON: There were already so many bands discussing the same old politics, so we just didn't want to talk about the same old things anymore. I remember there was a big issue with the readers of *HeartattaCk* about Antioch Arrow and them supposedly not being political enough. Their music was more of an attempt at art than trying to convey some sort of message. I remember reading articles slamming them and saying, "Oh, they're just all about their image." At the same time I think people were just tired of the same old shit that wasn't going in any new directions. For the most part in hardcore it was all these privileged white kids who were just complaining about everything. We had a different perspective because all of us grew up in the ghettos or white trash areas. We'd also always been really politically active for several years and we worked with different organizations like Anti-Racist-Action and we were going to protests and getting involved. A lot of these other people would just sit around and complain but they wouldn't do anything about it. A band like Nation of Ulysses wasn't necessarily an overtly activist band, yet they were bringing up important issues and it was innovative and creative. The Ebullition crowd was so uptight and rigid about things—apparently you had to have a neck beard and cut-off camouflage shorts to be accepted. We were just like, "Forget that, if we want wear pants that fit us and get a haircut then what's so wrong with that?" We had just gotten out of high school but I felt like we were still in it due to these sorts of debates. To this day I think Kent McClard is an awesome guy and he's done a lot of really cool stuff for music and art, but a lot of people from that Ebullition scene were just so hung up on these style points and things. A lot of the criticism we got from the scene revolved around us supposedly "changing" and trying to look different. The only thing I did was get a haircut and that for some reason was an issue with people. [laughs] It wasn't like my hairstyle made me into someone who didn't give a shit. I was still a poor punk rock kid and still creating art. I suppose this reaction to us pissed us off and that was reflected in the way our sound developed.

JOSE PALAFOX: We all had similar political ideas and we wanted to address these issues in our music and at shows. There was a lot of anti-immigration sentiment in San Diego at that time and there were also racist skinheads coming to the shows and messing with kids. We wanted to do something different musically but continuing what we had done politically in Struggle, but in a slightly different way.

JOHN BRADY: By the time I joined Swing Kids, a lot of the things that had been major influences for me musically speaking had started to become a bit stale. I was studying sociology in college, and while the ideas I had come upon a few years earlier formed the basis of a lot of my opinions, I discovered that there was a lot more depth to those ideas than most hardcore or punk songs could convey. Like Justin said, I guess we didn't need to hear or repeat the same old chants against the police and the government and so on. At the time, we were amidst Clinton's presidency, and it seemed to me that so many people had forgotten that things were still fucked up in the world. I felt that bands like Swing Kids were the perfect antidote for the fantasyland that people were living in.

NAMESAKE

JUSTIN PEARSON: The film came out a couple years before we started. The name did come from the film but it wasn't necessarily directly about it per se, as opposed to some of the ideas that came up in it. I guess I identified with the film in that hardcore potentially represented the same thing as jazz or swing did in that time period presented in the film. I wouldn't want to compare our situation in punk with what real swing kids were doing or what revolutionaries in Uganda are doing in terms of fighting oppression, but at the same time the reason many countries are having to rebel is because of the impact of what western countries like America have done or are doing. It's like the whole argument of, "America is the best country in the world. If you don't like it then leave!" It's like, okay I'll leave and go to another country and still be affected greatly by America and how they treat everyone else. We do have it better than the swing kids in Nazi Germany who were fighting back, but at the same time we could relate to the message of the film.

JOSE PALAFOX: The movie was kind of cheesy, but it did show the importance of challenging everything that is screwed up in society. As individuals we want to change the structure of institutional power and domination. Sometimes as musicians and artists we have a way of raising consciousness that is equally as powerful as any sort of political revolution. Sometimes people on the left just want to take over the nation state but ideology and ideas are equally important. Having some kind of counter hegemony is important as well.

TESTING SONIC WATERS

JUSTIN PEARSON: We were trying to avoid playing metal hardcore. There were all these bands like Unbroken and Undertow and Strife who were already doing that. We still wanted to play intense music, but we wanted to be a bit more artistic about it than we had been in the past. When we first started we didn't know what we wanted to do, but it ended up coming out in this weird way when we started working on the songs that ended up being on the first seven-inch. Eric was really into Drive Like Jehu and Rocket from the Crypt, which you can also notice on the last Unbroken records. I didn't think we were all that original, but at the same time it was something different.

JOHN BRADY: There were a lot of influences going on at the start, and also throughout Swing Kids' development. Eric obviously came from Unbroken, and was influenced by hardcore bands that identified with straight edge. I remember that at the onset, he very much wanted to show those roots in what we were doing. Chain of Strength was a particularly strong influence at the beginning, but that didn't last very long. Jose is a jazz drummer, and brought that element into the fold. Justin has always been much more influenced by American punk bands than I ever was. Obviously other San Diego bands had an influence on our sound, but I think it went a lot further than that. We had pigeon-holed ourselves personally by punk and hardcore definitions for a long while before the band formed, and it seemed that as Swing Kids developed, we all grew beyond that and discovered that jazz and other types of music could convey meanings just as well, and help us translate our thoughts into something meaningful.

JUSTIN PEARSON: There [were] the obvious musical references like Drive Like Jehu, Joy Division, Shellac, and even artists like Cecil Taylor, but I think our true influences came from social politics, geographical location, economic and cultural back grounds, and family life. Another thing that steered us in the direction we went was the fact that we all wanted to shed the musical style that we all were part of before Swing Kids. So many people started doing that crap and doing second rate jobs, so we wanted out of there, and we took a route that I think led some of us to even more creative and interesting places. That was an important part for us as a band, where Swing Kids led us, and not just musically either.

AVANT-GARDE AMBITIONS

JUSTIN PEARSON: We played the Detroit Fest and a lot of the bands fit into these safe genres and there were all these workshops where everyone was just sitting around complaining and not getting up and doing anything. No one outside of Southern California had seen bands like us or Antioch Arrow play. We had arranged to get a bunch of horn players and I remember when we played it was so intense and it felt so much better than what we were doing with Struggle. There was so much more urgency, and it was more personal. People just seemed to connect with the intensity of the art and they took what they wanted from it, which was really cool.

JOHN BRADY: Well, I don't know that we really had ambitions to break new ground, and certainly don't think that we ever did. However, I think that we did a really good job of synthesizing something out of all the things that were important to us at the time, and kept it at least somewhat interesting.

JAZZ INFLUENCE

JOSE PALAFOX: I've been playing drums since I was about 13. I started playing in high school with big bands and jazz bands so that's where some of my playing roots are. All of us were really interested in learning about the free jazz movement and the chaos that surrounded it.

JUSTIN PEARSON: All of us were into jazz. What really got me into it was hearing about the social and political struggles that the musicians had to go through—being black and playing shows for all these white people and entertaining them but having to walk in and out the back door due to the separate but equal laws. We were all really big fans of swing because it had this upbeat feel to it, but we were also into modern stuff and people like John Thorne working with Napalm Death. We were just energized by a lot of different styles of art.

JOSE PALAFOX: I saw some bands combining jazz with hardcore or punk but it's like they would come up with a "punk" part and then force a "swing" part or something to fit next to it. My approach was not so much the style of playing swing but the whole cosmology and way of interpreting. We threw that quote of Cecil Taylor in the record that basically was discussing those critics who don't see him as a jazz musician and he replied back to them that his music was a reflection and reproduction of many different things taking place in society. If you look at what he was doing in terms of banging on a piano or getting up in the middle of a song and screaming his head off then you can get a sense of what he was trying to reproduce—a feeling and a natural outgrowth of what you're exposed to around you.

JOHN BRADY: I have to admit, I am not, nor have I ever been a huge fan of jazz. The whole resurgence in swing dancing in the mid to late-nineties was more annoying to me than anything else. However, I love the ideas of jazz, the background and what the music means to its audience and to the musicians who play it. With the exception of a few greats I have listened to (John Coltrane, Cecil Taylor, Albert Ayler), I certainly have been more influenced by other forms of experimental music.

POLITICS

JOSE PALAFOX: San Diego is this city where you have one of the poorest cities on the other side of the Mexican border about fifteen minutes away from a very wealthy city. We wanted people to be aware of the issues from the other side of the border. It was especially important to me because I was undocumented myself.

JUSTIN PEARSON: "Disease" was the first song I wrote and it was obviously political. I had been thinking about how people treat each other on a social and commercial level and how we are conditioned to be greedy and not think about personal feelings of others. I grew up with alcoholic parents and my father was murdered right in front of my house when I was a kid. We all have issues and we're trying to change things socially but we have all these personal obstacles we have to overcome. It was more of a dark, emotional side of our lives. I was just trying to be sincere and say, "This is our lives." It was also sort of a grim time in history—it was just after the first Gulf War and a lot of us weren't so sure about the future. Things felt sort of grim. It was a pretty intense time to grow up in and discover your place in life.

CHEMISTRY

JOSE PALAFOX: Everyone had input, but Eric came up with most of the guitar riffs. We all collaborated on the rhythms and everything else, though. We all knew each other pretty well and we knew each other's interests. Collectively, we just applied what we liked and what we knew and tried to come up with something unique.

JUSTIN PEARSON: It was hard to play with Jose because he was truly a jazz drummer and he'd change things up all the time. He'd get so wrapped up into the music and you'd have to really pay attention to where he was going. There were times where he'd split during the middle of a song — just get up and run away from his drums — and it would just be John Brady playing his bass line for a couple of minutes and then Jose would come back and finish the song. We'd be like, "What the hell was that about?" [laughs] Jose would get lost in the music and it was kind of a performance. You have to have chemistry to feel music like that and for whatever reason we just clicked.

JOHN BRADY: Justin, Jose and Eric are/were some of the most intelligent and caring people I have known, and people who feel strongly about injustices they see going on in the world often deal with internal strife. Many people sink into drugs, drink or depression to deal with the conflicts they come up against. Others find creative outlets with which to get their frustrations out. Music is an incredible outlet for personal conflict, and I think each of us used Swing Kids as a means to come to terms with our issues. If our music seems well thought out, I imagine it is because we are complicated people, and were looking for a way to articulate our feelings on the things that affected us at the time.

JOSE PALAFOX: I remember being overly intense. I hate to use that word but the music would get so intense at the time. Sometimes I just needed time out and needed to get away for a minute. [laughs] It was the power of getting into the songs as well as the emotions the songs brought up. In jazz, sometimes not playing is also a way of playing. The other guys would just keep going and it usually worked out.

JUSTIN PEARSON: Eric was so creative and he came up with amazing parts. He and I were really on the same page artistically, which made it easy to work with him. He was one of the most creative people I've ever worked with.

JOHN BRADY: What is really interesting is that very few people who like Swing Kids ever had the opportunity to see us live. I am convinced that if they had, we wouldn't have so many people care about the band today! Yes, the intensity mentioned by Jose and Justin was there, and I suppose that is a pretty powerful thing, but on the whole we were sloppy as all hell and with only a few exceptions never really played all that well live. I think that the main reason for the intensity was that Swing Kids, more than any other thing going on in our lives at the time, provided each of us with a release for all of our frustrations and disappointments. It is really tough to get four people together in a tight setting, develop an outlet such as the one that the band provided, and not have a tight bond come out of it.

CRITICISM

JUSTIN PEARSON: No one said anything about the border issues that Jose wrote about that we put in our record, which was super informative and it was very personal and listed people's names who were murdered by the U.S. Border Patrol. No one said shit about that which proves the hardcore community can often be so narrow minded. It's funny because we would sit there and think, "These critical people are the same folks who are going to get some shitty job and go work in a cubicle and shit out their 2.5 kids and die an unhappy life." [laughs]

JOSE PALAFOX: I think we learned that we have shit we're dealing with, too. The system isn't just out there; the system is us, too. It's a physical and mental thing. We didn't want to come off preaching because we wanted to discuss how all of us in this scene together could recognize our collective privilege and voice our concerns and emotions. We didn't back down about politics but we just wanted to try a different approach.

JOHN BRADY: I think that I was better able to ignore most of the criticism that came our way than the other three guys in the band. They all played in Struggle and I didn't, and I never felt like I had to live up to the expectations people had of what an ex-Struggle band should be. If anyone wants to blame me for the fact that we were less of an overtly political band than Struggle, go ahead. I know, however, what organizations we played benefits for, I know what personal actions we took that reflected our views, and I don't really care what anyone else thinks about those things. The only criticism that I remember feeling particularly stung by at the time was that stemming from divisions within the San Diego scene. That was so long ago though, and isn't anything I really care about now. As far as Swing Kids being consumed with a particular style, I don't think we were unique in that respect. Every group trying to find their voice outside of the mainstream attempts to develop an identity with which to recognize one another. Each sub-genre of youth culture has their own identity and style, including those who were particularly critical of Swing Kids and the people we associated with.

EUROPEAN TOUR

JUSTIN PEARSON: We did a final tour of Europe, which was a huge disaster. The booking agent had about two weeks of the tour fall through. In retrospect it was cool because we did get out there and play and people did see us, but it was pretty hairy for a while during the time we were there. I suppose none of us knew what the hell was going on in life. We were all loose cannons in so many ways. Maybe that is part of the reason why we were a band for such a short amount of time. I just remember wanting to get through each show as fast as we could. It was so awkward, in so many ways. Not until the end did it come together. [It wasn't until] we did a chunk of shows with Jimmy Lavelle playing second guitar, that we [had] more power, musically, sonically, or whatever. After we got back, Jose had a break from school and we ended up doing a couple of last shows. Things went downhill for Eric pretty fast after the band, but I'm glad we got to share those last shows with him.

JOSE PALAFOX: Europe was intense. [laughs] We arrived in England and no one was there to pick us up and it was our first time outside the country, so it was kind of an intense experience. Some people in Europe had a misconception about what we were trying to do with jazz. Many thought we were a punk band just trying to spice up our sound with swing or something, which wasn't our approach at all. [laughs]

JOHN BRADY: Yeah, the tour was kind of fucked up. I don't really feel like I need to go into the details behind why it got screwed up. It happened a long while ago, and it wouldn't be fair to drag someone's name through the mud over it. Admittedly, I too have to take some of the blame for it. What was really important about the tour was that we actually got to make the trip, and we met some really great people. Swing Kids was four guys who came from really poor and broken families in some of the worst neighborhoods of San Diego. Most people who grew up the way we did never get an opportunity to see how people live their lives in other parts of the world. I think we all learned a lot about ourselves and about our place in the world, and that far outweighs the fact that it was disastrous in other ways.

EMOTIONAL TURBULENCE/LESSONS LEARNED

JOHN BRADY: Aside from half of the shows falling through, and the fact that we had to rely on the kindness of the new friends that we had made, I imagine that a lot of it was simply where we were at in our lives. Like Justin said, we were in our early twenties, and were trying to find our places in the world. It is incredibly difficult to reconcile what one feels is the correct way to live, versus what is expected of someone coming out of his or her teens. Getting married and having kids, taking on debt, being a good consumer by accumulating worthless crap and doing all the things that are viewed as a part of being a normal American adult are things that I have questioned before and since that time. I am thankful today that I came from a very poor background, and was able to retain a humble value system and recognition of my basic needs. I know that that is largely because of my involvement in hardcore. I have found that many people who grew up in communities similar to the one I am from, try to mask their roots, and if they become "successful" they often become quite conservative. Coming to terms with rejecting many of the common values found in this country, can be extremely isolating when you are young. On a completely different note, I suppose the tour was particularly rough for me while we were in France because I got really sick and had to go to the hospital. I was scared. None of the doctors spoke English, and I don't speak French. I am sure that the experience framed a lot of my general mood for the rest of the tour.

PARTING WAYS

JUSTIN PEARSON: The band didn't last very long because Jose moved and we just couldn't replace him. At that time many of the bands that were out were only doing it for a couple of years and then moving along. Swing Kids was only really around for about two years. Jose moved away for a while for college and now he's a professor at Stanford so he went on to better things. He came back and we did a little bit more, but we couldn't do it much more with him being so far away so we decided to move on.

JOHN BRADY: I certainly would have liked it if Swing Kids had lasted a bit longer. We were still trying to carry things on while Jose was away at school, playing together while he was on break and so forth. We all seemed to have a lot of ideas that could have panned out into something even better than the limited catalog that we ultimately produced, but the chemistry we had with each other seemed to dissipate after being apart from each other. Eric, Justin, and I all lived together, but without Jose, Swing Kids was done.

ERIC'S LEGACY

JUSTIN PEARSON: I don't really like to talk about Eric like this in a public form; however, I'll answer as I feel it's important to Eric that this history pertaining to his music exists. His death was not that soon after Swing Kids stopped playing, but after that time when we were not playing anymore, Eric seemed to resort to drug and alcohol abuse to the point where he was having issues with his personal life, as well as his job and other outlets. So when Eric took his life, it did come as a surprise and hurt so many people, but looking back at this situation, it made sense. But I'd like to center on the positive aspects here. One thing that I have noticed is that Eric lives on in me. I'm sure he lives on in so many people, but for me, I can feel his influence in music I write, things I think about, and so on. He was one of my best friends, and even though he is gone physically, I will always have him with me.

HIGH/LOW POINTS

JUSTIN PEARSON: I'm not sure what the high and low points were to be honest. Being in that band in retrospect was fun. I love those guys and Eric in specific, but for the most part, it was short lived and pretty grim. Either we were ahead of our time or people didn't like us. There were some great shows, and a lot of duds. Tour sucked for the most part, just one disaster after another, but there were tons of stories… anything from us crossing into Canada and getting in a fight in the van and Jose setting the inside of a borrowed van that we were in on fire, or arriving in London to start a European tour with nobody to pick us up, and then after doing the U.K. leg of the tour being sent to France and finding out that there was no tour booked, pre Internet, of course. Most of the shows were crummy or we were the odd band out. Some shows that stand out are ones with awesome bands like T Tari, Man is the Bastard, and Angel Hair. We met and saw great bands in that era, which was an awesome thing in itself. The infamous IEPER Fest that we played was great. That show for us had "magic" or whatever you call that stuff. It was so brutal. We became one with the audience and I feel that as a band and as individuals in that band, we transformed. Man, we were all a mess back then, just a total wreck. I suppose some of us are still.

JOHN BRADY: Michigan Fest and touring with Still Life was a lot of fun. I met a number of people on that trip who are still friends of mine today. I already mentioned that the shows were sloppy, but intense. I don't know what else I can add that hasn't already been said. Two funny things that happened do stand out in my mind though; First, Jose somehow ripped the side door of Still Life's van outside of Gilman Street, and second, I will never forget the look on Jose's face after he was fucked with when coming back into England from Belgium. I suppose the second one isn't so funny, but it was interesting to see how a Mexican national can travel all the way to Europe, and still have issues with immigration officers.

FINAL THOUGHTS/IMPACT OF BAND ON MEMBER'S LIVES

JUSTIN PEARSON: It was a turning point in our lives and it also coincided with a lot of things that were happening socially and politically. Maybe it was just the fact that we were in our early twenties and we were growing up and trying to figure ourselves out, but it just seemed like such a crazy and interesting time. I think Swing Kids started to fit into its own skin at the time we broke up, which was somewhat part of the band's beauty, if we actually had any.

JOSE PALAFOX: Artists reflect what is going on society but they also have the responsibility to re-imagine the world in a different way. I think there was so much stuff going on in the world in the early nineties, and I can only speak from my experience but I just got my citizenship papers a few years ago. I originally came here undocumented. All of us in the band dealt with a lot of different things whether it be society, school, parents or whatever, but we tried to connect it to larger things that were taking place in the world.

JOHN BRADY: Two things come to mind; don't take your inter-personal relationships for granted, and no matter how much I think I may have things figured out, I really don't. There truly are injustices in the world, and I applaud those who dedicate themselves to fighting those injustices. However, things are not always so black and white, and everyone is fucked up in their own way.

JUSTIN PEARSON: What I learned about myself [through Swing Kids] in a nutshell was that I'm a mess on so many levels. I try to avoid some bullshit tag like "emo," but out of all honestly, I'm not mentally stable for the most part. I have issues and I think a lot of that stems from my childhood as well as the culture I grew up in. But when I was in Swing Kids, maybe it was being in the band, or maybe it was just my age and time of change, but I was so confused about life. Nothing made sense and nothing seemed correct. I suppose I still feel this way, but I'm older and more set in my ways. Nonetheless, it was an odd time for us all; I know this for a fact. As far as how it impacted my life, I suppose I could just say that it was some sort of support system, be it the members of the band or the fact that we had some sort of artistic outlet and the ability to do something that we felt was important to us. I'm not sure I miss anything about the band to be honest. It served its purpose. It was short lived like some things should be and it is something that we can be somewhat proud of. I suppose I miss just being a vocalist in a band.

SELECT DISCOGRAPHY:

Self-titled (7", Kidney Room, Repress on Three-One-G, 1996)
    Pearson, Allen, Brady, Palafox

Split 10" with Spanakorzo (10", Three-One-G, 1997)
    Pearson, Allen, Brady, Palafox

Discography (CD, Three-One G)

TEXAS IS THE REASON

Vocals/Guitars: Garrett Klahn   Bass: Scott Winegard
Guitars: Norman Brannon   Drums: Chris Daly

New York's Texas Is The Reason formed when three friends and hardcore veterans — Norman Brannon (Fountainhead, Shelter, Ressurection), Chris Daly (108, Ressurection), and Scott Winegard (Fountainhead) — wanted to take on different musical challenges. Although they all grew up listening to and playing hardcore, they wanted to incorporate other musical influences. They enlisted with former Copper bassist Garrett Klahn to handle vocals for their new band which is when their signature sound — a blend of Brit-Pop, post-hardcore, and melodic rock — took shape.

They captured the scene's attention with their self-titled debut EP on Revelation Records in 1995. Some loved the band's emotional post-hardcore-meets-rock sound, while others felt that because they were among the bands that were playing a less abrasive form of music they were trying to leave the hardcore scene behind. But the fact that they elicited strong reactions one way or the other was a testament to the power of their music. The members felt that hardcore was about maintaining integrity and they didn't really care so much about where their music fit genre-wise, regardless of how reviewers and others described them.

Texas' next release was a split seven-inch with Pennsylvania's Samuel. At this point, the band began a period of constant touring and also started writing what would be their only full-length record. The album, *Do You Know Who You Are?*, found Texas Is The Reason embracing all of their non-hardcore/punk influences, while also moderating their tempos and time signatures slightly. The members felt it was a more mature and personal record on both musical and lyrical fronts and they were excited with the results.

Even before the album was released there were several major labels interested in signing the band. In the post-Nirvana and Green Day world of that time, the majors were looking for the "next big thing." Members of the band, who lived in New York and had friends at both independent and major labels, were familiar with the industry and skeptical of most of the attention. They agreed to meet with certain people they respected.

In the wake of *Do You Know...* major interest in the band intensified as Texas continued to be wined and dined by several of the biggest labels. The situation stressed the band, but the members enjoyed the experience for what it was, allowing the labels' employees to buy them dinner and put them up in lavish hotels. But at some point, the game — which is how the band saw the whole situation — grew tiresome. As the group was in talks to sign a seven-figure deal with Capitol after what would have been their second full-length for Revelation to fulfill their contractual obligations, the friendship among the members — the impetus for the band in the first place — became strained. Hoping to avoid any permanent damage to their relationships with each other, they ended the band, but not before releasing a final split seven-inch with The Promise Ring on Jade Tree Records.

Texas Is The Reason created their own unique path alongside their nineties brethren and as a result are viewed by many as one of the most intriguing post-hardcore bands of the nineties. Their music has gone on to influence much of the post-hardcore and emo sound that has become more popular in the years since the band ended. Although the members have all gone in different directions with their lives, their memories of what they created in just two years with Texas proved powerful enough for them to get back together for two nights of shows in New York City in 2006. There were, and still are, differences among the members, but they still smile when one asks a question about their story, their records, and their seemingly endless days on the road. Though they don't want to dwell on the past, they can't help but be proud of what they accomplished.

DESIRE TO DO SOMETHING DIFFERENT

NORMAN BRANNON: Musically speaking, hardcore was the furthest thing from my mind by the time 1991 rolled around. Even though I had joined Ressurection and 108, and Shelter later on, I played with them because they were my friends and I liked what they did. I enjoyed it, but as far as my own musical statement went, I knew hardcore wouldn't be the direction I would ultimately remain. I played in Fountainhead in 1990 and we were all into doing something different even way back then. If you listen to the Fountainhead record it's essentially a post-hardcore record. By the time 1993 rolled around, Shelter and 108 were on tour together — Chris Daly was in 108 and I was in Shelter. We both felt this desire to do something different. The bands we were playing in at the time didn't sound like anything we were listening to. So, we wanted to try to make some different kind of music together. After Shelter petered out in my life and I started working more on *Anti-Matter*, I was able to work from home, and so I was able to play my guitar a lot and figure out what I wanted to play. In late 1994, the first idea of Texas started to solidify. Scott from Fountainhead came on board, so Chris, Scott, and myself decided we wanted to make a band. We didn't know what it was going to sound like yet, but we knew it wouldn't be hardcore. We just needed to find a singer, which was incredibly difficult. Knowing we didn't want to play hardcore, finding a singer who could actually sing but who also came from the scene and understood the ethics and idealism we already had and wouldn't embarrass us on stage was really hard. [laughs]

CHRIS DALY: Norman and I were on tour with Shelter and 108, respectively, and we were tired of playing in confrontational bands with a heavy message. We wanted to unashamedly "rock out" and the time seemed right to do so. Scott was there from the get go, and Garrett came aboard after fate would land him in New York City.

SCOTT WINEGARD: We were definitely hardcore kids and we met through the scene. But we were getting into different music and wanted to play what we liked rather than do what everyone else was doing. We heard Quicksand, Sunny Day Real Estate, and Shudder to Think and we wanted to be more like those bands in their sense of dynamic songwriting, but at the same time we wanted stay in the world of hardcore and with our friends, most of whom were from the scene. Norman and I had played together in the past in Fountainhead, so we were on the same page in terms of where we wanted to go musically. And when we saw Chris play drums we knew he'd be amazing to play with. When it all happened that we were all able to play together we just rolled with it.

GETTING GARRETT IN THE BAND

NORMAN BRANNON: It didn't solidify until Garrett got kicked out of Copper. Copper was a band on Equal Vision Records. At the time I lived at the Equal Vision Records loft, so when Garrett was kicked out of Copper I overheard Steve Reddy on the phone in the next room freaking out and saying, "What do you mean you kicked him out?!" [laughs] I had known Garrett a little bit from the Buffalo hardcore scene. So, when I knew Steve was talking to Garrett I whispered to Steve if I could talk to him when they were done. I got on the phone and told him how terrible it was that they kicked him out and said that he should just leave Buffalo. [laughs] Before long I asked him if he wanted to try the band we wanted to do.

SCOTT WINEGARD: We went to see Into Another, Quicksand, and Seaweed at C.M.J., and Snapcase was in town and Garrett was with them. I met him several years back at a Dayton Hardcore Fest and he seemed like a cool guy. Meeting up with him again was cool and I felt like I got to know him a little better, and we all seemed to have similar ideas about the music we wanted to make. He was like, "Man, I wish I could join your band."

[laughs] Not too much time passed and Norm called me one night and said Garrett got kicked out of Copper. So, here was an opportunity presenting itself to give him a shot.

GARRETT KLAHN: Before the band started I was still living in upstate New York and putting on hardcore shows with my friends, which we had been doing since I was 17. My mother was never home so my house turned into the punk rock hotel. [laughs] We did all kinds of shows there, one of which Endpoint and Ressurection played, who Chris and Norm were playing with at the time. So, that's when I first met them. We stayed in touch and I eventually went on tour with Endpoint for two weeks. The whole time I had a girlfriend in Baltimore, so after the Endpoint tour I was headed to go see her and I had a two hour layover in Manhattan on the way, so Norm picked me up at the train station and he told

me they'd been jamming and asked if I was interested in playing with them. I liked the idea, but I had to catch my train, so we decided to keep talking about the possibility later. So I went to Baltimore and my girlfriend said she didn't want to see me anymore, so I called Norm and came back to Manhattan and hung out with them for a while. We hung out and practiced and things just clicked. It was like someone had some sort of greater plan in mind the way everything fell into place. I'm still friends with that girl and she jokes and says she's the reason Texas started. [laughs]

SMOOTH BEGINNINGS

NORMAN BRANNON: We didn't practice that often because it was so hard for us to get together when you are broke and living in Manhattan. We'd go to Daly's house in New Jersey every Saturday and have these marathon writing sessions. Everything with that band was both easy and difficult. The easiness of a lot of the things made the difficulties bearable.

GARRETT KLAHN: Things came together with the band really fast. We definitely did the grind around New York. We played everywhere and there were so many places to play back then. But all the songwriting happened on weekends. We never played during the week. We didn't have enough money to rent rooms plus Chris was living in New Jersey. So we'd all work during the week and a friend of ours had a car and we'd all go out to Chris's house and we'd hang out, have barbecues, and practice.

SCOTT WINEGARD: Norm and I had a few riffs and song skeletons we played with Chris once or twice before Garrett. But once Garrett joined, one of us would come up with an idea and Chris would roll out a drum beat idea and it would just flow together. We never had issues putting stuff together. We never had major discussions over how to cram one part into another; it seemed to gel and we were really excited with what was coming together.

NON-IDEOLOGICAL STANCE

NORMAN BRANNON: The first practice we ever did the music just came out immediately. We never had some sort of philosophical discussion about it. The only thing in the back of our minds was we wanted to rebel from this theology gone awry movement in the hardcore scene. Obviously we were all coming from that — Shelter and 108 being two extremely theological bands. At the time there were tons of other bands too that were blasting their paradigms down people's throats and that brought a whole new line to the whole thing. We were reacting not only to what was happening in the scene but what had happened in our past. We wanted to be political on an active level as opposed to a verbal level.

GARRETT KLAHN: I didn't give a shit about the debates of the time. [laughs] At first, because Norm was so heavily involved in the ethical aspects of hardcore, we automatically got mistaken for a mixture of that stuff. To me, it was just fun to play music and we enjoyed each other's company. Norm did all the interviews and answered all those burning questions the kids had. I guess it just didn't matter to me that much.

INFLUENCES/SOUND

NORMAN BRANNON: There were two types of music we could all agree on in terms of what we enjoyed listening to such as the British music happening at the time like Blur and The Verve. There was also everything from D.C. like Jawbox, Fugazi, and Shudder

to Think. On a musical level those were the things that informed what we were doing, which were all being filtered through growing up as hardcore kids.

SCOTT WINEGARD: I really loved My Bloody Valentine and Jawbox. Quicksand was also definitely a major inspiration too as here were people from the hardcore scene doing this amazing new sound that still had elements of hardcore. I was also really into Girls Against Boys. I think the British era of Texas was more attitude than songs. [laughs] We'd already written the songs a while before and just before *Do You Know...* we had just started listening to Oasis. So, those British influences were there, but they weren't quite as apparent in our sound. But listening to bands like Seem and Seaweed, more melodic, indie bands was a major influence.

CHRIS DALY: Maybe I'm delusional, but, live, I feel Texas was just as loud and heavy as any other bands that we did. It just wasn't angry sounding. It was a natural progression to that sound, and without a doubt Texas is the band that will always hold the biggest place in my heart — no disrespect to anything else I was involved in.

GARRETT KLAHN: Back then I guess we all listened to a variety of stuff. I don't know how much of a role it played in us writing the songs. We only had about 14 songs total! [laughs] There wasn't a big catalog of material and we weren't that prolific. As far as what I was listening to, I was really into a lot of The Beatles and was really into The Verve, as well. But it's not like we did our psychedelic record and our blues record because the band wasn't meant to last that long, which I felt from the start. All those songs were really written around the same time. The only real success we had was touring. That's all we did, which was good and bad. We did so many cool "firsts" together. I had never been west of Ohio, so the first time I hit the West Coast was with [Texas Is The Reason]. At the same time, we didn't really have time to write any new songs. It was a busy two years with not a lot of downtime. It was doomed from the start, though. [laughs] It never felt like a long term, cemented kind of thing to me. I always had the feeling that the band wouldn't be together forever. I felt like we were of that time and I don't think we could have topped ourselves, whatever people think that "top" is. It happened so fast that I hardly remember any of it.

NAME OF THE BAND

SCOTT WINEGARD: A lot of people who were die-hard hardcore fans and heard the name of our band were like, "Fuck them! They took the name of a Misfits song and are playing music that sounds like that?" [laughs] But we didn't care. We were finally doing something we really wanted to do and something about the name just fit.

NORMAN BRANNON: None of us really cared about the Misfits that much; we just thought it was a cool name. It actually came from a conversation with one of the guys from The Van Pelt. One night Scott and Garrett were hanging out with these guys and we were trying to come up with a name. We had a show coming up and we were desperate, so they asked the guys in The Van Pelt what their name would have been if it wasn't the one they chose. They said it was between The Van Pelt and Texas Is The Reason. So, I got a phone call and they told me the name and I said, "I hate it." [laughs] They told me what it was and I hated it even more. [laughs] But it started growing on me. The final factor in it was I was going to talk to a couple of old-school hardcore people and tell them that's the name we were thinking of and see if they made a direct connection, because I didn't want to be a band that made everybody think of The Misfits. I remember asking Mark Ryan from Supertouch, who had been going to shows since 1981 and he was from New Jersey so if anyone knew The Misfits it would be him. So, I ran the name by him and he said it was pretty weird, but he didn't make an immediate connection. So, it was just enough out of the context to be its own thing. Once I realized that the name stuck.

MOTIVATIONS

NORMAN BRANNON: With Texas I wanted to be as apolitical as possible. I didn't want us to side up with any of these factions. When people called us a post-hardcore band I didn't mind it so much because we were from the scene, but we were doing something else.

REV EP

NORMAN BRANNON: I remember "If it's Here…" being one of the most exciting things about our first practice because it just came out of nowhere. I just started playing it and everyone started playing along and it was almost as if it had already been written and we were covering it. It just came together so ridiculously easy, and it was one of the solidifying moments of the beginning of that band. Even the lyrics are a patchwork of different things. There was a line that says "We hate you all and that's for free" and that comes from a flyer we saw in Chris Daly's basement for a show in New Jersey. That was one of the first things Garrett saw at our practice so that was one of the first things he sang and it just stuck. If that type of thing doesn't happen to your band early on then you're pretty much a sinking ship. We had written those three songs pretty fast and as soon as we had decent boom-box versions of them we decided to demo them. We knew Brian McTernan for a while and we heard he was recording stuff in his house in Massachusetts. We had no money and he was into doing it, so it just came together. We did the entire recording of those three songs in one weekend and we paid $100 for it. That demo was what first started going around. Pretty much everyone we played it for on an indie level thought it was good enough to release as a seven-inch. We thought it was just a demo, but it became our first record and I'm glad it did. It definitely has a certain raw, youthful, enthusiastic energy to it that wouldn't have been there had we re-recorded it. When we wrote it we joked that we didn't want to be a hardcore band but we had to have at least one song where people could mosh. Not really so people could mosh but because we thought it was funny. That seven-inch was the perfect way to introduce ourselves to scene we were from while also marking new territory.

GARRETT KLAHN: We wrote the EP in a weekend, I think. I had never been to Boston before and we recorded with Brian McTernan. I remember I didn't own a guitar for the first six months I was in the band, so I had to borrow one for the recording. I played violin when I was a kid but hadn't really played much guitar. When I moved to New York City everyone had guitars, so they just showed me stuff and I put it together. I was happy with the EP. It was just a demo to us, and I don't remember how it made it to Revelation, but I remember wanting to be on Jade Tree as it was such a cool label. They all wanted Revelation, though. [laughs] I think people would have looked at Revelation as the premiere hardcore label at the time and Norman saying he didn't want to be affiliated with straight edge or political stuff and then he wanted to be on Rev, which was a straight edge hardcore label, and that was a bit confusing. But I remember Revelation bought us some gear and that changed our minds about them. I bought Walter Schreifels' Marshall head and his guitar. I remember being excited about the case for the head because it said Quicksand on it and we were all big fans of Quicksand at the time.

SCOTT WINEGARD: We all crammed into Chris's Toyota — the "Champagne Supernova" as he called it. [laughs] We drove to Brian McTernan's tiny studio in the basement of his house where all these hardcore kids lives. I didn't know Brian well at that point, but he was fun to work with. It was supposed to be a demo and we just didn't know anything about recording at the time. But after getting the tape and listening to it on the way back home, we were really proud of it. We decided to send it to Jordan Cooper from Revelation, as well as to some other labels, just to check out. Jordan felt it was good enough to put out as a seven-inch, and we liked the recording, too. It was like one day at Brian's and all of a sudden we had a record. It was simple — bam, it was done and out.

PRESSURE

NORMAN BRANNON: The only pressure I remember being under wasn't in regards to the quality of the music. We're four of the most opinionated people in the world. If we all liked a song then we were confident it was good. But when we met The Promise Ring I remember feeling a bit of pressure. I remember we played with them in Madison and we asked specifically to have them on the bill with us. When we met those guys their demo had just come out and their first seven-inch came out not too long after. When I came home from tour I gave Tim Owen from Jade Tree a copy of their music and that got the wheels rolling for them in terms of getting on Jade Tree. Once they signed to Jade Tree it seemed like there was a new Promise Ring record out every ten minutes! [laughs] I was

worried that we weren't putting out enough stuff. We put out the Revelation EP and the Simba record and we wrote the album pretty quickly after so there wasn't a lot of time to get too worried about it.

GARRETT KLAHN: Once things started happening I just wanted to go on tour. I was enjoying being young. I didn't feel any pressure, and the scene stuff didn't make a difference to me. When we met The Promise Ring I just remember feeling honored to be linked up with them. The first tour we did with them I was embarrassed because we were headlining and they were moving mountains back then. But we instantly all became best friends after the first night of that tour. Lots of stuff happened on that tour. It was really long and covered the whole U.S. It was a traveling circus! We played a house party on New Year's Eve in Indianapolis and that night there was a gunfight down the street from where the show was. All kinds of events like those seemed to be happening and it was just this great adventure. It was this idyllic, perfect excursion and we felt like a "band of brothers" as cheesy as that might sound. [laughs]

SCOTT WINEGARD: We were never competing with anyone or trying to sound like the best "ex-hardcore" band. It was just what we sounded like. It was what just came out naturally. We definitely wanted someone who sang, but aside from that we just wanted to do something a bit more rocking. None of the music was ever a conscious decision. It was just how it was and what came out.

AUDIENCE ENJOYMENT

NORMAN BRANNON: We wanted to create a sense at our shows where everyone could equally enjoy the show whether they stood in the front, back or middle. Part of enjoying a show to me is not necessarily about having someone step on your head or run into your back. Hardcore is a style of music that might incite that type of physical response, but I don't feel we were playing that exact style of music. It seemed like there was a time when kids were unsure what to do because for so many years they were told the way you express your excitement about a band was in a physical way. People were confused about what to do at shows. On one hand there was this hardcore tradition, but on the other hand the music was eschewing that same tradition. It was about reinventing hardcore. I remember saying in *Anti-Matter* that hardcore is the way we live our lives and therefore only we can define it. The reason I said that was because we don't have to follow the tradition; punk is about railing against tradition and not going along with the norm. At the time, dancing was irrelevant to what we were doing. The music in the scene had changed and the mainstream had co-opted it. You could see slam-dancing in Toadies videos and they had nothing to do with Agnostic Front or the Cro-Mags. I thought the new hardcore ethic should be to learn how to respect each other on every level, including a physical level. It was also about destroying the hierarchy at a show where only the strongest can be up front, as well as getting women up front and enjoying the show the way they wanted to. It was important to us to stop playing whenever anyone started moshing and to explain that we don't have to do these things and we can express ourselves in other ways, so let's do that. The first time we went to Europe we had to have someone come out before we played and explain that we were about respecting each other and part of that was we didn't want people jumping on top of each other during the show. We just wanted you to be here in the moment for what it is and not get in the way of another person's enjoyment of the show. Eventually we didn't have to stop that often and people got it.

SCOTT WINEGARD: We never wanted stage-diving and all that, because we felt like it wasn't a part of what we sounded like. We took Fugazi's influence there as they would get on kids for dancing too hard. I'm kind of a big person and I've done my share of stage dives. [laughs] There's a time and place for it, but there are also other people who want to see music, and I don't think most of the people wanting to see us wanted to be jumped on. Could you imagine coming to see Texas and Sensefield and people bragging about, "I got the mic for the chorus" or "Did you see my flip off the monitor?" [laughs]

GARRETT KLAHN: I never experienced much weirdness from the crowds in terms of our sound. I remember Norm was so worried about the whole moshing thing, but we ended up playing to a different crowd, so ultimately there wasn't a need to worry about it so much. Once we were able to sort out who we were playing with and where we were playing things just fell into place... except for Europe. They'd go apeshit! [laughs] The smaller the town, the crazier they would go. [laughs] Back then it seemed like Europe had a greater appreciation for music in general. They didn't care what you stood for; they were there to have a good time.

MAJOR LABEL COURTSHIP

NORMAN BRANNON: New York's an industry town so even back then it wasn't out of the ordinary to know people in the industry. At our first show there were a few people there that worked for major labels — they weren't there doing their jobs, though. They were old friends and acquaintances. After we played and people started hearing the demo there was major label interest alongside the indie interest. A lot of our friends in Quicksand and Sick of it All and Orange 9mm were on majors at the time. I remember bringing Matt Cross from Orange 9mm a copy of the demo because he wanted to hear it. I made him a tape copy of it and he accidentally erased it. So, he said we could meet at his manger's office and we could make a copy off the DAT. He introduced me to his manager and we put in the DAT and his manager is looking at his desk reading something and within two minutes of the first song he puts his magazine down and says, "Who is this?" Matt said, "It's Norm's band." He just looks at me and says, "Do you have a record deal?" [laughs] So, that brought about some interest. We were all in our early twenties and only knew major labels as this abstract thing. We didn't want to be a part of it and that wasn't our objective on an individual level. At the time the only indie labels that were interested were Art Monk Construction, Jade Tree and Revelation. We loved Art Monk but they were really, really small. Jade Tree was pretty small at the time, too. If we were going to stay on an independent label then we needed to go with a place that had a little muscle at the time and that ended up being Revelation. We signed to Revelation almost as a symbolic way of telling the majors that we weren't interested, we just signed a three record deal with Revelation. But they never went away. They started following us wherever we went and flew to every show we played. We actually started to become friends with some of them. Sure, some of them were total losers but the others were really nice people. At the same time, we were signed to Revelation so were like, "Look, if these guys want to fly us around and take us out to dinner then fine. We're still signed with Revelation at the end of the day." [laughs] Toward the end of the album cycle it started crossing our minds a little more. The full-length did pretty well and the shows were bigger than we anticipated. We were all pretty ambitious about what we wanted our next record to sound like. We only received about $7,000 to make *Do You Know...* we figured we wouldn't be able to do that with our second record on Revelation. The idea of a label coming in and buying our contract from Revelation was introduced and we started to consider it. We got sick of labels following us around and we wanted to make a decision. The only viable options at the time were Interscope and Capitol. Interscope ended up dying a fiery death and Capitol seemed like a decent place to go. *OK Computer* had just come out and they also signed Sparklehorse. I remember a guy from the label saying, "We have our Everclears to pay the bills — we want more Radioheads and Sparklehorses." That idea was really appealing. In the end the contracts with Capitol were drawn up but we ended up breaking up.

SCOTT WINEGARD: It was just so surreal that it was happening to us. I remember thinking, "Wow, this really happens. Bands really do get flown around and free food and put up in nice hotels." [laughs] It would have been interesting to see what would have happened had we signed, but looking back it was just really funny. Out of all the people I met from those big labels, I only talk to maybe one and I knew him before Texas. It's amazing to see how "real" those people really were and how great friends they were of mine, as they claimed to be. [laughs] Yeah, it's sure nice to know you all these years later. [laughs] It was funny walking out of a hotel in Hollywood and there was a big limo to take us around. We actually talked to five labels in one day, hearing the same story over and over again. Chris Daly fell asleep at the meeting with Hollywood Records. The president of the label threw pencil at him and said, "Wake up, kid." Chris threw the pencil back at him. [laughs]

CHRIS DALY: Being flown out to L.A. was fun. We were put up in bungalows at the Hollywood Roosevelt and managed to drum up a $500 phone bill calling our friends back home. The Cardigans were staying there at the time, and we watched the singer do laps in the swimming pool outside our rooms. What can I say? We were young and stupid, but it was fun nonetheless.

GARRETT KLAHN: I remember avoiding [the major label courtship] for a long time, but back then that's when a lot of the majors were looking at bands from the underground. At some point it became unavoidable, so we went with it. And we realized if you went out to lunch with them they'd give you a free box of promo CDs, so we had a lot of fun with it, and I went to a lot of those lunches to eat and get CDs to trade in. [laughs] Capitol seemed to make the most sense for us because [the deal] would have been for a couple of records. But I just looked at the whole situation like if it was going to happen, then it would happen. I just let Norm deal with those guys on a business level. But it wouldn't have lasted even if we went forward with everything. We would have broken up before writing a new record. At that point a year and a half went by and we were different people living different lives than when we started. The friendships had run their course for certain people in the band, and it was becoming more of a burden than anything else. If there wasn't pressure before there sure would be after signing for us to write a new record and stay together. They were offering bands tons of money. But thankfully we cut it short before it happened.

D.I.Y. DILEMMAS

NORMAN BRANNON: When you read in zines that every major label is evil then you believe it. Do I think every major label is good? No. But I've been screwed over by indie labels. If anyone's going to screw me over then we might as well get an advance. [laughs] Bands used to get a lot of crap because pretty much the standard answer to signing is you want more people to check out your music. Hardcore kids typically say that's bullshit, but

when you're in a band you do want your records to be in stores and you want the opportunity to play to different people. I was aware that The Ramones weren't on Dischord and The Sex Pistols weren't on Touch and Go, and if it wasn't for those bands then where would I be? Now that's not to say that every band should sign to a major, as long as the indie labels don't keep mimicking the major label model. That's the problem I think people need to address. It's not as simple as indie vs. major anymore. It's about business models. Indie record business models are worse in some ways than major label models because copying major models end up spending so much money without giving the band any. So, all of a sudden you're a band that sells a lot of records but never made a royalty and you're just surviving on playing concerts and that's not fair. I just felt there was more of a chance we were going to screw them than them screwing us. What were the real chances we were going to sell a million records? Our opinion was they were crazy. If they want to give us a million dollars then that's cool because we're not going to sell a million records. [laughs]

SCOTT WINEGARD: Some people were mad at us from various directions in the scene for not fitting into whatever mold they saw us fitting into. We were playing with like Samuel and the Art Monk Construction types of bands and bands like Chamberlain, but we were on Revelation and some of the kids from that scene thought we weren't cool because we were on a "hardcore" record label. And of course the hardcore kids sometimes got on us for not being "hardcore" enough. We never really seemed to fit in, yet we always did fine. If being on Revelation was a mistake, well, all these people got our records somehow. But there will always be people who have problems with you no matter what, so you just have to do what you feel is right.

EARLY ENDINGS

NORMAN BRANNON: There was a changing dynamic in our friendship that I don't think we were comfortable with. We started the band as friends and we wanted to end it as friends. It started to change a bit though and it revolved around pressures we didn't know how to deal with. We were treating each other badly and we were beginning to get delusions of grandeur to some extent. I felt like it was only going to get worse. The money and everyone blowing smoke up our ass wasn't that important to me at the time. When we broke up it was kind of a huge shock because it was just at the point where everyone seemed to be into it and we were just about to sign a seven figure record deal. People were losing their minds about it and telling us we were crazy. But ten years later I don't regret it and I feel totally sane about it. [laughs] The fact we were able to end it when we did allowed for some healing to take place and we're all friends to this day, which is far more important than a contract.

GARRETT KLAHN: A good chunk of the end came about after all the touring. We toured for about nine months off and on and we broke up a few times during the course of it. I left a couple of tours. I remember we did a three or four week tour with Sensefield and then drove across the country to fly to Europe and then we were in Europe for four or five weeks and that's when we broke up. Had we taken a break… who knows? But it was way too much for way too long. Norm and I never saw eye to eye on many things. I remember speaking with him and from what I've gathered he was plotting to quit the band during that final tour unbeknownst to me, but it ended up being a mutual thing. I got a phone call in a hotel room and that was it.

SCOTT WINEGARD: It felt like it needed to end. We were on full throttle the whole time. I think we maybe turned down two shows in two years. We were just around each other too much and we needed a break. I always felt like I was the band mediator, which drove me nuts. [laughs] Everyone would come to me about a problem with the other guy. But we were young and all had our own ideas of what we wanted. It got to the point when we just needed to take a break. I remember flying home from Europe and Norm was talking to me about it. It wasn't like we were miserable, but it definitely had this vibe of being a bit overbearing at a certain point. There was something missing all of a sudden. People not getting along affected how we acted toward each other. I never had a falling out with anyone in the band, but I didn't trust that we could continue on as a band and be honest with ourselves and what we wanted to do. What we had was something cool, though. It took me a few years to realize how exciting the band was. I'm really happy with the records and I'm happy to be a part of what we accomplished.

CHRIS DALY: We figured it would be better to break up and save our friendships than sign and be miserable and break up within a year anyway. It was a success, because we all live with in miles of each other and are still great friends. Our ten-year anniversary shows in New York City in November 2006 were absolutely two of the best nights of my life, and to share that with Norman, Garrett, and Scott was something almost too special for words. It was just absolutely amazing to play with those people and I am honored to say they are still my dearest friends in the world.

GARRETT KLAHN: Texas was and always will be a huge reference point in my life. Most of my "firsts" happened with those guys. Anything I've done musically since is always compared to Texas and I'm totally okay with that as I'm happy with what we accomplished. I was a lunatic at the time. [laughs] I didn't have any cares back then. But doing those recent reunion shows was a great opportunity to go back, and it helped us put things in perspective. All those people who came to those shows were a good reminder of what once was.

SELECT DISCOGRAPHY:

Texas Is The Reason (7"/MCD, Revelation, 1995)
   Klahn, Brannon, Winegard, Daly

Texas/Samuel Split (7", Simba, 1995)
   Klahn, Brannon, Winegard, Daly

Do You Know Who You Are? (CD/LP, Revelation, 1996)
   Klahn, Brannon, Winegard, Daly

Texas/Promise Ring Split (7", Jade Tree, 1996)
   Klahn, Brannon, Winegard, Daly

THREADBARE

Vocals: Brian Lovro
Guitars: Chad Dziewior
       Carl Skildum

Bass: Dustin Perry
Drums: Mike Paradise

Minnesota's Threadbare created an experimental, thematically rich post-hardcore sound that became a staple for other nineties hardcore bands that wanted to create hardcore that was honest but also musically challenging. Inspired by the sounds of Burn and Quicksand, as well as the noisier and progressive epics of heavy rock acts like Neurosis and Rollins Band, they created complex hardcore that blended many different genres. These influences came together to form a sound that was often overlooked because of the band's Midwestern locale.

Early in the Minnesota winter of 1993, Threadbare formed over a love for music that went beyond the confines of genre. Bassist Dustin Perry, drummer Mike Paradise, and guitarists Chad Dziewior and Carl Skildum all knew each other from playing in previous Minnesota hardcore bands (Bloodline, Reach, Downside, Switch, and Krakatoa, among others). Lovro, meanwhile, came from nearby South Dakota and met the others at various shows. Getting together proved difficult at first with Lovro and Perry commuting from different locations to the Twin Cities, where the other members lived. Nonetheless, they took every opportunity to flesh out their concoction of heavy though subtly melodic guitar riffs and groove-laden rhythms. After coming up with a few songs that were deemed acceptable, the members would then mail a tape to Lovro so he could work on lyrics while toiling away at college. Lovro eventually moved closer, which allowed Threadbare to play more shows and helped them secure label interest. In 1994, they released their first record on Watermark Records.

Although Threadbare was not able to tour regularly due to school and work, word spread about the group as prominent hardcore bands like Snapcase and 108 came through the Midwest and were impressed by the band's intensity and musicianship. They achieved even more notoriety after getting a slot at the More Than Music Fest and having tracks on Ebullition's *XXX* straight edge compilation and Norman Brannon's *Anti-Matter* compilation.

Feeling Older Faster, their Doghouse Records debut, is viewed as a fairly ambitious nineties hardcore record. Instead of rushing things, they took their time in the studio and worked on organically developing each song, allowing for pauses between change-ups, extending build-ups, and adding layers of noise to their already frantically dissonant riffs, which probe for a balance between heaviness and melody. The record is a document of twenty-somethings looking for meaning and purpose. Judging by the angry sounds created by the band, it was a difficult journey for them.

Facing many of the same problems that many in their mid-twenties face — post-graduate careers, steady relationships, and bills — the band broke up in the summer of 1996, just when they were putting the finishing touches on *Escapist*, their highly anticipated follow-up to *Feeling Older Faster*.

Although the projects the members have since been associated with have received some notoriety, a funny thing has happened the past decade: Threadbare's legacy has slowly burrowed into the minds of music fans, journalists, and musicians due in part to their re-analysis of *Feeling Older Faster*. Bands like Snapcase, Cable, and Cave In also helped spread the word in the years after Threadbare split up. In turn, respect for what they accomplished increases every year.

ORIGINS

CHAD DZIEWIOR: The original sound was somewhat different than the recorded band in that it was much more melodic. When the band finally settled on the "concrete" lineup, we had already become more dissonant and heavier, especially with Brian singing.

DUSTIN PERRY: We gave up on being a formula band and wanted to do something that had an emotional impact. I was never into the retro old-school stuff because I feel like every generation should have their own sound, so why would you want to do things that have already been done? When we put Threadbare together we seemed to somehow arrive at the sound we wanted. We wanted the music to have feeling and we played with feeling. We were afraid of doing something dumb, which gave us the motivation to work really hard on the songs. [laughs]

BRIAN LOVRO: We were all Quicksand freaks and into a lot of the early-nineties Revelation stuff. I was also really into Rollins Band, which had a big impact on me. We were all just really into music and I'm sure a lot of our various influences creeped in to our sound.

CARL SKILDUM: We wanted to basically just create near chaos and sound like the end of the world. I think there was also a lot of influence from Black Flag in that we wanted to replicate that sort of car-crash destructive sound, and we wanted to be the exact opposite of the positive message, clean-cut approach.

MIKE PARADISE: It wasn't like we were a bunch of angry guys. Threadbare was an outlet for the negative energy that we had, and I think it was a natural thing for people that age to experience. We didn't play by any rules. We just felt that when we're done doing what we have to do then the song is over.

DIVERSE MIXTURE OF EMOTION AND SOUND

DUSTIN PERRY: Everyone in the band had common musical ground, but we all had different tastes as well. I didn't want Threadbare to be a metal band, which might sound kind of strange because we had some really heavy parts. But I wanted to write songs that were tasteful and conveyed some kind of an emotional power.

CARL SKILDUM: We thought of ourselves as a hardcore band for sure, although we were all fans of different kinds of music outside of what was traditionally known as hardcore at the time. Hardcore was kind of our lifestyle and our philosophy, but we all learned a lot about music and our instruments by listening to and learning how to play lots of other stuff besides hardcore. I think I had lofty goals about wanting to push hardcore forward and expand the definition of hardcore

LYRICS

DUSTIN PERRY: At the time we felt that a lot of music didn't have any soul or purpose, so we always felt we wanted to challenge that mindset. Brian was really feeling those emotions when we played.

BRIAN LOVRO: I was out of high school and I didn't know where I was supposed to take my life. I tried not to make it a whiny thing because it wasn't like I lived some hard life, but a lot of it centered on frustrations with relationships and other people and yourself. Even though I liked a lot of those bands that sang about friends turning their back on you, a lot of my lyrics were aimed inward at the stupid things we do.

CARL SKILDUM: Brian wrote all of the lyrics and they were very personal, but we all felt we could relate to them. They were very much about alienation, loss, and regret. I remember at the time we all sort of rallied around this banner of being fed up with what we perceived as lies that "society" was feeding us. We didn't want to have the kind of scolding, posi-core lyrics that a lot of other bands had at that time, but rather have a more personal perspective

DEBATES

CARL SKILDUM: We were all interested in many of the various movements and agendas that sort of moved through hardcore at the time. I suppose we were associated with straight edge for a while, although that wasn't an agenda that we ever pushed. We were never really an agenda band, and never really wanted to take a position of telling people what to do, which was one thing that really was a big turnoff for us when other bands spent a lot of time issuing decrees and proclamations on how you should act.

DUSTIN PERRY: Around the time of Threadbare we felt the Minneapolis scene turned away from us. I don't know if they didn't like the fact we were on Doghouse or if they were jealous of that, but it was really disheartening to me. I was always really positive about the scene so the criticism was hard to take. We were always an open minded band.

MIKE PARADISE: When I think about that time period there was so much negativity and people battling about these topics. Subconsciously, I think some of that tension probably fed into our sound. We just had the music speak for it instead of having to spell it out for people.

TITLE OF "FEELING OLDER FASTER"

DUSTIN PERRY: It really was a reflection of the idea that, hey, we aren't kids anymore. I was just about done with school and was engaged at the time of the recording and was thinking about settling down and having kids and getting into the typical lifestyle, which was kind of depressing for me. I think the record was kind of us rallying against those pressures.

BRIAN LOVRO: I just remember driving back out to school in Spearfish and being kind of isolated and frustrated. I wasn't feeling right about a lot of things. I tried to write the lyrics in a way so it didn't come off like teenage angst, but now looking back on it I think it was teenage angst. [laughs]

ATMOSPHERE OF "FEELING OLDER FASTER"

CARL SKILDUM: We were all really on the same page in terms of writing. The songs were all more or less written collaboratively by all five of us in the same room at the same time. I think the sound of that record also had a lot to do with Tommy Roberts, the engineer, and the studio where we recorded it. It was in the basement of this old warehouse in a run-down part of downtown Minneapolis. The studio was only accessible by this big freight elevator, which led down into the bowels of this building, where you then had to follow these dark, twisting corridors to get into the studio. We did a lot of late nights and it was an ominous, disorienting place to do the recording. I remember taking breaks and walking down these halls and hearing the record playing back from the control room echoing through the halls and it was really bizarre and a bit oppressive, and we wanted to keep that, so we asked Tommy to replicate some of that starkness and "haunted" feeling with the mix and some of the things we added, like the music box at the end of "Midas." We had done the first seven-inch at that same studio, and I think both of those recordings feel like they are from a slightly darker place.

BRIAN LOVRO: There was a lot of improvising going on. I know I must sound like a Rollins geek, but we were really influenced by some of the Rollins Band stuff, like *Hard Volume*, and some of the jammed up stuff on that record where shit would just get hellish. Sometimes you just had so much hate and anger inside you, we'd just want to unleash it all while we were playing and take it as far as we could. Sometimes the music would just overtake us.

DUSTIN PERRY: We wanted the record to be like a bomb going off — a huge, cathartic release. We never wanted to be a band for people to dance to.

LIFE TURMOIL/MUSICAL CATHARSIS

DUSTIN PERRY: I was really impacted by Minneapolis somewhat turning against us, which fueled us in a way. [laughs] The weird thing about the band was that we didn't feel like people really cared about us that much, but now over the years I've had people come up to me when I was playing in Snapcase and say, "Man, you were in Threadbare? I loved that band!" These reactions have made me feel really good in that there were a few people that did care, because at the time we sure didn't feel like there were. [laughs]

MIKE PARADISE: I don't think the final outcome was intentional. We were lucky enough to complement each other musically and I think the final result is just the natural chemistry between us.

CARL SKILDUM: The funny thing is that even at the point when we did that record, I thought we all seemed relatively well adjusted; we could joke around with each other and we weren't these maudlin, self-pitying, angry guys all the time. However, we wanted to make records that were uncomfortable and really dwelled on raw feelings. Once we decided that was where we were going with the band I think we all got swept up in it.

"ESCAPIST"

CHAD DZIEWIOR: [*Escapist*] was done after we had already decided to call it quits. Our music was very personal to each of us, and as time went on it became increasingly difficult to find common ground. I think it was pretty hard for us when it came to writing songs because we all had such strong opinions and were very critical. It took a lot of work to complete a song because it was constantly going through new ideas and changes.

MIKE PARADISE: We wanted to break out of what we did on *Feeling Older Faster*, but I don't think it came together as naturally. Some people wanted to change the way we were working and inject more melody and more traditional song structures and it just didn't gel. The original idea for Threadbare was all about spontaneity and by the time Escapist came about it just wasn't happening creatively.

CARL SKILDUM: We spun our wheels for a few months trying to write together. Mike and I started working on stuff before the other guys would get to practice, and by the time everyone else showed up, we'd have something new, but it wasn't as collaborative as before.

BRIAN LOVRO: Half the band wanted to go in a more melodic direction and the other half wanted to go somewhere else. I felt stuck in the middle and wasn't sure what to do. Everyone else seems to like that record but I hate it. [laughs] Those guys did a great job with the music, but I just wish I wasn't even on it. I was kind of bumming because the whole thing was sort of unraveling and to have to make a record under those circumstances made me rush the lyrics.

DUSTIN PERRY: We ended up recording the instruments separately due to splitting time between two studios and it took a while to finish it. We tried some different things; we were unsure of a lot of the songs and did some experimenting with different effects and writing patterns, but it all ended up sounding pretty cool.

END OF THE BAND

CARL SKILDUM: We tried really hard to respect each other and from the start we had an unofficial mission statement that if one person left the band... that was it. There were some disagreements about direction and sound towards the end. I'm sorry to say there were no sordid tales or major scandals that brought it to an end; it was more an acknowledgement that we had run our course and it wasn't enjoyable anymore. Yet, I felt like there was more we could have done.

BRIAN LOVRO: Everybody had strong personalities and you could imagine how that might get weird at times. I sometimes felt like I didn't fit in because these guys had known each other for years and I was kind of the outside guy. People started changing and moving in different directions by the end of it, which I think is natural. I think what happened with us probably happened with most of the bands from that era.

DUSTIN PERRY: I never felt like we stopped because we didn't want to do the music anymore or because we didn't get along; rather, we just got kind of frustrated with it since we weren't really sure if the band mattered to anyone but us.

LOOKING BACK

CHAD DZIEWIOR: I am very happy I had the chance to play with such awesomely talented friends and create music people still care about. Threadbare will always have a special place in my heart and the memories of the time are priceless. My best friends came from the hardcore scene and that says it all.

MIKE PARADISE: When you're younger you're trying to figure out who you want to be and I began to feel comfortable in my own skin, which is how I look back on that period.

DUSTIN PERRY: The best part of it is that people still care about it. It means a lot to us that people appreciated what we did… like the band wasn't done in vain. [laughs] We never expected to be popular; we did it because we wanted to have an impact. I still feel really proud of what we accomplished.

CARL SKILDUM: I'm not really the same person I was [over] 10 years ago, but I still remember that time clearly. Threadbare was the only thing that was going right for me or even worth remembering from that time and it may have kept me sane in a lot of ways.

BRIAN LOVRO: Not to sound melodramatic, but I wish I had as much passion about something in my life right now as I did for Threadbare during its time.

SELECT DISCOGRAPHY:

Self-Titled (7", Watermark, 1994)
    Lovro, Dziewior, Skildum, Perry, Paradise

Feeling Older Faster (LP/CDEP, Doghouse, 1995)
    Lovro, Dziewior, Skildum, Perry, Paradise

Escapist (CD/LP, Doghouse, 1997)
    Lovro, Dziewior, Skildum, Perry, Paradise

FIGHT: THE NINETIES HARDCORE REVOLUTION IN ETHICS, POLITICS, AND SO

TRIAL

Vocals: Greg Bennick
Guitars: Timm McIntosh
    E.J. Bastien
    Josh Freer
    Brian Johnson

Bass: Brian Redman
    Derek Harn
Drums: Alexei Rodriguez
    Nick Platter
    Mike Green

Washington state's Trial combined insightful lyrics with a sound that merged the spirit of late-eighties straight edge bands like Youth of Today and Judge with a more experimental approach of bands like Burn and Inside Out. Perhaps most importantly, Trial got the crowd to break down their personal barriers and feel united in the shared suffering of the human condition.

After meeting at an Inside Out reunion show in California in 1993, vocalist Greg Bennick and guitarist Timm McIntosh bonded not only over a common love for hardcore, but also because they felt that music should be a personal and emotional experience. They believed music was primarily an avenue for communication, not one way communication, but a dialogue between the artists and the audience. It was this attitude that convinced McIntosh to relocate from California to Washington to form a band with Bennick that expressed these ideas. They started the band under the name Headline in 1994, but after their first show they changed their name to Trial.

Musically, the members loved Bad Brains, Youth of Today, and the Cro-Mags, but they also were inspired by what many late eighties/early nineties bands like Burn, Beyond, and Integrity were doing. Mixing classic hardcore and metal influences, they created something that was unique even among other experimental bands of the time that also mixed genres.

Although Trial put out several records and played countless shows, their most memorable creation was their lone full-length, *Are These Our Lives?* This record stands as a testament not only to the band's diverse social and political viewpoints, but also provides a powerful document of their musical growth. The record includes classical overtures placed between songs and their most complex song structures and rhythm patterns. The music provides an anchor as Bennick's lyrics speak to the listener in a way that is informative without being moralizing.

Trial was one of a handful of nineties hardcore bands to cover a very broad range of political and social issues such as human rights, animal rights, gender and racial empowerment, and corporate imperialism. While some activists in the hardcore scene were preaching about these causes without actually maintaining a personal investment in the issues, Bennick was directly involved in some personal way with the majority of the causes he discussed. Whether it was helping to counsel rape victims, people battling depression, or working with Native American tribes in an effort to maintain their rights, Bennick was always active in a variety of missions, which made his lyrics genuine.

Regardless of one's feelings about activism, straight edge, Native American rights, or any of the issues Trial was passionate about, the band left quite an impact on hardcore. Their energetic music prompted discussions before and after the shows, much of it punctuated with the humor that Bennick used to get his point across. Those performances left strong feelings in the hearts of those who were there.

ORIGINS

GREG BENNICK: Trial formed in 1995 under the name Headline. We wanted to create a band that would pull no punches in terms of chasing the core elements of political and social issues and the depths of personal emotions and the psychology of human interactions. We hit that stride, but it took a few records to get there. *Are These Our Lives?* is where it all came together, though the earlier records had songs that were in the zone, too ("Scars," "500 Years," "In Closing").

TIMM MCINTOSH: I met Greg and Derek [Harn] at an Inside Out reunion show in Sacramento, California, where I grew up. We became friends and kept in touch. After the passing of my father, Greg and Derek asked me to move to Seattle and start a band with them. It was actually 1994 when I moved up to Seattle and Headline was formed. I hated the name Headline and we changed the name to Trial after our first show. One of the meanings in the dictionary for the word Trial was "an attempt, an effort." I don't think there was any name that could fit us better. Trial was our attempt, our effort at making a difference in the world we live in.

GREG BENNICK: I was friends with Timm McIntosh and Derek Harn who were living in Seattle up the street from me. The three of us talked and realized that we all wanted to play hardcore like the kind we grew up with: fast and aggressive with big breakdowns and solid lyrics about topics and ideas that really mattered. We started practicing and, one by one, used every drummer currently alive on the Earth over the years we were together as a band.

LINEUP

GREG BENNICK: I was friends with Timm McIntosh and Derek Harn who were living in Seattle up the street from me. The three of us talked and realized that we all wanted to play hardcore like the kind we grew up with: fast and aggressive with big breakdowns and solid lyrics about topics and ideas that really mattered. We started practicing and one-by-one used every drummer currently alive on the Earth over the years we were together as a band.

DIFFERENCE BETWEEN EIGHTIES/NINETIES HARDCORE

GREG BENNICK: Hardcore in the eighties is defined for me by the photo on the cover of Youth of Today's *Break Down the Walls* record, and I am not talking about the beauty and power of Ray Cappo's nipples. In that picture, we see kids of all different kinds singing along from in front of the stage. There are punk kids and hardcore looking kids and metal kids. There was a much greater feeling of unity, to use a vastly overused word, back then than we had in the nineties where we saw punks go their own way, straight edge kids go their own way, and metal kids go their own way. In the eighties, the scene and the people in it were more diverse, but there was more of a collective bond between people. With that in mind, I will go out on a limb and say that what made the nineties unique was how fractured the music scene became. Trial always wanted to play to kids of all different kinds and we loved playing with bands like The Pist, who drew in punk kids in droves. One of my favorite shows ever was Trial and Whorehouse of Representatives at a house in Seattle. Before the bands played it felt like all the punks and edge kids were just staring at one another in a pre-riot type situation, but when the bands played everyone just had a blast making fun of one another in such a positive way and enjoying our differences. I remember introducing every single Trial song as a cover by some famous punk band and each was different. "This one's called 'The List' by Filth" and then we'd just play one of our own songs. It was just silly and it was a great time. Trial also played with Modest Mouse once in San Francisco and that was another night where any one member of the crowd couldn't have been more different than the person standing next to them. This was a unique opportunity for people to learn from people who were more similar to themselves than different if they just were to give them the chance.

TIMM MCINTOSH: The hardcore of the nineties seemed to be a progression of what the eighties had started — a higher conscience of ideas, beliefs, politics, and even spirituality.

The eighties opened up the table to new ideas that punk rock wasn't addressing. Nineties hardcore took those ideas and blew it wide open by pushing the envelope and really getting to the core of expression and free thought. Bad Brains, Youth of Today, 7 Seconds and Cro-Mags all touched on the spiritual side of things...and the nineties embraced and rejected those ideas at the same time. Eighties hardcore seemed to be more introverted while nineties hardcore felt more extroverted. The nineties encompassed all that hardcore should have been — a diverse collective of people working towards a better world through their ideas and music. It wasn't centered on the bands, but completely centered on the hardcore/punk community. The kid in the band was as important as the kid doing a zine, putting on a show, a distro at a show, speaking between bands, tables of literature published and written by the kids, this was hardcore. From my perspective, nineties hardcore was the peak of, and culmination of, all that hardcore should have been, a vehicle for expression, change, and self-awareness.

STRAIGHT EDGE

GREG BENNICK: We always wanted Trial to be a band which had a reach beyond the hardcore scene, and I am not just talking into "metal" and other genres. We wanted Trial and the ideas we were exploring to reach into non-hardcore and non-musical realms as well. With that in mind, aside from the fact that we had made individual choices to not drink and just enjoyed sharing that fact with people, there was the support that not drinking lent to our arguments in conversations as we went through the world. People have a solid stereotype of punk, hardcore, and metal listeners as being drug crazed and drunken fools. When I would start a conversation about punk rock or the band with someone outside of the scene, they would always assume that my being in a punk band meant that I was drunk most of the time and that I spent my time ranting and raving about how much I hated my parents. When I would tell them that we were all drug and alcohol free and vegan, their attention would suddenly focus. Conversations about the issues the band covered would be taken far more seriously. This was always important to us, because if the ideas within the music only have value within the scene — meaning if they can't be shared outside the scene as well — then we would have managed only to create a secret language with a limited reach. Ideas like the ones Trial covered, from sexual assault survivor psychology to native land rights issues and how they are affected by desire for gold, are for everyone to consider, not just punks and hardcore kids. Being straight edge helped further that cause along.

TIMM MCINTOSH: Trial was obviously a straight edge band. We weren't preachy about it though. Plenty of bands had one message — that message was straight edge. We had other ideas beyond straight edge that we felt were just as, if not more, important than the message of straight edge. Everyone already knew about straight edge. What were we going to say that was any different? At times it felt that the title of straight edge band would deter non-edge people from listening to us. I'm happy this wasn't the case.

ANIMAL RIGHTS

GREG BENNICK: Trial was never openly expressive about animal rights. The closest we came was a song called "Cycle of Cruelty," which was more about human rights and suffering overall as a concept. In terms of dealing with suffering itself, Trial was extremely effective in getting people thinking and talking about what hurt and scared them most. I know for sure that the band had that effect on me. At the same time, I will say that by the time of our reunion shows in 2005 some of our closest friends had been arrested as members of the SHAC 7. We support the struggle faced by members of the SHAC group who are currently imprisoned essentially for speaking their mind.

TIMM MCINTOSH: A huge focus of the nineties was animal rights. Being very passionate about animal rights, it was always a disappointment for me that we didn't have any songs that dealt directly with the subject. When the band was started we were all vegan except our drummer, Mike Green. "Cycle Of Cruelty," which dealt with the suffering of all living things human and animal, was the closest that we could come to the topic as not to be hypocrites. A band should stand as a collective for what's being purveyed through their lyrics, to have a song that dealt directly with the subject would have been misleading. If there was one thing that I wished would have carried over from the nineties into today's hardcore it would be a focus on animal rights

SOUND

GREG BENNICK: We always played music that made us feel like we could tear apart sheets of steel. It was all about us playing what made us stoked first and foremost and hoping that others would come along for the ride. The old school faster stuff is what we had grown up with and the heavy slower parts or the overall crunch was just what made us excited. I love the heavy stuff and so does Timm and when we were working on *Are These Our Lives?* all of those influences came into play.

TIMM MCINTOSH: My introduction into hardcore was through bands like Youth Of Today, Side By Side, Gorilla Biscuits...the "Youth Crew" bands. My biggest influences, though, came from bands like Burn, Beyond, and Inside Out. Bands that maintained that aggressive fast pace of the "Youth Crew" era and then laced them with breakdowns. Those breakdowns that made you want to kill anyone who was next to you. Without a doubt I tried to mimic the music that Gavin Van Vlack created with Burn. Whenever I wrote something, I wanted it to carry itself with emotion, to make me feel something. Couple that with Greg's lyrics and it was inevitable.

EARLY SHOWS

GREG BENNICK: It is important to note that Trial was a deeply intense band that inspired raw reactions in people at our live shows. Trial was real: every show was raw life, laid bare for anyone brave enough and willing to embrace it, including ourselves. That's important to note; we put the ideas out there — talking about the inalienable right of people to suffer, for example — and to accept and embrace and try to understand what that means is a challenge I continually tried to live up to and face along with those who were watching, listening to, and experiencing our shows and our music. We had near riots break out at our shows, and we had sets where a huge part of the audience seemed to end up in tears. It was always explosive. One night in Montreal, we were playing for an almost sold out crowd. The place was totally packed. We were just about to play our song "500 Years" which is a song written in support of Native struggles, most specifically the Dineh and Western Shoshone Nations in the Western United States with whom we had had direct contact through the 1990's. I decided that night to talk instead about local (to Canada) Native politics instead of trying to convince the Canadians that they needed to care about American Natives. I talked for about two minutes about a standoff that took place years ago in Quebec between Mohawk natives at Oka and the Sureté du Quebec (the police). At the end of this rant, I finished speaking with a suggestion of support for the Mohawks and their land rights position. The moment I finished, the room was silent. I had enough time to think, "Holy fuck...what have I done?" I was thinking that maybe I had overstepped my bounds and become, in the minds of the audience, the American who thinks he has all the answers for every other country in the world. I was always conscious of trying to speak on behalf of the whole band and thought for a moment that maybe I had screwed up somehow. There was a full couple moments of silence and then the place just fucking exploded. People started cheering and screaming and clapping and when we started the song and I thought the audience was going to tear the walls down. After the show, kids came up to me and said that they had been amazed that an American band actually cared about Canadian politics enough to say anything at all. Another moment of unleashed emotion was this one night in Holland. We had a song called "When There's Nothing Left to Lose," which is about claiming your right to suffer. All people suffer, yet we shield and mask that suffering all day every day with a veneer of calm, layers of perfection. I suggested to the audience that maybe just for one night, one song, we could give up guilt, give up shame, give up fear and anxiety about not being perfect and just admit and accept the fact that we were imperfect and desperate creatures and just share in that together. We told the audience to let out everything, to scream along whether they knew the words or not. When we started playing, there was an emotional explosion unlike anything I have ever experienced. The entire room let go. A girl came up to me after the show and told me that she had just stood in the back corner of the room, by herself in shadows, letting go, just screaming as loud as she could at the top of her lungs and crying. It still gets me choked up just thinking about that.

INTEREST IN SOCIAL/POLITICAL ISSUES

GREG BENNICK: I wasn't politically involved until I was 18 or so when I started talking to Native people about land rights. From there, just from reading and paying attention to the world, I got more and more involved with issues and the ideas, emotions, and people that went along with them. For me hardcore was and always will be about the intersection of vibrant energy and vital ideas. Trial strived to make music that mattered. We wanted to engage our audiences not only in terms of having them connect to the intensity of the music, but also in terms of their minds as well. Trial was always about bringing together the heart and the mind.

TIMM MCINTOSH: My interest stemmed mainly from the music I listened to. Music is such a powerful force and one of the greatest tools for change. I listened to heavy metal in the eighties and it was definitely great music, but lyrically it said nothing to me about the world I was living in. It didn't even say anything about me. The music that I got involved in was punk and hardcore and exposed me to issues that I may have never thought about. The music sparked my interest, but the ideas and opinions of my peers that did zines drove me to become more active and aware of the world I was living in.

GREG BENNICK: We identified the fact that we all suffer, for various reasons, and this [fact] needs to be embraced rather than denied or diverted. We need to come to understand our suffering and to feel it deeply. We need to identify this process as a vital part of being alive. When we suffer, it shows that we are feeling something, anything. Without feeling, we are dead, both inside and out. So to be wounded, alienated, abused, isolated...all of these things and more are elements of life itself. Trial wished to dive into and explore life and pain as deeply and intimately as possible.

INFLUENCE TO MAKE ISSUES A PART OF TRIAL'S SHOW

GREG BENNICK: If you have a pulse, it is impossible to ignore the political and social forces that are at work in the world. You don't have to be "politicized" either, meaning that you don't have to be an activist, or a protestor, or a voter, or anything to be affected and affected deeply by the world around us. With that in mind, Trial looked at deeper issues on our full-length: what is the nature of suffering? What motivates our fear and anxiety as we go through life? Why are we violent and what can we hope for in the midst of a violent world? How does our mortality play into all of this? When you start looking at the answers to those questions, you quickly realize that the day to day issues people encounter, from the war, to terrorism, to politics, and on and on, are all closely if not integrally tied in. You can't have a world absorbed in suffering without power struggles. Usually one would expect to hear that idea phrased the other way around: that you can't have power struggles (or government, or commerce, etc) without there being suffering. But what Trial looked at was that it is the suffering first that affects us, and that everything else branches out and is developed and built, by us, from there. We create religion and culture and politics *from* our suffering, they don't get created from nothingness and cause our suffering.

"ARE THESE OUR LIVES?"

GREG BENNICK: The Trial record I connect most with is the full length: *Are These Our Lives?*. That is the record on which we really hit our stride. The music is intense, and the lyrics are razor sharp, as a result of having tons of time to refine them. We finally got to the point we had been aiming towards musically and lyrically and listening to that record, even now six years later, feels amazing. That the record exists at all is a miracle. Three members of the band quit the summer prior to our recording and the songs on the record weren't fully finished yet. Timm and I spent the year finishing the record on our own and crafting the songs into what we wanted them to be. We got a bassist, Brian, to record with us in the studio and to join the band, but still needed a drummer. We called Jesus L. Pecador from Catharsis, the most dangerous band ever, to see if he'd be willing to play. He was, and flew out for a manic week of learning the songs in rehearsals followed by a week of recording. Recording was split up over two countries and three weeks. We did additional vocal tracking in Canada and then mixed and mastered there as well. I remember the last session when we mastered the record. We finished at six in the morning just in time to drive back to the States to get to work. Timm and I drove in silence all the way back to Seattle....it was a three hour drive, just the two of us. We listened to that record from beginning to end over and over again, feeling so very satisfied, like we had really accomplished something important and significant for ourselves, and hopefully for others too.

TIMM MCINTOSH: [This was] a record that almost didn't happen. After the departure of three members, my mindset was one of defeat as well as determination. Three people I shared so much time with, three people who became the closest friends I have ever known...just leaving the band without a word to me. It was heartbreaking. I felt defeated. Even though the songs weren't anywhere near what I wanted them to be, I was determined to finish up the songs that I had already put so much of my time and energy into. I remember sitting in my room making adjustments to the songs without a drummer to work out the changes. It was frustrating; I had all these ideas and no way to work them out. Greg kept pushing me and encouraging me that it could be done. I'd say that it's my proudest accomplishment. I don't know that I will ever write a record like *Are These Our Lives?* again. I'll never forget the morning that we drove back from Vancouver listening to the record. I was happy with it, but I wasn't sure what people that loved Trial from *Through The Darkest Days* and *Foundation* would think of it. It was heavier, dark, intense and politically charged. It was a progression and departure at the same time. We pushed ourselves beyond what we were really capable of.

CLASSICAL INTROS/OUTROS

GREG BENNICK: The classical parts on the *Are These Our Lives?* full length were Timm's idea. He started thinking about what it would be like to have one piece of music that took parts of all the other songs and combined them into one. He took the main guitar riffs from each of the songs on the album, transposed them to acoustic guitar and then imagined the strings, too. I found us some string players and we rehearsed a couple times, and then in the studio, it all came together. Without Timm, and the creativity and ability of the string section, those parts would never have happened. I love those parts because we can give the record to someone who hates the music and the songs and have them listen to that final "Seems Serene" track by itself while reading the lyrics and they will have a similar experience to if they had listened to the songs themselves.

TIMM MCINTOSH: Originally my idea was to have violin and cello on the song "Are These Our Lives?" only. After working it out and thinking about it more, I decided a full piece would be a good way to link the songs on the record together. Give the record a feel of being a solid unit. This was a frustrating process because I can't write sheet music, can't play violin or cello and, overall, I'm not a musician, really. I hear things in my head, I play my guitar and what comes out is what comes out. I wrote the parts on guitar, which are a combination of the melodies from each of the songs. After I completed that, I got together with a violin and cello player and directed them in the way I wanted it to sound. I'm sure this was frustrating for them since they were classically trained and usually played off of sheet music. They did an incredible job of converting my crazy humming into actual strings. I honestly didn't expect that it would have made it to the studio. I'm happy that it did, though. I think it opens people up that don't normally listen to hardcore to the ideas on the record.

GROWTH

GREG BENNICK: Being in a band is like dating four other people at once. You grow and change over time. We all learned to communicate better by the end of the band, but of course the things that drove us crazy about one another also grew by the end of the band! The musical progression is obvious from the demo through the album, but I had little to do with the actual mechanics of that. Timm got more focused in terms of what he wanted and more able technically to actualize what he was hearing in his head.

TIMM MCINTOSH: Anyone who listened to Trial from the beginning to the end will notice the change in the complexity of lyrics and music. We pushed ourselves to do the best we could, to not only challenge those around us, but also to challenge ourselves. I think that *Are These Our Lives?* was a realization of those changes. I wonder what we could have done next...was there any more room to grow?

TOUR STORIES

GREG BENNICK: One night, late, after a show in Philadelphia, Timm decided that it would be a good idea to shoot off bottle rockets into the air out on the street. After five minutes, this guy yelled out of a tenth floor window for Timm to stop. Timm yelled back that he would, but then kept setting off the fireworks. About three minutes later, this muscular construction worker guy with arms like tree trunks comes tearing around the corner out of the building and heads straight across the street, arms outstretched like a zombie, straight at Timm. No shirt, no shoes, just shorts on. As he got closer, he growled: "I am going to ask you nicely one time to stop" and as he did, he grabbed Timm by the throat and started strangling him. I grabbed the guy's forearm as he wrapped it around Timm's neck and started squeezing trying to pull it from Timm's neck, but it was like iron. My first thought was: "Oh well, Timm's going to die" because I was pulling on that guy's arm with all my might and couldn't move it even a millimeter. We were all over the guy, trying to get him to let Timm go, and eventually he did let go and backed off, leaving Timm choking and pissed off but thankfully alive. We calmed the guy down and he went home. We thought about lighting off more fireworks just to see what would happen, but decided against it. Timm was always creating tour magic. [Laughs] Another tour experience, though a bit different, came in 1998 when we toured for a weekend with Catharsis and that was amazing. The bands totally complemented one another and the crowds that came to see us were diverse enough to be interesting, but similar enough to make for amazing shows. Every night, there was fire juggling, drumming, and primal mayhem in the pit with the entire audience participating and letting go of inhibitions. We need more of that sort of thing in hardcore/punk/music in general. Music is so primal, and we need other similar forms of expression to come together with the musical angle we are used to taking.

TIMM MCINTOSH: I liked to have a lot of fun on tour. When you're in a van for hours and hours with four other guys...you get cabin fever. When that van stops and you have a chance to jump out...you get crazy. At least I do. My favorite story, though, didn't happen on tour, it happened at our first or second show. I can't remember exactly. If you know Greg, you know he's very diplomatic. Always willing to talk to you and discuss different points of view. We had a show at a teen center in Bremerton, Washington. There was a punk rock kid who was drinking outside the hall. During our set Greg addressed the consequences of someone drinking at a teen center, how it could lead to someone reporting it to the police, the police then shutting down the show and no more shows at the teen center for good. From the stage an argument begins and it's back and forth between underage punk rocker and Greg about the drinking. It gets heated and Greg finally gets so frustrated that he says, "Well...yeah, I'm right and you're wrong, so fuck you!" I will never forget that, it's a side of Greg that you don't get to see that often and so out of character. San Diego on our first tour was a good time, too. Wandering naked into random doughnut shops and asking if they had a job for me...I was a glazer and wanted to know if there was any donuts I could glaze. There was a big guy in the 7-11 that didn't find it that funny, good thing I was wearing shoes at least. I'm sure I could go on and on... but, those are our stories to recite to each other when I call Greg in 50 years and say, "Hey, remember that time when you..."

END OF THE BAND

GREG BENNICK: Trial broke up due to disagreements and frustrations amongst the members. Nothing too spectacular, actually. We just reached a point where moving forward artistically was going to be a challenge because of artistic and ideological differences and stagnating wasn't an option because of the desire of everyone to keep moving forward. To be honest, I question whether or not I would be able to write any better lyrics than I had on *Are These Our Lives?*, not because I am a lyrical genius, but rather because I had covered so much of what I think and feel on that record and I wasn't sure what was left that would fill a new full-length record with words of that potency. I miss Trial every day, especially when I endure empty small talk, see people hiding behind walls, when I feel that people aren't fulfilling their potential, or when I long for real connection. The reunion shows were perfect though, and I will always be thankful to everyone Seattle, London, Budapest, and every city from which people came to see us from around the world for their support and contribution. It would not, by any stretch of the imagination, have happened without each and every one of you.

TIMM MCINTOSH: The end of the band...man. I can only speak from my perspective. Frustrations had grown tremendously on our European Tour in 1999. Greg and I are like

brothers, actually, we're as close to it as you can be without sharing a parent. We'd often find ourselves in arguments about petty things. After we returned from the tour we all got together to talk about the upcoming tours that we wanted to do. Greg, at that time, wasn't feeling the same way about touring as he originally planned. Greg had other things in his life that he wanted to focus on. I think another big part of it is that Greg had dealt a lot with losing his voice on tour. We as humans never want to admit that we're fragile, I know that Greg had a hard time dealing with the fact that he was destroying his voice and not being able to give 100% to the band every night. We talked about me singing on the tours that he wasn't able to do, and this seemed like a good idea to keep the band going until Greg was able to focus 100% on the band again, but we know it wouldn't have been the same. The frustrations just became too much and we called it quits.

LOOKING BACK

GREG BENNICK: I would say by far that the biggest successes we had with the band on a social level, in my opinion, was with the expression of new angles and thought on the nature of suffering. We wanted to normalize suffering — not diminish it but make it okay and very human to be hurting deeply. We hit that mark with the song "Reflections." I love the fact that tons of bands are covering that song these days. I feel bad for their drummers as Jesus L. Pecador is the direct descendent of a hyperactive child and an octopus, but all the bands I have heard play it have done a great job with it so far. Another huge area where people benefited was with sexual assault survivors worldwide. Our song "Scars" was a catalyst for profound healing in individuals. I know this because I trained after our first tour as a crisis counselor for rape victim/survivors and would counsel people at our shows after we played. I am still in touch with many of these people and know that the work was cathartic. On the 107.7 KNDD interview, Timm and I talked about rape and sexual assault, and we both got supportive and widespread feedback after that interview. It is incredibly powerful when art and life not only intersect and reflect one another, but embrace and nurture one another. "Scars" was such an instance: the words in the songs, and our willingness to connect with those who were hurting, validated their pain. We also talked about sexually transmitted diseases that night and to this day we've had a continuing flow of people contact us either through our My Space page or directly in order to ask questions, share experiences, or offer encouraging words. There is more to come... without a doubt.

TIMM MCINTOSH: If I could do it all again, I would. Trial was my everything! I put all of my time and energy into the band. I shared time with people that I truly loved. I made connections that I would have never thought possible. I found out things about myself I never would have ever explored. I miss that. I miss that there will never be another Trial for me. It was a special time in my life that I shared with Greg and the others. It's surreal to have been a part of something that has had any sort of effect on anyone outside of the band. I don't know that I could ever wrap my head around that. The reunion shows were a bittersweet experience, the end to a band that I gave everything to and the realization that I was part of something that did make a difference in others lives, the way I was affected, no matter how small that difference was.

SELECT DISCOGRAPHY:

Through the Darkest Days (CD/7", Crimethinc, 1996)
    Bennick, McIntosh, Harn, Green

Foundation (CD/7", New Age, 1997)
    Bennick, McIntosh, Harn, Johnson, Green

Are These Our Lives? (CD/LP, Equal Vision, 1999)
    Bennick, McIntosh, Redman, Rodriguez

FIGHT: THE NINETIES HARDCORE REVOLUTION IN ETHICS, POLITICS, AND SO

UNBROKEN

Vocals: David Claibourn
Guitars: Eric Allen
       Steven Andrew Miller

Bass: Rob Moran
Drums: Todd Beattie

Known for their introspective, emotional lyrics, a sound that drew from Slayer, Integrity, Black Flag, and Drive Like Jehu, as well as a family-like bond that helped the members get through many difficult times, California's Unbroken were among the most enigmatic of the nineties hardcore bands.

The group was inspired by hardcore and straight edge as much as they were by the somber melodies of eighties post-punk bands like The Smiths and Joy Division. Unbroken formed after guitarist Eric Allen and drummer Todd Beattie of Flatline met bassist Rob Moran and guitarist Steven Andrew Miller to discuss forming a new hardcore band. Eventually, Midwest transplant David Claibourn joined on vocals and the band started to play shows around San Diego and Southern California.

Originally Unbroken's sound was reminiscent of other early-nineties Southern California straight edge hardcore bands like Outspoken, which was a blend of traditional hardcore with slight metal influences. By the time of their first full-length, *Ritual* (1993), the band took on a darker edge both musically and lyrically; the combination would eventually become a trademark for them. Their next record, *Life. Love. Regret.* (1994), was arguably among the defining full-lengths of nineties hardcore. By this point, the band had developed an emotionally turbulent hardcore sound that was technical, energetic, and therapeutic (for both the band and their fans alike). But what really made the record special was the deeply personal nature of the lyrics, which were contributed by several band members. Songs like "D4," "Final Expression," and "Curtain" were harrowing tales of frustration with relationships, personal failings, and dire social/political situations. As much as people enjoyed the music, many connected even more with their lyrics.

Unbroken toured cross-country on both *Ritual* and *Life. Love. Regret.* and slowly built up a following due to their captivating performances and unique fashion style. In a live setting, the band would often style their hair in the way their idol Morrissey would wear his and even sometimes wear dress shirts and ties. Some criticized them for daring to step outside the fashion norms of the scene, while others adored them for it.

After *Life. Love. Regret.*, Allen became less satisfied with their metallic sound and focused his songwriting more toward punk and noise. Inspired by San Diego bands like Drive Like Jehu and Rocket From The Crypt, Allen wrote a barrage of new riffs that comprised the band's final two seven-inches: *And/Fall on Proverb* and *Crushed On You*. These final songs were more frantic sounding than their previous records, but they were just as cathartic and sonically potent. As time has passed, many fans view these final two records collectively as their best work, though that is debatable as *Life. Love. Regret.* is quite impressive.

Around the release of the final two seven-inches, Unbroken decided to break up citing stagnancy in songwriting. Essentially, they felt they had done as much as they could with their sound and sought other musical possibilities. Soon, Allen joined forces with ex-Struggle members Justin Pearson and Jose Palafox to form Swing Kids. Miller and Moran went on to form emo/rock group Kill Holiday, while Claibourn moved home to St. Louis and started Johnny Angel. Beattie became focused on other aspects of his life outside the scene.

In 1998, Allen committed suicide. The rest of the band decided to play a reunion show to help Allen's family with funeral costs. Fans all over the country and even as far as Europe flew in to San Bernardino, CA for the show.

Although they were respected by many during their lifespan, Unbroken became even more popular after their 1995 break-up. Like many artists that are somewhat ahead of their time, Unbroken's muse was different. So, what made these Smiths worshipping, pomade wearing, splendidly dressed gentlemen so different? To put it simply: emotion. The kind of emotion that ignites revolutions in both mind and spirit. It is this pure emotion struck on every chord and heard in every scream that makes Unbroken so important to their fans and the many bands they influenced. Their songs conjure happiness, sadness, tragedy, and inspiration — a unique panorama of sounds, lyrics, and experiences that inspire people to this day.

ORIGINS/INSPIRATIONS

STEVEN ANDREW MILLER: Before we got into punk rock, we were all into British bands like The Smiths, Joy Division, and New Order. I learned how to play guitar by listening to The Smiths. I guess we all came into punk in our own ways. For instance, Eric Allen, our other guitarist, met up with Justin Pearson and got together and formed Struggle. Eventually, Unbroken was started by Eric Allen, Todd Beattie, and another singer.

ROB MORAN: I had met Todd and Eric at a Born Against show around 1990. We had met via various friends and just kind of new each other. Brian, the first singer, was doing a band with Eric and Todd called Flatline. Their bass player quit, so Eric and Brian had asked me if I wanted play bass and I said sure. I was doing this very dumb cover band at the time called X-Cellent Covers and we would do just all the New York City youth crew and hardcore bands as well as O.C. bands, too… stuff like Bold, Project X, Chain of Strength… God, this is a skeleton I had kind of forgot about! [laughs] Anyway, we got together in late 1990 and changed the name to Unbroken. Brian just stopped coming around to practice and New Age had wanted to do a record with us and we no longer had a singer. We also wanted to make our sound a little heavier so Steven Miller, a friend of Eric and Todd's, was asked to play second guitar. He added a whole new dimension to the band — he was just a little kid that came to our shows and ended up being a big part of the band. Dave was then asked to sing, as he used to sing a long to our demo and was a nice guy. Everything else just kind of fell into place.

DAVID CLAIBOURN: I moved to San Diego from the Midwest. I used to run into these guys as shows at the Che Café. I liked the band with their original singer. [laughs] Actually, it's kind of funny… when Rob originally asked me to sing for the band I thought he was kind of joking with me. So, basically, I told him to fuck off. [laughs] But when I found out he was serious I was like, "Yeah, of course I'll do it!" Not too long after that we recorded our first seven inch for New Age Records and we were pretty much a band from then on. I don't really think we got to our "sound" for a while, though.

TODD BEATTIE: I basically started playing drums only because being in an upper middleclass family I was the only one who could afford a drum kit. I got into the very accessible punk bands like The Sex Pistols and The Ramones and started playing punk songs with Steve and Eric. We would go out all day and skate, come back to the house, watch skate videos with a lot of skate punk shit, and try to play it. I think Steve was the first to start writing original songs. My brother was semi-abusive at times and was into drugs so we would write silly songs about being drug-free even before we had heard our first Minor Threat song.

METAL/HARDCORE CONCOCTION

ROB MORAN: The only two things that stick out in my mind was coming to practice with an Integrity cassette single on Progression Records and having that be a wake up call of how to be a hardcore band with metal influences. We were so different from everyone in hardcore in every way. Why not say fuck it and take it to the next level? So, we did.

STEVEN ANDREW MILLER: None of us were really into metal except for Rob. [laughs] I grew up listening to commercial metal like Black Sabbath, Ozzy and Def Leppard, but nothing that was super fast and heavy. I think at the time the heaviest record I owned was Judge's *Bringin' it Down*, which we thought was the toughest it got. In terms of our sound, we were really influenced by Downcast and Mean Season. I guess we were starting to get into metal to some degree after that, but not really knowing it. [laughs] I think we were getting sick of playing the typical 1-2-3 Go! hardcore of that time.

ROB MORAN: *Ritual*, our first full-length, was written, but half way through the writing process we discovered Drop D tuning and had written a song or two that end up being on *Life. Love. Regret.* as they just didn't fit with *Ritual*. We went ahead and finished *Ritual* and weren't too happy with it. People hated us so much because we just didn't fit in. We sounded more metal, we looked like rockabillys and we talked about topics other than straight edge.

DAVID CLAIBOURN: I'd say when we started we were kind of trying to be more like Outspoken or bands like that. Eventually, I think we just wanted to go for a more intense sound, which I think was something we were all feeling at the time. Steve and Eric were both great guitar players and they really pushed each other in good ways while also complementing each other. I think there were also bands — Drive Like Jehu and Helmet, for instance — that showed us that you could be intense without being just metallic.

TODD BEATTIE: Ever since my first concert — Bon Jovi and Cinderella — I dreamed of playing metal. I just couldn't convince Dave to grow a sweet mane of hair and whip it around in a circle on stage like all the rock gods were doing. No, seriously, I think it was an Integrity song that kicked me in the nuts and made me go out and buy a double bass pedal that I never really could play. After that first seven-inch on New Age Records we started to take on that nineties metal edge to hardcore music and it wasn't until much later that we really dialed into a truly original sound.

STEVEN ANDREW MILLER: I look back on *Ritual* with fondness, but I also view it nothing that was that great. It was definitely a record that was thrown together really fast and kind of incomplete.

EMOTIONAL TENOR

ROB MORAN: Everyone in the band was emotional. We cried on stage, broke up on stage in D.C. one time, fought, and all of it, I think, just translated into the music. Even if there were words on the music, we felt that those songs could convey emotion on their own. Dave just added to it and was an incredible liaison between the music and the words that were associated with it.

DAVID CLAIBOURN: Just being involved in the hardcore scene at the time you would hear the same banter night in and night out like "everything's so great." But life just isn't really like that. I think we started to talk about these kinds of things. I also think that since each band member was allowed to write lyrics to songs we were all allowed to vent our emotions in a way we weren't able to before.

STEVEN ANDREW MILLER: In my opinion, one of the things that opened us up the most was the fact that we started to get away from the typical lyrical content of what was expected of a straight edge band. A lot of bands might have had their animal rights song, their drug free song, their anti-sexism song, which was great, but it definitely got redundant. We were guilty of it, too. But the thing about hardcore was that it was supposed to be about youth crew this and that; everyone having a good time. At the same time, it was totally oblivious to the angst of being a teenager; the alienation of growing up wasn't addressed at all. None of us were happy kids. We definitely had issues of depression and thought about things of a darker nature.

TODD BEATTIE: It was after we had written all the typical "anthems" that every hardcore straight edge band was doing that we just got fed up. It was so ridiculous to see these preaching bands — us included at one time — to be singing this shit to an audience of other straight edge hardcore bands that were singing the same crap. It was then when we started to dig deeper.

"LIFE. LOVE. REGRET."

DAVID CLAIBOURN: I think we recorded the whole thing for like $800, which is nothing by today's standards. [laughs] I remember it being a fun time, but also a very intense one. I was even writing lyrics to a couple of songs as they were being recorded. I like the fact that everyone in the band had their voice on the record somewhere. I remember listening to it in the car after we got our copy and really feeling a sense of accomplishment that we didn't necessarily come away with after *Ritual*.

STEVEN ANDREW MILLER: *Life. Love. Regret.* was definitely a concept record. It was planned out from the artwork on down. Musically we recorded a diary and published it for everyone to see. It was just us being us. That record completely defines us as people during these years.

ROB MORAN: That was a tough time in our lives. Eric had quit and come back, there were girlfriend issues, people we knew died, there was a big fistfight in the studio. All of that helped to shape what that album was all about. I think that's why we were, are and always will be proud of that record. It just captured everything we were going through. Demons were exorcized and real tears and blood were captured on the record. Even on "Final Expression," you can hear Eric literally crying when he does his back up parts. It was a turbulent, real, yet fun time.

TODD BEATTIE: This was the first time that we weren't trying to be some band that we saw somewhere at some time at some show that we thought was the shit. We were being totally honest and coming out with toughest sounding shit we could musically and lyrically. We knew that this was something special when we were recording it. As Dave was saying, we did it for $800 and I really don't think we needed any more money to do it. It was so honest and it just happened like that, tears and all.

INNER TURMOIL

DAVID CLAIBOURN: I'll never forget having a guitar bounce off my head during a show in D.C. [laughs] Eric had quit in the middle of a tour. He had a chemical imbalance and if you put that in a stressful, cramped touring environment it can sometimes lead to problems. It was definitely a rough trip out there and by the time we got to D.C. he really missed his girlfriend and was just frustrated. It's funny, in the liner notes of the original *Life. Love. Regret.* release he put a sheet of paper in his section with his bus itinerary. He took a bus from D.C. all the way back home to San Diego, which had to suck.

ROB MORAN: We were so young and confused at this stage in our lives. It was that crossroad into adulthood of, "Do I go to college and do what is expected?" or "Do I tour in bands and experience the world for what it is?" I feel a lot of that translated into our music, and that was how we dealt with those questions. We knew deep down this was a dead end road as far as the society ladder went, so I think it was that take it for everything it is worth attitude that allowed us to be so real with what we were doing.

STEVEN ANDREW MILLER: I was 18 when we recorded *Life. Love. Regret.* Life was so simple then to some degree. For instance, I didn't have to pay rent; I had a girlfriend, worked part time and played music as much as possible. It was a very naïve and confusing time of my life, I'd say.

DAVID CLAIBOURN: We definitely all had our own sets of problems, but this, at times, seemed to help us bond together. I guess my philosophy is that the people who are really fucked up in this world are the ones who don't think they are fucked up at all. I think everyone has problems and you just have to work through them with time and experience. Unbroken was kind of like my version of psychotherapy. [laughs] Any time I had to deal with stuff I was able to get it out through recording a record or playing a show. I'm indebted to my bandmates and anyone who ever came to see us to allow me to have that outlet. That band was medicine for me that I needed at the time.

TODD BEATTIE: I was just kind of getting sick of the whole hardcore scene. We would be so close to each other for months on tour being cramped in a tiny van that when we would finally get back home we wanted nothing to do with one another. Night after night watching all these cloned bands, "Who has the fattest X on their hand?" Fuck that shit. The last tour I bleached my hair and wore some sweet Daisy Dukes to protest that tough guy jock look. I think there must be some pictures of my balls on drum stools out there. Yeah, I was mixed up. I think my inner turmoil was in my pants!

"AND"

STEVEN ANDREW MILLER: To be honest, there are two bands that influenced our later sound: Rocket From the Crypt and Drive Like Jehu. We were also huge fans of a lot of the Gravity bands like Antioch Arrow and Heroin. We were probably more into "punk rock" than the average hardcore kid. [laughs] There are kids into hardcore that seem to have no idea how revolutionary punk rock was in the early 80s. Like why were there straight edge bands in the first place? Why was there a need for someone in the punk rock community to say, "I'm not going to drink or do drugs"?

DAVID CLAIBOURN: The diversity in the San Diego music scene was really inspiring at the time. It wasn't uncommon for us to play a show with bands from a whole variety of different music styles. This really opened us up and exposed us to a lot of sounds that had an impact on the later era of Unbroken as well as the bands we did after we broke up. I think a lot of kids might remember us as just this straight edge hardcore band, but we were, first and foremost, a San Diego band.

ROB MORAN: We recorded the *And* seven inch in D.C. on the *Life. Love. Regret.* tour. We were at a good place, I think. There was nothing chaotic going on; we just wanted to try something different. What helped is I remember being on that tour and listening to "Wolverine Blues" by Entombed. I think it was a combination of Entombed and Drive Like Jehu that may have given our later seven-inches that angry sound. [laughs]

DAVID CLAIBOURN: I think I had tried to get Eric to listen to Drive Like Jehu for a long time, and he finally listened to them and got it. [laughs] He was the force behind a lot of that later material.

TODD BEATTIE: Yes, this was a true departure from our previous material. We were tired and jaded at a lot of crap that we heard and really didn't care what people would think about it. We liked it and we rocked it.

"WE LIVE AND DIE WITH OUR OPINIONS"

DAVID CLAIBOURN: I remember we'd go on tour and we'd see these stickers that said, "Go vegan or go fuck yourself." In the liner notes for *Life. Love. Regret.*, Todd basically said, "I'd rather do the right thing for the right reasons then do the cool thing for no reason at all." At that point, straight edge became very fashionable. If you had the Schism long-sleeve you were cool. The thing I'm happy I said, and I still mean it to this day, is "We live and die with our opinions." To me, this states that a lot of times in the hardcore scene we have similarities, but many kids focus on the differences. Let's not focus on the little differences. We have them in life and death and they'll always be there. But when you have a small scene like hardcore there doesn't need to be this further separation of people. It should be more open-ended. The ideological discussions should be there and you can agree to disagree, but why not try to see the commonalities between each other?

WINDING DOWN

DAVID CLAIBOURN: Eric and Steve were the main songwriters and they seemed to feel that the well was eventually tapped out; that there weren't any more songs in them for this style of music. In retrospect, I think every band has a certain kind of maturity process. I think *Life. Love. Regret.* was really the sound of Unbroken. Everything before was our process getting up to that point. But I had to respect their decision and the fact that they said they didn't have it in them anymore.

ROB MORAN: I think we were on tour in Europe, and decided that it had kind of run its course. We said we would do another East and West Coast tour then call it quits. It was nothing bad, it was just the newer songs we were writing, which I thought were awful, just didn't sound like us anymore. We sounded more like Rocket From the Crypt than Unbroken.

STEVEN ANDREW MILLER: The end came about because the band had run its course. We did all that we could possibly do. We had no aspirations of being on a big label or making tons of money. I think the best way to go out is to when you're still on top of your game because you can't tarnish it. I'd rather someday say "I wish that band would have kept playing" than "this band should have been done years ago." [laughs] It was also cool that during our recorded history we never once changed band members and also kept the same spirit and ethic alive for the duration of our existence.

TODD BEATTIE: I think it was the first time I saw "Clap Dancing" that I knew the end was near.

SUBSEQUENT INFLUENCE OF UNBROKEN

STEVEN ANDREW MILLER: To be honest, I'm not as familiar with most present hardcore. When we were doing Unbroken, we weren't concerned with what anyone else sounded like. The thing about hardcore is, of course, is that every single straight edge kid thinks the prime era of hardcore is the era that they are a part of. [laughs] In retrospect, *Life. Love. Regret.* has become bigger after our band's death than during our existence. Unbroken is a far bigger band now than when we were playing. I'm not bitter about it, but it is ironic that when we did our tours there was always somebody else that people seemed to be more concerned about. People would come up to me during this time and say, "Hey, what's going on with Strife?" Basically, anything other than what had to do with us. [laughs] It was weird to find out years later that people actually looked at Unbroken as an influential band. I wish we could have seen that more during our existence.

DAVID CLAIBOURN: I'm honored that people still really like Unbroken. My new band, Stabbed By Words, recently played a show in Syracuse and I was blown away when some people came up to me and showed me their "Life. Love. Regret." tattoos. I guess I can remember a time going to shows and screaming along to lyrics of other bands that I felt meant more to me at that time than they did to the band itself. I was always honored when we would play and some kids seemed to have the same reaction to us. I was just a kid screaming into a mic like anyone else could, so I'm flattered that people took it to heart.

TODD BEATTIE: I'm totally blown away when I meet someone from this era of hardcore who knows of Unbroken. I see an Unbroken shirt in passing or a sticker and immediately I'm taken back to the Che Café playing in front of 30 people. It's such a strange feeling to see someone with a tattoo of this band I was in 10 years ago.

THE PASSING OF ERIC

STEVEN ANDREW MILLER: Eric's death was very unfortunate. I had been friends with him since we were very young. I don't have any brothers in my family, but he is the closest thing I've got to a brother. We were all depressed kids at different points in our lives and Eric, with all due respect, wasn't the most emotionally stable guy at times. He disappeared and I eventually found out he committed suicide. I don't know what drove him to it, but I know his head wasn't clear going into those final days.

DAVID CLAIBOURN: When Eric passed away I was flat broke and I couldn't even get a ticket out there for his funeral, and that really sucks. I'm not bitter at anyone in particular, but I wish I would have had the opportunity to be at that funeral. I wasn't really able to say goodbye to him until we played the reunion benefit show for his family.

ROB MORAN: I got call at 8 a.m. from a very good friend of ours named Don. I thought he was fucking around and I told him it wasn't funny. Then Steve called me up crying an hour later and my heart just sank. The worst part about it for me was that [Eric] had called me a couple days before to go out to dinner, but I couldn't go. Two days later he killed himself. What hurts most about Eric's passing is that it was probably best for him. It is sad when you know someone close to you is in pain and beyond help. Another aspect of this that hurts is what great music he might have created if he was still alive. To this day [Eric was] one of the most talented people I have ever played with.

TODD BEATTIE: I was working with him at a warehouse job at the time. He got hooked on pain meds and did some really strange shit at work like slice box cutters into his shoulder and arm because he would say that he was numb to pain. I would walk by later and he would be passed out on the floor. He would show up to work sometimes totally out of his mind speaking about crazy shit that was happening to him. It was so scary. He would disappear for weeks at a time and when I finally got the call, I was totally relieved. I can remember when we were kids and Steve, Eric, and I would be skating at some school and he would say that he hated grownups and that he would never grow old, he would never live to be 30. I think this is what he truly wanted. As tragic as that sounds, he is happier now.

DAVID CLAIBOURN: I remember the last conversation I had with him. When I talked to him, I got a sense that he had accomplished everything he set out to accomplish. He mentioned that there were some things bothering him, but we just didn't get into it. I remember telling him how awesome Swing Kids were and how I wished I had stayed out there and could have possibly played with them. I also told him, "Eric you are simply one of the most genuine people I've met in my life." He thanked me and said that was one of the nicest things anyone had told him in a while. We said goodbye and that was basically it.

MEMORIAL SHOW

STEVEN ANDREW MILLER: Eric's family didn't have a lot of money. I can't remember who thought of the idea; I think it was Rob. He said that we should have Unbroken get back together for one show and have all the money go to Eric's family. At first, I thought it was a great idea, but the more I thought about it I didn't want to do it. It felt wrong to me for some reason. Aside from Eric not being there to play, some of us weren't straight edge anymore, and we were just kind of different people. I didn't know if we would be cheating people. I didn't have a good feeling about it. Anyway, a friend of mine drove me to the show and I saw hundreds and hundreds of kids in the place and the atmosphere was positive and somehow it just triggered a really good feeling. I was awestruck to some degree.

DAVID CLAIBOURN: It was a strange night. It rained all day, which is kind of rare in Southern California. There were around 1,500 kids there, which was unbelievable! Since Eric wasn't there it wasn't quite the same, but as we practiced our songs the nights before it was almost as if nothing had changed. It was still fresh. For myself, I needed to say goodbye to Eric. The way I needed to do it was to make every person in that room shut up for a minute and think about him because I needed to think about him. It was very hard to play those songs in front of all these people without him. So, we just thought about him and played our hearts out.

LOOKING BACK

STEVEN ANDREW MILLER: I remember coming to towns on our first U.S. tour and some of us had greased hair and pompadours and things like that due to our affinity toward Morrissey and people looked at us like, "What the hell are you doing? Are you guys gay?" [laughs] I also remember hearing that Strife, who was also from southern California, was saying things like, "Unbroken isn't a straight edge band because they dress nice and wear sweaters and have cuffs on their jeans." [laughs] This was funny because when we went back on tour in 1994 people in the scene all over the country had started dressing this way. As much as people say *Life. Love. Regret.* was influential, the only influence I noticed us have while we were playing was our impact on scene fashion. [laughs]

ROB MORAN: All we ever wanted to do was release a seven inch and we would have been happy. We had no idea it was going to turn into tours and an LP! We had no clue what we were doing, but it was fun. To hold an LP in your hands when all you wanted to do was release a seven inch was a huge deal! I'll never forget that feeling! Everything was fun; no expectations or anything else for that matter. It was just friends and sometimes adversaries creating something special.

STEVEN ANDREW MILLER: I'm happy to have had to do the opportunity to do all of the things I did with that band. Some people judge things in terms of how many records you sell and what not but that's just bullshit. That's not why we did this band. It wasn't about making money. It was about hanging out with some great friends and playing music. I was also able to meet so many people across the country and even from other parts of the world.

TODD BEATTIE: Our personalities would often collide and we would go months without speaking, but when we were on stage playing our music we couldn't have been closer. I'm older now, losing my hair, working a store designer job like that gay guy named "Hollywood" in the movie *Mannequin*, but you mention Unbroken and I'm 18 again fucking shit up on stage with my friends.

DAVID CLAIBOURN: I don't have any blood siblings, but if I've ever had brothers in my life it [has been] the guys in Unbroken.

SELECT DISCOGRAPHY:

You Won't Be Back (7",New Age, 1992)
   Claibourn, Allen, Miller, Moran, Beatti)

Ritual (CD/LP, New Age, 1993)
   Claibourn, Allen, Miller, Moran, Beatti)

Life. Love. Regret. (CD/LP, New Age, 1994)
   Claibourn, Allen, Miller, Moran, Beattie

And/Fall On Proverb (7", Three-One-G, 1995)
   Claibourn, Allen, Miller, Moran, Beattie

Crushed On You (7", New Age, 1995)
   Claibourn, Allen, Miller, Moran, Beattie

It's Getting Tougher to Say the Right Things (CD Discography, Indecision, 2000)

The Death of True Spirit (CD Discography, Indecision, 2003)

FIGHT: THE NINETIES HARDCORE REVOLUTION IN ETHICS, POLITICS, AND SO

UNDERTOW

Vocals/Bass: John Pettibone
Vocals: Joel DeGraff
Guitars: Mark Holcomb
Seth Linstrum

Bass: Demian Johnston
James Stern
Drums: Ryan Murphy

Seattle's Undertow created a sound that combined the rapid-fire eighties hardcore of bands like Brotherhood with a metallic, groove-oriented approach reminiscent of Inside Out, Absolution, Burn, and Beyond. Known for their heavy, rumbling verses and anthemic choruses that built and built until they were ready to burst, Undertow's songs had a distinct explosive sound that was unique but didn't stray too far outside the realm of what hardcore fans liked. They were on a similar path as Integrity, 108, and their California blood-brothers Unbroken in conjuring a dark and imposing atmosphere in an effort to illustrate their personal and political feelings and frustrations.

Undertow started as a reaction to the constantly hazy skies that filled the atmosphere in Washington. The area's depression and suicide rates are high because of these factors, and when you grow up feeling a bit "different" than those around you — a feeling everyone in Undertow had in common — it makes your teenage years all the more challenging. But once the members found hardcore, the music's rebellious nature stirred something inside of them and built some much needed self-confidence. A fan of legendary eighties Seattle straight edge hardcore group Brotherhood, John Pettibone was inspired by their positive anthems and eventually befriended the band. Just as Brotherhood was coming to a close at the end of the eighties, a young band named Refuse — comprised of future Undertow guitarist Mark Holcomb and drummer Ryan Murphy — was just beginning. After some member shuffling, Refuse asked Pettibone to replace original bassist James Stern, but then transferred him to vocals with the arrival of bassist Demian Johnston. Pettibone's voice was so loud and booming that he hardly needed a microphone to scream over their amps. Now united as a solid four-piece, they sought to help keep the Seattle hardcore scene thriving in the absence of Brotherhood. After playing with nearly every area punk and hardcore act, as well as a variety of touring groups, Undertow gathered momentum and hit other places.

As they were cutting their teeth in the world of touring — complete with several runs up and down the West Coast and eventually a jaunt out east — they put out their debut seven-inch, *Stalemate*, which contained one of their best known crowd movers, "Cutting Away." During their formative time as a band, the members were broadening their minds and learning about the world. Although the group was never a firmly issue-oriented outfit, the lyrics in many of their songs covered topics that were heavily analyzed in hardcore at the time such as straight edge, animal rights, racism, and homophobia. Pettibone in particular was often outspoken about such issues on stage.

At Both Ends, Undertow's only full-length, found the band progressing as musicians as they attempted to incorporate elements of metal and noise alongside their heavy hardcore riffs. This trend continued and reached its peak on the band's final EP, *Control*. Along with groups like Ressurection, Coalesce, Groundwork, and Deadguy, Undertow were forerunners in utilizing a noise/metal-laden approach to their brand of hardcore, which would fully manifest in some of the members' later bands (in particular, Johnston with Kiss it Goodbye and Playing Enemy; Pettibone with Himsa).

The fact that their sound evolved led to some problems maintaining the band as a functioning unit as the members were pulled in different personal and artistic directions. At the same time, the nineties Seattle straight edge scene Undertow helped build was bigger than ever, but its popularity also brought violent elements to shows, which the band saw as a disgrace. Ultimately these factors took a toll on the group, and they broke up in 1995, though they would soon do a brief reunion tour in Europe and a couple of final shows on the West Coast.

Undertow's story mirrored the tale of many involved in nineties hardcore, which is perhaps what made them so easy to identify with. They grew up in a confusing world and attempted to find their own place within the chaos that often engulfed their lives. They fell in love with a sub-culture only to be disappointed by its perceived limitations. Despite

their occasional differences, Undertow's members remained friends, learned a lot about themselves, each other, and society and used the scene as an outlet to express their feelings the only way they knew how — through some of the heaviest, emotional, and intense hardcore of the nineties.

INCEPTION OF THE BAND

JOHN PETTIBONE: In the late-eighties there were very few shows going on in Seattle because of a teen dance ordinance. As soon as [the cops] found out about a show they shut it down. But there was a place that was a ferry ride across from Seattle which was this old movie theater where they did shows. Everyone that came through played there but very few hardcore bands came through at that time. Brotherhood played and they talked about straight edge and the values of straight edge and unity and being involved and I totally connected with that. I bought their demo and t-shirt and I fell in love with it. I remember I wrote a letter to the address on the demo and about a week later I got a letter back from Ron Brotherhood, the singer, and he said, "Hey, we're playing this show; you should come and hang out." He took on a big-brother role with me. He instantly became a hero. I was kind of naïve and I thought it was so surreal I was friends with someone in a band that I liked so much.

RYAN MURPHY: Undertow started as a band called Refuse. Mark Holcomb and myself started Refuse in the fall of 1988 with a kid named Joel who was the first singer for Undertow. In 1990, Refuse changed the name to Undertow and we had John Pettibone playing bass at the time and a kid named Seth Linstrum on guitar. Eventually, we got rid of Seth and Joel and had John move to vocals. Demian came on board in 1992.

MARK HOLCOMB: We eventually kicked out Joel. Joel, Ryan, and I all went to high school together, so we had known each other for a long time. Ryan and I started to dislike Joel and his singing style — he really got into Morrissey and we were listening to Judge. [laughs] We basically broke up the band, but later that day we just decided to keep it going with other people. We got John to sing because he wasn't that good of a bass player. [laughs] We stole a bass player from our friend's band and our second guitarist moved from San Diego.

JOHN PETTIBONE: I met those guys and totally got along with them and felt this connection with them. When Refuse played I felt like this was something I wanted to be a part of. I was never really accepted in junior high and high school and it seemed like I had now found a home as well as some great friends. So, I stayed in contact with those guys and eventually they kicked the bass player out because he wasn't straight edge anymore and they asked me to play. That's how Undertow started. We were always involved in the punk rock scene because not a lot of hardcore bands came through town.

Then there was this place in Seattle called Washington Hall that started up. Brotherhood had turned into a band called Resolution and you could slowly see their interest in being a part of the community dissolve. At that time Undertow was starting to play and we started to make a name for ourselves. We played house shows almost every weekend and we made so many relationships with other kids who felt the same way as us about straight edge, they just weren't really aware of what it was due to a lack of exposure. We finally got up to Bellingham and also played in Vancouver and this scene started to happen in the northwest.

RYAN MURPHY: The early days of the band are essentially high-school memories. I don't remember much about school, but I remember a lot from Undertow. We would practice every Tuesday because our high school had half day Tuesdays. One year we ended up playing a show at John's high school which was really weird. It was funny around Seattle back then, there wasn't a big scene. As a matter of fact the scene was really small and if 50 kids showed up that was huge. One thing I remember about Undertow, and am still proud of, is that we would play *any* show. We played shows wherever we could and with any band. We actually got our first show at 924 Gilman with M.D.C., Final Conflict, and Filth. The crowd at that show hated us; we were four 15-year-old straight edge kids who had somehow infiltrated their crusty scene for the night. But at the end of the show, people were fired up on us and Gilman gave us a show whenever we needed one.

DEMIAN JOHNSTON: I joined after the band had been together for a couple years. I was just a fan who played bass guitar. I know they wanted to be in a band like Brotherhood. And they were great from the get-go.

FORMATION OF THE SOUND/EARLY DAYS

MARK HOLCOMB: We listened to everything we could get our hands on. All of us were writing music. I remember Ryan wanted to play faster stuff. When the Inside Out demo and eventual seven-inch came out that blew my mind! I loved the sound of Chain of Strength's vocals, too. It wasn't this "I've been riding the subway and I'm pissed off growly" type of New York thing, it was from the soul—Zack [from Inside Out] screamed his brains out. The first time I heard "Burning Fight" I thought it was the best song I'd ever heard. We started to realize that everything didn't have to be fast—it could be mid-tempo or slow, which might sound pretty obvious, but we were still young and trying to put it all together. [laughs] We played some shows in California and recorded a demo and then the band fell apart again.

RYAN MURPHY: A funny little fact about us: when we first started playing together, we wanted to sound like The Accused. We wrote a couple of shitty thrashy-sounding songs, and then went and saw Brotherhood play, came back, and were a full-on straight edge band. In the early days Youth of Today, Bold, and Brotherhood were big influences. We didn't know what we were doing for the most part and would just write a bunch of parts, then put them all together. As the band progressed we all got a little better at playing our instruments and different bands began influencing us more. Swiz was probably the band that had the biggest influence.

JOHN PETTIBONE: Our only real goal was to play shows with bands we loved. We played with Headfirst, Neurosis, and even Poison Idea pretty early on, which was pretty inspiring. We recorded a demo and Ron Brotherhood was willing to put it out on his label, Overkill Records. We were more metallic sounding, but our influences were pretty broad. Our first tour of the West Coast was with Jawbreaker, believe it or not, just before *Unfun* came out. We wanted to sound like a mixture of Burn and No Escape. We were getting into heavier sounds and wanted to incorporate that into our songs.

MARK HOLCOMB: When we were about 15 we'd play basement shows with about four songs under our belt. But then for a while there was nowhere to play after Brotherhood broke up. There was a law in Seattle for a long time called the Teen Dance Ordinance that said you couldn't have all-ages shows at venues that sold alcohol, which were pretty much the only places that could put on shows. If you had an all-ages show the insurance was so crazy; plus, they weren't allowed to sell alcohol so venues didn't see anything in it for them to put on all-ages shows. If there was a show somehow, no matter what type of sound, you went to it, so consequently that kind of united the scene a bit as there weren't really "all punk" or "all hardcore" showcases. All these different types of bands had to play together. We just kept on playing wherever we could. Eventually the city realized it made a mistake because when kids don't have a place to go they often end up causing trouble—throwing rocks into windows or whatever. If they had a place to go then maybe something positive could come of it. So, this church had shows for a bit and then there were shows that started cropping up in other places.

JOHN PETTIBONE: I remember I was at any early Green Day show and there was this kid up front and he turned around and looked at me and said, "Hey, you're in Undertow, right?" He started telling me about himself and how he was really into hardcore and he was a bass player and I said, "Funny you should say that. We're looking for a new bass player because our old one left, and if we don't find one we're going to break up." He said he'd love to play with us and he turned around and fainted during Green Day's set. [laughs] I helped him get outside and gave him some water and it turned out to be Demian. He became an integral part of the band and that's when the band really got going. He helped solidify what the band was.

DEMIAN JOHNSTON: Before me [Undertow's primary influence] was Inside Out. Once I came into the band we started to want to sound more like Burn with a touch of Integrity. I borrowed a Sunn Concert head and a Sunn 2 x 15" cabinet and I was embarrassed of it. I wanted a Crate or something stupid. Well, the bass was really loud in Undertow — I had that Sunn set-up for most of Undertow's career — and that helped make us try to make the bass more important.

CHANGES/TENSION

MARK HOLCOMB: Nirvana and a bunch of other bands in Seattle broke and all of a sudden the people who thought we were weird in high school thought we were cool. They wanted to see if we were like Nirvana, so a ton of people from our high school started to come out, which was weird. We started playing shows with bands like Sparkmarker and all of a sudden there was a scene in Seattle. At the time we were probably the only straight edge band [in the area], but I started to see other straight edge kids starting bands, too. We thought this was cool and it would finally put Seattle on the map again [in hardcore]. But then everyone started to not get along and shows became kind of cruddy, and to top it off everyone in the band was pissed at each other. We were going to play two last shows in Canada with Strain—the first show was awful and we almost just called it quits and went home. But the next show wasn't as bad. The city of Redmond opened up a venue to do shows and we got on one with Seaweed, which sold out at about 1,500 people. Most of the people were there to see Seaweed, but a bunch of our friends showed up and sang along and it really pumped us up. We figured, "Well, there's this cool new venue, people are coming to shows, why not keep it going?"

EMOTION

JOHN PETTIBONE: Seattle is so far up in the corner of the U.S., and it's a very dark and bleak city in some ways. It rains here over 200 days a year and it's just so gray. It has this feeling of depression and the suicide rate is actually pretty high. I grew up as a punk kid getting picked on all the time. I had two friends throughout high school. I got the shit kicked out of me all the time, so a lot of the emotion stemmed from those experiences early in our lives, as the rest of the guys could also identify.

DEMIAN JOHNSTON: A bunch of boys in their late teens and early twenties are going to be filled with emotion. It seemed like a lot of lyrics had to do with how messed up hardcore was or the problems with relationships and the occasional song about burning and how the fire is inside or whatever. We were messed up kids and loved to scream. What else could we say?

MARK HOLCOMB: We got into a lot of West Coast hardcore like Chain of Strength because it was a dude screaming his fucking brains out. It just made me feel more connected to the intensity of the music. There were also other bands that also showed us you didn't have to just be screaming about straight edge. You could tell when some of these guys were singing that they were putting their soul into it; you could almost feel how life was cracking them down. It was always about emotion. John could scream like the best of them. And we didn't have to be screaming about getting pushed around in Thompkins Square; I'd get pushed around by jocks and we'd just sing about our daily lives. We just wanted Undertow to be a reflection of our lives.

RYAN MURPHY: What's funny is that I just came across an old VHS tape of Undertow shows and started watching some of it. I could actually remember some of the shows and what it was like playing them, and it gave me goose bumps. The one thing about hardcore is that for the most part it is completely honest. We were not amazing musicians, but we poured everything we had into making those songs. We did not need the crowd to go ballistic; we just needed to get behind the instruments and play our songs together. I remember always being fired up to play shows and we would feed off of each other's energy. Towards the end we stopped feeling that same energy and it began to feel like we were going through the motions more and more. I think once we felt that sincere energy begin to fade, we had to stop doing the band. Thinking back on it, I would have to say that [the emotional release] was being part of something so sincere and sharing that experience with my close friends.

JOHN PETTIBONE: [The emotional release] was just natural for us. I always try to put so much personality into what I sing about. Seattle is a very depressing place. I come from a good family, but I grew up in a small, backwards town in the way they think of the rest of the world, and I felt like I was never a part of that mindset ever. Being able to go into the city and catch a glimpse of city life at such a young age was amazing. My parents gave me the freedom to expand my mind by going out on the weekend, provided I kept up with my schoolwork. I was able to see both sides of the world—the small city life as well as the big city. With Undertow I wanted to connect with the kids in front of me. A lot of us come from that same mindset or feeling in that we didn't fit in with mainstream society.

"STALEMATE"

MARK HOLCOMB: *Stalemate* started as a demo. We were supposed to do a record with Overkill Records, but the label was kind of wishy-washy about it. He wasn't really into our demo. Later our friend Dave from Excursion said he'd put our demo on a seven-inch; he couldn't give us any money for the recording, but he said he'd press it. We just wanted something to come out, so we went along with it. This was right when John started singing. I was starting to have my way in terms of songwriting. I was a late bloomer as far as social life; I was consumed with playing guitar while the other guys had girlfriends and were into other things. Toward the end of high school I became the main songwriter and had a specific vision for how I wanted the band to sound. We were really into Burn, Neurosis, and Inside Out. I can point to songs where we ripped off parts from those bands that we really liked. [laughs] We might have a Burn type of riff, but then we'd speed it up, change it up, try and make it our own.

RYAN MURPHY: With *Stalemate*, we just wanted to get something out there that represented what we were doing right then. John recently started singing for us and with *Stalemate*, for me anyways, I just wanted to hurry up and move past the first version of the band. I do remember being fired up once we played our first shows with it out.

LYRICAL CONTENT

MARK HOLCOMB: All of us had a typical suburban life in some ways. Nobody talked deeply about what was going on, but we were all fairly messed up whether we were neglected or just had other issues. We bonded over the fact that none of us got along with our families and hardcore and straight edge gave us a family. I didn't think I'd live to be 30. I didn't want to be a doctor or an architect, so hardcore became my life for a while. Some people go to college or do other stuff, but Undertow really was our first step toward learning about the world and finding ourselves as individuals. We were pissed-off because we felt like there was no one else in the world supporting us other than the guys in the band and our friends in bands like Unbroken—this became our family.

JOHN PETTIBONE: A lot of our songs were personal, but we also wrote about sexism, racism, and homophobia. At that time those subjects were brought up but not really pushed. A lot of times I felt like, "Yeah, I'm on stage and kids are screaming along, but are they getting it?" There were times when I was very preachy. I guess my stance reflects where I came from with my small town background. I remember there were only about two black families in my hometown and I remember hearing constant stories about them being humiliated. It was so farfetched for me; why are people treating other human beings like this? I wanted to bring out the emotion out in every song whether it was about something that angered me or something that inspired love or passion within me.

MARK HOLCOMB: We never really had a straight edge song. A lot of people thought "Control" was a straight edge song but actually it wasn't. Around that time Demian and I were getting sick of the straight edge mentality because Undertow had gotten a bit bigger as did hardcore. When some of our friends went out east and brought back kickboxing to Seattle, it sickened us. Seattle used to be this awesome place where all the bands of all types could play with each other, but around this time when we'd play people would start kickboxing and bringing out the macho element that wasn't really there before.

JOHN PETTIBONE: We were a straight edge band, but we never forced it on anyone. When Undertow started really cranking there were about 300 straight edge kids within the Seattle area and there were all these bands starting. There were so many of us but all the kids just weren't into straight edge hardcore. We played shows with Victory bands and even Ebullition bands like Struggle or groups like Heroin. We did have a slight political agenda, but we weren't a preachy band. We brought up topics we felt were important such as homophobia. Also, it might sound corny but everyone goes through personal trauma at times, and a lot of our songs were about just that—getting those negative feelings off our chest.

TOURS

MARK HOLCOMB: We went on a two month U.S. tour with Sparkmarker. Dave Excursion put out *Stalemate* and supported us. We were stoked to go. It was the best time of my life. When we left we were pretty naïve about what the rest of the country would be like. I remember Demian only had a couple pairs of socks that were supposed to last him for two months. The pair he was wearing when he first got in the van stunk so bad we told him we'd buy him new socks with our own cash and we threw them out the window. [laughs] We didn't know if the van was going to make it. The guitar player from Sparkmarker and I booked the whole tour through *Book Your Own Fuckin' Life*, and I remember you had to call 10 people to get a hold of the 11th. [laughs] Our guarantee was $50. If you didn't have money to eat you didn't eat. Looking back, I loved that part of it as it was a challenge. You'd play some shows and there would be two kids there. I remember kids asking me to give them a shirt because they didn't have enough money. I just remember thinking, "You've got to be kidding me! We had to borrow money to make 50 shirts; you think we're just going to give you one?" [laughs] I remember pulling up to a show and this guy told us a guy got shot at the venue the previous week and the police were supposed to be arriving because they expected a gang war over retaliation

for the incident. Seattle at the time was a quiet town whereas the East Coast was a real eye-opener. Some shows were amazing while other shows... I remember we had three shows cancelled in one week, our van broke down and this mechanic said he would come in on a Sunday and work on the van for us. He gave us the keys to his car and told us to go the lake with his family. [laughs] I think the guy's name was Maynard or something and he was awesome!

RYAN MURPHY: Our first tour was only a West Coast tour. We took off at the beginning of our spring break during our sophomore year of high school (it was John's senior year). We drove John's Ford Escort and his girlfriend's truck. We made these ridiculous tour passes that were pink and they said "Beaverhunt 1990" on them. Meanwhile, half of us weren't old enough to have a driver's license at the time and were too scared to talk to girls. [laughs] The tour with Sparkmarker in 1993 was perhaps the best time I ever had with Undertow. That was our first full U.S. tour, which was about eight weeks. We must have played every basement in the Midwest and South on that tour. One of the best memories was when our van broke before we even left for tour in the summer of 1994. I had an old '86 Honda Civic Hatchback and the four of us plus a roadie piled into the thing and hit the road. Two and a half hours later, my engine seized. We got picked up by a friend, hung out for a few days, and then decided to take Mark's 1979 Oldsmobile 88 on tour. We drove 44 hrs straight to Detroit in order to catch up with Unbroken. We called that the "Sticks and Picks tour." [laughs]

"AT BOTH ENDS"

MARK HOLCOMB: We had a deadline to record *At Both Ends* and it was kind of a free for all. We were kind of burnt out on each other at the time. We didn't have any feel as to how we wanted the record to come out. Everything just came from the heart. I remember writing about my experience hating the government, but it turned into an expression of my feelings. John broke up with his girlfriend and he wrote a song about that. It's not that we were over straight edge, but the idea of writing a song about being straight edge or vegetarian just wasn't what we wanted to share with people. There were some political themes, but they weren't direct. We tended to write about these things via our own experiences and how these events made us feel as opposed to trying to make a speech about it.

"CONTROL"

RYAN MURPHY: *Control* was fun to write. I just remember writing those songs in a day or two. We definitely found our stride with *Control*. I think we were all at the age where girls were warping our minds a little bit and adding stress to our lives. Speaking for myself, I had dealt with the murder of my grandfather and deaths of a couple other relatives all in one year. I think those events had me in a place where writing music was therapeutic in some sense.

PROGRESSIONS/SEATTLE STRAIGHT EDGE

MARK HOLCOMB: The straight edge scene in Seattle totally blew up. A lot of kids became straight edge because they were skating and it was kind cool at the time. All of a sudden there were 300 straight edge kids and a lot more people came out to shows. Before we went on tour we started to record *Control*. At this point we were pretty confident as a band. We got to a point where our generation of straight edge started picking up and everyone was helping each other out. I wanted the quality [of *Control*] to be good and I wanted to push myself on guitar. I remember being really optimistic and we'd practice and share ideas. At the same time more straight edge bands started coming up like Botch. So, all of a sudden there were all straight edge shows. In one way it was cool because it was rewarding to see the scene coming up that we helped build. On the other hand we were preaching to the converted. It became a popularity contest. We were popular because we were in Undertow, but now we had to live up to it. There was optimism on one hand but also some cynicism as to what was happening in the scene. Plus, we were all at different places in terms of where we wanted to go sonically.

RYAN MURPHY: Unfortunately, violence did end up hurting our scene. The last show we played before our hiatus was, in my opinion, a complete disappointment due to fights that had broken out throughout our set. I mean, we are talking about Seattle, the place where kids would sit down or stand in place while doing the weird bob-your-head-while-firmly-holding-your-back-pack-straps. The most aggressive a show ever got prior to the mid-nineties was a circle pit and a few stage dives. Then all of a sudden kids, including some of us, started to emulate some of the East Coast style of dancing, which I suppose was inevitable to some degree. In any case, fighting was not what Undertow endorsed, especially during our sets. I actually moved away from Seattle during the mid-nineties and the big growth spurt the scene went through during that time. I remember coming through Seattle with Ensign from 1997 to '99 and seeing so many new faces and not knowing any of them. It was cool to see Seattle growing, but at the same time I was sad that I missed out on that part of it.

DEMIAN JOHNSTON: We had a problem with popularity. It eventually ended us. We started to be more about "hardcore" and "straight edge" as we got bigger. We started to appease more but never in the way that new school hardcore bands are doing it by covering Gorilla Biscuits songs still. Yeah, by the way, if "Cats and Dogs" gets the biggest response of your set, you suck... a lot! [laughs]

JOHN PETTIBONE: We always had somewhat of a difference of opinion within the band regarding the sound we wanted to go with. Mark was really getting into Helmet and Quicksand and wanted to play a heavier style of rock sound. The rest of us wanted to play heavier music.

WINDING DOWN

DEMIAN JOHNSTON: What brought about the end of the band? Fights at shows. That lame kickboxing dancing that kids did. Xs on hands in 1995. It just wasn't fun. Mark ended it after a pretty big show in Redmond, Washington. He had just had enough. Mark never did something he didn't want to. We did a European tour after that with Ignite. It seemed a little weird to tour after breaking up, but with Ignite it seemed like the perfect thing to do.

MARK HOLCOMB: Our van broke down a week before we went on tour. We got in touch with Unbroken and just jumped in my car and shared their equipment. We toured from the back of my car for four weeks and we actually all had five dollars to eat every day. People knew who we were now so the shows went pretty well. We got back and we started to see how some of the other bigger bands like Strife were doing well and getting a bit more money and were able to tour a couple of times a year in a way that was feasible. But the violence and cliquishness in Seattle was still getting to us. We were all still friends but we were just kind of sick of being together all the time. [laughs] We decided to take a three month break and if anyone wanted to do another band that would be fine and we would just come back after a break. We played one more show in Seattle and it was the most

violent show we'd ever played. Kids were getting beat up and knocked around. There were bouncers pushing kids around and I had just had it with it all. It was supposed to be about community and having a good time, but now we were this band that people moshed to and got pushed around by bouncers, which wasn't why we did the band in the first place. We pretty much decided to end it after that. We did get back together to do a European tour and a final Seattle show but that was it. Ignite invited us on tour and it was awful, but we all bonded over the fact that each one of us hated someone different from Ignite. [laughs]

RYAN MURPHY: It's funny because right when we hit this stride in music writing, we ended the band. I remember talking with everyone about going out on top and that we should never be a band that drags it out trying to "make it" or something. It was just an unspoken agreement that we shouldn't do the band if it didn't feel sincere anymore. It was after a show in Redmond, Washington that we all just felt like we were going through the motions and were bummed on playing that we decided to put the band on hiatus. We all kind of knew that it was the end. We just wanted to be sure about it. Mark and Demian were doing a band called Dempsey, John and Demian were doing Nineironspitfire, then Demian and I started a band called Nothing Left. With all of us content with doing other things it felt like it was time to end Undertow.

LOOKING BACK

RYAN MURPHY: Man, I totally love every aspect of Undertow. We all got to participate in something great for a few years of our lives. I have continued to play and enjoy hardcore for almost 20 years now and have got to say that I feel fortunate to have gotten the chance to contribute to the hardcore scene with Undertow. As far as favorite memories go, I think the early days when we would hang with all the Chula Vista kids [were my favorites]. We were all still in high school and literally didn't give a fuck about anything, which always made for some fun times on tour. Later, when we met Dave Mandel and would always stay with him at his parent's house and have BBQs and pool parties. I could go on for days with all the cool friends we made while doing Undertow, but what I am trying to say is that it was about enjoying life, meeting new people, and bonding over similar interests whether it was politics, sports, your fucking diet, or whatever. We were all part of the same thing—hardcore.

DEMIAN JOHNSTON: I just loved doing it. I was in high school when I was in Undertow. First U.S. Tour at 17-years-old! It seems hilarious now. I got to meet a bunch of nice girls and boys. I got to get out of Seattle. I love it here, but doing Undertow made me feel like that maybe the whole world was my home. Or at least could be. I got to lose the anchor. I am proud of that. We were quite a freak magnet back then. I think the blue hair, dreadlocks, and Madonna t-shirts just attracted an odd crowd. It was great. I still keep in touch with a lot of the freaks. [laughs] I grew up a lot in that band. I am now a lot more bitter and paranoid, but I can remember seeing the Atlantic Ocean for the first time, with a naked Kevin Egan in it, like it was yesterday.

SELECT DISCOGRAPHY:

Stalemate (7"/MCD, Excursion, 1992)
　　Pettibone, Holcomb, Stern, Murphy

Undertow/Struggle split (7", Bloodlink, 1992)
　　Pettibone, Holcomb, Stern, Murphy

At Both Ends (CD/LP, Excursion, 1993)
　　Pettibone, Holcomb, Johnston, Murphy

Control (7"/MCD, Overkill, 1994)
　　Pettibone, Holcomb, Johnston, Murphy

Everything (CD Discography, Indecision, 2004)

VEGAN REICH

Vocals/Guitars: Sean Muttaqi   Drums: Jon Ewing
Bass: Dom Ehling   Andy Hurley
     Ray Titus   Aaron Sperske
     Sergio Hernandez

Vegan Reich is among the most controversial bands in the history of hardcore. Although they formed in 1987 and had broken up by 1992, their impact reverberated throughout the nineties, influencing prominent vegan straight edge outfits like Earth Crisis, Abnegation, Raid, and Day of Suffering while helping make animal rights a fixture in hardcore.

Formed by longtime anarchist activist and hardcore veteran Sean Muttaqi, Vegan Reich started as a reaction to what he viewed as apathy and inconsistency within the hardcore scene. Strongly influenced by the anarcho-punk and hardcore aesthetic of British bands like Crass and Conflict, Muttaqi was determined to take his rejection of jingoistic and oppressive mainstream American values to another level. Having made connections in the early eighties with both American and British radical groups, Muttaqi became active inside the underground anarchist movement. In conjunction with his interest in human rights, he was also an early animal rights activist and environmentalist. During this period, he made contact with British anarchist and punk rocker Rat (founder of militant bands like Statement and Unborn) whose vegan drug free lifestyle was highly influential and provided a framework for Muttaqi's eventual artistic and political vision for Vegan Reich, as well as the hardline movement he helped organize in 1990.

Although Muttaqi was in solidarity with most positions advocated by anarchists, he saw contradictions in the way their movement was carried out. For instance, at one particular national anarchist gathering, Muttaqi grew frustrated with the intoxication and sexual behavior exhibited by some attendees, which he felt negated what the movement was attempting to accomplish. Also, while anarchists claimed to be against of all forms of oppression, they still served meat and dairy products at most of their meetings. As a committed vegan, Muttaqi felt the goal of human life should be to free *all* forms of life. In turn, Muttaqi voiced his concerns in an artistic expression that incorporated his aforementioned musical inspirations, as well as diatribes against environmental and societal ills.

Vegan Reich was a divisive call to arms aimed at punk and hardcore that caused controversy right from the beginning. The band's moniker itself provoked arguments as many in hardcore were pacifists. However, Muttaqi claimed the name was a sarcastic response to critics in the anarchist and hardcore scenes who attacked him and his friends as "vegan fascists" due to their uncompromising stances on issues pertaining to environmentalism, animal rights, and politics.

Musically, Vegan Reich combined their militant messages with a mixture of U.S. hardcore ala Bad Brains and Cro-Mags, and U.K. anarcho-punk bands like Conflict. Vegan Reich's first recorded song, "Stop Talking—Start Revenging," appeared on the Animal Liberation Front (A.L.F.) benefit album titled *The A.L.F. Is Watching and There's No Place to Hide.* The track drew dispute due to its advocation of direct action against corporations that supported animal experimentation *"We must put them out of commission/Break their cycle of oppression/ Burn down their laboratories/And if they too get burnt/Well, they've had their warnings."*. The band furthered its cause in 1990 with their debut seven-inch on Muttaqi's own Hardline record label. The label also coincided with the start of the Hardline Movement, which demanded respect for all life, including the unborn, as well as following the dictates of the "natural order." The movement also turned a critical eye toward the intake of alcohol and narcotics in addition to what they considered "sexual deviancy."

As word spread about hardline, many venues Vegan Reich attempted to perform in across the country became either a forum for heated debate or brought about show cancellations due to threats of fire-bombs and even death. The F.B.I. put the band under surveillance due to their personal alliances with groups such as the A.L.F. Many zines would not even accept ads form Muttaqi's band and label.

As hardline surged in various places — in particular, Memphis, Tennessee and Salt Lake

City, Utah — Muttaqi found himself nearly powerless to participate in any type of direct action due to F.B.I. surveillance. Since the band wasn't able to play in most cities, Vegan Reich halted their touring. In the meantime, they went back to the studio to record a follow-up EP, *The Wrath of God*, which was a metal-tinged mini-opus (think Cro-Mags meets Iron Maiden) that touched on the band's interest in the spiritual and political ideologies that permeated Rastafarianism, Taoism, and Islam.

Although Vegan Reich had basically come to a halt by 1992, their influence impacted a huge swath of the hardcore scene as bands like Earth Crisis spread the vegan straight edge message throughout the remainder of the nineties, even if it was in a less militant manner than their predecessor. Hardline also remained a permanent fixture in the scene, albeit only in small pockets.

Muttaqi eventually handed over the reins of hardline to Indiana native Ryan Downey in 1993 (due to feeling a cultural disconnect with many who got into the movement in the early to mid-nineties) and went on to play in the band Captive Nation Rising (which started as a hardcore reggae fusion group, but ended up as an orthodox reggae outfit completely remove from the hardcore scene). He later joined forces with Chuck Treece for the punk band Pressure. Muttaqi converted to Islam in 1995 and ceased any full-time musical efforts. In 1999, he organized a short Vegan Reich reunion and recorded a final EP, *Jihad*, as well as a notable appearance at that year's Indiana Hardcore Fest. Not too long after the show, Muttaqi gave his backing to the remaining hardline movement leadership in the decision to put the movement to rest.

To some, Vegan Reich represented everything that was wrong with the sometimes overly sensational political debates in hardcore. Others, however, saw the band as pioneers as they encapsulated environmental, political, and spiritual perspectives into one unique, if over-the-top, creative vision. Good or bad, Vegan Reich left a lasting impact on hardcore.

EARLY INTEREST IN ANIMAL LIBERATION/VEGETARIANISM

SEAN MUTTAQI: A lot of people who get into animal rights and vegetarianism seem to have a predisposition to those issues, an innate compassion that makes them open to the concept. I was no different. I remember, even as a kid, going fishing, and then refusing to eat the fish I had caught, as I had made the connection that what was on the table had been alive. As soon as I was old enough to understand where meat came from it just didn't sit right with me. Once I got into the punk rock scene in the early eighties I also got involved in a lot of political activity from anti-nuke marches to the "U.S. Out of El Salvador" protests. With an increasing political awareness, the issue of vegetarianism was certainly growing on me. Coming into contact at that time with the first Flux of Pink Indians *Neu Smell* seven-inch helped propel me to making a firm commitment to becoming vegetarian. I think that was around 1981. Later on, Conflict became a *major* influence as well in my developing a more militant approach both in terms of animal liberation as well as my politics. Basically, it was never an issue I had to be overly convinced of. It always seemed like a natural thing to get into. Once I realized there were concrete movements based around animal rights, and an actual vegetarian lifestyle that was feasible, I was eager to become a part of it. Moving from vegetarianism to veganism required a little more education in seeing that there were issues with dairy products. But it was a pretty easy switch over. When I first got involved in animal liberation issues it was about the same time that the A.L.F. and movements like that got going in England. At a certain point that stuff started to spread over here, too. As people found out more what was going on over there, a lot of activists just saw it as a logical place to head with their activism….

IDEOLOGICAL INSPIRATIONS

SEAN MUTTAQI: Vegan Reich was basically a vehicle for me to express my long-held political views. I had played in other bands for years, but I always wanted to put a band together that expressed my ideas. I was exposed to a variety of things at a fairly young age ranging from Malcolm X's autobiography, to Native American political resistance, anarchist books from my father, and getting exposed to political and spiritual influences from reggae. We started a band and were doing it for the sole function of making ideology first. We wanted to create this entity even before there was music, so we put out radical veganism and political articles at shows before we even played and put the name "Vegan Reich" on them to try and raise some awareness. We wanted to get the message out to more people so we decided to start the band. Vegan Reich started before hardline started, so my initial goal was to spread a militant animal liberation message, as well as revolutionary political messages.

"VEGAN REICH"

SEAN MUTTAQI: The band name came about because some local people in the anarchist scene in our area basically called our crew "Vegan Reich," because we were so militant in our views, especially in regard to anarchist principles, such as you couldn't really be an anarchist if you were oppressing animals. We were coming from the perspective that if you were really an anarchist then you were being hypocritical; if you were eating animals because you were talking about total freedom and the right to not be oppressed, but if you don't believe in oppression then you can't be oppressive to animals by eating them. This view, and our notoriety surrounding it, greatly spread when we stirred up an enormous amount of controversy during the 1986 Anarchist Convention in Chicago. It was a catered event and they basically had it catered with pork ribs and spent a ton of money, everyone's money that had showed up for the gathering on this extravagant banquet. So, we staged a protest and I wrote an article and mass produced it and we called everyone out on the hypocrisy of doing that. They in turn were calling us fascists and Nazis because we were trying to tell them what to do, to limit their "freedom." Basically, we took that name for the band as a way to shove the issue in people's face. [laughs] It wasn't a full time band at first; it was more of a project that started in about 1987. It started some controversy, but we hadn't really branched out to the next level yet. The real controversial stuff happened later when we were playing out more.

EARLY SOUND

SEAN MUTTAQI: The real early stuff was influenced by Conflict and anarcho-punk type stuff. By the time we did the *Hardline* seven-inch, it still had anarcho-punk elements but we had become more of an American hardcore band. We were advancing in musicianship. We were somewhat similar to Bad Brains in that we had complex chord structures, some solos here and there, without being metal. A kid now might not see it as complex. [laughs] But in the context of the time it was pushing some boundaries. I was a musician before I was even into hardcore or punk. I grew up playing blues and rock when I was a kid and then I got interested in reggae. I think what made a lot of eighties hardcore stand out was that so many of us were coming from different musical backgrounds and then plugging those influences into a hardcore approach.

VIOLENT LYRICS/IMAGERY

SEAN MUTTAQI: We got a lot more flak from around the country than we did back home. I grew up in the early eighties with a lot of gang stuff going on in Southern California. From the long standing Black and Mexican gangs, to the punk gangs that sprang from many of the same neighborhoods and general gang culture — from the Suicidal Tendencies stuff, and Circle One, to punk rock gangs like L.A. Death Squad (The LADS), and The League. Our scene was really violent. People were getting stabbed and shot. Even as I got older and involved in the anarchist movement, we were always about guns, and fighting with Nazi skinheads. So, to me, being violent was sort of second nature, so it just came out in our lyrics. If you merge politics with what was already an aggressive approach in life then you've got the Vegan Reich *Hardline* record. [laughs] But of course, especially looking back on it, I can see how it was so shocking to people in other parts of the country who didn't have the same issues in their scenes. We were also very influenced by radical political groups such as The Black Panthers, which often used guns and those types of symbols on their literature.

BEGINNINGS OF HARDLINE

SEAN MUTTAQI: There was a certain core group in the beginning [of hardline] and we all brought different influences to the table. There were people from an anarchist background, from straight edge backgrounds, from Rasta backgrounds. I also had a fairly strong background of Liberation Theology, Black Power and Indigenous Rights struggles influencing me. I was really impacted by groups like M.O.V.E., as well. A lot of things were coming into play, but a lot of people we knew had spent years in anarchist or other left-wing backgrounds or groups, and one of the things people were getting fed up with from the anarchist movement was that at least in the U.S. at that point, the movement had moved away from its more historical IWW [Industrial Workers of the World] working-class type of revolt into a more individualistic, un-political type of movement. Nothing was getting done. People would end up arguing for hours about, say, someone sitting in a chair higher up than someone else and how that represented patriarchy or just bizarre things like that. [laughs] People would have stances about not oppressing human beings, but then they'd go out and get lunch at McDonalds, which whether you're talking about animal rights or third world exploitation, there was some definite issues with supporting corporations like that. We just wanted to do something that was not hindered by so much dogma. We didn't have a problem creating an organization or structure with an actual platform, though we kept it non-hierarchical. Going back to probably about 1987 a different group of people from the anarchist circle who happened to be vegan and drug-free were the first group that tried to organize what would eventually be called hardline. Eventually, that group merged with some straight edge kids who were getting into veganism and politics. At first we started throwing around the term "vegan straight edge" as a catch-phrase for this new group of people. But the missing component was that there were people who were vegan straight edge in our group who were also doing some questionable things in their lives in terms of personal character. The people coming together were pretty idealistic about trying to form almost an elite group that was not hindered by any sort of contradiction. Everyone was fed up with the contradictions they had seen from their respective scenes. A feeling came about that there had to be a component of character development. Some of the vegan straight edge people didn't seem to be militant about their views or about the need for revolutionary action. So, we coalesced into a new group, and that's when hardline really started. The hardline moniker had been used in both left and right wing circles to describe a person who was militant about their cause, unwavering in their ideological conviction. We used it unto itself, not related to left or right wing agendas, and in fact I think there were clearly elements that we had in common with both sides of the political spectrum.

"NATURAL ORDER"

SEAN MUTTAQI: At the time, the natural order, in terms of that being used as a phrase, was an attempt to find a non-alienating term to describe people's view of what was beyond the physical realm. Hardline definitely stopped short of trying to align to one religious view or another. It certainly had an overall spiritual tone to it, but hardline had kids coming from Christian backgrounds, Buddhist backgrounds, Jewish backgrounds, Rastas, Taoists, Muslims. In the literature, we were trying to be inclusive of all these different perspectives — finding unity not on what the nature of God is or isn't, but on the end resulting spiritual order that exists in the physical realm and the universal laws played out in nature. In retrospect there was a little too much emphasis placed on natural order because you can use nature as an excuse to do anything. You can find examples of all sorts of things in nature. One thing that defines religious belief, whether you're Christian, Muslim, Hindu, Jewish, Buddhist and so on, is that nature is not the be all/end all of your argument. Someone can say "in nature this happens," but religion is trying to push you beyond the physical realm. Some religions are trying to find a balance between spiritual and physical, such as Taoism, which was actually probably one of the main original influences in hardline in terms of our effort to be at one with the laws of nature, notions of consequence and effect, and if you go to extremes in certain areas it creates an imbalance.

"RULES"

SEAN MUTTAQI: There was a set of rules [in hardline], but we got the accusation of being fascist for having too many rules. There were anarchist roots to a lot of things in hardline, so there was always this internal friction between rules and not creating a hierarchy. In general, the main tenets were to strive against injustice and oppression, wherever it might be. Hardline always supported national liberation movements, animal liberation, and environmental causes. There were general rules about behavior in terms of striving for notions of purity such as being vegan and not doing drugs. But at the same time in an organizational structure, it was very decentralized, which actually led to some of the problems that hardline eventually experienced, because there wasn't enough of a hierarchy and it enabled a lot of disparate ideas to come in to where the movement almost lost control of itself. Years later you had all sorts of people taking on the name hardline who had nothing in common with each other aside from being vegan or drug-free. In the beginning there was cohesion about general beliefs. For instance, you could *not* be a right-wing Republican hardline person. I actually had to step in years later after I left and help some people clear things up and kick some people out because there were some weird groups later that had nothing to do with what the original goals were.

ORIGINAL OUTLOOK OF HARDLINE

SEAN MUTTAQI: Hardline was a revolutionary movement in everything that term can mean. The end goal was to create a new revolutionary society. It wasn't just an "improve yourself" straight edge scene with some extra rules tacked on. It was revolutionary in the same way that you can say how it is with anarchists or communists or radical Muslims. That manifested in different ways. There were people who had a different focus. It wasn't meant to be an animal liberation movement before other causes, but that's where most of the militancy seemed to take place. It was also millenarian in that we expected drastic changes to occur shortly. We tried to temper that with realism, but a lot of the younger kids who got involved felt that it was going to happen overnight, which led to a lot of disillusionment later on.

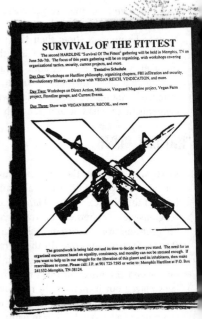

SURVIVAL OF THE FITTEST

The second HARDLINE "Survival Of The Fittest" gathering will be held in Memphis, TN on June 5th-7th. The focus of this years gathering will be on organizing, with workshops covering organizational tactics, security, current projects, and more.

Tentative Schedule

Day One: Workshops on Hardline philosophy, organizing chapters, FBI infiltration and security, Revolutionary History, and a show with VEGAN REICH, VINDICATION, and more.

Day Two: Workshops on Direct Action, Militance, Vanguard Magazine project, Vegan Farm project, Frontline groups, and Current Events.

Day Three: Show with VEGAN REICH, RECOIL, and more

The groundwork is being laid out and its time to decide where you stand. The need for an organized movement based on equality, consistency, and morality can not be stressed enough. If you want to help us in our struggle for the liberation of this planet and its inhabitants, then make reservations to come. Please call: J.P. at 901 725-7595 or write to: Memphis Hardline at P.O. Box 241532-Memphis, TN-38124.

MEDIA APPROACH/RESPONSE

SEAN MUTTAQI: Hardline was a well-oiled propaganda machine. It was clearly modeled after a lot of existing vanguard movements. We were very successful with what we were doing. We were getting constant exposure all the time. The responses were huge. I can only speak for the inception and the first few years because I was done by 1993, but in its heyday when Vegan Reich was going we were going to the post office every couple of days and getting a huge army sack of letters from kids from all over the world. Of course we received our fair share of hate mail, too. [laughs] But most of the responses were supportive.

VEGAN REICH SHOWS

SEAN MUTTAQI: Local shows were never too much of a problem because we had the same circle of friends in the scene and they all knew where we were coming from. But nationally the majority of our gigs would get cancelled because people would phone in threats to the clubs. People had the impression over the years that we were fascist. On one of our tours, a 60-day-tour, we only made it to about 11 shows on that tour because we'd get to a city and club owners would apologize but say they couldn't do the show because of threats from people to burn down the club. We had made so many enemies that there were a wide variety of people threatening us. There were people in the meat or animal exploitation industry itself. This is also going on in the context of a lot of direct action happening in different places. On one level we had enemies from the higher-up realm getting stuff shut down, and there was also another level of kids complaining and getting shows shut down.

MILITANCY

SEAN MUTTAQI: I don't think people liked having a band come out on militant issues. By the time Earth Crisis hit its high point the majority of the straight edge scene had become vegan. We were going against the grain of everyone when we started though — we were infusing drug-free ideology with veganism plus radical politics. The straight edge kids were pissed because we were saying they should look into veganism and the anarchists were pissed because we said they shouldn't do drugs. At that point in time everything we talked about rubbed most people the wrong way, one way or another. Obviously we had our supporters, but clearly the majority was always opposed to us.

DEBATE

SEAN MUTTAQI: If you hit a message really extremely then it forces the issue. People who didn't agree with us couldn't even really hold an argument with us at the very start; for instance, the abortion issue. Someone right off the bat might say, "We think that you're off base." We'd just say, "Do you eat meat? Well, how can you even argue about anything concerning whether we're oppressing people with our beliefs when your actions are oppressing animals?" The debate was so hot at the beginning that people actually became vegetarian for consistency purposes. Eventually a lot of the basic points won through. By the time the kids into us started bands they toned down a lot of the issues and made it more palatable and in turn it got a lot more people into the issues. Eventually it ran its course kind of like the sixties. You had a bunch of kids who were kind of burned out on social activism and it seems like it's the 1970s all over again with its excesses and lack of social concern.

SCENE HYPOCRISY?

SEAN MUTTAQI: We felt there was a lot of hypocrisy in people supposedly being so-called activists but not taking any actual action. Now in retrospect it seems like a hotbed of cautiousness compared to what is going on today in hardcore. [laughs] But at the time it was total frustration with everything that was going on whether it was the first Gulf War, environmental issues, or animal liberation stuff. There always has to be different ways to approach these issues. For instance, people look back at India gaining its independence and say it was all Gandhi. Of course Gandhi was a good focal point for people to look at pacifists getting gunned down by the British and getting the world's attention, but the British didn't leave India because of Gandhi himself, they left because there were other radical groups that were firing guns at British troops. Our whole thing was that in order to get people to pay attention to the issues you have to hit them over the head with it. Eventually it got hard to maintain that level because our shows got cancelled and we got banned in lots of areas, but for what we were trying to do it served its purpose for the time.

VIOLENCE

SEAN MUTTAQI: When we got to meet and talk with people they would see we had a case to present, whether or not they agreed with it, and that we weren't reactionary. That said, we got in our fair amount of fights back then. A lot of us had come from the older hardcore scene where it was the norm. If you were into punk back in the day you almost had to fight daily against jocks and rednecks. A lot of us had come from violent backgrounds long before we even got into punk and hardcore. Another thing that was weird for people to understand with the group was not only our willingness to use violence but also our violent imagery. For us we'd grown up in a very violent scene going to Suicidal Tendencies shows and everything was gang-oriented out here. We saw people fighting Nazis, people getting stabbed and a host of other crazy stuff. Violence was kind of second nature for us, so it wasn't a weird thing to put in the context of a band.

REVOLUTIONARY RHETORIC

SEAN MUTTAQI: Some people charged that we were a cult, but that would definitely be a stretch of the imagination. Cults usually have some sort of central figure who wants to create a centralized form of allegiance. Hardline had people from a Buddhist, Christian, or Judaic framework, and we weren't trying to get anyone to erase whatever sort of cultural milieu they were coming from. It did see revolutionary change ahead, not necessarily in a someone-floating-down-in-the-sky type of way, but just a change in the world ahead. And actually a lot of that has come to pass. The world is in a much more confrontational state now than it was during hardline, so much so that it made a lot of people who liked to mouth revolutionary things either put up or shut up, which is why you see a lot less people doing so now. [laughs] Some of the things that have happened in the world recently showed that revolution is real and bloody and it's not fun. It brought a reality to it that you can't just go around mouthing bloody, violent revolution either without understanding the consequences of that. Not to say that I've gone full-circle into just believing in pacifist struggles, but you can't take either approach lightly. To some extent there is more sobriety with people now as far as how they view the world situation, and it's a lot more complex than how people viewed it 15 or 20 years ago.

METAL INFLUENCE ON "WRATH OF GOD"

SEAN MUTTAQI: I had always been into different types of music, which included a bit of metal. In present times people are playing straight-up metal and calling it hardcore, but back then people seemed to through a metal phase because they were looking for ways to challenge their musicianship. Plus there was so much flak in hardcore with what we were doing that it was a bit easier for us to operate in the metal scene than it was in hardcore.

MYSTICAL/SPIRITUAL ELEMENTS OF VEGAN REICH

SEAN MUTTAQI: The mystical element was always there in Vegan Reich. It became more pronounced in our lyrics as we went on. I had always spent time around a lot of Rastafarians, was exposed to Islam, and I was always heavily into martial arts so there was a strong Taoist and Buddhist influence on me. I also met some of the people from M.O.V.E. who had actually fled after that whole thing went down. Basically, I was always

into religious studies and my lyrics reflected some Old Testament and Quranic influences in terms of structure.

SURVEILLANCE

SEAN MUTTAQI: There were shows we played where shit got burned down within blocks of where we played. There was sort of a wake of destruction around our shows, which is where I think a lot of the fear came from. There was a lot of F.B.I. surveillance and harassment and it got to the point where it became nearly impossible to keep the band going. Some of our influence was good but some of it was bad. I mean, Salt Lake City got so out of control that I don't know anyone who was too happy with that legacy. There were kids that were getting stabbed for drinking and shit like that, which was never a part of our ideology at all. There were always people who supported us or our views who weren't straight edge and we never had an issue with that. Things clearly started to unwind as it went on, though.

END OF VEGAN REICH/LEAVING HARDLINE

SEAN MUTTAQI: The biggest reason for leaving was that I felt conflicted because during hardline and with the problems we used to face I felt there was a big cultural disconnect between what a lot of the white, suburban hardcore kids were interested in and my own background. People would say, "Oh, Vegan Reich — a bunch of rich, white, vegan straight edge kids." But our band was always a majority Mexican entity. Not that it would have mattered if the whole band was white, but it was just weird having these perceptions from people who didn't know us and seeing how wrong they were. Also, hardline in its very early days had people from different ethnic backgrounds who were influenced by different things, but as it went on it clearly became more of what people were criticizing it for — a white, male group of kids who were into veganism, with a couple of extra things thrown in there almost for political points. For me, personally, I just couldn't take it anymore. So, Vegan Reich broke up, I left hardline, and I just started playing reggae and removed myself from hardcore for a while.

UNRAVELING OF HARDLINE

SEAN MUTTAQI: Hardline, in its mid-life to its end, clearly unraveled. It eventually split into two factions and I had to come in and officially give weight to one side over the other in terms of saying, "I'm here to tell you that this is not what we started hardline out to be." Hardline lost any aspect of militancy and was all-consumed with minute details or inward shit. It was like how minutely introspective can you get about where something was grown or whether a chocolate bar had an ounce of caffeine in it? It got absurd to the point where they weren't getting anything done. The original version of hardline was trying to promote a holistically healthy diet and tried to discourage people from eating processed sugars and being strung out on junk food culture. But eventually it became like, "Oh, you ate some white sugar so you're not hardline." That was never part of what hardline was from the get-go.

CAPTIVE NATION RISING

SEAN MUTTAQI: It was becoming impossible for Vegan Reich to function as a group. Tours were getting cancelled; I was getting fed up with the scene in terms of hardcore becoming kind of a white only type of hardcore scene. I just burned out on everything and called it quits. Everything stayed the same for me after that in terms of I still did the vegan, drug-free thing after that. I started playing in a reggae band and grew dreads and people would ask if I was a stoner. [laughs] I was still very political and drug-free but just in the reggae context. Captive Nation Rising was interested in using elements of hardcore and punk with reggae, but that band eventually just became a straight-up reggae band and we opened up for a lot of the big touring reggae groups. We were interested in doing music in a new realm with a horn-section, keyboards, and the whole thing.

INFLUENCE ON VEGAN STRAIGHT EDGE

SEAN MUTTAQI: A lot of the vegan straight edge kids started off as kids being into bands like Vegan Reich who started their own groups, so there was a continuous chain from, say, Vegan Reich to Earth Crisis. Vegan Reich pulled no punches. We were up-front and militant in regards to everything we were about, but at a certain point we could only go so far with that. Earth Crisis was, in a sense, a more palatable Vegan Reich. They had aspects of militancy but not too crazy and toned down the gun thing to a more general militant view. They honed vegan straight edge down to being a more environmentalist message, which was more palatable, and they accomplished some great things with that approach in that they took their message to more people.

1999 REUNION SHOW

SEAN MUTTAQI: The reunion was kind of a spur-of-the-moment thing. There was a fest in Indianapolis and the promoter contacted me and said he'd always wanted to see us play and asked if we'd consider doing it. He gave us six months notice, so we talked about it and we thought it would be cool. We did an EP basically just for the show and that was the only show we played since our breakup.

LEGACY OF VEGAN REICH

SEAN MUTTAQI: Vegan Reich's legacy ultimately exists more outside of music or hardcore than a lot of our contemporaries. We were relatively short lived, so it has more to do with things that came out of Vegan Reich and our part in helping develop the animal liberation and environmentalist movements in the formative years of their current context. What I mean is, there have been vegetarians and environmentalists for ages, but in terms of the modern movements, we had a key role in building what is continuing to this day, whether directly or through fans of the band who went on to have key roles within the bigger animal liberation and environmentalist groups. Likewise, with people in our early anarcho-vegan crowd, as well as the vegan straight edge scene and/or hardline, many of them went on to do all sorts of things connected to the same issues, whether it's starting

businesses that are vegetarian or eco friendly in nature, or raising a new generation of kids with similar ethics, home schooling their children and so on. It's not that everyone has stayed into exactly the same things — after 20 plus years since our inception, a lot of people have changed in various ways, progressed, or regressed depending on how some may look at it — but the fact is, overall, when I hear from people from back in the day, or run into someone randomly that was into Vegan Reich, so far at least, it seems to have predominantly been a positive influence on them. Even in my own life, being in Vegan Reich enabled me to meet some of the most interesting people one could hope to come into contact with. Some of my closest friends are people I met through being in Vegan Reich. Not to mention, being on the frontlines of debate back then, dealing with hassles from the authorities, and so on, only helped strengthen me for bigger struggles that were to come later, dealing with F.B.I. harassment after 9/11 and so on. I wouldn't change any of it for the world.

SELECT DISCOGRAPHY:

Hardline (7", Hardline, 1990)
   Muttaqi, Hernandez, Ewing

The Wrath of God (7", Hardline, 1992)
   Muttaqi, Ehling, Titus

Vanguard (CD Discography, Uprising, 1995)

Jihad (MCD, Uprising, 1999)
   Muttaqi, Hurley

FINAL THOUGHTS

I assembled *Burning Fight* as a glimpse into what felt like an overlooked era in hardcore. The music, ideas, and people in the nineties hardcore scene changed my life. To me, hardcore did not die when the first wave ended — it was just beginning a new phase. The nineties were, of course, indebted to and impacted by previous eras, but there was an important story that needed to be told about a period that came after the first influential eras of hardcore.

I wasn't sure where to go with the project at first. All I knew was that I felt the need to talk to people about their memories of nineties hardcore. I spoke with people about their experiences, the bands that meant something to them, and what debates they found the most compelling. Initially, I thought these interviews would be a hassle for those involved. It felt like I was cajoling people for thoughts and stories from a time which they now perhaps felt differently about. To my surprise, the conversations generated interest and enthusiasm. What resonated most with people were the ideas that fueled the music and the overall consciousness that existed during that time. There was an active dialogue prevalent in the scene that inspired us to think seriously about issues we may have never been exposed to. These discussions acted as a catalyst for personal and political exploration that completely changed the direction of our lives.

There were, of course, humorous moments of reflection about these times. Looking back, many felt that perhaps people took themselves too seriously as arguments sometimes turned into screaming matches and personal rivalries. Nonetheless, the dialogue from this time was educational, even if it sometimes taught people how not to act.

The ideas and music inspire me to this day. I am still moved when I think about seeing some of the amazing bands at basement shows or V.F.W. Halls. I remember passionate dialogue with people I had just met who eventually became my close friends. I remember feeling for the first time in my life that I belonged to a community. I remember screaming lyrics filled with angst as I drove my first car around late at night, wondering if the trajectory of my life would change. I remember these bands, these people, these ideas acting as an emotional salve as I struggled to become an adult. Most people probably feel as passionate about the era of hardcore they grew up within; this just happened to be the decade that I belonged to.

After six arduous years of interviewing, writing, and editing, the book finally feels like the document I intended it to be — a document that covers a time period that meant so much to so many people. I know I missed some things. Many important debates are left unexplored. Dozens of influential bands and people are not included. Nonetheless, I tried my best to present as many of the ideas and bands that played a vital role during this era.

If nothing else, I hope the testimony collected in *Burning Fight* demonstrates that people possess the power needed to make changes — not only to their own lives, but to the lives of others.

While I struggled with the final words to close this book, the lyrics to Endpoint's "Brown County" struck me. To me, these lyrics capture the spirit of hardcore about as well as anyone could.

We've got to learn what's down inside, we've got to learn to turn the tide.
We've gotta be free.
We've gotta share desire, we've gotta fight the liar
We've got to be free.
We've got to stand together through dark and stormy weather.
We've gotta share desire
We've gotta fight the liar
We've got to be free.

-Brian Peterson, March 2009

FOR MORE INFORMATION ABOUT *Burning Fight*,
THE TOPICS DISCUSSED IN THE BOOK, THE AUTHOR,
& A COMPLETE LIST OF BIOGRAPHIES FOR EVERYONE INTERVIEWED,
PLEASE CHECK OUT THE FOLLOWING SITES:

burningfightbook.com
myspace.com/90shardcore
revelationrecords.com

THE AUTHOR CAN ALSO BE REACHED AT 90SHARDCORE@GMAIL.COM

P.O. BOX 5232, HUNTINGTON BEACH, CA 92615
REVELATIONRECORDS.COM

PHOTOGRAPHY

Photographs taken or provided by...

MARK BEEMER: *p. 18- Ashes, 67, 190, 192, 198, 212, 219, 222, 225, 312*

ANDREW BOTTOMLEY: *p. 13, 21*

PETER BOTTOMLEY: *p. 243, 408, 412, 414, 456*

SEAN CAPONE: *p. 6, 10, 69, 158, 228, 240, 244, 247, 262, 266, 268, 288, 290, 296, 338, 342, 345, 348, 368, 375, 400, 460*

JUSTIN CORBETT: *p. 197, 270, 314, 318*

DANIELLE DOMBROWSKI: *p. 7, 52, 54, 77, 167, 177, 248*

BRANDON EBEL: *p. 129, 135*

JEAN-PAUL FRIJNS: *p. 9, 80, 216, 325, 406, 442, 446, 449, 450*

JOSH GRABELLE: *p. 15, 18- Turmoil, 19, 23, 59, 61, 321, 326*

CARL GUNHOUSE: *p. 11, 18-Falling Forward, 21- Ink&Dagger, Hatebreed, 50, 72, 154, 161, 178, 187, 206, 250, 308, 331, 335, 380, 383, 388, 420, 434, 438*

CURTIS LEHMKUHL: *Matt Davis pictures on dedication page*

DAVE MANDEL: *p. 1-Hanging out, 82, 157, 165, 182, 254, 257, 278, 293, 301, 304, 328, 332, 360, 372, 376, 387, 392, 424, 468, 470, 475, 478*

HOLLY MANN: *p. 126, 131*

VIQUE MARTIN: *p. 1-Greyhouse, 29, 31*

JOHN MCKAIG: *p. 99, 445*

MARK MILLER: *p. 273, 274, 277, 423, 431, 432, 453*

JUSTIN MOULDER: *p. 8, 48*

SEAN MUTTAQI: *p. 489, 491*

BRETT NOBLE: *p. 499- Brian old school, Rose today*

MICHELLE NOLAN: *p. 499- Brian's Present day Bio shot*

CELESTE PETERSON: *Title Page Crowd shot, p. 47*

OLE CHRISTIAN PETTERSON: *p. 1- Snapcase, 138, 143, 145, 148, 150, 152, 356, 363, 366, 492, 494*

DUSTY PILGER: *Overlayed crowdshot- starting on p. 24, Back cover photograph*

TODD POLLOCK: *p. 162, 168, 200, 396, 427, 454*

ADAM TANNER: *p. 166*

MALTE TERBECK: *p. 283, 284*

BIBLIOGRAPHY

All Ages: Reflections on Straight Edge, compiled by Beth Lahickey (Revelation Books).

American Hardcore: A Tribal History, by Steven Blush (Feral House).

The Anti-Matter Anthology: A 1990s Post-Punk and Hardcore Reader, by Norman Brannon (Revelation Books).

The Bhagavad-Gita As It Is, by A.C. Bhaktivedanta Swami Prabhupada (Bhaktivedanta Book Trust).

Check the Technique: Liner Notes for Hip-Hop Junkies, by Brian Coleman (Villard Books).

Conversations With Punx: A Spiritual Dialogue, by Bianca Valentino, (House Of B - limited edition run).

In Defense of Reality: Conversations Between Ray Cappo and Satyaraj Das (Equal Vision Records).

Dance of Days: Two Decades of Punk in the Nation's Capital, by Mark Andersen and Mark Jenkins (Akashic Books).

Diet for a New America, by John Robbins (HJ Kramer).

Evolution of a Cro-Magnon, by John Joseph (PUNKHOuse).

Our Band Could Be Your Life: Scenes from the American Indie Underground 1981- 1991, by Michael Azerrad (Little, Brown and Company).

My First Time: A Collection of First Punk Show Stories, edited by Chris Duncan (AK Press).

Post: A Look at the Influence of Post-Hardcore 1985 — 2007, by Eric Grubbs (iUniverse).

Radio Silence: A Selected Visual History of American Hardcore Music, by Nathan Nedorostek and Anthony Pappalardo (MTV Press).

Straightedge Youth: Complexity and Contradictions of a Subculture, by Robert T. Wood (Syracuse University Press).

Straight Edge: Clean-Living Youth, Hardcore Punk, and Social Change, by Ross Haenfler (Rutgers University Press).

We Owe You Nothing: Punk Planet: The Collected Interviews, edited by Daniel Sinker (Akashic Books).

ACKNOWLEDGMENTS

Burning Fight would not have been possible without insight, feedback, and all around assistance from all of the individuals interviewed in the book. These people took a lot of time to talk about their memories of this era. Without them, *Burning Fight* would not have happened.

Thank you to Jordan Cooper and everyone at Revelation Records for believing in *Burning Fight*.

Major thanks to Dave Stein for his advice and time spent helping me find the right publisher for the book. Without his help, these chapters would be nothing but Word Documents.

Vique Martin, Ghazal Sheei, and Greg Bennick played significant roles in helping me edit and proofread the book. Also, thank you to Ryan Hoffman, Rich Jacobs, Adam Tanner, Ian MacKaye, John Porcelly, Dave Agranoff, Sean Muttaqi, Anthony Pappalardo and Rob Moran for providing some added insight, feedback, and informational assistance with the Straight Edge and Animal Rights chapters.

Thank you to everyone who shared photos, flyers, and all around enthusiasm for the project. I wasn't able to use all the amazing images that were sent, but a hearty thanks must be given for their time, dedication, and talent: Ole Christian Petterson, Dave Mandel, Sean Capone, Mark Beemer, Jean-Paul Frijns, Vique Martin, Greg Straightedge, Dusty Pilger, Mark Miller, Franklin Rhi, Sean Muttaqi, Adam Tanner, Jose Palafox, Eric Rumpshaker, Celeste Peterson, Troy Trujillo, Justin Corbett, Steve Lovett, Fred Hammer, Carl Gunhouse, Dave Gagne, John McKaig, Jason Hellman, Danielle Dombrowski, Andrew and Peter Bottomley, Ati Moran, Kim Nolan, Andrew Kline, Patrick West, Curtis Lehmkuhl, Justin Moulder, Grace Bartlett, Kyle Even the Score, Kelly Missell, Chase Corum, Carl Skildum, Luke Stemmerman, Mike King of the Monsters, Steve from Pennsylvania, Samantha Samsone, Ben Roe, Holly Mann, Brandon Ebel, Scott from Pennsylvania, Michelle Nolan, Greg D'Avis, Chrissy Piper, Angela Boatwright, David "Igby" Sattanni, Micah Panzich, Malte Terbeck, and many others. Apologies if I forgot anyone. Special thanks to Don Irwin (*Punk Life* Fanzine) for his archival help and his amazing array of flyers.

Not enough words can be said for the friendship, encouragement, advice, love, and support I've been fortunate enough to receive from the following people: my amazing wife Lisa (who helped immensely with editing and had to endure way too many hours of conversations about hardcore than should be humanly possible!), the entire Peterson, Larcombe, and Quintero families, Brett and Rose Noble and family, Aaron and Amy Veikley and family, Mickey Nolan, Dylan Lee and family, Jeremy and Brandy Welvaert, Jim Grimes, Vique Martin, Ghazal Sheei, Caitlin Lipinski, Neeraj Kane, Sean Muttaqi, Dan Binaei, Brent Decker, Duncan Barlow, Rob Pennington, Betul and Ihsan Cicek, Alex Ferguson, Mani Mostofi, David Lewis, Al Collins, Greg Thompson, Bianca Valentino, Danielle Ramirez, Greg Bennick, Jes Steineger, Rob Moran, David Claibourn, Lisa Root, Andrew and Peter Bottomley, Aaron Burgess, Anne Elizabeth Moore, Dan Sinker, Norman Brannon, Ray Cappo, Ian MacKaye, Eric Grubbs, Pat Stolley, Sean Leary, Jeremy Matherly, Jeremy and Candy Heider, Brendan DeSmet, Justin Pearson, Dusty Fecht, Mitch Fecht, "The Burg," Livewire Board, the students and staff at Northtown Academy, Moline High School, and Bennett Community School, Vernon Stading and family, Grant and Annie Upson, Corey Fineran, Andy Round, and my beloved hometown: Minot, North Dakota.

Special thanks to Robert Fish for writing the Foreword and to Aisha Praught for her help in the transcription of some of the interviews.

I would not have attempted to write anything were it not for the following people:

NORMAN BRANNON and his amazing *Anti-Matter* Fanzine, which inspired me to write in the first place.

ERSKINE CARTER, who taught me how to write, read, and think in ways I never thought possible.

RYAN DOWNEY, who gave me some of my first writing opportunities and provided encouragement over the years.

PAUL CERVINSKI, who always provided an example of practicing what you preach.

JOHN CARPENTER AND STEPHEN KING—Carpenter's films and King's stories were among the first to really capture my attention at an early age and injected that creative "spark" in me.

AUTHOR & DESIGNER

BRIAN PETERSON was born in Minot, North Dakota, and moved to the Quad-Cities (Illinois/Iowa border) in his mid-teens where he became active in the Midwest hardcore scene, which impacted his life in innumerable ways. He has written about music and film for a variety of publications such as *Thrasher*, *Punk Planet*, *Skyscraper*, *Copper Press*, and *American Music Press* since 2001. He is also a high school English teacher. Aside from his freelance writing he is also working on several short stories and novels. He and his wife, Lisa, currently live in the Chicago area.

ROSE NOBLE, a Moline, Illinois native, was first introduced to hardcore in her mid-teens. Since then hardcore has played many significant roles in her life and has influenced how she embraces and creates art. She works as a graphic designer but spends as much time as she can creating fine artwork for bands, friends, and charities. Rose, her husband Brett, and their three children now reside in Galena, Illinois. *{ ladynoble.wordpress.com }*